Maria Del Sapio Garbero's concern with ruins is profoundly scholarly, blending as it does an impressive knowledge of Shakespeare with an intimate knowledge of Rome, its ruins and Renaissance humanism. Yet the project resonates beyond itself with the postmodern aesthetic of an artist such as Anselm Kiefer whose style might be characterized as a destructive gouging or shattering or alternatively a thick impasting or palimpsesting of the artwork's surface. Though refraining from so explicit a link, Del Sapio treats the text of Shakespeare's Roman works in much this way. The ruin (in Benjamin's words, "the form which things assume in oblivion") interrupts the narrative of history, threatening to smother it at birth. If historical narrative is called forth by what Benjamin called the "heliotropism" of the present, then the ruin threatens to return history to its tumbled ground, where in Nietzsche's words, "with an excess of history man again ceases to exist". The process is announced in *Titus Andronicus*, where tropes of ruin – burial, mourning, dismembering, remembering, palimpsesting – threaten to collapse the present to a traumatic heap. Yet ruins also beget the Humanist idea of rebirth and the project of modernity; it is the threat of ruin that translates desire into a language and artistry capable of inheriting the future.

John Gillies, University of Essex

Shakespeare did not have to leave England to know that he was living amid the ruins of Rome. He and his contemporaries constantly encountered the physical remains of the ancient conquerors, their stillstanding bridges, uncannily straight roads, baths, walls, and half-broken battlements; their fragmented statues and coins, perfume bottles and monumental inscriptions routinely unearthed from the loam. Still more, anyone with a grammar school education was steeped in the cultural remains of Rome, the language, history, stories, and underlying beliefs that had once ruled much of the world. Maria Del Sapio Garbero's book focuses on the remarkable succession of plays, along with the narrative poem *The Rape of Lucrece*, in which Shakespeare directly engaged with Roman themes. Richly learned, probing, and intellectually generous, *Shakespeare's Ruins and Myth of Rome* is an essential guide to these works. But it is also a brilliant guide to what it means here and now to think creatively with the traces of the shattered past. This book itself is what it says of its great subject: "A field of possibilities springing out of a field of ruins."

Stephen Greenblatt, Cogan University
Professor of the Humanities at Harvard University

Shakespeare's Ruins and Myth of Rome

Rome was tantamount to its ruins, a dismembered body, to the eyes of those—Italians and foreigners—who visited the city in the years prior to or encompassing the lengthy span of the Renaissance. Drawing on the double movement of archaeological exploration and creative reconstruction entailed in the humanist endeavour to "resurrect" the past, "ruins" are seen as taking precedence over "myth", in Shakespeare's Rome. They are assigned the role of a heuristic model and discovered in all their epistemic relevance in Shakespeare's dramatic vision of history and his negotiation of modernity. This is the first book of its kind to address Shakespeare's relationship with Rome's authoritative myth, archaeologically, by taking as a point of departure a chronological reversal, namely the vision of the "eternal" city as a ruinous scenario and hence the ways in which such a layered, "silent", and aporetic scenario allows for an archaeo-anatomical approach to Shakespeare's Roman works.

Maria Del Sapio Garbero is Professor Emerita of English Literature in the Department of Foreign Languages, Literatures, and Cultures at Roma Tre University (Italy).

Anglo-Italian Renaissance Studies
Edited by Michele Marrapodi

Shakespeare and Renaissance Literary Theories
Anglo-Italian Transactions
Edited by Michele Marrapodi

Shakespeare, Politics, and Italy
Intertextuality on the Jacobean Stage
Michael J. Redmond

Italian Culture in the Drama of Shakespeare and His Contemporaries
Rewriting, Remaking, Refashioning
Edited by Michele Marrapodi

Theatre, Magic and Philosophy
William Shakespeare, John Dee, and the Italian Legacy
Gabriela Dragnea Horvath

Shakespeare's Poetics
Aristotle and Anglo-Italian Renaissance Genres
Sarah Dewar-Watson

Shakespeare, Caravaggio, and the Indistinct Regard
Rocco Coronato

Shakespeare's Ruins and Myth of Rome
Maria Del Sapio Garbero

For more information about this series, please visit: www.routledge.com/ Anglo-Italian-Renaissance-Studies/book-series/AIRS

Shakespeare's Ruins and Myth of Rome

Maria Del Sapio Garbero

Figure 0.1 Igor Mitoraj (1944–2014), bronze sculpture
Source: Photo Luca Pizzi, courtesy of Atelier Mitoraj

 Routledge
Taylor & Francis Group

NEW YORK AND LONDON

First published 2022
by Routledge
605 Third Avenue, New York, NY 10158

and by Routledge
2 Park Square, Milton Park, Abingdon, Oxon, OX14 4RN

Routledge is an imprint of the Taylor & Francis Group, an informa business

© 2022 Taylor & Francis

Library of Congress Cataloging-in-Publication Data
A catalog record for this book has been requested

ISBN: 978-0-367-55910-6 (hbk)
ISBN: 978-1-032-19542-1 (pbk)
ISBN: 978-1-003-25967-1 (ebk)

DOI: 10.4324/9781003259671

Typeset in Sabon
by Apex CoVantage, LLC

MIX
Paper from
responsible sources
FSC
www.fsc.org
FSC™ C013985

Printed in the United Kingdom
by Henry Ling Limited

To my grandchildren Giorgio and Enrico

Contents

Acknowledgements

First of all I would like to thank the series editor Michele Marrapodi for the privilege of being hosted for the second time in the Anglo-Italian Renaissance Studies Series.

This book has a long story and owes many debts. It has its origins in a research project on "Shakespeare's Rome" I launched and directed for many years at Roma Tre University, and it has benefited from the right atmosphere of friendly collaboration and scholarly exchange provided by the colleagues of my home institution (Viola Papetti, Masolino d'Amico, Gilberto Sacerdoti, Paola Faini, Maddalena Pennacchia). With Maddalena, the current director of the "Shakespeare's Rome International Summer School" (SRISS), I have shared the intellectual challenge and the rewarding hard work of many compelling initiatives on Shakespeare's Rome. For continuous support of my research project, I must thank my Department of Foreign Languages, Literatures, and Cultures.

My great debt is to the stimulating inputs and feedback of the many scholars that over the years have participated in conferences and seminars organized at Rome Tre on the Roman Shakespeare. Some of them have offered durable and inestimable friendship and expertise: Manfred Pfister, Stephen Greenblatt, Michael Neill, John Gillies, Andrew Hadfield, Ramie Targoff, Rui Carvalho Homem, Patricia Harris Stäbler Gillies, Keir Elam, Iolanda Plescia, Laura Di Michele, Claudia Corti, Michele Marrapodi, Alessandra Marzola, Coppélia Kahn, Lisa Hopkins, Márta Minier, Nicoleta Cinpoes, Domenico Lovascio, Nathalie Vienne-Guerrin, Victoria Bladen, and Gary Watt.

This book has also benefited from a positive context of formal and informal collaboration with a number of institutions and the intersection with a diverse range of projects and critical approaches: the Socrates-Erasmus European Project on "Interfacing Science, Literature, and the Humanities" (Vita Fortunati, Manfred Pfister, Gilberta Golinelli, Mariangela Tempera); the Stratford-upon-Avon Shakespeare Institute (Michael Dobson); the London Shakespeare's Globe (Patrick Spottiswoode); the British School in Rome (Christopher Smith); the Royal Netherlands Institute in Rome,

KNIR (Harald Hendrix); the European Shakespeare Research Association, ESRA (Ton Hoenselaars, Rui Carvalho Homem): the University of Verona (Silvia Bigliazzi); Sapienza University of Rome (Rosy Colombo, Nadia Fusini, Paola Colaiacomo); the University of Rome "Tor Vergata" (Daniela Guardamagna); and the Roma Tre Research Centre for the Study of Rome, CROMA (Carlo Maria Travaglini).

First drafts of some of my volume's chapters were presented as papers in ESRA and Stratford-upon-Avon conferences. It would be difficult to list all the convenors or respondents who contributed to enriching or rethinking my line of thought: but some of them, like Ivan Lupic, Rui Carvalho Homem, and Kay Stanton, remain unforgettable for the passionate, thoughtful, and joyful way of interpreting their role in dialogical engagement.

For insightful comments on the manuscript I would like to thank Iolanda Plescia, who saw it grow. Michael Neill who has read the manuscript in its final configuration has generously provided invaluable response and inspiring suggestions. Many thanks to him! For timely bibliographical help at a final crucial moment, I would like to thank Michela Compagnoni. The debt I owe to the scholars who have passed away in recent and not-so-recent years is acknowledged in the pages of my volume. Errors and flaws I acknowledge as only mine.

Research for this book has been carried out at the British Museum Library (London), the Shakespeare Institute Library (Stratford-upon-Avon), the Cambridge University Library, the Fondazione Franco Besso Library (Rome), the Biblioteca Casanatense (Rome), the Folger Shakespeare Library, and the University of London Senate House Library, whose staff has been marvellous in facilitating my access to rare books. Among friends Anna Maria Tomassini has been a constant interlocutor. I would like to thank her for always having in store the right book at the right moment.

For permission to republish revised or expanded versions of previous works I would like to thank Routledge and Michele Marrapodi (for an article on *Coriolanus* published in his edited *Shakespeare and the Italian Renaissance*, 2014); V&R Unipress (for an article on *Julius Caesar* published in my co-edited *Questioning Bodies in Shakespeare's Rome*, 2010); Pacini editore (for an article on *The Rape of Lucrece* published in my edited volume *Shakespeare and the New Science in Early Modern Culture*). I would also like to thank Ashgate (now Routledge) for letting me recontextualize in this volume portions of the introduction and interchapter of my edited book *Identity, Otherness and Empire in Shakespeare's Rome* (2009). Finally, but not least, I would like to thank the commissioning editor of this book, Michelle Salyga, my editorial assistant Mitchell Manners, my project manager Rajalakshmi Ramesh, my copy editor Tracy Gath, and the editorial and production staff at Routledge for allowing me to devote more time than initially programmed to the writing of my book and for ensuring patient and expert assistance all along.

The city of Rome—with its ruins and beauties, and the daily visual vertigo of conflated temporalities—has provided an inspiring context to my work. Thank you Rome! And thanks to the city council for often making available breathtaking venues for conferences on the Roman Shakespeare, thus adequately responding to the place Rome holds in Shakespeare's world. Thanks also to the people of the Gigi Proietti Globe Theatre Silvano Toti, Rome (Carlotta Proietti, Daniele Salvo, Loredana Scaramella) who together with Maria Teresa Toti, the president of the Silvano Toti Foundation, have ensured productive collaboration between practitioners and scholars at my home institution.

Shakespeare's Rome has often been the subject of my graduate and postgraduate courses and lectures at Roma Tre University and elsewhere. I would like to thank my students for helping me discover each time the inexhaustible and engaging actuality—the "heliotropism" (Benjamin)—of this theme, and for the joy of sharing it with them. In dedicating this book to my beloved grandchildren Giorgio and Enrico, I like to think that they are ideally part of that circle, young though as they still are.

Figures

Abbreviations

Ant.	*Antony and Cleopatra*
Be	*Between Past and Future* (Arendt)
Birth	*The Birth of Tragedy* (Nietzsche)
Brit 1	*Britannia* (Camden, 1610)
Brit 2	*Britannia* (Camden, 1695)
Cor.	*Coriolanus*
Cym.	*Cymbeline*
Ham.	*Hamlet*
JC	*Julius Caesar*
Lives	*The Lives of the Painters, Sculptors, and Architects* (Vasari)
Met.	*Metamorphoses* (Ovid)
Orat.	*The Orator* (Cicero)
Origin	*The Origin of German Tragic Drama* (Benjamin)
Specters	*Specters of Marx* (Derrida)
The Rape	*The Rape of Lucrece*

Note on Texts

Quotations from Shakespeare's Roman works and sonnets refer to the following Arden editions.

Antony and Cleopatra, ed. John Wilders (London: Bloomsbury Arden Shakespeare, 2005).

Coriolanus, ed. Peter Holland (London: Bloomsbury Arden Shakespeare, 2013).

Cymbeline, ed. Valerie Wayne (London and New York: Bloomsbury Arden Shakespeare, 2017).

Julius Caesar, ed. David Daniell (London: Bloomsbury Arden Shakespeare, 1998).

Sonnets, ed. Katherine Duncan-Jones (London: Bloomsbury Arden Shakespeare, 2010).

The Rape of Lucrece, in *Poems*, ed. Katherine Duncan-Jones and H.R. Woudhuysen (London: Thomson Learning, 2007).

Titus Andronicus, ed. Jonathan Bate (London: Thomson Learning, [1995] 2003).

All other quotations are from *The Norton Shakespeare—Third Edition*, ed. Stephen Greenblatt, Suzanne Gossett, Jean E. Howard, Katharine Eisaman Maus and Gordon McMullan (New York: W. W. Norton, 2016).

Introduction

Part 1 "Ruin Hath Taught Me Thus to Ruminate"

"Ruin hath taught me thus to ruminate", Shakespeare writes in sonnet 64.11, conjuring up, in this and in a number of related sonnets (among them 65, 55, 125), an imagery redolent of Renaissance architectural visions of the collapsing glory and pride of past ages ("down-razed" towers, arches, monuments, besmeared marbles and brass): a privileged early modern ruinous scenario—incontrovertibly Roman—for a meditation on time and decay.[1] Shakespeare's commitment in his sonnets was to contrast the wreckage of Time—if not, latently, the very notion of eternity traditionally associated to ancient Rome—with a search for immortality that he pursued in the monumentality of *his* art. Rome, however, is never mentioned in his sonnets, even though a modern poetics of ruins in Western civilization emerges with the humanist archaeological discovery of the ancient fragmented colossus. And yet, interestingly, in sonnet 64, the inextricable interconnection between ruins and Rome and their meaning of both eternity and mutability surfaces as a pun favoured by the early modern pronunciation of Rome as "room". To meditate on poetry, time, and decay is to R(o)*m*inate. But what other lesson did Shakespeare draw from "outworn buried age" (son. 64.2), and how may such a "*romination*", which he rephrased as "fearful meditation" in sonnet 65, have influenced the historical or pseudo-historical setting of his Roman works (*Titus Andronicus*, *The Rape of Lucrece*, *Julius Caesar*, *Coriolanus*, *Antony and Cleopatra*, and *Cymbeline*)?

The early nineties of the sixteenth century, when Shakespeare supposedly wrote most of his sonnets, were also the years in which he started his confrontation with Rome with two works: one of them, *Titus Andronicus*, was a tragedy, his first, whose Q1 head title also advertises as specifically "Roman", *The Most Lamentable Romaine Tragedy of Titus Andronicus*; the other one, *The Rape of Lucrece*, was a poem worthy of tragedy. Both texts draw on ruins as a collapsed architecture, a bodily condition, and a metaphor, epitomized as they are by the themes of the destroyed city and the violated body and their lasting inscription in the Trojan symbolism:

DOI: 10.4324/9781003259671-1

the Fall *per antonomasia*. How were Rome's ruins ruminated and digested into the mythical, if "fearful", dramatic imagination of Shakespeare's Roman works? This is the question from which this volume originates.

In Shakespeare's time, the alimentary and nutritional connotations of the verb "to ruminate" were still tremendously active in their medieval suggestiveness: as the analogue of "to meditate", "to ruminate"—in its monastic habit and meaning connected with Biblical learning (while eating)—was physically related to reading as a prolonged act of ingestion, chewing, and transforming, namely to a notion of knowledge understood as a bodily process of incorporation and fully domesticated wisdom. In this sense it provided a formidable anatomical description, as best highlighted by Mary Carruthers,[2] of the experiential processes involved in memory and in memorizing and learning from tradition and the past. But the nutritional and incorporating metaphor also inscribed the issue of classical ancestry, and the related processes of reception or imitation, into a transnational, dynamic process of mobility, transfer, and re-signification. Substantially subsumed in the ways of learning/teaching methods of contemporary grammar schools,[3] Shakespeare seems to be fully alert to the metaphor's dramatic potentiality. And in fact, the relation between ruin, reading, eating, and memory will deserve some more reflection when I shall go on to address Shakespeare's peculiar, displacing use of his sources, especially in my first chapter on *Titus Andronicus*, but not only.

But what about antiquity, as the classical past was called in Shakespeare's time? And what about Rome? The centrality of Rome in England's early modern culture has been highlighted by many, and most efficaciously in works by Robert Miola, Maurice Charney, Geoffrey Miles, Clifford Ronan, Coppélia Kahn, Vanna Gentili, Warren Chernaik, and Patrick Gray, just to quote a few. As well remarked by Miola, "the ubiquity of the classical presence in Elizabethan and Jacobean literature should humble any surveyor of English Humanism", and in Shakespeare's time, "no form of literature was more steeped in classical example than the drama".[4]

Ronan lists 82 extant English Roman plays for the period 1497–1700, with an amazing, accelerated growth in the Elizabethan and Stuart years 1589–1642 (from four to 41, not counting 18 lost plays), before stabilizing in the following years 1643–1700 on the number of 37.[5] One cannot help noticing that the explosion of the Roman concern coincides with both the nascent imperial ambitions of the nation and an inversely proportional crisis of the concept of sovereignty (respectively marked by the Elizabethan defeat of the Spanish Armada and the explosion of the civil war between Royalists and Parliamentarians).

But the way Rome is appropriated, as I argue in this volume, is grounded on a discovery of the ancient City that the European Renaissance humanists understand, literally and metaphorically, as a "disinterment" or "unearthing", as Thomas M. Greene (*The Light to Troy: Imitation and*

Discovery in Renaissance Poetry, 1982) and Leonard Barkan (*Unearthing the Past: Archaeology and Aesthetics in the Making of Renaissance Culture*, 1999) have underlined in their major books respectively centred on literature and the visual arts, but both devoted in their different fields to highlighting the relation of mutual engendering that exists between Rome and Renaissance culture.

In Renaissance European culture Rome was *the* past—a past which encapsulated the heritage of the Trojan-Greek culture—and yet a past of an especially uncertain status: a mostly interred landscape of mute ruins which stood for the visible and yet ghostly signifier of a "buried age" (Shakespeare, son. 64.2) awaiting discovery.

"The Middle Ages had left antiquity unburied and alternately galvanized and exorcised its corpse", Panofsky has suggestively observed, whereas "The Renaissance stood weeping at its grave and tried to resurrect its soul. And in one fatally auspicious moment it succeeded".[6] Thomas Greene was brilliantly Panofskian when in his groundbreaking book he incisively pointed out that the "disinterment" literally involved stones as well as texts:

> The image that propelled the humanist Renaissance and that still determines our perception of it, was the archaeological, necromantic metaphor of *disinterment*, a digging up that was also a resuscitation or a reincarnation or a rebirth. The discovery of the past led men literally to dig in the ground, and the recovery from it of a precious object needed only a touch of fancy to be regarded as a resurrection. But the resurrection of buried objects and buildings could not be distinguished from the resurrection of literary texts as they were discovered, copied, edited, disseminated, translated, and imitated by the humanist necromancer-scholar.[7]

It is my contention in this book that Shakespeare's re-creation of Rome was cast in the same set of concerns, drives, and vocabulary. However, this was worked out not in a Hegelian-like dialectic of ruin and (overcoming) rebirth, that is, according to a progressive ("motion forward") vision of culture and civilization, but rather according to a critique grounded on anatomical scrutiny; one in which the ghostly and "fearful" sight of ruins is permanently and interrogatively part of the reflection on life, history, and modernity.[8]

What is particularly meaningful to my view and the purposes of this volume is that Shakespeare made Rome's "ruins" speak by first staging, in *Titus Andronicus*, the "most lamentable" (or mournful) spectacle of Rome itself breaking into pieces; namely, a Rome captured in the *finis imperii* act of interring itself and its many children, thus dramatizing, together with the coeval running trope that "Rome seule pouvoit à Rome ressembler / Rome seule pouvoit Rome faire trembler" ["*Rome* only might to *Rome* compared bee, / and onely *Rome* could make great *Rome* to tremble", son 6, vv. 9–10] (Du Bellay),[9] the audience's own posthumous, archaeological, and anatomical gaze on Rome: the temporality of a burdened and scrutinizing posterity, which is the mark of modernity.

Whether this play was the achievement of a single or collaborative authorship, the possibilities offered by the triple-layered form of the Elizabethan stage in this play's opening scene—gallery or upper stage, main stage, the "cellerage" accessible through a trapdoor—are fully exploited here by the playwright. As remarked by many, the actors' entrances and exits are carefully orchestrated with tribunes and senators entering the upper level, and the two yearning contenders for the emperor's title, the brothers Saturninus and Bassianus, entering and exiting the main stage from the two opposite lateral doors. The visual impact of a longed-for crown being handed over by the tribune Marcus aloft, and of Rome as a site of unremitting fratricidal struggle for power—performed below on the main stage—is powerful in the way it is meant to speedily introduce the familiar, self-destructive theme related to the Roman theme. However, as soon as the general Titus enters the main stage in triumphal procession, with the unburied bodies of his sons who have died in war for the glory of Rome, it is as if the very act of burial should take centre stage from this point onwards: the Andronici's tomb becoming a forceful theatrical prop in catalyzing Rome's self-destructive impulse, which corrodes its equally strong will to power at the very core.[10]

"Make way to lay them by their brethren" (1.1.92), Titus orders, followed by the stage direction: *They open the tomb*. As for the "tomb", in the absence of any specific stage directions in either Quarto or Folio copies of the play, editors tend to suggest that it "could have been represented by the discovery-space at the back of the stage or the trap-door downstage" (Jonathan Bate), or even a movable "structure representing a tomb" (Stanley Wells).[11] Each of these hypotheses may be plausible for the convenience of specific theatrical productions. However, I prefer the suggestiveness of a movable structure (a "monument" as Titus calls it, 1.1.354) communicating with the trapdoor, for the closeness it shares with burial as a ceremony of interment and for the symbolism it reverberates on the rest of the play and, overall, on the corpus of Shakespeare's Roman works. In fact, once opened at Titus's order at the outset of the play, it seems as if its (trap) door, leading to a descent, should remain wide open all along the play, eagerly expecting the gradually interred, amputated humanity depicted by the playwright—as the proper backdrop of the hospitable or inhospitable funereal rites which Shakespeare will disseminate all along this and the rest of his Roman plays.

The word "tomb" in Shakespeare's works occurs 57 times within 21 works: nine times in *Titus* (second only to *Romeo and Juliet* where it occurs ten times), in conjunction with "grave" (ten times) and "monument", which occurs three times as the equivalent of tomb. One certainly doesn't need to wait for either the last act, with the anachronic ruins of a monastery mentioned by an unnamed Goth (5.1.21), or for Lucius's very last lines (added in Q2–3, F) on the re-edified order of the state—with his admonishment, "That like euents, may nere it ruinate"[12]—to grasp that the play is about ruins and ruination. The butchery underwent by most of its characters, the profusion of tombs and acts of entombment, to say the least, concur conspicuously to make it so.

To Titus—the harbinger of family values—the tomb is a *sacrarium*, the "sumptuously re-edified" monument of ancestry and memory:

> This monument five hundred years hath stood,
> Which I have sumptuously re-edified.
> (1.1.355–56)

Monument (with the relevant meanings of edification and lasting memory) and tomb (with those of death, interment, and oblivion) coincide in the way they participate, from the outset of the play, in defining the parable of Rome herself. Indeed "re-edification" itself is a tricky word. It immediately gestures towards memory and *pietas*. But it is underwritten by oblivion, a cyclical succession of ruin and rebuilding, which immediately cooperates in foregrounding the tomb as a problematized icon of identity in the belated temporality of the play. In the first burial scene, the tomb is mentioned as a "sacred receptacle", a "sweet cell", quickly turning, however, into a voracious "store"-house, jealous of what will never be given back.

> O sacred receptacle of my joys,
> Sweet cell of virtue and nobility,
> How many sons hast thou of mine in store
> That thou wilt never render to me more.
> (1.1.95–98)

In a matter of just four lines, the tomb quickly turns from a monument (repository and memorial) of virtue and *pietas*, into a swallowing chasm, a ravenous underworld, an indifferent hoarding agent of death, from which nothing is "rendered" or heard but the blood-thirsty "groan" of unappeased shadows asking for blood (1.1.129): the uncanny "*lament* from history" (my emphasis), we might say borrowing from Walter Benjamin,[13] which Shakespeare lets us hear as if rising from the earth, and which perfectly corresponds to the theatrical dispositive of the trapdoor. In fact its prominence, as a reservoir and releaser of disturbing meanings, grows as it later changes into a pit (Act II)—a wild cave of fragmenting drives and desires—and an instrument of punishment and torture, a hole, for procuring death by gradual interment (when it comes to the moor Aaron); or, conversely, a space impiously denied as a place of burial (whether it is Titus's own offspring Alarbus, at the opening of the play, or Tamora Queen of the Goths, in the [Q1] very last line of the play): "And being dead, let birds on her take pity" (5.5.199). "Like Seneca" (in his *Troades* and *Phaedra*), Robert Miola has pointed out, "Shakespeare employs the tomb as a setting for dramatic action and ironic commentary".[14] In fact, from the very first scene, the tomb is invested with the pivotal role of showing and commenting on the swift and ineluctable fragmentation of ancient Roman values, almost as if they were scarred archaeological remains accruing all about it as the action of the play progresses.

More widely its door, leading downwards, functions as a threshold which causes the audience to fluctuate between life and death, inside and outside, the visible and the invisible, piety and impiety, wholeness and fragmentedness, continuity and discontinuity, bodies and phantasms, self and otherness, words and groans, thus forcefully theatricalizing the condition of the ruin in *Titus Andronicus*. It also predicates, archaeologi-cally—or Virgil-like, but anatomically—as I argue in this volume, the very relationship of the playwright with ancient Rome as a process involving the double movement of interring (retrieving the city's Fall and apoca-lypse, walking among the debris) and disinterring (excavating, anatomiz-ing, making it speak) its hewed and only half-seen colossal fabric, whether that be bodies, places, marbles, or texts.

Drawing attention to the double movement of archaeological explora-tion and creative reconstruction entailed in the humanist endeavour to "resurrect" the past, and underlining the fact that this was "localized above all at the site of Rome and around the legend of Rome", Thomas Greene has incisively written:

> One of the reasons the enterprise of Renaissance Humanism proved to be so fecund is that its scrutiny of the past tended to imply a latent pressure upon the present and future. Although it contained any number of antiquarians in the narrow, Nietzschean sense of the term, the enterprise as a total phenomenon was not antiquarian, not pedantically confined to the accumulation of isolated things and facts in and for themselves. Humanism was so powerful and attractive an initiative wherever it appeared because its study of antiquity was understood to carry implications for modern creativity. . . . Human-ism is an untidy object of knowledge because its activities arrange themselves on a spectrum situating at one end scholarly disciplines like archaeology and philology and at the other end creative arts like architecture and poetry.[15]

Yet, the pendulum between the two poles could hardly be conceived as an opposition, but rather as a juxtaposition in the face of the disciplinary permeability which characterizes the Renaissance culture and episteme.[16] Greene discards any polarity or temporal sequentiality between scholarly concern and creativity to underline instead the concomitance of the two impulses, which he aptly prospects as "a single, complex moment".[17] I couldn't agree more, in so far as this approach allows for a reconsideration of Shakespeare's Roman canon as "an untidy object of knowledge"; a canon, I argue, which finds in *Titus Andronicus* the prologue for an understanding of Roman history which goes beyond philological or dramatic generic accuracy, to grasp what, at the core of Rome's myth, is catastrophic and spectral.

And hence, I suggest, we can rescue *Titus Andronicus* from the still persevering critical attitude that considers it an anomaly in terms of genre or historical soundness—a patchwork badly or hardly fitting the Plutarchan canon of Shakespeare's Roman plays—if, taking as a point of departure Greene's notion of humanism as an "untidy" way of "resurrecting" the past, we look at this play as an utterly "untidy" artefact, an amphibious play epitomizing Shakespeare's (overall) complex experiment with Rome as history *and* tragedy. Arguably, this is a play in which the term "Roman" holds in so far as we assume that Rome in this play is present as history *and* memory, antiquity *and* the intertwined creative recalling of what, to Shakespeare's European contemporaries, appeared in the amputated and interrogative form of the ruin—or as Walter Benjamin might say, "in the form which things assume in oblivion".[18] In fact, in relation to the long-standing trope of "Rome forgotten" in medieval and Renaissance culture (which is the object of my following section),[19] one may well invoke Benjamin's way of "plumb[ing] the depths of language" *and* history[20] by pursuing a notion of memory which, as in his essay on Kafka, is prospected as a search grounded on oblivion, as if we were digging and "recall[ing] to mind something that [we] had forgotten". And,

> What has been forgotten . . . is never something purely individual. Everything forgotten mingles with what has been forgotten of the prehistoric world, forms countless, uncertain, changing compounds, yielding a constant flow of new, strange products. Oblivion is the container from which the inexhaustible intermediate world in Kafka's stories presses toward the light.[21]

We might conjure up Clarence's nightmarish drowning dream in *Richard III* as a striking theatrical enactment of Benjamin's comment on Kafka, an example which is particularly fitting, especially if we consider that *Richard III* (1594) and *Titus Andronicus* (1593–94) are almost coeval (in Jonathan Bate's convincing reconstruction).[22] As in Benjamin's "Kafka" and in Shakespeare's *Richard III*, I would like to suggest, the materials of memory and history in *Titus Andronicus* occupy an intermediate world, a sphere between the unfathomable and the real, the human and its fragments or ruins, long lost to knowledge. Significantly, burial, mourning, pietas, time, remembering, the retrieving of a traumatic past—recurrent motifs in Shakespeare's Roman works (especially in *Titus Andronicus*, *The Rape*, *Julius Caesar*, and *Coriolanus*)—are also the topics which mostly undergo, with different degrees of distortion in each play or work, the process of interrogation and transformation of things forgotten. We might call it a process of "active forgetting", adopting Christine Buci-Glucksman's comment on Benjamin's philosophy of history, a process which is "peculiar to memory and the infinite capacity of reopening a past which the 'science of history' claimed to be over and done with".[23]

In fact, against historicism, Benjamin problematizes what it means "to articulate the past historically" by considering the crucial role played by memory, or remembrance, namely the capacity that memory has of "recognizing" and "seizing hold" of the past not "the way it really was" and not so much in terms of laws and continuity as rather in terms of shocking interruptions and as "it flashes up in a moment of danger". By which the philosopher meant the moment a layered memory or "image of the past"—by him defined as a dialectical constellation of meanings—urges upon the present "as one of its own concern".[24] He translated this concept into a beautiful poetical statement when he wrote, "As flowers turn towards the sun, by dint of a secret heliotropism the past strives to turn towards that sun which is rising in the sky of history".[25] We can give concrete substance to this illuminating insight by summoning the disruptive role played by the many images, first interred over the centuries and then all of a sudden re-emerging into the light thanks to the nascent archaeological concerns of Humanist culture, thus marking a turning point in the course of Western civilization. As Leonard Barkan observes, "The objects, as it happens, are not new, but they are radical, which is to say that they appear literally and figuratively at the root level of the civilization that unearths them and provide a fundamental alternative that must be encountered".[26]

As I show in the next section, ancient Rome's ruinous landscape pressed upon the troubled transnational sky of European Renaissance history, with the force of an enigmatic conglomerate of semi-interred memories begging to come to light as a question of the present, as well as an anticipation of the future. And Shakespeare was the interpreter who with his theatre and poetry, better than anybody else in his own troubled Elizabethan times, was able to "recognize" Rome's "heliotropism": that is, her exceptional actuality. Not, then, as a historian would have it—in an age, however, when there was no such thing as a scientific notion of history—but rather by "seizing" and bringing into light, in his own terms, all the momentous and dialectical relevance of Rome's ruinous dimension. For, as Nietzsche helps us to observe in his *Untimely Meditations* ("Uses and Disadvantages of History for Life"), it is

> only through the power of employing the past for the purposes of life and of again introducing into history that which has been done and is gone—did man become man: but with an excess of history man

again ceases to exist, and without that envelope of the unhistorical he would never have begun or dared to begin.[27]

And Shakespeare? "Untimely" (Nietzsche) and paradoxical as it may seem, in order to radically "articulate historically" (Benjamin) his Rome— a Rome *of* and *for* his own time—Shakespeare gets rid of any immediately recognizable historical context or source, in his first "Romaine Tragedy", and as if anarchically associating and reciting episodes and limbs of an alien ancient Rome by heart, he anatomically descends into her archaeological profundity—namely the ruinous romanity of a layered, long-lost city—to make it release her inner disruptive meanings.

Is such an experiment left behind as an isolated and concluded episode when Shakespeare passes on to his Plutarchan plays? No: my contention is that it isn't, or that it is only apparently so. My argument in this book is that such a way of articulating the Roman past affects, even though with a less blatantly culinary and distortive perspectivism, the inner stuff of each of his Roman works. Some of the hints to this are the "ill-disposed" temporality and troubled hermeneutics engendered by a dissected and murdered fatherhood in *Julius Caesar*; the uncanny suspension of the human body between the paradigm of man and engine, organic and inorganic, in the archaeologized scenario of forgetful humanism and disowned bonds of *Coriolanus*; the fascination of ruin and the tragic belatedness of the two lovers in *Antony and Cleopatra*; the way the temporality of trauma and mourning in a violated woman corrodes the logic and linearity of a capitalized notion of History in *The Rape of Lucrece*; and last but not least, the disquieting excess of time and intended anachronisms that characterizes *Titus Andronicus* as well as *Cymbeline*, Shakespeare's first and last Roman play, by means of which the playwright stages, in a bifurcated tragic and comic mode, the ghosts of ancestry and a layered, if aporetic, notion of history.

And yet Shakespeare's art strongly interacts with history in the way it hosts and makes "echo" in his theatre and poetry what modern historiography would gradually learn to suppress, namely desultory modes of remembrance and the cry of suffering that is the "'lament' from history", as I feel appropriate to say borrowing from Benjamin:

> The "scientific" character of history, as defined by positivism . . . is secured at the cost of completely eradicating every vestige of history's original role as remembrance [*Eingedenken*]. The false aliveness of the past-made-present, the elimination of every echo of a "lament" from history, marks history final subjection to the modern concept of science.[28]

This depth, which Shakespeare achieves through memory, that is, through memory's act of digging into oblivion—a process akin to distortion and critique, in Benjamin's acceptation—is the point in which history at the theatre, by means of the triangulation provided by the "now" of the audience's gaze, meets and looks at itself—the primal stuff history is made of. As Buci-Glucksman remarks:

> The approach which awakes the forgotten is . . . archaeological and interpretative; its scanning of historical time bases itself upon an acute consciousness of crises and catastrophe, making time capable of being seen and thought. This is precisely what theatre does by catalyzing an essence of time which cannot be reduced to the physical, mechanistic, empty time of chronology, or to its expression in the event. "No empirical event can entirely register the determining force of the historical form of time." But theatre can do this: "Historical grandeur can be represented in art only in the form of tragedy". And, what is more, in the form of modern tragedy which is the "drama" of Shakespeare, Calderón and seventeenth-century German baroque *Trauerspiel*.[29]

It is to such a complexity that we are referred to, first and foremost, by *The Most Lamentable Romaine Tragedy of Titus Andronicus*: a complexity or hybridism which has considerably delayed its inclusion in the canon of *the* Roman plays and still causes scholarship to oscillate between those who unreservedly subscribe to its "Romanness"—precisely because, I would say, there is an excess of "Rome" (a Rome brought to its very limit)—and those who are still somehow under the spell of historical soundness voiced long ago by Terence Spencer when he derogatorily wrote, "the author seems anxious, not to get it all right, but to get it all in".[30]

Advisedly, one might argue. In fact, the playwright doesn't seem to want "to get it all right", neither in this first Ovidian Roman play, where his creative imagination outrageously revels in tearing to pieces and creatively transforming all his grammar school (or later) classical learning, nor in his three subsequent plays (*Julius Caesar*, *Antony and Cleopatra*, and *Coriolanus*), where, Plutarch at hand, he seems to be positively showing off subservience to his authoritative source and philological correctness. Arguably, what Shakespeare seems to be concerned with, starting with *Titus Andronicus*, is to present his audience with a sense of history experienced in the form of catastrophe and mourning, namely in a form akin to the *Trauerspiel* expounded by Benjamin: literally a play (*Spiel*) of mourning or sorrow (*Trauer*), and by him conceptualized as different from classical tragedy. "The object of [tragedy]", the philosopher writes, "is not history, but myth", whereas that of the *Trauerspiel*, which originates as the expression of the "provocatively worldly accents of baroque", is the immanence of history and its bodies. But what history? "The baroque knows no eschatology", Benjamin explains. And "is haunted by the idea of catastrophe", deriving from a crisis of sovereignty and the ensuing "theory of the state of emergency", a concept that would influence Benjamin's overall vision of history.[31]

My contention in this volume is that, starting from *Titus Andronicus*, the myth and bodies of ancient Rome undergo a similar "worldly" treatment in Shakespeare's universe, or in other words, a similar process of re-signification prompted by a revision of notions of national identity and sovereignty: an issue of great concern for Shakespeare if we consider that in those same early decades as a playwright he was also deeply engaged with national history (see the *Henry VI* plays, *Richard III*, and *Richard II*).

The amount of writing on the Roman Shakespeare is far too abundant to list. But it can be useful to start from M.W. MacCullen's important *Shakespeare's Roman Plays and Their Background* (1910), with the caveat that the plays selected as "Roman" are only the three so-called Plutarchan plays (*Julius Caesar*, *Coriolanus*, and *Antony and Cleopatra*), as is still the case in Maurice Charney's *The Roman Plays*, 1961. It is also useful to recall that it was only much later that the canon of the Roman plays was extended to include *Titus* and *Cymbeline*, thanks to John W. Velz's authoritative article in *Shakespeare Survey* (1978).[32] The thematic approach marked by Robert Miola's groundbreaking focus on the city (*Shakespeare's Rome*, 1983) can also boast the merit of having naturalized the enlargement of Shakespeare's Roman canon to *The Rape of Lucrece*, *Titus Andronicus*, and *Cymbeline*. Since the time of M.W. MacCullen, and on the background of a somewhat latent and unresolved scholarly disagreement regarding the degree of "Romanness", or "historicity", of *Titus* and *Cymbeline*, quite a few book-length studies and collections and a plethora of essays have been devoted to these plays. The assessment of Shakespeare's classicism on the basis of source studies methodologies, or jointly, with an attention devoted to the semiotics of theatre or the larger environment of methods and uses of classical learning in Elizabethan England, has been a constant concern.[33] The influence of new historicism and cultural studies has increasingly played a role in extending the study of the Rome's topic to its cultural uses in Shakespeare's age and beyond.[34] Such Roman themes as politics, forms of government, republicanism and empire, and Romanness and stoicism have been often addressed.[35] Questions regarding identity and otherness, in their relation with gender, masculinity, Romanness, and the issue of colonialism, have been variously focused upon and explored.[36] Shakespeare's Rome, in conjunction with its intermedial afterlife, is increasingly discovered as our contemporary.[37] As a result, traditional, influence-oriented studies have increasingly been revised and rebalanced in favour of Shakespeare's conscious or unconscious use and misuse of the meanings of Rome in the light of the agenda of his and our own present critical concerns. Marked by H. James's influential study, *Shakespeare's Troy: Drama, Politics, and the Translation of Empire* (1997), questions related to the appropriation of legitimizing founding myths, cultural heritage, and memory have also been frequently tackled.

My work is deeply indebted to critical approaches dealing with questions of inheritance and cultural transmission. But I take as point of departure a chronological reversal, namely the vision of the "eternal" city as a ruinous scenario—which was in fact the Renaissance standpoint—and hence the ways in which such a scenario allows for an archaeo-anatomical approach to the entire corpus of Shakespeare's Roman works.

Interestingly, Shakespeare mobilizes and strengthens the signifying agency of his ruined classical bodies when, contradictorily, he bestows on Hamlet, in the form a sceptical churchyard meditation on recycled dustiness ("Imperious Caesar, dead and turned to clay, / Might stop a hole to keep the wind away. / Oh, that that earth which kept the world in awe / Should patch a wall t'expel the water's flaw", *Ham.* 5.1.193–96), what in the previous play (*Julius Caesar*), in the hands of Antony's consummate rhetorical art, had just been shown as a powerful cultural material in determining the course of history: "But were I Brutus, / And Brutus Antony, there were an Antony / Would ruffle up your spirits and put a tongue / In every wound of Caesar that should move / The stones of Rome to rise and mutiny" (3.2.219–23).

In my way of dealing with Shakespeare's Rome, ruins come first. They are assigned the role of a heuristic model. As such, starting from the title of my volume, "ruins" take precedence over Rome's "myth", a precedence aiming at underlining the place they have in articulating the relationship between past and present and the role they play in problematizing Shakespeare's belated memory of Rome and its bodies.

In this respect *The Light to Troy* (1982), Thomas Greene's magisterial understanding of imitation as inextricably linked to ruins in Humanist and Renaissance Europe, has been a source of great inspiration, in conjunction with Foucault's methodological proposal of an "archaeology of knowledge". Greene views the whole matter of creativity in Humanist and Renaissance Europe as hinging on the archaeological master metaphors of excavation and the awakening of the dead, the latter entailing a culture capable of assuming "historical responsibilities, one which remembers, preserves, resuscitates, and recreates". For this, the critic has used the apt category of "heuristic imitation" to refer to the textual tactics—keyworded as subreading, subtext, latency of sense, anachronism—worked out by the Renaissance imitative artists (Petrarch as their forerunner) in order to negotiate their modernity, which he views as a state of "conditional independence". This involved, as he says, "a myth of origin and a myth of modernist growth away from the origin", sometimes resolved in the creation of a conciliatory "bridge" between past and present, other times by opposing the estrangement of a past alien culture with radical antagonism and violent forms of appropriation.[38]

In more recent years the reflection on the European Renaissance as grounded on ruins and a layered awareness of Rome and the past has been enriched by the contribution of an important group of books which cut across disciplinary boundaries. Concentrating on "objects that actually *did* emerge from the ground into the light of day", Leonard Barkan has strengthened the epistemic relevance of such a Renaissance fascination with ruins in his wide-ranging volume *The Unearthing of the Past* (1999) by devoting exhaustive attention to the role played in plastic arts by the unsystematic if disruptive Renaissance nascent archaeology.[39] Alexander Nagel and Christopher S. Wood in their *Anachronic Renaissance* (2010) have theorized the "anachronic" as substantial to Renaissance visual art and its plural and palimpsestic temporality: "The new work, the innovation, is legitimated by the chain of works leading back to an authoritative type. But the chain also needs the new work. It is the new work that selects the chain out of the debris of the past".[40] Continuing on the comparative and cultural perspective pursued by Greene, Andrew Hui's *The Poetics of Ruins* (2016) efficaciously documents the cogency of the ruin topic for any study of Renaissance Europe.[41] As for Shakespeare's own fascination with ruins, criticism has mostly concentrated on his sonnets and its relevant preoccupation with Time as a devouring agency, a theme well known (*tempus edax rerum*) to ancient authors such as Ovid and Horace.[42] One exception is Philip Schwyzer, who in his *Archaeologies of English Renaissance Literature* (2007) draws attention to the plays *Romeo and Juliet*, *Hamlet*, and *Titus* by mostly concentrating on charnel knowledge and concrete images of mortuary archaeology.[43]

I am indebted to all of these studies and, in ways that I am not able to quantify, to many other books not directly connected with my theme but methodologically crucial in the way they have contributed over the years to shape my cross-cultural topic—Shakespeare's Rome—in terms of "permeability", "spectrality", and "cultural mobility" (Greenblatt), as well as in terms of fracture, discontinuity, and juxtaposition (Benjamin, Nietzsche, and Foucault).

Shakespeare's early modern time was an epoch shaken by all sorts of historical and epistemic fractures brought about by the "new science" and the urge it posed for a reappraisal of reality and the human. Among those who underlined its cogency was Francis Bacon, who notably resumed the state of art in his encyclopedic *The Advancement of Learning* (1605). John Dee on his part went so far, in his famous *Mathematicall Preface to Euclid* (1570), as to envisage an "Arte of Artes" that he called "Anthropographie"—what nowadays we would appreciate as a transdiscipline—a way of learning which, by capitalizing on old and new "Artes", interestingly conceptualized an inclusive and integrated approach to the understanding of human beings.[44]

Theatre was not an effect but an integral part of the process, thanks to its daily staging for a large and hybrid audience of how, in the clash between old and new, the very notion of modernity was produced. In such a context ancient Rome (with all its familiar meanings of *Caput mundi* and *Teatrum mundi*) constituted, for Shakespeare and the Elizabethans, the privileged scenario on which to project the ambitions of a nascent empire in a logic of *translatio imperii*, but also, I contend, for questioning the nature of bodies and their location in a new universe, for interrogating the relation between past and present and hence for renegotiating the relation with myth and memory.

Pivotal in this context of shifting paradigms is the "immanence" of the body—both male and female—and the way its bemusing, layered corporeality is discovered and theatrically displayed as an object of interrogation by the early modern culture, aptly defined by Jonathan Sawday as a "culture of dissection".[45] As I will show in this volume, the dissected body takes centre stage in Shakespeare's Roman works. Indeed, his theatricalized Roman bodies—Titus, Lavinia, Caesar, Coriolanus, Antony, and Lucrece—provide some of the best examples of bodies menaced by the spectre of ruination (or Fall) as one of reduction and fragmentation—a loss of themselves—thus embodying, literally or metaphorically, the condition of the ruin as well as that of a renewed dramatic self-knowledge.

Taking its cue from the ruinous scenario of fragmented institutions and maimed bodies of *Titus Andronicus*, my volume aims at reassessing the myth and role of Rome in Shakespeare's world by adopting a critical perspective which is grounded on the "wordly" new science of anatomy as well as on an emergent archaeological consciousness of the past: a knowledge with "no eschatology" (Benjamin) and which, in the Foucauldian understanding of the "archaeological", includes layers, fractures, void, aporia, or, in other words, an attention for "phenomena of rupture" and "discontinuity".[46]

Advisedly (via Virgil's *Aeneid*, Horace's *Odes*, and Ovid's *Fasti*), Shakespeare's Rome is obsessively remindful of Troy, the burning city, the Ur-ruin. Indeed, the Humanist archaeological discovery of Rome as made up of a layered and disrupting temporality—something that Freud will later compare to a mental entity and to the functioning of memory itself[47]—was one that enveloped and subsumed the Trojan-Greek culture, in a way that made evident that it had been transmitted and preserved by means of a fractured and contaminating process of appropriation and *translatio*. In Salvatore Settis's underlining of the "classical" as a dynamic and changing mechanism rather than a static and concluded phenomenon, the construction of our contemporary "image of the Greek history" as "universal" for Western civilization, "needs the Romans not simply for their quality of cultural mediators, but mostly for the institutional, military, and administrative scaffolding by means of which the Roman empire created the context for it to take root and spread out in space and time". But, with what degree of purity and intangibility, Settis argues, in the extraordinary variety of cultures that cohabitated in the classical world?[48]

The Roman ruins in Humanist and Renaissance Europe stand for the globalized process of such a dynamism and mutability, and as such they provide a way for understanding the interaction of cultural systems in terms of hybridized *translatio imperii*. They also stand for a longed-for full, if elusive, meaning of Rome: a meaning which is tantamount to its emergent "archaeological hermeneutics", proposed and discussed by Greene as "an interplay of entities that resist total description".[49] Ancient Rome has always been considered a compendium of city and world, a catalyzing archive of political strife and different forms of government, the epitome of glory and fame, but also, as I argue in this book, a petrified display of history as a "catastrophe", entailing civilization and grandeur, as well barbarism and ruins—the stuff of progress in Benjamin's philosophy of history:

> There is no document of civilization which is not at the same time a document of barbarism. And just as such a document is not free of barbarism, barbarism taints also the manner in which it was transmitted from one owner to another. A historical materialist . . . regards it as his task to brush history against the grain.[50]

Whether advisedly or not, Shakespeare seems precisely to have taken up this task as his own.

In the rest of my Introduction and the six chapters of my book, I explore the ways in which an emergent archaeological consciousness of Rome and its ruins (both in Italy and England), together with the epochal knowledge of dissection provided by the new science of anatomy, are brought to bear on structure, bodies, characters, and motifs of Shakespeare's Roman works and made them matter for his (and our) own modernity. The chapters are organized according to the chronology of their composition. In my first chapter on *Titus Andronicus*, which I see as a sort of "Manifesto", I deal with its oneiric, layered temporality, its prevailing amputating and self-amputating protocol, and the way it affects the playwright's appropriation of the library and memory of ancient Rome. In my chapter on *The Rape of Lucrece*, the long-drawn self-dissecting mourning action of the violated Lucrece in front of the "skillful" Troy painting takes centre stage as a theatricalized process of self-knowledge grounded on the symbolism offered by Troy's ruins. Far from considering this as an aestheticized digression, I see Lucrece's transaction with the painting and precisely with the depicted sorrow of Hecuba ("In [Hecuba] the painter had anatomized time's ruin"), as an unsettling kind of performance art, a physical way of shaping her very body into a live and denouncing *tabula anatomica* of trauma and woe. In my third chapter on *Julius Caesar* I suggest a reading of Caesar's parable of glory and ruin as if it were a *pre-* and *post-mortem* dispute between two different kinds of orators coming to terms with the "Colossus" *par excellence* and its Fall ("O what a fall was there", 3.2.188): on one side of the amphitheatre Cassius, the deconstructive scientific anatomist, on the other Antony, the memorialist interested in gathering up Caesar's mangled body and in remythologizing it as a ghostly and sacred relic ("Thou art the ruines of the noblest man", 3.1.256). The fourth chapter deals with the construction of Coriolanus as an isolated clay giant, a monolithic if fragile archaeological embodiment of *Romanitas*, and the way the character is linked to a self-devouring and crumbling city. Drawing on our present concern for issues of otherness, hospitality, and gift giving, I explore the ways in which his atrophied sense of cohabitation is interwoven with the problem of memory and the catastrophe of a lost city and forgotten humanism. My last two chapters deal with the ways in which Rome's myth is renegotiated from the distant geographies of Britain (*Cymbeline*) and Egypt (*Antony and Cleopatra*), each entailing a different way of performing the idea of *translatio imperii*: one historically and ideologically mediated by the sense of Britain's growing self-awareness as an imperial country, the other imbued with loss and lasting desire. The chronologically inverted discussion of *Cymbeline* and *Antony and Cleopatra* is strategic. In deciding to conclude this volume with *Antony and Cleopatra*, I intend to bring to the fore what can be seen as Shakespeare's double way of coming to terms with the memory of Rome and classical humanism. Against the ideological and circumscribed nationalist framework of *Cymbeline*'s claim, I propose to view the geographically dilated, transnational, or global vision of *Antony and Cleopatra* as Shakespeare's everlasting fascination with Rome.

"Like the Limbs of a Mighty Giant": Archaeologizing Rome

In Salvatore Settis's insightful definition, ruins stand for fragmentation, yet paradoxically their meaning resides in their resilience, in the way they resist the passing of time:

> In the tradition of Western culture ruins stand for absence and presence at the same time: they exhibit, nay they *are*, an intersection of visible and invisible. What is invisible (or absent) is foregrounded by the ruins' fragmentation, their uselessness or even unintelligibility, their lost functionality (or if nothing less, their original functionality). Yet, well beyond the loss of their value-in-use, their obstinate, visible presence bears witness to the perdurability and eternity of ruins, their victory on the inexorable flow of time. The saying attributed to Bede ("as long as the Coliseum lasts, Rome does; and as long Rome lasts, the world does") didn't refer to the Coliseum in its full bloom—as an amphitheatre which could host tens of thousands of onlookers—but rather already (as is the case nowadays) as a gigantic wreck continuously dying, and yet still alive.[51]

Rome was tantamount to its ruins, a dismembered body, to the eyes of those—Italians and foreigners—who visited the city in the years prior to or encompassing the lengthy span of the Renaissance. "The public and private edifices, that were founded for eternity, lie prostrate, naked, and broken, like the limbs of a mighty giant; and the ruin is the more visible, from the stupendous relics that have survived the injuries of time and fortune". This is how ancient Rome appeared to the famous Italian humanist Poggio Bracciolini (1380–1459)—the author of *Ruinarum Romae Descriptio* [*Description of the Ruins of Rome*], the first of a four-volume work entitled *De varietate fortunae* (1448)—from the height of the Capitoline Hill, while walking among the ruins with his Latinist friend, Antonio Loschi, and carrying out, in the form of a *promenade erudite*, his meditation on ruins and on fortune as the engine of history. Rome was anthropomorphically identified as a skeletal and fragmented "mighty giant" (if we refer to the Englished parts of Poggio's *Ruins of Rome* provided by Gibbon in the concluding chapter 71 of his *Decline and Fall of the Roman Empire*, 1776–88, and from which I am quoting). More precisely, it was visualized as a gigantic "decaying corpse", if we follow Poggio's Latin original more closely: "[*Urbis Romae*] *iaceat instar gigantei cadaueris corrupti, atque undique exesi*".[52] The first book of Poggio's *De varietate fortunae* was widely circulated in Renaissance Europe as a separate volume (the rest would be printed only in 1723), both as a manuscript (of which many copies are extant) and a number of printed editions (Strasbourg 1510, 1511, 1513; Paris 1511; Basel 1538). Increasingly acknowledged as the first, revolutionary (if unsystematic) example of archaeological approach to the study of ancient Rome, it strongly contributed to establish a transnational imagery and lexicon in the way the Renaissance responded to Rome's ruins. *Ruinarum Romae Descriptio* strengthened the topicality of Rome as an epitome of "*de varietate fortunae*" ["the impermanence of fortune"]. But it also contributed to cast the early Renaissance discovery of the far-removed classical past, literally and metaphorically, as an act of digging and disinterment, as well as a finding that was archaeologically complex and elusive.[53] As Leonard Barkan has observed in relation to the discovery of the Laocoön sculpture in 1506 and other emergent artefacts,

> What places the unearthed object at the center of [the coeval] aesthetic debates is its specially elliptical quality. That the statue emerges from the ground, that it is to some extent deprived of physical and historical context, that it is imperfect—all these circumstances contribute to a sense that the image is in itself incomplete.

But what "re-enters" into the world is also explosive in the way it is revealed to be not "new" but "radical", as Barkan has it.[54]

Poggio, a transnational figure of erudite at the court of the popes, was famous for having devoted his life to the search of disappeared classical manuscripts all over Europe, England included—where he sojourned repeatedly, the first time for five years, on the invitation of the bishop of Winchester, Henry de Beaufort. Arguably, he cared very much for his English patrons if, before dedicating his *Ruins* to his humanist Pope Nicholas V, he first considered dedicating it to King Henry VI, he himself—allegedly—a patron of Italian humanism.[55] The list of Poggio's many finds includes quite a few works by Cicero and, notably, Lucretius's *De rerum natura*. But he was also acknowledged as a classicist of high standing for his transcriptions of ancient manuscripts and his groundbreaking work in deciphering Roman inscriptions, whose interpretation had been forgotten.[56] It is in terms of loss and mourning—mindful of a memory transmitted by ancient Roman literature—as well as those of distance, material discovery, and novel forms of interrogation, that his enquiry on Rome's ruins was led:

> This Tarpeian rock was then a savage and solitary thicket: in the time of the poet [Virgil], it was crowned with the golden roofs of a temple; the temple is overthrown, the gold has been pillaged, the wheel of fortune has accomplished her revolution, and the sacred ground is again disfigured with thorns and brambles. The hill of the Capitol, on which we sit, was formerly the head of the Roman empire, the citadel of the earth, the terror of kings; illustrated by the footsteps of so many triumphs, enriched with the spoils and tributes of so many nations. *This spectacle of the world, how is it fallen! how changed! how defaced!* The path of victory is obliterated by vines, and the benches of the senators are concealed by a dunghill. Cast your eyes on the Palatine hill, and seek among the shapeless and enormous fragments the marble theatre, the obelisks, the colossal statues, the porticos of Nero's palace: survey the other hills of the city, the vacant space is interrupted only by ruins and gardens. The forum of the Roman people, where they assembled to enact their laws and elect their magistrates, is now enclosed for the cultivation of pot-herbs, or thrown open for the reception of swine and buffaloes.[57]
>
> (my emphasis)

Field archaeology took its first steps by disclosing a theatrical, and utterly tragic, scenario which—around the meanings of a colossal and fragmented bodily image—merged landscape and limbs, organic and inorganic, visible and invisible. Poggio's recalling of Rome's *grandeur* from the height of the "defaced" Capitoline Hill, the heart and symbol of imperial power,[58] is one with the disproportion of its fractured and disseminated body and the enormity of its injuries and fall. As such it seems to resonate in Antony's words on Caesar's mangled body: "O what a fall was there!" (*JC*, 3.2.188), as if an anthropomorphic and archaeologized view of ancient Rome had added new language to figure out and explore, in terms of the colossal and the fragmented, Caesar's fall, the catastrophe, the ruin/relic/remain *par excellence* ("Thou art the ruines of the noblest man", *JC*, 3.1.256).

The attention that Poggio's work has received among historians, archaeologists, philologists, and culturalists, for the role it played in the development of a humanist and Renaissance culture grounded in the material discovery of the classical past, has been conspicuously increasing over the years.[59] However, it can be profitable in this context to pause a little on the particular attraction (often emphasized by critics) that his *Ruins* held for the eighteenth-century historian Edward Gibbon, who apart from translating and reporting excerpts of Poggio's dramatic beginning on the Capitoline Hill in the last volume of his *Decline and Fall*, rhetorically situated himself in the same highly symbolic ruinous place—the place where "the golden roofs of a temple" once stood—when in 1764, as he recounts, he started thinking of his work:

> It was among the ruins of the Capitol that I first conceived the idea of a work which has amused and exercised near twenty years of my life, and which, however inadequate to my own wishes, I finally deliver to the curiosity and candor of the public. Lausanne, June 27, 1787.[60]

By that time, as scholars have rightly observed, the wilderness of Poggio's Capitol had long changed into the *grand* square designed by Michelangelo which, together with a previous thirteenth-century Christian church, had completely effaced any sign of the ancient ruins.[61] And yet, Poggio's opening image of the city beheaded of its golden Capitol ("the head of the Roman empire, the citadel of the earth") proved to be a strong and lasting literary reminiscence of ruin, a trace indelibly impressed in the archaeology of mind and memory, one might say, if Gibbon deemed it expedient to conjure it up to symbolically frame the space of his historical narrative of Rome's "decline and fall". As a matter of fact, Gibbon's appropriation of Poggio was well suited to a project aiming at reconciling, as Patricia Craddock puts it, a "cautiously progressive philosophy of historical change with his elegiac and even tragic tone". For, as she concludes,

> As a narrative artist, Gibbon knew what as a philosophic historian he never articulated: all change including growth, implies death. Death may not be followed by immortality, but immortality never occurs, in history, until after death. The immortal Romes of the senators and the emperors were ultimately significant not in their fleeting triumphs, but in their declines and falls, in the lasting stones and shadows of their ruins.[62]

But this highlights all the more, I argue, the uncanny sense of fracture, rising from Poggio's aporetic Rome in his humanist and ensuing
Renaissance time, especially as it was epitomized by his chosen point
of departure, the height of the Capitoline Hill—a powerfully connoted
empty space, a presence without a presence—long since deprived of its
legendary and glittering golden temple and long since lost to sight. A
highly symbolic monument, more than once destroyed and re-edified by
a sequel of emperors, before being razed down for good in the Goths'
repeated sacks of Rome in the 410–450s CE, Rome's crowning temple of
Jupiter could only be evoked by Poggio with the words of Virgil's mythical
memory: "*Aurea nunc, olim siluestribus horrida dumis*" ("Golden now,
then bristling with woodland thickets", *Aeneid*, 8, 348).[63] Other "vacant
space[s]" were utterly unrecoverable to memory, framed by the ghostly
language of ruins, if any.

As it is well known, and as I have mentioned, the ancient written past
was also part of the ruinous picture. Meaningfully Petrarch, a precursor
of the archaeological concern in his own time, used the same term—
ruinae—to refer to surviving and maimed ancient texts, as if they were
relics which had escaped disaster or simply oblivion.[64] But Shakespeare
shows the same all-encompassing ruinous understanding of the past when
he has his Lucrece expand on Time as a whimsical dispenser of riches
and wreck. Also, as if endowed with her author's own archaeological
sense of cultural belatedness, she extends to the material life of books
Time's altering agency: "Time's glory is . . . / To ruinate proud buildings
with thy hours, / And smear with dust their glitt'ring golden towers; / To
fill with worm-holes stately monuments, / To feed oblivion with decay
of things, / To blot old books and alter their contents" (*The Rape of
Lucrece*, 939–48). Meaning itself and the assumed Horacian or Ovidian
eternity of the word are here on a par with physical architectures in being
exposed to the injuries of time and instability.[65] European Humanism and
Renaissance, which confidently grounded their enterprise on a rediscovered classic past, were also (from Poggio to Shakespeare) melancholically
haunted by the ruinous role of abandonment and forgetfulness and the
ways this could devour monuments as well as manuscripts. As Greenblatt
suggestively has it:

> Between the sixth century and the middle of the eight century,
> Greek and Latin classics virtually ceased to be copied at all. What
> had begun as an active campaign to forget—a pious attack on
> pagan ideas—had evolved into actual forgetting. The ancient
> poems, philosophical treatises, and political speeches, at one time
> so threatening and alluring, were no longer in anyone's mind, let
> alone on anyone's lips. They had been reduced to the condition of
> mute things, sheets of parchment, stitched together, covered with
> unread words.[66]

The ruined materiality of surviving literature and surviving stones underpins the discovery of Rome by means of what is visible as well as what is missing in the nascent archaeological endeavour of the fifteenth-century humanists to recover the long-lost memory of an original topographical order of the ancient City. "A fallen fragment was honoured with the name of Hadrian"; from afar, "Beside a bridge . . . he could discern, of the age of the republic, a double row of vaults", Gibbon comments, three centuries later, in resuming Poggio's search of Rome among her colossal body of ruins.[67] Gibbon's *Decline and Fall of the Roman Empire* was published in 1788, on the eve the French Revolution, when again the myth of Rome's glory—strongly imbued with the sight or memory of ruin—"heliotropically" turned (in the earlier discussed sense of Benjamin's) towards the present of European history with the urgency of a flashing and uncanny knowledge. Rome was not new: it was archaeologically "radical" (Barkan).

We might comment on this new episteme announced by the emerging discipline of field archaeology in the Renaissance with Foucault's distinction between "document" and "monument" and the way the two interacted in a period in which history was "primarily and fundamentally *memory*". "There was a time", he says, "when archaeology, as a discipline devoted to silent monuments, inert traces, objects without context, and things left by the past, aspired to the condition of history, and attained meaning only through the restitution of historical discourse".[68] In this memorializing endeavour of both "history in its traditional form" and archaeology, Foucault continues, *monuments* tended to be transformed into ideologized *documents*. We cannot be sure whether, in saying this, the philosopher was thinking of this very first humanist stage of archaeology and whether we may equate an early modern notion of history (hardly distinguishable as a discipline from other pre-existent and nascent forms of knowledge and learning) to what he means by "history in its traditional form". But the consequences of the archaeological method of analysis he proposes as a new way of understanding history are all there to be seen as part of the material unearthing of the past that was being started in Poggio's time. With Foucault we can say that chronology is broken by re-emerging, and intermingled, short if unexpected period strata of events and temporalities, with the consequence that "the notion of discontinuity assumes a major role", together with an uncanny pressure of "the raw material of history, which presented itself in the form of dispersed events": what an advancing historicism would learn to reduce, if not "to efface in order to reveal the continuity of events". More precisely, and seemingly agreeing with Benjamin, he adds, "Discontinuity was the stigma of temporal dislocation that it was the historian's task to remove from history. It has now become one of the basic elements of historical analysis".[69] In other words, for all its unsystematicity, Renaissance Roman archaeology announced the story of a progressively documented but hardly achievable completeness, which is akin to Foucault's acceptation of the idea of the archive and the archaeological.[70] This coincided with a burgeoning conceptualization of ancient Rome as symbolizing both the concept of totality or ecumenicity (*oikoumene* in Greek is the sum total of inhabited lands)[71] and what I would call an ever-changing rhizomatic space that could not be reduced to a fixed and complete physical form.

A disciple of Coluccio Salutati and a friend of Niccolò Niccoli, the most passionate collectors in Florence and Europe of rediscovered ancient books and disinterred statues,[72] Poggio was not alone in his endeavour to fathom the form of the shapeless "giant" once he moved from Florence to Rome, where he went to serve as apostolic secretary at the court of the popes. In an environment which included men of erudition (or antiquarians, as they were then called) as important as the Latinist Antonio Loschi, the epigraphist Cyriaco d'Ancona, and the architect Leon Battista Alberti, another renowned humanist—Flavio Biondo—had also undertaken the task of collecting the limbs of the "mighty giant" in his *Roma instaurata* (1444–46) ["Rome Restored" or "Revived"], translated from Latin into Italian (together with *Italia Illustrata*) by Lucio Fauno in 1542. But more than being interested in documenting and archaeologically describing ruins as such, eventually within the philosophical framework of a reflection on the variation of fortunes and the instability of kingdoms and empires, like Poggio's project, Biondo's was propelled by a broader memorializing intent: that of making Rome's ancient topography reacquire its history, namely by "writing Rome into existence", as some might put it.[73] Drawing on his highly esteemed scholarly knowledge of ancient sources, Biondo recomposed Rome's imposing topography by recollecting and reassigning names to its ancient walls, gates, obelisks, emperors' houses and gardens, public spaces, forum, temples, arches, baths, and theatres and amphitheatres, thus making it live again in all its extension and monumentality. "Many reasons, your Holiness, lead me to undertake the task of harking back to the memory of Rome's ancient edifices; or better the ruins that we are left to see of the City which was once the mistress of the world", Biondo wrote at the outset of his dedicatory preface to Pope Eugenius IV.[74] But his project also aimed at comparing and reconnecting, in terms of continuity, the ancient and the new Rome,[75] which implied the celebration of the recent, gradual rebirth of the city by drawing attention on the early Renaissance "fabrics", which the popes, prompted by many, were undertaking to build in the aftermath of their return to Rome after a long time of exile in Avignon.[76] Interestingly, he also wanted to highlight the role Rome might still claim as the Christian "mistress of the world"—a Rome resurrecting from and being literally rebuilt upon her own ruins—according to an interpretation of *translatio imperii* grounded on a domestic *renovation*, which in that time could only coincide with Rome's primacy as the head of Christianity. For, even though "all memory of hers had disappeared with the legions, consuls, senate, the beauty and ornaments of the Capitol and the Palatine", Biondo argued,

> Rome can still boast to this day a magisterium upon realms and nations, for the maintenance and increase of which there is no need of armies, horses, or infantry . . . religion is enough. . . . Our emperor is not Caesar's successor, but the successor and Vicar of the fisherman Peter who is more than worshipped by all Princes of the world. . . . Most of Europe pays tributes to Rome in equal if not superior amount to that of ancient times.
>
> (60–61)

Rome is celebrated as a cosmopolitan site of cult worthy of being revered by a good part of the world which "by choice and willingly submits and bows to the authority of Rome" (62). It is clear that the humanist Biondo cannot advocate for the cause of the ancient pagan ruins to the ears of his Holy Patron, without taking on the cause of the Christian Rome. In his *captatio benevolentiae* rhetoric, Rome can triumphantly boast an infinite number of churches with sacred relics, teeming with thousands and thousands of pilgrims eager to admire and touch them, arriving yearly from the most disparate parts of the world. Biondo takes pains to list them one after the other, and notably, he concludes, from "the English island, however divided it is geographically from us" (62). It may be expedient to keep Biondo in mind when dealing with Shakespeare's same conflation of the two Romes in *Cymbeline*, and the role "tributes" play in keeping (and not keeping) them together in the perception of early modern England.

That Rome might kindle nothing like reverence in post-Reformation England is also interesting to notice. "I was at Pontius Pilate's house, and pissed against it", we are brashly informed by Jack Wilton, Thomas Nashe's imaginary traveller (1594).[77] As has been said by many, Jack is a mouthpiece for all sorts of popular prejudices about a corrupt, mischievous, and perilous Italy, or part of it (with Rome not the least part of it), but he is also a sensor for other forms of anxiety: regarding relics, for instance, or also sight and beauty.[78] True. To a Protestant the threat that the faithful may yield to the visual fascination of monuments, or opulent shrines, could be a good reason for travelling by keeping sight under surveillance. However, it is noteworthy in this context that, upon arriving in Rome, what seems to be not a small nuisance to Nashe's traveller is the encounter with an "overinscripted" place, an excess of historicity and memory, which he is eager to eliminate as hastily as possible. Rome's inhabitants are ridiculed for their obsession with records and memorials: "There was a poor fellow during my remainder there that, for a new trick that he had invented of killing cimex and scorpions, had his mountebank banner hung up on a high pillar, with an inscription about it longer than the King of Spain's style" (43). And not unsurprisingly he suffers with semi passivity his guided visit to Rome's antiquities. His Roman host had showed him "all the monuments that were to be seen, which are as many as there have been emperors, consuls, orators, conquerors, famous painters or players in Rome" (42–43).

> The chiefest thing that my eyes delighted in was the church of the seven Sibyls, which is a most miraculous thing, all their prophecies and oracles being there enrolled, as also the beginning and ending of their whole catalogue of the heathen gods, with their manner of worship. There are a number of other shrines and statues dedicated to the emperors, and withal some statues of idolatry reserved for detestation. . . . These are but the shop dust of the sights that I saw, and in truth I did not behold with any care hereafter to report, but contented my eye for the present, & so let them pass; should I memorize half the miracles which they were told me had been done martyrs' tombs, or the operations of the earth of the Sepulchre and other relics brought from Jerusalem, I should be counted the most monstrous liar that ever came in print. The ruins of Pompey's theatre, reputed one of the nine wonders of the world, Gregory the Sixth's tomb, Priscilla's grate, or the thousands of pillars areared amongst the rased foundations of old Rome, it were frivolous to specify, since he that hath but once drunk with a traveller talks of them.

Rome (first introduced as "the queen of the world & metropolitan mistress of all other cities", 42) is too often remembered and talked about to deserve specific record or remembrance. Or, if remembered, it is a matter doomed to be soon forgotten. Well before Freud, but humorously, Nashe's protagonist seems to be aware that Rome is an all-embracing "catalogue", the closest to what we might intend as an overwhelming and hybrid palimpsest of stones and inscriptions, which he airily laughs away (together with his funny inventor of bedbugs traps), as a sight-limited indulgence, or venial sin of sight, before veering abruptly to the tale of his own private disadventures: "Let me be a historiographer of my own misfortunes, and not meddle with the continued trophies of so old a triumphing city" (43).

It is difficult, after such a coarse version of Castiglione's *sprezzatura*, to go back to humanists like Poggio and Biondo, to whom we owe the beginning of what we might call Rome's augmented memory: actually a historicized turn in the way of addressing antiquities. And yet we must, if we want to add a concluding word on the role they played in fostering attention for Rome's ruins as both a question and a poetics. In Humanist and Renaissance Italy (and Europe), ruins emerged as a matter of cultural memory as well as the "Thing" (one might well say with Hamlet), the uncanny and unavoidable anteriority, in respect to which artists conceived of form and craved for their eternity of their art. Indeed, ruins were also pivotal in fuelling and relaunching the debate in the field of art theory and the visual arts. In an age in which the museum as an institution was far to come, the concern for ruins was also understood as a wider undertaking of documentation, on the part of painters and antiquarians like Mantegna, Raphael, Rubens, Pirro Ligorio, Cassiano dal Pozzo, which aimed at constructing a painted or a so-called paper museum (Cassiano dal Pozzo), while also marking the concomitant beginning of the phenomenon of antiquity collection, as recorded in Lorenzo Lotto's *Portrait of Andrea Odoni* (1527), acknowledged as the first testimony of such a topic in the visual arts.[79]

Humanists like Biondo, Poggio, Alberti, and others paved the way to all this. Taken together they represented a move beyond the medieval consideration of Rome's antiquities as mute *mirabilia*, while elucidating a difference marked by the emergence (with Bracciolini) of a new archaeological paradigm. Rome's ruins were part history, part myth; many were simply part of the unknown. But after Poggio, ruins are not only topographically restored to their names and places, if any, by means of their pre-existing monumentalizing written memory. They invade the eyes of the beholders not simply as materials which can be explained away by the ordering and monumentalizing memory of the knowledgeable classicist, but rather (ancient texts included) as a forgotten and damaged reservoir of documents calling for the—virtually interminable—deciphering and sceptical work of archaeology, epigraphy, and philology;[80] or, in some cases, reinventing poetry. Indeed, the shapeless and scattered form of the gigantic "decaying corpse" resists mythical comparisons with the surviving knowledge of the ancients because of an otherness, an unreadability, which calls for the work of new scrutinizing—eventually healing—disciplines. But such a "being-with" ruins (Derrida),[81] archaeologically nourishes a sense of history and of (one's) art as marked by the unsettling set of meanings that stem from "vacant spaces" and "dispersed events" (Foucault), namely from the confused and catastrophic chronology of ruins. And yet ruins also referred to a long temporality, a "cosmos", we might say with Panofsky, drawing on his distinction between document and monument: "These records have therefore the quality of emerging from the stream of time. . . . The cosmos of culture, like the cosmos of nature, is a spatio-temporal structure", but different from "evolutionary time".[82]

It was as part of a yearning, if frustrated, search for meaning and completeness that the discovery and appropriation of Rome also prompted a taste for fake inscriptions. As Peter Spring has written:

> Through inscriptions the antiquarian could look beyond buildings or monuments to the emperors who dedicated them or to the countless ordinary men and women of antiquity who were enshrined in them. Inscriptions gave voice to the tacit, and life to the inert. They turned

brick and stone into literate gestures of commemorations, whether heroic or poignant, and communicated them to posterity. . . . So emotional was the response they evoked, that the appetite for them eventually found vicarious satisfaction in fakes.[83]

When visiting Rome in 1580–81, where he sojourned for five months, Montaigne showed that digging into oblivion, craving for a full meaning of the collapsed "mighty giant", had partly exhausted its humanist pathos, if not its projectuality, leaving additional space for scepticism. In the face of more than one generation of antiquarians, poets, and architects (Du Bellay and Palladio among the latest) who attempted to conjecture from one ruined detail the shape of an entire building or culture,[84] Montaigne marked a difference when he declared it was useless to try to fathom the depth of Rome's ruins, declaring his preference for an "abstract" idea of the ancient city. To his valet and scrivener to whom (in the third person), he dictated a good part of his *Journal de voyage en Italie,*

> He observed: that there is nothing to be seen of ancient Rome but the sky under which it had risen and stood, and the outline of its form; that the knowledge he had of it was altogether abstract and contemplative, no image of it remaining to satisfy the senses; that those who said that the ruins of Rome at least remained, said more than they were warranted in saying; for the ruins of so stupendous and awful a fabric ["*si espouvantable machine*"] would enforce more honour and reverence for its memory; nothing he said remained of Rome but its sepulchre. The world in hatred of its long domination, had first destroyed and broken in pieces the various parts of this wondrous body; and then, finding that, even though prostrate and dead, its disfigured remains still filled them with fear and hate, they buried the ruins itself.[85]

In the same logic, what they purposely destroyed and buried forever, Montaigne argued, was "that which was finest and most worthy of preservation in the imperial city" (572). Montaigne was not an unprepared or hasty consumer of ruins. Once in Rome he bought quite a few books and maps which he used to read overnight before undertaking his daily tours. We are not told their titles and authors, but it is likely that Poggio's and Biondo's works (which he was able to read in Latin) were both among his purchases. His reflections on the grandeur of Rome's dead body owes much to Poggio's fragmented "mighty giant" (*Ruins of Rome*), and Montaigne followed him almost *verbatim* when he said, "He fully believed that an ancient Roman, could one be brought back, would not be able to recognize the place" (573).[86] However, differently from Poggio, or Biondo, or other archaeologically minded humanists, Montaigne suspended interpretation, or "subreading", in the words of Greene,[87] of what remained. For, he said,

> in truth, many of the conjectures which one has formed from pictures of the ancient city, are not at all borne out, when you get there, for even the site has undergone infinite changes; some of the valleys are filled up . . . by the gradual agglomeration of the ruins of old Rome; so, the *Monte Savello* is nothing but the heaped-up ruins of part of the theatre of Marcellus.
>
> (572–573)

Indeed, the mass of ruins piled up by diggings "had attained the height and size of natural mountains". Hence it was in the excess of their quantity rather than in their indiscernible quality, he seemed to say, that their grandeur resided—"a strange and amazing proof of grandeur"—which was in itself arresting, one which made the world understand "how surpassing was the glory and pre-eminence of the city against which they had conspired" (572). Montaigne's vision of Rome's ruins is the spectacle of how a search for the topographical original order of the ancient city was met with the production of further ruins. Ruins were no path to knowledge. Ordering meant further disorder, he seemed to suggest.

Montaigne showed more concern for the ways in which modern Rome was intermingled with the ancient one, but such a Rome didn't appear to him as an achieved "*Roma instaurata*" (Flavio Biondo), a restored and newly rising Rome built or reconstructed on the basis of the authoritative models of the ancients, but rather as a "bastard Rome", the product of a bizarre continuity dictated by chance. He observed

> that the buildings of this bastard Rome, which the moderns were raising upon, or appending to, the glorious structures of the antique world, though they sufficed enough to excite the admiration of the present age, yet seemed to him to bear a close resemblance to those nests, which the rooks and the swallows construct upon the roofs and walls of the churches in France, which the Huguenots have demolished.
>
> (572)

And still, emphasizing the process of entombing and the agency of chance:

> The modern architects never think of looking for any other foundation for their houses than the tops of old building, the roofs of which ordinarily form the floors of modern cellars . . . they securely base their own structure upon the ruined tops of the structure below, just as chance has happened to dispose them during the lapse of ages.
>
> (573)

Rome as it appears to Montaigne is not so much the humanist Rome of memory and recollection of its ruins as rather, sceptically, the Rome of fragmentation and casual and outrageous reuse, a city whose inhabitants are daily engaged in stepping on the edifices of their ancestors: "the modern Romans walked on the tops of the houses of their ancestors . . . almost everywhere you see beneath your feet the tops of ancient walls which the rain and the coaches have laid bare" (568). And so, while shunning the excavating and conjectural procedures of the rising Renaissance archaeology, what Montaigne brought to the fore was exactly the anxiety which was at the core of archaeology, the confused chronology of its objects of study and the prospective failure of its reordering projectuality, which he condensed in the hallucinatory verticality of a solitary pillar experienced through the upside-down perspective provided by excavation: "It has more than once happened that, after digging a long way down, the workmen have come to the top of some high column, which still remained standing on its base far beneath" (573).

Voyage to Italy remained unknown to readers until 1774. Had it circulated in Shakespeare's time we might have inferred that Shakespeare had learned from Montaigne this sceptical, modern way of dealing with the bodily and textual fragments of Rome in *Titus Andronicus*, but also his "undulating" manner of handling ruins, memory, ancestry, and the heritage of Rome in *Julius Caesar*, *Antony and Cleopatra*, or *Hamlet*. But since this was not the case, one may conclude that they were simply contemporaries.

"Not Marble, nor the Gilded Monuments": Ruins and Poetical Power

The attraction of ruins—an "afflatus" in Margaret Ferguson's recasting of the traditional pathos associated with ruins[88]—has always been equal to the drive of poets to prevail on the menace of destruction and death, or also ambiguous temporality, with the eternity of their poetry. The theme is as old as Horace and Ovid, who are customarily conjured up in relation to the resonances we may feel in Shakespeare's so-called sonnets of immortality, and especially in sonnet 55 (in conjunction with sonnets 15–19, 81, 107, 115, 123, 125).[89] Let us consider Horace's famous verses: "I have finished a monument more lasting than bronze and loftier than the Pyramids' royal pile" (*Odes*, 3.30.1–2).[90] The opposition between architectural and written monuments is similarly implied in Ovid/Golding's closing lines of his *Metamorphoses*: "Now have I brought a work to end which neither Jove's fierce wrath / Nor sword, nor fire, nor fretting age with all the force it hath / Are able to abolish quite" (VX, 984–86).[91] But both the Augustan poets, anxiously (or eulogistically), link the durability of their poetry to the destiny of Rome. Here is Ovid (*Met.*): "For look how far so ever / The Roman empire by the right of conquest shall extend,

/ So far shall all folk read this work. And time without all end / (If poets as by prophecy about the truth may aim) / My life shall everlastingly be lengthened still by fame" (XV, 991–95). And here is Horace: "On and on shall I grow, ever fresh with the glory of after time. So long as the Pontiff climbs the Capitol with the silent Vestal" (3.30.7–9). Virgil is on the same line when he writes, "If aught my verse avail, no day shall ever blot you from the memory of time, so long as the house of Aeneas shall dwell on the Capitol's unshaken rocks, and the Father of Rome hold sovereign sway!" (*Aeneid*, 9.446–49).

Poetic immortality finds an imaginable measure in the incommensurability of Rome. But when we come to *Tristia*, the work Ovid wrote during his exile in Tomis (on the Black Sea), it is as if the author's ruin, that is, his exclusion from Rome as a fatherly centre of power,[92] had, conversely, proved empowering for his poetry ("Little book, you will go without me", 1.1.1), which can now envisage its (and the author's) eternity as relying, solely, though perhaps more reassuringly, on the strength of an everlasting, if contingent, chain of reading:

> What a memorial I have reared to thee in my books, O my wife, dearer to me than myself, thou seest. Though thy fate may take much from their author, thou at least shalt be made illustrious by my powers. As long as men read me thy fame shall be read along with me.
>
> (V.XIV.1–5)[93]

Is this passage of power and durability from monarchs or realms to authorship and readership ("As long as I am read") what may have proved attractive to Shakespeare? But also, was the Renaissance vision of Rome as a ruinous scenario (of texts and stones) avoidable, considering the fact that a prevailing rebirth (through imitation/appropriation and transmission) stemmed precisely from an impulse to make sense of ruins?

Now that Latin poets had already made the rivalry between marble and word a well-worn trope is largely known. Less obvious is the fact that antiquaries and topographers could claim the same role as poets in the eyes of posterity when, in the Italian "Quattrocento", they began the monumental work of piecing together the fragmented "mighty giant". In fact, they were well aware that the written memorization of Rome was aimed at constructing a monument more durable than stones. A case in point is Flavio Biondo, the already mentioned author of *Roma instaurata*, who in offering Pope Eugenius IV his work, which he presented as a gift in the process of a Rome being built anew, also revived the ancient trope of rivalry between kings and poets, word and masonry, written and physical cities. Interestingly, he left to posterity the task of judging whether the resurging Rome—in its process of being "remade", "readjusted", "renewed" ("*rifatta*", "*riconciata*", "*rinovata*") by the papal masons and architects—was destined "to be more stable and enduring by means of works of marble, stones, bronze or rather by means of literature and writing" ("ad esser più stabil[e], & a durare per piu tempo, per questa via d'opera di calcie, pietre, di bronzo, che per la via de le lettere, e de la scrittura").[94] Du Bellay will make recourse to the same trope in the concluding sonnet of his French *Ruines of Rome*: "Hope ye my verses that posteritie / Of age ensuing shall you ever read? . . . / If under heaven anie endurance were, / These moniments, which not in paper writ, / But in Porphyre and Marble doo appeare, / Might well have hop'd to have obtained it. (son. 32.1–8).

It is tempting to think that Biondo's "written Rome", the first systematic and monumental guide to Rome's ruins and topography, which was certainly familiar to early modern English travellers such as William Thomas who, unlike Nashe, visited Rome—perhaps in the more accessible 1542 Italian translation provided by Fauno (who enlarged it to include Biondo's geographical *Italia illustrata*)—may have been browsed by Shakespeare too—since, allegedly without ever setting foot in Rome or any other part of Italy, he contributed to write or rewrite such places so indelibly into existence in his own works. Be that as it may, Shakespeare is definitely assimilating an early modern way of discovering and coping with ruins to an ancient trope of poetical immortality, when in his sonnet 55 he meditates on collapsing architectures and constructs, in the face of their mortality, an empowering personal myth of eternity.

> Not marble, nor the gilded monuments,
> Of princes, shall outlive this powerful rhyme;
> But you shall shine more bright in this contents
> Than unswept stone, besmeared with sluttish time.
> When wasteful war shall statues overturn
> And broils root out the work of masonry,
> Nor Mars his sword, nor war's quick fire, shall burn
> The living record of your memory:
> 'Gainst death, and all oblivious enmity,
> Shall you pace forth; your praise shall still find room
> Even in the eyes of all posterity
> That wear this world out to the ending doom.
>   So, till the judgement that you yourself arise,
>   You live in this, and dwell in lovers' eyes.

In the context of this volume, the question worth posing is up to what extent Rome is present in Shakespeare's sonnets. As I have said, Rome is never mentioned. Yet, we hear the city resonate in the way its very vocabulary, beheaded of its subject (Rome), pervades Shakespeare's more general meditation on Time, Time declined with Ovid as "devouring time" (son. 19), but also Time as a paradigm of a natural cycle of "increase" and "decrease" (son. 15), as well a historical agent of proud monumentality and fragmentation (son. 55, 107). More specifically, might the image of vulnerable "gilded monuments" in the opening line of sonnet 55 (customarily understood as princely tombs) be taken as a reference to Rome's golden temple (or temples) of the Capitoline Hill made legendary by Virgil as well as Pliny, Ovid, and Seneca, among others, and most notably (for their destruction by fire during the AD 69 civil war) by Tacitus (*Histories*, 3.71–72)?[95] This is supported by a similar image occurring in Lucrece's reflection on Time whose "office", she laments, is "To ruinate proud buildings with thy hours, / And smear with dust their glitt'ring golden towers; / To fill with worm-holes stately monuments" (*The Rape*, vv. 945–46); an occurrence signalling perhaps a contemporaneity in writing and, more importantly, a broader concern for Rome's ruinous imagery which started early in Shakespeare's career, permeating his works as both a poet and a playwright.

In fact other images in sonnet 55 remind us all too rapidly of the "quick fire [s]" ignited by those internecine wars that (from *Titus Andronicus* to *Julius Caesar*) the playwright proves to be very good at staging, while also referring us (under cover) to his own post-Reformation times, hardly lacking in "wasteful wars" and "statues overturn[ed]" (line 5). But take also the aforementioned oblique assonance between Rome and "room" hinted at in lines 9–11 ("'Gainst death, and all oblivious enmity, / . . . your praise shall still find room / Even in the eyes of all posterity")—an assonance waiting to be perfected and played upon in *Julius Caesar* ("Now it is Rome indeed, and room enough", 1.2.155). In sum, in light of such an unmistakably Roman cluster of images, phonetic allusions, and travelling meanings, sonnet 55 might well have both Rome/"room", or the fair youth, indistinctively, as its addressee, I dare suggest. In the sense that ancient Rome functions not just as an unnamed set backdrop of mortality but rather, in accordance with the role played by the poetics of ruins in Renaissance Europe, as a haunting term of comparison in testing the standard and durability of art—no matter how distancing, iconoclastic, and self-confident, or reverence-, anxiety-, and melancholy-inducing this may have been in the responses it produced in Shakespeare and a coeval "re-naissance" culture conscious of its own belatedness.

And in fact the impermanence of the architectural setting conjured up to frame the context of the poet's reflection on time and its injuries is again incontrovertibly classical in sonnet 65 ("Since brass, nor stone, nor earth"), the sonnet in which the self-confident and triumphal accent of sonnet 55 is made less assertive and the poet's "fearful meditation" also interrogatively invests the longed-for eternity of "rhyme" with a vulnerability and a scepticism which can find solace only, if at all, in the improbability of a miracle: "who his spoil o'er beauty can forbid? / O none, unless this miracle have might: / That in black ink my love may still shine bright" (65.12–14). It may be observed that the grounding of this sonnet in the current imagery of classic ruins is only announced, limited as it is to the first half part of the opening line, to be rapidly channelled into a more general sense of mortality thriving on inexhaustible and less connoted wars and ever-crumbling rocks and gates.[96] Yet, even though wrought as a haunting and soon hastily abandoned note, such imagery is important, for it allows for a conjunction of ruins past and present, and the thematization (only obliquely hinted at in the sonnets) of the rivalry between the weight of an authoritative cultural giant—in ruins though it may be—and the poet's individual capacity to "engraft [things] new" (son. 15, v. 14), or better, as is put forward in other sonnets, to monumentalize the living voice (son. 81). Did the poet work such a miracle? The answer is not all that easy as sonnet 55 (for instance) might let us think. "For we which now behold these present days / Have eyes to wonder, but lack tongues to praise", Shakespeare also wrote in sonnet 106 (13–14), the sonnet in which he overtly, and sceptically, addresses the difficulty of actualizing the past, as well as the present.

Within this context, as the complex embodiment of the defacement that Time assumes in its ruination, when "Time in time shall ruinate" (Du Bellay/Spenser, 7.10), ancient Rome turns out to be the effaced but underwritten text in Shakespeare's *Sonnets*, the uncanny trace, as omnipresent and lasting as the poetry he aims to build in "war with time" (son. 15.13).

Mobile Ruins; or, Awakening the Dead

Mixed though major reasons, as is now evident—questions of ancestry and power, the transfer or mobility of cultural authority (as Greenblatt might have it), of tributes and currency among ages and nations, not to mention issues of faith and warlike schisms—coalesce around the transnational topic of Rome's ruins, which travels through Europe imbued with the relevant dialectics between fracture and continuity, oblivion and memory. But first and foremost it involved literary genealogies, namely a theory of imitation understood as a search for individuality aggressively or anxiously pursued as an exercise in repetition and difference.

Notably, this issue in Renaissance Europe—namely the anxiety of being contemporary and original by equalling the excellence of a collapsed, if haunting cultural "giant"—had been catalyzed and problematized at its best by Joachim Du Bellay in his sonnet sequence *Antiquitez de Rome contenant une generale description de sa grandeur, et comme une deploration de sa ruine: plus un songe ou vision sur le mesme subject*, the result of his sojourn in Rome from 1553 to 1557, published together with his *Songe* in 1558.

As Greene has remarked, Du Bellay's works on the topic were "not so much about the Roman ruins as about an individual responding to ruins, trying in the already well-worn image to resurrect them".[97] Such an endeavour, in *Antiquitez de Rome*, considerably marked by a competitive belatedness and consistently imagined as an uncovering of tombs and awakening of the dead, is exploited from the outset of its ingratiatory sonnet devoted to the king of France who, in a logic of *translatio studii* (namely the transfer of cultural authority from one nation and language into another),[98] is invited to accept the poet's work (a "*petit tableau*", a poetical "picture" of the sacred "*poudreuses reliques*") as a conquest and an increase of cultural power.

> Ne vous pouvant donner ces ouvrages antiques
> Pour vostre Sainct-Germain, ou pour Fontainbleau,
> Je vous donne (Sire) en ce petit tableau
> Peint, le mieux que j'ai peu, de couleurs poëtiques.
> Qui mis sous vostre nom devant les yeux publiques,
> Si vous le daignez voir en son jour le plus beaux,
> Se pourra bien vanter d'avoir hors du tombeau
> Tiré des vieux Romains les poudreuses reliques.
> (1–8)[99]

Ruins, as we see, are being discovered as an invaluable and transferable cultural capital, *pace* Montaigne who, with a different kind of *pietas*, would prefer them well sealed off in their Roman tomb. If only it were possible to physically transfer Rome's antiquities right into the king's palaces and gardens! Du Bellay wistfully suggests . . . tongue in cheek, perhaps. However, by favouring with his intellectual patronage this special kind of exhumation wrought in the language of His Majesty, the king would certainly be credited with the merit of rebuilding the grandeur of ancient Rome in France ("*rebastir en France en telle grandeur*", line 10).

Interestingly, Du Bellay's own Roman ruins enjoyed further expendability in Europe, either in his own mournful if agonistic tenor, or—in an anti-papist mood more in tune with the Revelation—to show them, apocalyptically, as emblems of the past and present corrupted City and its predestined fate, as was the case in the illustrated miscellany of poems edited by the Dutch exile Jan Van Der Noot, *A Theatre Wherein Be Represented as Wel the Miseries & Calamities That Follow the Voluptuous Worldlings as Also the Greate Ioyes and Plesures Which the Faithfull Do Enioy* (usually shortened as *A Theatre for Voluptuous Worldlings*).[100] Van Der Noot's *Theatre* included a good part of Du Bellay's *Songe*, a sequence of 15 visionary sonnets on Rome's doom Englished anonymously by a very young Edmund Spenser, but for the occasion four of these were omitted to be replaced by others inspired by themes from Revelation, and which will be useful to resume when we come to *Antony and Cleopatra*. Introduced by a long and sumptuously laudatory dedication to the Queen Elizabeth—Phoenix, Astrea, the champion of European Protestantism—enriched with emblematic woodcuts by an unknown artist (*picturae*) and prose commentary on the poems which outweighed the poems themselves, *A Theatre for Voluptuous Worldlings* was published in London in 1569, the year before Elizabeth was excommunicated by Pope Pius V: "a time of international crisis, when the Protestant cause in Europe seemed close to defeat".[101] Two different editions in French and Dutch, accompanied by more refined copperplate etchings attributed to Marcus Gheeraert the elder, had been published in London the previous year. A further would be published in German in 1572: an instance of how the discourse on Rome's ruins could be catalyzed as an argument which mattered in an international context and for a variety of causes.

"As a theory of history, as a hermeneutic tool, and as a linguistic practice, translation is at the heart of Du Bellay's and Spenser's meditations on Rome", Margaret Ferguson has written in remarking the complexity of the topic.[102] Richard Mulcaster (c. 1531–1611), Spenser's teacher and the influential headmaster of Merchant Taylors' School and St. Paul's School in London, contributed to spread interest for this author in England: not surprisingly, for he fervently shared the nationalist side of Du Bellay's argument on questions of imitation and translation from other languages and the past as a way of testing and affirming one's national language and literature. And in so doing he was successful, we should say, for Du Bellay's "ruines" were widely circulated by a receptive Spenser, who apart from revising and completing the translation of the *Songe* sonnets he had Englished for Van Der Noot's collection when he was hardly 17, also undertook the rewording of *Antiquitez de Rome* for inclusion (respectively as *The Visions of Bellay* and *Ruines of Rome: by Bellay*) in his 1591 *Complaints*,[103] a collection of poems deeply concerned with issues of imitation and creativity, in their connection with the *topoi* of vanity and mortality. Rome was a huge, all-encompassing, and controversial argument, as shown by Du Bellay's sonnet 25 (1–3).

> O that I had the *Thracian* Poets harpe,
> For to awake out of th'infernal shade
> Those antique *Caesars*, sleeping long in darke.

Spenser vividly acknowledged the immortality Du Bellay deserved for having revived "Old Rome out of her ashes" and given "a second life to dead decays" in "L'Envoy" (sonnet 33.5–6), which he devised as a close to his version of Du Bellay's *Ruines of Rome*—a form of immortality, as one may well say, they both achieved by working with ruins. But I suspect it is only as a translator, and behind the screen offered by another language, that Spenser was willing to share Du Bellay's pathos in front of the "tragick sights" of Rome (see sonnet 7). Meaningfully, Spenser opened his *Complaints* with a work of his own on the ruins topic, *Ruines of Time*, which represented his own English (and distancing) counterpoint to Du Bellay's elegiac and regretful *Antiquitez*. And in fact, Rome's ruins, as Spenser re-fantasized them in the opening sonnet of his *Ruines of Time*, have already undergone—physically and emotionally—the ineluctable final effacement of Time only prospectively feared by Du Bellay.

Arguably, resurrection in the name of Rome's lasting *allure* could find little room in Spenser's program, and this comes as no surprise considering the declared Protestant projectuality of Spenser's mature literary agenda.[104] If anything, his "complaint" is for Britain's ruins. And in fact, as has been remarked, his *Ruines of Time* was meant to be "a manifesto for a renewed English poetry founded on the ruins of the past, a new life springing forth on the funeral monuments of the dead", but free of the tutelage of Rome, or of more recent writers—Petrarch, for instance, and Du Bellay himself.[105] One might say that there is no drama in Spenser's way of abandoning/forgetting Rome, a "false idol", like the ones destroyed by Artegall in the *Faerie Queene* (book V) but not quite. As observed by Andrew Hui, "Spenser's iconoclasm purifies completely, leaving no traces except for its own words. . . . but writing cannot defeat idols without reproducing them".[106]

In sum, if only to be obliterated, this state of affairs bears witness to the extent to which Rome's ruins mattered to modern creativity, or any other form of appropriation of Rome in Shakespeare's time. As Thomas Greene has insightfully shown, the complex cluster of meanings revolving around the topic of Rome's ruins remains central to humanist and Renaissance European culture, and Du Bellay, who had addressed it in his treatise *Deffence et Illustration de la Langue Françoyse* (1549) before resuming it as a poetical theme in *Antiquitez de Rome* and *Songe*, was exemplary in the way he cast it as "the central humanist drama": "He discovered in Rome the fragmented, deciduous majesty of the ancient past; he encountered the heartbreaking inscrutability of history; he measured the difficulty of calling the dead back to life and faced the subtle frustrations of artistic emulation". In the end, Greene continues, he was "obliged to recognize only the disorderly contiguity between the past and an uncontrollable European future already actualized hatefully in the Roman present".[107]

But what concerns us equally in the context of this volume is the language—announced by Du Bellay's title *Antiquitez*—which as a poet he shared with the coeval so-called antiquarians (an appellative which in early modern European culture designated historians, archaeologists, classicists, philologists, and epigraphists). For them all the discovery of a past "*qui n'est plus*" (Du Bellay, sonnet 5) meant contradictorily (literally or metaphorically) the uncovering of tombs, the unearthing of ruins and relics, the encounter with cadavers, shades, traces, and ghosts of a demanding memory and unachievable model; an anxiety that Shakespeare casts as a family romance when he obliquely assigns to Brutus (to his being gripped by Caesar's phantasm) as well as Hamlet (his being haunted by fathers as well as historical figures like Caesar and Alexander), his obsessive own confrontation as an author with ghosts of authoritative fatherhood.

Meaningfully, the same creative act in the *Ruines* first sonnet is imagined according to a double-faced paradigm of descent, both mythical and archaeological: one in which the subtext of Orpheus's plunge into the unfathomable abyss of the underworld is problematized by the material chaos of crumbled stones and walls prospected by the superimposed new and concrete excavating enquiry of archaeology.

> Ye heavenly spirites, whose ashie cinders lie
> Under deep ruines, with huge walls opprest,
> But not your praise, the which shall never die
> Through your fair verses, ne in ashes rest:
> If so be shrilling voyce of wight alive
> May reach from hence to depth of darkest hell,
> Then let those deep Abysses open rive,
> That ye may understand my shreiking yell.
> Thrice having seene under the heavens veale
> Your toombs devoted compasse over all,
> Thrice unto you with lowd voyce I appeale,
> And for your antique furie here doo call,
> The whiles that I with sacred horror sing
> Your glorie, fairest of all earthly thing.

The ceremony, aptly viewed as "necromantic" by Thomas Greene,[108] is both religious and necessarily sacrilegious in its modern inquisitive intentions and effects. The invocation of a poetical power ("Fury"), which may be equal to the unsurpassed glory of the city and its lasting literature ("her brave writings", 5.12) that the poet wants to sing and emulate, is fantasized as a panic-stricken descent into hell and a profanation of tombs. It is cast as an Orphic ritual of descent into darkness and of bringing back the dead to light by means of the enlivening power of the human voice—a "shreiking yell" which rhymes with hell (in the second quatrain of the first sonnet)—or else a "lowd voyce" (1.11), thrice proffered by the poetical subject on the tombs of the past. But poetical power is also metaphorically rendered (as again in sonnet 25) as masonry skill, able to mend, repair, and accord what is disjointed. Such skill is modulated as a material capacity to bring back to order—Amphion-like, by means of the art of music—the stones of the city's crumbled walls. The image is mythical, but it is revisited with a spirit that is both sceptical and archaeological: "O that I had the *Thracian* poetes harpe, / For to awake out of th' infernal shade / Those antique *Cæsars*, sleeping long in darke, / The which this auncient Citie whilome made: / Or that I had *Amphions* instrument, / To quicken with his vitall notes accord, / The stonie joynts of these old walls now rent . . . Or that at least I could with pencill fine, / . . . To builde with levell of my lofty style, / That which no hands can evermore compyle" (25.1–7).

Not differently from the humanist Poggio, Rome for Du Bellay is a cadaver, an uncanny archaeological vision of a "disjointed" architecture and disarticulated temporality. Great art, magic, is needed to draw its body out of its tomb and make it whole: "Rome n'est plus, & si l'architecture / Quelque umbre encore de Rome fait revoir, / C'est un corps par magique sçavoir / Tiré de nuict hors de sa sepulture" (5.5–8). But such a Rome—the object of a nocturnal digging ritual—will only "yeeld a seeming sight" of its "architecture" (rendered with "Body" in Spenser's rewording of these lines), to those who undertake to write it into life: "Rome is no more: but if the shade of *Rome* / May of the bodie yeeld a seeming sight, / It's like a corse drawne forth out of the tombe / By Magicke skill out of eternall night").

Du Bellay's ruinous, nocturnal, and spectral Rome, as it was reworded and appropriated by Spenser, may not have escaped the attention of Shakespeare as a playwright. Suffice it to think of the crumbling architecture of kingship in his Roman plays and his major tragedies, the way such a vulnerability is imagined as an anatomy of illness and fragility in *Julius Caesar*, *Coriolanus*, and *Antony and Cleopatra*. But let us also think of the collapsed and layered temporality of *Titus Andronicus*, his first Roman tragedy. And the extent to which the spectre of a ruinous temporality—"a strange-disposed time" in *Julius Caesar* (1.3.33)—insidiously affects this play and other major non-Roman plays. *Hamlet* for instance: and not in the sense hinted at by Horatio ("I am more a Roman"), but rather in the way memory (a central and contiguous theme to that of the "questionable shape" of fatherhood and ancestry in these two plays) is tragically intertwined with an unmendable perception of Time, Power, and History: "The time is out of joint. O cursed spite, / That ever I was born to set it right" (1.4.43 and 1.5.196–97).

That Shakespeare knew Du Bellay, likely via Spenser, appears clear to many critics. However, these have mainly drawn attention to Shakespeare's sonnets and the way they are obsessed by a similar ruinous and ravishing image of time that, in Du Bellay/Spenser, is epitomized in sonnet 7 (8–11): "The peoples fable and the spoyle of all: / And though your frames do for a time make warre / 'Gainst time, yet time in time shall ruinate / Your workes and names, and your last reliques marre". Such a debt was first signalled and extensively analysed by A. Kent Hieatt,[109] who concluded that the impermanence of the fair youth's beauty and virtues, namely the feared image of the fair youth's beauty about to be injured and cancelled by the work of time, is actually wrought by means of a "poetic metamorphosis of Du Bellay and Spenser's Rome".[110] The critic was right in perceiving what until that moment had gone unnoticed. However, preoccupation with lexical similarities, based on a mere one-to-one relationship among source studies, is pushed so far as to overshadow Shakespeare's broader transaction (conscious or unconscious as it may have been) with tradition, namely a pre-existent European intertextual and intercultural reflection on ruins. After all, Spenser himself, I would like to remark, seemed to be interested in situating his rewording (or remake) of Du Bellay within a cultural continuum which brings us back to Poggio's *Ruinarum Romae Descriptio* [*Description of the Ruins of Rome*], when he chose to translate "Antiquitez" with "Ruines" and not "Antiquities" (however interchangeable the two terms were at the time), thus confirming, whether deliberately or not, their dramatic epistemological potential.

Archaeology of the Tragic Emotion

"Ye sacred ruines, and ye tragick sights" (son. 7): Du Bellay/Spenser's ruins of Rome appeared clad in the lore of exceptional dramatic pathos, and it is this that may have proved inspiring to Shakespeare the playwright in his early career and in years in which (both in his dramatic and non-dramatic poetry) he was testing, interrogating, and problematizing the power and archaeology of the tragic emotion for his own time and to his own dramatic ends: the emotion of Titus and Lucrece. But also later Hamlet's—"Give me that man / That is not passion's slave, and I will wear him / In my heart's core" (3.3.71–73)—which he explores mostly through the precedent of Troy and the figure of Hecuba. Surely it is this that he achieves in his first (Roman) tragedy; the tragedy in which he makes Rome's ruins speak first and foremost by recasting the scarred body of the "mighty giant" as the bodily ruin of his chopped humanity.

Thus, if Rome as a name is removed from the "fearful meditation" on ruins which takes place in Shakespeare's sonnets, vice versa, but in parallel, its disfigured "*poudreuses reliques*" (Du Bellay's dedicatory sonnet, line 8), "Which only do the Name of Rome retain" (son. 7.2), are awakened and restored to their full and tragic size and name in his Roman plays. Which is not to say that they are reanimated and staged in their wholeness or truth, but rather in a form (or temporality) which remains radically "worm-hole[d]"—as we might say borrowing from Lucrece (*The Rape*, v. 945), and radically "disadjusted"—as we might say with Hamlet mediated by Derrida.[111] As with ruins and spectres, the shape of Rome is necessarily equivocal, uncertain, aporetic, enthralling, and deceptive; deceptive like the unearthed frescoes fantasized about in Fellini's film, *Roma* (1972), soon vanishing like phantasms in contact with air. Starting from *Titus Andronicus*—Shakespeare's own outrageous contribution to the Renaissance poetics of ruins, I argue—the "worm-hole[d]" form (or temporality) of the colossal stature of Rome's ruined bodies of edifices or statues coalesces in his Roman plays with the fissured body of the tragic hero or heroine and its demand for interpretation.

But it is in *The Rape* that Shakespeare provides the key. For it is in this poem (to which I will return in a chapter devoted to it) that the word "ruin" occurs in association with the digging and dissecting procedures of the new science of anatomy, which indicates an understanding of the Roman world and the past (customarily overlooked by critics) that, early in his career, Shakespeare overtly situates in the explorative episteme of modernity, thus outlining a *critique* which goes well beyond his Roman works to invest the way history, bodies, and emotions are addressed in his dramatic universe. The lines I am referring to are the famous ones of Lucrece's post-rape ekphrasis when she finally finds in a "well-painted piece" of Troy the correlative for her doleful condition as violated woman: "To this well-painted piece is LUCRECE come, / To find a face where all distress is stell'd. / Many she sees where cares have *carved* some, / But none where all distress and dolour dwell'd" (vv. 1443–47). But then she "comes" to Hecuba:

> In her the painter had anatomiz'd
> Time's ruin, beauty's wrack, and grim care's reign;
> Her cheeks with chops and wrinkles were disguis'd:
> Of what she was no semblance did remain.
>
> (1450–54)

In his ekphrasis, Shakespeare intertwines body and architecture, female body and city in the name of Troy—the fall/ruin *per antonomasia*. "As PRIAM [Sinon] did cherish, / So did I TARQUIN, so my TROY did perish" (vv. 1546–47). One term (Troy) is commented upon by the other (Lucrece) and vice versa. This has been well noticed by critics. What has gone fairly unnoticed is that Shakespeare doesn't limit himself to reasoning (scholastically) by means of similes and syllogisms. For when dealing with Hecuba and her face rendered unrecognizable by sorrow, exactly as her down-razed Troy has been made by war, the argument undergoes a substantial twist, and a further, complicating question is foregrounded: that of representation. That is to say, the problem of how a wounded female body can or cannot reach knowledge through a process of recollection of a spectral anteriority. Or in other words, the problem of how a far-removed and devastating "woe" can be made plastically present in its tragic nudity up to the point of triggering and becoming somebody else's (Lucrece's) feeling, as well as a traumatic instrument of self-knowledge. "Here feelingly [Lucrece] weeps Troy's painted woes" (v.1492).

As will be shown in Chapter 2, this is the question which, early in his career, Shakespeare foregrounds when he transforms a well-known and long-practiced ekphrastic procedure into a sophisticated and actualized theatre of memory and knowledge, its actors (in the very theatrical space opened up by his poetic ekphrasis) being a mournful violated woman, a mother figure's painted wreckage, and a painter. A new kind of painter though, mind you, one who is able to anatomize ruin—that is, ravage and "dissemblance"—and to reproduce it plastically on Hecuba's face as pure substance. In fact, the disguising skeleton-like nudity which identifies ruin as well as the anatomized body is depicted on Hecuba's face—to be then transferred onto Lucrece's living face—as if it were a disfigured rubble of meaning, a marred layer of inorganic colour resisting as well as looking for a voice and interpretation. "Her cheeks with chops and wrinkles were disguis'd: / Of what she was no semblance did remain" (vv. 1453–54). Hecuba's face as depicted by Shakespeare's skilful painter, I argue in Chapter 2, is a complex construct which produces meaning by means of its process of decomposition. Her face has been peeled of its identifying surface and anatomically de-structured and dis-(as)sembled "in chops and wrinkles", in order that its inner meaning—a lump of woe—may be grasped at. And it is now that Hecuba's "no semblance", a catalyst of the meanings of the whole painting, visually stands for pure, achieved sorrow. And what a striking achievement, we might well say: a "document in distress" wrought in a way that foretells its future in the yet-to-come art of Picasso's denouncing *Guernica*, or Munch's *Cry*.

For the violated Lucrece, Hecuba's painted woe functions as a symbolic mediation for a sorrow that the painter has made anatomically visible and assessable. But it doesn't serve the intentions of an unproblematic transcendent meditation (or allegory) on death and transience. For ruins, as Benjamin helps us to say, belong to the "realms of things" and the time of history.[112] Or, as the playwright might add, to the all-too-earthly physiology of bodies and their affections, the stuff of theatre. And in fact what Shakespeare's skilful painter provides is an anatomy, a document, and not an allegory, or emblem of ruin: an exploration of ruinous bodies and tragic emotion, I maintain, that even though contrived and put to the test in a narrative poem, while waiting for the longed-for anticipated reopening of London theatres, has a forceful heuristic bearing on Shakespeare's coeval *Titus Andronicus* as well as on his ensuing Roman and non-Roman dissecting tragedies. Let us remember that public theatres in London were repeatedly closed and reopened because of the plague from 1592 to 1594.

"Woe" is the meaning Lucrece "comes to". "To come"—a verb which significantly occurs again in *Hamlet* in relation to Hecuba—means to arrive, fall by, fall in, as well as reach, attain, *happen*. In *The Rape* Lucrece "comes" to Hecuba as if suddenly succoured *in extremis* by the grace of a reminiscence ("At last she calls to mind where hangs a piece / Of skilful painting", vv. 1366–67). But from the moment she stumbles upon the picture, we see her at work to make the painted tragic ruin and emotion *happen*, performatively, on her own living body: "I'll tune thy woes with my lamenting tongue / And drop sweet balm in PRIAM's painted wound, / And rail on PYRRUS that hath done him wrong, / And with my tears quench TROY that burns so long / And with my knife scratch out", vv. 1465–69). Announced and emphasized by an insistent use of modal verbs,[113] Lucrece's performance of woe, as I call it, a bodily *copia*, emerges as an inextricable intersemiotic cluster of bodily and verbal language, past and present time.

Similarly, in *Hamlet* the Trojan queen comes alive as a by-product of a mediated memory: a seemingly obsessive fragment of a lost if first-rate play on the Virgilian matter of Troy, which takes on flesh and passion with the arrival of the players in Elsinore (HAMLET "I heard thee speak me a speech once, but it was never acted, or if it was, not above once", 2.2.358–59). The object of a shared exclusive knowledge between Hamlet and first player, the play—an anterior story of grief and revenge—remains untitled and far removed from the audience. It is evident that Hamlet's urging priority is to lead the player to the precise excerpt ("'t was Aenes' tale to Dido") and line he wants to hear ("especially when he speaks of Priam's slaughter. If it live in your memory, begin at this line", 2.2.369–71). Residual as the untitled play may be, such a passage (or textual "ruin") is indelibly living in the "tablet" of his mind, invested as it is with the power of a mnemonic trace archaeologically pressing for response, connections, and action.

Dealing with one's ancestry and memory involves self-engagement, coming to terms, with the tragic kernel of an originary scene: "In Troy, there lies the scene", the Prologue announces in *Troilus and Cressida* (1.1.1). Hamlet, like Lucrece, feels the same impellent call "coming" from Hecuba's tragic grandeur (however disguised and jeopardized this may be by the distancing, parodic framework of the scene) when he impatiently urges the actor: "Say on; come to Hecuba. / FIRST PLAYER "But who, ah woe, had seen the mobled Queen–"/ HAMLET "The mobled Queen"! (*Ham.* 2.2.423–25). But only to discover that he—a "coward"—is miserably unable to reach the emotional symbiosis the actor has got "in fiction". "And all for nothing! / For Hecuba! / What's Hecuba to him, or he to her, / That he should weep for her" (2.2.476–79). Differently from the actor, and differently from Lucrece with whom, however, he shares his unequalled capacity to dilate the time of his plaintive condition, Hamlet is unable to make that passion *happen* on him. Not in that way. And in fact this will not be the play "Wherein [he]'ll catch the conscience of the King" (2.2.524). For such a goal, and for the hardly mythical King of Elsinore, Hamlet has in store an updated, "knavish piece of work", *The Mousetrap*, of which he mockingly underlies the highly metaphorical potential, when he adds, "how tropically!", perhaps also hinting at its "topicality" (3.2.220–23). That the originary scene is irremediably lost in its epic or tragic size shouldn't come as a surprise. Shakespeare writes *Hamlet* soon after *Troilus and Cressida* (1600)—an unmediated reappraisal of the Troy matter. Here, in fact, the problematization of Trojan-Greek ancestry comes full circle in terms of authority as well as genre instability, "the goal" of this play being rather "self-deformation", as Heather James has incisively remarked.[114]

"There is tragedy, there is essence of the tragic only on the condition of this originarity, more precisely of this preoriginary and properly spectral anteriority", Derrida writes commenting on Hamlet's cursed destiny to do what he cannot do: "to put time on the right path".[115] And in fact tragedy is interrogated—acquiring metatheatrical relevance in the Hecuba's scene—as a consequence of Hamlet's perception of his impotence. "Hamlet is no Hecuba", Tanya Pollard has argued.[116] But Lucrece is, I maintain: however, not without raising other (gender-coded) questions (as I show in Chapter 2), and while at the same time anticipating Hamlet in so many aspects—mostly for soliloquizing proficiency in a long-drawn self-analysis of emotions as well as for a proclivity in taking issue with one's own "spectral anteriority", which also meant putting to the test the very means of representation. One wonders why Shakespeare didn't craft a tragedy out of her story instead of an epyllion. By which I mean that the epyllion as a genre is as questionable for *The Rape* as tragedy is for *Hamlet*. In this the Trojan queen was pivotal in both texts. An obsession for Shakespeare himself, as is evident, Hecuba—the epitome of a gender-coded ruinous body and sufferings in *The Rape*—far from being a sacred relic, an untouchable monument of tragic grandeur, appears rather as a figure invested with heuristic potentiality: a haunting and spectral under-text, I argue, which more than calling for unquestioned identification, asks for its anatomy.

Ruins—and the ruins of memory—are essential to the humanist and Renaissance idea of rebirth and *translatio imperii*, as well as to any theory of modernity.[117] The story of Troy—the burning city—and of Aeneas who arrives as an exile, or refugee, on the Latium coast to found a new Troy, is at the origin of Rome's founding myth. As a paradigm of destruction and reconstruction it was destined to proliferate in Europe in a number of other, similar national appropriations of Troy's ancestry based on a fantasized diaspora of Aeneas's progeny. Britain's "Troynovant" and its claimed descend from Brutus is not the least among them (and it did not go uncontested). But such a travelling and empowering story of noble heritage and dislocated re-edification of Troy's glory, variously allud-ing to Virgil's *Aeneid*, Ovid's *Fasti*, Horace's *Carmen*, Livy's *History of Rome*, and Lucan's *Pharsalia*, was tragic at the core, indelibly marked as it was by the disquieting memory of a constitutive *vulnus*: the enormous beacon-fire that signalled from afar that Troy was burning and which, erasing the ancient city forever, transformed it into a city without ruins. Troy's fire, in the way it ominously underwrites and prophesizes Rome's destiny as a return of the same—the iteration of a Vichian pattern of glory and destruction—lies at the core of Greek-Latin civilization (see Horace's *Odes*).[118] It identifies the nexus as an act of violence. And the Trojan queen's mythical tragic grief stands exactly at that juncture, enjoy-ing the popularity of the sight and comment *par excellence* on the fall *per antonomasia* in Renaissance European imagination.

In Shakespeare's works Hecuba becomes a movable signifier in the way her originary aura is conjured up to serve a variety of causes. So much so that more than being the "mobbled" (Q2, Q1) or "inobled" (F) queen

(2.2.497–98)—terms of a still unresolved philological crux—we might well say with Ivan Lupic's plausible suggestion that she is "mobile" and "mobilizing".[119] As a mother of many sons lost in war and an example of fierce and relentless revenge, she underwrites the similar incommensurable disgrace and determined enmity of the eponymous *Titus*'s protagonist, a play that, as Heather James has remarked, was already "establishing the Troy legend as a ground for ideological contestation in the theater".[120] In *Coriolanus* Hecuba inspires Volumnia's depiction as a mother capable of breeding martial and unflinching masculinity. She is a test for tragic failure, in *Hamlet*. In *The Rape*, as I see it, the "spectral anteriority" and authority of her disfiguring woe gives palimpsestic (and conceptual) depth to the destructive distress of a violated woman: it is thus that it becomes relevant as a complicating factor in understanding history and its foundational myths. Together, Hecuba and Lucrece—with their denouncing female bodies—give bodily visibility to history as an archaeological ruination of wound upon wound. In such a reciprocity Hecuba stands for the originary ruin, the Ur-ruin, on which Lucrece's devastating woe lays and relies in order that other silenced female cries may be uncovered and heard from the interstices of history—Philomela's first of all but also Echo, Lavinia, the fictional character Shakespeare is creating in his coeval *Titus*. In this sense Lucrece's final ruinous image of herself encompasses time, bodies, feelings, texts, silences, and words: words which she articulates as a protracted and endless mourning, a cry, "the [female] lament from history", as we might say going back to Benjamin's words discussed earlier in this Introduction.

Would Shakespeare recognize himself as one of those who played a part, and with skill, in the great Humanist and Renaissance endeavour of disinterring/unearthing the dead, while being at the same time modern? It is likely he would, if we trust the blustering Aaron ("Oft have I digged up dead men from their grave", 5.1.135) in his first Roman play, as well as Prospero's final renunciation of his "so potent art", which he summarizes as an awe-inspiring and terrifying set of prodigies, as well as a necromantic act of uncovering of tombs: "graves at my command / Have waked their sleepers, oped and let 'em forth / By my so potent art. But this rough magic / I here abjure . . . / I'll break my staff, / Bury it certain fathoms in the earth, / And deeper than did ever plummet sound / I'll drown my book" (*Tempest*, 5.1.48–57).

Comments on the Italian duke's concluding speech on his "art" customarily signal its blatant debt to Medea's invocation of Hecate in Ovid/Golding's *Metamorphoses* (Ovid, 7.192–209/Golding, 7.258–76),[121]—an often exploited *locus classicus* in English Renaissance literature dealing with sorcery—and hence the way this identifies Prospero's magic art as contradictorily intertwined with Sycorax's black magic. Moreover, critics often record as an incongruence the couple of lines on graves and the awakening of the dead (48–50) if considered in relation to Prospero's concrete actions in the play;[122] almost as if, perhaps for the sake of an impressive final climax, the playwright had taken more than he needed from his source text. Jonathan Bate goes against the grain in drawing attention to the intentionality of such a set piece: "Sixteenth-century models of reading were always purposeful". In fact, as he underlines, this was a skilful and carefully edited "piece of Renaissance imitation", which the playwright carried out by using the Elizabethan translation as well as the Latin original and by preferring Ovid to Golding, especially when he came to the couple of lines on "graves", which he translates, following Ovid's "*man-esque exire sepulchris*", in a way that physically emphasizes "the ghosts actually coming out of their tombs",[123] rather than Golding's: "I call up dead men from their graves" (7.275). Bates also underlines the sacrilegious pagan overtones of this last part of the duke's speech and its conflicting relevance in a Christian era. And it is precisely in this that he perceives the purposefulness of the Medea passage, in the fact that it "marks a movement away from the pagan world towards Christian "kindness. . . . Medea's powers are summoned up not so that they can be exercised, but so that they can be rejected".[124] I couldn't agree more if we follow the main line of the plot and we believe that the burial of Prospero's book (or books) is enough to restore him and his characters (and audience) to a world of shared Christian pacification. But considering the complex suggestiveness of the play and its ending, I would also see the intentionality of the Medea excerpt in the way it proclaims a kinship with a coeval theory of creativity (or imitation) grounded—as Greene might say, and as it was epitomized by Du Bellay's ruins—on a "quintessential humanist rite" of descent.[125] In fact, the Medea piece describes an encounter with the pagan deities of the underworld, which is experienced as a panic-stricken profanation, while exhibiting it as a modern gesture of blatant appropriation.

In the primitive, displaced context of *The Tempest*, and in the hands of Prospero—the Italian duke who, like a new Virgilian Aeneas, is placed in the condition of founding a new city with the relicts of a realm which has escaped the deluge (books being among the salvaged objects)—the Ovidian Medea's speech, set piece as it is, emerges, archaeologically, as a surviving and terrifying old mark of a far-removed classic past, as well as a devoutly collected textual ruin, or relic. Shakespeare chose to exploit it as a signature, when he placed it, almost as a double end, at the closure of his play—not a classical but still very Ovidian sort of play—where it stands, controversially, as Prospero's dropped role. Indeed, together with Prospero's pagan *masque*, it comes to prominence with the disturbing force of an anachronism: an anachronism finely wrought as an utterly visible *copia* and invested with the important function of summarizing Prospero's magic as well as (metaphorically) Shakespeare's powers as an artist, his very capacity of "beeing-with" ruins, to give flesh and voice to shades, or (else) to make "the sleepers" walk out of the darkness of their tombs.

Situated as it is in a structurally pivotal point of the play, Medea's speech stands out as a seal not just on Shakespeare's profoundly Ovidian *Tempest* but on his whole career as a poet and playwright, even though it is consigned to the erasure—albeit always uncertain—of things abjured. Did the speech spring out of the very book Prospero is plunging into the water? Books partake of the same condition of *ruinae* (Petrarch) in the disanchoraged economy of the play. They are and remain a relict from beginning to end. Ovid is one of them, on Prospero's distant oceanic/ Mediterranean island, standing for a paradigmatic story of *translatio*, a story whose movement is one of iterative ruination, burning palaces, migrations, shipwrecks, encounters with Otherness, drifting, salvaged, travelling and transformed books, and highly ambivalent rebirth. In this sense Prospero's island may well be viewed as a "Troynovant", or a new Rome, not the physical city, but the city as paradigm of a catastrophic history and an archive of Western civilization.

The cinema (Greenaway) as well as contemporary productions of the play (most recently Daniele Salvo at the Silvano Globe Theatre in Rome) are just a few examples of how forcefully these characteristics of Shakespeare's ideal last play call for archaeological hermeneutics and representation.[126]

Notes

1. Quotations from the sonnets are from *Shakespeare's Sonnets*, ed. Katherine Duncan-Jones (London: Bloomsbury Arden Shakespeare, 2010). But I have also consulted the bilingual Shakespeare's *Sonetti*, ed. and transl. Alessandro Serpieri (Milano: Rizzoli, 1991/1998).
2. Mary Carruthers, *The Book of Memory: A Study of Memory in Medieval Culture [1990]* (Cambridge: Cambridge University Press, 2013), pp. 202–212.
3. On learning and antiquity see for all Colin Burrow, *Shakespeare and Classical Antiquity* (Oxford: Oxford University Press, 2013), pp. 21–50.
4. Robert S. Miola, *Shakespeare's Rome* (London and New York: Cambridge University Press, 1983), pp. 9 and 8.
5. Clifford Ronan, *"Antike Roman": Power Symbology and the Roman Play in Early Modern England* (Athens: University of Georgia Press, 1995), p. 180.
6. Erwin Panofsky, *Renaissance and Renaissances in Western Art* (Stockholm: Almqvist & Wiksells, 1960), p. 113.
7. Thomas M. Greene, *The Light to Troy: Imitation and Discovery in Renaissance Poetry* (New Haven and London: Yale University Press, 1982), p. 92.
8. See Hegel's *Philosophy of History* (1837): "The sight of the ruins of some ancient sovereignty directly leads us to contemplate the thought of change in its negative aspect. What traveller among the ruins of Carthage, of Palmyra, Persepolis, or Rome, has not been stimulated to reflections on the transiency of kingdoms and men . . . But the next consideration which allies itself with that of change, is, that change while imports dissolution, involves at the same time the rise of a *new life*—that while death is the issue of life, life is also the issue of death". Transl. J. Sibree (New York: Cosmo Classics, 2007), pp. 72–73. For further insightful comment on the dialectics of ruin, progress, and modernity in Hegel, see Todd Samuel Presner, "Hegel's Philosophy of

World History via Sebald's Imaginary of Ruins: A Contrapuntal Critique of the 'New Space' of Modernity", in Julia Hell and Andreas Schonle, eds, *Ruins of Modernity* (Durham and London: Duke University Press, 2010), pp. 193–211.

9. Joachim Du Bellay, *Les Antiquitez de Rome*, 1558, translated by Edmund Spenser as *Ruines of Rome: by Bellay*. Quotations (hereafter indicated as authored by Du Bellay/Spenser), refer to Edmund Spenser, *The Yale Edition of the Shorter Poems*, ed. William A. Oram et al. (New Haven and London: Yale University Press, 1989).

10. On *Titus*'s funerals, see Michael Neill's indispensable reflections in *Issues of Death: Mortality and Identity in English Renaissance Tragedy* (Oxford: Oxford University Press, 1997, rpt 2005), pp. 288–292 *et passim*. For a discussion of funeral monuments as stage properties and producers of social and symbolic meaning in Shakespeare's tragedy, see pp. 305–327.

11. Jonathan Bate, "Introduction", in *Titus Andronicus*, The Arden Shakespeare (London: Thomson Learning, 2003), p. 4, n. 1, p. 127, n. 92.1, p. 133. Stanley Wells, *Re-editing Shakespeare for the Modern Reader* (Oxford: Clarendon Press, 1984), Chap. 4, "The Editor and the Theatre: Act One of *Titus Andronicus*", p. 108.

12. Here is the (Q2–3, F) closing variant in full: "And being so, shall haue like want of pitty. / See iustice done on *Aron* that damn'd Moore, / From whom, our heauie haps had their beginning. / Then afterwards, to order well the state, / That like euents, may nere it ruinate". Jonathan Bate's Arden edition, n. 191. See also Stanley Wells and Gary Taylor, *William Shakespeare: Norton Textual Companion* (Oxford: Oxford University Press, 1997), p. 215.

13. Walter Benjamin, "Paralipomena on the Concept of History", in *Selected Writings*, vol. 4, 1938–1940, transl. Edmund Jephcott et al. (Cambridge, MA: The Belknap Press of Harvard University Press, 2003), p. 401.

14. Robert S. Miola, *Shakespeare and Classical Tragedy* (Oxford: Clarendon Press, 1992), p. 21.

15. Thomas M. Greene, "Resurrecting Rome: the Double Task of the Humanist Imagination", in P. M. Ramsey, ed., *Rome in the Renaissance: The City and the Myth*, vol. 18 (Binghamton: Medieval and Renaissance Texts and Studies, 1982), p. 41, but see also his *Light to Troy*, chapter 11, pp. 220–241.

16. I am here extending Greenblatt's notion of "permeability" (addressed as an "unresolved struggle between competing representational discourses", *Shakespearean Negotiations: The Circulation of Social Energy in Renaissance England* [Berkeley: University of California Press, 1988], p. 8) to the interacting dynamics of different forms of knowledge. See Maria Del Sapio Garbero, ed., *Shakespeare and the New Science in Early Modern Culture* (Pisa: Pacini, 2016), pp. 5–24.

17. Greene, "Resurrecting Rome", p. 44.

18. Walter Benjamin, "On Franz Kafka", *Illuminations*, ed. and with an Introduction by Hannah Arendt, transl. Harry Zorn (London: Pimlico, 1999), p. 129.

19. See later pp. 16–28.

20. Hannah Arendt, "Introduction" to Benjamin, *Illuminations*, p. 52.

21. Benjamin, *Illuminations*, pp. 52 and 127.

22. Bate, "Introduction", pp. 69–79.

23. Christine Buci-Glucksmann, *Baroque Reason: The Aesthetics of Modernity* (London: Sage Publications, 1994), p. 67.

24. Benjamin, "Theses on the Philosophy of History", in *Illuminations*, pp. 247–248; but see also "Paralipomena on the Concept of History", pp. 401–403.

On the state of emergency and the way it is related to the crisis of sovereignty in the seventeenth century, prompting a sense of impending catastrophe, see also *The Origin of German Tragic Drama* (1928), transl. John Osborne, Intro. George Steiner (London and New York: Verso, 2003), p. 65 and 74. This affects Benjamin's conceptualization of his *Trauerspiel*, but also, pervasively, his whole vision of history.

25. Benjamin, "Theses on the Philosophy of History", in *Illuminations*, p. 246.
26. Leonard Barkan, *Unearthing the Past* (New Haven and London: Yale University Press, 1999), p. XXI.
27. Friedrich Nietzsche, "On the Uses and Disadvantages of History for Life", in *Untimely Meditations*, transl. R. J. Hollingdale (Cambridge: Cambridge University Press, 2007), p. 64.
28. Benjamin, "Paralipomena", p. 401.
29. Buci-Glucksmann, *Baroque Reason*, p. 67.
30. Terence John Bew Spencer, "Shakespeare and the Elizabethan Romans", *Shakespeare Survey*, 10 (1957), 27–38 (p. 32). But see also Geoffrey Miles who, years later, in excluding *Titus Andronicus* and *Cymbeline* from his analysis, observes, "their fictional plots and fairy-tale vagueness of chronology, seem to belong to a different species, using Rome as an archetype of civilization and empire rather than as a subject whose history and ethos are of interest in their own right" [*Shakespeare and the Constant Romans* (Oxford: Clarendon Press, 1996), pp. vii–viii]. He thus deprives himself of a character, Titus, who in the framework of his book might have proved worthy of being discussed.
31. Benjamin, *The Origin of German Tragic Drama*, pp. 62 and 65–66. Expanded discussion of *Trauerspiel* is offered by D. Messina, in R. Campi, D. Messina, M. Tolomelli, *Mimesi, origine, allegoria* (Firenze: Alinea, 2002), pp. 162–170.
32. John W. Velz, "The Ancient World in Shakespeare: Authenticity or Anachronism? A Retrospect", *Shakespeare Survey*, 31 (1978), 1–12. For a recent assessment of the state of art, see Miola's authoritative and indispensable article "Past the Size of Dreaming? Shakespeare's Rome", *Shakespeare Survey*, 69 (special issue on *Shakespeare and Rome*, ed. Peter Holland (2016), 1–16. But see also D. Lovascio, "Introduction: Visions of Rome in Shakespeare", *Shakespeare*, 15:4 (2019), 311–315.
33. See Alessandro Serpieri, Claudia Corti, and Keir Elam, eds, *Nel laboratorio di Shakespeare. I drammi romani* (Parma: Pratiche Editrice, 1988); Charles and Michelle Martindale, *Shakespeare and the Uses of Antiquity* (London and New York: Routledge, 1990); Charles Martindale and A.B. Taylor, *Shakespeare and the Classics* (Cambridge: Cambridge University Press, 2004); Lynn Enterline, *Shakespeare's Schoolroom* (Philadelphia: University of Pennsylvania Press, 2012); Burrow, *Shakespeare and Classical Antiquity* (Oxford: Oxford University Press, 2013).
34. Over the years the shift of approaches and theoretical perspectives has been signalled by a conspicuous group of important collections: John Drakakis, ed., William Shakespeare, *Antony and Cleopatra* (Houndmills: Macmillan New Casebooks, 1994; Graham Holderness, Brian Loughrey and Andrew Murphy, eds, *Shakespeare: The Roman Plays* (London: Longman, 1996); Richard Wilson, ed., William Shakespeare, *Julius Caesar* (Houndmills and New York: Palgrave New Casebooks, 2002); Peter Holland, ed., *Shakespeare and Rome*, thematic issue of *Shakespeare Survey*, 69, 2016; Domenico Lovascio, ed., *Shakespeare: Visions of Rome*, special issue of *Shakespeare*, 15, 2019; Domenico Lovascio and Lisa Hopkins, eds, *The Uses of Rome in English Renaissance Drama*, thematic issue of *Textus: English Studies in Italy*,

29, 2016. But see also among monographs: Lisa Hopkins, *The Cultural Uses of the Caesars on the English Renaissance Stage* (Farnham: Ashgate, 2008, rpt London and New York: Routledge, 2016); Warren Chernaik, *The Myth of Rome in Shakespeare and His Contemporaries* (Cambridge: Cambridge University Press, 2011); Domenico Lovascio, *Un nome, mille volti. Giulio Cesare nel teatro inglese della prima età moderna* (Roma: Carocci, 2015).

35. See Vanna Gentili, *La Roma antica degli elisabettiani* (Bologna: Il Mulino, 1991); Geoffrey Miles, *Shakespeare and the Constant Romans* (Oxford: Clarendon Press, 1996); Andrew Hadfield, *Shakespeare and Republicanism* (Cambridge: Cambridge University Press, 2005); Patrick Gray, *Shakespeare and the Fall of the Roman Republic* (Edinburgh: Edinburgh University Press, 2019).

36. See Janet Adelman's *The Common Liar* (New Haven: Yale University Press, 1973) and her many chapters in *Suffocating Mothers* (New York: Routledge, 1992), and elsewhere; Coppélia Kahn, *Roman Shakespeare: Warriors, Wounds, and Women* (London: Routledge, 1997); Arthur L. Little Jr., *Shakespeare Jungle Fever: National-Imperial Re-Visions of Race, Rape, and Sacrifice* (Stanford, CA: Stanford University Press, 2000); Ania Loomba, *Shakespeare, Race, and Colonialism*, 2002; Maria Del Sapio Garbero, ed., *Identity, Otherness and Empire in Shakespeare's Rome* ([Farnham and Burlington: Ashgate, 2009] rpt London and New York: Routledge, 2016); Maria Del Sapio Garbero, Nancy Isenberg, Maddalena Pennacchia, eds, *Questioning Bodies in Shakespeare's Rome* (Göttingen: V&R Unipress, 2010); Domenico Lovascio, ed., *Roman Women in Shakespeare and His Contemporaries* (Kalamazoo: Medieval Institute Publications, 2020).

37. See Maddalena Pennacchia, *Shakespeare intermediale. I drammi romani* (Spoleto: Editoria & Spettacolo, 2012); Nathalie Vienne-Guerrin and Sarah Hatchuel, eds, *Shakespeare on Screen: The Roman Plays* (Mont-Saint-Aignan: Publications des Universités de Rouen et du Havre, 2009); Daniela Guardamagna, ed., *Roman Shakespeare: Intersecting Times, Spaces, Languages* (Oxford: Peter Lang, 2018); Maria Del Sapio Garbero, ed., *Rome in Shakespeare's World* (Roma: Storia e Letteratura, 2018).

38. Greene, *The Light to Troy*, pp. 41–42.

39. Barkan, *Unearthing the Past*, p. XXI.

40. Alexander Nagel and Christopher S. Wood, *Anachronic Renaissance* (New York: Zone Books, 2010), p. 11.

41. With Greene he "believe[s] that a single word contains within itself a micro-history of ideas, resonating with overtones beyond its literal sense". Following Georges Didi-Huberman's notion of "surviving image", Hui invites us to regard ruins as something that "has lost its original value and meaning", yet spectre-like and haunting with its latency of sense, "assumes a new monument-function as a sign of a former glory, stubbornly fixed to its geographical habitus", *The Poetics of Ruins in Renaissance Literature* (New York: Fordham University Press, 2016), pp. 17 and 23.

42. See for all A. Kent Hieatt, "The Genesis of Shakespeare's *Sonnets*: Spenser's *Ruines of Rome: by Bellay*", PMLA, 98:5 (1983), 800–814.

43. Philip Schwyzer, *Archaeologies of English Renaissance Literature* (Oxford: Oxford University Press, 2007).

44. John Dee, *Mathematicall Preface to Elements of Geometrie of Euclid of Megara* [1570], The Project Gutenberg Ebooks, 2007, pp. 41–43.

45. Jonathan Sawday, *The Body Emblazoned: Dissection and the Human Body in Renaissance Culture* (London and New York: Routledge, 1995), p. 2.

46. The archaeological approach in Foucault's conceptualization is characterized by a turning away from linear successions and a concern for "discoveries in

depth" and "sedimentary strata", each strata presenting its "own peculiar discontinuities and patterns", its "epistemological acts and thresholds", and raising a series of questions: "What link should be made between disparate events? How can a causal succession be established between them? What continuity or overall significance do they possess? Is it possible to define a totality, or must one be content with reconstituting connexions?" *The Archaeology of Knowledge and the Discourse of Language*, transl. A.M. Sheridan Smith (New York: Pantheon Books, 1972), pp. 3–4.

47. Sigmund Freud, *Civilization and Its Discontents*, transl. Joan Riviere (London: The Hogarth Press, 1930), p. 17 *et passim*. For more on this see Maria Del Sapio Garbero, "The Illness of Shakespeare's Rome: An Introduction", in Del Sapio Garbero, ed., *Rome in Shakespeare's World* (Roma: Edizioni di Storia e Letteratura, 2018), pp. vii–xxii.

48. Salvatore Settis, *Futuro del 'classico'* (Torino: Einaudi, 2004), pp. 13–14 and 17. My transl.

49. Greene, *The Light to Troy*, pp. 94–95.

50. Benjamin, "Theses on the Philosophy of History", p. 248.

51. Settis, *Futuro del 'classico'*, p. 85. My transl.

52. Poggio Bracciolini, *De fortunae varietate et Urbis Romae & de ruina eiusdem descriptio*, 1448. Quoted in Edward Gibbon's *The History of the Decline and Fall of the Roman Empire* [1788–89], in 12 vols, ed. J.B. Bury (New York: Freed De Fau & Company Publishers, 1907), vol. 12, chapter 71, p. 183. The Latin text is here quoted according to the Latin-French edition, *Les Ruines de Rome. De Varietate Fortunae*. Livre I. Texte établi et traduit par Jean-Yves Boriaud. Introduction by Philippe Coarelli and Jean-Yves Boriaud (Paris: Belle Lettres, 1999), pp. 12–13. Gibbon probably translated from the complete text published in 1723, which presents several variants with respect to the print editions of the first book, published in different editions starting at the beginning of 1500.

53. The idea of elusiveness as specific to the archaeologist humanist discovery of the past as aforesaid is well underlined by Greene (*The Light to Troy*). Strangely, Poggio is overlooked in his book; to be sure he is mentioned only once and not for his *Ruines*.

54. Barkan, *Unearthing the Past*, pp. 7 and xxi.

55. See Peter Spring, *The Topographical and Archaeological Study of the Antiquitie of the City of Rome, 1420–1447* (University of Edinburgh, unpublished PhD thesis, 1972), p. 244.

56. See Philippe Coarelli and Jean-Yves Boriaud, "Introduction" to *Les Ruines de Rome. De Varietate Fortunae* I, pp. XI–LXXI.

57. Thus translated and quoted in Gibbon, *The History of the Decline and Fall of the Roman Empire*, p. 183. But see also the Latin-French text established by Coarelli and Boriaud, *Les Ruines de Rome. De Varietate Fortunae*, pp. 38–39 (and Introduction, p. LXVII).

58. For a discussion of the Capitol symbolism in relation to Rome as head of empire, see Catherine Edwards, *Writing Rome: Textual Approaches to the City* (Cambridge: Cambridge University Press, 1996), pp. 82–88.

59. See Stephen Greenblatt, *The Swerve: How the Renaissance Began* (London: The Bodley Head, 2011). But see also Roberto Weiss, *The Renaissance Discovery of Classical Antiquity* (Oxford: Basil Blackwell, 1969).

60. Gibbon, *The History of the Decline and Fall of the Roman Empire*, vol. 12, p. 213.

61. Patricia B. Craddock, "Edward Gibbon and the 'Ruins of the Capitol'", in Annabel Patterson, ed., *Roman Images* (Baltimore and London: The John

Hopkins University Press, 1984), pp. 64–67. See also Edwards, *Writing Rome*, pp. 73–74 and 89–95.

62. Craddock, "Edward Gibbon", pp. 63, 79.
63. Bracciolini, *Ruinarum Romae Descriptio* (*De varietate fortunae*, Libri primi), quoted according to the Latin-French text established by Coarelli and Bori-aud, p. 13. Ensuing mentions of Virgil's *Aeneid* are from The Loeb Classical Library, English translation by Henry Rushton Fairclough, revised by G.P. Goold (London and Cambridge, MA: Harvard University Press, 1999).
64. See Greene, *The Light to Troy*, pp. 92 and 148–179.
65. For a recent archaeological discussion of the book not simply as a text and a subject matter, but materially as a property and as a place of historicized reading and how this questions the stability of the early modern text, see Stephen Orgel, *The Reader in the Book: A Study of Places and Traces* (Oxford: Oxford University Press, 2015).
66. Greenblatt, *The Swerve*, p. 43.
67. Gibbon, *The History of the Decline and Fall of the Roman Empire*, pp. 183–184.
68. Foucault, *The Archaeology of Knowledge*, pp. 7–8. For "an ontology that declares open borders" between monument and document to the end of a new approach to the study of humanities, see John Guillory, "Monuments and Documents: Panofsky on the Object of Study in the Humanities", *History of Humanities*, 1:1 (2016), pp. 9–30.
69. Foucault, *The Archaeology of Knowledge*, p. 8.
70. The epistemological fracture introduced by growing documentation and the birth of the Foucauldian notion of the archive can be best appreciated in light of our own digital forms of memory and modernity. As media theorist Wolfgang Ernst has written,

> the archival method of memory (record management) is a non-narrative alternative to historiography, in the best tradition of early twentieth century avant-garde which "questioned all models of memory (especially narrative ones), favouring openly dynamic, discontinuous forms contiguous with modern means of technological reproduction—especially photography and film" (Ernst 2010). An archival collection of photographs as accumulation (different from private photo albums) does not yet constitute a meaningful story; on the contrary, it rather deconstructs narrative.

"Radically De-Historicising the Archive. Decolonising Archival Memory from the Supremacy of Historical Discourse", in *Decolonising Archives* (L'Internationale Online, www.internationaleonline.org, 2016), p. 12.
71. As Salvatore Settis points out, the universality subsumed in the term *oikoumene* is also proper to the 'classical' (*Futuro del classico*, p. 12).
72. See Greenblatt, *The Swerve*, especially the chapter "Birth and Rebirth", pp. 110–134.
73. I am borrowing from Edwards, *Writing Rome*, pp. 6–8. But see also, with the same implications of discovery and making things exist through writing or remapping, Richard Helgerson's monumental *Forms of Nationhood: The Elizabethan Writing of England* (Chicago: The University of Chicago Press, 1992), p. 13.
74. Flavio Biondo, *Roma instaurata* (1444–46). Quotations are from the Italian translation by Lucio Fauno, *Roma ristaurata, et Italia illustrata di Biondo da Forlì* (Venezia: M. Tramezino, 1542). Further pages are given directly in the text. The translation from Italian into English is mine.

75. For more on Biondo see Spring, *The Topographical and Archaeological Study*. But see also Angelo Mazzocco, "Rome and the Humanists: The Case of Biondo Flavio", in Paul A. Ramsey, ed., *Rome in the Renaissance: The City and the Myth* (New York: Center for Medieval & Early Renaissance Studies, 1982), pp. 185–193.
76. On the transformation of the city undertaken by the popes see David Karmon, *The Ruin of the Eternal City: Antiquity and Preservation in Renaissance Rome* (Oxford: Oxford University Press, 2011). See also Yvonne Elet, *Architectural Invention in Renaissance Rome*, especially the chapter, "Reviving the Corpse" (Cambridge: Cambridge University Press, 2018), pp. 15–32.
77. Thomas Nashe, *The Unfortunate Traveller or The Life of Jack Wilton*. Printed by T. Scarlet for C. Burby, (London, 1594), p. 43. Further pages directly in the text.
78. Andrew Hadfield usefully links Nashe's *Unfortunate Traveller* to Jan Van Der Noot's *A Theatre Wherein Be Represented as Wel the Miseries and Calamities That Follow Voluptuous Worldlings* (1569), William Thomas's *The Historie of Italie* (London, 1549), and others, for the way it contributes to give us an idea of how Rome was perceived as a "city of startling contrasts" in Tudor England. See his "Renaissance England's View of Rome", in Maria Del Sapio Garbero, ed., *Rome in Shakespeare's World* (Roma: Edizioni di Storia e Letteratura, 2018), pp. 127–146.
79. Salvatore Settis, "Arte classica, libertà, rivoluzioni", *Sei lezioni di Salvatore Settis*. RAI cultura. Terza lezione: https://www.raicultura.it/arte/articoli/2020/06/Winckelmann--ebc1eef9-20f3-421f-813d-04fde0f00130.html.
80. See in Poggio's *Ruines* his disappointment in discovering that even such an erudite writer as Petrarch had negligently mistaken the Pyramide Cestius's tomb for that of Remus's, notwithstanding the fact that the engraved epigram was still intact. *Les Ruines de Rome. De Varietate Fortunae*. Livre I. p. 19.
81. As Derrida points out in his reflection on spectrality: "this being-with specters would also be, not only but also, a politics of memory, of inheritance, and of generations". *Specters of Marx* (New York and London: Routledge, [1993] 2006), p. XIX.
82. Erwin Panofsky, "The History of Art as a Humanistic Discipline", in *The Meaning of the Humanities* (1940). Quoted in Guillory, "Monuments and Documents", p. 17.
83. Spring, *The Topographical and Archaeological*, p. 109.
84. See Greene, *The Light to Troy*, p. 234.
85. Michel de Montaigne, *The Complete Works of Michel de Montaigne*, 4 vols, edited by William Hazlitt (transl. Charles Cotton); *Comprising His Essays, The Letters; The Journey Through Germany and Italy* (now first translated); *A Life*, by the editor (London: John Templeman, 1842), p. 572. Hereafter page mentions are directly in the text.
86. Poggio Bracciolini, *"ut, si quis reuiuiscat ex priscis illis antiquae urbis ciuibus, alios homines intueri, aliam se longe urbem incolere asseueret, ita eius specie et ipso solo subuersis, ut nihil fere recognoscat, quod priorem urbem repraesentet"*, *Les Ruines de Rome. De Varietate Fortunae*. Livre I, p. 15.
87. Greene, *The Light to Troy*, p. 238.
88. Margaret Ferguson, "'The Afflatus of Ruin': Meditation on Rome by Du Bellay, Spenser, and Stevens", in Annabel Patterson, ed., *Roman Images*, pp. 23–50.
89. For the way they resonate in Shakespeare's sonnets, see Jonathan Bate, *Shakespeare and Ovid* (Oxford: Clarendon Press, 1993), pp. 92–96. But see also Alessandro Serpieri, *I sonetti dell'immortalità* (Milano: Bompiani, 1975), pp. 46–54. For an enlarged discussion of the poetical immortality topos to classical and Renaissance literature, see Hui, *The Poetics of Ruins*, pp. 27–51. But see also Edwards, *Writing Rome*, pp. 6–8.

90. Horace, *Odes*, transl. Charles E. Bennet [1914], Loeb Classical Library (London and Cambridge, MA: Harvard University Press, 1964).
91. Ovid, *Metamorphoses*. Quotations are from Arthur Golding translation, ed. Madeleine Forey (London: Penguin Books, 2002). Hereafter mentioned as Golding's *Metamorphoses*.
92. Shakespeare hints at Ovid's disfavour in *The Taming of the Shrew*, 1.1.33 ("As Ovid be an outcast quite abjured").
93. Ovid, *Tristia*, Loeb Classical Library, tansl. Arthur Leslie Wheeler, [1929] (London and Cambridge, MA: Harvard University Press, 1965).
94. Biondo, *Roma ristaurata*. The last lines of the "Dedicatory Preface" in the Italian translation by Lucio Fauno with the title *Italia Illustrata*.
95. For more on the Capitol "in ruins" and "in flames", see Edwards, *Writing Rome*, pp. 70–82.
96. On the topicality of tombs in post-Reformation England and the way this affected poetical elegy and Shakespeare's construction of one's eternity, see John Kerrigan, "Shakespeare. Elegy, and Epitaphs *1557–1640*", in Jonathan Post, ed., *The Oxford Handbook of Shakespeare's Poetry* (Oxford: Oxford University Press, 2013), pp. 225–244.
97. Greene, *The Light to Troy*, pp. 221–222.
98. On the specific theme of imitation and *translatio studii* see Jean-Claude Carron, "Imitation and Intertextuality in the Renaissance", *New Literary History*, 19:3 (1988), 565–579. For a recent discussion of Du Bellay's circulation in England and its incidence on Shakespeare according to a transnational understanding of imitation see Line Cottegnies, "Of the Importance of Imitation: Du Bellay, Shakespeare, and the English Sonnetteers", *Shakespeare Studies*, 48 (2020), 41–47. For a post-millennium notion of mobility and its revisionary agency see Steven Greenblatt et al., eds, *Cultural Mobility: A Manifesto* (Cambridge: Cambridge University Press, 2010).
99. Joachim Du Bellay, *Les antiquitez de Rome* et *Les regrets* (Genève Lille: Droz Girard, 1960). This dedicatory sonnet was omitted when Spenser's translated *Les Antiquitez* to be included in his *Complaints* (1591) as *Ruines of Rome*.
100. Mentions refer to the EEBO edition: https://quod.lib.umich.edu/e/eebo/A08 269.0001.001/1:4?rgn=div1;view=fulltext.
101. Tom MacFaul, "A Theatre for Worldlings (1569)", in Richard A. McCabe, ed., *The Oxford Handbook of Edmund Spenser* (Oxford: Oxford University Press, 2010), p. 150. See also Bart Westeweel, ed., *Anglo-Dutch Relations in the Field of the Emblem* (Leiden and New York: Brill, 1997), pp. 50–62 and Andrew Hadfield, "Edmund Spenser's Translations of Du Bellay in Jan van der Noot's *A Theatre for Voluptuous Worldlings*", in Fred Schurink, ed., *Tudor Translation* (Basingstoke: Palgrave Macmillan, 2011), pp. 143–160.
102. Ferguson, "The Afflatus of Ruin", p. 25.
103. See the two sections of *Complaints* and *Theatre for Wordlings* in Spenser, *The Yale Edition of the Shorter Poems*, pp. 215–484.
104. As Margaret Ferguson underlines, translating Du Bellay's *Antiquitez* was, however, important in Spenser's progress as a poet. It allows us to understand "not only Spenser's portrait of Duessa in the *Faerie Queene* but also his ambivalence toward his own act of bringing Du Bellay's poems about ancient Rome to Protestant England", "'The afflatus of ruins'", p. 30.
105. Hassan Melehi, "Antiquities of Britain: Spenser's *Ruines of Time*", *Studies in Philology*, 102:2 (2005), 159–183 (p. 159). For a discussion of the role played by Du Bellay and Spenser in the history of early modern concern for ruins see also, by the same author, *The Poetics of Literary Transfer in*

Early Modern France and England ([Farnham: Ashgate 2010] rpt Abingdon: Routledge, 2016). On transference (or *translatio studii*), see also Carron, "Imitation and Intertextuality".

106. Hui, *The Poetics of Ruins*, p. 210.
107. Greene, *The Light to Troy*, p. 221.
108. Greene, *The Light to Troy*, p. 220.
109. See Hieatt, "The Genesis of Shakespeare's *Sonnets*". But see also Tom Muir, "Without Remainder: Ruins and Tombs in Shakespeare's *Sonnets*", *Textual Practice*, 24:1 (2010), 21–49; and Anne Lake Prescott, "Du Bellay and Shakespeare's Sonnets", in Jonathan F.S. Post, ed., *The Oxford Handbook of Shakespeare's Poetry* (Oxford: Oxford University Press, 1916), pp. 134–150, who more recently has enlarged the role played by Du Bellay in fostering what she calls a "ruinish" dialect (of which she over-accentuates the modish side, at the expense of its epistemological potential). She also devotes a "Coda" to *Titus Andronicus*.
110. Hieatt, "The Genesis of Shakespeare's *Sonnets*", p. 802.
111. Derrida, *Specters of Marx*, p. 21.
112. Benjamin, *The Origin of German Tragic Drama*, p. 178 *et passim*.
113. For a discussion of modal verbs in Shakespeare's language, see Iolanda Plescia, "Expressions of Futurity in Early Modern Dramatic Dialogue: A Case Study", in Gabriella Mazzon and Luisanna Fodde, eds, *Historical Perspectives on Forms of English Dialogue* (Milano: Franco Angeli, 2012), pp. 99–115.
114. Heather James, *Shakespeare's Troy: Drama, Politics, and the Translation of Empire* (Cambridge: Cambridge University Press, [1997] 2006), p. 91 (pp. 85–118).
115. Derrida, *Specters of Marx*, cit. p. 24.
116. Tanya Pollard, "What's Hecuba to Shakespeare?" *Renaissance Quarterly*, 65:4 (2012), 1060–1093 (p. 1082).
117. Hell and Schonle, *Ruins of Modernity*, pp. 193–194.
118. "If Troy's fortune revive again, it shall be under evil omen, and her doom shall be repeated with dire disaster, I, Jove's consort and sister, leading the conquering hosts. Should her walls thrice rise in bronze with Phoebus' help, thrice shall they perish, destroyed by my Argive warriors; thrice shall the captive wife mourn her husband and her children" (*Odes*, 3.3.61–68).
119. Ivan Lupic, "The Mobile Queen: Observing *Hecuba* in Renaissance Europe", *Renaissance Drama*, 46:1 (2018), 25–56.
120. James, *Shakespeare's Troy*, p. 84.
121. The reference is to Ovidio, *Metamorfosi*, Latin-Italian edition, ed. Piero Bernardini Marzolla (Torino: Einaudi, 1979) and Arthur Golding, *Ovid's Metamorphoses*, ed. Madeleine Forey (London: Penguin, 2002).
122. See for all the Arden edition of *The Tempest*, eds. Virginia Mason Vaughan and Alden T. Vaughan (London: Bloomsbury Arden Shakespeare, 1999), notes 48–49, p. 266.
123. Bate, *Shakespeare and Ovid*, pp. 8–9.
124. Bate, *Shakespeare and Ovid*, pp. 251–252.
125. See Greene, *The Light to Troy*, pp. 222–223.
126. The coincidence between *The Tempest* and the archive of Renaissance culture and civilization, civility and ruins, was beautifully brought to the fore by Greenaway in his very Foucauldian film *Prospero's Books*. It has been insightfully exploited by ensuing theatrical adaptations of the play. Among these a recent Italian production by Daniele Salvo for the Gigi Proietti Globe Theatre Silvano Toti in Rome (25 September 2018).

Introduction

Part 2 The Ruins of England

In his *Britannia* (three Latin versions after 1586, a couple of European editions, English translation in 1610), in the section devoted to the "Romans in Britain", seen as the only beginning of England's written history, William Camden presents Caesar's expedition to the island in 54 BC more as a gesture pursued for the "sake of glory", an act of propaganda which enabled him to boast an enlarged perimeter of the Roman world, than as an immediate project to actually subdue the land.

> When Fortitude and Fortune were so agreed, or Gods appointment rather had thus decreed, that Rome should subdue all the earth, Caius Iulius Cæsar, having now by conquests over-runne Gaule, to the end, that by a successive traine of victories atchieved both by land and sea, he might joyne those Lands together which nature had severed, (as if the Romane world would not suffice) cast an eie unto the Ocean; and in the four and fiftieth yeere before the incarnation of Christ, endevoured to make a journey into Britain.
>
> (*Brit* 1, 34)[1]

To the eye of the local inhabitants Caesar paraded his "journey" with the terrifying spectacle of 80 transport ships for his legions and about 18 more just for horses—a number of ships strikingly increased to hundreds (800) in the second expedition of the following year. But he left to others who would come after him (Augustus, Caligula, Claudius, Vespasian, Adrian, Constantine) the task of really transforming the island into a Roman province—which they did by creating hostility among Britain's several kings and conquering their lands one after the other. Nevertheless, as shown by his "Commentaries", extensively quoted by Camden (*Brit* 1, 34–38),[2] Caesar was ingenious in framing his two British campaigns as a "conquest" especially when, faced with landing coasts which were hostile to his fleet and the indomitable belligerence of the local population, he thought it expedient to go no further than the territories across

DOI: 10.4324/9781003259671-2

the river Thames. These comprised a region roughly coincident with the early modern counties of Middlesex and Essex—a region inhabited by people Caesar mentions as the Trinobantes: a name probably deriving from "towns in a valley", "a city in a wood", or "a city of ships", as the ancient local etymology of Londiniun might also indicate, and not Troja Nova, the "reedified" city, as the "fabulous writers" maintain, Camden argues in his philological speculation. (*Brit* 1, 417, 421; *Brit* 2, 307, 311).[3] But returning to Caesar's hyperbolic "journey to Britain", it is likely that his only intention was to force princes of the local population to surrender and pay tributes to Rome (the name of Cassivellaun or Cassibelin occurs in this instance, *Brit* 1, 36–37). In all cases, for Caesar to be able to return to Rome as a conqueror, it was sufficient for him to establish favourable peace deals with individual princes and warleaders. It was even more important though to show Britain to the Romans (as in fact he did in writing as well as by showcasing hostages brought back to Rome for his triumph). Indeed, it was crucial to the end of his legend that he could enlist the conquest of that last northern bastion in the annals of his achievements. Years later, Tacitus in *Agricola* aptly invited a distinction between discovery and conquest: "he [Cæsar] discovered onely, but delivered not unto the Romanes, Britaine" (*Brit* 1, 38).

That said, in Camden's work Caesar, as well as coeval Latin authors, are given the merit of having inscribed Britain into history; or, in other words, of having written its first inhabitants into existence, at a time when they were still lacking the writing instruments and books necessary to transmit their own memory to posterity. For Camden the Latin reports on their culture, houses, manners, apparel, war tactics, Druidic religious rites, memorable actions, and speeches as proud barbarous warriors—which he accounts for both in *Britannia* and the ensuing *Remains Concerning Britain* (1605)—were just one instance of this truth. Then, "From his time [Caesar's] and no further off, must the Writer our Historie fetch his beginning, of his worke" (*Brit* 1, 34), Camden suggests; for as Varro had authoritatively stated in defining the historical age, "the Acts therein done, are contained in true Histories" (*id.*). This is Camden's *vademecum*, while pursuing his Roman path back to Britain's origins as "highly" as possible[4] based on the amazing documentation drawn from Latin and later authors; a method that he defines as radically distinct from the "fabulous", undocumented mode prompted by the followers of Geoffrey of Monmouth, the author of *Historia Regum Britanniae* (ca. 1136), the book in which the story of Brutus and Britain's Trojan descent first appears, with no previous traceable source whatsoever, as Camden takes pains to demonstrate.

Among those that in Tudor England subscribed to Monmouth's story of the island as a Troja Nova (Caxton, Bale, Holinshed, Drayton, Stow) was the most assertive Richard Harvey, the discussed author of *Philadelphus, or A Defence of Brutes, and the Brutans History* (1593), who had revitalized the issue in the 1590s at the cry of: "We are not Brittons, we are Brutans" (for more see chapter on *Cymbeline*). Not that Camden himself didn't perceive the empowering role that ennobling legends had in national foundation myths from time immemorial. In fact, he explains, the story of Brutus may have originated as an effect of imitation in the European competition for noble Trojan origins.[5] Nor was it likely that he could have ignored the corporate interests that intervened in the defence of such an ancestry (ahead of the Roman Britannia *Augusta*) in the anti-papist England of post-Reformation time. These were elements that turned the matter of origins and belonging in general into a problematized and utterly passionate issue in Elizabethan culture. But as a pursuer of truth, as he was keen on regarding himself, Camden insisted on the separation of fables from facts, by claiming a method based on the comparison of written sources and a topographical re-collection of the "remains" of an English past buried under centuries of oblivion: a past which—subtly contrasting with ideologized Tudor notions of an inviolable and unviolated England—he looked at through the prevailing lens of recurrent ruination and an emerging archaeological consciousness of the island's Roman and post-Roman past as a buried presence to be unearthed and anatomized in depth, as human bodies were in the resurgent coeval anatomy. Information and other perspectives on Roman-British relations in antiquity could also be found elsewhere, starting from Holinshed's *Chronicles*.[6] But Camden's project as a would-be historian and chorographer was rooted, advisedly or not, within the same excavating episteme which encouraged Poggio Bracciolini and his humanist colleagues, not to mention Petrarch before them,[7] to search for modernity in a buried and aporetic past.

"In the fields of which suburbs, while, I was first writing these matters, there were gotten out of the ground many urnes, funeral vessels, little Images, and earthen pots", Camden wrote, referring to finds brought to light in the new suburbs north-east of London,

> wherein were final peeces of mony coined by Claudius, Nero, Vespa-
> sian etc. Glasse vials also and sundry small earthen vessels, wherein
> some liquid substance remained which I would thinke to bee either of
> that sacred oblation of wine and milke, which the ancient Romanes
> used when they burnt the dead, or else those odoriferous liquors that
> Statius mentioneth.

The same event will be recounted more extensively by John Stow in 1598 in his *Survey of London*. Camden also explained,

> This place the Romanes appointed to burne & burie dead bodies,
> who according to the law of the xij. tables carried coarses out of the
> Cities, and entered them by the high waies sides, to put passengers in
> mind that they are, as those were, subject to mortalitie.

(*Brit* 1, 433–434)

The *disjecta membra* of Poggio Bracciolini's "mighty giant" were reappearing, with no need of travelling to Rome, from beneath the soil tread by domestic perambulatory antiquarians like Camden and shown as subterranean objects of astonishment and wonder. Coincidentally, suburbs north and south of London were also those liminal places—within and outside the jurisdiction of the city (the so-called Liberties)—where playhouses were rising, in the last two decades of the century, and enjoying, in Mullaney's words, their

> culturally and ideologically removed vantage point . . . a freedom, a range of slightly eccentric or decentered perspective, that gave the stage an uncanny ability to tease out and represent the contradictions of a culture it both belonged to and was, to a certain extent, alienated from.[8]

Here, without travelling, Elizabethans were offered the vicarious experience of "strange things" and temporal as well as geographical elsewheres (in Platter's often quoted report), "learning from plays what is happening in other lands".[9]

England's Roman ruins similarly belonged to mixed territories and liminal knowledge. As tangible fragments of a surviving past, ruins were discovered as temporally alien and geographically contemporary. In fact, they pertained to a topography that the antiquarians increasingly disclosed as a layered field of visibility and spectrality. A case in point was that of St. Paul's Cathedral: a sacred place whose subterranean finds revealed, as inhabited by alien and unsettling forms of devotion and secret knowledge, a layered and aporetic profundity, a depth, the depth of time, which opened up to its bemusing materiality and to conjectural and uncanny speculation: "That there stood of old time a Temple of Diana in this place some have conjectured, and arguments there are to make this conjecture good", Camden argues.

> While Edward the First reigned, an incredible number of Ox-heads were digged up, as we finde in our Annals, which the common sort at that time made a wondering at, as the Sacrifices of Gentiles: and the learned know, that *Taurapolia* were celebrated in the honour of Diana.
> (*Brit* 1, 426)

Visible and spectral as they presented themselves, ruins partook in the same spectacle of ambivalence and liminality which defined the space of the playhouses. Indeed, ruins were both within and outside the "legality" of the prevailing cultural discourse, precisely as the myth of Rome was in post-Reformation time and as Shakespeare articulates it in *Cymbeline*, problematically conflating as it did the ancient and the "papist" Rome. Equally (as in Shakespeare's uncanny resurrections of his late plays),[10] ruins could foster suspicion when collected as relics and regarded with the devotion of a reappearing numinous past. More recent ruins—such as those caused by the Tudor dissolution of monasteries and stripping of the altars, left with whitewashed walls and defaced or interred sacred statues—made cogent and overconnoted this ambivalent condition. Indulging in the view of ruins might involve idolatry when iconoclasm and forgetting had become the "central sacrament of Reform" (Eamon Duffy), and when the hardly defined demarcation between image-meaning and word-meaning in the knowledge of divine reality had kindled a divisive epistemological dispute which went well beyond the theological field to invest ways of knowledge *tout court* (Stuart Clark).[11] If anything, Reformist iconoclasm complicated with yet another layer of ruins and meanings the process of renegotiation of England's relation with its Roman past, within the larger framework of Renaissance process of self-fashioning, as Greenblatt might say.[12]

Shakespeare's theatre builds upon what one might call the spectral concreteness of the ruin, in the way it is persistently underwritten by an unsettling sense of crisis and loss and in the way this problematizes at the core his anatomy of reality. Did the antiquarian pursuit have any part in his sharpened capacity to listen to and visualize the pressure coming from the groan of a ruinous past? Spenser's imagination thrived on this, when iconoclastically in his *Ruines of Time* he constructed his Camden-inspired "Verlame" (see vv. 169–75), as a *tabula rasa* suspiciously enveloped and suspended in the issue of its memory.

> I was that Citie, which the garland wore
> Of *Britaines* pride, delivered unto me
> By *Romane* Victors, which it wonne of yore;
> Though nought at all but ruines now I bee,
> And lye in mine owne ashes, as ye see:
> *Verlame* I was; what bootes it that I was,
> Sith now I am but weedes and wasteful gras?
> (36–42)[13]

Verulam, the ancient city of Roman Britain rediscovered by the antiquarians, is here transformed into a powerful personified allegory of mournful remembrance, but paradoxically with no ruins worthy of being remembered or mourned ("To tell my forces matchable to none, / Were but lost labour, that few would believe, / And with rehearsing would me more agreeve", 89–91). For the antiquarian, on the contrary, ruins could be both effaced and surfacing in their capacity to foster conjecture, meaning, and interpretation.[14] Unlike Spenser, for Camden, Verulam's ruins were still endowed with such a pressure when he restored them to their "Antiquity", or memory:

> But returne we now to places more within the Country, and of greater antiquity. From Hertford twelve miles Westward, stood

VEROLAMIUM, a Citie in time past very much renowned, and as greatly frequented, Tacitus calleth it VERULAMIUM . . . Neither hath it as yet lost that ancient name, for commonly they call it Ver-ulam, although there remaineth nothing of it to be seene, beside the few remains of ruined walles, the checkered pavements, and peeces of Roman coine other whiles digged up there. . . . Whereby it was guessed that this was the very same towne of Casibelaunus fortified with woods and marishes, which Caesar wan. In Nero his time it was counted a MUNICIPIUM . . . These Municipia were townes endowed with the right of Romane Citizens . . . But whether this Municipium or towne enfranchised were with suffrages or without, a man cannot easily affirme. . . . I have seene old antiquities of mony stamped, as it seemeth here, with this inscription TASCIA, and on the reverse VER. Which that learned searcher of Venerable antiquity David Powell, Doctour in Divinity interpreth to be Tribut of Verulamium.

(*Brit* 1, 408–409)

We might perceive germs of this acting in both *Titus Andronicus* and *Cymbeline*, in the way confusing fragments of an archaeological, enig-matic Rome are brought home in each play to imagine the encounter with the otherness of one's past, entailing the questioning of history and originary myths. As later in Webster's theatrical invention of a voice, an "echo" coming from the fault lines of a layered past, ruins provided the occasion for an uncanny confrontation with history that gestured towards conflated geographies and temporalities: "This fortification / Grew from the ruins of an ancient abbey", Delio says in *The Duchess of Malfi*'s grave-yard scene, "And to yon side o'th' river lies a wall, / Piece of a cloister, which in my opinion / Gives the best echo that you ever heard, / So hol-low and so dismal, and withal / So plain in the distinction of our words, / That many have supposed it is a spirit / That answers" (5.3.1–9).[15] The "echo" cooperates in transforming into lamentation the sorrow of the living. Ruins, and the attention on responsive ruins, also prospected an idea of history (or memory) physically if archaeologically experienced as "depth", with one's feet. "I do love these ancient ruins", Antonio says on the rebound, "We never tread upon them but we set / Our foot upon some reverend history" (5.3.9–11). As in Shakespeare's "Bare ruined choirs" (son. 73), ruins emerge as residual if troubling affectivity.[16]

The second half of the sixteenth century in England was characterized by a deep historical concern for the nation's origins, testified, as scholar-ship has extensively shown, by an extraordinary intellectual investment in the study of antiquity and updated topography (or chorography). It engaged a conspicuous number of antiquarians, surveyors, and county mapmakers, as well as philologists, classicists, poets, and playwrights in Elizabethan times (Saxton, Camden, Stow, Daniel, Drayton, Spenser, and others), resulting, as Helgerson has remarked, in a massive new geographical "writing" of the nation and national identity. This assumed significant relevance in Speed's *Theatre of the Empire of Great Britain* (1611–12) where the illustrated mapping of the counties of Britain—his *cartes à figures*—was often enriched with the counties' emerging archaeological past. As in the maps of Cornwall, Cumberland, Essex, and Northumberland, remains of Roman columns, altars, inscriptions, and coins encircle the centrality of the county's land, rearticulating—as its interrogating marginalia or *parergon*—the relationship between space, borders, and history. Cumberland, the county of the well-signalled Hadrian Wall (or "Picts Wall" as Speed calls it), is theatricalized by two imposing classic medallions functioning as banners. The first, on the left, parades the county's antiquity: "CUMBERLAND and the Ancient Citie CARLILE Described with many Memorable Antiquities therein Found Observed"; as we read in a framed square below, this is the city "where many monuments and Altars, with inscriptions to their Idole Gods, for the prosperity of their Emperours and themselves, many of them yet remaining in divers places there, are to be sene, and some of them according to their true forms here expressed". The second medallion, on the right, chronicles the history of the Wall:

> The ancient and utmost limits of the Roman Empire, was first made of Turffs and Stacks by Hadrian the Emproure. Afterwords by Severus much strengthened and extended through the Maine even from Sea to Sea, a worke soe famous, that the title Britannicus was given as Surname to the Emproure. And lastly in the declining estate of that Empire. It was built of firme stone, etc.[17]

As pointed out by Helgerson, the problematized relationship between chronicle and topography, time and space, also marked a shift of attention from the power residing in the chronicles of kings and dynasties (see Hall and Holinshed in the wake of Monmouth) to the binding agency residing in the materiality of the land, or places.[18] William Camden was well aware of his commitment when in addressing the readers of his *Britannia* he highlighted the paradoxical circumstance of persons who might be "strangers in their owne soile, and forrainers in their owne City" (*Brit* 1, "To the Reader", n.p.).

Marking the birth of the Society of Antiquarians, the publication of *Britannia* in 1586 was a landmark in redefining the state of antiquarian studies. As has been said, it "gave all future research a starting point and a base of reference. Here was a comprehensive work of inquiry into national origins and a description of the land unprecedented in its fullness and detail".[19] But in a way, I suggest, that was not simply topographical but newly archaeological, in the sense that time and space, and the English language itself, were not simply considered in their linear and horizontal succession, but (as the bodies of contemporary anatomy) taken on in their layered and bemusing profundity. Rewritten by time and its injuries, the land was discovered as a spectral geography, in the same ways in which, vice versa, history and origins appeared as rooted in the elusive condition of the ruin.

Like Rome in Du Bellay/Spenser's *Ruines of Rome* (sonnet 7.2), Camden's Verulam "onely doo the name of [Verulam] retaine". Nonetheless, scant as they were, its ruins are still visible and meaningful to him, in the sense that they can still stand for England's Roman past, and paradoxically for Rome's durability as a paradigm of the eternity of ruins, namely of a cyclical and traceable history of destruction and rebirth:

> In the reigne of the same Nero, when Bunduica or Boadicia Queene of the Icenes in her deepe love of her country, and conceived bitter hatred against the Romans, raised bloudy and mortall war upon them, it was rased and destroyed by the Britans, as Tacitus recordeth ... Neverthless it flourished again and became exceeding famous.
>
> (*Brit* 1, 409)

Not differently from ancient Rome in Italian humanist and Renaissance culture, England was being discovered and written into existence by means of a tension introduced not just by the land, but also by the land considered through the lens of time and its ruins. Significantly, history is objectified as "remain" in Camden's ensuing *Remains Concerning Britain* (1605), as if to indicate a careful work of collection and reconstruction (or *renovatio*) on the part of the nascent historian. Camden's enterprise began with a view of Britain's Roman ruins and was imbued with no less humanist empathy. As shown in the previous pages, from Poggio to Du Bellay in humanist and Renaissance Europe, Rome's ruins affect the viewer with the pathos of a tragic sight ("ye sacred ruines, and ye tragick sights"; sonnet 7). Even though in different degrees, the gaze of antiquarians, poets, and playwrights in early modern England seems to be similarly affected in the discovery of their own ruins. Camden didn't conceal his pathos, especially when he came to the end of the Roman rule and the ensuing invasions of the Anglo-Saxons of the fifth and sixth centuries: a moment felt as a brutal and traumatic fracture in early modern historiography,[20] to which he draws attention by means of the denouncing, overheated accents of the sixth-century monk Gildas, the author of *De exicidio et conquestu Britanniae* ("On the Ruin and Conquest of Britain"), usually referred to as *The Ruin of Britain*.

I will return to this in my chapter on *Titus Andronicus*. But how were Shakespeare's Roman (*and* history) plays interacting with this novel, inquisitive way of bringing to light the profundity of the past?[21] And could Roman ruins—or more precisely its ruinous myth—provide a viable discourse in addressing England's more recent troubled past? Francis Bacon interestingly ascribed antiquities to "defaced history" when, in ordering history into three types ("memorials, perfect histories, and antiquities"), he compared them to pictures: "For of pictures or images, we see some are unfinished, some are perfect, and some are defaced". Thus, with respect to perfect history, if memorials (mostly reports and documents) are simply "preparatory history", "antiquities are history defaced, or some remnants of history which have casually escaped the shipwreck of time".[22] As a matter of fact, antiquarian studies were doing much more. And Camden, a scholar connected to continental new historiography, had set an example of how the "remains" of Britain could be "restored" to their "Antiquity", namely how they could contribute to capitalized History, thanks to scrupulous philological scrutiny and interpretation.[23] And in fact there was no appeal for scrupulousness in Bacon's notion of "defaced history", were it not for a thinly disguised uneasiness with the fortuitous, damaged, and residual condition of its materials; the terms of an "epistemological uncertainty", in Adrian Hui's comment.[24] In Foucault's conceptualization of history as knowledge grounded in discontinuity, overlapping and sedimentary strata, the surviving object—what he calls the "dispersed event", the event which is archaeologically displaced, unintelligible, and hence unthinkable by traditional history—would be given the influential status of "one of the basic elements of historical analysis".[25]

Shakespeare's art, from beginning to end, makes "perfect" stories out of shipwrecked and defective/defaced materials. From *Titus*, to *Pericles*, to the *Tempest*, the imagery of the shipwreck and its relicts is pivotal in signalling itself as the *locus* of crisis and productive meaning. In *The Tempest*, as already observed in the first part of this Introduction, everything—the material and the immaterial, characters, memory and books, kings, slaves and servants, clothes, kingly signs of power, stories, myths, and the form (s) of the play itself—is (literally and metaphorically) disruptively confronted with the ruinous condition of the relict which has escaped the shipwreck. But what is equally important to highlight is that, soon in Shakespeare's career, both in the early Roman works and in the history plays of his first tetralogy (*1 Henry VI, 2 Henry VI, 3 Henry VI, Richard III*), ruin and its isotopic term "deface" (variously declined as defaced, defacing, defacer), occur as words that matter significantly, alternatively triggering an anatomizing and self-anatomizing process, or a denouncing *ekphrastic* procedure. Hecuba's disfigured face in *The Rape* conflates both. In *Richard III* (the last history of the first tetralogy), such a lexicon acquires the theatrical force of a cursing voice as in the vision of impending catastrophe prophetically evoked by Queen Elizabeth:

> Ay me! I see the downfall of our house.
> . . .
> Welcome, destruction, death, and massacre;
> I see, as in a map, the end of all.
>   (2.4.52–57);

or of an *ekphrastic* mournful meditation, as in the anthropomorphic "defaced" image of England provided, as if out of completion, by Buckingham:

> This noble isle doth want her proper limbs,
> Her face defaced with scars of infamy,
> And almost shouldered in the swalling gulf
> Of blind forgetfulness and deep oblivion.
> (3.7.116–19)

England is unveiled here, archaeologically, as an amputated and disfigured statue—a noble monument menaced in its integrity by self-generated and self-devouring malignant scions. One might hear echoes of Spenser's Roman Verlame: "But whie (unhappie wight) doo I thus crie, / And grieve that my remembrance quite is raced / Out of the knowledge of posteritie, / And all my antique moniments defaced? . . . / Forgotten quite as they were never borne" (*The Ruines of Time*, 176–179). But shifting from poetry to theatre, the language of ruins and forgetfulness is charged and shared with the force of a *critique* of power. It is also obliquely charged with only half-concealed allusions to a not-too-remote Reformist iconoclasm, when Richard's England is denounced not just as a butchery but also as a place of "defaced" sacred images: "your waiting vassals / Have done a drunken slaughter, and defaced / The precious image of our dear Redeemer", King Edward cries out (2.1.119–21). As a noun, "defacer" is invested with a final catalyzing role when it is referred to Richard, whose contingent identity as a character increasingly disappears behind the prevailing image of a miscreation, a dog—a "foul defacer of God's handiwork"—or a devastating boar (used again for Aaron, *Titus*, 4.2.140), a "wretched, bloody, and usurping boar, / That spoiled your summer fields and fruitful vines, / Swills your warm blood like wash, and makes his through / In your embowlèd bosoms—this foul swine" (5.2.7–10).

This conflation of a time of ruin, beastly imagery, and domestic vampirism is in keeping with a play which, by unanimous critical agreement, exceeds the confines of the histories to veer towards the condition of tragedy.[26] It is also clear that Shakespeare is already thinking of his first "*most Lamentable Romaine Tragedy*" and its similarly menacing scenario of growing fear and compulsory amputation—both plays securing him a rightly earned reputation as the "shake-scene" (Robert Greene) of contemporary London theatre. Arguably he needs a chorus, a collective figure, to channel such an excess of emotional temperature of both actors and audience. In *Richard III* he ingeniously provides one by summoning the presence of Queen Margaret (a character present in all of the four plays of the first tetralogy), whose alien and alienating cursing voice gradually joins into a single and swelling tragic chorus the curse of the other female characters of the play—Queen Elizabeth, the Duchess of York, and Queen

Anne—Richard's derogatorily "tell-tale women". Thus Shakespeare provides a "lament from history" (in the already discussed sense used by
Benjamin) worthy of the Furies. Interestingly, Queen Margaret in this play
is both a remnant and a revenant. She occurs as a sign of interruption and
repetition in the spectral geography of the court, gradually transformed as
she is into a returning and denouncing anachronism, the representation
of a "spectral anteriority", as we might say borrowing from Derrida.[27]
As we know, Queen Margaret is confined to France at the end of *3 Henry
VI*, her native place, where she died in real life in 1482. But the French
queen reappears in *Richard III*—almost archaeologically I would say—as
a Cassandra-like prophetess of total catastrophe, and with Hecuba's same
role as teacher of cursing, a task which she performs, as has been noticed
by Fernando Ferrara, with the refinement of a virtuoso.[28] "The time will
come" (she warns Elizabeth in the first act), "that thou shalt wish for
me / To help thee curse" (1.3.241–42). And Elizabeth later in the fourth
act: "O thou, well skilled in curses, stay awhile / And teach me how to
curse" (4.4.110–11). Precisely this Margaret does, but metatheatrically,
almost as if—shifting role with her director or playwright—she "stopped
awhile" to impart a Stanislavskian drama lesson on how to psychologi-
cally strengthen the passion (woe and anger) which is being conveyed into
acting and words.[29]

> MARGARET Forbear to sleep the night, and fast the days.
> Compare dead happiness with living woe.
> Think that thy babes were fairer than they were,
> And he that slew them fouler than he is.
> Bett'ring thy loss makes the bad causer worse.
> Revolving this will teach thee how to curse.
> ELIZABETH My words are dull. Oh, quicken them with thine.
> MARGARET Thy woes will make them sharp and pierce like mine.
>
> (4.4.112–19)

Let all the words of calamity "have scope", they chorally cry out, and
although with no other effect than to "easy the heart" (124–25), let them
be as "copious" and deafening as to prevail on the competing noisy
"trumpets" and "drums" of the tyrant. KING RICHARD: "A flourish,
trumpets! / Strike alarum, drums! / Let not the heavens hear these tell-
tale women / Rail on the Lord's anointed. Strike, I say! (4.4.142–44).
Interestingly, Shakespeare creates the same female choral and roaring
effect when in the almost coeval poem *The Rape* he similarly conjures up
Hecuba and Philomel to strengthen the long-drawn cursing lament of the
raped Lucrece.[30]

It is my intention in this section to underscore Shakespeare's early
concern for Rome's anteriority, or parable of glory and ruin, as critically
intermingled with the agenda of a national historiography, especially

in his first tetralogy covering the civil war of the Two Roses, and markedly in the way it culminates in *Richard III*. In fact, no less than in *Titus Andronicus*, this was a play characterized by a crisis of sovereignty and the anxiety of a permanent state of emergency (4.4.416)—a constitutive condition of tyrannical rule in Benjamin's vision of history (discussed earlier in the first part of this introduction)—whose effect is that the court, together with its symbolic places of power, easily turns into a suicidal "slaughterhouse", a place of progressive severed family bonds and limbs. "Go, hie thee, from this slaughterhouse/Lest thou increase the number of the dead, / And make me die the thrall of Margaret's curse, / No mother, wife, nor England's counted Queen" (4.1.38–41), Queen Elizabeth cries, while prompting one of her sons to flee Richard's carnage. She is by now aware that she might not escape the dreaded prospective of taking on the unnatural residual condition of Margaret—a remnant and a revenant, a ruin, a living relict surviving her name as a Queen, a wife, a mother—as Margaret had admonished in the first act: "Long mayst thou live to wail thy children's loss, / And see another, as I see thee now, / Decked in thy rights, as thou art stalled in mine. / Long die thy happy days before thy death, / And, after many lengthened hours of grief, / Die neither mother, wife, nor England's queen" (1.3.200–205). Spectral queens who survived their role, though, sometimes, not their title (as in the case of Catharine of Aragon, for instance) were a not-too-remote memory in the mind of Shakespeare's Elizabethan audience.

Richard III's fourth act is also the act where Margaret—an unsettling and admonishing monument of gradual spoliation and waste—at last (and for good) takes her leave from Shakespeare's first tetralogy, almost as if to make space for the plethora of ghosts of the present which the playwright enlists for the finale of his fifth act. But she does so not without sharing her awareness with the audience that what we have witnessed so far is just a prologue, "a dire induction" (4.4.5–7) to the play's impending bloody ending. Perhaps she is also ventriloquizing the playwright's announcement of his ensuing fratricidal "*Most Lamentable Romaine Tragedy*". The ominous funereal equipment (grave/tomb) which has physically occupied the entirety of the first act of *Richard III* to sacrilegiously set the tone of the whole play is ready to be handed over to *Titus Andronicus* (its proper sequel) as an overdetermined theatrical prop. If only subliminally, Shakespeare's audience is prepared to immediately perceive it as a sign of foreshadowed defaced rituality, when in continuity with *Richard III*, it similarly and immediately takes centre stage.

The first tetralogy is teeming with images of destruction or self-destruction which tend to be fixed in memory as menacing *ekphrastic* visions of state and history ruination. For Shakespeare's audience, ancient Rome and England's traumatic past comment on each other and gesture towards a no less gruesome present.[31] Arguably in that first decade of his career as a playwright, Shakespeare had understood that the one could make emblematic what in the other was contingent, Rome playing the role of both the same and the other in such a process of self-knowledge. It may also be useful to remember that the dire metaphorical connotations of the term "cannibal" are first exploited in Shakespeare's first tetralogy, occurring twice in *3 Henry VI*, out of a total of five, before being visualized as a proper anthropophagous banquet in *Titus Andronicus*.

Shakespeare overtly showed his interest for what the antiquarians were doing in terms of discovery of their own land when he literally brought a map on stage in both *1Henry IV* (3.1) and *King Lear* (1.1). But his concern was also manifested as speculative in kind when in *Richard III* he turned the architectonical silhouette of the Tower of London into a central and questioned protagonist: a layered and incumbent repository of still open wounds and haunting memories, as the murdered King Henry VI's admonishes when he returns as a ghost, Caesar-like, on the night before the battle: "When I was mortal, my anointed body / By thee was punched full of deadly holes. / Think on the Tower and me" (5.3.123–25).

Towers, as a place and a symbol of power and woe, occur frequently in Shakespeare's spectral time *and* topographies: 71 mentions in 13 works, but 26 times (the maximum) in *Richard III*. The tower's name has already occurred as a sinister place of imprisonment and slaughter in the course of the play, when it comes to prominence, oddly but interestingly in Act 3, as an object of scrutinizing antiquarianism leading to Caesar as a legitimizing if simplistic founding figure. This occurs when the hereditary Prince Edward asks Richard, Duke of Gloucester, where he will be hosted while awaiting his coronation, and he receives the answer that he "shall repose . . . at the Tower" (3.1.65–93):

> PRINCE I do not like the Tower, of any place.
> Did Julius Caesar build that place, my lord?
> BUCKINGHAM He did, my gracious lord, begin that place,
> Which since, succeeding ages have re-edified.
> PRINCE Is it upon record, or else reported
> Successively from age to age, he built it?
> BUCKINGHAM Upon record, my gracious lord.
> PRINCE But say, my lord, it were not registered,
> Methinks the truth should live from age to age,
> As 'twere retailed to all posterity,
> Even to the general all-ending day.
> . . .
> GLOUCESTER I say, "Without characters fame lives long".
> [*Aside*] Thus like the formal Vice, Iniquity,
> I moralize two meanings in one word.

We know (as Shakespeare's audience might or might not have known) that such a popular Caesarean claim in relation to the origins of the London Tower was being dismissed as groundless in Shakespeare's time. Camden had set things right by informing his readers that this was a fortress marking the eastern end of the city walls built much later by Constantine the Great.[32] And John Stow in his *Survey of London* (1598) would refer to the matter as to a dated issue before providing a reliable list of English kings who in time had contributed to strengthen the tower architectonically as well as making it famous as a "slaughterhouse", among these Richard III and Henry VIII. "It hath beene the common opinion: and some haue written (but of none assured ground)", Stow writes in his chapter on towers and castles,

> that *Iulius Cæsar*, the first conquerour of the Brytains, was the originall Authour and founder as well thereof, as also of many other Towers, Castels, and great buildings within this Realme: but (as I haue alreadie before noted) *Cæsar* remained not here so long, nor had hee in his head any such matter, but onely to dispatch a conquest of this barbarous Countrey, and to proceede to greater matters. Neither do the Romane writers make mention of any such buildings erected by him here. And therefore leauing this, and proceeding to more grounded authoritie, I find in a fayre Register booke containing the acts of the Bishops of Rochester.[33]

But naïve and eccentric as Shakespeare's chat may appear at first glance, the passage is replete with meaning and *double entendre*. Richard makes the mention of Caesar resonate ominously with allusions to fratricidal and patricidal events that Shakespeare has been staging in his first tetralogy (and which in *3 Henry VI*, 2.5, we find epitomized as an F stage direction—"Enter a SON that has killed his father at one door and a FATHER that has killed his son at another door [with their bodies]"). The passage also highlights the epochal appropriative logic proliferating around places and monuments as a matter of familiar controversy, while foregrounding the proclivity of British monarchs (and/or naïvely aspiring princes) to imagine themselves in the garments of Caesar and in the authoritative act of turning the knowledge of places into self-celebratory maps. In fact, Caesar is summoned up as both a murdered governor and an admired "conqueror": the historian of his own fame, one who was capable of marking places for posterity with an unequalled lasting imprint.

PRINCE That Julius Caesar was a famous man:
With what his valour did enrich his wit,
His wit set down to make his valour live.
Death makes no conquest of this conqueror,
For now he lives in fame; though not in life.

. . .

> And if I live until I be a man,
> I'll win our ancient right in France again,
> Or die a soldier, as I lived a king.

More in general the passage foregrounds a concern which, tongue in-cheek, Shakespeare wants to share with his Elizabethan audience.[34] So much so that one is tempted to visualize the relation between the chorographic awareness fostered by contemporary antiquarianism and Shakespeare's own theatrical representation of England in the form of an ongoing conversation among playgoers on their way to Shakespeare's theatre: a conversation that may have started in front of the copy of a momentous book (Camden's?) advertised in one of the city's book-shop windows, or pausing by sites described as milestones (for instance the London-stone)[35] or made memorable by reports of unexpected and astonishing diggings (Spitalfield, St. Paul Cathedral's churchyard). The conversation continues as the playgoers make their way north up to the scaffolds of a playhouse in Shoreditch or south across the river in Southwark. Imbued with the right ironical distance, Shakespeare allows us to hear the oral vitality of a conversant community around themes and discoveries of common concern for kings, aristocratic elites, and commoners of different ranks.

Critics do not exclude Shakespeare's sympathy for the circle of the Earl of Essex (executed in 1601), including the group of playwrights and historians interested in dissenting Tacitism, Seneca, and antiquarianism, "with Ben Jonson's teacher and friend William Camden at the heart of the movement".[36] Tacitus, the critical historian of late imperial Rome, is a favourite source in Camden's *Britannia*. And Shakespeare may have come across Camden's *Britannia* by the time he wrote the plays of his first tetralogy—the plays which chronologically intersect with his first Roman play, *Titus Andronicus*. In fact it seems as if he had ironically absorbed the reorientation of discourse displayed by Camden in his search for a past (or a Rome) "of one's own": an empirical way of dealing with truth, history, and documents which was also archaeological at the core. British-ness and myths of origin were part of this changing historical paradigm, as is well shown by the author of *Britannia*, the acclaimed "Varro, the Strabo, and Pausanias of Britain".[37] Interestingly, Shakespeare's piece of antiquarianism in *Richard III* alludes to the theme of the Roman origins of Britain, by playfully turning it into an issue, an excavating if ironic reflection on memory and its ideologized forms of control, in an epoch in which the growth of available historical documentation, we might say with Foucault,[38] was both questioning and questioned by Tudor history writing, according to a teleological and legitimizing myth of pacification and national prosperity.[39] Shakespeare's Elizabethan audience could hear it voiced by Richmond, in the play's final speech, and interestingly, almost in parallel (1593), by Lucius in *Titus Andronicus*'s final speech, but as its displaced and very questionable version.

Camden's *Britannia* was not commissioned by a king. It was the fruit of an international scholarly concern. And it shows, both in the way its author repeatedly affirms his claim to intellectual independence and in the way he brags about the environment of its germination. As he states in the first lines of his address to the reader, the work was solicited very "earnestly" by his friend, "*Abraham Ortelius* the worthy restorer of Ancient Geography", with the (often quoted) objective to "restore antiquity to Britaine, and Britaine to his its antiquity". This involved a methodology, though, "which was as I understood, that I would renew ancientrie, enlighten obscuritie, cleare doubts, and recall home veritie by way of recovery, which the negligence of writers and credulity of the common sort had in a manner proscribed and utterly banished from among us" (*Brit* 1, "To the Reader", n.p.). And thus, "in war with time" (as we might say borrowing from Shakespeare, sonnet 15), he started his memorializing project by first restoring names to land and vice versa, but with no intention of affirming what is uncertain or discarding what is probable:

> Truly it was my project and purpose to seeke, rake out, and free from darknesse such places as Cæsar, Tacitus . . . and others antique writers have specified and TIME hath overcast with mist & darknesse by extinguishing, altering, and corrupting their old true names. In searching and seeking after these, I wil not a vouch uncertainties so I do not conceale probabilities.
>
> (*Brit* 1, "To the Reader", n.p.)

The linguistic discovery of one's land is imagined in the form of an archaeological excavation. Indeed, names are taken care of as if they were objects injured by time—smashed, changed, corrupted—and in need of being literally "scraped" out of their dust. They are addressed with the same European lexicon of loss, discovery, and reparation used for ruins. What is also highlighted, though, is a contemporary tension between a drive towards integrity which characterizes the early modern projectuality of cultural memory and the typical transnational Renaissance awareness that such a task begins with a challenge arising from the ghostly resistance of surviving and curtailed "remains", as is made clear by Camden's ensuing *Remains of Britain* and its composite list of contents: *Languages, Names, Surnames, Allusions, Anagrams, Armories, Moneys, Impresses, Apparel, Artilleries, Wise Speeches, Proverbs, Poesies, Epitaphs.*[40] This makes up a promiscuous if untimely reservoir of cultural knowledge.[41] Yet, Camden's untimely "remains", which he gathered by meticulously surveying county after county, were part of a program which was huge in scope. It spanned the material and the immaterial—land and language, landscape, monuments, coat of arms, tombs, epitaphs—and it included documents as well as the memory deposited in the layered etymology of names and words, the memory of a nation marked by an "inundation of forraine people", as he writes in addressing the readers of his *Britannia*. The notion of "monument" itself (a recurrent term in *Britannia*) included things and the act of recollection embedded in things remembered, in line with its contemporary composite intersemiotic meaning. In Thomas Cooper's *Thesaurus* (1565): "a remembrance of some notable art: as sepulchers, books, images, a memoriall, a token, a testimonie, A token pledge of love, chronicles, histories of antiquie".[42]

But Camden complicated the definition of his venture when he enlarged the framework of uncertainty that characterized the "corrupted" state of his materials to the matter of British origins. Perhaps precluding, for this reason we suspect, any award or patronage on the part of Elizabeth, even though as a scholar he could boast a profile of high international standing and a major role in the birth of the "Society of Antiquarians". "I am not ignorant", Camden wrote, "that the first originalls of nations are obscure by reason of their profound antiquitie, as things which are seene very deep and farre remote". Origins are defined by profundity, distance, and obscurity. They are figured visually as an objectified and alien Other, a far removed picture blurred by the rust of time or, also, as the intricate and curtailed map of great rivers whose "courses, the reaches, the confluents, and the out-lets . . . are well knowne, yet their first fountains and heads lie commonly unknown" (*Brit* 1, "To the Reader").

The prevailing revisionist outlook of the Elizabethan chorographic historiography is condensed in the set of questions which, overtly or covertly, it raised, thus incisively highlighted by Helgerson: "What is British history the history of? What is the element of continuity in that history? What holds it together?" But,

> The more the antiquaries learned, the less easily they could say that their histories told the story of a single British people or a single governing dynasty stretching back to Brut and his Trojan warriors. As the imagery of both Drayton's frontispiece and the frontispiece of Speed's *Theater*, suggests, quite different peoples have occupied and ruled Great Britain.[43]

Parry is on the same line when he remarks:

> A great deal of intellectual energy was expended in dispersing the accumulated legends generally known as the British History that filled in the vacant stretches of the remote past with shining princes from Troy and a long line of sturdy British kings that included such familiar names as Locrine, Lud, Lear, and Cymbeline.

But once you had done away with Brutus and other Spenserian deeply rooted if fabulous ancestry, "what was one to put in their place?"[44]

Camden included a growing interest for the first barbarian populations reported by Caesar and other Latin authors and, increasingly in the progressive enlarged versions of his *Britannia*, for the ensuing culture of the Anglo-Saxon invaders—the savage authors, in early modern imagination, of ethnical cleansing and an almost total destruction of the ancient late Roman-Christian Britain—who, however, were to be acknowledged as the true German progenitors of modern England. "This English tongue is extracted, as the nation, from the Germans, the most glorious of all now extant in *Europe* for their moral, and martial vertues", Camden wrote in *Remains Concerning Britain*[45] published in 1605, after James I's access to the throne and his prospective unification of the reign under the ancient restored name of Britain.

Unionism and the pacification with one's origins, however, could not efface the wounds, namely the fact that the identity of modern England was grounded on discontinuity, hybridization, repetitive occupation, and conflict among Britons, Romans, Picts, Scots, Anglo-Saxons, Danes, and Normans, with the Anglo-Saxons as the cruellest occupiers of them all: an indelible trauma, in Gildas's sixteenth-century record of their "wolfish" invasion at the fall of the Roman Empire. As said, Camden relies mostly on Gildas's "most lamentable ruine and downfall of Britain" for his pages on the "The Downfall or Destruction" of ancient Britannia. "When we shall read these reports", Camden observed on commenting his *Ruin of Britain*,

> let us not be offended and displeased with good Gildas, for his bitter invectives against either the vices of his owne countreymen the Britans, or the inhumane outrages of the barbarous enemies, or the insatiable crueltie of our Fore-fathers the Saxons. But since that for so many ages successively ensuing, we are all now by a certain engraffing or commixtion become one nation, mollified and civilized with Religion, and good Arts, let us meditate and consider, both what they were, and also what we ought to be: lest that for our sinnes likewise, the supreme Ruler of the world, either traslate other nations hither, when we are first rooted out, or incorporate them into us, after we are by them subdued.
>
> (*Brit* 1, 110)

In Camden and other antiquaries' new narrative of origins, early modern England appears as a nation born out of a catastrophe as a mixture of ethnicities and languages, at the special historical conjuncture in which its citizens (or intellectual elites) are engaged in a crucial process of self-making.[46] Looking for a legitimizing if documented classical antiquity of the "ancient Island" was part of the process. But "an acceptable national self" entailed "self-alienation", as Helgerson has argued, and "models of civility were to be found elsewhere. . . . In this sense to be English was to be other".[47]

Interested in staging the process more than the accomplishment, Shakespeare interestingly reshuffled the implications of the relation between self and other, civility and barbarity when, blatantly and unexpectedly, he chose to address the myth of Rome (let alone the myth of Troy in *Troilus and Cressida*) by starting not from its imperial splendour but from the oneiric and desacralizing end of its decay, thus transforming both terms of the opposition into the object of a radical if bemusing anatomy of origins and the past. But he also shortened the distance between past and present in the process. In fact, what unites Rome and Britain, or better the author of the Roman plays and that of some of his history plays, is the tension introduced by an excess of power and its crisis, or else the centrality of the ruin.

As in the nightmarish chasm of inextricable "fearful wrecks", experienced by Clarence in his dream of drowning (*Richard III*, 1.4.9–36), confrontation with one's past, especially in Shakespeare's first decade as a playwright, takes the form of a descent into its own tomb/womb. Shakespeare's audience is asked to descend into the layered depth of a past which is conceived as both alien and familiar, and variously imagined (already in *Richard III* and, significantly, by Richard himself) as a primal voracious scenario of beastly appetites, a vortex of "Death, desolation, ruin, and decay" (4.4.409). "It means to go down in history. . . . it is a matter of depth. . . . as Schwyzer has it.[48] It entails the encounter with violent primal scenes and traumas, as Thomas P. Anderson has suggested, and the issue of "what it means" for poets and playwrights, "to inherit and bequeath the memory of crisis, which is marked . . . not by simple knowledge, but by the ways 'it simultaneously defies and demands our witness'". "English history and the national subject", Anderson observes,

> emerge in the symbolic space where immediate understanding remains elusive. During the early modern period, this symbolic space becomes the stage of the theater, as Shakespeare constructs a version of national history from wounds that do not close and from cries that echo in the "tongueless caverns of the earth".
>
> (*Richard II*, 1.1.105)[49]

My concern in this section has been to highlight the ways in which the construction of England's national myth is involved in the matter of Troy and Rome—namely the question of origins, inheritance, and memory— via the problematizing discursivity of ruins and their intrinsic meaning of catastrophe and discontinuity. How was the early modern topographical "writing" of England (as Helgerson has aptly called it) affected by the tension introduced by the heuristic potential embedded in the Renaissance discovery of ruins? And, can we understand the early modern antiquarian excavation of national origins among the wreckage of history—not least the more recent dregs left by Tudor fratricidal conflicts among dynasties and faiths—as being intertwined with Shakespeare's uses of a ruinous Rome?

Certainly the reflection on "remains" and on history as made up of ruins and hybridization was on the agenda of Shakespeare's contemporary England. And Rome's parable of glory and ruin, death and rebirth—a Rome which imperially encapsulated the Trojan-Greek legacy—provided its paradigmatic and legitimizing classic version: a Rome desired in the act of being anatomized, refunctionalized, rewritten, rejected. Classical antiquity, but not yet the (sacralized) "classical" as it will be understood and called in the next centuries,[50] is the Humanist's and Renaissance's discovery and invention. Grounded on ruins, it contained within itself the key to its deconstruction and transformation or, in other words, the seeds of its questioning, which simultaneously "takes the form of a . . . myth of modernity", or "conditional independence".[51]

Notes

1. William Camden, *BRITANNIA: A Chrorographicall Description of the Most Flourishing Kingdomes, ENGLAND, SCOTLAND, and IRELAND, and the Ilands Adioyning, Out of the Depth of ANTIQUITIE, Written First in Latine by William Camden, Translated Newly into English by Philémon Holland* (London: Georgii Bishop and Ioannis Norton, 1610). Mentions directly in the text abbreviated as *Brit 1*. I have also consulted Camden's Britannia, Newly translated to English by Edmund Gibson (London: F. Collins, 1695) mentioned as *Brit 2*.
2. See Caesar, *The Gallic War*, Books IV and V (Cambridge, MA: Harvard University Press, 1917). For a consideration of Caesar's adventure as an "exorbitant" gesture, an act of hybris (for Latin authors) in transgressing the mythical oceanic boundaries, see John Gillies, *Shakespeare and the Geography of Difference* (Cambridge: Cambridge University Press, 1994), pp. 10 and 20.
3. He also extends his speculation on Londinium.
4. As Graham Parry has observed in his chapter on Camden's antiquarian endeavour, "The principal intention was to describe Britain as a province of the Roman Empire (hence the simple classical title) and to locate the towns and camps of the Romans as fully and accurately as possible. *The Trophies of Time: English Antiquarians of the Seventeenth Century* (Oxford: Oxford University Press, 2007), p. 23.
5. Camden thus sums up the issue of Britain's origins and the belated Virgilian search for a Trojan ancestry: "Tacitus . . . a thousand and foure hundred yeers ago, who searched diligently into these particulars, wrote thus, 'What maner of men the first inhabitants of Britaine were, borne in the land or brought in, as among barbarous people is not certainly knowen'. Gildas, being himselfe a wise and learded Britaine, who lived a thousand yeers since, had not one word of this Brutus". Bede, Camden continues, "and as many as wrote elven hundred and Threescore [1160] yeers since, who seeme not once to have

heard of Brutus his name; so silent are they of him in all their owne writings
... before that in a barbarous age, and amid the thickest clouds of ignorance,
one Hunibald a bald writer, fabled and feined, That Francio a Trojane, King
of Priams sonne, was the founder of the Frenche nation. Hence they collect,
that when our country-men heard once how the French-men their neighbours
drew their line from Trojans, they thought it a foule dishonour, that those
should outgoe them in nobilitie of Stocke, whom they matched every way
in manhood and proësse. Therefore, that Geffrey Ap Arthur of Monmouth,
foure hundred yeers agoe, was the first, as they thinke, that to gratifie our
Britains produced unto them the Brutus, descended from the gods, by birth
also a Trojane, to be the author of the British nation" (*Brit* 1, 6–7).

6. See, for all Miola, *Shakespeare's Rome*, pp. 1–18.
7. Petrarch's earlier concern for Rome's ruins and their reading has been brilliantly highlighted by Thomas Greene in *The Light to Troy*, who interestingly
traces back to Petrarch the birth of a new "archaeological hermeneutic" which
challenges—while interacting with it at the same time—a medieval "allegorical hermeneutic". Two different activities are involved, Greene explains, "the
bridging of time" against "the piercing of a veil". The older (allegorical)
presupposed "no cultural distance" from the past, the same "universe of
discourse" and a "fullness of knowledge" that could be "unlocked by a single
operation"; the new (archaeological) presupposed distance and an interplay
of elements that foreclosed "total description" (pp. 93–96).
8. Steven Mullaney, *The Place of the Stage: License, Play, and Power in Renaissance England* (Ann Arbor: The University of Michigan Press, [1988] 2004),
pp. 30–31 and 20–23.
9. Platter (quoted by Mullaney, *The Place of the Stage*, p. 75).
10. For a Shakespearean gender-coded treatment of themes of iconoclastic
interment and resurrection, see Del Sapio Garbero, "'Be Stone No More':
Maternity and Heretical Visual Art in Shakespeare's Late Plays", in *Actes des
congrès de la Société française Shakespeare*, 33 (2015), 1–13, http://shake-
speare.revues.org/3493.
11. See Eamon Duffy, *The Stripping of the Altars* (New Haven and London: Yale
University Press, 1992), p. 480 *et passim* and Stuart Clark, *Vanities of the
Eye: Vision in Early Modern European Culture* (Oxford: Oxford University
Press, 2007), pp. 161–203. But see also the more recent Stewart Mottram,
Ruin and Reformation in Spenser, Shakespeare, and Marvell (Oxford: Oxford
University Press, 2019). For a discussion of Shakespeare's *Sonnets* in the context of the post-Reformation suspicion of ruins, relics, and idolatry, see Tom
Muir's analysis of sonnet 105 in his "Without Remainder", pp. 26–30.
12. In *Renaissance Self-Fashioning: From More to Shakespeare* (Chicago and
London: The University of Chicago Press, 1980), in defining self-fashioning
as a process governed by "the principle of regenerative violence" (p. 188 *et
passim*), namely the destruction of what is alien or other (as such inevitably
productive of ruins, the ruins of the Other), Greenblatt singles out three main
cultural and historical phenomena that in Renaissance England characterize
its accomplishment: the regimentation of pleasure in the name of a source of
authority, the colonization of the New World and Ireland, and the Reformation iconoclasm, all of them well epitomized by Spenser. It is clear, he also
underlines, "that any achieved identity always contains within itself the signs
of its own subversion or loss" (p. 9).
13. Edmund Spenser, *The Ruines of Time*, in *The Yale Edition of the Shorter
Poems of Edmund Spenser*, p. 234.
14. For more on Spenser's contradictory issues raised by his Verlame, see Rebeca
Helfer, *Spenser's Ruins and the Art of Recollection* (Toronto: University of

Toronto Press, 2012), pp. 139–145. But see also Hui, *The Poetics of Ruins*, pp. 190–194.

15. John Webster, *The Duchess of Malfi*, ed. J.R. Brown, The Revels Plays (London: Methuen, 1964).

16. Ruins in Webster's play also gestured towards Elizabethan colonial maps of discovery and conquest. A case in point is Richard Bartlett's tragic story as the cartographer of a conquered Ireland (1600–1603) and the author of maps describing the conquest in progress, with sites of faith and ritual power destroyed and re-emerging, configuring the space of a militarized country but also of spectral if resistant archaeological remains. See the O'Neill Crowning Stone in Bartelett's "Tullahogue and Dungannon" map finely commented by Michael Neill in its relation with the responsibility of mapmaking and history. *Putting History to the Question: Power, Politics, and Society in English Renaissance Drama* (New York: Columbia University Press, 2001), chap. 14.

17. John Speed, *The Counties of Britain. A Tudor Atlas (The Theatre of the Empire of Great Britain*, 1611–12), eds, Nigel Nicolson and Alasdair Hawkyard (London: Pavilion, 1995), Cumberland map, pp. 58–59. I am grateful to Michael Neill for drawing my attention to Speed's maps and Webster's *Duchess*.

18. See Helgerson, *Forms of Nationhood*, especially, chap. 3 "The Lands Speaks", pp. 120, and 105–147. On examining the two terms of "chorography" and "chronicle", Helgerson writes, "Though the two terms and the practices they represent inevitably contaminate one another, chorography defines itself by opposition to chronicle. It is the genre devoted to place, as chronicle is the genre devoted to time. The opposition was not, however, necessarily antagonistic" (p. 132). Helgerson's attention to the empirical early modern geographical turn doesn't contrast with John Gillies's concern for cultural geography, or what (drawing on Vico) he has called a "poetic geography" or "typo-geography", a "typology of place . . . more concerned with *loci* than with area as such". In fact, when we come to Shakespeare, we find that he is "conversant with quite a variety of geographic discourses and a variety of cartographic genres". *Shakespeare and the Geography of Difference*, p. 49.

19. Parry, *Trophies of Time*, p. 3.

20. On the revised genocidal version of the Anglo-Saxon conquest in early modern England, see Schwyzer, *Archaeologies of English Renaissance Literature*, pp. 42–43.

21. As Helgerson has observed in relation to the cultural construction of identity, "points of origin and originating agents are many. Texts, nations, individual authors, particular discursive communities—all are both produced and productive, productive of that by which they are produced". *Forms of Nationhood*, p. 13.

22. Francis Bacon, *The Advancement of Learning* [1605], in *The Advancement of Learning and New Atlantis*, ed. Arthur Johnston (Oxford: Clarendon Press, 1974), p. 71.

23. See Frank Smith Fussner, *The Historical Revolution: English Historical Writing and Thought* (London: Routledge, [1962] 2010), pp. 72–74. "The purpose of the discourses written by antiquaries", he writes, "was to investigate the antiquity of the laws, customs, and institutions of England. The antiquity of Parliament and of the Christian religion in England were matters of immediate concern to both the sovereign and the subject. James no less than Elizabeth perceived a fearful symmetry between past and present". "No money came to the College and hence nothing came of it as an institution" (p. 77). For more on the notion of history in Shakespeare's times, see Patrick Collinson, "History", in Michael Hattaway, ed., *A Companion to English Renaissance Literature and Culture* (Oxford: Blackwell, 2003), pp. 58–70.

24. Hui, *The Poetics of Ruins*, p. 192 *et passim*.
25. In relating the dispersed event to a new notion of history grounded in discontinuity, Foucault writes, "For history in its classical form, the discontinuous was both the given and the unthinkable: the raw material of history, which presented itself in the form of dispersed events—decisions, accidents, initiatives, discoveries; the material, which through analysis, had to be arranged, reduced, effaced in order to reveal the continuity of events. Discontinuity was the stigma of temporal dislocation that it was the historian's task to remove from history", *The Archaeology of Knowledge*, p. 8.
26. See for all Phyllis Rackin, "History Into Tragedy: The Case of *Richard III*", in Shirley Nelson Garner and Madelon Sprengnether, eds, *Shakespearean Tragedy and Gender* (Bloomington and Indianapolis: Indiana University Press, 1996), p. 39. But see also Jane E. Howard and Phyllis Rackin, *Engendering a Nation: A Feminist Account of Shakespeare's English Histories* (London and New York: Routledge, 1997).
27. Derrida, *Specters of Marx*, p. 24.
28. Fernando Ferrara, *Il teatro dei re: saggio sui drammi storico-politici di Shakespeare* (Bari: Adriatica Editrice, 1995), p. 255. The critic writes extensively on the "Megaera" role of Margaret (whom he likens to Medea) and the other female characters of the play, underlining their classical derivation and rehabilitating them from the stereotype of "tell-tale women".
29. I am here using Peter Brook's Brechtian acceptation of alienation: "It was out of respect for the audience", he writes "that Brecht introduced the idea of alienation: alienation is cutting, interrupting. Holding something up to light, making us look again". *The Empty Space* (London: Penguin Books, [1968] 1990), p. 81. Margaret's "interrupting" and choric presence, her being both character and playwright, works in all senses according to a technique involving at the same time emotional involvement and alienating, reflexive distance.
30. For reasons which will appear clear in my chapter on *Lucrece*, in saying this I decisively differ from James R. Siemon, when on comparing the "joint outcry" of *Richard III*'s women with Lucrece's complaint, he all too easily discards the latter as ineffective "lonely pathos": "Violated Lucrece, in keeping with the popular genre of female complaint, lyrically expresses the lonely pathos of self-punishment; she submits to the definition of pollution determined by the male order, leaving death her only 'remedy'. . . . By contrast with Lucrece, Joan and the Margaret of the *Henry VI* plays, Elizabeth and the Duchess neither kill themselves, lead armies nor direct campaigns. But they turn the stereotypes allotted them . . . to use against the tyrant". "Introduction", *King Richard III*, Arden edition (London: Bloomsbury Arden Shakespeare, 2009), pp. 26–27. In my view, Lucrece does much more in Shakespeare's poem than surrender to suicide—which, of course, as a historical character she could not avoid.
31. This is also true for the rest of his history plays. As Giorgio Melchiori has pointed out, "Shakespeare . . . relies on the Roman history when he decides to address according to a new perspective the moral issues raised by the complicated period of English history he had chosen to dramatize in his second tetralogy, including *Richard II* and *Henry V*. His main problem was how to justify a king's killing, as in the case of *Richard II*"; but also that "he found himself in the condition of paying tribute to the greatest and most glorious king that England had ever had, as Henry V; who, however, was Henry IV's direct offspring, the king who was responsible for Richard's deposition (and death)". *Shakespeare. Genesi e struttura delle opere* (Bari: Laterza, 1994), p. 392 (my transl.). On issues of interaction between Rome and Shakespeare's

history plays, see also Franco Marenco, *La parola in scena. La comunicazione teatrale nell'età di Shakespeare.* (Torino: UTET, 2004), pp. 102–108.

32. Camden, *Britannia* (*Brit* 2, pp. 312–313): "At each end of the wall that runs along by the river, there were strong Forts; the one towards the east remains to this day, call'd commonly the Tower of London".

33. John Stow, "Of Towers and Castels", in C. L. Kingsford, ed., *A Survey of London: Reprinted From the Text of 1603* (Oxford: Clarendon Press, 1908), pp. 44 and 44–71. *British History Online*, www.british-history.ac.uk/no-series/survey-of-london-stow/1603/pp44-71. Stow was familiar with Camden and his work, which he mentions as an authoritative precedent in his "Epistle dedicatory" (p. xcvii). It is likely that Shakespeare consulted both, in the course of his interacting concern for national history and ancient Rome.

34. Curiously, Shakespeare seems to have forgotten the irony of this piece of fake antiquarianism when he writes *Richard II*'s last act where, perhaps for the sake of a tragic effect, he has Queen Isabel mention the tower of London unequivocally as the "Julius Caesar'ill erected Tower" (5.1.2), intermingled with other highly rhetorical *topoi* of Fall. Her dethroned and imprisoned king is "the model where old Troy did stand!" and his prison/tomb "a beautiful inn" partaking of an "alehouse guest" (5.1.1–15).

35. The London-stone, Camden wrote, "which I take to have been a *Milliarie*, or *Mil-marks*, such as was in the mercat place of Rome: From which was taken the dimension of all journeys every way, considering it is in the very mids of the City, as it lieth in length" (*Brit* 1, 423).

36. See Burrow, *Shakespeare and Classical Antiquity*, pp. 186–187.

37. Edmund Gibson, "Preface to the Reader", in his 1695 translation of William Camden's *Britannia* (*Brit* 2, n.p.).

38. See Foucault on the growing importance of the document in our contemporary historiography and what he discusses as a changing relationship between document and the monument, that is, between documentality and the memorializing selected monumentality of traditional historical material. *The Archaeology of Knowledge*, pp. 6–7.

39. For more on these issues see Laura Di Michele, *La scena dei potenti. Teatro politica spettacolo nell'età di W. Shakespeare* (Napoli: Istituto Universitario Orientale, 1988). On Shakespeare's performance of history, see Phyllis Rackin, *Stages of History: Shakespeare's English Chronicles* (Ithaca: Cornell University Press, 1990); Fernando Ferrara, *Shakespeare e le voci della storia* (Roma: Bulzoni Editore, 1994); Paola Pugliatti, *Shakespeare the Historian* (London: Palgrave Macmillan, 1996). On issues of nationhood and appropriation in time and space, see Graham Holderness, *Shakespeare Recycled: The Making of the Historical Drama* (New York and London: Harvester, 1992); Ton Hoenselaars, ed., *Shakespeare's History Plays: Performance, Translation, and Adaptation in Britain and Abroad* (Cambridge: Cambridge University Press, 2004). On the representation of the common people and the similar way they define the urban environment in the History and the Roman plays, see Carlo Pagetti, "Shakespeare's Tales of Two Cities: London and Rome", in Del Sapio Garbero, ed., *Identity, Otherness and Empire*, pp. 145–155.

40. William Camden, *Remains Concerning Britain* [1605], eds. John Philipot and W.D. Gent (London: Charles Harper, 1674).

41. For a theoretical discussion of early modern untimely objects and their role in prospecting a hybrid temporality, see Jonathan Gil Harris, *Untimely Matter in the Time of Shakespeare* (Philadelphia: University of Pennsylvania Press, 2009).

42. Quoted in Hui, *The Poetics of Ruins*, p. 195.

43. Helgerson, *Forms of Nationhood*, pp. 120, 140.
44. Parry, *The Trophies of Time*, p. 9.
45. Camden, *Remains Concerning Britain*, p. 27.
46. Among those who underlined the element of discontinuity, there is Samuel Daniel. For more on this see Helgerson, *Forms of Nationhood*, p. 122 *et passim*.
47. Helgerson, *Forms of Nationhood*, pp. 242–243.
48. Schwyzer, *Archaeologies of English Renaissance Literature*, p. 1.
49. Thomas P. Anderson, *Performing Early Modern Trauma from Shakespeare to Milton* (Aldershot and Burlington: Ashgate, 2006), pp. 6, 86.
50. See on this, Settis, *Futuro del 'classico'*, pp. 91, 54–61 and Burrow, *Shakespeare and Classical Antiquity*, p. 3 *et passim*.
51. Greene, *The Light to Troy*, p. 43.

1 Starting With the Debris of *Finis Imperii*

Titus Andronicus

"Hail Rome, Victorious in Thy Mourning Weeds": Rome Entombed and Unearthed

While I was writing this chapter, Italian newspapers published the unexpected results of one of the many ongoing Roman archaeological digs, faced every day with layered centuries of history and the task of making sense of what emerges as untimely and as urgent in its demand to be understood. This particular piece of news was the reappearance of the remains of Emperor Titus's triumphal arch dating back to 81 CE, the second of the two devoted to him, in the course of an archaeological campaign that aimed to restore the Circo Massimo hemicycle: an unimaginable tangle of pedestals, beheaded columns, stones, and elliptic inscriptions that archaeologists promised to rearrange—but not immediately; you need money to do that!—into the vestiges of a stately architecture and the imaginative force of an imperial icon of the past. Meanwhile, as the ruins of Titus's arch remained momentarily visible to be hopefully composed into the graphically imagined ancient monument—a triumphal arch, the monument under which the processions of victorious generals paraded before heading towards the temple of Jupiter on the Capitol—visitors would be content with enjoying the sight of the unearthed stones, from the "extraordinary" vantage point of the adjacent medieval tower of Torre Moletta (*La Repubblica*, 17 May 2015).

Well, this seems to me an inspiring allegory of heritage and memory in the making. As beholders of such a landscape we are paradoxically promised a "perfect" view of what is fragmentary and only half seen: paradoxically, in so far as the perfection of the view rests on a position which is grounded on, and yet temporally distant from, those remains—precisely like the case of the medieval tower presumably erected with some of the materials taken from the same settlement.

The remains of Titus's triumphal arch at Circo Massimo, in conjunction with the sight provided by the medieval Torre Moletta, may well serve as a suggestive, petrified representation of the way Shakespeare, the playwright, began his trafficking with ancient Rome: a traffic which, as

DOI: 10.4324/9781003259671-3

if starting from the end, he launched with *Titus Andronicus*—a visionary play with no direct classical source and which could be set in the span of time encompassing the fourth and fifth centuries CE, on the eve of the deflagration of the Roman Empire, culminating in the repetitive sacks inflicted by the Goths in 410–450.

Shakespeare's *Titus Andronicus*, more than any of his ensuing Roman plays, urges us to observe a similar archaeological or geological articulation of the playwright's relationship with Rome and its memory: one which (as I have anticipated in my Introduction) absorbs the distance or difference of a belated point of observation; but also, and more importantly, one which entails inheriting the past at the point of its ruin and inchoate transformation, or metamorphosis, into something else.[1] As a matter of fact, Shakespeare seemed to refer his audience to an even broader span of time—one subsuming the whole parable of imperial Rome (27 BCE–476 CE)—if we consider Titus's mention, at the outset of the play, of the five hundred years of Andronici's tomb ("this tomb / This monument five hundred years hath stood", 1.1.350;[2] see earlier, Introduction, pp. 4–6) and the way it is symbolically invested with the ineluctable role of entombing Rome's past and present in layers of self-devouring glory and bodies: "Why, foolish Lucius, dost thou not perceive / That Rome is but a wilderness of tigers? / Tigers must prey, and Rome affords no prey / But me and mine. How happy art thou then / from these devourers to be banished" (3.1.53–57). As for the barbaric sacks launched from the outside, these were not a thing of the past in sixteenth-century Rome. For those in Shakespeare's audience who had a memory of the traumatic reprise of 1527 carried out, ironically, by the Landsnecht, the mutinous troops of Holy Roman Emperor Charles V, this was enough to justify as well as reinforce the hallucinatory scenario of a city repetitively oscillating between glory and barbarity, aggression and self-aggression. As in the visual perception and memory of the play which Henry Peacham in the 1590s in his famous drawing notably sketched as a syncretic mixture of costumes and ages, Shakespeare works at making events, ages, and bodies precipitate into one mixed heap of limbs, temporalities, and perspectives. The playwright also makes every effort to encapsulate the belated, layered perspective of a scrutinizing posterity.

Needless to say, the historical Titus of my incipit (the general who was emperor of Rome in the brief span of time going from 79 to 81 CE), has nothing to do with the fictional character imagined by Shakespeare, even though similarities might be drawn between Titus, the famous destroyer of the temple of Jerusalem, and the widely reprehended religious impiety of the Shakespearean Titus Andronicus on the part of the Goths. But this is just an instance of the prismatic quality—often compared to that of cubist painting[3]—which characterizes this play. Indeed, it emblematically stages a perception of Rome as a "floating signifier", as linguists, anthropologists, and psychoanalysts might help us to say, namely "a void of meaning", or better "an undetermined quantity of signification", in the words of Lévi-Strauss, which is "apt to receive any meaning". As such it signals "a relation of inadequation . . . between *signifiant* and *signifié*", a loss of reality—as deeply felt as the effort at bridging the gap one finds in the thought of Lévi-Strauss himself,[4] who developed these notions as an anthropologist experiencing his own encounter with the otherness of the Amazonian natives and his personal frustration in coming to terms with the elusiveness of their signifying system.

In his first Roman play, Shakespeare deals with Rome as if he were invested in an endeavour similar to that of Lévi-Strauss—coping with an ungraspable referent. Rome is a catastrophic, unsituated and yet overconnoted body, to whose memory the playwright as well as his audience or readers—like Lévi-Strauss's *bricoleur*—are called to contribute by playing inventively at what has been viewed as a "Rome effect", a "'Rome' as an anthology of stories".[5] "Rome": which Rome, whose Rome? This is what one is bound to ask, if we take as a point of departure the unsituated ruinous scenario of *Titus Andronicus*, namely Shakespeare's point of departure. It is no coincidence that Titus's opening triumph is one with a protracted funeral rite, a visual enactment of the self-neutralizing terms which make up the oxymoron pronounced by Titus upon entering the stage: "Hail, Rome, victorious in thy mourning weeds" (1.1.73). Equally meaningful is the fact that the first place to be mentioned is the Capitol, where the triumph takes place—the overinscripted heart of empyreal power as well as an erased and lost place, the nostalgic epitome of "*de varietate fortunae*" in the European humanist imagination: "the temple is overthrown, the gold has been pillaged . . . and the sacred ground is again disfigured with thorns and brambles", writes the already quoted Poggio.

> The hill of the Capitol on which we sit, was formerly the head of the Roman empire, the citadel of the earth, the terror of kings; illustrated by the footsteps of so many triumphs, enriched with the spoils and tributes of so many nations. *This spectacle of the world, how is it fallen! how changed! how defaced!*
>
> (see Introduction, p. 18)

Shakespeare begins his dealings with Rome by locating himself in the same empty space. As is the case for the European humanists, his first theatrical picture of Rome is born out of absence and desire. Indeed, *Titus's* Rome holds up as a signifier in so far as we share with the playwright such an emptiness, a loss of reality, and yet its excess. An excess staged by the playwright, together with the violence of the plot, as an extraordinary if floating and nightmarish "quantity of signification": arguably a condition that cinema, more than theatre, will be able to handle and enact at its best, as Julie Taymor's *Titus* (1999), a film not incidentally produced at the end of a millennium, stands to prove. Ancient Rome stood as such as the petrified representation of an ontological crisis in Shakespeare's time. As best catalyzed in sonnet 3 by Du Bellay (Englished by Spenser), Rome was the lost referent *per antonomasia*. It stood as the allegory of the "World's Inconstancy", impermanence being its only ontology.

> Thou stranger, which for Rome in Rome here seekest,
> And nought of Rome in Rome perceiv'st at all,
> These same old walls, old arches, which thou seest,
> Old palaces, is that which Rome men call.
> Behold what wreake, what ruine, and what Waste,
> And how that she, which with her mightie powre
> Tam'd all the world, hath tam'd her self at last,
> The pray of time, which all things doth devoure.
> Rome now of Rome is th' only funerall,
> And only Rome, of Rome hath victorie;
> Ne ought save Tyber, hastening to his fall,
> Remaines of all: O worlds inconstancie.
> That which is firm, doth flit and fall away;
> And that is flitting, doth abide and stay.

Rome's "fleetingness" is its only "firmness", a self-neutralizing coincidence of opposites which in the closing couplet is worked out and strengthened by rhyme (away/stay) as well as chiastic inversion (fleetingness/firmness). In Du Bellay/Spenser's *Ruines*, Rome has prevailed upon itself and now, with the display of its entombed landscape, it endlessly celebrates its own spectrality before the eyes of posterity. Shakespeare's *Titus* allows us to experience the same loss, the same anxiety, at the very moment in which the city was being discovered in Renaissance Europe. Also, the playwright deliberately showcases his own expertise in gathering and reshuffling the sources he needs in order to envision that spectrality.

Indeed, looking for Rome in Renaissance Europe involved a search for a city which lay disseminated in a palimpsest of stones, vegetal life, and only gradually re-emerging ancient texts: an almost geological conglomerate of ruined architectures and elliptic memories—a remembrance, more than a reality. And this is all the more important to keep in mind if we consider that the reconstruction of an assumed integral space of the imperial ruins—as we have come to know it first of all in contemporary Via dei Fori Imperiali—was yet to come. In fact, this was mostly the result of the large-scale excavating project launched by Mussolini in the 1920s with the aim to make it stand as an instance of *Romanitas*, well suited to reappropriating the imperial pride of the nation.[6]

Had Shakespeare read Du Bellay/Spenser's *Ruines of Rome* (published in *Complaints*, 1591) by the time (late 1592 according to some critics, late 1593 according to others) he contrived his visionary, unsituated Rome in *Titus Andronicus*? He might have, as I anticipate in my Introduction (pp. 32–38) and as has become clear to critics of Shakespeare's sonnets. Even though, in the face of the long time-honoured and transnational cherished poetics of ruins in the Renaissance, I would avoid searching for evidence in lexical similarities when we come to *Titus* (for all its sometimes startling resemblances), to emphasize rather the influence the French poet may have had in fostering a deeper but more abstract notion of the eternal city as a "flitting" entity: one that was culturally and widely shared and according to which, as Du Bellay put it, "That which is firm, doth flit and fall away; / And that is flitting, doth abide and stay" (3.13–14). Certainly, an authoritative and long-standing reflection on Rome as inextricably linked to its ruins had made the playwright alert—skilful "shake-scene" that he already was—to their dramatic potentialities. Such a dramatic force was mightily epitomized by the opening verses of Du Bellay's sonnet 7:

Ye sacred ruines, and ye tragick sights,
Which onely do the Name of Rome retaine,
Old moniments, which of so famous sprights
The honour yet in ashes do maintaine:
Triumphant Arcks, spyres neighbours to the skie,
That you to see doth th' Heaven it selfe appall,
Alas, by little ye to nothing flie,
The peoples fable and the spoyle of all.

As has been gradually acknowledged, *Titus Andronicus* was Shakespeare's first and most explosive experiment with tragedy and not the least or less learned of his Roman plays. Appeared in print in 1594 (Q1), *Titus* was one of the 1593 new plays produced at the Rose according to Henslowe's *Diary*, granted that we can rely on its uneven and rather debatable chronology.[7] Be that as it may, it was box office success. Henslowe, landlord and manager of the Rose, recorded it as among the best of the season. Notably, it was Peter Brook who began to show *Titus*'s innovative power in 1955 when he insightfully picked it up for representation in Stratford after a century of prudish oblivion, let alone the modernist aesthetic repulsion expressed by T.S. Eliot's famous "one of the stupidest and most uninspired plays ever written"; one which "would have made the living Seneca shudder with genuine aesthetic horror".[8] After years of (enduring) scholarly squeamishness with this play, it was Jonathan Bate who consistently contributed to assess its importance in Shakespeare's canon in his 1995 Arden edition. Shakespeare had written—or continued to write and revise—his play in years afflicted by insurgent plague, unremitting death and contagion, and short-lived reopening of the London theatres. As Bate has suggested, Shakespeare had profited from the long periods of closure of the theatres for inventing himself as a non-dramatic poet. He wrote *Venus and Adonis* and began writing *The Rape of Lucrece*. "These works took him to Ovid and to Roman history, quite possibly for the first time since his schooldays" and prompted "a new play based on his classical reading—a Roman tragedy which has exceptionally strong stylistic and thematic links with *Lucrece*". It revealed to be "*the* pivotal play in Shakespeare's early career", as Bate has it, a bench test, the play which allowed him "to go back to English history [and the yet unpublished *Richard III*] but with a new tragic intensity".[9]

In the course of that learned leisure time (mentioned as "idle hours" in *Venus and Adonis*'s dedication), so tragically imbued of all-too-real sights of defacing illness and sorrow, Shakespeare may also have come across Spenser's *Complaints* and the "tragic sights" of Du Bellay/Spenser's *Ruines of Rome*. But the bearing on *Titus Andronicus*, if I may insist, is more a question of profound insight than of lexical similarity. In fact, there is no need to wait for any explicit mention of ruins to understand that the play's topic is "ruin", the ruin of city, state, family, bodies, in a word the fall of a civilization—as Heiner Müller decisively fixed it in the title of his remake (*Anatomy Titus Fall of Rome*, 1985)—and that this had paradigmatic relevance for Shakespeare's Elizabethan theatregoers.[10] Suffice it to remember the aforementioned interrelation of *Titus Andronicus* with the internecine and no less gory scenario of Shakespeare's coeval first tetralogy (mostly) devoted to the domestic 30-year war between the two houses of York and Lancaster; an interrelation overtly signalled by the way coffins and litigious funerals migrate from one play to another—*1 Henry VI*, *Titus Andronicus*, *Richard III*—as the setting and theatrical equipment in each of their opening scenes. In both plays, in fact, they soon take centre stage as signs of offended rituality and announced, self-destructive violence. But let us also consider the similar feud on questions of legitimacy and succession which theatrically opens both *3 Henry VI* and *Titus*, the latter functioning as a catastrophe metaphor, remindful of the other.

The allegorical use of the ruins of Rome as a familiar trope to refer to the fragile nature of kingdoms and power in early modern European culture is well known. As Vanna Gentili has remarked, "the ruins of Rome are among the favourite emblems for a representation of the past which is both allegorical and historical".[11] In fact, allegorically, ruins tell the story of a Fall. But the historical approach aiming at rescuing Rome's ruins from their silence in order to make them stand as a decipherable instance of an abandoned, authoritative past to emulate or challenge is equally active.

Within the sphere of the visual arts, as outstandingly shown by Giorgio Vasari's *Lives* (1550), Rome's parable of glory and ruin is essential to Vasari's own notion of "renaissance" and the elaboration of an idea of art history that, precisely drawing on Rome, he understands (without Vico)[12] as a cyclical succession of excellence, decline, and rebirth, "namely, the rise of the arts to perfection, then decline and their restoration or rather renaissance".[13] The question of imitation, that is, the issue of how artists could "imitate the old in making the new" (8), is tantamount to the question of Rome,[14] but Vasari complicates it by drawing attention to the way such a passage from excellence to decay and rediscovery of ancient models was cut across by and intermingled with phenomena of destruction and pillage, as well as processes of recycling hybridisms and transformations. Indeed, in the same solicitous if emulative spirit of his humanist predecessors (Poggio Bracciolini, Flavio Biondo), Vasari devoted much of the "Preface" to his *Lives* to raising the question of Rome's decay. Which for him was mostly the question of how the conditions of what remained, or was only surfacing or unachievable, determined the attendant issues of model and imitation: or "restoration". As for destruction, pillage, and decline, this process had begun, he wrote, "even before the coming of the Goths and other barbarous and foreign nations who combined to destroy all the superior arts as well as Italy" (7). And continued even more harmfully, he took pains to underline, with the iconoclastic "fervent zeal of the new Christian religion" (10). So that ancient Rome, and what was identified with Rome—"marvelous statues, sculptures, paintings, mosaics and ornaments of the false pagan gods . . . but also the memorials and honours of countless excellent persons"—(*ibidem*), ended up dispersed as dismembered and recycled material in the churches of the new Christian Rome, when not "buried under the débris" of the destructive fury of its external enemies (11). However, Italian Christian churches represented the sites where the complex strata of heritage and memory of Rome, appropriating phenomena of the heathen Pantheon included, could be seen laid bare:

> the church outside the walls of Arezzo, built to St. Donato . . . has eight sides, and was built of the spoils of the theatre, colosseum and other buildings erected in Arezzo before it was converted to the Christian faith. No expense was spared, and it was adorned with columns of granite, porphyry and variegated marble taken from ancient buildings.
>
> (9)

But Christian churches were also the place where many good things had been swallowed up and saved for imitation: "A good illustration . . . is afforded by the church of the chief of the apostles in the Vatican, which is rich in columns, bases, capitals, architraves, cornices, doors" (8).

The history of the Renaissance, as has been variously observed, is a history of hybridisms, anachronisms, and palimpsestic temporalities. As in those many Renaissance paintings in which ruined classical arches and architectures are absorbed as a recurrent element or backdrop of the subject matter, the aim to disinter and give shape to a dispersed classical past is displayed as coexisting with its ruinous and aporetic side. "As soon as the reconstruction of fantasy is produced it undergoes a dismantling. The process of construction and destruction that occurred in historical time, is here, on the virtual level, rehearsed with no time lapse at all."[15] The ruins or dust of Rome were perceived as part of a process of metamorphosis and transformation, as well as of fractured and overlapping temporalities, a hybridism which, in different ways, I argue, the Renaissance or baroque Shakespeare overtly staged in *Titus Andronicus* and *Cymbeline*, at the beginning and end of his trafficking with Rome.

It is indeed this Rome, left "destitute of shape and life" in Vasari's words (11), a Rome where what is "flitting" is the only permanence (Du Bellay/Spenser), a Rome broadly perceived as something to be archaeologically searched for amongst its early modern ruins and conglomerates, that I want to conjure up as a landscape, in order to see how it affects—in conjunction with the profoundly revolutionary drive of the playwright's own Reformist times—Shakespeare's dismembering protocol in *Titus Andronicus*, his first and long-held indecorous and "non canonical" Roman play. But what sense of aporia and discontinuity is brought to bear on his general way of looking at Rome? And are we to recognize the same sense of cultural instability when we later come to Antony's auspices? "Let Rome in Tiber melt, and the wide arch / Of the ranged empire fall" (*Antony and Cleopatra*, 1.1.33–34).

Titus Andronicus, I would like to suggest, makes us enter the Shakespearean Roman world (*Julius Caesar, Antony and Cleopatra, Coriolanus*) *à rebours*, as if amongst the stones of a ruined triumphal arch, but also at the point of contact with times to come: a belated archaeologically envisioned temporality where bodies, their history, and textuality must be searched for in their fragments, if not waste material.

Such a "ruinous" peculiarity of Shakespeare's play was derogatorily captured by Edward Ravenscroft when, in motivating his pruned adaptation carried out in 1687, he observed:

> [*Titus Andronicus*] is the most incorrect and indigested piece in all his works; It seems rather a heap of rubbish than a structure. However as if some great building had been design'd, in the removal we found many large and square stones both useful and ornamental to the fabrick, now modell'd.[16]

Ravenscroft's negative architectural metaphor—one which conflates content and textuality—helps us raise an opposite stance in this chapter. For it is exactly in this "being with ruins", or in "this–being with spectres [or ghosts]" (as Derrida might put it),[17] that we perceive the modernity of Shakespeare's way of tackling the topic of Rome in *Titus Andronicus*, one which radically and "heliotropically" (Benjamin) interrogated his own times. Arguably his Rome could be felt as utterly contemporary in Tudor post-Reformist England when men and women were widely experiencing the anxiety if not the trauma of broken and overlapping temporalities, whether this regarded the permanent issue of succession and legitimacy after the death of Henry VIII or the similarly permanent issue of confessional change or loyalty to which the former was inextricably interrelated. Tudor England was marked by "a crisis in prospect or in *potential*", Peter Lake has observed. And Elizabeth's lack of an heir made the anxiety last for her entire reign: "Catholics and protestants alike—remained obsessed with what was going to happen if and when the queen died; which explains why questions of marriage, succession and Mary Queen of Scots remained such hot-button issues throughout the reign".[18] In the course of a historical conjuncture defined more by a sense of discontinuity than continuity, the very notion of memory had undergone successive reform and a problematization induced by regimes of enforced "social amnesia".[19] This was made materially manifest in 1535 by the dissolution of monasteries and their libraries—the custodians of textual heritage—which caused the entire English library, namely "the treasure houses" of the nation's memory, to undergo a process of destruction and reconstruction, "bibliographical oblivion" and Reformist bibliographical rebuilding.[20]

Was Shakespeare's *Titus* answering the suspending void of all-too-near ruins with the suspended temporality of his oneiric Roman ruins? As criticism is increasingly willing to recognize, the method Shakespeare used in *Titus* was profoundly experimental, but this is precisely because, I suggest, the temporal continuum is replaced by a broken or "suspended" temporality: a "non-time-space", which following Hannah Arendt's conceptualization is kept in existence by filling the gap with a conflict of intermingling "particles" of past and future. Arendt writes,

> time is not a continuum, a flow of uninterrupted succession; it is broken in the middle, at the point where "he" [Kafka's man] stands; and "his" standpoint is not the present as we usually understand it but rather a gap in time which "his" constant fighting, "his" making a stand against past and future, keeps in existence.[21]

The "standpoint" and the present of which Hannah Arendt was thinking while writing these pages was the gap that had been created by the atrocities and debris of the Second World War, when the link connecting generations had been broken and the past, she writes quoting Tocqueville, had "ceased to throw its light upon the future" (*Be*, 7). It was the fractured time (not the only one in history, and in fact we are in the very middle of a similar phase) when a whole generation of writers and men of letters "were sucked into politics as though with the force of a vacuum" (*Be*, 3).

Indeed, it is the political acceptation of what Arendt calls a "non-time-space", a "battlefield and not a home", that it can be useful to keep in mind in defining the "present" of Shakespeare's characters and the theatrical experience of his audience. This is the present of a crisis of memory and a *critique* of history, where the past represented by Rome is not a given, something that can "be inherited and handed down", but a genealogy to be "unearthed" (in the philosopher's words), something to be questioned, and "ploddingly" discovered and reinvented (*Be*, 13).

This is impressively dramatized in Shakespeare's first Roman play, a tragedy characterized by a "disintegrative rhetoric" and a disintegrative manner of inheriting Rome's cultural authority, as Heather James has insightfully observed.[22] Indeed, we have hardly entered Rome as beholders of the triumph of the general Titus, the embodiment of Romanness and the Roman *virtus*, that his integrity together with the scenario of bodies and places around him undergo at incredible speed the process of their explosive fragmentation into what I perceive as a multilayered and hybrid archaeology of Romanness. Such a process can be emphasized by conjuring up the coeval, anthropomorphized, collapsed geography of Rome provided by Du Bellay/Spenser, one which is archaeologically displayed through the image of a self-entombing city. In sonnet 4.5–14, "Jove fearing, lest if she should greater growe, . . . / Her whelm'd with hills, these seven hills, which be nowe / Tombes of her greatness, which did threate the skies; / Upon her head he heapt Mount Saturnal, / Upon her bellie th' antique Palatine, / Upon her stomacke laid Mount Quirinal". Du Bellay's subsequent sonnet 5 reinforces such an image with that of a self-enwombed body: "The corpes of Rome in ashes is entombed, / And her great spirite rejoined to the spirite / Of this great masse, is in the same enwombed" (9–11). The city's written heritage though, uprising from or as if breaking out of its marble ruins, is there to be literally and metaphorically excavated, copied, interrogated, rewritten. A challenge to all: "But her brave writings, which her famous merite / In spight of Time, out of the dust doth reare, / Do make her Idole through the world appeare" (12–14).

Exploiting the metaphoric proximity of body and citadel, Shakespeare seems to have transferred onto Lucrece's sieged Roman body the suggestive imagery of hills and body parts. This happens twice in *The Rape*: in v. 390 ("Between whose hills her head entombed is") and 679 ("[Tarquin] Entombs her outcry in her lips' sweet fold"). Other single occurrences of verb "to entomb" are in *Macbeth* (2.4.9), *Troilus and Cressida* (3.3.184), *Coriolanus* (2.1.86), and interestingly in sonnet 81 ("When you entombed in men's eyes shall lie / Your monument shall be my gentle verse", 8–9), the most famous among the sonnets of immortality, where the poet's protracted meditation on time and decay, so pervasively underwritten by Rome's glory and ruin (see Introduction, pp. 28–32), is challenged, in significant emulative forms, by the monumentalization of his poetry. But how is this worked out in *Titus*?

Bodies in Times of Ruin

Sacrifices as feasts or feasts as sacrifices open Shakespeare's first Roman play, in a barbaric scenario of *finis imperii* characterized by an anxiety to reaffirm, by means of hostile bodies turned into communal food, a shared imperial sense of identity. This represents the climax of Titus's triumph: the way Rome spectacularizes its system of exchange with the conquered foreigner (or Other) in the expanded multicultural space of the empire.[23] The burning limbs and entrails of the eldest son of Tamora, Queen of the Goths, should serve that purpose in Lucius's mind, the winning survivor of the Andronici, who at the end of the play will be given the triumphal task of summing up, with a repetitive revengeful strategy, past and future, Rome and the Goths. Burning the bodies of the enemy or foreigner is figured out, first of all, as variously said by many, as a public unifying ritual in a family-grounded performance of memory ("*Ad manes fratrum*" / ['to the shades of our brothers']", 1.1.101). Funereal rites are "the most conspicuous form through which memory is performed (or suppressed)", Michael Neill has observed.[24] Indeed, on a private and internalized level this should serve "to appease" the "groaning shadows" of the dead (1.1.129), as both Titus and Lucius erroneously believe, thus preserving those who are alive from being exposed to (and "disturbed with") the "prodigies on earth" (1.1.103–104): by which they mean perhaps the violence which is buried with the dead and which surfaces from among the fractures of the world they inhabit, its fault lines, disturbing the sleep of many with bad dreams (as in *Julius Caesar*). But this is only the beginning of a reciprocating dynamic of violence which soon transforms bodies and Romanness into fragments and a growing cohort of ghosts.

As a matter of fact, Shakespeare's Rome, as aforesaid in the Introduction (pp. 4–6), is already a world of "remains", mourning, and memorials when he designs Titus's opening triumph (*Aeneid*, Book 6 at hand) as mostly a burial of his own ancestry. It is no case that since the outset, and up to the end of the play (see 5.3.79–86), Rome's glory should be constitutively haunted by the violence archetypically encapsulated in the "Ur-narrative" of Troy's fall—Rome's (and England's) originating myth— thus telling the story of a city obsessed by the cyclic return of the same, or better, by the underwritten tale of a destroyed and resurgent City, but not in the same place:[25]

> Romans, of five-and-twenty valiant sons,
> Half of the number that King Priam had,
> Behold the *poor remains*, alive and dead:
> These that survive, let Rome reward with love;
> These that I bring unto their latest home,
> With burial amongst their ancestors.
>   (1.1.82–87; my emphasis)

Coherently, the play enacts from the very start (and however "piously" understood at the beginning) the condition of a Rome which is, Du Bellay–like, literally and metaphorically, tomb/womb of itself; a condition which resounds as a haunting threat in Quintus's comment on the cavity of Bassanius's death, the first in a retaliatory and precipitating series of atrocities: "I may be plucked into the swallowing womb / Of this deep pit, poor Bassanius' grave" (2.2.239–40). Interestingly, Du Bellay's aforementioned anthropomorphized vision of an enwombing and self-entombing Rome (sonnets 4 and 5) also resonates, I suggest, as a pervading figure of archetypical female voracity in Shakespeare's complex construction of otherness within the hybridized context of *finis imperii*; one which, as with Tamora's foreign body, is uncannily in and out, incorporated as well as incorporating, in a process defined, as often observed, by an agency of mutual othering.[26]

Such an opening of the play may well have been written by, or together with, George Peele, the playwright who authored *The Battle of Alcazar* (produced ca. 1589, printed in 1594), a hit, as it is acknowledged, in the genre of staged disembowelling anatomy.[27] But Shakespeare is supreme in the way he draws consequences. The play becomes, structurally and coherently, the place of a permanent "state of emergency"—we might say with Benjamin[28]—the place of an endless chain of mutual violence, variously remindful of the fact that the originating myth of Rome was a narrative of war and destruction: the tale of Troy's fall, the "brightburning Troy" in Titus's words (see also later 5.3.86). It is not for nothing that Revenge, the revenant *par excellence*, and the very protagonist of the play, is sumptuously portrayed at the end of the play as a live and threatening Allegory, performed by Tamora: the abstract embodiment, a masque, of the perfectly orchestrated "violent orderliness"[29] of the play. Accordingly Rome (likely cast with Tacitus's lacerated Rome as its main historical inspiration)[30] is turned, in brief, into a *corps morcelé*, a world of progressively mutilating and self-mutilated bodies, a world of body parts—hands, heads, tongues—which predicate the dissolution of Rome's institutions—as well as the problematization of its legacy.

Meaningfully, this is epitomized by Lavinia—"the greatest spurn" (3.1.102)—a female body raped and mutilated by Tamora's Gothic sons, but remindful of a violence and a trauma which is inscribed in Rome's language and its foundation myths. "*Stuprum—Chiron—Demetrius*" (4.1.77), the learned Lavinia tragically writes in the sand with a stick in the identification scene, "*Magni dominator poli / Tam lentus audis scelera, tam lentus vides?*" ["Rulers of the great heavens, are you so slow to hear crimes, so slow to see?"] (4.1.82), as if positing her last denouncing act between the permanence of a lasting Senecan inscription and the impermanence of the material on which it is carved. But in the *finis imperii* racially and culturally hybridized context contrived by Shakespeare, this is also ironically brought to the fore by the equally learned, Machiavellian Aaron—a blackmoor, the counsellor and lover of a Gothic queen, who demonstrates he is also menacingly knowledgeable in matters of Roman history and myths—when he plots the rape of Lavinia according to Roman "precedents" and Ovidian patterns: "Take this of me: 'Lucrece was not more chaste / Than this Lavinia'" (1.1.608–609). Even Demetrius—a rough and the less educated Goth in the play—does his best to show up as no less Romanized when he emphasizes his rapist fire with Horacian and Senecan inserts (1.1.633–35).[31]

Indeed, violence is written indelibly on Lavinia's flesh, "carved in Roman letters", as we might say borrowing from Aaron's sacrilegious way of remembering the dead (5.1.135–40). But those letters lie dismembered scattered on the soil, undecipherable, as the elliptic fragments of a broken Roman inscription. What remains of her is an illegible "map of woe" (3.2.12), one which to Titus's soldierly sight appears, topographically, as a ravished and silent field of destruction:

> Thou map of woe, that thus dost talk in signs,
> When thy heart beats with outrageous beating,
> Thou canst not strike it thus to make it still.
> Wound it with sighing, girl, kill it with groans.
>   (3.2.12–15)

Before dying Lavinia has come to share with the dead (see opening scene 1.1.129) the disarticulation of her own language, its transformation into a naked surviving lament—a spectral blood-thirsty groan—which her father elicits, uncannily, as an anesthetizing therapy, a way to harden her doleful heart.[32]

But Titus and his brother Marcus themselves contribute, with similar images of amputation and petrification (or "stony image[s]", 3.1.259), to the hallucinatory and ruinous landscape of the play. "O, here I lift this one hand up to heaven / And bow this feeble ruin to the earth (3.1.207–208), Titus utters, as if imagining himself in the petrified shape of a smashed ancient monument, a dimidiated "torso", we might say, like the famous *Torso of Belvedere* (first century BCE), the Greek sculpture discovered in Rome in the 1430s to which the acquisition in the papal Belvedere collection of the Vatican in the 1530s had earned the fame of a masterpiece worth copying, and circulated in a variety of Renaissance drawings as a fragmented instance of the heroic Herculean posture (among these that of the Trinity College Cambridge Sketchbook executed around 1550).[33]

This is not to say that Shakespeare may have come across one of those drawings, but Lucius's representation of the dead Titus as a "trunk", in his final farewell to him (5.3.151), seems to concur to this prevailing scenario of bodies as a defaced and fragmented monumentality. The play of emotions on- and offstage seems to follow suit. For such a petrified landscape is also meant to be astounding and petrifying for the beholders, as shown by Marcus, seemingly at pains to define the emotional temperature of the play as one of horrified stupor and gelid numbness and stillness.

Figure 1.1 Torso del Belvedere, Musei Vaticani
Source: © Musei Vaticani

Arguably, it is not just Titus that he refers to when he argues that life overdoes dreams in being a nightmare:

> Thou dost not slumber. See thy sons' heads,
> Thy warlike hand, thy mangled daughter here,
> Thy other banished son with this dear sight
> Struck pale and bloodless, and thy brother, I,

Even like a stony image, cold and numb.
Ah, now no more will I control thy griefs:
Rend off thy silver hair, thy other hand
Gnawing thy teeth, and be this dismal sight
The closing up of our most wretched eyes.
Now it is a time to storm. Why art thou still?
(3.1.255–64)

The audience response is incorporated in what is being constructed onstage—"this dismal sight"—deictically (thy, I, here, now) by way of a finely wrought positional transaction of images and gaze, namely a prescription of what we should fix our eyes upon and how we should experience it, within a circularity, or "sympathy in owe" (3.1.149), in which each subject is interactively the object of the others' sight. Like the characters of the play, the onlookers are first of all supposed to be "still", as the audience at a tragedy should, "Struck pale and bloodless", before obliquely receiving the injunction to explode, with Titus, into an angry and shattering emotional outburst. But to no avail for now: "Why art thou still?" The response elicited by Marcus is returned by persistent "stillness", the emotional release being unexpected sarcastic laughter, Titus's disturbing (uncomfortable) laughter, the disintegration of dramatic decorum in Jonathan Bate's words: "As the decorums of Roman honour disintegrate, so do the decorums of dramatic expectation".[34] And yet, whether or not we join in Titus's laughter, if we want to share the play's grief, we have to take on the responsibility and uneasiness of such an anti-tragic laughter. It's not by chance that any Shakespearean at theatre feels compelled to take notice of how the audience members around him or her are affected by and comply with this momentous point of the play.

In the no more than scarcely ten lines that the playwright assigns to Marcus in this instance, he also dictates an oneiric and prevailing sight, or anatomy of Rome as a hallucinatory heap of mangled bodies and discrete, severed limbs ("See thy sons' heads, / Thy warlike hand") hanging in the void as if against a Caravaggesque black backdrop, before parading in front of the audience in view of the final revengeful banquet; an effect which Shakespeare will exploit again in the envisaging of Macbeth's hallucinations, with the difference that what Titus and the audience are invited to see is all too real.

Indeed, limbs and their owners in Shakespeare's play are turned into objectified—almost inorganic—wrecks, hurled around by a storm, which is continually evoked and mentioned as the agent propelling the action of the play and the past into the future. The storm is evoked first of all by Titus who, significantly, pictorially emblematizes his own story as that of one who "stand[s] . . . upon a rock, / Environed with a wilderness of sea" (3.1.94–95), foreboding the incumbent completion of his misfortune. In fact he is, in every sense, a castaway. And if for a while he and a few others of his family survive the "deluge" (3.1.230)—a connected, pervasive image in the play—it is only to accomplish the task of burying, if not murdering, their own progeny and to confront an appearance of themselves, uncannily and dreamlike, as mute phantasms of a "dumb show" (3.1.132): the image of their own cheeks mirrored back to them "stained like meadows yet not dry, / With miry slime left on them by [the] flood" (3.1.125–27). One might say that they are posthumous to themselves and to their own time, in the way they look back at their own bodies as if these were already mingling with, and becoming indistinguishable from, the surrounding muddy landscape and its chalky post-flood colour.

We can only invoke the view of Benjamin's angel of history to account for such an archaeological way of conceiving the course of history, one in which past and future are bound into "one single catastrophe".

> His face is turned toward the past. Where we perceive a chain of events, he sees one single catastrophe which keeps piling wreckage upon wreckage and hurls it in front of his feet. The angel would like to stay, awaken the dead, and make whole what has been smashed. But a storm is blowing from Paradise; it has got caught in his wings with such violence that the angel can no longer close them. The storm irresistibly propels him into the future to which his back is turned, while the pile of debris before him grows skyward. This storm is what we call progress.[35]

The storm, variously and metaphorically articulated as a swallowing surge, flood, fire, wind, is what drives the past into the future in *Titus Andronicus*, but also what shatters the linear "chain of events" and piles up in one single multilayered and culturally hybridized conglomerate, past, present, and future: Romanness and Gothicism, Titus and Tamora, but also Titus, Tamora, and Lucius, in the way these three characters together recapitulate the time—or indistinct territory—which, from Rome, looks backward to Troy and onward to the Goths, at the turning point in which Rome is becoming medieval. An excess of history at a moment of crisis, we may well say, when the old and the new interpenetrate, and the old emerges or returns with the haunting and dreamlike quality of a revenant.

Shakespeare will assign to Clarence, a character of his coeval *Richard III*, the dream version of such a way of experiencing history as a collapsed temporality:

> Methought I saw a thousand fearful wrecks,
> Ten thousand men that fishes gnawed upon,
> Wedges of gold, great anchors, heaps of pearl.
> Inestimable stones, unvalued jewels.
> Some lay in dead men's skulls, and in those holes
> Where eyes did once inhabit there were crept—

As 'twere in scorn of eyes—reflecting gems,
Which wooed the slimy bottom of the deep
And mocked the dead bones that lay scattered by.
                                            (1.4.23–31)

Then came wand'ring by
A shadow like an angel in bright hair
Dabbled in blood, and he squeaked out aloud:
"Clarence is come, false, fleeting, perjured Clarence,
That stabbed me in the field of Tewkesbury.
Seize on him, Furies, take him to your torments!"
                                            (1.4.49–54)

Indeed, what happens in Clarence's drowning dream is a descent into time's womb or grave: a world of disanchoraged "fearful wrecks", an undifferentiated territory of human and non-human, beauty and horror, organic and inorganic which he experiences with the typical hallucinatory confusion and distortion that characterizes the reappearance of "discarded" or "forgotten objects" (Benjamin).[36] But his is also an updated Virgilian underworld (*Aeneid*, Book 6) of wandering and vengeful shadows.

Wrecks, ghosts, storms, and shipwrecks are strictly interwoven in the way Rome was addressed in Shakespeare's time. And this has a bearing, I argue, on *Titus*'s increasingly spectral and self-observing, or self-reflexive, characters. In Du Bellay's *Ruines*, ghosts are envisaged as activating a self-referential visual regime, which makes them both part and posthumous beholders of their catastrophe: "Ye pallid spirits, and ye ashie ghoasts" . . . "Do you not feele your torments to accrewe, / When ye sometimes behold the ruin'd pride / Of these old Romane works built with your hands, / Now to become nought else but heaped sands?" (sonnet 15, 1 and 11–14). This is the same split condition which we can observe in Du Bellay's cherished image of the shipwreck as a metaphor of Rome's destiny, a pictorial image which we might well include in Blumenberg's views of shipwrecks "with spectator":[37] "Like as ye see the wrathful Sea from farre, / In a great mountaine heap't with hideous noyse, / Eftsoones of thousand billowes shouldred narre, / Against a Rocke to breake with dreadful poyse; . . . So whilom did this Monarchie aspyre / As waves, as winde, as fire spread over all, / Till it by fatal doom adowne did fall" (sonnet 16.1–4 and 13–15). Looking from afar implies a meditative distance which is functional to knowledge and allegorization (the shattered vessel becomes an allegory of life). But it also prospects a spectator who can be coincident with the seafarer, namely a spectator who is in and out of the storm. The maritime imagery is exploited again by Du Bellay when (in sonnet 21:10–14) Rome's self-destroying drive is imagined as a shipwreck in one's own port: "Her power it selfe against itselfe did arme, / As he that having long in tempest sailed, / Faine would arrive, but cannot for the storme, / If too great winde against the port him drive, / Doth in the port it selfe his vessell rive".

In Shakespeare's *Titus*, we find a similar shipwrecked perception of Rome's destiny and the human existence. Pervasively (see 1.1.73–76; 3.1.69; 1.94–99; 3.1.220–32) we are confronted with the seafarer and castaway motif. The seafarer motif is soon announced in the protagonist's initial entry, when he compares his military campaign to a "bark" which safely "Returns with precious lading to the bay / From whence at first she weighed her anchorage" (1.1.75–76). But it will be once Titus has set foot victoriously on the firm land of his Rome and in the larger span of the play's timeframe that he will experience the vicissitudes of adverse wind and shipwreck.

> For now I stand as one upon a rock,
> Environed with a wilderness of sea,
> Who marks the waxing tide grow wave by wave,
> Expecting ever when some envious surge
> Will in his brinish bowels swallow me.
>
> (3.1.94–99)

Here Titus is in the grip of the tragic knowledge he has acquired. He is one with it, the shipwreck being so absolute as to blur the boundaries between subject and storm or wave: "I am the sea", he outcries shortly thereafter (3.1.226). By now, Rome's vessel is catastrophically one with the wind propelling it towards the future of its destruction.

The nautical metaphor has received large philosophical attention as a condensation of humanity's shipwrecked existence. Suffice it to mention Schopenhauer quoted by Nietzsche in *The Birth of Tragedy* (1872):

> Just as the boatman sits in his little boat, trusting his fragile craft in a stormy sea which, boundless in every direction, rises and falls in howling, mountainous waves, so in the midst of a world full of suffering the individual man calmly sits, supported by and trusting the *principium individuationis*.[38]

But Titus's risky position "upon a rock" on the verge of being swallowed by the swelling sea cannot serve a "freeing illusion" by means of a distantiating and pacificatory contemplation of the stormy sea of life, as we might add, with Lear's aspiration in mind (in 5.3.8–19). Titus is far from transcendence. On the contrary, "he is the sea". He "doesn't sit quietly" on his rock trusting in his possibility to come to terms with the form and meaning of his existence, a condition that in Nietzsche's complex vision of the tragic form pertains to the Apollonian capacity to transcend the Dionysian originary sorrow.[39] For that—for the dramatization of an achieved Apollonian art of survival among the billows of life—we shall

have to wait for the fable-like narrations of Shakespeare's late plays—
Pericles, The Winter's Tale, Cymbeline, The Tempest—the late dreams
of the "naïve artist", as I have argued elsewhere, drawing on Nietzsche's
problematized notion of *naïveté*.[40] In *Titus* the spectator (Titus) is knowingly one with the enormity of his tragedy, distance being represented,
only and terribly, by the awareness of its uselessness: "If there were reason
for these miseries, / Then into limits I could bind my woes" (3.1.220–21).
And it is from such a sense of repetitiveness and colossal purposelessness
that his irrepressible and disturbing laughter originates (3.1.265): a disturbance quite similar to Joker's compulsory laughter in the waste land
of Gotham City in the recent eponymous film directed by Todd Phillips
(2019). Gaunt is lapidary in *Richard II*: "Misery makes sport to mock
itself" (2.1.85).

"How Can I Grace My Talk, / Wanting a Hand to Give It Action?": The Fragmentation of the Father's Tale

> Speak, Lavinia, what accursed hand
> Hath made thee handless in thy father's sight?
> What fool hath added water to the sea?
> Or brought a faggot to bright-burning Troy?
> (3.1.67–70)

Titus asks, conjuring up ancient narratives of submerging floods together
with a primal burning city; a city which seems to be replicated by Rome
with redoubled flames. Is there still a tongue to tell this story of "further
misery" for "time to come"? He also asks,

> Or shall we cut away our hands like thine?
> Or shall we bite our tongues and in dumb shows
> Pass the remainder of our hateful days?
> What shall we do? Let us that have our tongues
> Plot some device of further misery
> To make us wondered at in time to come.
> (3.1.131–36)

One might feel a ventriloquist's presence of the playwright in these lines,
voicing for his own age the "misery" stemming from the flames, the
broken images, the enforced forgetfulness of his own "hateful" post–
Reformation time. But how is he to tell his story, in what form?

Criticism has authoritatively shown that "Titus is a figure of Aeneas
as well as of Priam" (Miola).[41] It has also insightfully observed that the
epic genre which, through Aeneas's lineage, had "consecrated the imperial origins of Rome and offered a model of self-containment to Titus",
is an exhausted "fortifying resource" (James).[42] What I am interested in

bringing to the fore is the question of Titus's shattered tale and the way it is pervasively interwoven with maimed bodies and broken bonds among generations. Forcefully emerging as a central issue in Act 3, this is, as I take it, the question we hear resonating persistently in Titus's words, the Roman general who throughout the play is haunted by the "precedent" of Troy, the burning city—the Ur-ruin—but who is also famous in his family for being a storyteller of "sad stories chanced in the times old" (3.2.84; see also 5.3.161–65).

Which stories and which times are the audience referred to? The question remains open until the end of the play, when resuming the Troy motif announced from its very beginning we are explicitly referred to Aeneas's epic and the moving narration of its fall to a "sad-attending" Dido (5.3.79–86): a desiring and empathic figure—a listener in love, enthralled by that tale—in the Virgilian storytelling scenario (*Aeneid*, Books II–III). Placed almost at the closure of the play, such a mention retroactively unites Aeneas and Titus, structurally foregrounding with the mark of pervasiveness and metadramaticality the importance of such a theme in the play. But can the Virgilian epic form of those "old tales" tell the horror of Titus's own time? Can Titus's Rome "Speak . . . as our ancestor" ("Speak, Rome's dear friend, as erst our ancestor"?). Can it ventriloquize "his solemn tongue" (5.3.79–80)? No, Shakespeare's early modern audience might well answer, if those "old tales" identified Troy as a world of Gods, heroes, heroism, and, mostly, empathic "sad-attending" listeners. In this light the mention of "Dido's sad-attending ear" at the end of the play is not only called to "fulfill a narrative of social renewal" for those who, after Lucius's coup, have a vested political interest in reassembling the dismembered body of the state[43] but, as I see it, reverberates backwards on the whole play troubling the entire fatherly scenario of narration, listening, and shared compassion.

Troy is a contradictory tale in Shakespeare's *Titus*. Immediately summoned up at the outset of the play in order that it may favour a fatherly and ennobling kinship between Titus and Priam, both heroic fathers of many sons lost in war, Troy's ancestry is soon perverted into barbaric funeral rituals. Troy is also a field of contentious appropriation by both Romans and Goths. It is conjured up by Tamora, Queen of the Goths, to project into a pleasant, fulfilling tale—that of Aeneas and Dido—her passion for Aaron (2.2.21–29), while being at the same time the premonitory tale of a burning city for Titus (3.2.27–28). The motherly figure of Hecuba in turn is evoked to serve a variety of purposes by both Goths and Romans: Tamora's revenge on the one hand, (1.1.135–41); the adverse fate of persons, like Titus and Lavinia, on the other, "[run] mad for sorrow" (4.1.20–21). It also (latently) inspires the feminizing characterization of Titus's suffering face, excavated by tears: "witness these crimson lines, / Witness these trenches made by grief and care" (5.2.21–22); a face which is, infratextually, very similar to the anatomized ruin of Hecuba's face in the coeval *Rape* (vv. 1443–56).

But what is lacking and dramatically debilitating in the production of an accomplished and hence persuasive tale is Titus's own public Roman body, the male oratorical body of a leader who is typically invested with *Romanitas*—*virtus* as well as grace, eloquence, authority—by means of the very solemn posture which guarantees the rhetorical delivery: "No not a word; how can I grace my talk, / Wanting a hand to give it action?" (5.2.17–18), he cries. As we know, students like Shakespeare were taught in grammar schools (via Cicero and Quintilian) that the combination of talk and action—namely the performance of speech through a masterful, passionate use of voice and gesture ("actio")—played an essential part in the production and efficacy of meaning.[44] Roman *ars oratoria*, as witnessed by marble statuary, was iconically clear on this. You needed a toga *gracefully* laying its folds on one of your arms, while leaving the other free to properly translate into comely "action" ("actio"/"acting"), the movement of the body and the emotional nuances of the voice. "All these emotions must be accompanied by gesture . . . but the movements of the hand must be less rapid, following the words and not eliciting them with the fingers; the arm thrown out forward, like an elocutionary missile", Cicero recommends in *The Orator* (Book III.220),[45] the treatise which, ironically, features among the properties of the Andronici's library in this play. The "manly throwing out of the chest" and arm, in its ballistic posture codified by Cicero, is the gear which fastens together the weapon of eloquence.

But by the third act—a turning point in the emergence of the theme of jeopardized speech and empathic storytelling—Titus has already lost one of his hands, thus becoming very similar to some of those ruined statuary of Roman orators (generals, governors, moral philosophers, authoritative fatherly figures) of which only an archaeological and maimed posture is left, a toga without heads, and hands, and hence without "*actio*". "For by action the body talks" ["*Est enim actio quasi sermo corporis*"], Cicero writes (Book III.222).[46] Lacking one of his hands—an auxiliary but no minor protagonist in Cicero's *actio*, Titus is in no condition to properly perform his words.

On the contrary, he seems to be dramatically aware of his having become the scornful embodiment of a fragmented *ars oratoria*: the manly art of eloquence and persuasion, as he should well know given the Andronici's familiarity with Cicero's treatise. Hence, his amputated hand assumes crucial deconstructive significance in the context of the play, especially when we consider that he hasn't lost it heroically on the battlefield. His loss is rather the co-product of a grotesque mockery: an exchange of hand with heads. But Shakespeare goes even further when, before Titus amputates his hand to save his sons, he contrives his oratorical speech in their defence in the utterly humiliating posture of a pleader or a beggar.

Figure 1.2 Marble statue, Curia romana
Source: Public domain

As from Quartos and Folio stage directions, after his first 11 verses, Titus must assume a prone position: "*Andronicus lieth down, and the Judges pass by him*" (3.1.11). In the absence of any further direction as to his prostrate posture, editors of the play have him rise some 50 verses later, after he has been repeatedly reminded that nobody is listening to him: "O noble father, you lament in vain: / The tribunes hear you not, no man is by, / And you recount your sorrows to a stone" (3.1. 27–29).

Accordingly, his initial self-assuring use of metaphor—a central rhetorical figure in the ancient conceptualization of a moving and successful rhetoric—undergoes ineluctable disintegration, as shown by the nautical metaphor which solemnly marks his entry on stage, soon pessimistically perverted into that of "one who stands upon a rock" (3.1.94) waiting for the final blow. What remains is the unfeasible tale of his raped/amputated children and a smashed rhetorical posture, a dumb-show enacting the failure of language, as critics have variously observed[47]—or, as I would add, sticking to the gender-coded linguistic context of the play—the alienated condition of a language deprived of the guarantee of a whole and authorizing father. This will be contradictorily replaced by the baroque, electrified linguistic exuberance of Titus's protracted mourning and what is being (obliquely) denounced: Marcus's (Petrarchan) anatomical blazon of Lavinia, an embarrassing aestheticizing tale of a female violated body,[48] which marks and unmasks the obscenity of metaphor and the violence of the father's library. "THE DAUGHTER IS HAUNTING ROME HER HOME / FIGHTS HER FIGHT AGAINST THE BLACK AND WHITE / OF LITERATURE IT IS THE MURDERER'S PIT"—Heiner Müller has written in one of the illuminating glosses to his anatomizing remake of the play—"THE VERSE IS RAPE AND EVERY RHYME A DEATH / SWEEPS THE BOOKS OFF THE SHELVES WITH HER STUMPS / BURNING CANDLES CLENCHED BETWEEN HER TEETH / APPLAUDED BY THE ORPHANED GRANDSON / BURNS THE LIBRARY ON THE PARQUET FLOOR / AND BATHES HER STUMPY ARMS IN THE FLAMES / MEANWHILE THE GRANDSON PISSES IN THE FIRE".[49]

In Shakespeare's play, Titus's library (which as a stage space materializes in Act 4.1 and Act 5.2) contains ideally all the books that have been written as well as the script of Lavinia's life and death, her beauty, her horror, her sorrow, her fate; and—as for the plots of revenge Titus is contriving in that secluded and meditative space—he will not let it "fly away"; "for what I mean to do / See here in blood lines I have set down, / And what is written shall be executed" (5.2.11–15).

As has been remarked, "The Andronici are the bearers of the language of the fathers, especially the texts of the fathers".[50] But such a knowledge stored in Titus's library undergoes an earthquake as an effect of Lavinia's rape ("the greatest spurn" for her father), one which shatters to the extreme Titus's self-confidence in his own art as a storyteller, namely his capability of transforming that knowledge into a viable tale. In a context highly determined by acts of reading, writing, and speech,[51] the returning motif of storytelling—remindful of Aeneas's seductive profile as a storyteller—draws attention to its importance in the ongoing process of remembrance, and hence to the performativity of memory. And not simply because storytelling makes written words come alive, but because it iconically foregrounds the bodily gesture of reaching out which ties generations together, and hence the past to the present and to the future. In this sense Lavinia's (often noted) praised art of reading and teaching is relevant, but primarily, in the context of my argument, because it gives centre stage to a troubled connective posture in the controlled fatherly performance of memory. Her gendered intermediary role is visually highlighted by Marcus when in his post-rape and pre-mortem elegy he compares her to Cornelia—the Roman mother proverbially careful in reading "to her sons" (4.1.12–13). Such a motherly reproductive "care" is indirectly reaffirmed again when the young Lucius mentions some of his books as a motherly gift: "Grandsire, 'tis Ovid's *Metamorphosis*; / My mother gave it to me" (4.1.42–43). Significantly Lavinia is also praised for excelling in handling a cross-gendered typology of texts including poetry and prose, tales as well as the manly art of rhetoric: "Sweet poetry and Tully's *Orator*" (4.1.14).[52]

But Lavinia's reading and teaching role is as crucial as the fracture and the sense of loss, which she introduces early in the play with her maimed, silenced, and finally murdered body. Indeed before dying, and for most of the play, she stands for a lost connective icon, the mournful loss of a shared and unifying tale. She also stands, I argue, agreeing with Katherine Rowe, for the "contingent loss of self-representation".[53] And yet "the play feeds on her femininity".[54] In fact, Lavinia's loss of hands to handle books, reading, and writing literally consigns her to the hands of the two father figures, Titus and Marcus, who, after her silencing rape in Act 2.4, are given full control of her image and language. From now on theirs is the task of speaking for her (MARCUS: "Shall I speak for thee?" 2.4.33), as well as *reading her* (a "map of woe", 3.2.12), and *reading for her* (TITUS: "Lavinia, shall I read?" 4.1.47), but in a scene (4.1) whose content is the performed repetition of a story of ferocity and horror. In such a context, I argue, the mention of *The Orator* in Act 4 can only feature, ironically, as an object detached from its use, a fatherly *ruina*—as books and words are in the coeval *Rape*—the sign of decayed knowledge and a difficult legacy. For, by now, Lavinia is of a piece with Rome's exploded *ratio* and her father's fragmented oratorical body: or even worse, she has been definitively swallowed into the library of the fathers as an image of horror and shame. The field of representation is, irreparably, a ruinous and fatal scenario "patterned . . . for murders and rape" (4.1.58; 5.2.45). Ironically, the theme of storytelling—doubly highlighted in its testamentary importance by Lavinia's absence—returns to mark with its exclusive male-gendered reconfiguration, and as if forgetful of its underwritten trauma, the contradictory ending of the play.

LUCIUS [*to his son*]

Come hither, boy, come, come and learn of us
To melt in showers. Thy grandsire loved thee well:
Many a time he danced thee on his knee,
Sung thee asleep, his loving breast thy pillow;
Many a story hath he told to thee,

And bid thee bear his pretty tale in mind
And talk of them when he was dead and gone.
                    (5.3.159–65)

Storytelling, as an agent of memory and the instrument thanks to which
ties among generations can be constructed, or reconstructed, is undermined by Lavinia's expunction and her unreconciled ghostlike, monstri-
fied presence. Drastically cancelled from the linguistic tissue of the play in
Act 2, she remains visible on stage until her murder in the play's last act
(5.3.45), but to signify a deeper gender-coded set of issues which involve
her father's destabilized sight—his vomit-inducing woe (3.1.232)—and
more largely the order of representation.

As feminist theory has argued in the last five decades or so, and particularly Irigaray in *Speculum* and *Marine Lover*, woman's body in Western
thought and culture occurs as the object—and medium—of a male artist's
(or philosopher's) search for a specular and fulfilling construction of reality.[55] The capacity to *properly* reproduce the female figure is a measure, or
guarantee, of their capacity to grasp reality. Lavinia's violated body (like
that of the coeval Lucrece) disturbs to the point that she must be slaughtered by her father, such a female role in the scopic framework of cultural
representation and in a fatherly controlled vision of a reassuring reality.
Like Lucrece, no matter whether in a different story and context, she shatters the untroubled mirror of "re-semblance", or *mimesis*, with a broken
glass, namely with a knowledge (as I argue in my following chapter on *The
Rape*), which is utterly dispossessing for the male subjectivity. Revealingly,
this is dramatically voiced by Lucrece's father, Lucretius, when he cries,
"O, from thy cheeks my image thou hast torn" (v. 1762); a loss of specularity which (for both Lavinia and Lucrece) is tantamount to an unappealable
sentence of death proffered in the (Lacanian) "name-of-the-father".

Thus, true, Lavinia's mangled body stands for a dismembered Rome,
as is customary and rightly remarked, at least since Waith ("The rape and
mutilation of Lavinia is the central symbol of disorder, both moral and
political"),[56] but it also stands, as often happens in Shakespeare's works
(no matter whether intentionally), for an underwritten *critique* of the patriarchal order of representation and the failure of a shared and fatherly guar-
anteed heroic-epic tale. Anticipating the scene among Lear and Cordelia
(5.3.8–19), such a tale survives as the mere fantasy of a father's deranged
mind, "one who takes false shadows for true substance" (3.1.81):

Come, take away. Lavinia, go with me;
I'll to thy closet and go read with thee
Sad stories chanced in the times of old.
Come, boy, and go with me; thy sight is young,
And thou shalt read when mine begin to dazzle.
                    (3.2.82–86)

In this Shakespeare went against the grain, *pace* Philip Sidney, who in taking side with the cause of Poetry against those (the "Poet-haters")[57] who were fiercely abusing theatre and poetry, had forcefully defended the role of the "Heroicall" (and heroic tragedy) as what ensured memory, namely tied time and generations together:

> The incomparable *Lacedomonians* did not only carry that kinde of Musicke euer with them to the field, but euen at home, as such songes were made, so were they all content to bee the singers of them, when the lusty men were to tell what they dyd, the old men what they had done, and the young men what they would doe.
>
> (178)

"But if any thing be already sayd in the defence of sweete Poetry", Sidney continued, "all concurreth to the maintaining the Heroicall", which he deemed "the best and most accomplished kinde of Poetry":

> Only let *Aeneas* be worne in the tablet of your memory; how he governeth himself in the ruine of his Country; in the perseruing his old Father, and carrying away his religious ceremonies; in obeying the Gods commandements to leaue *Dido*, though not onely all passionate kindnes, would haue craued other for him; how in storms, howe a fugitiue, how victorious, how besiedged, howe to strangers, how to allyes, how to enemies, how to his owne; lastly, how in his inward selfe, and how in his outward gouernment.
>
> (179–180)

Epic and heroic literature is acknowledged as a cohesive model of individual and civic virtues by Sidney. But the classical/humanist library provides no comfortable pedagogy in Shakespeare's first Roman play. In fact, Titus is no Aeneas. On the contrary, Sidney at hand, Shakespeare seems to be knowingly working at constructing a character which for his audience should sound as a decayed version if not a reversal of the Trojan hero: the refugee who is nobly destined to navigate through the Mediterranean seas with the gift of his salvaged religious ceremonies and a moving, heroic, and instructive tale of rebirth, guided by the gods. Differently from the Virgilian hero, Titus laments the loss of both. "*Terras Astraea reliquit*; be you remembered, Marcus, / She's gone, she's fled" (4.3.4–5), Shakespeare has him cry, likely deriving from Tacitus (apart from Ovid) such a world of absent if retributive Gods: "For never was it more fully proved by awful disasters of the Roman people or by indubitable signs", Tacitus writes in his *Histories*, "that the gods care not for our safety, but for our punishment".[58] Also, what the aged Titus laments in front of the violated Lavinia is the loss of his accomplishment as a storyteller, the possibility for him to translate into a "plot" an untranslatable reality, and which he leaves encapsulated and suspended for his audience in a sequel of questions and prospective self-amputating resolves: "Shall thy good uncle and thy brother . . .? / Or shall we cut our hands . . .? / Or shall we bite our tongues . . .? / What shall we do? Let us that have tongues / Plot some device of further misery / To make us wondered at in time to come" (3.1.121–36). Decidedly Titus (and the playwright with him) is beyond Sidney's belief in the "heroical". Nor will the "heroical" be reinstated by the victorious Lucius at the end of the play, when the "solemn tongue" of Aeneas's tale will be conjured up to define nothing but the vanishing aura of a very questionable ending. As Heather James has written,

> Ovid dominates the central acts of the play at a direct cost to Vergil as a source of cultural decorum . . . No sooner is Vergilian authority installed through the ritual events and ceremonious speeches of the first act than it is deposed by a specifically Ovidian insouciance, marked by the once humorless Titus' laughter.[59]

Yes, the classical past refuses to be contained within its original mythical form, as Shakespeare demonstrates to the utmost when later he directly addresses the Troy matter in *Troilus and Cressida*, to transform it into a play of untragic ruins, a play without tragedy, without heroisms, and unresolvedly, without a generic status. And yet, as I am showing, the Virgilian motif of Aeneas's tale persists all along *Titus* as the symbol of a "lamentable" shipwrecked tie between past and present and among generations, the underwritten nostalgia of the play, its mourning.

Titus's Mourning

Titus's manner is not the "heroical", I want to argue, but filtered through Seneca and Tacitus's pessimism, the "most lamentable" baroque mode of the *Trauerspiel*, in all the postures enhanced by the ruined body and deranged mind of the protagonist Shakespeare has invented: a Roman body with very Benjamin-like "creaturely" heart and entrails. As has been observed, Benjamin's *Trauerspiel* has increasingly become relevant in the reading of Shakespeare and in defining Shakespearean tragedy as different from ancient tragedy. In discussing Shakespeare's classical inheritance, Richard Halpern has recently assessed its role in retroactively highlighting or shedding new light on the Senecan baroque nature of Shakespeare's tragedy, after more than two centuries of prevailing, unmediated Greek comparisons.[60] Assuming as implicit the great work which (at least since Miola) has been done in foregrounding the Senecan inheritance,[61] my concern in this section is to address Titus's mournful manner and the way it stands for a body secularly projected onto a modern landscape of ruins and earthbound awareness of its own frailty and mortality.

In Heiner Müller's version of the play, "THE GENARL IN PEACETIME
. . . BURROWS IN THE LABYRINTH OF THE BOWELS / LOOKING
FOR THE SEAT OF SOULS WITH HIS KNIFE".[62] We don't know whether
he finds it. But we do know that his pain and his subject matter is sorrow
and that he will put an end to it by using that knife against Lavinia and her
unbearable shameful sight: "Die, die, Lavinia, and thy shame with thee / And
with thy shame thy father's sorrow die" (5.3.45–46). Meanwhile, "Character in the usual sense of the word disintegrates completely. What we see is a
personified emotion", Waith incisively remarked decades ago.[63] Titus undergoes a feminizing "liquefaction", we also might say, exploiting a suggestion
stemming from Marion Wynne-Davies's feminist reading of the play.[64] Titus
weeps, sighs, prays, he shoots messages to the gods with an arch, he vomits,
he is run mad. He accepts to become the prey of a sorrow corporeally felt
and theatrically anatomized and exhibited in front of the audience in all its
inundating and consuming agency, and with a set of images, I take it, that
Shakespeare (as Benjamin might well say) will later spend only "for love".
It is indeed in *Antony and Cleopatra*'s overflowing passions that the playwright will powerfully resume again those images of infinitude and bound-
lessness. Like the river Nilus, Titus's sorrow "disdaineth bounds" (3.1.72).
He lets it submerge him, with eyes wept to "ancient ruins [urns]" (3.1.24).[65]
He also wants them to be like a copious fountain—in order that he may sate
nature's greediness with tears instead of blood ("So thou refuse to drink my
dear sons' blood", 3.1.22)—while linguistically amplifying, at the same time,
the dishonour of that mournful condition. "For two and twenty sons I never
wept / because they died in honour's lofty bed. . . . / And let me say, that
never wept before", he repeats, as he ruinously surrenders to his unheroic
lamenting passion, one which interestingly conflates body and language:
"My tears are now prevailing orators" (3.1.10–26). When we come to his
famous "overflowing" speech in front of the violated Lavinia, he is one with
that aquatic and drowning drift:

> If there were reason for these miseries,
> Then into limits could I bind my woes,
> When heaven doth weep, doth not the earth o'erflow?
> If the winds rage, doth not the sea wax mad,
> Threatening the welkin with his big-swollen face?
> And wilt thou have a reason for this coil?
> I am the sea. Hark how her sighs doth blow.
> She is the weeping welkin, I the earth.
> Then must my sea be moved with her sighs,
> Then must my earth with her continual tears
> Become a deluge overflowed and drowned,
> For why my bowels cannot hide her woes
> But like a drunkard must I vomit them.

> (3.1.220–32)

Titus's boasted expertise in the practice and metaphor of navigation and anchorage (the very first imagery upon which, in his entry onstage, he bestows the task of defining his *Romanitas* and his male capacity to prevail upon nature and its storms) belongs to a remote and shipwrecked picture.

In Benjamin's conceptualization of early modern *Trauerspiel*, as anticipated in my Introduction (p. 10), the difference between history and myth marks the distance of early modern drama from ancient tragedy. For the object of the latter "is not history but myth";[66] a distinction which is worth resuming in this chapter in relation to the dismissed heroism and triumphant mourning of the Roman Titus. *Trauerspiel*, as understood by Benjamin, is profoundly historical as well as profoundly mournful. It is rooted in "the baroque cult of the ruin" and in a vision of history mournfully experienced as catastrophe and decay. As for myth, this occurs as a remnant objectified dispersal: "a broken pediment" or "crumbling columns" (*Origin*, 178–179), a decayed stage prop, exactly as the broken up and floating Latin textuality in Shakespeare's play. Benjamin visited Rome in the fall of 1924 while he was writing his *Origin* completed in 1925. The colossal view of its ruins may have had quite a bear on his plastic classic envisioning of the "objects" of the *Trauerspiel*; a form of tragedy in which language itself, as he remarks—often characterized by set speech—has the same decayed physicality of things.

The "bombastic" language of mourning, in his view, far from being simply stereotypical as in fact it was, is tragically and paradoxically representative of a protagonist who "asserts . . . creaturely rights" (210), namely the jeopardized rights of a fallen and dimidiated creature. "It is fallen nature which bears the imprint of the progression of history" (180), he observes. And the figure who best epitomizes this "creaturely" condition in early modern culture is the monarch: "The sovereign, the principle exponent of history, almost serves as its incarnation". . . . "He holds the course of history in his hand like a sceptre" (62 and 65), but he is deprived of heroic allure. Rather, his power as a tyrant is as absolute as his flaws and deficiencies are in the embodiment of his role. He thus condenses (like most of Shakespeare's tragic figures)[67] the "complementarity" of tyranny and tyrannicide, tyrant and martyr, persecutor and victim. "In the baroque the tyrant and the martyr are but two faces of the monarch. They are the necessarily extreme incarnation of the princely essence", Benjamin argues. "In the drama of the baroque [the monarch] is a radical stoic, for whom the occasion to prove himself is a struggle for the crown or a religious dispute ending in torture and death" (69 and 73).

In a way that is neither eschatological nor transcendent, *Trauerspiel* is imbued with the contingency of early modern history, a historicity which brings together many parts of Europe—in the way it is marked by the violence of military and no less brutal cultural and religious conflicts—in a persistent "state of emergency" (*Origin*, 65–66). The mournful

discursivity of *Trauerspiel*—a play of sorrow—"a playing at and a dis-
playing of human wretchedness", in George Steiner's apt synthesis,[68]
supplements with lasting and ostentatious linguistic exuberance the sense
of loss of characters staged in their condition as creatures held in the grip
of their secular and historical contingency, imprisoning physicality, and
solitude.

> Mourning is the state of mind in which feeling revives the empty
> world in the form of a mask, and derives an enigmatic satisfaction
> in contemplating it. Every feeling is bound to an *a priori* object, and
> the representation of this object is its phenomenology. Accordingly
> the theory of mourning, which emerged unmistakably as a *pendant*
> to the theory of tragedy, can only be developed in the description of
> that world which is revealed under the gaze of the melancholy man.
> For feelings, however vague they may seem when perceived by the
> self, respond like a motorial reaction to a concretely structured world.
>
> (*Origin*, 139)

And yet mourning in Benjamin's terms seems to be more than a feeling,
it is an intention:

> It is determined by an astounding tenacity of intention, which, among
> the feelings is matched perhaps only by love and that not playfully.
> For whereas in the realm of the emotions it is not unusual for the rela-
> tion between an intention and its object to alternate between attrac-
> tion and repulsion, mourning is capable of special intensification, a
> progressive deepening of its intention.
>
> (139)

For Benjamin, the relationship between mourning and ostentation is to be
searched in this "progressive deepening of its intention".

"I am the sea" (3.1.224), Titus laments, as he lets himself drown in his
own flood, with a Benjaminian "astounding tenacity of intention". Titus's
phenomenology of his pain—in line with early modern psychological
materialism brought to the fore and explored by a fast-growing scholarship—is a psychophysiology.[69] Titus holds firmly in his hand the dissecting
knife of anatomy. His heart, he proclaims, "all mad with misery, / Beats in
this hollow prison of my flesh" (3.2.9–10). And his misery is as corporeal
as its psychic awareness and the paraded figurative construct on which
it thrives: "my bowels cannot hide her woes / But like a drunkard must I
vomit them" (3.1.231–32).

Shakespeare's sense of immanent, or more specifically, visceral and
perturbed interiority could rely on ancient humoral theories of the body
as well as the coeval resurgent science of anatomy. Anatomy helped in
the fathoming and dissecting of early modern emotions. And his Titus

is dramatically clever in finalizing to his own anguish the re-interrogated relationship between body parts and embodied "affections", or self-knowledge;[70] but he is also rhetorically exhaustive in proclaiming his mourning without limits and without end: including as it does that which is linguistically precluded to his tongueless Lavinia ("Speechless complainer, I will learn thy thought", 3.2.39).

Starting from *Titus*, I argue, Shakespeare seems compelled to enlist in his agenda, in the form of a failed or unaccomplished act of interpretation, a fatherly promise to translate into intelligible meaning a daughter's "martyred signs" (3.2.36; see also 3.1.83,108; 3.2.36). "Thou shalt not sigh, nor hold thy stumps to heaven . . . / but of these I will wrest an alphabet" (3.2.43–44), Titus solemnly promises, anticipating the same frustrating endeavour to gather and heal—or "botch up"—Ophelia's pitifully wounded, disordered, and disordering language: "Her speech is nothing, / Yet the unshaped use of it doth move / The hearers to collection" (*Ham.* 4.2.7–9).[71] In *Titus*—where words are meant to be things and deeds, and playing with them turns into tragic parody—the problem is that even for such a binding commitment there are not enough hands "to *hand*le it" properly (3.2.29). In fact, Titus's one hand is hardly sufficient to "tyrannize"—namely to violently sedate—his imprisoned rebellious heart. "This poor right hand of mine / Is left to tyrannize upon my breast" (3.2.7–8), he laments, thus politicizing the perturbed internal scenario of his body, as well as the proclaimed will to a new "alphabet". But as things are, a new "alphabet" can only be a message to the future, enclosed in a drifting bottle: a suspended wishful thinking, like the gentlemen's abortive "aiming at" Ophelia's disseminated "half sense". Indeed, while functioning as a powerful incitement for future generations of men and women to take on that task (or "aiming at"), Titus's mourning passion stops at the level of a *grand*, doleful anatomizing endeavour in the "now" of the play, the enormity of Lavinia's mute martyrdom (see 3.1.83, 108; 3.2.36) playing as the overturned mirror and climax of his own Benjaminian over-loquacious "martyr-drama".[72]

"Our Inheritance Was Left to Us by No Testament"

The ostentation of Titus's grief—a Senecan "insisted passion", a sanctification, in Miola's words[73]—is inversely proportional to the possibility of being heard, let alone shared. Its physical and human environment is a deaf and unanswering landscape of stones, and "yet plead I must / And bootless unto them. / Therefore I tell my sorrow to the stones" (3.1.35–37). But no longer in the shape of an epic tale. "Ah, wherefore thou dost . . . bid Aeneas tell the tale twice o'er / How Troy was burnt . . .?" (3.2.26–28), Titus cries, refusing to ventriloquize the ancient Virgilian tale. He knows that the tale is no gift if it lacks a listener and a storyteller, and yet, compulsory, he reiterates the tale of his sorrow, because repetitive and inescapable are the causes of his misery. In such a double bind, the tragedy of a prevailing mechanic repetition discloses its "comic potential". "In revenge tragedy", Kerrigan observes drawing on Bergson's *Le rire*,

> the point of maximum stylization is often the moment of repetition. It is also that phase of an action in which characters most behave like puppets. . . . This "mechanism" can be humanly contrived, but often, as *Le Rire* intuits, comedy springs from a sense that providence itself reduces person to puppets.[74]

Significantly, Titus's refusal to repeat the ancient epic tale occurs in conjunction with the obsessive question of hands, namely the maimed and decayed posture of Titus as an orator. The tales of the classical past in *Titus*—tales without bodies, or proper bodies, to take them on—seem to lay broken and malignant among the stones, as the lost tie among generations, and yet ready to emerge with the fatal signature of the "precedent"—as, most fatally, in the case of Lavinia's physical cancellation at the hand(s) of her father, or the classically over-proficient recipe of Titus's cannibal banquet.

"The play's persistent emphasis is on woeful speeches aimed at arousing pity, as the drama enacts and re-enacts scenes of dysfunctional persuasion", Lynne Magnusson has observed in her linguistic discussion of Shakespeare's rhetoric of grief. Against a repeated denial of pity, the play continues to keep "constantly in play the imaginative possibility of a moral, community-building dialogue of lamenting plea and answering efficacious pity".[75] Right. But what made the "dysfunctional" issue recognizable as a relevant one—at least to Shakespeare's educated audience—is the way it is metatheatrically foregrounded by the ubiquitous presence of the Virgilian motif of storytelling. Most of *Titus*'s significance, I contend, lies in its underwritten motif of a fragmented epic tale and the way this is tragically interwoven with the more general issue of a crisis of inheritance: of what this means—gender-coded as it is—for the life of a whole community of men and women.

Tragedy began, Hannah Arendt observed at the aftermath of the Second World War, when a group of intellectuals discovered that there was no generation poised to gather the tale of history and complete it, or more precisely,

> when it turned out that there was no mind to inherit and to question, to think about and to remember. The point of the matter is that the "completion", which indeed every enacted event must have in the minds of those who then are to tell the story and to convey its meaning, eluded them;

by which she meant that what they had to cope with was a fractured tradition, manifesting itself in no easy continuity between past and present and in a lost adherence between thought and reality. "[A]nd without this thinking completion after the act", she continued, "without the articulation accomplished by remembrance, there simply was no story left that could be told" (*Be*, 6). But had any such thing as the naming and transmission of the inheritance ever happened? Incisively she saw the question and the answer condensed in an aphorism by the French poet and writer, René Char, "*Notre heritage n'est précédé d'acun testament*" ("our inheritance was left to us by no testament"), which she placed at the opening of her Preface to *Between Past and Future*, to mark the essence of an epoch in which the legacy of the past and its memory had been problematized not only by war, but by the breakdown of an entire tradition of thought. And yet, without the questioning and combative procedures of remembrance ("which is only one, though one of the most important, modes of thought", *Be*, 6), no reconciliation with the past was possible. Benjamin had raised a similar set of issues when, addressing the topic from the side of a completing and pacifying memory (an idealistic vision for some), he wrote, "Memory is the epic faculty *par excellence*. Only by virtue of a comprehensive memory can epic writing absorb the course of events on the one hand and, with the passing of these, make its peace with the power of death on the other".[76]

Making peace "with the power of death" (Benjamin), or the "groaning shadows" of the dead (Shakespeare): is there any such epic possibility for memory in *Titus Andronicus*? Certainly not for Titus, who, in the throes of an increasing number of threatening ghosts asking for revenge, becomes a victim of his own vengeful action: "these two heads do seem to speak to me / And threat me I shall never come to bliss / Till all these mischiefs be returned again" (3.1.272–74). But is there anybody else—this is the question Shakespeare still presses at the end of the play—who can inherit, like Aeneas with his burning Troy, the responsibility of telling an epic and "completing" tale for Rome? "Speak, Rome's dear friend, as erst our ancestor / When with his solemn tongue he did discourse / the lovesick Dido's sad-attending ear / The story of that baleful burning night / When subtle Greek surprised King Priam's Troy. / Tell us what Sinon hath bewitched our ears, / Or who hath brought the fatal engine in / That gives our Troy, our Rome, the civil wound" (5.3.86).

Editors of the play are divided as to whether the "dear friend", the man who should inherit the tale, namely the responsibility of memory, is Marcus or the prospective new emperor Lucius. It depends on a set of textual choices to be made about who pronounces what, and who should be invested with what, but such a textual indecision created by the different versions of the play,[77] I argue, perfectly befits, with its mark of undecidability, Shakespeare's problematized thematization of the theme of succession, or (in my perspective) inheritance. In the end it is Marcus who decides for Lucius's succession: "*here's Rome's young captain: let him tell the tale*, / While I stand by and weep to hear him speak" (5.3.93–94;

my emphasis). But is Lucius an exile or renegade who, like Coriolanus, is entering Rome with the help of the enemy's Gothic army, a trustful candidate for that task? Shakespeare doesn't say. But what is telling is the fact that Lucius is not the person who inherits the ancestors' art of story-telling. His is the Empire, and a cursory report of its latest ruinous events: alas, the same which loom large on its ambiguous and unstable survival. Instead, it is a boy, the young Lucius and his generation—precisely those who have been left with no inheritance (in Arendt's terms)—who are invested with the mandate of taking care of the tale as such: namely, as I am suggesting in this chapter, a tale which "waits to be completed" with an understanding of "what happened"(*Be*, 8) and which, if anything, becomes political (e.g. socially significant) by means of the very performative and bridging gesture that makes it possible: "Many a story hath he [Thy grandsire] told to thee, / And bid thee bear his pretty tale in mind / And talk of them when he was dead and gone" (5.3.163–65).

As for the newly nominated emperor Lucius, the emperor who, "meed for meed" (5.3.65), at the end of the play, resumes Rome's barbaric obliteration of its alien bodies (Tamora, Aaron), he seems rather to undo what Marcus pretends can be "knitted" again (5.3.69): an ending which startlingly duplicates the play's catastrophic beginning. Horror, aiming at recovering a lost sense of bond and imperial identity (regardless of Rome's hybridized humanity), has no end: as, unfortunately, is the case with the widely reacknowledged contemporaneity of *Titus* in our present times. Hence, as often with Shakespeare, we had better search for an answer to the queries he raises not so much in the ending of his plays (or what appears to be such), as rather in what he does before.[78] And what he does, in his post-Reformation times and in his first Roman play, I argue, is to situate the tale of his tragedy in a void, in the terms conceptualized by Arendt, among the ruins that fill up the gap between the past and a time *á venir*, and where the subject is dramatized as he laments the loss and strives to keep alive—albeit with the wrong means and in vain—the call for memory: "What shall we do? Let us that have our tongues / Plot some device of further misery / To make us wondered at in time to come" (3.1.134–36).

In such light the unexpected sight of a ruined monastery—a glimpse of a ruinous future in the chronology of the play—might be considered, perhaps, less of an anachronism than it seems.

"One Mixed Ruine": The Troubling Memory of Monasteries

The Goth's sight of the "ruinous monastery" ("Renowned Lucius, from our troops I strayed / To gaze upon a ruinous monastery", 5.1.21), as has been remarked by many, "brings a Reformation context into the play",[79] even though at this point of the story, Lucius with his army of Goths should be in Rome or nearby—Rome, already a city of ruins at the conjectured historical time of the play—where, however, there were no "ruinous monasteries" to be seen. So, such a mention, undoubtedly allusive to the Tudor dissolution of monasteries, but also perhaps, I take it, suggestive of Anglo-Saxon destructions of proto-Christian monastic sites, displaces us with a figure of dislocation which seems to be geographically anatopic, as well as (but only questionably) temporally anachronic. Critics continue to interrogate its unsettling apparition. Was it meant to sound as a hint to an achieved *translatio imperii*, a dislocated symbol of a winning Gothic and Reformist North, as some maintain (Bate); or rather as a critique of domestic, long-standing ruinous landscapes which at the end of the play cast the light of contemporaneity on the endless chain of desecrating acts which marks Shakespeare's first Roman play? Perhaps both ways of experiencing that mention were possible to Shakespeare's audience. Perhaps what the onlookers were brought to perceive was an effect of "one mixed ruin", as I will argue in a while, borrowing suggestions coming from the already mentioned sixth-century monk, Gildas, profusely reported in Camden's *Britannia*.

In his two mentions of a ruinous monastery (*Titus Andronicus* and sonnet 73), Shakespeare makes it "the prism through which we view the wider scene", Schwyzer has observed. In *Titus Andronicus*, it stands for an "emblem of ambiguity" in a play that as a whole refuses "to be aligned in a clear and unified perspective".[80] True. It does so by both inviting and resisting interpretation, I underline, namely with the ambivalence, incongruity, and resilience of an apparent desituated object. But sticking to my prevailing argument of the play's layered temporality, I would like to underscore the way it stands for the obfuscating shadow of ruins to come, one which deconstructs the final conceit of a constructive and accomplished "weaving" of the nation. In this it intriguingly seems to reverse the (aforementioned, pp. 85–86) palimpsestic mode of Renaissance painters of framing their subject matter with glimpses of past classical ruins, by problematizing the scene with a glimpse of future ruin.

Interestingly, the briefness and unexpectedness of the monastery's apparition—one might liken it to an *agitprop* incursion—also betrayed a coeval post-Reformation anxiety in tackling the topic of dissolved monasteries. "The dissolution had been a textual as well as an architectural disaster, countless irreplaceable manuscripts having been lost in the wanton devastation of the monastic libraries", Schwyzer has observed.[81] And their defaced silhouette, when still extant, remained as the material mark of many acts of forced erasure and razed down memory in the "massive attempt at social, emotional, and spiritual reprogramming", as Mullaney puts it, that characterized Tudor Reformation. Like churchyards and ossuaries, they were part of "every day landscapes of memory", what the critic calls "affective" landscapes;[82] the places which for centuries before their destruction had mediated the link and the form of one's intimate relationship with the dead, the way their afterlife was imagined and remembered, and yet not exactly the ruins to deal with in Elizabethan England.[83]

William Camden, well known by now to the readers of this book (see pp. 54–61), the chorographer of his "Britannia", and hence, as we may well say, the constructor and "restorer" *per antonomasia* of an "affective" landscape in Shakespeare's times, was one of those who felt compelled to overtly take on the responsibility of their memory, however troubling that task could be for some of his readers, as he underlined in his address to the reader.

> There are certaine, as I heare who take impatiently that I have mentioned some of the most famous Monasteries and their founders. I am sory to heare it, and with their good favour will say thus much, They may take it impatiently, and per adventure would have us forget that our ancestoures were, and we are of the Christian profession when as there are not extant any other more conspicuous, and certaine Monuments, of their piety, and zealous devotion toward God. Neither were there any other seed-gardens from whence Christian Religion, and good learning were propagated over this isle, howbeit in corrupt ages some weeds grew out overranckly.[84]

Was Shakespeare inspired by or siding with Camden when in his first Roman play he produced his piece of unsituated and troubling architecture? Certainly in the context of an issue that Camden made his readers perceive as still lacerating for many, Shakespeare's theatricalized incursion acquired the same political untimeliness. Nay, ambivalent as it was, it knowingly participated in the same displaced form of resistance embodied in the Tacitism attributed to Camden's entourage.[85]

Camden showed how monasteries contributed to national history and landscape as custodians of a layered story of learning as well as an instance of repetitive ruination and rebirth;[86] a story that was startlingly emerging as a bemusing archaeology: one that brought together, in the form of a collapsed and confused chronology, a long span of time encompassing Rome and ancient Britain, old and recent ruins, old and new ashes of the dead, but also one that exemplified an image of the library as an interrogative space of coexistence of pagan and Christian books, remote and new languages, old and new traumas. As he wrote, reporting on the diggings recorded by an ancient historian dating back to the tenth century:

> Ealdred the Abbot, in the reign of *K. Edgar* [about the Year 960], searching out old subterraneous vaults of Verulam, broke them all down. . . . This he did, because these were ordinary lurking places of thieves and whores. . . . *Eadmer* his Successor went forward with the work which *Ealdred* had begun, and his diggers levelled the

foundations of a palace in the middle of the old city, and in a hollow place in the wall, contrived like a finall closet, they happen'd upon books having covers of oak, and silk strings to them; one whereof contain'd the life of St. Alban written in the British language; the rest certain Pagan Ceremonies. And when they had open'd the earth to a greater depth, they met with old stone-tables, tiles also and pillars, pots, and great earthen vessels neatly wrought, and others of glass containing the ashes of the dead, &c. And at last, out of these remains of old *Verulam*, Eadmer built a new Monastery to St. *Alban*. Thus much as to the Antiquity and Dignity of Verulam.

(*Brit* 2, 299)

It doesn't matter if reports like this are archaeologically correct in the light of the revising research that since then has been devoted to the origins of the monasteries and the way they controversially partake in the history of both proto Roman-British Christianity and later Anglo-Saxon Christianization.[87] Here, as elsewhere in this section, what concerns us is the early modern "structure of feeling" (as Raymond Williams might put it)[88] in matters concerning acts of destruction and memorialization of the national past. And Camden's archaeological conglomerate of Verulam-St. Albans ruins is strikingly interesting in the way it shows how everything can be simultaneously present to the eye of the belated early modern witness: namely uncannily remote, displaced, untimely, and yet familiar, as in the case of anachronism. Camden in turn brought everything home to the present with his updating closure on more recent Reformation contexts of transformation, cancellation, and readapted surviving architectures:

Verolanium at this day being turned into fields: The towne of Saint *Albans* raised out of the ruins thereof flourisheth; a faire towne and a large, and the Church of the Monasterie remaineth yet for bignesse, beauty and antiquity, to be had admiration: which when the Monkes were thrust out of it, was by the townsmen redeemed with the summe of 400 pound of our mony, that it might not be laid even with the ground, and so it became converted into a parish Church.

(*Brit* 1, 412)

The Blackfriars Dominican monastery in London shared the same story of sites having partly escaped the deluge, only to be converted into a space for revels and gradually a theatre, the theatre of Shakespeare's Company, the Chamberlain's Men, by 1596.

Titus's ruinous monastery similarly seals the archaeological collapsed temporality of the play with its residual, mute affectivity. The audience were called upon to emotionally contribute to it with their own emotions and memories, as well exemplified by John Speed's later comment on the destroyed abbey at Bury St Edmund (Suffolk): "Whose ruins lie in the dust, lamenting their fall, moving the beholders to pity their case"[89]. But to which age can we refer *Titus*'s monastic remains?

Opening the Holland version of Camden's *Britannia* at page 107, our attention is drawn by a phrase which can be no less than attractive to students of Shakespeare's *Titus*; a phrase which thus emphasizes the section devoted to the end of Roman Britannia: "this most lamentable ruine & downfall of Britain". It can be useful then not to part company with this work for a while to underline how ruins in the early modern construction of England articulated the very origins of the nation, marked as they were—and as Camden in particular takes pain to underline—by the bloody events which stained the passage from Roman Britannia to Anglo-Saxon England, and which Camden commented upon as times of contiguity as well as traumatic discontinuity between the two worlds. In this he was not dissimilar from most of his contemporaries "who looked back at the arrival of their ancestors in Britain with a mixture of pride and horror".[90] But Camden's appears as a specific concern in understanding this moment in the larger context of the fall of the Roman world: a point of transit in history in which the confusing series of emperors and events that built up to the shocking first sack of Rome in 410 CE, at the hands of the Goths led by Alaric, was intertwined with the cancellation of ancient Britannia and the beginning of a violently Anglicized England at the hands of the Anglo-Saxon. Whether ideologically tinged with Romanism, as some of his contemporaries thought, or not, Camden's image of a nation violently born of a catastrophe could be dramatically suggestive for a playwright, perhaps inspiring the very title of his first Roman tragedy. Vice versa, dealing with Rome's bloody, confused, and hybridizing events of decay, as in *Titus*, could be meaningful to a nation that in Shakespeare's time was reflecting on its own origins and identity, discovering them as historically close to that same world of fractures, wounds, ruins, and hybridized new beginnings.

Interestingly, what also emerged in Camden's narration of this tragic conjuncture in history was a tale of abandon. Threatened by domestic civil wars and extended attacks of barbarian populations from the North, Camden writes, Rome had deemed it necessary to concentrate its forces to defend itself, and after something like five centuries of government in Britannia (476 years in his calculation), the Roman garrisons were taken out of the island and

> having transported their forces . . . for the defence of France, and buried their treasure within ground, left Britaine bereft of her youth, wasted with so many musters and levies, dispoiled of all succour and defence of garrison, unto the cruell rage of Picts and Scots.
>
> (*Brit* 1, 87)

Petitions for help like the one addressed to Aeitius, thrice Consul of the Roman Senate, intriguingly entitled "The Groans of the Britains"

(107), were destined to remain unanswered. "The Empire drooping with extreme age, lay along maimed, dismen bred, and as it were, benummed in all the limnes and parts thereof" (86).

The fate of Rome was the fate of the world, St. Jerome lamented after the sack of Rome in 410, "Romani imperii truncatum caput!", "the head of the Roman empire was cut off, and, to speak more truly, the entire world perished with that single city".[91] In his *Britannia*, Camden entrusts Gildas with the task of speaking the contradictory "melancholy" of "abandon", one which we would nowadays recognize as typically postcolonial:

> to the fearfull people they [the Romans] gave good instructions, and exhortations to play the men, and left unto them paternes, showing them how to make armour and weapons. Upon the coast also of the Ocean, in the tract of the South countrey, what way they had ships . . . they planted turrets, and bulwarks with convenient spaces distant one from another, yeelding farre and faire prospect into the sea: and so the Romans gave them a final farewell never to returne again.
>
> (*Brit* 1, 86)

One wonders whether Shakespeare browsed through Camden's useful pages on "Britannia Romana" (and "Romans in Britain") and whether this may have been inspiring when he depicted the scene of Prospero's final departure from Caliban's island.

What followed (in Camden's reconstruction) was a series of successive, devastating invasions of Picts, Scots, Anglo-Saxons, and Danes, which he accounts for under the telling heading: "The Down-Fall or Destruction of Britain" (107). The picture of Britain's ensuing two centuries of invasions and destruction is similarly conveyed through the apocalyptic and highly dramatic accents of Gildas in Camden's fractured and discontinuous view of English history.

> In such wise, as all the Colonies by force of many engines, and all the Inhabitants together with the Prelates of the Church, both Priests and People, by drawne sword glittering on every side, and crackling flame of fire, were at once laid along on the ground: yea, and that which was a piteous spectacle to behold, in the mids of the streets the stone works of turrets, and high walles, rent and torne in sunder from aloft the sacred altars, and quarters of carcases (covered with imbossed works of imagerie) of a bloudy hue, were seene *all blended and mixed together (as it were) in a certaine horrible wine-press*, neither was there any Sepulcher at all abroad, save one onely the ruins of buildings, and the bowels of wilde beasts and fowles.
>
> (*Brit* 1, 110; my emphasis)

In Gildas's passionate and poetically inspired invective, the "ruine" is body and stone, moral and architectural fall, ash and dripping blood, limb and fragment, rubble and cadavers, human and nonhuman. It is "one mixed ruine": an image inspired by Edmund Gibson's rendering of this passage in his later translation of *Britannia* (1695), and which I found more suitable than Holland's "all blended and mixed together" to the end of my argument, and as a title of this section (they are both italicized in the two versions here reported).

> All the Colonies were overturned with Engines, and the inhabitants, together with the Bishops, Priests, and all the People, cut off by fire and sword together. In which miserable prospect, a man might likewise see in the streets, the ruines of towers pulled down, with their stately gates; the fragments of high walls; the sacred altars, and limbs of dead bodies, with clots and stains of blood *hudled together in one mixt ruine, like a wine-press*: for there was no other graves for the dead bodies, than what the fall of houses, or the bowels of beasts and fowls gave them.
>
> (*Brit 2*, CIV; my emphasis)

We are compellingly reminded of *Titus*'s lexicon by this disturbing image of "one mixed ruin", let alone of the play's very last lines ordering Aaron's atrocious death by semi-interment and Tamora's "no funeral rite, no man in mourning weed", thrown "forth to beasts as birds to prey" (5.3.195–97).

It doesn't matter in this context that Camden's mediated vision of Saxon invasion has been revised by subsequent historiography. Furthermore, we don't know whether Shakespeare ever read the high medieval author. However, it is plausible to speculate that he had come across Gildas through Camden's Latin version of *Britannia*, namely before its English translation produced by Philémon Holland in 1610. Be that as it may, one might well say that Gildas's powerfully oneiric catalyzation of England's origin as "one mixt ruine" or "wine-press", has entered Shakespeare's *Titus*—and settled there—as its inner dramatic motor or engine. It thus unites Rome and Britain—aptly disguised as Rome and the Goths—at a moment of crisis and transformation, traumatically marking their respective end and beginning as a collapsed temporality: when "Time in time shall ruinate" (Du Bellay/Spenser, 7.10).

As Neill has argued, the success of tragedy, and the revenge tragedy in particular, in Elizabethan culture has much to do with the "rage of the dead" and the anxiety engendered by unsatisfied or defectively satisfied duties of memory. "The role of the revenger is essentially that of a 'remembrencer'", and "revenge drama shows vengeance to be no more than memory continued by other means".[92] Revenge tragedy's proliferating and resentful ghosts asking for remembrance, as shown also by

Greenblatt's discussion of *Hamlet*'s Purgatory, culturally originated in the massive suppression of rites and "rights of memory" undertaken in Protestant times,[93] which entailed a truncated affective relation with one's dead, seemingly placed "beyond the help or intercession of their survivors".[94] In *Titus* their memory devours Titus's mind like a "gnawing vulture" (5.2.31). But they also originated, I would like to add, in the fissure of older bleeding wounds, wounds which had marked the very origins of England and which still claimed to be remembered. Poets, playwrights, and antiquarians in early modern England seemed to be equally haunted, one way or another, by an image of their past as a traumatic "one mixt ruine", and equally explored, with different means, the way this past could be faced and elaborated, namely remembered and historically transmitted to posterity.[95]

Interestingly in *Titus*, it is the learned Aaron who provides the desacralizing version of it all when he boasts that he has literally used the bodies of the dead as a weapon in the vindictive dynamics of the play's story and its underwritten complex picture of memory and forgetting.

> Oft have I digged up dead men from their graves
> And set them upright at their friends' door,
> Even when their sorrows almost was forgot,
> And on their skins, as on the bark of trees,
> Have with my knife carved in Roman letters,
> "Let not your sorrow die though I am dead".
>
> (5.1.135–40)

Among Aaron's many villainies there is also his behaviour as a necromantic archaeologist: one practising a disinterring "potent art" which brings him close to Prospero, the magician/playwright. And vice versa. Shakespeare performed the task of memory and its traumas in the symbolic space of theatre, where knowledge, as I have already mentioned agreeing with Anderson's understanding of the language of trauma,[96] is not immediate but displaced and elusive, excessive and lacking, inviting as well as defying our witness. Interestingly, witness is a recurrent word in the play, but whose witness is it? "Witness this wretched stump, witness these crimson lines, / Witness these trenches made by grief and care, / Witness the tiring day and heavy night, / Witness all sorrow" (*Titus*, 5.2.21–22), Titus persistently urges up to the end, in spite of the awareness he does have that he is speaking to the wrong addressee. In fact, how could Revenge (which he recognizes as being Tamora in the guise of Revenge)—an enemy mockingly disguised as a friend—be trusted as a testimony and a healer of his doleful body and mind? "I am Revenge, sent from th'infernal kingdom / To ease the gnawing vulture of thy mind" (5.2.30–31), Tamora seductively announces, within a communicative framework which has irreparably gone awry at this point of the play.

But it is part of the peculiar capacity of the play to shift from tragedy to tragi-comedy, that its unyielding call for a witness (or tending towards a compassionate sharing of sorrow, "all sorrow") should be met with a series of hilarious equivocations and mistaken deliveries, as in Titus's undelivered or hijacked messages to the gods (4.3.1–86). Indeed *Titus Andronicus*'s message sending (scrolls, apostrophes, interpellations, pleas, petitions) seems rather to thematize the Derridean philosophical concept of the *envois* (envoy, mail delivery, call on) discussed in *La carte postale*: it claims a destination, "*il se tourne vers quelqu'un*", an addressee, a *réception*, but to whom, and with what outcome?[97] "News, news from Heaven! Marcus the post is come. / Sirrah, what tidings? Have you any letters? . . . What says Jupiter?" Titus asks to no avail (4.3.77–78), and yet spasmodically and persistently.

The sight of the monastic ruins resists the attention it calls for with the same force of the mute, if bleeding and "most lamentable", traces excavated on *Titus*'s bodies. In this it intermingles with the "thingness" of the play's classical textuality and its ruinous custodian, the library: no longer the place of a weaving tale among generations, but of a memory gone berserk and acting with the malignant agency of a killer.

Using Sources as Misused *Ruinae*

"The Renaissance explores the universe; the baroque explores libraries" (*Origin*, 140), Benjamin has observed. The library is given architectural presence in Shakespeare's *Titus* to increasingly become, literally and meta-phorically, the dwelling place of a "remembrancer" haunted by an over-inscripted, problematized ancestry and grappling with the hatching-out of fatal recipes in a short-circuited vindictive crescendo. When we come to the fifth act, Titus's "I'll Play the Cook" (5.3.204) definitely catalyzes such a space as that of a kitchen: one in which the activity of reading and working with texts is indistinguishable from Titus's all-too-real halluci-natory exercise in carving and cooking; but Titus does not settle in it as its only dweller. As a matter of fact, such a library (or cookery) is ideally shared by all in the play, used as it is as a staged archive and promptbook for most of the violent action being performed along the play. Suffice it to mention the way the contents of the classical library inspire both Aaron's planning of Lavinia's rape (on behalf of its less-learned Gothic executors) and her slaughter at the hand of her father.[98] However, and importantly, the overlapping roles of Titus as a cook and a philologist direly literal-ize the coincidence between bodies and bodies of text, which in their chopped, mingled, and (digestively) "ruminated", or [Ro]minated form, pervade the whole play ("knock at his study, where they say he keeps / To ruminate strange plots of dire revenge", 5.2.5–6).[99]

Titus's narrative thus theatricalizes the well-trained art of its con-struction, one that, following Renaissance patterns, "invents the new by imitating the old" (Vasari), but playfully defines its novelty by over-exhibiting its artful inner machinery and the involved muscular activity of fragmentation and pillage deployed all along the play. In this the playwright, who was just establishing his reputation as a "shake-scene", was simply blatantly exposing the fact that in his time creative invention was one with the theory of imitation and its rhetorical strategies—and one could adroitly make quite a lot of those.[100] As a grammar school student Shakespeare had been thoroughly trained in the field, according to a pedagogy which, as in Ascham's *Schoolmaster* (1570) and other coeval teaching manuals, aimed to lay bare not "what is done" as rather to "teach you how it is done". Ascham had worked his method out—Cicero, Plato, and Aristotle at hand—by surveying/comparing/evaluating a vast amount of coeval literature devoted to this topic (Dutch, German, and largely Italian) and by sharing with his European colleagues a definition of imitation which was structurally based on chiastic transmutations ("*dissimilis materiei simili tractatio*; and, also, *similis materiei dissimilis tractatio*, as *Virgill* folowed *Homer*: but the Argument to the one was *Ulysses*, to the other *Aeneas*") and a reordering of the *loci*—"either *praeponendo*, *interponendo*, or *postponendo*".[101]

Shakespeare seems to perfectly follow suit in his first experiment with Rome and tragedy. As a matter of fact he outdoes him—or any imaginable grammar school's over creative practice of imitation for that matter—with what we might call a Barthesian playful textuality, which (explosively from Act 4) unites in a drift of anarchic readerly/writerly activity (Barthes's *jouissance*), both the playwright and his audience.[102] Indeed, using his sources as shreds, or un*author*ized and autonomous *ruinae* (to conjure up Petrarch's term for surviving written ancient past),[103] he transforms the ancient classical text into a field of menacing ambiguity: a field of dispersed and floating objects detached from any easily recognizable source or meaning which his Titus (but Aaron is no less skilful in this) manoeuvres aggressively as weapons in a cruel theatre of interpretation. This was no coincidence. By the time Shakespeare contrived his reckless *Titus*, he was thoroughly engaged in parodying an apish practice of imitation in his coeval *Love's Labour's Lost* (see 4.2.60–66; 112–119), and seemingly intentioned to show, in his "tardy-apish nation" (*Richard II*, 2.1.18–23), what he was able to do in the context of his inaugural Roman play, namely at the very heart of Rome and its burdensome classical heritage. With this in mind, perhaps, he undertakes a massive "reification of the idea of the text itself through linked stage business and language".[104]

It seems functional to this objectifying project that the playwright, sarcastically—with the sound of Titus's disturbing laughter in his audience's ears—installs in the place of the imitator's apish activity that of the "vivisector" and the cook", thus channelling his prevailing rhetoric of fragmentation into that of a grotesque culinary economy; a protocol which invests with distortive effects the play's textual tissue, as well as its characters and the world of their values and beliefs. In fact, characters are accordingly conceived as multilayered artefacts, their bodies literally caught at the moment of their deflagration, when they are releasing traces of a previous life while embedding elements of their future, according to an archaeology of the subject which is made evident by the imploded textuality of the play.[105] Indeed, the whole system of signification is involved in such a dilapidating and reshuffling dynamic of text(s) and bodies. Shakespeare thus threads a tale which blatantly exhibits its posthumous status, a fractured story born of a memory of violence and ruins, persistently wrought with the mutilated limbs of a ravished classic library, which we see hurled around (in rags and tatters) with the *ston*iness and ambiguity of archaeological objects—Ovid, Virgil, Cicero, Horace, Seneca, Livy: the debris of humanism at the dawn of a new humanism, we might say, tentatively. Indeed, Shakespeare shows how true what Thomas Greene has said of the Renaissance theory of imitation is: "The process called imitation was not only a technique or a habit; it was also a field of ambivalence".[106] The General and the Moor, as Müller has it, "WHILE THE SPADES OF ARCHAEOLOGY CLANK", may well dance together "ON THE ASHES OF ROME".[107]

In such light, *Titus Andronicus*, more than being simply a visionary allegory of the Fall, more than being historically or philologically incorrect, far from being simply an early-career popular revel in celebration of carnage, allows us to enter Shakespeare's laboratory, a laboratory where more explicitly than in the ensuing Roman plays, but with a deep impact on them, I argue, he unfolds a sort of *manifesto* of how he intends to deal with inheritance and memory. In such a laboratory, or cookery, what matters is not what is linear and settled, but—as Benjamin or Foucault would put it—what is fractured, unpredictable, untimely, unspeakable, forgotten, residual, and only half-seen. *Titus Andronicus* is a tragedy where the *past* surfaces from the fault lines of history with the uncanny side of Rome's foundation myths, the raped women, the burning city, the spectral and threatening agency of "broken limbs" (5.3.7), the cannibal banquets, the killing potential of the letter and quotations without an owner, or context.

Titus Andronicus is also a tragedy where the future can appear—flashing up and unexpectedly—with a question embedded in the unconcluded if epiphanic tale of a blackmoor child crying under the ruined walls of a monastery (5.1.20–26). Benjamin would say,

> The concept of progress is to be grounded in the idea of the catastrophe. That things "just go on" is the catastrophe. . . . Redemption looks to the small fissure in the ongoing catastrophe. . . . The question is to be pursued as to what extent the extremes to be grasped in redemption are those of the "too early" and the "too late".[108]

Notes

1. I am grateful to Stephen Greenblatt and Michael Neill for encouraging me to pursue this line of thought during the Roman Shakespeare conference (Rome, 2016) when I presented a very first draft of this chapter.
2. Quotations from *Titus Andronicus* refer to Jonathan Bate's Arden edition (London: Thomson Learning, 1995/2003). Translations from the play's Latin phrases into English are from this edition.
3. "This play is to chronology as Cubism is to photography", Anne Lake Prescott has written. "Du Bellay and Shakespeare's Sonnets", in Jonathan F.S. Post, ed., *The Oxford Handbook of Shakespeare's Poetry* (Oxford: Oxford University Press, 2013), p. 148. But see also Schwyzer, *Archaeologies of English Renaissance Literature*, p. 101.
4. Claude Lévi-Strauss, "Introduction à l'oeuvre de Marcel Mauss", in Marcel Mauss, ed., *Sociologie et Anthropologie* (Paris: Presses Universitaires de France, 1950), p. 46. Qtd in Jeffrey Mehlman, "'The Floating Signifier': From Lévi-Strauss to Lacan", *Yale French Studies*, 48 (1972), 10–37 (p. 23).
5. See Katharine Eisaman Maus, "Introduction" to *Titus Andronicus*, in Stephen Greenblatt et al., eds, *The Norton Shakespeare*, 3rd ed. (New York and London: Norton, 2016), pp. 492 and 493. But see also Manfred Pfister, "The Romes of *Titus Andronicus*", in Maria Del Sapio Garbero, ed., *Rome in Shakespeare's World*, p. 149, and Naomi Conn Liebler, "Scattered Corn: Ritual Violation and the Death of Rome in *Titus Andronicus*", in Liebler, *Shakespeare's Festive Tragedy: The Ritual Foundations of Genre* (London and New York: Routledge, 1995), pp. 131–148.
6. See Graham Holderness, "*Julius Caesar*: Shakespeare and the Ruins of Rome", in Michele Marrapodi, ed., *Shakespeare and the Visual Arts. The Italian Influence* (Abingdon and New York: Routledge, 2017), pp. 341–355 (pp. 341–342).
7. See Philip Henslowe, *The Diary*, 1591–1609, ed. J. Payne Collier (London: The Shakespeare Society, 1845), pp. 33–34, and Philip Henslowe, *The Diary*, 1591–1609, ed. Walter W. Greg (London: A.H. Bullen, 1904), pp. 16–17.
8. T.S. Eliot, "Seneca in Elizabethan Translation", in *id.*, *Selected Essays* (London: Faber and Faber, 1934), pp. 82 and 79. For a historical survey of the play's criticism until 1995, see Philip Kolin's introductory article "*Titus Andronicus* and the Critical Legacy" to his edited Titus Andronicus: *Critical Essays* (New York and London: Garland Publishing, 1995), pp. 3–58.
9. Bate, "Introduction", pp. 78–79.
10. As underlined by Jonathan Bate, who refers us to George Puttenham for this (*The Arte of English Poesie*, 1589), the past is understood as paradigmatic, in Shakespeare's time, when "the example of the past gathers probability of like success for the present". But *paradigma* for Puttenham, he points out "is not dependent on recognizable *imitatio*". Bate, *Shakespeare and Ovid*, pp. 92 and 85.
11. Vanna Gentili, *La Roma degli elisabettiani* (Bologna: Il Mulino, 1991), p. 8 (my transl.).
12. Giambattista Vico, *New Science. Principles of the New Science Concerning the Common Nature of Nations* [1744], transl. David Marsh (London: Penguin Book, 2013). See section 14 on "The Course of Nations", and "The Resurgence of Nations", pp. 448–480.
13. Giorgio Vasari, "Preface" to *The Lives of the Painters, Sculptors and Architects*, transl. A.B. Hinds, 4 vols (London and New York: Dent, 1980), vol. 1, p. 6. Ensuing pages directly in the text.

14. The history of humanism and Renaissance was crowded with artists who in visiting Rome, like Brunelleschi (recounted by Vasari), "at the sight of the grandeur of the buildings, and the perfection of the churches was lost in wonder, so that he looked like one demented. . . . He had noted and drawn all the vaulting in the antique, and was continually studying the subject, and if pieces of capitals, columns, cornices and bases of buildings were found buried he and Donato set to work and dug them out to find the foundations. From this a report spread in Rome, when they passed carelessly dressed, and they were called the men of the treasure, for it was believed that they were studying necromancy in order to find the treasure" (*Lives*, vol. 1, pp. 274–275).

15. Nagel and Wood, *Anachronic Renaissance*, p. 309. But see also Greene, *The Light to Troy* (chapter on "Imitation and Anachronism"), pp. 28–53; and Benjamin, *The Origin of German Tragic Drama*, p. 178.

16. Edward Ravenscroft, "To the Reader", in Kolin, ed., Titus Andronicus. *Critical Essays*, p. 375. For the political implications of Shakespeare's plays' massive remaking in Restoration times, see Michael Dobson, *The Making of the National Poet: Shakespeare, Adaptation and Authorship, 1660–1769* (Oxford: Clarendon Press, 1992).

17. Derrida, *Specters of Marx*, p. xviii.

18. Peter Lake, *How Shakespeare Put Politics on the Stage: Power and Succession in the History Plays* (New Haven and London: Yale University Press, 2016), pp. 17–18.

19. See Christopher Ivic and Grant Williams, eds, *Forgetting in Early Modern English Literature and Culture* (London and New York: Routledge, 2004), "Introduction", pp. 1–17. But see also Garrett A. Sullivan, *Memory and Forgetting in English Renaissance Drama* (Cambridge: Cambridge University Press, 2005), pp. 1–24.

20. Jennifer Summit, "Reading Reformed: Spenser and the Problem of the English Library", in Christopher Ivic and Grant Williams, eds, *Forgetting in Early Modern English Literature and Culture*, pp. 165–166.

21. Hannah Arendt, *Between Past and Future: Eight Exercises in Political Thought* (New York: The Viking Press, [1954] 1961), p. 11. Pages of ensuing mentions directly in the text as (*Be*, page).

22. James, *Shakespeare's Troy*, p. 43.

23. Maria Del Sapio Garbero, "Fostering the Question 'Who Plays the Host?'", in *id*, ed., *Identity, Otherness and Empire*, p. 91.

24. Neill, *Issues of Death*, p. 261.

25. For the conflation of the two cities in Shakespeare's imagination via Virgil's *Aeneid* (Books I–II) and the centrality of the Latin author in grammar school curricula, see Miola, *Shakespeare's Rome*, pp. 30–31. For an extensive exploration of the inheritance of the Troy legend in Shakespeare's works and the way it is intertwined with Tudor ideology and the notion of *translatio imperii*, see James, *Shakespeare's Troy*. For the relation between *translatio imperii* and the tragic reversal introduced by tribal violence, see Silvia Bigliazzi, "Romanity and *sparagmos* in *Titus Andronicus*", in Del Sapio Garbero, ed., *Rome in Shakespeare's World*, pp. 87–106.

26. For more on the play's regime of female bodies, see Marion Wynne-Davies, "'The Swallowing Womb': Consumed and Consuming Women in *Titus Andronicus*", in Valerie Wayne, ed., *The Matter of Difference: Materialist Feminist Criticism of Shakespeare* (Ithaca and New York: Cornell University Press, 1991), pp. 129–151. On issues of alterity othering and racialization, see Little, *Shakespeare Jungle Fever*, pp. 1–67; Loomba, *Shakespeare, Race, and Colonialism*, pp. 75–90; Gilberta Golinelli, *Il testo shakespeariano dialoga con i nuovi storicismi, il materialismo culturale e gli studi di genere* (Bologna: Emil, 2012).

27. See Richard Sugg, *Murder After Death: Literature and Anatomy in Early Modern England* (Ithaca and London: Cornell University Press, 2007), pp. 17 and 24.

28. Walter Benjamin, "Theses on the Philosophy of History", VIII, in *Illuminations*, p. 248.

29. John Kerrigan, *Revenge Tragedy: Aeschylus to Armageddon* (rpt Oxford: Clarendon Press, [1996] 2001), p. 196.

30. Among ancient Rome's historiographers, Tacitus enjoyed specific popularity in England in the last years of Elizabeth's reign. And he is by far the best author to be considered when looking for a disenchanted chronicle of the disastrous events which heralded the image of a city consistently threatened by the fragmentation of its ancient values as well as its stately architecture. In fact, in what remained of his *Historiae* (mainly revolving around the epoch of the three emperors and the AD 69 civil wars) as well as the *Annales*, the reader found ample witness of events relating to the post-Augustan tyrannical regimes of the first century CE which, both because of internecine civil strife and increasing problems of military control in the northern provinces of Germania and Britannia, concurred to construct the image of a city on the brink of collapse, repeatedly transformed into a tragic scenario of razed down sacred buildings. Among these was the legendary golden temple of Jupiter on the Capitoline Hill—a symbol of imperial power—destroyed at the hands of opposed imperial factions. The history of his translation (the *Historiae* and *Agricola* by Henry Savile in 1591; the *Annales* and *Germania* by Richard Greenway in 1598) deserves specific interest in the context of this volume, for the way the archaeological textual reparation of Tacitus's surviving works is intertwined with emerging forms of resistance to monarchic absolutism during the last year of Elizabeth. As has been said, the translation of classics was already a politicized activity in Tudor England when Savile, apart from historically reconstructing missing parts of Tacitus's survived work, completed it with an essay on the Machiavellian art of war. Rome was domesticated to serve Tudor policy. But in this case people knew that the Earl of Essex (see the 1601 Essex rise against Elizabeth) had an interest in Tacitus and "Tacitism". David Womersley, "Sir Henry Savile's Translation of Tacitus and the Political Interpretation of Elizabethan Texts", *The Review of English Studies*, 42:167 (1991), 313–342. But see also Hadfield, *Shakespeare and Republicanism*, pp. 43–47. On Tacitus's influence (in conjunction with Sallust and Montaigne) in Tudor and Stuart theatre, see Chernaik, *The Myth of Rome*, pp. 17–25.

31. See Shakespeare, *Titus Andronicus*, ed. Jonathan Bate, notes lines 633–635, pp. 165–166.

32. For a reading of Lavinia's rape in the light of sexuality and politics in Elizabethan culture, see Leonard Tennenhouse, *Power on Display: The Politics of Shakespeare's Genres* (New York and London: Methuen, 1986), pp. 106–108.

33. Barkan, *Unearthing the Past*, pp. 189–201.

34. Bate, "Introduction", p. 11.

35. Benjamin, "Theses on the Philosophy of History", in *Illuminations*, p. 249.

36. Benjamin, "Franz Kafka", in *Illuminations*, p. 129.

37. Hans Blumenberg, *Shipwreck With Spectator: Paradigm of a Metaphor for Existence*, transl. Stephen Rendall (Cambridge, MA and London: The MIT Press, [1979] 1997).

38. Friedrich Nietzsche, *The Birth of Tragedy, or Hellenism and Pessimism*, transl. Shaun Whiteside (London: Penguin Books, 2003), p. 16.

39. In resuming the nautical metaphor (inspired by Schopenhauer) Nietzsche writes, "With sublime gestures he [Apollo] reveals to us how the whole world

of torment is necessary so that the individual can create the redeeming vision, and then, immersed in contemplation of it, sit peacefully in his tossing boat amid the waves". *Idem*, p. 26.

40. See Maria Del Sapio Garbero, "Shakespeare's Maternal Transfigurations", in Karen Bamford and Naomi J. Miller, eds, *Maternity and Romance Narratives in Early Modern England* (Farnham and Burlington: Ashgate, 2015), pp. 112–113; and *Il bene ritrovato. Le figlie di Shakespeare dal* King Lear *ai* Romances (Roma: Bulzoni, 2004), pp. 81–137.

41. Miola, *Shakespeare's Rome*, p. 46.

42. James, *Shakespeare's Troy*, pp. 69–70.

43. Heather James, "Dido's Ear: Tragedy and the Politics of Response", *Shakespeare Quarterly*, 52:3 (2001), 360–382 (p. 368). In this compelling essay, James addresses the theme of sympathetic passions and the power they have in creating an uncontrollable—and hence dangerous—alliance, or "consent", at theatre between representation and audience. Underwritten by the Virgilian "Dido's ear", she shows how from *Titus Andronicus* to *The Tempest* the issue of "response", or "consent", is a constant concern for Shakespeare. But no attention, however, is drawn on Titus's shattered tale and the implications of his unheard of pitiful plea for response, which is the main focus of my approach to the play. In dealing with *Titus*, James sticks to the play's last scene where the lord's evocation of "Dido's sad-attending ear" occurs as a sedating appeal for shared compassion for the sake of the nation. In my analysis, Dido's capacity of response reverberates backwards on the whole play as Titus's frustrated achievement.

44. See in Bate's edition of *Titus*, the specific footnote n. 18 (p. 253). For an extensive discussion of the symbolic relevance of hands in early modern culture and the relation between rhetorical "actio" and theatrical "acting", see Michael Neill's groundbreaking essay "'Amphitheatres in the Body': Playing With Hands on the Shakespearean Stage", *Shakespeare Survey*, 48 (1996), 23–50. But see also Katherine A. Rowe, "Dismembering and Forgetting in *Titus Andronicus*", *Shakespeare Quarterly*, 45:3 (1994), 282 and 279–303, and Gary Watt, "The Art of Advocacy: Renaissance of Rhetoric in the Law School", *Law and Humanities*, 12:1 (2018), 116–137. On grammar school verbal rhetorical training and its bearing on Shakespeare's theatrical treatment of passions, see Enterline, *Shakespeare's Schoolroom*. But see also Burrow, *Shakespeare and Classical Antiquity*, pp. 21–50. On hands and the problematization of classical past, see Stephanie L. Pope, "Gestures and the Classical Past in Shakespeare's *Titus Andronicus*", in Lovascio, ed. *Shakespeare: Visions of Rome*, 326–334. For a larger discussion of action as a theatrical practice see David Bevington, *Action is Eloquence: Shakespeare's Language of Gesture* (Cambridge, MA: Harvard University Press, 1984).

45. Cicero, The *Orator* (Book III), in Cicero, *The Oratore* (Book III), *De Fato, Pradoxa Stoicorum, De Partitione Oratoria*, transl. H. Rackham, Loeb Classical Library (London and Cambridge, MA: Harvard University Press, 1948).

46. Interestingly hands are termed as "the *Spokesman* of the Body", in John Bulwer's statement of a few decades later than Shakespeare's play. Qtd in Neill, "Amphitheatres", p. 30 (Bulwer, p. 2). John Bulwer was an early modern explorer of human communication and the author of *Chirologia: Or the Natural Language of the Hand and Chironomia: Or, the Art of Manual Rhetoric* (London, 1644).

47. See for all S. Clark Hulse, "Wresting the Alphabet: Oratory and Action in *Titus Andronicus*", *Criticism*, 21:2 (1979), 106–118; Mary Laughlin Fawcett, "Arms/Words/Tears: Language and the Body in *Titus Andronicus*", *ELH*,

50:2 (1983), 261–277; Gillian Murray Kendall, "'Lend Me Thy Hand':
Metaphor and Mayhem in *Titus Andronicus*", *Shakespeare Quarterly*,
40:3 (1989), 299–316; Jane Hiles, "A Margin for Error: Rhetorical Context in *Titus Andronicus*", in Kolin, ed., *Titus Andronicus: Critical Essays*,
pp. 233–248.

48. On the pornographic structuring of Lavinia's mutilated body, see Cynthia
Marshall, *The Shattering of the Self: Violence, Subjectivity, and the Early
Modern Text* (Baltimore: The John Hopkins University Press, 2002), pp. 106–
216. But see also Mariangela Tempera, "*Titus Andronicus*: Staging the Mutilated Roman Body", in Del Sapio Garbero et al., eds, *Questioning Bodies*,
pp. 109–119.

49. Heiner Müller, *Anatomy Titus Fall of Rome* (1985), transl. Carl Weber and
Paul David Young, in *Heiner Müller after Shakespeare: Macbeth and Anat-
omy Titus Fall of Rome* (New York: Paj Publications, 2012), scene 10, p. 140.
For more on the way Müller "lays bare the complicity between the violator
and the poet", see Pfister, "The Romes of *Titus Andronicus*", pp. 157–158.
Pfister's essay was first presented at the Conference "Shakespeare 2016. The
Memory of Rome" held in Rome on April 2016. But see also Francesco
Fiorentino, "Introduzione" to Heiner Müller, *Anatomia Tito Fall of Rome.
Un Commento Shakespeariano*", ed. Francesco Fiorentino (Roma: L'Orma
Editore, 2017), pp. 7–35. For more recent rewritings of Lavinia which pro-
vide her with a voice and an" alternative historiography", see Márta Minier,
"The 'Contemporary Past' in Retakes on the Roman Plays", in Del Sapio
Garbero, ed., *Rome in Shakespeare's World*, pp. 234–235.

50. Fawcett, "Arms/Words/Tears", p. 269.

51. See Philip Kolin, "Performing Texts in *Titus Andronicus*", in *id*, ed., Titus
Andronicus: *Critical Essays*, p. 249.

52. For a more general discussion of Lavinia's learning, see Sara Eaton, "A
Woman of Letters: Lavinia in *Titus Andronicus*", in Shirley Nelson Garner
and Madelon Sprengnether, eds, *Shakespearean Tragedy and Gender* (Bloomington and Indianapolis: Indiana University Press, 1996), pp. 54–74.

53. Rowe, "Dismembering and Forgetting in *Titus Andronicus*", p. 295.

54. Marshall, *The Shattering Self*, p. 108.

55. In these works Luce Irigaray engages in a conversation with Western thought,
from Plato to Freud and Nietzsche, addressing the issue of femininity as
a male construct. *Speculum With the Other Woman*, 1974, transl. Gillian
G. Gill (Ithaca: Cornell University Press, 1985); *Marine Lover of Friedrich
Nietzsche*, 1980, transl. Gillian G. Gill (New York: Columbia University
Press, 1991).

56. Eugene M. Waith, "The Metamorphosis of Violence in *Titus Andronicus*"
(1957), rpt in Kolin, Titus Andronicus: *Critical Essays*, p. 106.

57. Philip Sidney, "An Apologie for Poetry" (written 1579 ca; pbd, 1595), in
G. Gregory Smith, ed., *Elizabethan Critical Essays*, vol. 1 (London: Oxford
University Press, 1950), p. 181. Ensuing pages directly in the text.

58. Tacitus, *Histories*, Book I.3. Trans. Clifford H. Moore, The Loeb Classical Library, 5 vols (London and Cambridge MA: Harvard University Press,
1925–1937), vol. 2.

59. James, *Shakespeare's Troy*, pp. 43–44.

60. This has helped "replacing the somewhat speculative relation between Shakespeare and the Greeks", Halpern writes (entering the arena of a rekindled
vexed question), "in favour of the more 'scholarly, 'responsible' account
of his influence by Seneca", or, more exactly, he persuasively argues, it
has allowed for what may be taken as a more plausible consideration of

Shakespeare's relationship with the Greeks, one mediated by the relevance of Seneca in his plays. "The Classical Inheritance", in Michael Neill and David Schalkwyk, eds, *The Oxford Handbook of Shakespearean Tragedy* (Oxford: Oxford University Press, 2016), pp. 23–24. Among those who have devoted extensive work to Shakespeare and *Trauerspiel*, see (with specific attention to *Hamlet*) Hugh Grady, *Shakespeare and Impure Aesthetics* (Cambridge: Cambridge University Press, 2009) and (with specific attention to *Richard II*) Zenòn Luis-Martinez, "Shakespeare's Historical Drama as *Trauerspiel*: *Richard II* and After", *ELH*, 75 (2008), 673–705.

61. See for all Miola's book-length study, *Shakespeare and Classical Tragedy*; but see also Martindale and Martindale, *Shakespeare and the Uses of Antiquity*, pp. 29–44, and Burrow, *Shakespeare and Classical Antiquity*, pp. 162–201.

62. Müller, *Anatomy Titus Fall of Rome*, scene 10, pp. 138–139.

63. Waith, "The Metamorphosis of Violence", p. 109.

64. Wynne-Davies, "The Swallowing Womb", p. 144.

65. As pointed out by Bate (in his edited *Titus*, p. 191) 'ruins' is emended with 'urns' in Thomas Hanmer's eighteenth-century edition of Shakespeare's works (*The Works of Shakespeare*, 6 vols, Oxford, 1743–1744). They are both plausible to me if we think of both in terms of eyes turned into holes by consuming tears (e.g. wept to holes). We are helped in this by Clarence's "those holes / Where eyes did once inhabit" (1.4.27–28) in the coeval *Richard III*. They also make me think of one of those fountains in Rome emerging from ancient ruins.

66. Benjamin, *Origin*, p. 62. Ensuing pages directly in the text.

67. In defining the rules of German *Trauerspiel*, Benjamin (with mainly Hamlet in mind) took pains to remark Shakespeare's originality: "The finest exemplifications of the *Trauerspiel* are not those which adhere strictly to the rules, but those in which there are playful modulations of the *Lustspiel*. For this reason Calderòn and Shakespeare created more important *Trauerspiele* than the German writers of the seventeenth century, who never progressed beyond the rigidly orthodox type". He then quoted Novalis on the desirable symbolic combination of *Lustspiel* and *Trauerspiel* and the way "this demand was fulfilled by Shakespeare": "In Shakespeare there is indeed an alternation between the poetic and the anti-poetic, harmony and disaharmony, the common, the base, the ugly and the romantic, the lofty, the beautiful, the real and the imagined: in Greek tragedy the opposite is true" (*Origin*, pp. 127–128).

68. George Steiner, "Introduction" to Benjamin, *Origin*, p. 17.

69. As stated by Gail Kern Paster, "For the early moderns, the power of the passions was a function of the affect-producing organs—the blood-making liver, the hungry heart, the angry gall bladder, and the melancholy spleen. Affects had specific locales, specific points of origin". *Humoring the Body. Emotions and the Shakespearean Stage* (Chicago: The University of Chicago Press, 2004), p. 12. But see also David Hillman, *Shakespeare's Entrails: Belief, Scepticism and the Interior of the Body* (Houndmills and New York: Palgrave Macmillan, 2007), pp. 47–48; David Hillman and Carla Mazzio, eds, *The Body in Parts: Fantasies of Corporeality in Early Modern Europe* (New York and London: Routledge, 1997); Michael C. Schoenfeldt, *Bodies and Selves in Early Modern England: Physiology and Inwardness in Spenser, Shakespeare, Herbert, and Milton* (Cambridge: Cambridge University Press, 1999); Gail Kern Paster, Katherine Rowe and Mary Floyd-Wilson, eds, *Reading the Early Modern Passions: Essays in the Cultural History of Emotions* (Philadelphia: University of Pennsylvania Press, 2004).

70. This is particularly evident in the characterization of Leontes where, as I have argued elsewhere, sight takes anatomical centre stage in the spectacle of his hallucinatory affections. Maria Del Sapio Garbero, "A Spider in the Eye/I:

The Hallucinatory Staging of the Self in Shakespeare's *The Winter's Tale*", in Ute Berns, ed., *Solo Performances: Staging the Early Modern Self in England* (Amsterdam: Rodopi, 2010), pp. 133–155.

71. Maria Del Sapio Garbero, "Translating *Hamlet*/Botching Up Ophelia's Half Sense", in Harold Bloom, ed., *William Shakespeare's Hamlet*, New Edition (New York: Infobase Publishing, 2009), pp. 135–150.

72. In Anderson's Foxean reading of *Titus*, Lavinia's "martyred signs" stands for the violence lurking in the interval between words and deeds (or signified and signifier) which is made wide in post-Reformation time and which regards the religious as well as the secular culture, and specifically Rome's legacy: "In Shakespeare's hands . . . Roman inheritance is not a *thing* already passed on to England and possessed by its citizens. Instead, the inheritance resembles a promise still to be completed, a transaction that can, therefore, go violently and unpredictably awry". *Performing Early Modern Trauma*, p. 33. But for *Titus's* relations with John Foxe's *Acts and Monuments*, see also Peter Lake, "Tragedy and Religion. Religion and Revenge in *Titus Andronicus* and *Hamlet*", in Neill and Schalkwyk, eds, *The Oxford Handbook of Shakespearean Tragedy*, p. 172.

73. Miola, *Shakespeare and Classical Tragedy*, pp. 20–21.

74. Kerrigan, *Revenge Tragedy*, p. 202.

75. Lynne Magnusson, "Shakespearean Tragedy and the Language of Lament", in Neill and Schalkwyk, eds, *The Oxford Book of Shakespearean Tragedy*, pp. 127–128. For an overview and discussion of the dynamics of the tragic emotion in Shakespeare, in the light of the focalizing notion of "affect", see David Hillman, "The Pity of It. Shakespearean Tragedy and Affect", in Neill and Schalkwyk, eds, *The Oxford Handbook of Shakespearean Tragedy*, pp. 135–150. But see also Drew Daniel, *The Melancholic Assemblage: Affect and Epistemology in the English Renaissance* (New York: Fordham University Press, 2013).

76. Benjamin, "The Storyteller", in *Illuminations*, p. 96.

77. See Bate's unresolved choice (note 79 to Act 5.3, Arden edition, p. 270) compared to Norton's and the other editions' different choice of having Lucius invested with this task.

78. As Lisa Hopkins has written, "the play is less interested in endings than in transition", *The Cultural Uses of the Caesars*, p. 31.

79. Bate, "Introduction", p. 19.

80. Schwyzer, *Archaeologies*, pp. 104, 101.

81. Schwyzer, *Archaeologies*, p. 80.

82. Stephen Mullaney, "'Do You See This?' The Politics of Attention in Shakespearean Tragedy", in Neill and Schalkwyk, eds, *The Oxford Handbook of Shakespearean Tragedy*, p. 159.

83. For an extensive archaeological treatment of this topic and its bearing on early modern poetry, see Schwyzer, *Archaeologies*, pp. 72–150. For a discussion of questions regarding the dead's afterlife and the relation with Shakespeare's tragedy, see Neill, *Issues of Death*, especially the chapter "Accomodating the Dead", pp. 243–261, and Stephen Greenblatt, *Hamlet in Purgatory* (Princeton: Princeton University Press, 2001).

84. Camden, *Britannia* (Address 'To the Reader', n.p.). Ensuing mentions directly in the text (as *Brit* 1 for the 1610 Holland translation and *Brit* 2 for the 1695 Gibson's translation).

85. On Tacitism, see earlier n. 30. But for a reconstruction of Camden's entourage revolving around the Earl of Essex (executed in 1601) and including Ben Jonson, George Chapman, hypothetically Shakespeare, and their concern for Latin authors like Seneca and Tacitus (the critics of tyrannical power and moral decline in late imperial Rome), see also Burrow, *Shakespeare and Classical Antiquity*, pp. 186–187.

86. Indeed it marked the beginning of monastic history. See Parry, *The Trophies of Time*, p. 10. But see also Margaret Aston, "English Ruins and English History: The Dissolution of the Sense of the Past", *Journal of the Warburg and Courtauld Institutes*, 36 (1973), 231–255.

87. For more on this see for all, see Schwyzer, *Archaeologies*, pp. 54–57 and 40–43.

88. Raymond Williams, *Marxism and Literature* (Oxford: Oxford University Press, 1977).

89. John Speed's commentary on the reverse side of the Suffolk map, quoted by Nicolson and Hawkyard in their edited John Speed, *The Counties of Britain*, p. 168. John Speed's commentary printed on the reverse of each map, is omitted in this edition.

90. Schwyzer, *Archaeologies*, p. 40.

91. Qtd in Edwards, *Writing Rome*, p. 89.

92. Neill, *Issues of Death*, p. 247.

93. Greenblatt, *Hamlet in Purgatory*, pp. 102–204. For a historical and cultural exploration of the issue of purgatory in the passage from Catholicism to Reformation, see Duffy, *The Stripping of the Altars*, pp. 338–376.

94. Neill, *Issues of Death*, p. 244.

95. Camden's reuse of such poetical modes of memory as Gildas's allows for an early modern recovery of a traumatic past that, subjective and biased as it may appear to our present historiography, was able to voice its silences and the haunting "groans" of the dead (*Titus*, 1.1.129).

96. Anderson, *Performing Early Modern Trauma*, p. 6 (see my Introduction, p. 0).

97. Jacques Derrida, *La carte postale* (Paris: Flammarion, 1980), p. 8.

98. Indeed, as Albert H. Tricomi observed long ago polemicizing with T.S. Eliot's harsh opinion of the play, it is precisely the "cool distance" and "ways in which the figurative language imitates the literal events" that "makes *The Tragedy of Titus Andronicus* a significant dramatic experiment". "The Aesthetics of Mutilation in 'Titus Andronicus'", *Shakespeare Survey*, 27 (1974), 11–20 (pp. 14 and 11). See also his "The Mutilated Garden in *Titus Andronicus*", *Shakespeare Studies*, 9 (1976), 89–105.

99. For such a suggested homophony between 'rumination' and 'Romination', see my Introduction, p. 1.

100. For an extensive discussion of Shakespeare's treatment of his sources, see John Kerrigan, *Shakespeare's Originality* (Oxford: Oxford University Press, 2018).

101. Roger Ascham, *The Schoolmaster*, in G. Gregory Smith, ed., *Elizabethan Critical Essays*, vol.1, pp. 19, 8, 15. Ascham is often referred to as the main promoter of a practice of learning (e.g. imitation) grounded on double translation (from Latin into English and vice versa), one which may have been "intimidating and liberating in equal measure", Burrow has observed, sometimes resulting in rewarding "creative imitation" or "inspired misremembering". "Shakespeare and Humanistic Culture", in Charles Martindale and A.B. Taylor, eds, *Shakespeare and the Classics* (Cambridge: Cambridge University Press, 2004), pp. 13–14. But see also Enterline, *Shakespeare's Schoolroom*, chapter 2, pp. 33–61.

102. See Roland Barthes, *The Pleasure of the Text*, transl. Richard Miller (New York: Hill and Wang, [1973] 1998). The text of bliss (*jouissance*) for Barthes is one which allows for fulfilment as well as loss, shock, disturbance (p. 19).

103. See my Introduction, p. 20.

104. Kolin, "Performing Texts in *Titus Andronicus*", p. 259.

105. Suffice it to mention Lavinia whose wounded and traumatized body is sadly reminiscent of Philomela's as well as of the body of Lucrece, in the same way in which Lucrece's mournful and self-anatomizing body, in the coeval *Rape of Lucrece,* is reminiscent of Hecuba and Philomela, but also, in her case, proleptically, of her future life in the world of representation.
106. Greene, *The Light to Troy*, p. 45.
107. Qtd and transl. by Pfister, "The Romes of *Titus Andronicus*", p. 157. As Pfister has written in commenting this passage, "This does not only give greater agency to [Aaron], the immigrant and racial Other, but invests him also with a heightened meta-dramatic awareness of the theatricality of power politics".
108. Walter Benjamin, *Central Park* (1938–1939), transl. Lloyd Spencer with Mark Harrington, *New German Critique*, 34 (1985), 32–58 (p. 50).

2 Lucrece's Pictorial Anatomy of Ruin

By the time Shakespeare wrote *Titus Andronicus* and *The Rape of Lucrece*, Rome's ruins in European Renaissance culture had achieved the status of a *paradigm*: they were exploited for any meditation on time, history, beauty, or realms. Archaeologically underwritten by the imagery of the burning Troy, the semantics of ruins defines all tropes of invasion, conquest, destruction, and appropriation, in Shakespeare's Roman canon: "Tell us what Sinon hath bewitched our ears", the unnamed Lord-orator laments in *Titus*, as the play heads towards its conclusion. "Or who hath brought the fatal engine in / That gives our Troy, our Rome, the civil wound" (5.3.84–86). Ruins also shape the sorrow of two raped women—Lavinia and Lucrece—in the two Roman works that Shakespeare writes during the severe resurgence of the plague (1592–94), in times of contagion and death: a female sorrow which problematizes the Virgilian imperial destiny of Rome as well as his own concern for the Roman theme and the classical past. Together, Lavinia and Lucrece get in the teleological discourse of history with a deadlock, a lump of grief, which forces to interrogate in depth the sense of history as well as the order of signification. Shakespeare's two characters cooperate in this. If Lavinia's rape literally coincides with her Ovidian silenced body and ruinous male acts of interpretation, Lucrece supplements that silence with an excess of language: the flow of her own *pre-mortem*, interminable mourning, which is as unsettling, I argue, as Lavinia's horrible spectacle of her disabled voice and gestuality. As shown in this chapter, ruins in *The Rape of Lucrece* are discovered as a heuristic tool, an instrument of self-anatomizing knowledge for Shakespeare's two protagonists, as well as the means through which the poet overshadows history (the contextual transition from monarchy to republic) by foregrounding the "lament from history" (Benjamin). But let us enter the poem from the end, namely from the mourning of Lucrece's kinsmen over her dead body.

DOI: 10.4324/9781003259671-4

"One That Was a Woman, Sir, But Rest Her Soul, She's Dead" (*Hamlet*)

Mourning is an act of possession in Shakespeare's *Rape of Lucrece*, the competitive contest of a sanitized form of appropriation after Lucrece has washed away her "stain" with a suicidal gesture (v. 1752):[1]

> Then son and father weep with equal strife
> Who should weep most, for daughter or for wife.
>
> The one doth call her his, the other his,
> Yet neither may possess the claim they lay.
> The father says "She's mine", "O, mine she is,"
> Replies her husband: "do not take way
> My sorrow's interest, let no mourner say
>   He weeps for her, for she was only mine,
>   And only must be wailed by COLLATINE."
>   (1791–99)

Without her gesture, the continuation of previous forms of patriarchal and lawful ownership of her female body within the family would have been culturally problematic. One has only to think of the way Lavinia's violated body is cleared of her stain in *Titus Andronicus*. Death inflicted on her by her own father is the result of a sort of communal briefing: an improvised macabre session on the "shame" of daughters and on the "sorrow" of the fathers as well as on the justice of wiping off both—shame and sorrow—following a law sanctioned by custom. "Was it well done" on the part of the centurion Virginius, Titus asks his guests, "To slay his daughter with his own right hand, / Because she was enforced, stained and deflowered?" (5.3.36–38); this, before offering his interlocutors, then and there, a spectacularized re-enactment of Livy's narrative of that episode.[2] Titus's gesture—like most of the action in *Titus Andronicus*—is "performed" with books at hand, that is by conforming to what is called "A pattern, precedent, a lively warrant" (5.3.43). Remembering Rome, claiming its inheritance, being a Roman in that play of *finis imperii*, means becoming a butcher to one's own children, participating in a disquieting dismembering of Rome. But it is also evident that in addressing and read-dressing the theme of women's rape in those same years 1593–94, Shakespeare was interested in mapping the irresolvable tangle of cultural issues embedded in the violation of women, as well as exposing the paradox of an exit that necessarily involved the death of the victim by murder.

But "rest her soul" (*Ham.*, 5.1.120), Lucrece did the deed herself—thus complying with the only other cleansing option traditionally available to women. As a result, her family can reappropriate her alienated body by means of a sanitized, if self-exonerating form of mourning. Lucrece's husband and father can go so far as to construct their woe in terms of a compensatory rhetorical agon in Shakespeare's Roman poem; an agon which is not exempt of a parodic twist in the way the poet handles the two men's respective claims to have an "interest"—a right, or a better title—to the expression of woe for the death of their beloved.

The suicide, however, which—culturally overdetermined as it may be—Lucrece protractedly advocates to herself as the *will*/ful gesture of a woman in control of her own destiny ("I am the mistress of my fate", v. 1069), undermines the masculine appropriative claim with an anxiety which is soon voiced by both father and husband:

> "O," quoth LUCRETIUS, "I did give that life
> Which she too early and too late hath spilled."
> "Woe, woe," quoth COLLATINE, "she was my wife;
> I owed her, and 'tis mine that she hath killed."
> "My daughter" and "My wife" with clamours filled
>   The dispersed air, who, holding LUCRECE' life,
>   Answered their cries, "My daughter" and My wife".
>   (1800–06)

Such a rhetorical "strife" for the *post-mortem* possession of Lucrece's body, through mourning, anticipates a similar scene between Hamlet and Laertes, lover and brother, which Shakespeare would recreate a few years later around Ophelia's grave, soon after the suicidal body of the young woman has been interred, by night, with a "maimed" Christian burial (5.1.198). "Is she to be buried in Christian burial when she *will*fully *seeks her own salvation*?" (5.1.1–2; my emphasis) asks the Grave-digger at the opening of Act 5, faced with a gesture whose intentionality is ambiguously both affirmed and denied by the curtailed religious service.[3] Again, suicide[4] as well as the funereal appropriation of a female body—a correlate of the well-established poetic mode of the blazon—are made into an issue. Who loved her most? Here stands Laertes who, disdainful of the priest's waspish restrictions, bombastically tries to perform his *carmen* in a Petrarchan mode, by exploiting the long-standing transfiguring equation of woman and flower and translating Ophelia's terrestrial flesh into a heavenly body: "Lay her i' th' earth, / And from her fair and unpolluted flesh / May violets spring. I tell thee, churlish priest, / A minist'ring angel shall my sister be / When thou liest howling" (5.1.217–21). And here stands Hamlet—"the Dane", as he pugnaciously presents himself—who, as if in a tournament and forgetful of the suffering inflicted on his beloved when alive, is determined to be no less of a man in such a funereal profession of love. "Why, I will fight with him upon this theme". "I loved Ophelia. Fourty thousand brothers / Could not with all their quantity of love / Make up my sum" (5.1.245–50), he cries, as he purports to emulate with equal if not superior weight, or "emphasis", as he terms it, the spectacle of Laertes grotesquely leaping into the grave to fully accomplish the show of his sorrow:

> What is he whose grief
> Bears such an emphasis, whose phrase of sorrow
> Conjures the wand'ring stars and makes them stand
> Like wonder-wounded hearers? This is I,
> Hamlet the Dane.
>
> (*Ham.*, 5.1.233–37)

As shown in some of his highly metatextual sonnets, Shakespeare was well aware that the fame bestowed upon the object of love by the "virtue" of either tongue or pen is typically funereal, if self-creating for the surviving lyric subject: "Or I shall live your epitaph to make / Or [etc. etc.] / Your monument will be my gentle verse" (son. 81, 1–9; but see also 101). Widely exploited in Petrarch's influential *ars poetica*, such a trope was mythically condensed in the ancient story of Apollo and Daphne and beautifully recounted by Ovid, where the empowering myth of the God as a laurel-crowned poet is grounded in the stillness of Daphne's body meta-morphosed into that very plant. Indeed, we hear the same trope resound-ing in the graveyard, in the words of those who promise Ophelia "a living monument" (5.1.276). Only, we are not given the time to hear Hamlet's epitaph. For the two—Hamlet and Laertes—will soon come to hands, in a scene which is intriguingly remindful of *The Rape*'s epilogue. Contempo-rary well-read theatregoers may have perceived a similar parodic concern that Shakespeare had shown earlier, in the way he depicted the rhetorical fight to the finish between father and husband in *The Rape*—with Colla-tine who "bids LUCRETIUS give his sorrow place", and strives to exceed his father-in-law's woe with his mask of blood achieved by theatrically plunging into his wife's blood: "And then in key-cold LUCRECE' bleeding stream / He falls, and bathes the pale fear in his face, / And counterfeits to die with her a space" (vv. 1773–76).

As Nancy Vickers has remarked, "Shakespeare's [*Lucrece*] closes as it opened, as men rhetorically compete with each other over Lucrece's body". Starting from Collatine's improvident rhetorical display of his lady's beauty in front of Tarquin,

> [i]n *Lucrece*, occasion, rhetoric, and result are all informed by, and thus inscribe, a battle between men that is first figuratively and then literally fought on the fields of woman's "celebrated" body. . . . a male rivalry, which positions a third (female) term in a median space from which it is initially used and finally eliminated.[5]

Aptly, Vickers strengthens her argument by broadening her point to some of Shakespeare's coeval sonnets, where Petrarchan celebratory love discourse, with its high-flown if untrue vocabulary, is disclaimed as "merchandised" love (son. 102), an appropriative gesture by means of which one's object of love is cast into a triangular economy of exchange: "So it is not with me as with that Muse, / . . . / Who heaven itself for ornament doth use, / . . . I will not praise that purpose not to sell" (son. 21). It is in the same anti-Petrarchan vein that Collatine is admonished by the narrator in *The Rape* for having ignited—with his Laura-like blazon of "LUCRECE the chaste" (v. 7), her face a contrast of "lilies and roses" (vv. 71–73)—Tarquin's devastating desire: "Why is Collatine the publisher / Of that rich jewel he should keep unknown / From thievish ears, because it is his own" (vv. 33–35).

Among those who have addressed the centrality held by the language of praise in *The Rape*, Vickers is the critic who has most insightfully highlighted the ways in which the poem unfolds the violent side of a poetics which thrives on "female matter for male oratory".[6] I am following the same line of reasoning when I say that *The Rape* may well be viewed as a critique of the Petrarchan code. But I also want to stress the fact that this is representative of the climax as well as the consumption of a genre, especially if one considers the ways in which the implied sexual politics of a well-established poetic code variously develops in Shakespeare's works into a fully-fledged "theme" which befits the plot of epic and theatrical genres: epyllion (*The Rape*), tragedy (*Hamlet*, *Othello*), as well as tragicomedy (*Cymbeline*). Meaningfully, Shakespeare's revisionist approach points towards a narrative in which, even though eventually physically and permanently interred, or fictionally and only temporarily erased, the female subject challenges, in an oblique yet radical way, the appropriative intentions inherent in the Petrarchan code. But to stay with Lucrece: is she fully "eliminated", or "trapped", as Vickers seems to maintain, in the competitive/appropriative logic of the male language which marks both the beginning and end of the poem?[7]

It is my intention in this chapter to address what constitutes the middle: namely the section in which Shakespeare makes his heroine capable of changing her status from that of a Petrarchan, dead-like "virtuous monument", offered to the inspection of Tarquin's predatory gaze (his "lewd unhallowed eyes", vv. 391–92), to that of a *pre-mortem* "monument" of herself as an image that actively troubles and displaces the male gaze of her kinsmen. My departure will be Lucrece's long-drawn ekphrasis of the Troy piece—a "piece of skilful painting" (vv. 1366–67)—which takes place after her rape: a vicarious exploration of the self through which, before putting an end to her life, she transforms her own face, by way of a fashioning *ars moriendi*, into a disquieting "anatomy of ruin": a living and revengeful *tabula anatomica*, as I would like to call it. I suggest to see this as an act of individuation and self-possession which, problematic and provisional as it may be, stands against the anonymity that lurks behind the entire male, self-regarding, rhetorical edifice of poetical blazons—the anonymity, so outspokenly and emblematically voiced on Ophelia's grave by the witty-tongued Grave-digger who, asked to reveal the identity of the person to be interred, simply utters: "One that was a woman, sir, but rest her soul she's dead" (*Ham.*, 5.1.120).

Other critics have addressed the talkative Lucrece we meet in the post-rape part of the story. Coppélia Kahn acknowledges that rape "grants" her a voice, but this is "the voice of the victim", she says. "The terms of her victimage do not constitute a vantage point distinct from the patriarchal ideology that generated Tarquin's act".[8] Yet others, in recent years, have made a different claim. In her Ovidian rereading of the poem, Lynn Enterline has insightfully addressed the relationship between rape and language as epitomizing the woman's voice. "In the Ovidian tradition, rape is the call that interpellates the female subject", she argues. Focusing on Ovid's violated women, variously evoked in the poem, she has foregrounded both the traumatic quality of Lucrece's "entry into the discursive orbit" (and hence, "the perverse logic of a violent pedagogical curriculum") and the complexity of such an entry, of what it means to be a woman and a self-authoring woman.[9]

My suggestion in this essay is that Lucrece's post-rape, self-possessing assertion of identity, Ovidian as it is in its founding mythological imagery, is underpinned by the new science of bodies or what has been called the new "culture of dissection".[10] In this light, the battle between men that, in a Petrarchan mode, "is first figuratively and then literally fought on the fields of woman's 'celebrated' body" (Vickers), can be perceived as part of a much broader contest of contrasting and overlapping modes of understanding/imagining/possessing bodies in early modern culture, of which Shakespeare's poem bears clear traces. In such a context, which entailed a problematization of early modern bodies, and a reappraisal/reinscription of female otherness,[11] Shakespeare's Lucrece, as a woman, I want to argue, is given the chance to erode not only the male reifying Petrarchan mode of representation of the female body, but also "stale" if popular forms of female complaint, thus creating a new space for self-knowledge.

"Pausing for Means to Mourn Some Newer Way"

Shakespeare's live "anatomy of ruin" takes form corporeally, as the result of a transaction: a process of exchange between subject and picture, worked out by way of a lengthy (from v. 1366 to v. 1568) description of a painting representing the greatest of all classical tropes of fall—the fall of Troy—which is intended to mirror *en abyme* Lucrece's "fallen" state. Through the intersection of the grieving heroine and the implicit narrator's action, the Troy-piece is attentively looked at and read in its various scenes, as well as in the way the painter has represented the posture and emotions of its characters in the precise moment when the besieged citadel falls under the attack of the Greek army. The ravished Lucrece is eagerly

looking for a figure that may reflect her distress, when she finds it "stell'd"
on Hecuba's face, the figure which is mythically one with woe—"Woe,
woe is me!"—she repetitively claims in Euripides's eponymous play.[12]

> To this well-painted piece is LUCRECE come,
> To find a face where all distress is stell'd.
> Many she sees where cares have *carved* some,
> But none where all distress and dolour dwell'd,
> Till she despairing HECUBA beheld,
>   Staring on PRIAM's wounds with her old eyes,
>   Which bleeding under PYRRUS' proud foot lies.
>
> In her the painter had *anatomiz'd*
> Time's ruin, beauty's wrack, and grim care's reign;
> Her cheeks with chops and wrinkles were disguis'd:
> *Of what she was no semblance did remain.*
> Her *blue blood chang'd to black in every vein,*
>   Wanting the spring that those shrunk pipes had fed,
>   *Show'd life imprison'd in a body dead.*
>   (1443–56; my emphasis)

The painter seems to have satisfied Hecuba's urge for an ethic of response,
or else a true understanding of her wretchedness; the one she invokes in
Euripides's eponymous play when she implores Agamemnon: "Be like a
painter", "Stand back, see me in perspective / see me whole, observe my
wretchedness".[13] What she lacks is voice in Shakespeare's poem: but this
raises the question of a knowledge which puts to the test the possibilities
of both pictorial and verbal language.

> On this sad shadow LUCRECE spends her eyes,
> And *shapes* her sorrow to the beldam's woes,
> Who nothing wants to answer her but cries
> And bitter words to ban her cruel foes;
> The painter was no god to lend her those,
> And therefore LUCRECE swears he did her wrong,
> To give her so much grief, and not a tongue.
>   (1457–63; my emphasis)

Shakespeare's implicit narrator is here using a verb, "to stell" (to portray),
which elsewhere the poet advisedly exploits to refer us—in the manner
of the favourite Renaissance *paragone* between the arts—to the painter's
envied capacity to visually capture and fix the exact form of things—a
condition for good *mimesis*: "Mine eye hath played the painter and hath
steeled / Thy beauty's forme in table of my heart" (son. 24). But the picture of Hecuba—the memory of a spectral, archaeological anteriority, as

I suggest in my Introduction (pp. 38–43)—belongs to no ordinary good portraiture. Compared with the other anguished faces of "this well-painted piece", Hecuba's seems to defy representation, her features disfigured by "chops and wrinkles". "Of what she was no semblance did remain": the reticulum of her blue veins is dried up and surfacing, as if the artist had descended into the depths of her face, to uncover the truth of something that was underneath and invisible, scarred skin featuring both as a marker of effacement—the effacement of what "she was"—and as a breach, an opening towards a deeper form of *mimesis*.

I would like to suggest that within the mass of bodies and colour in the picture of the fall of Troy, what for Lucrece comes into relief, catalyzing the meaning of it all, is an *écorché*: an exercise in the study and representation of the human body—familiar to both artists and anatomists in early modern culture—grounded in the dissecting episteme of the new science and a new anatomical awareness of the space and layers of the body interior. Meaningfully to my purpose, the *OED* reminds us that "to stell", in Shakespeare's time, also occurs in Haydocke's abridged translation of Lomazzo's *Trattato dell'arte della pittura, scultura ed architettura* (1584) published in 1598 with the title *A Tracte Containing the Artes of Curious Paintinge, Carvinge, and Buildinge*—a translation which marked a step beyond the phenomenon of sheer art collecting and the beginning of an interest in England for continental art theory. "Before you begin to Stell, delineat and tricke out the proportion of a man" [It. "*Prima che delinei, e disegni un'huomo*"], Lomazzo wrote, "you ought to know his true quantity and stature". In fact, it was only through a proper understanding of quantity, he argued, that the painter could imitate "by lines" the "rounde" "nature of the thing" on "the flat and plaine superficies" of a table.[14] Supported by Michelangelo's commanding precepts developed throughout years of anatomical studies, Lomazzo explained at the outset of his treatise how "quantity" ("breadth, length, and *thicknesse*"; my emphasis) was essential to "perspective light" and to the "motion" of the figure. More in general, what he authoritatively underlined was that "quantity" (the study of the body's volume and proportion among body parts) constituted the "matter" of art, and that such an understanding—the only and ultimate objective for the carver—was as preliminary as it was essential for the painter in order to achieve "quality" (specificity, similitude, resemblance) by means of colour ("the last forme & perfection to the figure"):

> But because to create the substances of things proceedeth from an infinite power, which is not founde in any creature (as the Divines teach) the Painter must take something in steed of matter: namely *Quantitie proportioned*; which is the matter of Painting. Here then the Painter must needs understand that *proportioned quantitie and quantitie delineated* are all one, and that the same is the materiall

substance of Painting. For hee must consider, that although hee be never so skillfull in the use of colours, and yet lacketh this delineation, he is unfurnished, of the pricipall *matter* of his arte, and consequently of the substantiall part thereof.[15]

The representation of despairing Hecuba in Shakespeare's ekphrasis seems to refer his readers to such a "materiall substance" of her state, an achromatic "substance" grasped by peeling her figure of its skin and colour—which however Shakespeare's imaginary painter has left there, in a withered and diatonic tangle of "chops and wrinkles"—as if to signal the work he had done to "carve" the flesh up to its blackened veins beneath. The effect might be imagined as the same one produced by a pencilled or chalked *tratteggio* as if, set on the background of "this well-painted picture", Hecuba's face had been left in a state of *non-finito*; an effect one sometimes observes in Renaissance paintings or frescos, or in preparatory cartoons.[16] Shakespeare himself seems to refer us to such a state of "work in progress" when he later elaborates on Hecuba's figure as "pencill'd pensiveness and colour'd sorrow" (v. 1497): as if Hecuba's figure had been left midway on its transformation from pencil to colour, abstraction to *mimesis*—and hence the line of drawing was still visible under the surface of few achromatic brushes of colour. In such a suspension—the suspension of a "studio"—it signalled a search for volumetric knowledge and a profounder, layered configuration of truth.

Interestingly, Hecuba's "sad shadow" seems to materialize, to Lucrece's eyes, as the enactment of an excavating project she herself engages with soon after her rape, in a painful ambivalence of truth and shame, exposure and concealment, and with the help of a lexicon intrinsically indebted to the coeval semantics of ruins as well as the visual arts: "My sable ground of sin I will not paint / To hide the truth of this false night's abuses" (vv. 1074–75).

Such a pervading intention encourages us to understand the relevance of Hecuba's unveiling anatomy of ruin by considering it in the context of the Renaissance distinction between "*pittura di colorito*" (colour painting) and "*pittura di disegno*" (design painting)[17]—a distinction variously pursued, for instance in the art of Michelangelo and Raphael—and which was subsumed in Lomazzo's discussion of "quantity" and "quality". In this light, Hecuba's portrait, I want to argue, emerges as a by-product of design, in the sense drawing was understood in the Renaissance Italian art theory: the "foundation" of both painting and sculpture for Vasari, "and the very soul which conceives and nourishes in itself every part of the [shaping] intelligence".[18] Because as a stage preparatory to painting, drawing was scientifically linked to the sciences of geometry, optics, perspective, and anatomy, and because as such, in dismembering and studying muscles, veins, and sinews, but also in perceiving proportions and connections among body parts, it pursued not simply a specific classificatory

Figure 2.1 Il Cigoli (1559–1613), Studio of Pictorial Anatomy, Galleria degli Uffizi, Firenze

Source: Galleria degli Uffizi, Firenze, D.L. 83(31.05.2014), art. 12 and 3

task but a broader heuristic project. Indeed, compared with the perfect conclusiveness of the *"pittura di colorito"*, Hecuba's face comes into relief and imposes itself to both the "perusal" of Lucrece's eyes (see v. 1527) and that of the poem's implicit narrator as a deconstructing if powerful mode of understanding both subject and world: "In her the painter had anatomiz'd / Time's ruin, beauty's wrack, and grim care's reign". It brings to the surface what is beneath. It emerges as a flayed figure—an *écorché*—thus referring us to the dismembering protocol of both anatomy and the art of drawing in the way they both cooperated in Renaissance culture (be it by means of the knife, pencil, or both), towards the understanding—or invention—of the body's volume and a new reappraisal of the human.

Such a transcendent projectuality—of gnoseological relevance for Roberto Ciardi[19]—was persistently highlighted by Vasari when focalizing the link between the art of design and the practice of anatomy in the work of his Renaissance artists and the story of his own cultural time. Leonardo is one of those who best exemplified such a dismembering epistemological concern; a concern for the layered structure of the body interior which he shared with philosophers and physicians:

> He . . . devoted even greater care to the study of the anatomy of men, aiding and being aided by M. Marcantonio della Torre, a profound philosopher, who then professed at Padua and wrote upon the subject. I have heard it said that he was one of the first who began to illustrate the science of medicine, by the learning of Galen, and to throw true light upon anatomy, up to that time involved in the thick darkness of ignorance. In this he was marvellously served by the genius, work and hands of Lionardo, who made a book about it with red crayon drawings outlined with the pen, in which he foreshortened and portrayed with the utmost diligence. He did the skeleton, adding all the nerves and muscles, the first attached to the bone, the others keeping it firm and the third moving, and in the various parts he wrote notes in curious characters, using his left hand, and writing from right to left, so that it cannot be read without practice, and only at a mirror. . . . Whoever succeeds in reading these notes of Lionardo will be amazed to find how well that divine spirit has reasoned of the arts, the muscles, the nerves and veins, with the greatest diligence in all things.
>
> (*Lives*, 2, 162–63)

Similarly, for Michelangelo, anatomy served a heuristic project—a yearning, in the words of Vasari—for "the arrangement and the method" of the human body (*Lives*, 4, 170), namely for its structure and laws in connection with the play of the "emotions and passions of the soul", which he fulfilled by bringing to perfection the "difficult" art of design (4, 141).

> Michelagnolo was devoted to the labours of the arts, seeing that he mastered every difficulty, possessing a genius admirably adapted to the excellent studies of design. Being perfect in this, he often made dissections, examining the ligatures, muscles, nerves, veins, and various movements, and all the postures of the human body, and even animals, especially horses, which he loved to keep. He liked to examine the arrangement and method of everything, and no one could have treated them better even if they had studied nothing else.
>
> (*Lives*, 4, 170)

As Vasari indicates, Michelangelo was in search of a pure, conceptual if shameless nakedness. And his works demonstrated the hard labour he had to face when he decided to look for all this not in the surface of colour, as other great masters "not so grounded in design" did (4, 143), but in the "profundity" of the body: the bodies of the dead and the living, the blessed and the damned. "Every human emotion is represented and marvellously expressed. The proud, envious, avaricious, luxurious", Vasari observes in front of the *Last Judgement*, as well as all "the divers gestures of young and old, men and women": a tremendous amount of "knowledge of the world such as is gained by philosophers by means of speculations and books" (4, 143). The achievement was unique: the painter Vasari stressed in his dazzling story of Michelangelo's life. It laid open the way to the "great style", or the "grand manner" in the painting of nudes (4, 141). And it radically changed early modern ways of seeing:

> O, happy age! O, blessed artists who have been able to refresh your darkened eyes at the fount of such clearness, and see difficulties made plain by this marvellous artist! His labours have removed the bandage from your eyes, and he has separated the true from the false which clouded the mind. Thank Heaven, then, and try to imitate Michelagnolo in all things. When the work was uncovered [1541] everyone rushed to see it from every part and remained dumfounded.
>
> (*Lives*, 4, 130)

Vasari's rapt ekphrastic pages on Michelangelo's works, especially those on the Sistine Chapel, remain unsurpassable in the way they announce the good news of Michelangelo's discovery of men's and women's new, dazzling nakedness. The entire world, he says, was thus made aware of such a revolutionary swerve in culture, the fact that it marked a passage in unveiling not simply unimaginable horizons of truth about the human body, but also new and extraordinary enabling possibilities of "seeing": what we may well take as a powerful mark of an epistemological fracture.

Was Shakespeare experimenting with his own "grand style" when, early in his career, he decided "to play the painter" (son. 24) and to "pen/cil" Lucrece's journey into the "nakedness" of her doleful heart *and* flesh, corporeally, by evoking the mighty figure of Hecuba and by means of a direct dialogue with the *method* of visual art and anatomy? Lucrece's self-anatomizing ekphrasis appears in none of Shakespeare's direct Latin sources (Ovid's *Fasti*, II, vv. 685–852;[20] Livy's *History of Rome*, I.57–60), and if we compare it to other ekphrastic occurrences in his works, we find nothing so imposing (some two hundred verses), in length and manner.[21] Be that as it may, I feel it is not too daring to say that Lucrece acquires a Michelangiolesque stature in the course of her mighty *corps-à-corps* with the painting, her "perusing" eyes wide open on her mirror-like "piece of skilful painting" (vv. 1366–67), her limbs and sinews involved in an extraordinary form of bodily *imitatio*. This is accomplished by the gradual, twofold transaction—which is worked out in the meantime: (a) the transaction between body and the epic topic of the painting, in an extreme enactment of *enargeia*, or identification[22] ("On this sad shadow Lucrece spends her eyes, / And shapes her sorrow to the beldam's woes"); (b) the one between surface and depth, a transaction highlighted by Vasari in relation to Renaissance reinvented bodies.[23] We should add a third, competitive level—that is, the transaction between word and image—but let us leave it out for a moment. For, what needs to be stressed in the first place is Shakespeare's awareness of what an anatomical understanding of the body was like, and the gender-coded anti-Petrarchan rhetorical strategies it might be put to serve in the discursive economy of his Roman poem. Let us consider more carefully the verses, quoted earlier, in which Lucrece describes Hecuba's figure:

> In her the painter had anatomiz'd
> Time's ruin, beauty's wrack, and grim care's reign;
> Her cheeks with chops and wrinkles were disguis'd:
> Of what she was no semblance did remain.
> Her blue blood chang'd to black in every vein,
>   Wanting the spring that those shrunk pipes had fed,
>   Show'd life imprison'd in a body dead.
>
> (1450–56)

The painter is said to have represented his character as if life were verging on death, or as if life were still perceivable in the state of death. Now this was precisely the liminal state of the anatomized body as it was reproduced in its relevant didactic illustrations. Sorrow has just broken Hecuba's heart (the "spring" of life) and "her blue blood chang'd to black in every vein", narrates the piteous if outrageous story of "life imprison'd in a body dead", as if in the posture of a moralized *écorché*. As such, in mirroring and bringing to light Lucrece's own inner state, Hecuba's picture serves a corporeal process of spoliation and self-knowledge.[24]

  This, however, becomes significant if observed in relation to the Petrarchan rhetoric of the woman's body of which it is a reversal. Indeed, the previously quoted stanza (vv. 1450–56) recalls and subverts Tarquin's anatomizing blazon, silently rehearsed on Lucrece's sleeping and passive body:

> Her lily hand her rosy cheek lies under,
> Coz'ning the pillow of a lawful kiss;
> Who, therefore angry, seems to part in sunder,
> Swelling on either side to want his bliss;
> Between those hills her head entombed is,
>   Where like a virtuous monument she lies,
>   To be admired of lewd unhallowed eyes.

Without the bed her other fair hand was,
On the green coverlet, whose perfect white
Showed like an April daisy on the grass,
With pearly sweat resembling dew of night.
Her eyes, like marigolds, had sheathed their light,
    And canopied in darkness sweetly lay
    Till they might open to adorn the day.

Her air, like golden threads, played with her breath,
O modest wantons, wanton modesty!
Showing life's triumph in the map of death,
And death's dim look in life's mortality.
Each in her sleep themselves so beautify,
    As if between them twain there were no strife,
    But that life lived in death, and death in life.
                                        (386–406)

Tarquin's blazon also indicates the aggressive nature of this rhetoric:

Her breasts like ivory globes circled with blue,
A pair of maiden world unconquered,
Save of their lord no bearing yoke they knew,
And him by oath they truly honoured.
These worlds in TARQUIN new ambition bred,
    Who like a foul usurper went about
    From this fair throne to heave the owner out.
                                        (407–13)

The female body is conceived according to the early modern colonial tropes of virginity, discovery, and conquest: a masculine scenario. It is "a world unconquered", all the more longed for if fantasized as a territory of competition, a battleground. It is within this context, in the presence of a fragmented female body, minutely inventoried by a masculine predatory gaze—cheek, head, hand, eyes, hair, breasts—that Tarquin, "in his will his wilful eye he tired", fuels his desire with a list of "false compare" (sonnet 130): Lucrece's "azure veins, her alabaster skin, / Her coral lips, her snow-white dimpled chin" (vv. 417–20). As Sawday has written, "In England in the last years of the sixteenth century and the early years of the seventeenth, the anatomic intensity of the blazon became a more overtly misogynist exercise, particularly in the hands of John Donne".[25] Shakespeare makes his Lucrece resist that ornamental if partitioning exercise.

"Painted flourish" or "painted rhetoric": thus, similar ways of creating women's beauty are often dismissed by Shakespeare, the playwright, with words remindful of Lucrece's scorn for the covering quality of "paint". The language of praise is criticized, often mockingly, for its counterfeiting excess as well as for its merchandising nature: "O, she needs it not. / To things of sale a seller's praise belongs (*Love's Labour's Lost*, 2.1.11, and 4.3.230–36; but see also *Twelfth Night*, 1.5.214–18). In *The Rape*, at an early stage of Shakespeare's career as a poet, anatomy serves an alternative project: nay, the blazon's masculine visual coding itself and its power relations are what is questioned and unsettled. In fact, the Troy piece's ekphrasis transforms his heroine from the unaware object of a masculine gaze, which she is in the first part of the poem, into someone who sees. Not only. By means of a gender-coded subverting parallelism and in a carefully orchestrated displacing mimetic strategy, Shakespeare makes Lucrece "[spend] her eyes" on the face of another woman: that of Hecuba's, a "sad shadow", a disquieting "no semblance". By so doing, Lucrece opposes surface with depth. She thus de-faces, I argue, the colourful, apparent reality of Tarquin's flat "map" with the bemusing complexity of the three-dimensional chart of the *écorché* into which she will literally transform herself (see vv. 1712–13).

Lucrece's ekphrasis of the Troy painting has attracted a good deal of criticism over the years. E.H. Gombrich has reminded us that the verbal rendering of visual artefacts was a very ancient literary phenomenon and that Philostratus's *Imagines* may have influenced Shakespeare.[26] Miola has referred us to Aeneas's description of the painting depicting the fall of Troy in Dido's palace (*Aeneid*, I); a tale which (together with the content of *Aeneid* II) had been "studied by generations of Elizabethan schoolchildren".[27] The fictive nature of the described work of art has also been stressed (by Meek), with the related argument of *ut pictura poesis*.[28] The ekphrastic visual figuration is itself a creation of language—so the argument runs; as such it is an intrinsic self-referential verbal procedure. Nevertheless, what Shakespeare may really have seen in relation to his depiction of the Troy painting has also been addressed as a theme of discussion, to be dismissed by others as a pointless argument, or sometimes continued with the even more groundless question of whether it is a painting or a tapestry.[29] Critics have also focalized the relevance of Lucrece's ekphrasis to say, "[t]he only power left to [her] is in the realm of art".[30] More recently others, like Marion A. Wells, have given psychoanalytic and cultural significance to such a power by underlining the ways in which, through Lucrece's ekphrasis, Hecuba becomes "an allegory of cultural mourning", one that "replaces 'Laura' at the center of the male gaze".[31] Lynn Enterline instead has importantly drawn attention to Lucrece's ekphrasis as a "transfer of affect", a practice which, through *prosopopeia* and *imitatio*, had specific pedagogical centrality in Tudor grammar schools.

> Both the narrative and dramatic encounters with Hecuba's grief have much to tell us about Shakespeare's reaction to the power and limits of classical *imitatio*—and much, too, about his habits for generating

effects of character and feeling, whether in narrative verse of for the stage.[32]

What has been fairly neglected (at least to my notice) is the broader epistemic significance of Lucrece's ekphrasis when considered in relation to the triangulation it establishes with the new science of bodies, and hence the ways this problematizes the entire order of representation in the poem, namely the very ways of understanding/possessing and repossessing bodies. This is emphasized as a turning point in the poem. Shakespeare stops the flux of Lucrece's words and he creates a "pause", an *interim*, an unnatural void in the poem's illusionism: a "pause" as long as the dilated time of her waiting for the messenger to return from Ardea with an answer to the painful message she has sent to her husband Collatine, during which the problem of representation emerges as such. It is not by chance that this part of the poem is introduced by Lucrece's need to search for "means to mourn some newer way":

> But long she thinks till he return again,
> And yet the duteous vassal scarce is gone.
> The weary time she cannot entertain,
> For now 'tis stale to sigh, to weep and groan:
> So woe hath wearied woe, moan tired moan,
>   That she her plaints a little while doth stay,
>   Pausing for means to mourn some newer way.
>   (1359–65)

So far, she considers, in a sort of free indirect speech, she has exhausted "woe" with woe, "moan" with "moan": a remark that we can take as an unsatisfied metatextual comment, on the debased woman's "complaint"— a popular literary genre in Shakespeare's time.[33] More importantly, she seems to be endowed with the more general awareness that so far she has given free rein to all those rhetorical ornaments of tropes and set pieces, which will often be adduced by critics as elements of the partial failure of an engaging poem.[34] A most censured instance of this is her apostrophe to Night, Opportunity, and Time, an exceedingly long-drawn rhetorical exercise which interestingly, however, she herself indignantly discards the very moment she has finished performing it, as poor stuff, matter for flat people ("shallow fools"), hardly worthy of even a routine performance by competing law students.

> Out, *idle words*, servants to shallow fools,
> Unprofitable sounds, weak arbitrators!
> Busy yourselves in skill-contending schools,
> Debate where leisure serves with dull debaters;
> To trembling clients be you mediators:

> For me, I force not argument a straw,
> Since that my case is past the help of law.
> $\qquad$ (1016–22; my emphasis)

Lucrece's mournful subjectivity emerges as if in a state of alienation from her emotional state, mediated as this is by the emptiness of phantom-like postures and words. She is literally haunted by their alien nature. She is equally haunted by the alien nature of words about her. Like Cleopatra after her, she is a woman with "stories" to watch out for. Consider the way Shakespeare makes her abhor the prospective endless proliferation of "rhymes" that history and time have in store for her. These are handled as wounding arms by Tarquin in the rape scene, when he threatens, "And thou, the author of [your husband's and kinsmen's] obloquy, / Shalt have thy trespass cited up in rhymes / And sung by children in succeeding times (vv. 523–25). They are later figured as the ultimate injury by Lucrece who, like Cleopatra, is made, proleptically, to take on the awareness of a different temporality—that of Renaissance culture, in which Lucrece's story was very popular—and more in general, that of the order of representation:

> The nurse to still her child will tell my story,
> And fright her crying babe with TARQUIN's name.
> The orator to deck his oratory
> Will couple my reproach to TARQUIN's shame.
> Feast-finding minstrels, tuning my defame,
> $\quad$ Will tie the hearers to attend each line,
> $\quad$ How TARQUIN wronged me, I COLLATINE.
> $\qquad$ (813–19)

This forcefully brings to the fore the complicating fact that in doing so Shakespeare makes her live at the same time the double metaleptic condition of life and its endless reproduction in the domain of representation. Indeed, "The History of Lucrece . . . comes to include the history of its textual repetition".[35] So much so that in figuring herself in the act of envisaging a "newer way" of mourning, she is actually drawing and acting her drawing—her mourning—almost as in Escher's lithograph (1948) of a hand iteratively drawing a hand, I suggest. To the extent that, as Genette remarks in his discussion of metalepsis,[36] the very possibility of distinguishing between different levels of diegesis, or else between real and unreal, the original and its endless reproduction, is lost. But this doesn't simply account for the self-reflexivity of the Shakespearean poem. As mentioned in the Introduction, starting from *Titus* and *The Rape*, Shakespeare's Roman characters are often shown as inhabiting the vertigo of an archaeological, hybrid temporality, one that conveys their past, their present, and their future, thus catalyzing a set of issues regarding the complex dynamics of cultural memory in its relation with history and mythmaking. Cassius and Brutus are shown as part of such an already "edited memory"[37] and spectral temporality when they rewrite Caesar's murder into a piece of viable collective memory ("How many ages hence / Shall this our lofty scene be acted over / In states unborn and accents yet unknown?" 3.1.111–13).

Lucrece's disavowing *critique* of the over-talkative Lucrece ("Out, idle words", v. 1016)—an interrogative modern subjectivity that Shakespeare will later catalyze in a character as loquacious and unsatisfied with words as Hamlet—full of contradictions as it may be, is essential and preparatory to her "pause", which she reaches by way of a gradual act of erosion and spoliation. In making his Lucrece look for "means to mourn some newer ways", Shakespeare has to make her enter the arena of art theory. But *ekphrasis* in turn—an aesthetic enterprise—becomes part of a declared project of alternative, if provocative, self-fashioning. She is evoking the Renaissance *paragone* among the arts when she says, "To see sad sights moves more than hear them told" (v. 1324).[38]

But is she simply looking for a medium different from the "stale" verbal one at her disposal? Or is she voicing something more: an authorial concern for the ways in which bodies and feelings were being rediscovered and reinvented by both science and the humanities? If so, this might be perhaps imagined as part of that "graver labour" Shakespeare had "vowed" he would undertake, the year before, in his dedication of *Venus and Adonis* to the Earl of Southampton.[39] Let us recall again that public theatres in London were repeatedly closed and reopened because of the plague from 1592 to 1594—the years of *The Rape*'s conception and writing[40]—and that these prolonged "pauses" may have given time to the playwright not only "to play the poet", but also to put to the test the "staleness" of traditional poetical tropes and look, more engagingly, for coeval "new" modes of understanding the human. The plague itself, the frequent physical sight of diseased and dead bodies in the streets of London, may have played a part in the anatomical shift we observe in Lucrece's lamentation or *meditatio mortis*. These external circumstances may have also been responsible for a certain wavering or fractured effect of Lucrece's mourning in this and other parts of her soliloquy. But as often happens in Shakespeare, the circumstantial can produce the epochal, a culturally significant effect of sense or manner: which in this case we can recognize as already Hamletic.

Lucrece's metatextual quarrel with words emerges as substantial to the soliloquizing young woman taking issue with herself and her own suicidal resolve in the ensuing stanzas.[41] "This helpless smoke of words doth me no right", she insists (v. 1027). Language, her own language, cannot help her. "Since that [her] case [of violated chastity] is past the help of law" (v. 1022), let alone the possibility to "report [her] and [her] cause aright / To the unsatisfied", we might add conjuring up, with a retroactive

suggestiveness, the pregnancy of Hamlet's last words to Horatio (5.2.317–
18). The Lucrece, "in mutiny" with herself, who doesn't know whether it
is better "[t]o live or die" (vv. 1153–54), who "cavils . . . with everything
she sees" and "[h]olds disputation with each thing she views" [v. 1093
and vv. 1101–102], testing and discarding comparisons for her sorrow, is
a subject enveloped in narratives that cannot help, consciously in search
of a posture and/or language which, as a woman, she can feel as her own.

She is a woman who loses her words as much as she inexhaustibly proffers them. "Sometime her grief is dumb and hath no words, / Sometime 'tis

Figure 2.2 Lucas van Leyden, *The Suicide of Lucretia* (ca. 1514), Rijksmuseum,
    Amsterdam

Source: Public domain

mad and too much talk affords" (vv. 1105–106). She is dispersed in what is too much and too little. In a sense she has already undergone a process of spoliation when she encounters her painting. She is already a nude, when she recognizes herself in Hecuba's *écorché*, "nakedness" being the contingent link between poetry and art, word and image: the thing that both literature and the visual arts, let alone science, were historically and theoretically looking for in the European culture of dissection.[42] Interestingly, nakedness is given an almost threatening height and assertiveness in some of Lucrece's Renaissance visual representations: as for instance in Dürer's oil painting (ca. 1518) hosted at the Alte Pinakotek (Münich), or in Lucas van Leyden's engraving (ca. 1514).

Such a search turns into a bodily performance for the early modern subjectivity that Shakespeare represents in the poetical context of *The Rape*.

"By Force of Mourning": Lucrece's *Tabula Anatomica*

Even though announced as the fruit of a "weary time" (1555), Lucrece's ekphrasis of the Troy piece is no "idle" digression. During her long-drawn mourning—in "some newer way"—the body is brought to the fore in a self-possessing if violent *nosce te ipsum*: it is shaped into a proof, theatricalized as a piece of evidence, constructed into a threat. It is explored and displayed as her own in the transaction Shakespeare activates between image and word, the stillness of the painting and the corporeal dynamism of Lucrece's reading action. She rails against the painter for giving Hecuba "so much grief, and not a tongue". She promises to complement the deficiency with her "lamenting tongue". In turn she takes on as her own Hecuba's "look" and that of all the other suffering figures of the painting, the One becoming the supplement of the Other, a composite construction.[43]

> Here feelingly she weeps TROY's painted woes:
> For sorrow, like a heavy-hanging bell,
> Once set on ringing with his own weight goes;
> Then little strength rings out the doleful knell.
> So LUCRECE set a-work, sad tales doth tell
>   To pencill'd pensiveness and colour'd sorrow:
>   *She lends them words, and she their looks doth borrow.*
>   (1492–98; my emphasis)

Indeed, her ekphrasis is not just a grandiose enactment of the conventional Renaissance *paragone* among the arts, an example of *ut pictura poesis*, of the extent to which poetry can compete with the mimetic force of visual arts, or vice versa. In this process of "lending" and "borrowing", as Shakespeare beautifully conceives it, Lucrece's act of reading, more than naively incurring the "error" of confusing art and reality as critics have sometimes argued,[44] wittingly articulates the transaction between the two different spheres of meaning (one pertaining to representation, the other pertaining to the live corporeality of emotions). Indeed, it is her project to do this by means of her own body, thus staging a self-anatomizing experience of the subject, which in our own times we would perceive as living performance art, a signifying practice which, in inter-locking different semiotic systems (image, word, body), aims at going beyond the limits of all—"to the extent that the possible attitudes of the subject in relation to his speech remain open", we might say borrowing from Kristeva's conceptualization of the "transfinite in language".[45] One might refer to our contemporary artist Karl Lakolak to find a rendering of

Étude pour "Lucrèce" - Bordeaux janvier 2011

Figure 2.3 Karl Lakolak, *Study for Lucrece*, Bordeaux
Source: © Karl Lakolak, 2011

what Shakespeare was perhaps hinting at, or looking for, when he made his Lucrece both explore and explode the limits of all forms of language available to her violated, hysterical body. In Lakolak's installation (2011), Lucrece is body, blood, painting, pencil, colour.

Indeed, what Shakespeare's Lucrece is lucidly doing before committing suicide is to transform herself into a complex corporeal text, a living construct of self and otherness. In respect to this the final bloodletting, even though proposed as a vengeful and disciplining gesture, will not disentangle the lethal double bind she embodies, as a testament made flesh, for her husband and community: "How TARQUIN must be us'd, read it in me: / Myself, thy friend, will kill myself, thy foe" (vv. 1195–96).

As such Lucrece's overinscripted and contradictory (female) self—one that remains both friend and foe—imitates and exceeds the knowledge hinted at by the self-exposing anatomized bodies of the new science. Let us remember that the bodies destined to the dissecting table of surgeons in early modern Europe were those of criminals or outcasts. These were

Figure 2.4 Berengario da Carpi, *Isagoge Breves* (1522)
Source: Wellcome Collection (London)

"torn apart, but no longer in an attempt solely, as Foucault describes the drama of public execution, to reconstitute 'a momentarily injured sovereignty'".[46] They also underwent a process of redemption in the ordering/disciplining hands of science. The anatomized body was an uncanny if docile body in the relevant books of anatomy. It was contrived as if participating with the scientist in its own dissection when it was shown, theatrically, in moralized postures or as holding the flaps of its own opened body. In Berengarius's *Isagoge Breves* (1522), the female body was shown as holding the veil of its unveiling: as if it were a curtain/shroud the owner herself was eager to lay open.

Shakespeare's defiled, soliloquizing, and self-examining Lucrece is located within the same self-inspecting theatrical episteme, but is shown—I contend—as engaged with a salvation of her own: which paradoxically she does by working at her own death, that is by literally sculpturing herself—before dying—into an identifying if unsettling monument of death.

How? "By force of mourning". As Derrida has written in an essay with this title,

> whoever thus works *at* the work of mourning learns the impossible—and that mourning is interminable. Inconsolable. Irreconcilable. Right up until death—that is what whoever works at mourning knows, working at mourning as both their object and their resource, working *at mourning* as one would speak of a painter working at painting but also of a machine working at such and such an energy level, the theme of work thus becoming their very force, and their term, a principle.[47]

Shakespeare's Lucrece indulges in mourning as if aware that mourning is her object, her resource, her force, her principle. But she also seems aware, as the philosopher would point out, that she is working at her own failure, that her energy is employed in "a work working at its unproductivity"; and that "[i]n order to succeed, it would well have to *fail*, to fail *well*".[48] In saying this, I differ from Marion A. Wells when she says, "Lucrece's absorption in Hecuba . . . serves epic's 'melancholic' conversion of mourning into political energy".[49] For, Lucrece is constructed in a way that makes her body foreigner to that very project, even though she eventually becomes the instrument and occasion for the final political rebellion of Rome against the Tarquins. By which I mean that the tangle of issues in which she is enmeshed as a violated woman—and Shakespeare is marvellous in making her a cluster of irreducible dilemmas—renders her radically resistant to the male intentionality of the poem. Granted, she wants to be revenged, but what she mostly wants is her mourning, mourning as a form of woeful self-possession. To this serves the archaeological and transhistorical juxtaposition of her face on that of Hecuba (see Introduction, pp. 38–43): to reconstruct a woeful, remembering, and denouncing body. In this light the notion of "unproductivity" offered by Derrida, as the goal in relation to which the mourner spends one's energy, can acquire specific significance in a poem in which the self works at its weaving by way of its unweaving, and in which the unweaving literally means working at death. How can working at one's "failing" be experienced as a way to succeed—an achievement valuable in itself?

As Neill has remarked in his compelling book on the relationship between death and identity in English Renaissance tragedy, death underwent a process of reinvention in early modern culture that "[brought] *terra incognita* into view by imposing a cultural template upon its shapeless 'emptiness'".[50] In that process, mortality was constructed into a discursivity that in important ways cut across the questions of identity and self-knowledge, let alone gender. Think of Cleopatra. Not differently from Cleopatra devising the setting of her own self-inflicted death, Lucrece is shown envisaging and presiding over the scene and form of her suicide, in the presence of the male spectatorship of the kinsmen whom she knows will gather round her in a while. She is shown working at "failing", but at "failing *well*". Wasn't Montaigne writing that "to dye . . . is the greatest work we have to doe"?[51] This takes special time and work in Shakespeare's poem, the time and work of Lucrece's long ekphrasis: the climax of a mourning by means of which her death, "her life's fair end" (v. 1208), as she terms it using Roman vocabulary, is prepared on her own terms as an unsettling if monumentalizing staging of the self.

Drawing on Freud's *fort-da* (*Beyond the Pleasure Principle*, 1920) and his late theory of mourning as an endless labour (mainly worked out in his Great War writings and beyond),[52] we can say that Lucrece's ekphrasis is the moment in which the materials of trauma—fantasized as a post-war destroyed citadel through the fall of Troy—are best intelligible to consciousness at the moment in which the loss, displaced and re-enacted by a fictive compensatory representation ("Here feelingly she weeps Troy's painted woes", v. 1492), is assimilated into the identification process. In fact, the Troy piece's ekphrasis is meant to be Lucrece's "means to mourn some newer way", the final jubilatory act of a repetitive elaborating gesture in Shakespeare's poem, one in which art hermeneutics and the critical agency of the I are on a par with the passions of the body (melancholy, shame, rage, groaning) and the hysterical experience of the presence/absence of meaning: "Sometime her grief is dumb and hath no words, / Sometime 'tis mad and too much talk affords" (vv. 1105–106). Subjectivity for Lucrece is produced in that tragic interval spanning the double loss inflicted by rape and death, and in the split and contradictory terms available to her.

Lacanian feminist theory would provide a word, *jouissance*, to cover this heterogeneous—bodily/mental/critical/aesthetic—experience of the subject, characterized by an irruption of the semiotic in the symbolic. Kristeva, perhaps, would say that Lucrece has "jouissance as [her] goal",[53] while she heads towards her expected Roman end. Her hair is "dishevelled", so as to be likened to a "grove" in which the Ovidian ravished Philomela, metamorphosed into a bird, can be given hospitality (vv. 1128–30). Her hair is indeed like that of Philomela herself after her rape, as we find it depicted in Ovid's *Metamorphoses*. But it is also, typically, like the hair of the community of women participating in the orgiastic festivals of Dionysus or Bacchus; rites during which Philomela and her sister Procne's vengeance took form.[54] There is something of the hysterical body of a Maenad in Lucrece's hair as well as in the way her eyes, and (supposedly) her body with them, run from one point to another of the painting, reading and voicing the woe of its figures, sharing their cry, cursing on their behalf with a "lamenting tongue": a supplement that conjures up Philomela's amputated tongue, which Ovid makes us see as a still animated, severed anatomical part, after Tereus has cut it—"quivering on the ground . . . as an adder's tail cut off doth skip a while" (VI, 711–13).

This makes us feel that the figure of Philomela, overtly quoted as simply the analogue of Lucrece's violated and self-victimizing person in the poem, is more pervasive and assertive than one would think,[55] emerging as it does, unmentioned, with the rebellious side of her traumatized body in Lucrece's mournful if enraged and jubilatory performance of her ekphrasis. As if in a deferred and displaced enactment of the disruptive potentialities connected to the Ovidian female character conjured up earlier in the poem, Lucrece's grief becomes, indeed, that of the vengeful Maenad. The same might apply to the active and vengeful side of Hecuba's story that similarly could have been read by Shakespeare in Ovid's *Metamorphoses* (Book III) and that seems almost to have been censored in his imaginary Troy piece. Tracts of the Ovidian Hecuba transformed by woe into a threatening barking dog, however, may be perceived in Lucrece's strength and grain of voice. Like Hecuba, whose "anger gave her heart and made her strong and stout", Lucrece engages in a muscular confrontation with the figures of her painting. Like her who, in Ovid's story, "Did in the traitor's face [Polymnestor's] bestow her nails and scratched out / His eyes",[56] Lucrece promises to "scratch out the angry eyes / Of all the Greeks" with her knife (vv. 1469–70), which she will soon do with her nails when she meets with the "mild image" of "perjur'd Sinon" (vv. 1520–21): "Here all enraged, such passion her assails, / That patience is quite beaten from her breast. / She tears the senseless SINON with her nails" (vv. 1562–64). Like Ovid's Hecuba, "enflamed with wrath", she rails, shrieks, shouts, curses, weeps, her shouts and her cry becoming pure sound, an enveloping, propagating roar, the funerary "tuning" element of her ekphrasis (see v. 1465).

In Lucrece's ekphrasis "the transfer of affect" (Enterline)[57] is not just a transaction between Lucrece and Hecuba's painted ruin. It co-opts, "feelingly", a chain of classical, suffering female bodies, on the model of the Trojan women in Euripides's *Hecuba*, and almost as Margaret does in the coeval *Richard III* (see Introduction, Part 2) by sharing the semantics of "curse" with other women of the play, if not (proleptically) with other marginalized subjects like Caliban. ELIZABETH: "O thou, well skill'd in curses, stay awhile / And teach me how to curse mine enemies"; "My words are dull: O quicken them with thine". / MARGARET: Thy woes will make them sharp and pierce like mine" (*Richard III*, 4.4.110–119).

During Lucrece's long reading of her Troy piece, as we see, Shakespeare translates into performance what is repressed or cannot be fully expressed by either the "piece of skilfull painting" or the poet's own language. Performance is the labour she needs to translate grief into knowledge. But what is more, she wants to be shaped by that reading, up to the point that her very body will be impressed by the knowledge she gains: her difficult legacy, for others to decipher. We discern the method and the creative skill of the artist who is also an anatomist in the way Lucrece's tears are deliberately and literally used by her as a scalpel to chisel and shape, on the anatomic model offered by Hecuba, her agonizing self. Held in check and concealed as a marker of shame, soon after the rape

> For they their guilt with weeping will unfold,
> And grave, like water that doth eat in steel,
> Upon my cheeks what helpless shame I feel;
> (754–56)

tears become wittingly the marker of a difference, during the encounter with the painting: the instrument or matter—the acid-like substance mentioned in the aforementioned verse 755—of an excavating labour. The "looks" she "borrows" from the painting are what her weeping "engraves" on her face: "She throws her eyes about the painting around, / And who she finds forlorn she doth lament" (vv. 1499–500). The face she obtains in the course of such an extreme form of transaction is "that map which deep impression bears / Of hard misfortune, carved in it with tears" (vv. 1712–13): a disquieting *tabula anatomica*, a live "anatomy of ruin", an unsettling, if self-authorizing map/image.

"Tear" (as a singular or plural noun) is a recurrent lemma in Shakespeare's poem. It is too persistently evoked to be an "idle" word or the obvious representative of an emotional state connected with the tropes of fall and lamentation. Reading attentively, we perceive that this is a word that matters. It is the matter with which Lucrece makes her body signify in her own bemusing terms. Interestingly, it occurs as both a noun (more than 20 times) and a verb (ca. 6 times) referred to a lacerating or self-lacerating action ("to tear"). As a verb and especially in its meaning of "being torn between contrasting feelings", it resonates in Lucrece's protracted, self-dissecting *nosce te ipsum*. In conjunction, noun and verb articulate a broader field of meanings connected with knowledge and self-knowledge. "To tear"—in its meaning of "tearing something", "bringing into light", "flaying", or "removing something forcefully"—is more than once materially performed by Lucrece with her nails: first as a form of self-punishment ("She, desperate, with her nails her flesh doth tear", 739), then as a defacing and unveiling gesture against the delusions of art and representation. For what Lucrece also learns during her ekphrasis is that art can reveal as well as falsify reality. Accordingly, art itself is the target of her destructive rage when Shakespeare has her scratch the well-painted image of false Sinon's tearful woe ("This picture she advisedly perus'd, / And chid the painter for his wondrous skill, / . . . / Here, all enraged, such passion her assail, / That patience is quite beaten from her breast. / She tears senseless SINON with her nails", vv. 1527–64). "To tear" is the verb that connotes Collatine's accusatory articulation of Tarquin's name after Lucrece's death, as if he wanted to tatter it into light: "Yet sometime 'TARQUIN' was pronounced plain, / But through his teeth, as if the name he tore", vv. 1786–87). Most importantly, "to tear" is the verb used by Lucretius, when as a father, he is forced to confront the last and cruellest disclosure: the end of a reassuring mimetic form of self-knowledge provided by one's progeny:

> 'Daughter, dear daughter', old LUCRETIUS cries,
> 'That life was mine which thou hast here deprived.
> If in the child the father's image lies,
> Where shall I live now LUCRECE is unlived?
> Thou wast not to this end from me derived.
>   If children predecease progenitors,
>   We are their offspring, and thy none of ours.
>
> Poor *broken glass*, I often did behold
> In thy sweet *semblance* my old age new born;
> But now that fair *fresh mirror*, dim and old,
> *Shows me a bare-boned death* by time outworn.
> *O, from thy cheeks my image thou hast torn,*
>   And shivered all the beauty of my glass,
>   That I no more can see what once I was'.
>   (1751–64; my emphasis)

Hecuba's "no semblance" (v. 1453) has been laboriously worked and transferred into Lucrece's marred "semblance" (vv. 1758–59): an appalling skeletal image, which her father suffers as a loss of specularity.[58] Lucrece has broken the smooth surface of her father's glass. She has turned on him a "dim" mirror, or a "Mirrour which Flatters not", as those which Shakespeare's readers could observe in familiar representations of *King Death* or also in the frequent figuration of the anatomist as one looking at himself in a mirror from which he mediates the knowledge of his interiority as an *écorché* or skull.[59] But there is more. "By force of tears", Lucrece has "torn"—she has flayed—the skin of re-"semblance" out of her face, and now the shocking Hecuba-like nakedness of that face—the only "semblance" she can deem her own—rewards her kinsmen's claim of possession with a knowledge which is utterly dispossessing. She has shattered the glass of an untroubled *mimesis*, thus dismantling the proprietary chain of a fatherly controlled myth of identity and sameness: "O, from thy cheeks my image thou hast torn" (v. 1762).

The sight of Lucrece splitting open her own heart with a knife is petrifying for the onlookers. They are "stone-still" (v. 1730), as the blood spurting out of her breast circles her body by separating into two rivers: "Some of her blood still pure and red remained, / And some looked black, and that false TARQUIN stained" (vv. 1742–43). Meaningfully, at this moment a man—Lucius Iunius Brutus—so far non-existent in the poem, takes control of her dying body and mostly of her knife which, "followed" by the furious spurt of blood it has provoked, he draws from her wound: "And from the purple fountain BRUTUS drew / The murd'rous knife, and as it left the place, / Her blood in revenge held it in chase; / And bubbling from her breast, it doth divide / In two slow rivers", vv. 1734–38). Not inadvertently for Shakespeare the playwright, I think, here we are provided with a scene of strong if pertinent visual ambiguity. With that knife "chased" by blood in his hand, Brutus appears for a moment as if completing Lucrece's murdering gesture. He also appears as if in the act of presiding over Lucrece's bloodletting and its canalization into a visible and disciplining dualism: one in which physiology is split into a clear-cut opposition of colours and moral connotations. Lucrece's conflictual interiority is thus externalized and resolved into a shared, medicalized, and healing spectacle: pure red *versus* stained black.

Looked at in this way, the scene conjures up the blood that in the myth is provided by the two veins of the beheaded Medusa—curative and restorative of life if coming from the right vein, unwholesome and lethal if coming from the left one: the blood which in two separate phials Athena hands over to Aesculapius and, through him, to the discriminative regime of control of medical science.[60] Lucrece may well have killed herself on her own, but like the female body of Medusa, she stands for a body to be killed, in order to be eventually re-signified as partitioned and instructive body parts.

Pervasively, and overtly in the epilogue of Shakespeare's poem, Lucrece's body functions as the personification of *Anatomia* itself, a self-flaying and flaying deity whose symbols in early modern culture were the mirror and the knife, an iconography derived from the myth of Perseus and Medusa. In one most learned allegorical reading of this myth in Shakespeare's time, the "Gorgonicall" stands (etymologically) for "earthlinesse", and the killing of Medusa, for which Perseus "atchieued, to have flown to heauen", stands for the "vanquishing" and "ouercomming" of "all bodily substance signified by *Gorgon*".[61] But Medusa's petrifying glare, as Freud and others remind us, also "stands for fear of interiority; more often than not, a specifically male fear of the female interior".[62] The spectacle of

Lucrece's interiority, disclosed by her "mournful and congealed face" (v. 1744) and her blood, renews that fear in Shakespeare's poem, the very moment she literally acquires the inert condition of a corpse.

Lucrece's Anatomy Theatre

As critics have increasingly argued in recent scholarship, physiology and psychology, body and psyche, matter and spirit, were still inextricably— or relatively—linked in the vocabulary of early modern culture. In an age in which no assertive philosophical conceptualization of the self as a separate entity—or psychologized science of interiority—was yet available, the new language of anatomy (often in anachronistic conjunction with the ancient humoral vision of the body) provided the discursive resources for imagining the body's "nakedness", or else the layered space of inwardness.[63] The scopic economy of the anatomy theatre, I would like to underline, with its double dynamic of concealment and exposure, was very much part of this Renaissance enactment of the old Delphic injunction *nosce teipsum*: the proclaimed philosophical imperative of the new anatomy and an inscription which stood out in anatomy theatres all over Europe. This is particularly true of Shakespeare's most scopic poem,[64] where the dramatization of an inspected and self-inspecting subjectivity, one in which the gaze itself becomes the object of representation and self-representation, is complicated by the question of gender and the related cogent issue of possession and self-possession.

What I find particularly suggestive is the fact that before addressing this issue of the body's "nakedness", namely of the body torn of its skin, with some of his more famous anatomized or self-anatomizing characters (Julius Caesar, Hamlet), as precisely the thing that problematizes and defines modernity, Shakespeare should first of all place a woman at the centre of his dissecting table: precisely as Vesalius had chosen to do on the frontispiece of his *De Humani Corporis Fabrica* (1543). Was Shakespeare, like him, impelled to explore at their point of contact the very principles of life and death? As Sawday has written in his beautiful comment on the bisected circular architecture and crowded scenario of Vesalius's frontispiece, "the anatomical universe revolves around the conjunction of the womb and the tomb":

> The opened centre of the female corpse, the womb, lies at the centre of this imagined circle. . . . With his right hand, [he] peels open the body to reveal the womb. The corpse, passive beneath her dissector's hand, gazes directly at [him] . . . What is depicted is no less than a demonstration—the principle of life concealed within the womb— Vesalius is about to open to our gaze. . . . But, ironically, rising pictorially out of the womb appears the skeleton. If the womb marks our point of entrance into the world, then Vesalius' own left hand, with

its finger raised in a gesture of signification as well as rhetoric, guides our attention back to the skeleton, our point of departure: "Nascentes Morimur"—we are born to die.

A drama of life and death is, then, being played out within the circular confines of the temple of anatomy which has been bisected for our instruction.[65]

Lucrece's feminine story of desire, rape, and death, which Shakespeare pins down as an "anatomy of ruin", matches the universalizing moral implication of the anatomy lesson epitomized in Vesalius's frontispiece. But knowledge of the female body in early modern culture, whether for sex or knowledge as such, was rhetorically grounded in what Sawday, in relation to Donne's appropriative language of praise and notorious "roaving hands" of Elegie XIX, has called a regime of "discovery" and "ownership". "It is with just such a proprietal gesture", he adds, "that Vesalius, on the great title-page of the *Fabrica*, had himself pictured placing his right hand on the dissected female body, in a gesture of ownership".[66]

This makes us notice that hands take centre stage in Shakespeare's poem. What is more, they are part of a dynamic of contentious "proprietal gestures". There is a clanking sense of power in the way the eroticized hand of Tarquin—first mentioned in the hospital context of his arrival at Lucrece's house (vv. 253–61)—replaces the eye in the nightly predatory conquest of Lucrece's body, with an insistence that makes it martially rhyme with "stand" and "land": "His hand, as proud of such a dignity / Smoking with pride, marched on to make his stand / On her bare breast, the heart of all her land" (vv. 455–41 and 463). There is a defiant assertion of identity in the way Lucrece's split person shapes and defend her "life's fair end"—her "failing well"—by persistently intimating to her own hand that it should perform the task of restoring her to herself: "Faint not, faint heart, but stoutly say 'So be it'; / Yield to my hand, my hand shall conquer thee: Thou dead, both die, and both shall victors be" (1209–11; but see also 1208 and 1722).

Reading attentively, we can observe that Lucrece's whole voyage beyond "superficiality" is such as to crosscut a palimpsest of competing cultural paradigms and a tangle of "proprietal gestures", a pervasive struggle for possession that characterizes the entire poem. This involves not only Tarquin's prying eyes and hands, but also the gaze of the new anatomical science, whether it is contrived as the gaze of the painter of the Troy piece, who seems to be also a natural scientist, or refers us more broadly to that of the author/poet himself, and which an argumentative Lucrece seems to both ratify and resist.

The relation between the inspecting gaze of the male Renaissance art of anatomy and the ways in which the female body was constructed as an object of knowledge is too vast to be examined here. But one cannot avoid underlining the fact, as Richard Sugg helps us to say, that knowledge of the female body was potentially pornographic, even though held in check by cultural constraints, or by "a much more complicated impulse" as Patricia Parker argues: "a desire both to see and not to see".[67] "Interestingly, that ambivalence neatly matches the dualistic psychology of anatomical proof", Sugg remarks, "The sudden plunge within, seeking a viscerally rooted confirmation of feeling or faith, is implicitly countered by a fear that looking to hard, one may fail to locate what is sought".[68]

These issues and the relevance they can have to my view in relation to Shakespeare's poem may be incisively evoked by means of one of the woodcuts which illustrated Estienne's book of anatomy, *De dissectione partium corporis humani* (1545), which followed by only two years Vesalius's *De humani corporis fabrica*. Significantly, in this table of anatomy the female reproductive organ is displayed by means of a metaphorical biblical referent—the story of Bathsheba spied upon by David—which, together with the square window cut open on the female womb interior, fantasizes the anatomical knowledge of the female body as a prying male gesture. As we are reminded by critics, this woodcut was one of "seven well-drawn nudes set before Renaissance architecture . . . all distinguished by the parted thighs obliged by gynecology and pornography". Revealingly, they had originally appeared as sex illustrations in Jacopo Caraglio's *Loves of the Gods*. "In the new series a literary pretext transforms pornography into genteel Humanist erotica, before a medical disembowelling cancels sexual allure".[69] Other tables featured Venus, Proserpina, and other goddesses. That of Venus in Estienne's book of anatomy (Figure 2.5) presents us with a framing of the female body which is interestingly similar to Titian's later figuration of Lucrece in the moment of being raped by Tarquin (v. 1571): an instance of the complex interaction between art, anatomy, and sex in early modern culture; but also an instance of how, in the realm of *anatomia*, knowledge of the female body was gained by conflating the new Renaissance scientific regime of observation with mythologized, if stereotyped, male-oriented focalizations of female corporeality.

The story of Lucrece was a topic that allowed for this ambiguous mixture of profanation, pleasure, and knowledge, yielding and resistance; a mixture which somehow bifurcated in the two opposed ways of representing that story in Renaissance visual arts, either as a male, violent entering into the space of secrecy and mystery (see Titian's theatrical rendering of this), or as a (sometimes) heroic female gesture of reappropriation of one's own destiny (see Dürer and Lucas of Leyden's statuesque rendering of Lucrece's suicide).[70] Shakespeare catalyzes all of these cultural intentions or drives in his poem, while situating his heroine at the centre of his anatomy theatre and making her claim an anatomy of her own.

Lucrece's self-killing may well be viewed as a patriarchally encoded gesture of self-cleansing. In fact, she thus regains the name of "chaste" in the consideration of her community—the name that initially exposed her to rape. "Chaste" is a word insistently pronounced by Brutus as he takes

Figure 2.5 Charles Estienne, *De dissection partium corporis humani* (1545)
Source: Wellcome Collection (London)

control, in manly fashion, not only of her body (from now on destined to become an exhibited relic, like Caesar's mangled body in Antony's funerary oration), but also of the masculine knife with which Lucrece has killed herself. That knife is now brandished by Brutus—he "who plucked the knife from LUCRECE's side" (1807), the poet repeats—to excite rebellion against the corrupted Tarquins. Awakened by Brutus to the values of *Romanitas*, Lucrece's citizens can now appropriate her corpse as a foundational cleansing body for the nascent Republic: it is upon these ruins that their new pact as a community is sealed. But this was a well-known inherited story, that Ovid in his *Fasti* (Book II, 685–856) had narrated in no more than 171 verses, and that Shakespeare (or somebody else) summarized in the one-page (or little more) opening "Argument".[71] What seem to matter, instead, in Shakespeare's long poem are the ways in which the Roman "argument" is used to serve another story: a story regarding an early modern battle for the reconceptualization or reappropriation of bodies. It is with a similar early modern concern that Shakespeare addresses the figure of Caesar just few years later. Yet in his puzzling dedication to the Earl of Southampton to whom he swore "love . . . without end", he presented the 1855 "untutored lines" of his endless poem as a "pamphlet without beginning", "a superfluous moiety". Concealed behind the virtuosity of a flattering tribute to his "lordship", the author was perhaps alerting his reader to a matter that, raising from an ex-centric temporality and "untutored" intentionality, had grown into an exorbitant if enthralling middle or half, an interim: the long "weary time" of the interval between rape and death, during which a woman, aware that History and textuality have already wrought the expected end, "set[s] a-work" (1496) at "failing well".

Notes

1. Quotations from the poem refer to the Arden edition of *Shakespeare's Poems*, eds. Katherine Duncan-Jones and H.R. Woudhuysen (London: Thomson Learning, 2007). I have also consulted the Cambridge edition of Shakespeare, *The Poems* (Cambridge: Cambridge University Press, 2006) ed. John Roe, and the Italian bilingual edition of *Lucrece* in *Poemetti*, ed. and transl. Gilberto Sacerdoti (Milano: Garzanti, 2000).
2. Livy, *The Rise of Rome: Book One to Five* (III. 44–48), transl. T.J. Luce (Oxford: Oxford University Press, 1998), pp. 185–190. Livy's work was translated into English in 1600 (*The Romane Historie Written by T. Livius of Padua*. Transl, by Philemon Holland. London: Adam Islip, 1600).
3. The legal, religious, and moral problems raised by suicide in Shakespeare's times are interestingly discussed in Michael McDonald, "Ophelia's Maimèd Rites", *Shakespeare Quarterly*, 37:3 (1986), 309–317.
4. Lucrece's suicide has been the object of much debate. For a broader discussion of the ways in which Lucrece problematizes her suicide, see Katharine Eisaman Maus, "Taking Tropes Seriously: Language and Violence in Shakespeare's *Rape of Lucrece*", *Shakespeare Quarterly*, 37:1 (1986), 66–82 (pp. 67–70). As this critic has rightly argued, Lucrece "makes her decision for suicide without consulting the men whom she supposes to be her owners", or better she refuses to accept their Augustine-like reasoning about her innocence. Thus, for Maus, "[f]ar from being the culturally acceptable thing to do in a patriarchal society, Lucrece's suicide shocks the Roman men; its supererogatory character is precisely what makes it seem both heroic and troubling, sublime and confused, to its witnesses and to the reader" (p. 69). In Maus's view, the problematization of one's actions is a feature of the poem and belongs alike to the other major character, Tarquin. See also on this Ian Donaldson, *The Rapes of Lucretia: A Myth and Its Transformations* (Oxford: Clarendon Press, [1982] 2001), pp. 40–49. For a different view, see Catherine Belsey, "Tarquin Dispossessed: Expropriation and Consent in *The Rape of*

Lucrece", *Shakespeare Quarterly*, 52:3 (2001), 315–335 (p. 330). For her, Lucrece's suicide is coherent with the perception she has of "her own place in the symbolic and cultural order", within which she is constructed as a "loyal wife". See also in the same line Kahn, *Roman Shakespeare*, pp. 27–45.

5. Nancy Vickers, "'The Blazon of Sweet Beauty's Best': Shakespeare's *Lucrece"*, in Patricia Parker and Geoffrey Hartman, eds, *Shakespeare and the Question of Theory* (New York and London: Routledge, 1991), pp. 108 and 96.

6. Vickers, "'The Blazon of Sweet Beauty's Best'", p. 96. But see also Patricia Parker, *Literary Fat Ladies: Rhetoric, Gender, Property* (London and New York: Methuen, 1987), especially the chapters "Rhetorics of Property: Exploration, Inventory, Blazon" and "Transfigurations: Shakespeare and Rhetoric". See also (with a different Lacanian-Derridean approach) Joel Fineman, "Shakespeare's *Will*: The Temporality of Rape", *Representations*, 20 (1987), 25–40.

7. Jonathan Bate is among those who have questioned such a view of Lucrece as simply a victim or a mediator of patriarchal language (*Shakespeare and Ovid*, pp. 78–79) by emphasizing instead the space she is given, alone of all other of Shakespeare's female characters, in establishing a sisterhood with other women.

8. Kahn, *Roman Shakespeare*, p. 38.

9. Lynn Enterline, *The Rhetoric of the Body From Ovid to Shakespeare* (Cambridge: Cambridge University Press, 2000), pp. 158–159.

10. See Sawday, *The Body Emblazoned*, p. IX.

11. This was very much fostered by the new science of anatomy. See for all Helkiah Crooke's early modern compendium of anatomy, *Microcosmographia: A Description of the Body of Man* (London: William Jaggard, 1615), and Gail Kern Paster, *The Body Embarrassed: Drama and the Discipline of Shame in Early Modern England* (Ithaca: Cornell University Press, 1993). In relation to this issue, it can be relevant to look at the debate raised by Thomas Laqueur's claim about a supposed still prevailing "one-sex model" in early modern medical science (*Making Sex: Body and Gender From the Greek to Freud* (Cambridge, MA: Harvard University Press, [1990] 1992). See on this Michael Stolberg's contention ("A Woman Down to Her Bones. The Anatomy of Sexual Difference in the Sixteenth and Early Seventeenth Centuries", *Isis*, 94:2 (2003), 274–299).

12. Euripides, *Hecuba*, transl. Edward P. Coleridge (London: G. Bell and Sons, 1910), The Internet Classical Archive, http://classics.mit.edu/Euripides/hecuba.html.

13. I owe this inspiring quotation to Ivan Lupic, the author of the already mentioned wide-ranging essay on Hecuba's circulation in the culture of early modern Europe, "The Mobile Queen", p. 47. I am grateful to him for letting me have a copy of his essay.

14. Giovanni Lomazzo, *A Tracte Containing the Artes of Curious Painting, Carvinge, and Buildinge* [1584], abridged transl. Richard Haydocke, 1598 (Facsimile) (Amsterdam and New York: Capo Press, 1969), pp. 16–17.

15. Lomazzo, *A Tracte*, p. 18.

16. As recorded by Vasari all along his *Lives*, preparatory cartoons supplemented the picture with a conspicuous amount of knowledge, and were treasured and circulated by artists and kingly patrons as valuable goods in the European Renaissance cultural ambience.

17. See Roberto Paolo Ciardi, "Il corpo, progetto e rappresentazione", in Roberto Paolo Ciardi and Lucia Tongiorgi Tomasi, eds, *Immagini anatomiche e naturalistiche nei disegni degli Uffizi, Secc. XVI e XVII*, (Firenze: Olschki, 1984), p. 12.

18. Vasari, "Preface to the Lives", in Vasari, *Lives*, vol. 1, p. 1. But see also his "Preface" to Part III, in vol. 2, pp. 151–155.
19. See Ciardi, "Il corpo, progetto e rappresentazione" (pp. 9–15), but also Sawday, *The Body Emblazoned* (p. 85 *et passim*).
20. Ovid, *Fasti*, transl. Betty Rose Nagle (Bloomington and Indianapolis: Indiana University Press, 1995), pp. 75–80.
21. The same is true for other possible sources. The story of Lucrece had often been told by medieval English authors. Among these Gower, in *Confessio Amantis*, and Chaucer (see his "Legend of Lucrece of Rome", in *The Poetical Works of Geoffrey Chaucer*, 10 vols (London: William Pickering, 1845), vol. V, vv. 1680–885.
22. See on this Marion A. Wells, "'To Find a Face Where All Distress Is Stell'd': Enargeia, Ekphrasis, and Mourning in *The Rape of Lucrece* and the *Aeneid*", *Comparative Literature*, 54:2 (2002), 175–198.
23. See earlier discussion on Michelangelo's new volumetric bodies (pp. 140–143).
24. The trope of flayed bodies is anticipated at vv. 1167–69 when Lucrece comments on her post-rape split between body and soul, comparing it to a flayed pine: "Ay me! The bark pilled from the lofty pine, / His leaves will wither and his sap decay; / So must my soul, her bark being pilled away".
25. Sawday, *The Body Emblazoned*, p. 202.
26. E.H. Gombrich, *Art and Illusion: A Study in the Psychology of Pictorial Representation* (London: Phaidon, 1962), pp. 176–177.
27. Miola, *Shakespeare's Rome*, p. 31.
28. See Richard Meek, *Narrating the Visual in Shakespeare* (Farnham and Burlington: Ashgate, 2009), pp. 72 and 55–79. But see also S. Clark Hulse, *Metamorphic Verse: The Elizabethan Minor Epic* (Princeton: Princeton University Press, 1981), pp. 175–194; Judith Dundas, "Mocking the Mind: The Role of Art in Shakespeare's *Rape of Lucrece*", *The Sixteenth Century Journal*, 14:1 (1983), 13–22; and Catherine Belsey, "Invocation of the Visual Image: Ekphrasis in *Lucrece* and Beyond", *Shakespeare Quarterly*, 63:2 (2012), 175–198.
29. For future and further speculations, let me remind the reader incidentally that the fall of Troy was a familiar topic in Renaissance visual art, and that Giulio Romano, the only artist to be mentioned in Shakespeare's works, had an entire room of the Mantuan Palazzo Te painted with "the history of the Trojan War", as Vasari made known in Renaissance Europe (*Lives*, vol. 3, p. 106). As such, even when considering as pointless the vexed question of a direct visual source for *The Rape*'s ekphrasis, Giulio Romano cannot be conjured up, as happens in Hulse's *Metamorphic Verse*, just to be too readily dropped as the uninfluential "waxworker of the *Winter's Tale* (See Hulse, *Metamorphic Verse*, p. 181). Hulse however draws consequences from entering such a "pointless" argument when "he vote[s] for a tapestry"—thus nourishing himself, on the basis of pure conjectures, the even more pointless doubt on whether Lucrece is looking at a painting or a tapestry.
30. Hulse, *Metamorphic Verse*, p. 192; see also Dundas, "Mocking the Mind", pp. 13–22.
31. Wells, "To Find a Face Where All Distress Is Stell'd", p. 99.
32. Enterline, *Shakespeare's Schoolroom*, pp. 92–94 and 127.
33. See John Kerrigan, *Motives of Woe: Shakespeare and 'Female Complaint': A Critical Anthology* (Oxford: Clarendon Press, 1991).
34. For a brief overview of criticism and revaluation of the poem see for all Maus, "Taking Tropes Seriously", p. 66. For a reconsideration of Shakespeare's "complaint poem", see Laura Bromley, "Lucrece's Re-Creation", *Shakespeare Quarterly*, 34:2 (1983), 200–211 (p. 201 *et passim*).

35. Jonathan Crowe, *Trials of Authorship: Anterior Forms and Poetic Reconstruction From Wyatt to Shakespeare* (Los Angeles and Oxford: University of California Press, 1990), p. 141.

36. Gérard Genette, *Figure III: discorso del racconto*, transl. Lina Zecchi (Torino: Einaudi, 1976), pp. 283–284.

37. Marjorie Garber, *Shakespeare's Ghost Writers: Literature as Uncanny Causality* (New York and London: Methuen, 1987), p. 53.

38. For a reappraisal of the Renaissance dialogue among the arts, see Michele Marrapodi, ed., *Shakespeare and the Visual Arts: The Italian Influence* (New York and London: Routledge, 2017). But see also Keir Elam, *Shakespeare's Pictures: Visual Objects in the Drama* (London: Bloomsbury, 2019), and Camilla Caporicci and Armelle Sabatier, eds, *The Art of Picture in Early Modern English Literature* (New York and London: Routledge, 2020).

39. "Right Honourable . . . only if your honour seem but pleased, I account myself highly praised, and vow to take advantage of all idle hours, till I have honoured you with some graver labour." *Venus and Adonis*, in Shakespeare, *Poems*, p. 128.

40. See Katherine Duncan Jones and H.R. Woudhuysen, "Introduction", in Shakespeare, *Poems*, pp. 13–15.

41. A link between *Lucrece* and *Hamlet* was soon seen in Shakespeare's time by Gabriel Harvey when he signalled them as both meant to "please the wiser sort", but has yet to be fully explored. Michael Platt, who mentioned Harvey at the opening of his "*The Rape of Lucrece* and the Republic for Which It Stands", *The Centennial Review*, 19:2 (1975), 59–79 (p. 59), gives ample reason for re-evaluating *Lucrece* as the result of the "graver labour" Shakespeare promised the Earl of Southampton in his dedication to *Venus and Adonis*, but does not propose by any means an approach aiming at exploring the affinity between the two characters.

42. I here share Leonard Barkan's argument when, after remarking on the typical Renaissance interconnection between literature and visual arts, he says, "[T]he fundamental job is to understand in theoretical terms the actual point of contact between the word and the image. . . . Once we have left behind the making of casual analogies as more opportunistic than revelatory, we are left with a small number of possible undertakings; in fact the usual suspects: theory and history." "Making Pictures Speak: Renaissance Art, Elizabethan Literature, Modern Scholarship", *Renaissance Quarterly*, 48:2 (1995), 326–351 (p. 329).

43. In rhetorical terms this is understood as *prosopopeia*, in Paul De Man's definition: "an apostrophe to an absent, deceased, or voiceless entity, which posits the possibility of the latter's reply and confers upon it the power of speech. Voice assumes mouth, eye, and finally face, a chain that is manifest in the etymology of the trope's name, *prosopon poien*, to confer a mask or a face (*prosopon*)". The definition is quoted in Barkan's *Unearthing the Past* (pp. xxiv–xxv), who suggests a consideration of *prosopopeia* as a master rhetorical figure in the Renaissance process of poetical reinvention of emerging stony figures and "historical—and transhistorical—dialogue": "the very basis of recuperating ancient sculpture that represented the human form was to endow the object with a voice. . . . Renaissance viewers responded not only by describing the works in their own voices but also by giving the objects voices of their own".

44. See Meek, *Narrating the Visual in Shakespeare*, pp. 78–79.

45. Julia Kristeva, "The Novel as Polilogue" (1977), in Julia Kristeva, *Desire in Language: A Semiotic Approach to Literature and Art*, transl. Leon S. Roudiez et al. (Oxford: Blackwell, 1989), p. 173.

46. Sawday, *The Body Emblazoned*, p. 55 and Michel Foucault, *Discipline and Punish: The Birth of the Prison*, transl. A.M. Sheridan Smith (Harmondsworth: Penguin Books, 1977), p. 48. On "flap anatomy" and the dramatic/didactic side of the anatomy show, see also Neill, *Issues of Death*, pp. 102–140. For a reformist moralizing attitude of anatomy, see Andrew Cunningham, *The Anatomical Renaissance: The Resurrection of the Anatomical Projects of the Ancients* (Aldershot: Scholar Press, 1997) (especially pp. 191–279).

47. Jacques Derrida, "By Force of Mourning", *Critical Inquiry*, 22:2 (1996), 171–192 (pp. 172–173).

48. Derrida, "By Force of Mourning", pp. 173–174.

49. Wells, "To Find a Face Where All Distress Is Stell'd", p. 118.

50. Neill, *Issues of Death*, p. 2.

51. Michel de Montaigne, *Essays*, Three Books, transl. John Florio (1553–1625), Book II.6, "Of Exercise or Practice". But see also II.13, "Of Judging of Others' Death" (University of Oregon, Renascence Editions online, 1999). https://scholarsbank.uoregon.edu/xmlui/bitstream/handle/1794/766/montaigne.pdf.

52. See Sigmund Freud, *Considerazioni attuali sulla guerra e la morte* (1915) and *Lutto e malinconia* (1917), in *Opere*, vol. 8 (Torino: Bollati Boringhieri, 1989). On Freud's revision of his mourning theory after *Mourning and Melancholia*, see Tammy Clewell, "Mourning Beyond Melancholia: Freud's Psychoanalysis of Loss", *Journal of the American Psychoanalytic Association*, 52:1 (2004), 197–223.

53. Kristeva, "The Novel as Polilogue", p. 172.

54. See Golding's *Metamorphoses*, Book VI, vv. 674 *et passim*.

55. For more on this see Jane O. Newman's insightful essay, "'And Let Mild Women to Him Lose Their Mildness': Philomela, Female Violence, and Shakespeare's *The Rape of Lucrece*", *Shakespeare Quarterly*, 45:3 (1994), 304–326. But I differ from her when she argues that in Shakespeare's text Philomela's violence is present as a "truncated story", an altogether repressed element (pp. 311 and 316–17, see also p. 325, n. 60).

56. Golding, *Metamorphoses*, Book XIII, vv. 669–677.

57. Enterline, *Shakespeare's Schoolroom*, p. 93.

58. As Joel Fineman has observed, for her father, Lucrece's "'broken glass' reflects the breaking, or the having-been-broken, of his specular identity". "Shakespeare's *Will*", p. 65.

59. See Ciardi, "Il corpo, progetto e rappresentazione", pp. 27–29.

60. See Robert Graves, *The Greek Myths* (London: Penguin Books, [1955] 1960), Vol. I.

61. John Harrington, "Preface to the Translation of *Orlando Furioso*, 1591", in G. Gregory Smith, ed., *Elizabethan Critical Essays*, 2 vols (London: Oxford University Press, 1950), vol. II, pp. 202–203.

62. Sawday, *The Body Emblazoned*, p. 3 *et passim*.

63. See Neill, *Issues of Death*, p. 140. But see also Schoenfeldt, *Bodies and Selves*, pp. 1–15. For a more recent reassessment of these issues, see David Hillman, *Shakespeare's Entrails: Belief, Scepticism and the Interior of the Body* (London: Palgrave Macmillan, 2007), pp. 2–11. On the link between humoral physiology and psychology, see Paster, *Humoring the Body*, pp. 1–24.

64. Kahn, *Roman Shakespeare*, p. 32.

65. Sawday, *The Body Emblazoned*, pp. 67–71. The lines from Donne's Elegie XIX: "Licence my roaving hands, and let them go, / Before, behind, between, below. / O my America! My new-found-land", commented at pp. 26–27 and p. 190 *et passim*.

66. Sawday, *The Body Emblazoned*, p. 27.
67. Patricia Parker, "Othello and Hamlet: Dilation, Spying, and the 'Secret Place' of Woman", *Representations*, 44 (1993), 60–95 (pp. 66–67) (quoted by Sugg).
68. Sugg, *Murder After Death*, pp. 113–114.
69. Benjamin A. Rifkin, "The Art of Anatomy", in Benjamin A. Rifkin, Michael J. Ackerman and Judith Folkenberg, eds, *Human Anatomy: Depicting the Body from the Renaissance to Today* (London: Thames & Hudson, 2006), p. 20. But see also Bette Talvacchia, *Taking Positions: On the Erotic in Renaissance Culture* (Princeton: Princeton University Press, 1999), especially chapter 8 on Estienne.
70. For a feminist discussion of the theme of Lucrece's suicide in Renaissance visual arts, see Linda C. Hults, "Dürer's 'Lucretia': Speaking the Silence of Women", *Signs*, 6:2 (1991), 205–237.
71. Given that in his dedication to Southampton, Shakespeare presents his poem as "a pamphlet without beginning . . . a superfluous moiety", it is likely to suppose, Joel Fineman has argued, that the poem's opening "Argument" was a late addition by somebody else ("Shakespeare's *Will*", pp. 26–27).

3 Anatomizing the Body of a King

Knowledge, Conspiracy, and Spectrality in *Julius Caesar*

Coliseus Sive Theatrum: The Anatomizing Space

In *Roma ristaurata* [1440] (Italian transl. 1542), Biondo's imposing reconstruction of Rome's ancient topography and defaced monuments—the work in which, as aforesaid (see Introduction), the Italian humanist "wrote Rome into existence"—the early modern traveller could find an important concern with ancient theatre: the physical form of stage and edifices as they emerged among the ruins, as well as the memory of its *histriones*, comedians, tragedians, Clodius Aesopus, Roscius, the most famous in Roman time and often quoted by Cicero, who held in due regard the relation between "*l'eloquentia e l'arte istrionica*". Pantomimes exert a particular kind of fascination on Biondo:

> their function was to enact, through contrived gestures, in the midst of comedies or tragedies, the compositions of poets . . . the pantomime was so called for his skill in simulating, accompanied by music, an inexhaustible variety of situations, cleverly expressed with his hands, face, and his whole body—so much so that one had the impression he had used his voice too. With that same body he could be Hercules, or Venus, he could change into a man, or woman, now a king, now a soldier, now old, now young, so that it really seemed that in being one he was many.[1]

The physical architecture of theatres, Biondo explains, had changed considerably in terms of the variety of spectacles they offered, as well as in terms of stateliness and magnificence, in the passage from republican to imperial Rome but, like the *thermae*, they had always featured as a popular view, an essential landmark in Rome's culture and the architectonical landscape. The circular form of the Coliseum—an amphitheatre, "*dove si possa d'ogni intorno vedere*" ("where you can see all around from wherever you are")—was the invention of the imperial Rome, in Biondo's early modern archaeological speculation:

DOI: 10.4324/9781003259671-5

The amphitheatre . . . is nothing more than two theatres bundled together, where you can see all around from wherever you are. According to Cassiodoro, it was Titus who first had the idea of realizing such an edifice, but Tacitus holds Caesar was the first, having built one in Campo Martio; this is confirmed by Svetonius who adds though that it was destroyed by Augustus when he decided to build his Mausoleum there.[2]

The surviving spoiled amphitheatre "which we see still standing" and "which we call Coliseo", "we think was called Arena" [*"c'hora veggiamo in pie"* and "which is now called Coliseo", *"crediamo che fusse chiamata l'Arena*], like the similar edifice in Verona, and this because of the soil, Biondo conjectures, which was spread on the ground during the gladiatorial games, and which served to both soften the ground and to reduce the slipperiness of the oiled bodies of the gladiators as they fought (see 49–50). However, the amphitheatre, which we tend to associate exclusively with the gladiatorial arts, hosted a variety of spectacles, Biondo points out. Indeed it was both arena and theatre. Spoiled, mangled, and colossal as it was, it had come to signify a form, the form of the Theatrum *per antonomasia* in Renaissance Europe, one, however, in which the gladiatorial space of the arena defined a common, subsumed dialectics: that of the battlefield, an open air space where, as in the similar circle adopted by the rising Elizabethan theatres, a variety of "pastimes" and "plays" were performed and where an agonistic activity aimed at the understanding of bodies and the production of meaning was enacted. I wouldn't exclude that a traveller like Johannes de Witt may have had in mind Biondo's rediscovered Roman amphitheatres, and especially the Coliseum, the amphitheatre par excellence with all its resonances of imperial history and defaced beauty, when he likened the Swan's marble-like columns to its decayed splendour.[3]

"Coliseus sive Theatrum" is the inscription of an engraving representing a classical theatrical structure that circulated in a 1511 edition of Plautus's *Comedies* and in a few other Venetian Renaissance editions of Latin plays. If, as some critics suggest, the illustrator of Vesalius's *De humani corporis fabrica* (1543) used that engraving as an inspiration for the amphitheatre of the title page, he implicitly brought under the same heading the new surgical display of the body interior. The amphitheatre stood for the form of the world and the set of Vitruvian geometric relations along which the human *fabrica*, architecturally conceived, was newly investigated from an anatomical point of view in humanist Europe. As such it was appropriated as a cognitive space.[4] A similar caption, with the same equation underscored *per antonomasia*, also appeared on the upper left side of a large etching of the Roman Colosseum itself, dating circa 1590 and published by the Flemish engraver Nicolas Van Aelst: "Theatrum sive Coliseum Romanum". Was Shakespeare aware that his characters were moving in this same highly paradigmatic circle when he produced his Roman plays? Interestingly, a Coliseum featured also majestically, as an archetypical theatrical space, on the upper side of the title page of Ben Jonson's 1616 in Folio edition of his *Workes*, apparently at odds with the human figures in modern dress below: a way, in Stephen Orgel's fine ekphrasis, of "defining drama in relation to its history and its kinds".[5] But also, we might add, a celebration of theatre's heuristic space and its power of conflating different geographies and temporalities.

Shakespeare's Globe Theatre has been considered by John Gillies as a sort of analogue for the "cosmographic imagination which produced the world maps of Ortelius and Mercator". He has also shown how nowhere more than in the Roman plays, and particularly in *Antony and Cleopatra*, is Shakespeare's playhouse, the "Globe", made to coincide with "a world map in its own right".[6] Nowhere more than in the Roman plays, I would like to add, is the universalizing claim entailed in the very name of Shakespeare's playhouse made to coincide with a globalized anatomizing arena, in a period when anatomy had championed and gained its space and dignity by presenting itself as a science combining empirical observation and philosophical speculation, *evidentia* and spectacularized oratorical production of its bodies, thus affirming itself as a sort of keyword, a pervading heuristic model for both science and humanities in early modern Europe. It is no coincidence that the (assumed) first play to be performed at the Globe in 1599 was *Julius Caesar*; the play in which a most powerful "process of dismemberment and reinscription"[7] takes place. It is my suggestion in my analysis that the dissecting method of anatomy belongs to Cassius. In this I differ from a customary tendency to concentrate on Antony regarding this aspect. Richard Wilson, the first, or one of the first, scholars to inspiringly suggest a relation between the anatomy theatre and Shakespeare's play, capitalizes on Antony's final anatomical show of "meat" and "blood" to underscore the intersections with the carnivalesque anatomy lessons and the way the play "reproduces the spectacular corporeality of carnival in the service of a new disciplinary order".[8] But if I see the anatomist mostly in Cassius, it is not because I dispute the anatomical mode of Antony's final forensic autopsy—for anatomical discursivity is pervasive in the play and it intercepts the purposes of more than one character—but rather because Cassius's preliminary, deconstructive scrutiny of Caesar is substantial, as I take it, to Antony's reinscription of Caesar's "ruins". In my reading, the one doesn't hold without the other.

Antony's role in remythologizing Caesar's dead body has often been commented upon. Timothy Hampton has emphasized the role he plays in reconstructing Caesar's "exemplary status": "Caesar's body, which signified public heroism when whole demands, when gashed, a language that will interpret or gloss its gashes. The exemplary body must be correctly interpreted if it is to have political or moral significance".[9] Taking my cue from an "exemplarity" of Caesar, that in the play is epitomized by both the tyrant and the martyr, and drawing on the fact that this emerges as the construction of opposed and interacting interpretive stances, my concern in the first half of my chapter is to focalize Cassius's anatomical preliminary lesson on Caesar's disproportion. My proposal is that Cassius's speculative language is underwritten by issues of epistemic relevance—in a way that, at least to my knowledge, has not so far been noticed[10]—one which Shakespeare himself seems to intend to overshadow with Antony's last words: "All the conspirators save only he [Brutus] / Did that they did in envy of great Caesar" (5.5.70–71).

But before entering Shakespeare's Roman dissecting arena with the anatomizing words of Cassius, I would like to give physical visibility to the heuristic space made available by the anatomists, with the guidance of Alessandro Benedetti, the author of *Historia corporis humani sive Anatomice*, first printed in Venice in 1502. Benedetti was a physician and anatomist at the University of Padua, "fair Padua, nursery of arts", where Shakespeare's Lucentio, in *The Taming of the Shrew*, purports to "institute / A course of learning and ingenious studies" (1.1.8–9). Padua is also appreciated in this play as a place where one can "practice rhetoric in your common talk", "The mathematics and the metaphysics" (1.1.35–37). However, Padua in Renaissance Europe was mainly the site of a groundbreaking resurgence of anatomical studies, the place where quite a few acclaimed European physicians and anatomists studied and taught: the Englishman William Harvey (the discoverer of blood circulation), and before him the Spanish anatomist Juan de Valverde, and the Belgian Vesalius, the author of the most famous *De humani corporis fabrica* published in 1543 in the same year when, as a parallel to this growing early modern cartographical conscience of the body, Copernicus (he himself linked to the intellectual ambience of Padua) announced the good news of a new map of the universe.

I don't know whether Shakespeare ever heard of the less famous Alessandro Benedetti and of his pioneering *Historia corporis humani sive Anatomice* published 40 years earlier, in 1502 (which circulated fairly widely in Europe in a Paris edition and four others in German-speaking countries), but here, in Benedetti's work, we find the first envisaging of a movable anatomy theatre and the proposal of dissection as an instructive (or "moral") theatrical performance worthy of attracting not simply physicians, but humanists, and governors like Maximilian I of Hapsburg (soon to be elected Holy Roman Emperor in 1508) and his Venetian imperial ambassador Christoph von Schrovenstein, both of them the dedicatees of Benedetti's highly esteemed book of anatomy. Benedetti's anatomy theatre, which he imagined, in a Roman gladiatorial style, as an amphitheatre, like those of Rome or Verona—which he mentions—to be installed for the occasion in a well-aired room, will be transformed at the turn of the sixteenth century, in Shakespeare's times, into a permanent indoor structure by Girolamo Fabrici d'Acquapendente, the explorer of the venous system, and he himself a surgeon and anatomist at the University of Padua where his anatomy theatre is still visible.

But let us follow Benedetti's instructions for the arrangement and use of his removable anatomy theatre, a sort of pre-Shakespearean "wooden O" (apparently designed with the Roman arena of Verona, his city of birth, in mind).

> the only corpses which may be legitimately claimed for dissection are those belonging to people of humble origins, or unknown persons, from faraway lands, in order to avoid offending neighbours and bringing shame on family members. The best bodies are those that have been hanged, preferably middle-aged, neither too lean nor too fat. . . . The best period to proceed is the coldest time of winter, so that the cadavers do not start to putrefy immediately. The best location for a dissection is a large, well-aired room, in which a temporary theatre will be set up, with seats placed round it in a circle (such as the ones which may be seen in Rome and Verona), big enough to contain the number of spectators and prevent the crowd from disturbing the wound surgeons, who are in charge of the dissections. They must be skilled, and they must have already performed frequent dissections. The seats will be assigned according to rank; to this purpose, only one warden will be present, who shall check and arrange everything. A number of custodians will be necessary, so that they may keep away the meddlers who will try to get in, and two trustworthy treasurers, who shall procure all that is necessary using the money collected. The dissection procedure will require razors, knives, hooks, drills and gimlets (the Greeks call them "chenicia"), as well as sponges to promptly remove blood during the dissection, scissors, and basins; torches must be on hand in case it should get dark.

And then finally in his opening one-page description of his theatre, and with the timing we would appreciate in a drama director and playwright, Benedetti turns his attention to the corpse, which he makes appear as a focal point in the middle of a series of concentric rings of benches, displayed and offered to the inspective gaze of the onlookers for a prescriptive theatrical time; the time established by the unappealable natural law of putrefaction—or else, the natural time elapsing from life in death and putrefaction—which alone decides, as in a sort of new Aristotelian unity, the type of conjunction between action and place.

> The cadaver shall be placed in the middle of the theatre, on a rather high table, in a well-lit and comfortable place for the dissectors. It will be necessary to establish a time for the beginning and the end of

appointments, so that the work may be completed before the body's putrefaction.[11]

For all its brevity, all is arranged as if with the care of a theatrical entrepreneur and with the awareness of a playwright: the architecture of the anatomy class, the disposition of spectators, the preoccupation with details such as the funding public, box office, personnel, time of production. Benedetti's refoundation of anatomical studies is tantamount to the construction of his theatre and to its Roman circular shape; a shape which implies publicity, the widening (although strictly regulated) audience of an amphitheatre; an amphitheatre which, while offering an arena-like view of the uncanny gladiatorial dissecting spectacle, orchestrates with its very circular form a forensic speculation on the human body, a moral philosophical dispute: that is, a comparison among different ancient sources and between the authority of classical or divine texts and direct observation.

In fact the anatomist, as he is presented by Benedetti, at the opening of the sixteenth century, and as it will be in Renaissance Europe for a good part of the seventeenth century, is both a physician *and* a philosopher. For him as it will still for Francis Bacon,[12] a century later, anatomy is a useful branch of natural philosophy, whether it be to confirm or gradually dismantle the epochal highly textualized order of the human body in its codified correspondences with the world and the universe. Anatomy "is grounded in philosophy", Benedetti writes, "if it wants to be of any use to medicine; in it we perceive the admirable, divine work of God our Creator". And "You", he says addressing his dedicatee, the emperor Maximilian of Austria, "will thus more readily turn your gaze towards the forms of the universe, of which man is but a smaller replica".[13]

Differently from later books of anatomy, Benedetti's work was not supported by illustrations. But Benedetti was an accomplished classicist and a physician highly renowned for his oratorical skills. He knew how to make space for his discipline, by exploiting the ennobling equivalence between the body interior and the God-like architecture of the universe:

> You should not find it objectionable . . . that I have invited you to observe a heap of entrails, since, as they say, there is nothing in nature that is not worthy of admiration and wonder. Indeed, Heraclitus himself, while sitting next to a stove to keep warm, urged those who were hesitating and standing back to draw nearer: "Do you not know—he said—that the immortal gods are here?" For it is certain that the divinity of nature is hidden in all places, and the soul pervades everything.[14]

Let us remember in passing that dissection, as Benedetti takes pains to point out, started from the belly with a first cross-like incision; and that the vision of entrails constituted the onlookers' first encounter with the body interior. Yet every body part was to be considered part of a hierarchical order replicating the providential design of nature and universe. Future illustrators of books of anatomy, such as those who worked for Vesalius or Estienne, will try their best to emphasize from a secular perspective the commonplace God-like structure of the human frame, "the beauty of / the world, the paragon of animals" in Hamlet's derisive words (2.2.267–68), by resorting to the ennobling cladding, or posture, of classic statuary.

In fact, if not the object of a religious/ideological contemplation, the still pulsating early modern human entrails were wrapped in their Renaissance Greek-Roman allure, as if in a common endeavour of artists and anatomists alike to maintain the difficult analogy, while probing into the body interior to be increasingly bemused by its complexity and by the skeleton within.

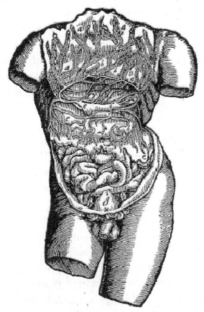

Figure 3.1 Helkiah Crooke, title page, *Microcosmographia* (1615)
Source: Wellcome Collection (London)

However, Helkiah Crooke in 1615 still celebrated in the very title of his late Renaissance compendium of European anatomy, *Microcosmographia. A Description of the Body of Man*, the ancient long-standing assumption that the human body was a *microcosmus*, "an abstract or model of the world", in the (obliquely) critical synthesis offered by Francis Bacon in 1605, "as if there were to be found in man's body certain correspondences and parallels, which should have respect to all varieties of things, as stars, planets, minerals, which are extant in the great world".[15] Caesar's body, in the complex and contradictory way it is constructed in Shakespeare's play, responds in everything to a body which both calls for and exceeds the set of symmetries which allowed for the analogy with universe.

As in Francis Bacon's *Advancement of Learning* (where the traditional *exemplar* position of human beings in the *scala naturae* is redefined in alimentary/nutritional terms), the highly textualized order of the early modern human body turns it into a territory of increasingly conflicting paradigms and shifting metaphors. The body turns into a battleground, as it has been variously shown in the last few decades by a fast growing scholarship on early modern bodies.[16] The epistemic inversion is brashly highlighted in Vesalius's frontispiece to his *Humani corporis fabrica* in the isolation of the onlooker concentrated on his book, while all the others are intent on looking directly at the real "fabric" of the human body as it is being deployed by the anatomist.[17]

Indeed, as may be seen in the painting "Skeletons" by Agostino Veneziano, painters and anatomists alike explored the undiscovered lands of the human body with a book in their hands, whether sacred or secular or both, while trying nonetheless to invert the hierarchy between ancient sources and direct observation, between the authority of ancient natural philosophy and dissection as the ultimate source of knowledge, and as the path towards the discovery of the "true cause" (*JC*, 1.3.62). Invested with meanings which are political in so far as they intersect the scientific and the philosophical, this becomes Cassius's Baconian challenging claim in Shakespeare's *Julius Caesar*, I suggest.

In the terms of the anatomists, this meant finding a way in territories which needed to be cartographized anew, or else remapped and renamed, as Benedetti, a contemporary of Columbian geographical discoveries, states, with an incisive navigational analogue in the very last paragraph of his treatise. But let's hear Benedetti's interesting last paragraph to understand the methodological challenge entailed in his conclusive navigational metaphor.

> I would encourage everyone, both students and expert doctors and surgeons, to go as often as possible to see these spectacles, which should be repeated at least once a year; for in the theatre we see things as they are, we expose them to observe them closely, so that the book

of nature may be opened before our eyes, and its work be observed as though it were alive.

   After all, writing is most similar to painting, an art which often awakens memory from indifference and clears away darkness from the soul. But, as Plato says, he who trusts in written testimonies without observing things well, and does not think over, within himself, what was described, will often convey more opinion than truth to the minds he wishes to address. The same thing happens to those learning about navigation when they read nautical maps, in which islands, gulfs, bays and promontories do not exactly match the real ones that are before their eyes.[18]

This also meant discovering in the dissecting and unmasking function of the theatre the potentiality of a new alliance with the demonstrative, ostensive space being invoked and devised by the new science, not only medicine with its fast-spreading European anatomy theatres, but also the new Renaissance cartography with its theatrical titles and frontispieces.

   Shakespeare is part of this revolutionized cognitive paradigm. He participates in it powerfully with the metaphorical mechanism of great cognitive potential which is the theatre. He too asks his spectators/readers to transform themselves into navigators and awed observers before the unexpected infinite theatre of the visible, while in his Globe he places them interrogatively in a circle around that all-too-human body, still to be explored, which holds the centre: "the beauty of the world, the paragon of animals", in the disenchanted anatomy of Hamlet, who breaks up the ordered symmetries of metaphysics, or theology, which held that man should be the measure of all things ("in action how like an angel, in apprehension how like a god")—a body which articulated the analogical exchange between heaven and earth, macrocosm and microcosm—to consign him instead to the observation of a secularized gaze, explorative and sceptical, "and yet to me what is this quintessence of dust?" (2.2.267–69).

In Shakespeare's Arena With the Words of Cassius: or, Julius Caesar's *Écorché*

In this section I intend to look at how in Shakespeare's *Julius Caesar* the arena, the part, and the method of the Renaissance anatomist belongs to Cassius, a modern "intellectual and an anarchist".[19] In this, in entrusting Cassius with such an important hermeneutical role, I argue, Shakespeare was doing nothing but acknowledging the reputation he enjoyed as a follower of the Epicurean philosophy in Plutarch's "Life of Brutus", the subject of customary entertainment with his Platonist friend Brutus. Let us consider the authority with which the Plutarchan Cassius delivers his lesson on imagination and its misconstructions after the ghost's apparition to Brutus at Philippi:

> In our secte, Brutus, we have an opinion, that we doe not always feele, or see, that which we suppose we doe both see and feele: but our senses are credulous, and therefore easily abused (when they are idle and unoccupied in their own objects) are induced to imagine they see and conjecture that, which they in truth doe not. . . . For our imagination doth upon a small fancie growe from conceit to conceit, altering both in passions and formes of thinges imagined. For, to say that there are spirits or angells, and if there were, that they had the shape of men, or such voyces, or any power at all to come unto us: it is a mockerye.

Figure 3.2 Michelangelo, *The Last Judgement*, detail, Musei Vaticani
Source: © Musei Vaticani

This is not just a lesson on the way imagination often builds upon false "conceits", a wisdom that Shakespeare capitalizes upon by ingeniously disseminating it throughout the play. It also encapsulates the lucid diagnosis of an enfeebled and surrendering melancholic subjectivity: "But yet there is a further cause of this in you", Plutarch's Cassius says to Brutus. "For you being by nature given to melancholick discoursing, and of late continually occupied: your wittes and sences having been overlaboured, doe easilier yeelde to such imaginations" (North's Plutarch, 1072).[20]

It comes as no surprise, then, that in Shakespeare's play Cassius is rewritten as a mirroring Other. From the very outset, in fact, he is mentioned in connection with the mirror: a recurring symbolic object, together with the flaying knife, in late Renaissance personifications of "Anatomia".[21] Interestingly, they were both alluded to in Michelangelo's self-portrait in his *Last Judgement* fresco for the Cappella Sistina, where the flayed skin of an entire body dangling from the left hand of Saint Bartholomew—his other hand brandishing a knife—stands as a forceful, if somewhat disquieting, instance of self-knowledge achieved through the speculative and denuding practice of anatomy.

In Shakespeare's *Julius Caesar* (but see also *The Rape* and *Antony and Cleopatra*), a mirror or the like appears in this Delphic "Nosce te Ipsum" ("Know Thyself") function—the proclaimed philosophical imperative of anatomy destined to become a familiar inscription in the anatomy theatres throughout Europe—when Cassius offers himself to be the mirror of Brutus's hidden and troubling "passions":

> Therefore, good Brutus, be prepared to hear.
> And since you know you cannot see yourself
> So well as by reflection, I your glass
> Will modestly discover to yourself
> That of yourself which you yet know not of.
> (1.2.66–70)

Cassius's deconstructive inspection of Caesar's body thus develops as part of a larger unmasking role that he seems to enact from the very outset of the play. Indeed, it is Cassius's task to perform with the gaze and the language of anatomy the preceding intellectual meditation that will make Caesar reveal his inner mortal frame, transforming him into a sort of Renaissance *écorché*: those that had been made famous by artists and anatomists alike (Leonardo, Michelangelo, Rosso Fiorentino, Berengario da Carpi, Vesalius, Valverde) and which, I would like to suggest, are visually close to the Caesar flayed by Cassius's words. For, all over Europe, anatomy, as Helkiah Crooke will summarize to his English readers in his *Microcosmographia*, had "a double acceptation":

> There is among Physitians, a double accepatation of Anatomy; either it signifieth the action which is done with the Hand, or the habite of

the Mind, that is the most perfect action of the Intellect. The first is called Practicall Anatomie, the latter Theoricall or Contemplatiue: The first is gained by experience, the second by reason and discourse: The first we attaine only by Section and Inspection, the second by the living voice of a Teacher . . . The first is altogether necessarie for the practice of Anatomy, the second is only profitable; but yet the profite is oftentimes more beneficiall than the use itself of Anatomy.[22]

In this sense Cassius's "contemplative" brand of anatomy may be considered as a sort of "profitable" first incision; an incision aimed at removing the mythologized layer of skin from Caesar's body, thus transforming

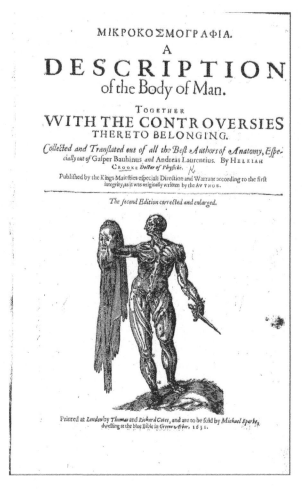

Figure 3.3 Helkiah Crooke, title page, *Microcosmographia* (1615)

Source: Wellcome Collection (London)

the body of a king into a secular ruinous body, the body of a convict. Such a task was likely to appear all the more necessary to the conspirators ("some certain of the noblest-minded Romans", 1.3.123), and to Shakespeare's audience alike, for being located in the austere republican places of the Senate, Pompey's Porch, Pompey's Theatre (1.3.125, 153), and against the festive offstage scenario of the city of which Caesar is a master. Indeed, it is from the bustling background of the Lupercalia that an echo of the approving shouts of the Roman plebs arrives, when a crown is "thrice" offered to Caesar by Antony to be "thrice" refused (1.2.220–30),[23] clearly demonstrating Caesar's skill in fuelling one's legend in front of the rabble as much as the necessity of Cassius's deconstructive pursuit. In addition to its being a popular anatomical illustration in Shakespeare's times, I feel that the suggestiveness of Valverde's *écorché*, dated 1556, provides, more than other images, the right visual analogue for the Caesar being flayed by Cassius's words. In England, the catalyzing force of that image, whose rich symbolism could be traced back both to its influential Michelangiolesque antecedent of the Cappella Sistina and to the mythical story of Marsyas flayed by Apollo, was confirmed by Helkiah Crooke when he reproduced it in the internal title page of his *Microcosmographia* in 1615.

As in the story of Marsyas narrated by Ovid, often subsumed in Renaissance anatomical *écorchés*,[24] we wouldn't be surprised if we heard a still alive Caesar screaming, "Why flayest thou me so?" while he is stripped of his skin and,

> Nought else he was than one whole wound. The grisly blood did spin
> From every part; the sinews lay discovered to the eye;
> The quivering veins without a skin lay beating nakedly.
> The panting bowels in his bulk ye might have numbered well,
> And in his breast the sheer small strings a man might easily tell.[25]

Cassius's words seem to aggressively flay Caesar alive up to the point of showing his "quivering veins" and "panting bowels", before turning into a knife. It may perhaps be of some import here to remember that "flayed", a highly charged anatomical term, is also expressly used by Shakespeare to give us a portentous martial image of Coriolanus. "Who's yonder / That does appear as he were flayed?" Cominius observes, after one of his battles against the Volscians: "O gods, / He has the stamp of Martius, and I have / Before-time seen him thus" (1.6.22–24). "Mantled" only in blood (1.6.29), he too does seem to be represented as a sort of frightful *écorché*.

Plutarch could have hardly provided a more suggestive image for the purpose of my argument when, in his "Life of Julius Caesar", he tells the story of the dictator referring to himself, metonymically, as "this skinne". He quotes Caesar as saying, "Brutus will looke for this skinne", when report had it that Brutus was conspiring against him, "meaning thereby, that Brutus for his vertue, deserved to rule after him, but yet, that for ambitions sake, he woulde not shewe him selfe unthankefull nor dishonourable".[26] As if complying with Caesar's belief, Shakespeare strengthens the role Cassius plays in the conspiracy by assigning to him, more than to Brutus, the conscience of the tyrannicide and hence the ideological questioning of Caesar's "skin". He thus takes centre stage as the person who triggers the fierce contentious process of inspecting Caesar's body that is at the core of Shakespeare's play.[27] Appropriately, Cassius is soon targeted as "a great observer" in Caesar's distrustful judgment (1.1.201).

Arguably, Cassius's proclivity to examine, far from simply being the outcome of an "envious" project, as it might appear if we take note of Brutus's anxiety of succession (2.1.177) or Caesar's dislike of him ("Such men as he be never at heart's ease / Whiles they behold a greater than themselves" [1.2.207–8]), alerted Shakespeare's audience to a larger context of drives and intentions. Those who were familiar with Stubbes's successful *Anatomie of Abuses* (1583) and his puritanical fustigation of the multifarious forms of public and private "vices", in which he also included festivities, idleness, and theatre, knew only too well where to find the word that would categorize Cassius's eagerness to pry and unmask. Indeed "anatomy" had become a fashionable word by the time the play was produced.[28]

But there was much more to be seen in his anatomy. Under Cassius's gaze Caesar's sacralized body is forced to become the early modern "penetrable" or "transparent" body fantasized by the anatomist,[29] a body whose volume, organs, and meaning lay open to the new evaluating regime of science. Coldly dismantled of his god-like skin, Caesar's body is gradually and relentlessly reduced before death to its mortal essence: a "piece of earth". It is shown as if it were that of a "sick girl", a physiology of feeble frame. It is not just a strategy of *captatio benevolentiae* that he has fallen down in a swoon in front of the Roman multitude. Caesar was unable to swim his way across the troubled Tiber to the opposite bank. He cried, "Help me, Cassius, or I sink", and Cassius helped him by offering his shoulders like Aeneas with his father Anchises. Cassius saw Caesar trembling with fever and crying for water during his campaign in Spain (1.2.90–130). Caesar's mythologized body, increasingly swollen by the acclaiming shouts of the plebs offstage (in Act 1.2), is at the same time debunked onstage by Cassius who first compares him to a Colossus: a disproportionate figure whose anatomy invokes the ordering discipline of perspective:

> CASSIUS Why, man, he doth bestride the narrow world
> Like a colossus, and we petty men
> Walk under his huge legs and peep about
> To find ourselves dishonourable graves.
> Men at some time are masters of their fates.

> The fault, dear Brutus, is not in our stars
> But in ourselves, that we are underlings.
> "Brutus" and "Caesar": what should be in that "Caesar"?
> What should that name be sounded more than yours?
> Write them together: yours is as a fair name:
> Sound them, it doth become the mouth as well.
> Weigh them, it is as heavy; . . .
> . . .
> When could they say, till now, that talked of Rome,
> That her wide walks encompassed but one man?
> Now is it Rome indeed, and room enough,
> When there is in it but only one man.
>
> (1.2.134–56)

The anatomy of Caesarism, which parallels the representation of the dictator's private persona as a diseased body, and precedes Caesar's final "shrinking" into the "little measure" of a corpse, to be mourned later by Antony (3.1.150), is first of all a lesson on perspective; an art, or science, which in Renaissance times, as it has been incisively stressed by Jonathan Sawday, developed as part of a culture of dissection, a branch of anatomy. Caesar's body politic seems to be first and foremost anatomized pictorially by Cassius as a body marring and offending the law of perspective, and the science of perspective, as it developed in Renaissance culture, and as we see in this passage, pertained to the representation of bodies in space. It involved volume and proportion, the understanding of the interior body space, the position of organs and limbs, and the measurement of bodies in relation to other bodies within space; which is what made the work of the anatomists coincide with the contemporary research of the artists. As Sawday has remarked with Serlio's treatise on architecture to hand,

> Any attempt at rendering surface convincing without an understanding of volume was to be content with the "bare shew of superficiencies" rather than the full complexity of the body functioning within space. Space, the positioning of the body within a three-dimensional matrix, was the key to anatomical understanding.[30]

As was also explained in Giovanni Lomazzo's *Trattato dell'arte, della pittura, scultura ed architettura* (1584), and as it was beautifully rendered in one of Richard Haydocke's illustrations for his abridged English translation published in 1598—only one year ahead of Shakespeare's *Julius Caesar*—bodies had to be geometrically measured and located in order to achieve volume and proportion.[31] They had to undergo the trial of scientific measurement, one might say, in order to acquire the measure urged by the Renaissance perspectival regime.

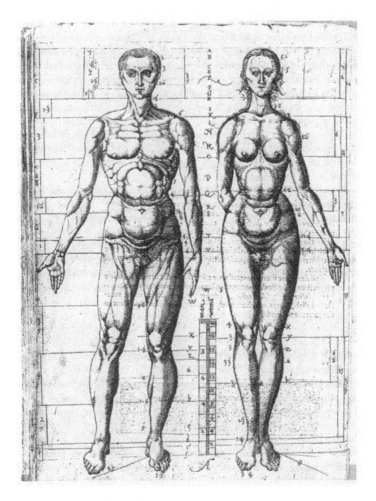

Figure 3.4 G. Lomazzo/R. Haydocke, "Of Proportion", *A Tracte Containing the Artes of Curious Paintinge, Carvinge, and Buildinge* (1584/1598)

Source: Wellcome Collection

"By a theory of proportions", or "anthropometry", in Panofsky's definition, "we mean a system of establishing the mathematical relations between the various members of a living creature, in particular of human beings, in so far as they are thought of as subjects of artistic representation".[32] Grounded in a growing acknowledged importance of sculpture and painting as part of the *artes liberales,* and hence the way they participated in the production of what Panofsky calls "metaphysical meaning", artists "tried to assimilate the entire scientific culture".

The theory of human proportions [the favourite discipline of Leon Battisti Alberti, Leonardo, Dürer] was seen as both a pre-requite of artistic proportions and an expression of the pre-established harmony between microcosm and macrocosm; and it was seen, moreover, as the rational basis of beauty. The Renaissance fused, we may say, the cosmological interpretation of the theory of proportions, current in Hellenistic times and in the Middle Ages, with the classical notion of symmetry as the fundamental principle of aesthetic perfection. . . . Perhaps only this theory—mathematical and speculative at the same time—could satisfy the disparate spiritual needs of the age.

(*Id*, 89–90)

In Shakespeare's play, the art of perspective and proportions, or anthropometry, seems to be turned into a heretical and dangerous knowledge. Indeed, it is one with Cassius's conspiratorial project. Caesar is figured as a giant straddling the Roman worldwide geography with his "huge legs"; a man who, with his colossus-like stature, visually dwarfs everything around him: space as well as the volume and height of all men surrounding him. Cassius's reference to the Colossus is not traceable to Shakespeare's Plutarchan sources. In depicting Caesar disproportionately, Shakespeare may have had in mind the *colossi* of the Roman statuary—or even more specifically the legendary colossal statue in bronze of Caesar mounted upon a globe which, according to ancient historians, was erected on the Capitol. As the historian Dio Cassius writes, the Senate "decreed that a chariot of [Caesar] should be placed on the Capitol facing the statue of Jupiter, that his statue in bronze should be mounted upon a likeness of the inhabited world, with an inscription to the effect that he was a demigod".[33] Also shown by the image of Octavian Augustus on some of his coins, this posture was increasingly adopted in the discourse of imperialism as symbolic of a Roman worldwide hegemony; a symbolism which, interestingly, as with all things Augustan, would prove very attractive to the future King James I and the Stuart dynasty.

"The statue is the characteristic expressive form of Rome", Ralph Berry has observed, and an instance of ancestry and of "the patriarchal grip".

It is hard, marble, an unrelenting assertion of the self that one has to accept or overturn. . . . Flavius and Marullus know that to have the Caesarean images disrobed is a vital symbolic challenge, just as Caesar knows that it must be met by having them "put to silence".[34]

A statue in fact occurs, as reminded by Berry, in other pivotal moments of the play as an assertion of identity and as a shared popular awareness that statues partake in a process of construction of a patriarchal lineage and stately "nomenclature". Think of the crowd's acclaim of Brutus: "Give him a statute with his ancestors" and "Let him be Caesar"

(3.2.50–51). In the same way the comparison between Caesar and the Colossus, which is customarily seen as a reference to the legendary bronze statue of Apollo (the Colossus of Rhodes), is crucial in Cassius's conspiratorial argument, and for more than one reason. What is worth noticing though in this context is that the Colossus of Rhodes often featured in Renaissance perspectival design of disproportion, and especially in the field of the nascent science of photometry. In one of Rubens's studies prepared for the illustrations of François d'Aguillon's treatise *Optics* dated 1613, we see a bearded philosopher portrayed in the act of visualizing with the aid of a surveyor's staff the optical lines departing from different points of the mythical statue, while a number of *putti* are fumbling about with cosmological and measuring instruments—an armillary sphere, a rule or level, a quadrant.[35]

Cassius's famous linguistic testing of Caesar's name is encased within the same comparative logic of measurement and proportion ("write them", "sound them", "weigh them") dictated by Renaissance perspective, to which in fact the inspective eye of Cassius returns to conclude his preliminary experiment with bodies, volume, and space: "When could they say, till now, that talked of Rome, that her wide walks encompassed but one man? / Now is it Rome indeed, and room enough, / When there is but one only man" (1.2.153–56). What should also be noted here is that Cassius's wordplay with "Rome" and "room" took advantage of the fact that "Rome" in Shakespeare's times was pronounced "roum", and as such the name of the city was all the more capable of being invested with connotations related to space *tout court*,[36] whether that be a constraining or expanding geography, as it is, for instance, alternately in *Coriolanus* and *Antony and Cleopatra*.

Caesar's disproportionate figure, as viewed by Cassius, disfigures a proper perspectival background. In Cassius's diagnosis (or "anthropometry"), Caesar has grown into a *monstrum*. In fact, as Cassius later states, he has achieved the quality of a fearful portent-like figure. Therefore, if Cassius wants to reduce Caesar to his contingent human measure, he first needs to give his conspirators a convincing lesson on proportion and perspective. He needs to enforce a new perspectival regime, or a new "ordering code", if we prefer the supportiveness of a Foucauldian category.[37] He has to divest Caesar of his Caesarean mythological skin, and lay bare his body-space beneath, thus unmasking and revealing his frail human interior, as in a Renaissance *écorché*, or as in the ripped classical statuary, with protruding organs and entrails, which one could see in Vesalius's, Estienne's, or Valverde's famous tables of anatomy, and of which the English public would find a generous sampling in Crooke's 1615 *Microcosmographia*. Indeed, as I have I have already said, Crooke's popular textbook exhibited in its very title page a reproduction of Valverde's *écorché*, thus providing a hint of how this early modern wide-spreading interest in the anatomized human figure may have pervaded the mode and imagery of the conspirators' inspecting endeavour in Shakespeare's play. In this light the disrobing of Caesar's statues prompted by Flavius, the tribune of the people, at the outset of the play appears as metaphorically isomorphic with Cassius's anatomizing stance or procedures.

"But If You Would Consider the True Cause": Questioning Bodies and Proportions

In commenting on the circular form of the Leiden anatomy theatre and the Vitruvian-like position of the cadaver at its centre, Sawday has written,

> Disposed on the anatomy table in a sacrificial pose, the cadaver suggests the Vitruvian figure once more. The right hand of the corpse is thrown out so that it nearly touches the innermost ring of the concentric circles. This somewhat inelegant suggestion of a Vitruvian figure reminds the onlooker of the old tradition of understanding the human image as a principle of proportional design.[38]

Disposed on Cassius's philosophical dissecting table, Caesar's figure with its splayed legs appears as a sort of Vitruvian man exceeding the proportions successfully illustrated by Leonardo as an instance of a symmetry coincident with the geometrical laws of nature. Caesar's colossal figure is no longer "a principle of proportional design" and correspondences with the universe. He seems to have obscured the traditional concentric rings of corporeal and cosmological correspondences with the elements, stars, and heavens, devised in contemporary English iconography to both exalt and hierarchically circumscribe the human frame, as we can see typically in the title page of Robert Fludd's *Utriusque Cosmi Majoris et Minoris* (1617).

I would argue that this is where Shakespeare's play turns into the most extraordinary anatomy of the king's "two bodies"; that is, in the way in which Cassius takes advantage of this underlying traditional way of conceptualizing the exemplary role plaid by the body politic in articulating the hierarchical relation with the universe,[39] in order to inject a new heretical, or secular, understanding of heavens, kingship, and human beings. Accordingly, as in Renaissance anatomy lessons, Cassius cannot avoid being a philosopher. As in Italian public dissections, or as in Crooke's distinctions between the two forms of anatomy, Cassius seems to be primarily the "lector" "whose task was to perform the lesson", that is, "to teach the public anatomy", both before and during the demonstrations—not an easy task to perform. In fact, as Giovanna Ferrari has remarked,

> This was a very special kind of course, shorter than the normal but much more demanding, and above all, very risky for the anatomy professor's reputation. For during the dispute the professor had to

answer, in public, questions put to him without prior warning by lectors from various different disciplines,[40]

but mostly medicine, philosophy, theology, and the arts.

In one of his insightful essays on *Julius Caesar*, Alessandro Serpieri has argued that the hermeneutical paradigm pervades the structure of the play.[41] I would like to put forward that the heuristic mode of anatomy has a great bearing in determining the hermeneutical register of the play, with Cassius being the character that predominantly employs it. Significantly, he is the one who champions his cause against a god-like Caesar by advocating a rational non-mythological interpretation of natural phenomena and of the universe at large at the same time. Cassius cannot question and dissect the highly textualized body of Caesar without engaging with the world around him and with different modes of knowledge.

Let us consider the way in which Cassius addresses a fearful Caska on the night of conspiracy when a myriad of wonders seem to shake the order of the universe to its roots. Meaningfully, these portents narrated by Plutarch, as they are handled by Shakespeare, are turned into the amplified object of a dispute between Caska, represented as the womanish dupe of superstition, and Cassius, depicted as the champion of a masculine rational investigation of natural phenomena. What is more, this contention over truth and opinion is authoritatively, albeit briefly, anticipated by Cicero, a highly influential intellectual presence in early modern England and grammar school curricula, thus assuming significance as an epistemic fracture at a crucial historical juncture. "Indeed it is a strange-disposed time. / But men may construe things after their fashion, / Clean from the purpose of the things themselves" (1.3.33–35). When Cassius enters the stage soon after, almost like a grammar school student testing his acquired classical art of persuasion,[42] he seems to be endowed with the task of developing Cicero's elliptic and undisclosed argument. In front of him is Caska who, here as elsewhere in the play, is derogatorily depicted as if embodying "a Roman", a representative of the impressionable commoner, a "willing bondman" (1.3.113), despite the fact that he is a patrician.

CASSIUS   Who's there?
CASKA   A Roman.
CASSIUS   Caska, by your voice.
CASKA   Your ear is good. Cassius, what night is this?
CASSIUS   A very pleasing night to honest men.
CASKA   Whoever knew the heavens menace so?
CASSIUS   Those that have known the earth so full of faults.
    For my part, I have walked the streets,
    Submitting me unto the perilous night,
    And thus unbraced, Caska, as you see,
    Have bared my bosom to the thunder-stone . . .

        (1.3.40f.)

With a crucial rhetorical move, Cassius first turns Caska's subjugated eyes from the heavens' ill disposition to the reality of the earth he inhabits. He then addresses the "Roman" as he used to be and as he should be:

> You are dull, Caska, and those sparks of life
> That should be in a Roman you do want
> Or else you use not. You look pale, and gaze,
> And put on fear, and cast yourself in wonder
> To see the strange impatience of the heavens.
> *But if you would consider the true cause*
> *Why* all these fires, *why* all these gliding ghosts,
> *Why* birds and beasts, from quality and kind,
> *Why* old men, fools, and children calculate,
> *Why* all these things change from their ordinance
> Their natures and preformed faculties
> To monstrous quality . . .
>   (1.3.57–61; my emphasis)

"The true cause": as a philosophical category this was both a Baconian and a Stoic founding concern. The Stoic acceptation of cause was extensively discussed in Cicero's *De Fato*, where the reflection on causality is dated back to the Greek philosopher Crisippo. In Crisippo's definition, "A cause is that which makes the thing of which it is the cause come about" (XV.34),[43] but not all causes could be known. This is the reason for which the issue of causality involved fatalism and determinism—the Stoic "all-controlling" world of "necessity" (XX.48)—as well as, contradictorily, an individual "free from the necessity of fate" (XVI.38), for, even though the cause could be both false and true, "the act of assent" is "in our power" (XIX.43). Significantly, it will be only later, when the early modern new science takes on the task of studying the causes of natural phenomena, physically and unreservedly, that—as Cassius does—it will be possible to invoke the "true cause" as a real possibility of freedom from fear and the Stoic "necessity of fate". It is when, as Bacon in *Novum Organum*, natural philosophy is understood, physically, "as the 'Inquiry of Causes'".[44]

The Baconian undertaking to look for "the true cause", in connection with the question which activates the research, is what concerns us here in relation to Shakespeare's Cassius: his appeal to interrogate the "why" of natural phenomena, the "why" we hear resonate anaphorically, and five times in a row, while he continues to conflate knowledge, power, and visual proportion in his reasoning. For, received knowledge, not differently from undisputed power, and not differently from the unquestioned body of Caesar grown into the exceeding measure of a "colossus"— "prodigious grown", he says, "And fearful, as these strange eruptions are" (1.3.77–78)—is what transforms men into tremulous "female" bodies and natural phenomena into nightmarish monstrosities, "instruments of fear and warning", as during that night of conspiracy; a night teeming with inexplicable disruptive events and fantastic apparitions as in a painting by Bosch.

Cassius's masculine-connoted "scientific" claim cannot go unnoticed. Anatomy, and its aggressive pretence to open up bodies in order to penetrate them and lay bare the nature of things, implied a project of control on nature which was rooted in a rhetoric of masculinity and conquest. This is made clear by the language adopted by Bacon in presenting his method for the "advancement" of learning.[45] But it had also been iconically and paradigmatically fixed in the frontispiece of Vesalius's *De Humani Corporis Fabrica* (1543), where the body to be opened up and explored by the exhibited firm hand of the anatomist and the prying, circling ring of male gazes is literally and symbolically that of a woman: the predated if bemusing knowledge *per antonomasia* ever since. As aforesaid in the previous chapter on *The Rape*, the knowledge and control of the woman's body was the first testing territory for an episteme defined by a masculine rhetoric of "discovery" and "ownership".[46] In Cassius's anatomy of Caesar and natural phenomena, femininity features as the effeminating and enervating agency to which a powerful father is reducing the Romanness of his sons. It is the underwritten anxiety of a normative masculine knowledge. Cassius is the person entrusted with the task of maintaining the sexual difference, by first heralding the distinction between truth and opinion, wonders and reality—a topic issue in the nascent Renaissance science; one which entails the choice, in Cassius's perspective, between feminine subduing fear and masculine freedom. In Gail Kern Paster's reading of the play, Caesar's murder and the complex gender-inflected discursivity on blood and bleeding is what enhances the conspirator's project in profundity, by disclosing "the shameful secret of Caesar' bodiliness", namely that of a female leaking body; the body that Antony is all too ready to reinscript according to his own political programme.[47]

But before that, it is Cassius's preliminary task to engage on a large-scale interrogation of natural phenomena; an interrogation which, for its radicalness, deserves attention in itself. The prodigies of the night of conspiracy are not simply presages to him, a premonitory corollary of an incipient kingly assassination (and of course they theatrically function as such). He invites to look at them as phenomena demanding investigation and a reordering according to a rational regime. Cassius cannot divest Caesar's body of his mythology without conjuring up the heavens. He also cannot question Caesar's body as both a man and a body politic without engaging in depth with questions of volume, place, and proportion. In brief, Cassius cannot downsize Caesar as a body politic without shaking the highly codified relation between bodies, geography, and cosmology; and Rome offered the proper global or expanding space to make his endeavour resonate as purposeful to Shakespeare's early modern times. In this sense, Cassius's anatomical role is of a piece with that of the new rational philosopher, looking for the "true cause"; even more so because it is connected with a nocturnal undertaking, a conjure, a secret.

Accordingly, he is portrayed as a perilous scholar. Cassius is "pale" and "leane", as Brutus is in Plutarch's "Life of Brutus" (North's Plutarch, 792). But Cassius's acknowledged reputation as a concerned student of philosophy in Plutarch is turned into Caesar's distrust and suspicion in Shakespeare's play: "He reads much, / He is a great observer, and he looks / Quite through the deeds of men". Also, "He loves no plays / As thou dost, Antony; he hears no music". And, "Seldom he smiles" (1.2.200–4). I would suggest here that we are also offered a dazzling synthesis of the two newly combined ways of reading sequentially *along* the flat surface of textbooks (e.g. old sources' knowledge on human beings) and, in depth, *into* the volume and secret of bodies. This is precisely what anatomists did and what new scientists (for example, Bacon) were increasingly advocating. Cassius indeed reads, observes, flays, probes into bodies.

I do not think, then, that it is too daring to say that it is this underlying broader questioning of a universe grounded in opinion (or mythology)— more than the overt cause for freedom—which in Shakespeare's play prepares the diminution of Caesar into a frail body and into the measure of a corpse literally fitting the measure of the anatomical table. Indeed, the cause of liberty and the enquiry into the "true cause" of natural phenomena, republican radicalism, and the inquisitive eye of science are gradually made to conflate in Cassius's stance. This assumes particular relevance, if viewed through the lenses provided by the coeval translation of Tacitus's *Annals* and *Histories* and the Earl of Essex's republican interest in it.[48] Tacitus's history of imperial Rome encouraged a view of Octavius's victory at Filippi as a watershed event which had changed the course of history and allowed for the beginning of Rome's imperial despotism, corruption, and decline.[49] Contrary to the growing concern of Tudor and Jacobean sovereigns in being celebrated as emperors of a nascent empire, Tacitus prompted a revision of imperial Rome. Tacitus also elicited (reinforcing Plutarch's portrait) a subterranean reappraisal of Brutus and Cassius—Cassius in particular—who (as in Plutarch's "Life of Brutus") is praised as "the last of the Romans" in Tacitus's *Annals*, but not only. "I am said to have praised Brutus and Cassius whose acts so many pens have recorded, whom not one has mentioned save with honour": so the dissident historian Cremutius Cordus defended himself in Tiberius's time, against an accusation which Tacitus records as an unheard of sort of crime to date, and which we may hold, perhaps, as the beginning of Brutus's and Cassius's suspicious reputation; the reputation which in due time will precipitate them straight into Dante's Hell. "Livy, with a fame for eloquence", Cordus claimed, "this very Cassius, this Brutus— not once does he describe them by the now fashionable titles of brigand and parricide, but time and again in such terms as he might apply to any distinguished patriots" (*Annals*, IV. 34).[50] Shakespeare's Brutus may have been warranted by both Plutarch and Tacitus when he reinstates Cassius to his initial honour: "The last of all the Romans, fare thee well" (5.3.99). In obliquely investing Cassius with the status of the scientist, Shakespeare by no means rehabilitates him. He subtly complicates his conspiracy, though, by updating his agenda with issues that relates him in a sophisticated way, namely controversially, to the early modern episteme of the "new science".

This reverberates on Antony's language itself. Meaningfully, if inadvertently, anatomy reveals to be a master metaphor in the soliloquy which he proffers in front of Caesar's dead body, before his speech at the market place. "O Mighty Caesar! Dost thou lie so low? / Are all thy conquests, glories, triumphs, spoils, / *Shrunk to this little measure*? Fare thee well. / I know not, gentlemen, what you intend / Who else must be let blood, who else is rank / If I myself" (my emphasis). Indeed, in his complaint, bloodletting stands for both murder and Cassius's speculative inspection that has reduced the king's body into a "shrunk" measure. Caesar's "rank" (e.g. "swollen") body features as both a malady and a quality of a disproportioned royal greatness, in the same ways in which bloodletting—a medical purging ritual—conflates the treatment Caesar undergoes as both a sacral and a secular, medicalized body.

Cassius in *Julius Caesar* raises a tangle of issues that the framework of the play cannot answer, among them the Baconian confrontation between scientific and divine knowledge, or else between rational knowledge and a knowledge driven by the force of impressions, opinion, and imagination; it had, as its corollary, the relationship between knowledge and power, an issue of no little importance in early modern England (let alone our present time).[51] But as we are aptly reminded by Foucauldian cultural theory, the entry of knowledge into discourse is always regulated by the institutions and the rules or limits posed by the order of representation.[52] And this is all the more true if, as in the early modern episteme, it is the body politic itself which dictates with its own hierarchically ordered properties and functions the order of any other body. As an aristocrat and a champion of liberty, a politician and a radical philosopher, a republican and a nostalgic of a (republican) old regime, Cassius is contradictorily ahead of as well as behind the present embodied by Antony. Cassius is in and out of History. Ironically, he, the anatomist/philosopher who has been so good in seducing Brutus and the select group of patricians into taking up the knife, will not be able to control the dispute over Caesar's dead body. Quickly marginalized to the borders of the play, he has no part in the crucial oratorical context which takes place at the market place. And Brutus—an appreciated orator—in asserting the cornerstones of the conspirators' political world vision ("the purity of the Idea", as Serpieri terms it),[53] is too honest to dare going beyond his favourite "brief compendious maner" (North's Pluatrch, 1056). All together the group of conspirators will be unable to administer politically, in front of the people, the "new" knowledge they have of Caesar's body which, symbolically, remains a nocturnal stuff. In fact, for all their ability to figure a reproportioned idea of bodies and space, their thoughts and words remain located in the aristocratic places of excellence and conspiracy. And once they have pursued theatrically their "noble" deed, they are not able to render adequate "public reasons" of Caesar's death (see 3.2.1–8). In brief, they are not able to move the 'anatomy lesson' out of the place where Caesar has been murdered—in Pompey's senatorial theatre, at the basis of his statue—to the larger theatre of the Forum. We now understand that it has not been by chance that Shakespeare has made us aware that "he [Cassius] doesn't like theatre".

But Antony does. "That's all I seek . . . / that I may / Produce his body to the market-place" (3.2.226–28), he claims in his negotiation with Brutus, well aware that the populace, used to Caesar's spectacular display of his body politic, is ready there in the Forum, to make the pendulum sway in favour of the best orator or actor.

Antony's Theatre of Passions and Recollection

"Why does Shakespeare select the middle of the third act for his murder, almost the precise center of the play, instead of locating it at the very end, as any 'normal' playwright would have done?", René Girard has asked, in his aim to shed light on what might be considered a disappointing mistake, a lack of aesthetic unity. In fact it seems as if "the hero dies in the 'wrong place'", and the play starts over again with another story, that of the murderers', which overlaps with that of Caesar's, actually stitching together two plays in one. The answer for Girard "is clear: *Julius Caesar* is centered neither on Caesar nor on his murderes; it is not a play about Roman history but about collective violence itself". What concerns its author is "how the murder of Caesar can be a source of disorder first, and then a source of order" and hence "the cyclical nature of sacrificial culture", the way "the end of one cycle (the Roman Republic)" leads to "the beginning of a new one (the Empire)", Girard suggests in his anthropological reading of the play.[54]

In this second part of my chapter, I would like to handle the issue raised by Girard in the culturalist terms of inheritance and memory. From the very outset the playwright has made clear that the issue in his play, more than Caesar, is Caesarism. "O that we then could come by Caesar's spirit / And not dismember Caesar", says Brutus in Act 2 (1.168–69) in his sacrificial envisaging of Caesar's murder, idealistically fantasized as a carving with no bloodshed (2.1.165–79). Cassius has taken a good deal of the play's first part to speculatively downsize the measure of a body which has grown to the disproportion of a menacing colossus. But now that the "bleeding business" has been done, as Brutus puts it (3.1.168), and Caesar's marred body is there bleeding at their feet, belying all good intentions, it all depends on the way the task of memory is accomplished, or more precisely, I argue, the way Caesar's ruins are "produced" or "re-produced" on the larger theatre of history. The problem is Caesar's inter-ment and his spectralization: a thing—the *thing*—that the conspirators will not be able to perform but as an internalized fear. On the contrary, this keeps Antony busy for most of the second part of the play and until its epilogue at Philippi. This is Antony's time, his play, the play in which he takes control of Caesar's "marred" body to transform it, through the "rhetoric of martyrdom",[55] from "a savage spectacle" (3.1.223) into a "piteous spectacle" (3.2.195–96).

As Jonathan Goldberg has written,

> Antony's role is to be the echo of Caesar, the fulfillment of his word, embodied in performance. Antony takes upon himself to extend him-self to represent Caesar. Antony's performance becomes history, as firmly as Cassius's lack of love for plays marks out his destiny.[56]

And yet, the conspirators' murder of Caesar is no less theatrically wise, one might argue. Nay, it is Cassius himself—he who doesn't love plays—who clads with the lore of a repeated and everlasting theatrical scene their tyrannicide: "Stoop, then, and wash. How many ages hence / Shall this our lofty scene be acted over / In states unborn and accents yet unknown" (3.1.111–13). As Richard Wilson has efficaciously observed in introduc-ing his edited New Casebooks on *Julius Caesar*, this is a play seemingly

> sure of the power of representation to pre-programme reality. . . . Whether dramatizing controversy about mass culture in the Col-osseum; conflict over public information in the Senate; contest for audience ratings in the Forum; or war conducted by surveillance and misinformation, this drama spoke directly to poststructuralist anxiety that there was nothing outside of texts and simulation.[57]

The mistake is to think, as Brutus does, that they can theatricalize their tyrannicide on the scene of history ("even to the [sight of the] market place") by separating their bloody arms and swords as defenders of "Peace, freedom, and liberty" from Caesar's remains; or that Caesar's body can continue to "bleed in sport" ("How many times shall Caesar bleed in sport") without resuscitating, in "spirit", the corpse "That now on Pompey's basis lies along, / *No worthier than the dust*" (3.1.114–16; my emphasis); or even presume that the action of their swords will not be followed by "added slaughter" (5.1.54) and generalized violence.[58]

Much has been said on Antony's consummate *ars oratoria* in his funeral eulogy and the extent to which Shakespeare is able to outdo most of the best treatises of the age, as well as Latin classics like Quintilian and Cicero.[59] However I would like to insist on this point in order to highlight Antony's handling of the crowd's passions and the role they play in enhancing the process of re-signification of Caesar's "dust", a goal which, as I take it, Antony achieves by replacing the cold if rational language of an exclusive anatomical theatre, with the highly affective and contagious temperature of a collective theatre of martyrdom and recollection. In so doing Antony's speech ends up contrasting not just Brutus's speech, I argue, but Cassius's arguments as well. As for passions, I deem it expedient to concentrate specifically on Cicero's *De Oratore*, the treatise that from the beginning of Shakespeare's career as a playwright seems to hold a special place in his concerns. It is no coincidence that it first occurs in his first Roman play, as a property of the Andronici's library and as one of Lavinia's inherited books: a *ruina*, though, as I argue in my chapter on *Titus Andronicus*, an obliquely denouncing item of a ruinous fatherly rhetoric in a play which is so catastrophically marked by Titus's amputated body as an orator. Then the treatise reappears, once again obliquely, in *Julius Caesar*, embedded in an elliptical if crucial and premonitory statement voiced by Cicero himself: "Indeed it is a strange-disposed time. / But men may construe things after their fashion, / Clean from the purpose of the things themselves" (1.3.33–35). As a matter of fact the historical Cicero—an authoritative presence in the standard curricula of Tudor grammar schools—had amply reflected in his treatise on the difference between truth and opinion, or between reality and perception: an inescapable defining question for the *ars oratoria* and the power it exerted on people's convictions and choices by exploiting exactly that difference.

> Now nothing in oratory, Catulus, is more important than to win for the orator the favour of his hearer, and to have the latter so affected as to be swayed by something resembling a mental impulse or emotion, rather than by judgement or deliberation. For men decide far more problems by hate, or love, or lust, or rage, or sorrow, or joy, or hope, or fear, or illusion, or some other inward emotion, than by reality, or authority, or any legal standard, or judicial precedent, or statute.
> (*Orat*. II.178)[60]

Indeed, these considerations defined the entire field of oratory as the terrain of opinion formation: "For, while art [science] is concerned with the things that are known, the activity of the orator has to do with opinion, not knowledge" (*Orat*. II.30).

Shakespeare's Antony seems to be all too aware of this when after Caesar's murder he immediately understands that Rome's political future and the course of history itself depends on how prompt he is in upturning one scenery (Pompey's theatre) into another (the market place), one range of feelings (judgement) into another (emotion), one set of topics (principles and abstractions) into another (facts and concreteness). Nay, in this he demonstrates he is a champion in "readiness": an ability—*celeritas*—highly fostered in Cicero's *Orator* (I.17), before being rewritten by Hamlet's bemusing "readiness is all" (5.2.194). Antony asks permission to bring Caesar's body to the market place and to speak after Brutus, which Brutus mistakenly permits against Cassius's (far-sighted and) predicting, "I like it not" (3.1.243). Meanwhile Decius's incitement to Cassius "to go to the pulpit" with Brutus and speak to the people has remained unanswered (3.1.84). There, in the Forum, Antony will take advantage of the fact that Cassius is given exit by Brutus, evidently at pains to divide more than keep the multitude together and closing ranks with Cassius for a univocal explanation: "Cassius, go you into the other street / And part the number: / Those that will hear me speak, let 'em stay here. / Those that will follow Cassius, go with him / And public reasons shall be rendered / Of Caesar's death". To which one of the plebeians answers: "I will hear Brutus speak"; and another: "I will hear Cassius and compare their reasons / When severally we hear them rendered" (3.1.3–10). We are not allowed to know what happens or what is said offstage.[61] But on stage Cassius's protracted deconstructive anatomy of Caesar's disproportioned body, which has long kept him busy so far, is already an echo, diluted and lost into Brutus's nudely, if honestly enounced argument of "peace, freedom, liberty". For when Antony's turn comes, he demonstrates not only that he is "a man who can speak in a way calculated to convince" (*Orat.* I.260), but also, as Cicero added in his instructions for the apprentice orator of his own present, that he is a man who knows how to speak to the masses: "For this oratory of ours must be adapted to the ears of the multitude, for charming or urging their minds to approve of proposals, which are weighed in no goldsmith's balance, but in what I may call common scales" (II.159).

As Cicero anticipates in the first pages of his dialogical treatise, this was the achievement of maturity (55 BC). Structured as a dialogue among a plurality of voices, it came out of an experience, which had been forged by an age of crisis and conflicts, and an urge to update the transversal art of oratory to the necessity of his present times:

> For in my early years I came just upon the days when the old order was overthrown [Cicero may have been eight at the outbreak of the civil war between Marius and Sulla]; then by my consulship I was drawn into the midst of a universal struggle and crisis, and my whole time ever since that consulship I have spent in stemming those billows which, stayed by my efforts from ruining the nation, rolled in a flood upon myself.
>
> (I.3 *et passim*)

Indeed, his was a world of transitions and a new order: the transitions which brought the republican Rome to the threshold of a vast and populated empire, an age in which oratory, the art of speaking and communication, needed to be understood and reassessed in the terms of the present times: namely according to the dynamics of the Forum, a prevailing (and unmediated) space in the relation between kings and people—and a fertile conjuncture for populism, as we would say nowadays. Shakespeare seems to be more than alert to this, with resonances that reverberate on his coeval *Henry V* and also hint at contemporary Elizabethan ways of handling the relation with the large community of the nation in early modern times.

Shakespeare's Mark Antony, as suggested in *De Oratore*, is "swift in invention, copious in exposition and embellishment, and steadfast and enduring in recollection" (I.114). And yet, as Cicero's Antonius (see I.208), he knows that art consists in dissimulating art: "I come not, friends, to steal away your hearts, / I am no orator, as Brutus is, / But, as you know me all, a plain blunt man / . . . For I have neither wit, nor worth, / Action, nor utterance, nor the power of speech / To stir men's blood. I only speak right on: / I tell you that you yourself know" (3.2.210–17). What Shakespeare's character also knows (via Cicero) is that a good orator "ought to feel the pulse of every class, time of life, and degree" (*Orat.* I.224), and that "in oratory the very cardinal sin is to depart from the language of everyday life, and the usage approved by the sense of the community" (I.12 and II.201). And in fact complying with his assertive denial of being an orator, Antony organizes his speech according to an attentively gathered list of "facts" aimed at disproving Brutus's abstract allegation of "ambition" with a concrete and collectively produced popular memory of Caesar ("I tell you what you yourself know").

Structured as a plurality of voices, the "either for or against" method (*Orat.* I.263) was both a practice and a pedagogy in Cicero's treatise: "By this time it is plain that the power to argue both sides of every question is abundantly furnished from the same commonplaces", Cicero wrote.

> But your opponents' proof must be countered, either by contradicting the argument chosen to establish it, or by showing that their desired conclusion is not supported by their premises and does not follow therefrom; or, if you do not so rebut it, you must adduce on the opposite side some proof of greater or equal cogency.
>
> (II.216; my emphasis)

Favoured by his position as a second speaker, Antony firmly adopts the dismantling possibilities provided by the contradictory option. Against Brutus's abstract allegation, ambition, he provides proofs "of greater or equal cogency" (for three times Caesar refused a royal crown; he replenished the State's coffers with riches he won in his campaigns; he was generous with the poor), but, faithful to the Ciceronian recommendation of using a reconciliatory style for highly emotional passages, he subtly dissimulates his intention as a compliant argument: "I speak not to dis-prove what Brutus spoke, / But here I am to speak what I do know" (3.2.101–102). / "The noble Brutus / Hath told you Caesar was ambi-tious: / If it was so, it was a grievous fault" (3.2.78–80). "He [Caesar] was my friend, faithful and just to me; / But Brutus says, he was ambi-tious, and Brutus is an honourable man" (3.2.86–88). But this is only to submit, concomitantly, the antagonist's only allegation, ambition, and its only warrant, honour, to a deflating repetition. Hidden behind a modesty strategically obtained by a hammering succession of litotes,[62] Brutus's allegation, ambition—with nothing to warrant it but Brutus's honour—is relentlessly evoked to be undermined by a parallel counter-enumeration of shared facts and memories: "what I do know" (3.2.102), "that which you yourself know" (3.2.217). There is no place in the Forum for Cas-sius's speculative anatomy, whose reasons, at this point, disappear in the background as things belonging to the secret world of conspiracy. Antony instead has free rein to deploy all the talent and the abilities that Cicero lists as indispensable to a good orator, and which Shakespeare makes him exploit unscrupulously, in order that the plebeians, as they ask, may be "satisfied" (3.2.19). In this the "arrangement" of topics—one of the five defining elements of the Ciceronian theory of oratory, together with invention, style, memory, and delivery (I.187)—is essential. Antony knows that in order "to stir men's blood", the objective that has been in his mind from the very beginning, it is essential that pieces of evidence be provided according to an order and a timing dictated by the effect they are meant to produce on his audience (see *Orat.* II.47–48). Evidence is handled accordingly: some proofs are immediately produced to win the goodwill of his audience, others, such as Caesar's will ("a kind of herme-neutic streap-tease" for Richard Wilson),[63] are announced and delayed with a perfect knowledge of the devices of amplification and with the lucid Ciceronian awareness that emotions can be gradually and more effectively aroused and controlled if giving the impression that one is prompting the opposite mood: "Lastly appeals, whether mild or passionate, and whether for winning favour or stirring the feelings, must be swept aside by exciting the opposite impressions" (*Orat.* II.216). And in fact Antony is a master in giving the impression that he is keeping his audience calm, while he is actually and consistently warming it up to the point of explosion and mutiny. "Have patience, gentle friends", he pleads in delaying the reading of Caesar's will. "I must not read it. / It is not meet you know how Caesar loved you. / You are not wood, you are not stones, but men: / And being men, hearing the will of Caesar, / It will enflame you, it will make you mad" (3.2.141–45).

Antony's "right moment" for the unfolding of his central and win-ning tangible evidence—Caesar's mangled body—is the construction of an astute and long-drawn "either for or against" manipulation of proofs, memories, and emotions. Indeed, he thus complies with the three conditions that Cicero indicates as necessary to the art of speaking and persuasion: "the proof of our allegations, the winning of our hearers' favour, and *the rousing of their feelings to whatever impulse our case may require*" (II.115; my emphasis). Antony tests and pursues this last achievement to its extreme consequences, his aim being not Caesar's burial, as he modestly declares at the beginning of his speech in front of the crowd, but the resuscitation of a spectral and vengeful "Cry havoc" Caesar, as he has sworn in his soliloquy on Caesar's "ruins"—"the ruins of the noblest man", the "ruins" par excellence—at the feet of Pompey's statue (3.1.256).

> O pardon me, thou bleeding piece of earth,
> That I am meek and gentle with these butchers.
> Thou art the ruins of the noblest man
> That ever lived in the tide of times.
> . . .
> Over thy wounds now I do prophesy
> (which like dumb mouths do ope their ruby lips
> To beg the voice and utterance of my tongue)
> . . .
> That a curse shall light upon the limbs of men:
> Domestic fury and fierce civil strife
> Shall cumber all the parts of Italy:
> Blood and destruction shall be so in use,
> And dreadful objects so familiar,
> That mothers shall but smile when they behold
> Their infants quartered with the hands of war:
> All pity choked with custom of fell deeds,
> And Caesar spirit, ranging for revenge,
> With Ate by his side come hot from hell,
> Shall in these confines, with a monarch's voice,
> Cry havoc and let slip the dogs of war,
> That this foul deed shall smell above the earth
> With carrion men, groaning for burial.
>   (3.1.254–75)

The body that Cassius has squeezed to measure in his pre-mortem anatomical lesson of proportions re-emerges as a disproportioned and terrifying (fatherly) figure in the second part of the play: a monstrous and destroying portent. In many aspects the violence summoned in this tirade is not inferior to those that Shakespeare generally assigns to his villains: take Aaron in his previous Roman play. But in the delivery of his speech Antony is simply insuperable in the art he is able to deploy in finely shaping and channelling this violence into a collective and emotional crescendo. Indeed he shows he knows only too well that, as in Cicero's profile of the good orator, "all the mental emotions, with which nature has endowed the human race, are to be intimately understood, because it is in calming or kindling the feelings of the audience that the full power and science of oratory are to be brought into play" (*Orat.* I.17, but see also I.165).

Like an orator, Antony is proficient in gathering, arranging, and memorizing his topics, but like an actor he is able to transfer such a mingle of love, sorrow, pity, compassion, indignation, and anger onto his audience. Which he does by constructing, as at theatre, and as in the Elizabethan wooden "O", a contagious and reciprocating circle of gazes, memories, and emotions. "Thy heart is big", he has previously said to one of his servants, "get thee apart and weep. / Passion I see, is catching, for mine eyes, / Seeing those beads of sorrow stand in thine, / Begin to water" (3.1.282–85). Passion is discovered as the contagious effect of mirroring eyes. Antony has practiced enough for the role he is going to play in a while, and he knows his art when he physically invites the crowd to design "a ring about the corpse of Caesar" for its final dramatic disclosure, the production of Caesar's body, whose body parts—wounds, blood—are shown as if they were "animated things":[64] "If you have tears, prepare to shed them now. / You all do know this mantle. I remember / The first time ever Caesar put it on. / 'T was on a summer's evening . . . / Look, in this place ran Cassius' dagger through. . . . / Through this, the well beloved Brutus stabbed, / and as he plucked his cursed steel away, / Mark how the blood of Caesar followed it. / . . . O, now you weep, and I perceive you feel / The dint of pity: these are gracious drops. / Kind souls, what weep you when you but behold / Our Caesar's wounded? Look you here, / Here is himself, marred as you see with traitors" (3.2.167–95).

As is well-known, ancient *ars oratoria*, the art of those who were in power, the art that as argued in this volume Shakespeare addresses as a fragmented fatherly posture in *Titus Andronicus*, was more than aware of its contiguity with theatre and acting. Cicero, who takes pains to differentiate "manly" oratorical *actio* from histrionic mimicry,[65] cannot avoid the example of theatre when he comes to the orator's empathy with one's argument and audience. "I give you my word", says the advocate orator Antonius in Cicero's treatise,

> that I never tried, by means of a speech, to arouse either indignation or compassion, either ill-will or hatred, in the minds of tribunal, without being really stirred myself, as I worked upon their minds, by the very feelings to which I was seeking to prompt them.
>
> (*Orat.* II.190)

The capacity to perform the emotion that the orator wants to transfer tangibly, through the eyes, onto the audience, which is essential in forensic pleading, is not different from that of an actor or poet, no matter if in this case theirs is the world of fiction, Cicero's orator argues, exemplifying his point with a few moving lines by the Roman poet and dramaturg Pacuvius:

> what can be so unreal as poetry, the theatre or stage-plays? And yet, in that sort of things, I myself have often been a spectator when the actor-man's eyes seemed to be blazing behind his mask, as he spoke those solemn lines. . . . I thought I heard sobs of mourning in his voice. Now if that player, though acting it daily, could never act that scene without emotion, do you really think that Pacuvius, when he wrote it, was in a calm and careless frame of mind?
>
> (II.193)

Shakespeare's Antony, like Cicero's orator, is able to reach and share with the crowd the same degree of pathos that good actors are capable of achieving in front of their audience. But such a Ciceronian reflection also touches us for being strikingly similar to Hamlet's set of concerns in matters regarding the "theatre" of passions and the wider sphere of dissimulation. Antony in *Julius Caesar* displays the same "monstrous" and envied capacity of empathy that, at Elsinore, Hamlet observes in the actor who impersonates Hecuba's grief: "A broken voice, and his whole function suiting / With forms to his conceit? And all for nothing! / For Hecuba! / What's Hecuba to him or he to her / That he should weep for her? (2.2.475–79).[66]

Antony's *actio*—the language of the body in Cicero's conceptualization (*Orat.*, III.222)—prevails on Brutus's because he is in perfect control of the dissimulative side of *ars oratoria*.[67] He grieves with the Romans, weeps with and for them. He gives a form to memory and a resuscitating tongue to Caesar's wounds. Brutus too weeps for Caesar's bleeding body. But compared with his clear-cut measure and partition of his first-person emotions ("As Caesar loved me, I weep for him . . . There is tears, for his love; joy, for his fortune; honour, for his valour; and death for his ambition", 3.2.27–28), Antony communicates the impression that the flow of his emotions grows together with the affected and swelling emotions of the crowd's. Before showing Caesar's body, the evidence that Antony produces are memories (of love, benefits, magnanimity) that gradually worm their way into the audience's permeable eyes and bodies.[68] He doesn't ask the people solely to "awake [their] senses, that [they] may the better judge", as Brutus does (3.1.16–179), nor does he engage with a discussion of Brutus's republican values of "piece, freedom, liberty". With his perfectly synchronized *actio* and *pronuntiatio*, he circumvents them by capturing his audience in the activation of a collective and contagious memory theatre which consistently affects their ear as well their sight with objects of memory "image"-natively recalled.

As a mnemonic technique based on a spatial division and disposition of one's subject matters in speaking, the technical art of memory, as shown by Yates and (in less distant years) by Carruthers, was a part of classical rhetoric. "From antiquity, *memoria* was fully institutionalized in education, and like all vital practices it was adapted continuously to circumstances of history. *Memoria* unites written and oral transmission, eye and ear, and helps to account for the highly mixed oral-literate nature of medieval cultures".[69] But even though the printed book had rendered most of its curious memory drillings obsolete, humanism had rediscovered it through Quintilian and Cicero, as essential to the increasingly important art of speaking. In Cicero's oratorical expounding, memory, like letters in a written script, functions as a storage of topics,[70] and the classification and arrangement of its contents is imagined as a field of positioned images and precedents. It is as if they were "gold hidden here and there in the earth, it should be enough for me to point out to [the apprentice orator] some marks and indications of its positions, which with knowledge he could do his own digging and find what he wanted" (*Orat.* II.174). We might imagine that Antony's acting of his eulogy on the scaffolds of Shakespeare's Globe is marked by a similar unfolding of theatrical localized topics. But the "the discovery of what to say is insufficient, unless you can handle it when found", Cicero recommended (II.176). Mnemonic techniques were useless, if you didn't "supplement all this with the torch of memory", with the bodily movement, "intonation" and "energy" involved in the delivery (e.g. *actio* and *pronuntiatio*) of your speech (II.149). If the candidate orator

> shall succeed in appearing, to those before whom he is to plead, to be such a man as he would desire to seem, and in touching their hearts in such fashion to be able to lead or drag them whithersoever he pleases, he will assuredly be completely furnished for oratory.
>
> (II.176)

In *Julius Caesar* the "torch"—"the torch of memory"—becomes, literally, the inflaming and contagious fire of violence that Antony throws among the crowd and which transforms Rome into a burning city, a Trojan beacon. 1 PLEBEIAN: "We'll burn his body in the holy place, / And with the brands of fire all the traitors' houses. / Take up the body". 2 PLEBEIAN: "Go fetch fire". ANTONY: "Now let it work. Mischief, thou art afoot: / Take thou what course thou wilt" (3.2.244–52). Interestingly if ironically, Shakespeare did not forget to mention that Cicero ("by order of proscription"), together with Cinna—a poet—were among the victims of that fire (4.3.174–77), even though omitting Plutarch's further piece of information (in "The Life of Marcus Antonius"), that Antony ordered those who had "been given commission to kill Cicero, that they should strik of his head & right hand, with which he had written invectives . . .

against him" (North's Plutarch, 979). But others were literally victims of that devouring and devoured fire (think of Portia), a fire that will be quenched only after Philippi's final carnage, presided over by Caesar's ghost.

Transforming Ruins Into Relics

The crowd's permeable body, namely its affectability, assumes even more relevance if we consider that in Shakespeare's play the temporal setting of the conspiracy against Caesar and his assassination conflates the (long noticed) two seasonal festivities of the Lupercalia (15 February) and the Ides of March (15 March). What was also significant for Shakespeare's audience was the quasi-temporal coincidence of the play's festive scenario with the Carnival, the period in which public anatomy lessons were allowed to be held in Renaissance Europe. Critics have provided insightful comment on the ways in which such a layered festive scenario underwrites the play, and the ways in which an atmosphere of celebration and carousal bears on the manipulation of the masses and their all-too-easy oscillation between ritual and rebellion.[71] Indeed, the play shows how festivities are favourable to the construction of the legend of those who are in power as well as the spread of contagious and indiscriminate violence.

Anatomy, with its mingle of violence and symbolic redemption, offered a background which was in line with this. As in the very popular public executions, from which came most of the bodies for dissections, the practice of anatomy fostered a ritualized (if commodified) perception of the inspected body. "The execution itself was a 'function', an event that was ritualized in such a way as to reorder its profound violence", Ferrari observes; an event during which the criminal body passing through the redemptive retribution of execution could be transformed into a relic.

> What was sought for above all was fat, but also blood, teeth, hair, burnt skull, the umbilicus, and other parts and substances of the body that possessed specific healing properties. Human fat . . . was generally extracted from the bodies of convicts by the executioner— sometimes as the last act of execution—purified, and then sold as a pain-killer. In England the mere contact with the cadaver of someone who had been hanged was considered to be therapeutic.[72]

The imagery used by Decius in interpreting Calphurnia's dream seems to be deeply indebted to the popular, ritualized practices which accompanied public executions or anatomy practices all over Europe:

> Your statue spouting blood in many pipes
> In which so many smiling Romans bathed
> Signifies that from your great Rome shall suck

Reviving blood, and that great man shall press
For tinctures, stains, relics and cognizance.
This by Calphurnia's dream is signified.

                    (2.2.85–90)

But it will be Mark Antony, "a masquer and a reveller" in Cassius's
words (5.1.62), the astutely demagogical politician trained, according to
Plutarch's story of his life, in "asiatik" eloquence,[73] who will be able to
capitalize on Caesar's body by moving the corpse, this "bleeding piece of
earth" (3.1.254), to the market place, and by turning Cassius's secular
anatomy into what might be seen as a form of "sacred anatomy",[74] a
ritualized and almost Christological understanding of Caesar's mangled
body, but as has been noted, in a context of perverted and commodified
rituals.[75] Interestingly, as if mindful of Henrician (1538) and Elizabethan
proscription of any form of worship for relics and the like,[76] Caesar's
memory and its transmission among generations is strengthened by the
prevailing register of a rhetoric which is prompted by withholding the
pagan (or papist) consuming of Caesar's Christological body (3.2.195).

> But here's a parchment, with the seal of Caesar.
> I found it in his closet. 'Tis his will.
> Let but the commons hear this testament—
> Which, pardon me, *I do not mean to read*—
> *And they would go and kiss dead Caesar's wounds,*
> *And dip their napkins in his sacred blood,*
> *Yea, beg a hair of him for memory,*
> And, dying, mention it within their wills,
> Bequeathing it as a rich legacy
> Unto their issue.
>
>   (3.2.129–38; my emphasis)

Caesar's body parts in Antony's hands—a drop of his blood, a hair—
are given a currency which lies undisclosed in Caesar's will and whose
delayed reading, with his charitable donations, is Antony's trump card:
"he gives, To every several man, seventy-five drachmas. . . . Moreover, he
has left you all his walks, / His private arbours and new-planted orchards"
(3.2.234–39). But he first invites the populace to circle around Caesar's
body and to look with tearful eyes at his wounded body which, in this
way, undergoes a reordering according to the symbolism of the martyred
body, a reordering which is later astutely sanctioned by Octavius when
Shakespeare has him readjust, anachronistically, the number of Caesar's
wounds: "three and thirty" (5.1.52), like Christ's years, and not 23 as in
the playwright's Plutarchan sources ("The Life of Caesar").

"An element of martyr-drama lies hidden in every drama of tyranny",
Benjamin observes. In examining the baroque drama we are confronted

with "a fundamental uncertainty as to whether this is a drama of tyranny or a history of a martyrdom", but "it has nothing to do with religious conceptions" (*Origin*, 73). It is such because

> The enduring fascination of the fallen tyrant is rooted in the conflict between the impotence and depravity of his person, on the one hand, and, on the other, the extent to which the age was convinced of the sacrosanct power of his role. . . . if the tyrant falls, not simply in his own name, as an individual, but as a ruler and in the name of mankind and history, then his falls has the quality of a judgement, in which the subject too is implicated.
>
> (72)

"O what a fall was there, my countrymen! / Then I, and you, and all of us fell down, / Whilst bloody treason flourished over us" (3.2.197), Antony pleads. With Antony's affective conflation of the tyrant and the iconography of a suffering man, Shakespeare brings to the fore precisely this historical and contradictory conjuncture. "Just as Christ", Benjamin writes, "the King, suffered in the name of mankind, so, in the eyes of the writers of the baroque, does royalty in general" (*Origin*, 73).

Antony's Caesar is as much a document (a document in butchery) as it is a monument (the sacralized memory) of a suffering body. But for the crowd, his place in history shall rely on the unhistorical remembrance of a body dismembered into disassembled and commodified objects of memory, wounds, a holed mantle, a tuft of hair, a blood-stained napkin, gifts, money: spoils all turned into relics if not, perhaps, *souvenirs*. As Benjamin suggests, "The *souvenir* (*Das Andenken*) is the relic secularized. The *souvenir* is the complement of the 'experience'".[77] Caesar's remembrance relies on the fragmentariness of a memory grounded in acts of commodified experience. It is connoted however by a permanence upon which Benjamin, elsewhere, elaborates by means of the Bergsonian notion of involuntary memory:

> Experience is indeed a matter of tradition, in collective existence as well as private life. It is less the product of facts firmly anchored in memory than of a convergence in memory of accumulated and frequently unconscious data. It is, however, not all Bergson's intention to attach any specific historical label to memory.[78]

In *Julius Caesar*, this is a permanence that Shakespeare's Antony constructs in terms of images forcefully impressed on and through the people's eyes as the guilt and memory of a collective unconscious. As such they are destined to return in many forms of unsettling spectrality: "You all know this mantle. I remember / The first time ever Caesar put it on. . . . / Look, in this place ran Cassius dagger through . . . / See what a rent . . . /

Through this, the well-beloved Brutus stabbed, . . . / This was the most unkindest cut of all: . . . / Mark how the blood of Caesar followed it / . . . / Look you here, / Here is himself, marred as you see with traitors" (3.2.168–95).

"I Come to Bury Caesar, Not to Praise Him": Caesar's Spectralization

"For there to be ghost, there must be a return to the body, but to a body that is more abstract than ever", Derrida argues.

> The spectrogenic process corresponds therefore to a paradoxical *incorporation*. Once ideas or thoughts (*Gedanke*) are detached from their substratum, one engenders some ghost by giving them a *body* from which ideas and thoughts have been torn loose, but by incarnating the latter in *another artifactual body, a prosthetic body,* a ghost of spirit, one might say a ghost of the ghost.[79]

Relics in Antony's funeral oration seem to participate in precisely such a construction of the ghost's prosthetic and self-reproducing corporeality.

After Antony's incomparable performance, a collective rite of spectralization, only a sceptical and Nietzschean philosopher to the core like Hamlet (the hero of the playwright's assumed next play), in league with an author capable of relentless self-deconstruction as Shakespeare was—the Hamlet who, however, is "confronted with an overplus, a superfluity" of ghostly fatherhood[80]—may still doubt the powerful agency of recycled dustiness ("Imperious Caesar, dead and turned to clay, / Might stop a hole to keep the wind away. / Oh, that that earth which kept the world in awe / Should patch a wall t' expel the water's flaw", *Ham.* 5.1.192–95). Thanks to Antony's oration, Caesar's corpse, the "bleeding piece of earth", is resuscitated to his spectral anamorphic shape, "a trap for the gaze" in Garber's Lacanian discussion of *Hamlet*.[81] The relic in *JC*, the part for the whole, by now has a life of its own. The relic opens up to all kind of substitution and more than one form of distortion or metamorphic apparition.

"The Latin word for civilization, *humanitas*, derives from the verb *humare*, to bury", Vico reminds us.[82] For Caesar—a disproportioned colossus in Cassius's debunking anatomy (1.2.135)—the playwright conjured up all his dramatic art to officiate the burial *par excellence* ("I come to bury Caesar, not to praise him", 3.2.75), as well as his spectralization:[83] namely his being turned into what is undecidable (BRUTUS: "Art thou some god, some angel, or some devil, / That mak'st my blood cold, and my hair to stare?", 4.3.277–78); as well as the experience of being haunted, being gripped by the terror announced by the iterability of his "monstrous apparition" as a ghostly "thing" (BRUTUS: "Why com'st thou?" GHOST: "To tell thee thou shalt see me at Philippi". BRUTUS: "Well: then I shall see thee again?", 4.3.280–82).

Roger Ascham likened him to a half hidden and ungraspable Venus in Shakespeare's time.[84] As a matter of fact, and as often noticed by critics (from Schanzer to Goldberg, Melchiori, Drakakis, and others), Shakespeare from the very outset of the play has worked at constructing his Caesar as an absent figure, namely, in Drakakis's words, as a ruler who is "beyond reach", "above the view of men". And if Caesar is the tragedy's subject, Melchiori has written, this is so

> not in his quality of conqueror and protagonist of history, but in that of a sovereign on the verge of becoming a tyrant. Dramaturgically his role is far from preeminent, but it is functional to the main theme and its dialectics. The true protagonists are Caesar's murderers and those who dispute the legitimacy of that act.[85]

Schanzer adds to this by asking: "But does not Shakespeare further anticipate Pirandello, by making us feel that perhaps there *is* no real Caesar, that he merely exists as a set of images in other men's minds and his own?"[86] Indeed, as we witness a conspicuous variety of conflicting opinions about him, we see relatively little of him onstage, and when we come to the self-theatricalized and self-promotional Caesar in front of the crowd, this takes place offstage as if to amplify the subjugating charisma his persona exerts on the people of Rome. Caesar is already a ghost and the "ghost writer" of Shakespeare's play itself in Garber's discussion of the spectrality of Shakespeare's canon.[87]

Performance has not ignored Caesar's pervasive ghostly nature, nor its constitutive, disproportioned, and "anamorphic" shape. Trevor Nunn in his memorable 1972 production for the Royal Shakespeare Company at Stratford-upon-Avon underscored the "danger" of Caesar's exorbitant and incumbent shape, by having onstage, for the entire duration of the performance, a colossal and menacing statue. In his finely stylized production at the Gigi Proietti Globe Theatre in Rome (2019), the Italian theatre director Daniele Salvo similarly assigned due relevance to Caesar's spectral disproportion, the target of Cassius's anatomy. In his *Giulio Cesare*, Caesar's murder gives way to the hallucinatory sight of a spectral gigantic substitute obtained with prosthetic stilts. Caesar's murder has generated a monster, the counter and interacting image of the conspirator's searched for "measure".

"Upon what meat doth this our Caesar feed / That has grown so great?" Cassius asks in the first act (1.2.148–49). But the play also invites to reflect on inheritance and memory, the ways in which "the "bleeding piece of earth" regains his colossal shape in the community's eye of the mind. Du Bellay's verses come to mind: "O that I had the *Thracian* Poets harpe, / For to awake out th' infernal shade / Those antique Cæsars, sleeping long

Figure 3.5 Caesar's ghost in Daniele Salvo's production of *Giulio Cesare* at the Gigi Proietti Globe Theatre Silvano Toti, Rome, 20 September–6 October 2019.

Source: Photo ® Marco Borrelli, courtesy of Borrelli and the Gigi Proietti Globe Theatre Silvano Toti Archive (Roma Tre University)

in darke, / The which this ancient Citie whilome made" (2.5.1–4). What also comes to mind is Spenser's praise of Du Bellay for reviving and giving "a second life to dead decayes" (Envoy, 3–6), as well as, ironically, the unresuscitated (but not less ghostly) mass of Roman "carkases" in his *Faerie Queen*, lying in the House of Pride's underground dungeon (I.V.49).[88] But here the connection with Du Bellay's necromantic art of resurrection can only serve to indicate how far and further Shakespeare forces his concern for Caesar's surviving spirit.

In Shakespeare's play, Caesar's "bleeding piece of earth"—"the ruins of the noblest man"—have grown to the shape of a ghost which fearfully swells beyond its Vitruvian defining limits. In fact, Antony's speech does not only manage to downsize Brutus's abstract allegations. He also and foremost manages to dismantle the very law of measure and proportion which has been incessantly voiced so far by Cassius in his republican/

(Tacitean) anatomy of the king, to inaugurate instead the disproportion and disproportioning visuality of the ghost. Announced by the wavering and deformed flame of Brutus's candle, to Brutus the ghost materializes as the effect of a contagion, an *ill*-conjunction of "thing" and "eyes", exteriority and inwardness, objectification and subjectification: "How ill this taper burns. Ha! Who comes here? / I think it is the weakness of mine eyes / That shapes this monstrous apparition. / It comes upon me: art thou any thing? / Art thou some god, some angel, or some devil, / That mak'st my blood cold, and my hair to stare? / Speak to me what thou art". "Thy evil spirit, Brutus", the ghost replies (4.3.273–80). It also *"begins by coming back"* ["Again", "Ay at Philippi"], Derrida observes. "One cannot control its comings and goings" (*Specters*, 11).

But Cassius is no less infected and haunted for being spared a real apparition. Indeed he is as much a prey of a condition ("As we were sickly prey", 5.1.86) that Derrida would call a "phenomenological reduction to the ghost" (*Specters*, 162). Marked by the disavowal of his Epicurean secular philosophy, the courageous and rational Cassius surrenders to "things that do presage" (5.1.78), namely to an overall spectralized landscape which fatally swallows up everything. Architectonically shaped by the eye-sky of the Globe, this is epitomized by the menacing "downward look" of ominous and proliferating "ravens, crows and kites": a watching "canopy" made up of beasts of prey which "Fly o'er our heads . . . / As we were sickly prey", and whose "downward look" has grown to the dimension of a confusing and fatal sky: "Their shadows seem / A canopy most fatal, under which / Our army lies, ready to give up the ghost" (5.1.83–88). Meaningfully, such a canopy / eye has been anticipated from the very outset (in 1.2.130) as the spectral visual form of Caesar's power, an "eye, whose bend doth awe the world".

In Cassius's death, Brutus reads the triumph of Caesar's unleashed vengeful spirit: "O Julius Caesar, thou art mighty yet. / Thy spirit walks abroad and turns our swords / In our proper entrails" (5.3.94–97). Messala and Titinius, his faithful lieutenants, instead refer us speculatively to a more pervasive kind of spectrality. They mourn Cassius's death as the child of error, that of a man fallen under the gloomy aegis of Melancholy, in the way he courts the spectrality of self-"engendered" misconstructions: "the things that are not" (5.3.59–71). As Derrida observes,

> the technique for having visions, for *seeing* ghosts is in truth a technique to *make oneself seen* by ghosts. *The ghost, always, is looking at me.* . . . Follow my gaze, the spectre seems to say. . . . Let us follow this gaze. Right away we lose sight of it: disappeared, the departed, in the hall of mirrors where it multiplies. There is not only one spirit watching You. Since the spirit "is" everywhere (*aus allam*), it proliferates *a priori*, it puts in place, while depriving them of any place, a mob

of specters to which one can no longer even assign a *point of view*: they invade all of space.

As mostly for Cassius, they are "non-localizable", they are "atopic", in Derrida's expounding on spectrality (*Specters*, 168).

In *Julius Caesar* the phantasm which—as a spectral embodiment of fatherhood and kingship—is already foreshadowing and rehearsing the role it will play in Shakespeare's imminent *Hamlet*, is everywhere; and with the undecidability of its form—"what art thou?"—contaminates everything: political beliefs, sky, gaze, thoughts. It has grown into a watching and enfeebling "canopy", and has muddled every perspective, symmetry, point of view. In this the ghost completes Antony's work. In fact, Caesar's disproportionate figure, that Cassius from the outset has viewed as a disfiguring component of a proper perspectival background, in Antony's hands has reacquired the quality of a fearful portent-like figure. Indeed, Caesar's *interment-as-disinterment* (as I would call it) gives way to his re-apparition, a remythologized *monstrum* which signals the end, I suggest, of the Renaissance theory of proportion that Cassius seems to have politicized so well in the first half of the play.

"The final development of the theory of proportions", Panofsky has written,

> corresponds, however, to the general evolution of art itself. The artistic value and significance of a theory exclusively concerned with the objective dimensions of bodies contained within definable boundaries could not depend on whether or not the representation of such objects was recognized as the essential goal of artistic activity. Its importance was bound to diminish in proportion as the artistic genius began to emphasize the subjective conception of the object in preference to the object itself.

In fact, the law of proportion was not independent of the prevailing cultural meanings which characterized the Renaissance episteme and the seeds of its mutations:

> The victory of the subjective principle was prepared, we recall, by the art of the fifteenth century, which affirmed the autonomous mobility of the things represented and the autonomous visual experience of the artist as well as the beholder. When, after the "revival of classical antiquity" had spent its momentum, these first concessions to the subjective principle came to be exploited to the full, the role of the theory of human proportions as a branch of art theory was finished. . . . The styles that may be grouped under the heading of "non pictorial" subjectivism—pre-Baroque Mannerism and modern "Expressionism"— could do nothing with a theory of human proportions, because for

them the solid objects in general, and the human figure in particular, meant something only in so far as they could be *arbitrarily shortened and lengthened, twisted, and, finally, disintegrated.*

(my emphasis)[89]

Placed at the point of the intersection between Renaissance and Baroque culture, Shakespeare's early modern appropriation of Caesar's ruins undergoes the discipline of opposed and interacting perspectival regimes; a moment which is also ideologically marked by a crisis of sovereignty and a state of emergency. Cassius's (republican) yearning for geometrical measure in Caesar, his perspectival and symmetrical world vision, breaks up against the relativistic episteme announced by Montaignian and Cartesian philosophy. In the play, as mentioned earlier, this is brought to the fore by Cicero's elliptical "But men may construe things after their fashion, / Clean from the purpose of the things themselves" (1.3.34–35), to be represented, in different ways, by Brutus's conflicting subjectivity, Caska's fearful "impressionism", Calphurnia's inexplicable nightmare, the soothsayer's oracular language, before becoming, knowingly, the ground of Antony's manipulating art of memory. I ask whether it is not more exact to put the matter in a slightly different way and say that Cassius's obsessive theory of "measure" is itself part of a framework in which "perspective" has already given way to "perspectivism": one in which, from the very beginning, the shape of the "absent" powerful father twists and shrinks and stretches itself at will according to the changing focal point of the viewer, before prevailing—like the wavering flame of Brutus's taper—as a disturbing visual experience: an anamorphic presence, an enfeebling interiorized phantasm, the illness of "things that are not" (5.3.69). Caesar's power—the constant "Northern star"—continues to "hold the place" (3.1.58–65), but as a returning and contagious sight: the contagion of spectralized things. As often noticed Shakespeare doesn't take sides. But framed by his amphitheatre, "*dove si possa d'ogni intorno vedere*" ["where you can see all around from wherever you are"] (Biondo), he shakes his audience, by urging them to live such a threatening optical (baroque) experience of power.

What Antony has finely worked at in his resuscitating eulogy is precisely this: the awakening of "Caesar's spirit, ranging for revenge" (3.1.270). And ever since that first "coming back . . . one cannot control its comings and goings" (Derrida). Yet Antony has only "come to bury Caesar, not to praise him" (3.2.76).

As Dobson has rightly written in observing the predicted actuality of this play, reviving *Julius Caesar* at theatre renovates the sad truth that

Rome is now and then and everywhere, a founding ideal of Western civilized world and progress that is also a perpetual wound, like the ones that ope their ruby lips to beg the voice and utterance of

Antony's tongue. In the theatre and beyond it, it is always both the Ides of March and the day of the battle of Philippi.[90]

Elicited by resurgent forms of Caesarism all over the world in our present days, the Italian theatre Director Andrea De Rosa, in an adaptation based on Fabrizio Sinisi's rewriting of Shakespeare's play (*Giulio Cesare. Uccidere il tiranno*, 2017), has insightfully transformed Antony's litotic statement ("I come to bury Caesar, not to praise him") into a stage direction which transforms Caesar's interment, or Caesar's "interment-as-disinterment" as I prefer to call it, into an activity that occupies the whole first half of his one-act production.[91]

Figure 3.6 Antonio's burial of Caesar, in Andrea De Rosa's production of Sinisi's *Giulio Cesare. Uccidere il tiranno*, Teatro Argentina, Rome, 12 May 2019

Source: Photo Andrea Savoia, courtesy of Daniele Russo's project

When the performance begins, Caesar is already a corpse, wrapped up in a shroud and placed, like a mummy, at the centre of the stage and of his own grave, ready to be interred. In the background, dangling from the sky, is an enormous balloon: we can take it as a world image. An anonymous man in modern clothes violently bursts the balloon open and a roaring mass of powdery earth breaks out to then continue slowly to fall; that same earth is collected by the man with a shovel and used to cover Caesar's mummy, with a to and fro motion, from the background to the proscenium and vice versa, which lasts monotonously for half an hour (out of the entire hour of the show). Concomitantly, as if emerging from a Virgilian underworld, the bodies and voices of Cassius, Brutus, and Caska rise from trapdoors and begin discussing Caesar and his killing. Brutus speaks first, representing all of the voices, mixed up. He now speaks like Caska (the common impressionable man) and he trembles like him in evoking horrendous apparitions and natural phenomena that are shaking the earth. He now speaks like Cassius in exposing his chest to the lightning. He now wavers to and fro (like who? Like Brutus?). Then the voices are separated, as they are in Shakespeare's text. But in first confusing the voices, Brutus seems to show not his complexity, as critical literature would have it, but rather his weakness. What does the director mean? That there is a Caska lurking inside even those who oppose tyranny? That the responsibility for Caesar's excessive power is to be shared?

The man with the shovel is Antonio. And when his turn comes, he says that he is there to bury the dead man, not to praise the man who was alive, and yet the buried man will live again many times, because Caesar is the enactment of the will of the "Majority", he says, and in times like these, "orphan of any grace or miracle", the power of the majority is God, "our only God".[92] Caesar is tyrant and father. Allusively referring to Fascism and later subtler forms of fatherly totalitarianism, Antonio reminds the audience of Caesar's old and new donations and great public works realized for the wellbeing of the people: drainage of marshes in the peripheries, lowering of taxes, care homes, gardens, sporting and entertainment arenas.

Caesar is the tyrant that people dread, desire, and love, and who, as such, is destined to return and triumph. And indeed, the second half of the play, marked by a microphoned and hammering "To Philippi", enacts such a ghostly nature of Caesar and his triumph as a returning Tyrant-Father: "To Philippi", Antonio shouts on behalf of the "Majority"—among the clamour of alarming and uncontrollable events, acoustically evoked by an amazing soundtrack. Caesar is the man who creates, with the help of those burying and immortalizing him, the state of emergency and its solution. And Philippi becomes the epitome of all wars: wars with arrows, spears, catapults, chariots, walls, and total wars fought with bombs, atomic bombs, nerve gas; that is his way of protecting his children. To Philippi! Antony shouts in his microphone, as he indulges in the pleasure of announcing and describing destruction and the rubble of the world that power and wars leave behind. This final television-like war scenario is presided by the unbearable din of an invisible helicopter which the spectator hears hovering above, uninterrupted. Until the moment when—together with the conspirators' self-killing—everything dies out in absolute silence, perhaps with one last shovelful of ash which Antonio (the common man, the war correspondent, but mostly the populist who engenders his own leader) lets fall on Caesar's body, and with the soothing promise of a world of well-monitored peace (or *pax*). In this, in eliciting the tangle of complicity between leaders and communities, domination and protection, love and terror, but also between democracy and violence getting out of hand and leading to reshaped reinforced authority, the layered memory of Shakespeare and Rome continues to urge "heliotropically" (Benjamin) upon our present with concerns of our own.

Notes

1. "i quali havessero avuto a dimostrare con gesti finti nel mezzo de gli atti de le comedie, o tragedie, le compositioni de poeti . . . il pantomimo detto cosi dal variare di tanti atti, imitando tanti, accordandosi col suono, cosi bene esprimea con le mani, col volto, e con tutt'l corpo quello che egli volea, che a punto s'intendeva, come s'egli con la voce l'avesse detto, e col medesimo corpo si facea hor Hercole, hor Venere, hor diventava maschio, hor femina, hora il vedevi Re, hora soldato, hora vecchio, hora giovane, tal che parea ch'egli essendo uno fusse molti". Biondo, *Roma ristaurata*, p. 47 (my transl.).
2. "l'anfiteatro . . . non vuol dire altro che duo teatri accozzati insieme, dove si possa d'ogni intorno vedere, e secondo Cassiodoro, il primo che pensò di fare questo edificio fu Tito imperatore ma Tacito non vuol, che fusse Tito il primo, pche dice che C. Cesare ne edificò uno nel cãpo Martio; il quale però dice Svetonio, che Cesare destinò di fare, ma che Augusto havendo da farvi il Mausoleo, il butto per terra". (Biondo, *Roma ristaurata*, p. 48, my transl.).
3. On de Witt, see Andrew Gurr, *The Shakespearean Stage, 1576–1642* (Cambridge: Cambridge University Press, 1992), p. 132. For a discussion of the relation between power and theatrical space in *Julius Caesar* and the Elizabethan theatres, see Richard Wilson, *Free Will: Art and Power on Shakespeare's Stage* (Manchester: Manchester University Press, 2013), pp. 146–161.
4. See Giovanna Ferrari, "Public Anatomy Lessons and the Carnival: The Anatomy Theatre of Bologna", *Past and Present*, 117 (1987), 50–106 (p. 84f); Franco Ruffini, *Teatri prima del Teatro. Visioni dell'edificio e della scena tra Umanesimo e Rinascimento* (Roma: Bulzoni, 1983), pp. 47–53; Sawday, *The Body Emblazoned*, p. 69f. Differently from others, Sawday has indicated Bramante's Tempietto as an alternative source of inspiration for Vesalius's title page.
5. Stephen Orgel, *Spectacular Performances: Essays on Theatre, Imagery, Books and Selves in Early Modern England* (Manchester and New York: Manchester University Press, 2011). p. 162.
6. Gillies, *Shakespeare and the Geography of Difference*, pp. 70, 90, and 99–122.
7. Richard Wilson, "Introduction to *Julius Caesar*", in Wilson, ed., *Julius Caesar* (New Casebooks), p. 17.

8. Richard Wilson, "'Is This a Holiday?' Shakespeare's Roman Carnival", in Wilson, ed., *Julius Caesar*, p. 71. But see also Ute Berns, "Performing Anatomy in Shakespeare's *Julius Caesar*" (in Del Sapio Garbero et al., eds, *Questioning Bodies in Shakespeare's Rome*, pp. 95–108). She equally concentrates on the anatomy of Caesar's dead body and hence on the final oratorical context between Brutus and Antony, in which she sees the evolution of the anatomical practice and the deployment of two different ways of knowing.

9. Timothy Hampton, *Writing From History: The Rhetoric of Exemplarity in Renaissance Literature* (Ithaca and London: Cornell University Press, 1990), pp. 221–222.

10. An earlier draft of this essay, where I first presented my proposal, was published in Del Sapio Garbero et al., *Questioning Bodies in Shakespeare's Rome*, 2010, pp. 33–56 ("Anatomy, Knowledge, and Conspiracy: in Shakespeare's Arena with the Words of Cassius").

11. Alessandro Benedetti, *Historia corporis humani sive Anatomice*, Latin/Italian bilingual edition, ed. Giovanna Ferrari (Firenze: Giunti, 1998), pp. 84–85 (my transl.).

12. See Francis Bacon's IX chapter of *The Advancement of Learning* [1605] ("Human Philosophy, or the Knowledge of Ourselves"): "And generally let this be a rule, that all partitions of knowledges be accepted rather for lines and veins than for sections and separations; and that the continuance and entireness of knowledge be preserved. For the contrary hereof hath made particular sciences to become barren, shallow, and erroneous, while they have not been nourished and maintained from the common fountain. . . . So we see also that the science of medicine if it be destitute and forsaken by natural philosophy, it is not much better than an empirical practice". *The Advancement of Learning and New Atlantis* (Oxford: Clarendon Press, 1975), p. 102. For more on Bacon and the language of anatomy, see Devon L. Hodges, *Renaissance Fictions of Anatomy* (Amherst: The University of Massachusetts Press, 1985), pp. 89–106.

13. Benedetti, *Historia corporis humani*, pp. 76–77.

14. Benedetti, *Historia corporis humani*, pp. 120–121.

15. Bacon, *The Advancement of Learning*, p. 105.

16. I am indebted to the following: the already quoted Hodges, *Renaissance Fictions of Anatomy* (1985), Giovanna Ferrari, "Public Anatomy Lessons and the Carnival" (1987), and Sawday, *The Body Emblazoned* (1995); Hillman and Mazzio (eds), *The Body in Parts*; Paster, *The Body Embarrassed* and *Humouring the Body*; Schoenfeldt, *Bodies and Selves*; Maurizio Calbi, *Approximate Bodies: Gender and Power in Early Modern Drama and Anatomy* (London and New York: Routledge, 2005); Hillman, *Shakespeare's Entrails*; Sugg, *Murder After Death*. But see also Del Sapio Garbero, "A Spider in the Eye/I"; and the essays included in the already quoted collection ed. Del Sapio Garbero et al., *Questioning Bodies in Shakespeare's Rome* (2010).

17. On these topics, see Sawday.

18. Bendetti, *Historia corporis humani*, pp. 350–351.

19. David Daniell, "Introduction", in Shakespeare, *Julius Caesar*, ed. David Daniell, p. 60.

20. Plutarch, *The Lives of the Noble Grecians and Romanes, Englished by Thomas North* (London: Thomas Vautroullier and Ion Wight, 1579).

21. See Ciardi, "Il corpo, progetto e rappresentazione", pp. 26–29, and Sawday, *The Body Emblazoned*, p. 183 *et passim*. As recalled by Sawday (p. 3), "Those attributes were derived from the story of Perseus, the mythical hunter of the *Medusa*. . . . The Medusa stands for interiority. . . . The attempt at

conquering the Medusa's realm with the devices of *Anatomia* involved a confrontation between an abstract idea of knowledge, and the material reality of a corpse".

22. Crooke, *Microcosmographia*, p. 26.
23. On the play's two public spaces, see Hampton, *Writing From History*, p. 212 *et passim*.
24. See Frederika Jacobs, "(Dis)assembling: Marsyas, Michelangelo, and the Accademia del Disegno", *The Art Bulletin*, 3 (2002), 426–448 (p. 429), and Sawday, *The Body Emblazoned*, pp. 185–187.
25. Ovid, *Metamorphoses*, transl. Arthur Golding, Book VI, vv. 490–498, pp. 188–189.
26. North's Plutarch, "The Life of Julius Caesar", *The Lives of the Noble Grecians and Romanes*, p. 792.
27. As Hodges has observed in a chapter on *King Lear*, "The anatomy of a body is . . . an act of destruction and revelation". Lear's anatomical prying into the nature of his daughters' hearts and the play's pervasive drive to go beyond the reality of appearance represent Shakespeare's attempt "to open up the constraining limits of dramatic form so that he can reveal the plenitudes of nature and truth. But what he discovers is that by stripping away empty masks in an effort finally to present solid and coherent truths, he participates in a fragmenting process of representation while trying to circumvent it. . . . By attempting to go beyond the dramatic order, Shakespeare like Lear, further collapses metaphysical values into empirical matter" (Hodges, *Renaissance Fictions of Anatomy*, chapter 5, "Anatomy as Tragedy", pp. 71 and 87).
28. Stubbes's book saw four editions before Nashes's counter *Anatomie of Absurditie* was issued in 1589.
29. I am borrowing these terms from Sawday's *The Body Emblazoned* (p. 87) and Ciardi, "Il corpo, progetto e rappresentazione" (p. 29).
30. Sawday, *The Body Emblazoned*, p. 86.
31. See Giovanni Lomazzo, *A Tracte Containing the Artes of Curious Paintinge, Carvinge, and Buildinge* [1584], transl. Richard Haydocke [1598], Facsimile (Amsterdam and New York: Capo Press, 1969), p. 36. See especially chapters on "proportion", "perspective", and "distance".
32. Erwin Panofsky, *Meaning in the Visual Arts* (New York: Doubleday, 1955), p. 56.
33. Dio Cassius, *Roman History*, 9 vols, transl. Earnest Cary, Loeb Classical Library (London, Heinemann and Cambridge, MA: Harvard University Press, 1961), vol. IV, p. 235.
34. Ralph Berry, "*Julius Caesar*: A Roman Tragedy", *Dalhousie Review*, 61:2 (1981), 324–336 (pp. 327–328).
35. See Michael Jaffé, "Rubens and Optics: Some Fresh Evidence", *Journal of Warburg and Courtauld Institutes*, 34 (1971), 362–366.
36. As Voltaire explained: "Il y a ici une plaisante pointe; Rome en anglais se pronounce *roum*, et *roum* signifie aussi *place*". Interestingly in translating Cassius's verses (1.2.155–56), he transliterated "Rome"-"room" as "Roume"-"room": "Ah, c'est aujourd'hui que Roume existe en effet; car il n'y a de roum (de place) que pour César". Quoted and commented upon in Philip E. Cranston, "'Rome en Anglais se prononce *roum* . . .'. Shakespeare Versions by Voltaire", *Modern Language Notes*, 6 (1975), 809–837 (p. 826). Intriguingly, one might add, for Elizabethan actors and playwrights, "Rome" stood also for theatrical space, "the Rome over the tyer-howsse" and "my lords Rome", by Collier glossed as "the best place . . . set apart for the patron of the company and . . . friends". Henslowe, *Diary*. 1591–1609, ed. J. Payne Collier, p. 16.

37. See Michel Foucault, *Le parole e le cose: un'archeologia delle scienze umane* [1966], transl. Emilio Panaitescu (Milano: Rizzoli, 1978), pp. 10–11.
38. Sawday, *The Body Emblazoned*, p. 73.
39. See on this Ernst H. Kantorowicz, *The King's Two Bodies: A Study in Mediaeval Political Theology* (Princeton: Princeton University Press, 1957).
40. Ferrari, "Public Anatomy Lessons and the Carnival", p. 88 *et passim*. It is useful to remember in this context that the doctor's syllabus in university courses was still similar in some aspects to that of literary scholars. In fact, it included logic and philosophy. It was precisely the dispute (or "contraddittorio") that made the public anatomy lessons of Padua and Bologna so popular all over Europe, attracting flocks of foreign scholars and students each year at Carnival, the period during which the "useful shows" (*utilia spectacula*), as they were called, or "gran fontione", were allowed to be held. Significantly, when the university of Bologna decided to build a new anatomy theatre in a more spacious chamber of the Archiginnasio in 1637, they architectonically reinforced the double focus of dispute and dissection. "Instead of revolving around its original central point, the dissecting table, the new theatre clearly had two focuses. The dissecting table was, as it were, counterbalanced by the cathedra from which the anatomy professor propounded and defended his theses". For all this, see Ferrari, "Public Anatomy Lessons and the Carnival", pp. 76, 86.
41. Alessandro Serpieri, "Prefazione", in William Shakespeare, *Giulio Cesare*, transl. Alessandro Serpieri (Milano: Garzanti, 1994), pp. XXXII–XLVII. For Shakespeare's theatrical transcodification of the play's Plutarchan source, see his *"Julius Caesar*. Presentazione, Tabulazione, Commento", in Serpieri et al., *Nel Laboratorio di Shakespeare. Dalle fonti ai drammi*, 4 vols (Parma: Pratiche Editrice, 1988), vol. 4, pp. 15–129.
42. On grammar school ways of learning from the classics see Enterline, *Shakespeare's Schoolroom* (2012), and Burrow, *Shakespeare and Classical Antiquity* (2013). "All the reading and translating of classical texts through which grammar-school boys slogged their way", Burrow observes, "was intended ultimately to enable them not to display mastery in reading a dead language, but to write" (p. 40).
43. Cicero, *De Fato*, in *id*, *The Oratore* (Book III), *De Fato, Pradoxa Stoicorum, De Partitione Oratoria*, transl. H. Rackham, Loeb Classical Library (London and Cambridge, MA: Harvard University Press, 1948).
44. In underscoring "Bacon's definition of natural philosophy as the 'Inquiry of Causes'" in *Novum Organum*, Brian Vickers has written, "Bacon's scientific theory had as its goal the discovery of the laws of nature and physical causes by a process that would rise gradually but inevitably from the particular to the general". "Francis Bacon and the Progress of Knowledge", *Journal of the History of Ideas*, 53:3 (1992), 495–518 (pp. 513 and 502).
45. See Hodges, *Renaissance Fictions of Anatomy*, p. 95 *et passim*.
46. Sawday, *The Body Emblazoned*, p. 27.
47. Gail Kern Paster, "'In the Spirit of Men There Is No Blood': Blood as Trope of Gender in *Julius Caesar*", in Wilson, ed., *Julius Caesar*, p. 151.
48. On Tacitism, see the first chapter on *Titus Andronicus* in this volume, note 30.
49. As Edwards has observed, if in Livy's case the historical approach is "a teleological account of the rise of Rome", in Tacitus's this is "an ironic account of its decline". *Writing Rome*, p. 72. For more on the relation of Tacitism with the conspiratorial Earl of Essex's entourage and the connection with the Shakespearean treatment of Brutus and Cassius, see Margot Heinemann, "'Let Rome in Tiber Melt': Order and Disorder in *Antony and Cleopatra*", in John Drakakis, ed., *Antony and Cleopatra: William Shakespeare* (Houndmills: Macmillan New Casebooks, 1994), pp. 173–177.

50. Tacitus, *Annals*, transl. J. Jackson, in *Works*, Loeb Classical Library, 5 vols (London and Cambridge, MA: Harvard University Press, 1937), vol. 4.

51. For more on these issues and the intersection with Shakespeare's works, see Del Sapio Garbero, ed., *Shakespeare and the New Science* and (by the same author) "Troubled metaphors".

52. See Michel Foucault, "The Order of Discourse", in Robert Young, ed., *Untying the Text: A Poststructuralist Reader* (London: Routledge and Kegan Paul, 1981), pp. 51–76, and the Preface in *Les mots et les choses* (Paris: Gallimard, 1966).

53. Alessandro Serpieri, "Reading the Signs: Towards a Semiotics of Shakespearean Drama", in John Drakakis, ed., *Alternative Shakespeares* (New York and London: Routledge, 1992), p. 130.

54. René Girard, *A Theatre of Envy* [1990] (South Bend, IN: St. Augustine's Press, 2002), pp. 223 and 224. But see also the chapter "Domestic Fury and Fierce Civil Strife", pp. 193–199.

55. Hampton, *Writing From History*, p. 222. For a discussion of the Tudor Reformist culture of martyrdom in the light of the popularity of John Foxe's *Acts of Monuments* (1565–1583) and its theatrical secularization, see Marshall, *The Shattering of the Self*, pp. 85–105.

56. Jonathan Goldberg, "'The Roman Actor': *Julius Caesar*", in Wilson, ed., *Julius Caesar*, p. 97.

57. Wilson, "Introduction" to his edited New Casebooks series, *Julius Caesar*, pp. 1–28 (p. 1). Marjorie Garber speaks of the play as a representation of representation, where "the so-called original is already a figure". *Shakespeare's Ghost Writers*, pp. 56 and 58. This is also a play, a political play, as underlined by Serpieri, where "most of the action is performed by the word: the symbolic word, the contentious word, the word of persuasion, the word of dissimulation". Notes to Shakespeare, *Giulio Cesare*, bilingual edition, ed. Serpieri (Milano: Garzanti, 1994), p. 223 (my transl.). On the pervasive theatrical register of the play, see for all Hampton, *Writing From History*, pp. 198–236. But see also Jack D'Amico, "Shakespeare's Rome: Politics and Theatre", *Modern Language Studies*, 22:1 (1992), 65–78.

58. For an in-depth contextualized discussion of the tyranncide issue raised by Shakespeare, see Robert Miola, "*Julius Caesar* and the Tyrannicide Debate", *Renaissance Quarterly*, 38 (1985), 271–289.

59. See above all Serpieri's fundamental rhetorical analysis both in his "Reading the Signs" and "Body and History in the Political Rhetoric of *Julius Caesar*", in Del Sapio Garbero et al., eds, *Questioning Bodies in Shakespeare's Rome*, pp. 219–236. But see also Pennacchia, who, in concentrating on Antony's theatrical and physical use of the Forum's space, interestingly expands on issues of shifting rhetorical media. "Antony's Ring: Remediating Ancient Rhetoric on the Elizabethan Stage", in Del Sapio Garbero, ed., *Identity, Otherness and Empire*, pp. 49–59.

60. Cicero, *De Oratore* (Books I–II), trans. E.W. Sutton and H. Rackham, Loeb Classical Library (London and Cambridge, MA: Harvard University Press, 1967). Mentions directly in the text. *De Oratore* was written in the form of a conversation among four acknowledged orators, but other younger followers of *ars oratoria* join in along the development of its three books.

61. In F lines 3–10 are omitted. The discrepancy is significant. It as if Shakespeare didn't know what to do with Cassius and his reasons at this crucial moment, after that, profiting from some hints at Cassius's solid and better philosophical education in the Plutarchan sources, he had assigned to him such a decisive role in deploying his secular anatomy of Caesar's body. In F we don't know whether Cassius remains silent on stage or whether he exits with the others and when. We hear of him as a fugitive from Rome (together with Brutus) in

3.2.258–59, before reappearing in 4.3 quarrelling with Brutus as they prepare their army for the last clash with Antony and Octavius at Filippi.

62. As shown by Serpieri, "Litotes of thought pervades the entire oration in its various articulations". "Reading the Signs", pp. 132–133.

63. Wilson, "'Is This a Holiday?'", p. 67.

64. Gentili, *La Roma antica degli elisabettiani*, p. 68 *et passim*. "E' da queste animazioni simboliche", Gentili suggests, "che scaturiscono i fatti, la rivolta popolare contro i congiurati" (p. 71). On Shakespeare's concern with tyranny and populism see Stephen Greenblatt, *Tyrant: Shakespeare on Politics* (New York and London: Norton, 2018), especially chap. 3 ("Fraudulent Populism").

65. "Emotions must be accompanied by gesture—not this stagy gesture reproducing the words but one conveying the general situation and idea not by mimicry but by hints, with this vigorous manly throwing out of the chest, borrowed not from the stage and the theatrical profession but from the parade ground or even from wrestling" (*Orat.*, III.220).

66. For a reading of these lines in the light of the theatricality of school training in classical rhetoric and the way this contributed to the education of passions in Tudor grammar schools, see Enterline, *Shakespeare's Schoolroom*, pp. 9–32 and 121–152.

67. On the specific aspect of Antony's cunning use of the theatrical space, see Pennacchia, "Antony's Ring", p. 57 *et passim*. But, as Pennacchia argues, "It is only by making his medium invisible, by presenting theatre as a 'transparent interface', a user-friendly tool, that Antony wins", p. 59.

68. For more on Shakespeare's anxiety about permeable bodies, see Del Sapio Garbero, "A Spider in the Eye/I", pp. 133–155.

69. Carruthers, *The Book of Memory*, p. 153. But see also Frances Yates, *The Art of Memory* (London: The Bodley Head, [1966] 2014), pp. 114–135.

70. "Just as a script consists of marks indicating letters and of material on which those marks are imprinted, so the structure of memory, like a wax tablet, employs 'topics', and in these stores images which corespond to the letters in written script", *De partitione oratoria*, VII. 26, transl. H. Rackham, Loeb Classical Library (London and Cambridge, MA: Harvard University Press, 1948).

71. See Wilson, "'Is This a Holiday?'". But see also Hampton, *Writing From History*, pp. 205–236 and Liebler, *Shakespeare's Festive Tragedy*, pp. 85–111.

72. Ferrari, "Public Anatomy Lessons and the Carnival", pp. 100 and 102. See also Piero Camporesi, *The Incorruptible Flesh: Bodily Mutation and Mortification in Religion and Folklore* (Cambridge: Cambridge University Press, 1988) and Katherine Park, "The Criminal and the Saintly Body", *Renaissance Quarterly*, 47 (1994), 1–33 (pp. 22–29).

73. North's Plutarch, "The Life of Marcus Antonius", p. 971. ("He used a manner of phrase in his speeche, called asiatik, which caried the best grace and estimation at that time, and was much like to his manners and life: for it was full of ostentation, foolishe braverie, and vaine ambition").

74. Here I am using this definition in a sense that can be loosely referred to the "sacred anatomy" discussed by Sawday, one which recuperated the theological side of ancient anatomy and that could be traced back to the medieval embalming or "division of bodies for religious ends" (*The Body Emblazoned*, pp. 98–99).

75. On the perverted ritual context of the play, see Naomi C. Liebler, who convincingly relates it to "an emergent market economy". We should not forget here that it is also Brutus's wish to envelope Caesar's assassination in the

language of religious ritual. But, as Liebler has rightly remarked, "Whereas Brutus invites the conspirators to bathe their arms in Caesar's blood, in a private in-gathering gesture of solidarity, Antony parcels out the body, along with seventy-five drachmas . . . like a feudal lord distributing largesse to the general populace". Moreover, "[Brutus's] desire to make Caesar's murder seem ritualistic is not the same thing as an attempt to make it an *actual* ritual, nor does he say anywhere outside the confidential circle of conspirators that it is one. His orations to the people do not refer to ritual (although . . . Antony's do); they only appeal to the commons' sense of republicanism" (*Shakespeare's Festive Tragedy*, pp. 102 and 105).

76. See Muir, "Without Remainder", p. 23, and Margaret Aston, *England's Iconoclasts: Laws Against Images* (Oxford: Clarendon Press, 1988), vol. 1, p. 278. As Greenblatt has observed in addressing the migrancy of sacred rituals (as well as clerical garments) from the church to the theatre in post-Reformation time: the "sacred sign, designed to be displayed before a crowd of men and women, is emptied, made negotiable, traded from one institution to another", "Shakespeare and the Exorcists", in Patricia Parker and Geoffrey Hartman, eds, *Shakespeare and the Question of Theory* (New York and London: Routledge, 1990), p. 71.
77. Benjamin, "Central Park", p. 48.
78. Benjamin, *Illuminations*, pp. 153–154.
79. Derrida, *Specters of Marx*, pp. 157–158. Further mentions directly in the text.
80. Garber, *Shakespeare's Ghost Writers*, p. 133.
81. Garber, *Shakespeare's Ghost Writers*, p. 135 *et passim*.
82. Giambattista Vico, *New Science*, p. 223.
83. Here in the terms discussed by Derrida, *Specters of Marx*, pp. 165 and 156–221.
84. "Caesar, for that little of him that is left unto us, is like the halfe face of a Venus, the other part of the head beying hidden, the bodie and the rest of the members unbegon, yet so excellently done by Apelles, as all man may stand still to mase and muse upon it, and no man step forth with any hope to perform the like". "The Schoolmaster", in Smith, ed., *Elizabethan Critical Essays*, pp. 44–45.
85. Giorgio Melchiori, "Il mito di Roma: *Julius Caesar*", in Melchiori, *Shakespeare*, pp, 401–402 (my transl.).
86. See, respectively, John Drakakis, "'Fashion It Thus': *Julius Caesar* and the Politics of Theatrical Representation", in Wilson, ed., *Julius Caesar*, p. 82, and Ernest Schanzer, *The Problem Plays of Shakespeare: A Study of Julius Caesar, Measure for Measure, Antony and Cleopatra* (Routledge: London and New York, [1963] 2005), p. 32.
87. Garber, *Shakespeare's Ghost Writers*, pp. 52–73.
88. "All these together in one heape were throwne, / Like carkases of beasts in butchers stall. / And in another corner wide were strowne / The antique ruines of the *Romaines* fall: / Great *Romulus* the Grandsyre of them all, / Proud *Tarquin*, and too lordly *Lentulus*, / Stout *Scipio*, and stubborne *Hanniball*, / Ambitious *Sylla*, and sterne *Marius*, / High *Cæsar*, great *Pompey*, and fiers *Antonius*". Edmund Spenser, *The Faerie Queene*, 1.5.49, ed. Douglas Brooke-Davies (London: J.M. Dent, 1997).
89. Panofsky, *Meaning in the Visual Arts*, pp. 105–106.
90. Dobson, "Nationalism, National Theatres and the Return of *Julius Caesar*", in Daniela Guardamagna, ed., *Roman Shakespeare: Intersecting Times, Spaces, Languages* (Oxford: Peter Lang, 2018), p. 54.

91. I am referring to the production held in Rome at the Teatro Argentina on 12 May 2019, together with an adaptation of *Titus Andronicus* by Daniele Russo. The two plays were conceived as two parts of a single performance in a project devised by Daniele Russo. The first performance of De Rosa's *Giulio Cesare. Uccidere il tiranno* was held in Naples at the Teatro Bellini in 2017 on the occasion of the Napoli Teatro Festival.

92. Fabrizio Sinisi, *Giulio Cesare. Uccidere il tiranno* (Gorgonzola, MI: Nardini Editore, 2017), pp. 51–52 (my transl.).

4 "My Memory Is Tired"

Coriolanus's Forgetful Humanism

Whether Coriolanus appears as a mechanism, an "engine" (5.4.18–19),[1] a deadly and reiterative war machine, or as an *écorché*, "a thing of blood" (2.2.107), his marked "physicalization" is increasingly regarded by criticism as well as performance as a crucial dimension of Shakespeare's play, producing as it does an iconicity of the character which "refuses to be contained within the boundaries of spoken languages". In this context, blood and wounds are commented upon as signs of membership, Coriolanus's only organic components. Together, they are substance and memory of what he has spilled for Rome: his blood.[2] Organic in this sense should refer us to a quality which is specific to blood: that of establishing a vital flux among body parts and making them whole. In fact, in the martial economy of the play, blood and wounds constitute Coriolanus's defining corporeal prerogatives, by means of which a bond should be iconically and instantly sealed with Rome's citizens. "He hath planted his honours in their eyes and his actions in their hearts" (2.2.27–28), one of his officers remarks. Accordingly, eyes (in conjunction with the parallel insatiable quality of mouths) are given full scopic relevance in the starving/voracious dynamic of the play (so brilliantly explored by Janet Adelman)[3] and, typically, in two strategic scenes: in Act I, scene 6, when soon after the victory over the Volscians, "mantled" in "blood", Coriolanus "appear[s]" to his general Cominius "as he were flayed" (1.6.22); and in Act 2, scene 1, during the warrior's ensuing triumph, when the enraptured paroxysm of the crowd acclaiming him in the streets is insistently foregrounded, metonymically, as that of an insatiable, "spectacled" collective eye. Rome is indeed a stratified gallery of eyes—on stalls, bulks, windows, roofs, walls—eager to see him (2.1.200–07).

Blood and wounds, however, as often said, are things that matter more as tokens of denial in *Coriolanus* than of sharing and fulfilment. We soon learn that Coriolanus's body, "a thing of blood", portentous and desirable as it might appear as a representation of Rome's best virtue—a representation in keeping with the republican Rome depicted by Plutarch ("in those days, valliantnes was honoured in ROME above all other vertues: which they called *Virtus*, by the name of virtue selfe")[4]—in Shakespeare's play

DOI: 10.4324/9781003259671-6

is rather a body that works at constructing itself as an object reluctant to being exchanged. Coriolanus remains an inedible body in the hungry and voracious landscape of the play.

Volumnia, his wolfish mother, a father-substitute, has invested all her energies in shaping the boy—who in his teens "might act the woman in the scene" (2.2.94)—into the warrior who holds "that valour is the chiefest virtue" (2.2.82).[5] Accordingly, he has transformed himself into a body fit only for war: a body primordially finalized to its belligerent technical use, we might say, with Giorgio Agamben (*L'uso dei corpi*, 2014).[6] Valiantness is in his arm for Volumnia, an almost detached body part, fixed in its operative and deadly movement, an automatism almost deprived of intentionality: "Before him / He carries noise, and behind him he leaves tears. / Death, that dark Spirit, in's nervy arm doth lie, / which being advanced, declines, and the men die" (2.1.153–55).

Meaningfully, Coriolanus, the she-wolf's son, *wears* his blood as if it were an externalized and inorganic element; a fluid that he seems to enjoy most as he feels it cooling down on its face to assume the cold consistency of painting (1.6.68–69; 1.9.47; 1.9.66; 1.9.92), or a terrifying mask, a second skin, a carapace. "Mantling", enveloping himself with the enemy's blood, protracting and parading that condition as, with ill-concealed complacency, he does on the battlefield, is the only exception to his otherwise reluctance to showcase his wounded body: "'Tis not my blood", he boasts, "Wherein thou seest me masked" (1.8.9–10). Shakespeare's text, perhaps remindful of the fact that in ancient Rome victors used to ascend in procession the path leading to the Capitol with their face painted red like the face of Jupiter's statue in the god's temple,[7] elicits performance and film adaptations to indulge on this. In Ralph Fiennes's film of *Coriolanus* (2011), we are made to observe a slaughtered enemy soldier who, before dying, in wriggling out of Coriolanus's grip smears his face with blood.[8] In Josie Rourke's 2013–14 theatrical production for the Donmar Warehouse (later filmed for National Theatre at Home), the statuary Tom Hiddleston who impersonates Coriolanus takes time, under the open air shower designed for the purpose, to wash away his incrusted blood, a cover in the director's intentions for what the warrior doesn't want to show.[9]

In Shakespeare's play the blood of his enemy, together with Caius Martius's added name ("Coriolanus")—a "robbery" in Aufidius's words—are Coriolanus's bark, his true reward, and what should suffice to construct his body into the epitome of a non-negotiable *Romanitas* to the eyes of his Roman citizens. "Who's yonder", says his general Cominius, "That thus appears he were flayed? O gods / He has the stamp of Martius, and I have / Beforetime seen him thus" (1.6.23). This is Coriolanus's statue, the monuments with which Rome rewarded its heroes: they could also be the most ephemeral, the first to be questioned, replaced, or destroyed in adverse fortune, as some of Shakespeare's audience might read in Tacitus's

Histories (see Book I.56–57, 78, 79), or elsewhere. Indeed, Coriolanus's second skin, his covertly ostentated congealed blood, symbolically defines his warrior's identity as that of a statue: a "stamp of", which is also an otherness that suspends his identity between the person and his masculine gruesome plaster impression.

My concern in this study is the way in which Shakespeare deploys the gradual fragmentation of Coriolanus's "stamp" in his play, and the way the colossus ("a broken Coriolanus", in Eliot's enigmatic mention)[10] discovers his human fragility as he gradually ruins towards his final tragic disintegration. My proposal is that this happens by means of the underwritten theme of hospitality—a forgotten virtue in the bleak dehumanized landscape of the play—and the challenge it tragically raises in relation to Coriolanus's uneasiness in coping with its attendant obligations of memory, exchange, gratitude, and reciprocity.

The Hospitable Canon

On acknowledging defeat at the hand of Coriolanus, Aufidius, the Volscians' general, swears unquenchable hate towards him and eternal war, even at the risk of treading on obligations made holy by such places as temples, the home, Capitol, the sites of shared rites and founding pacts, "Embargements all of fury". Among such obligations, the ruins or leftover of "rotten privilege and custom", in Aufidius's blasphemous words, we find the law of hospitality, or "the hospitable canon" as it is called by Aufidius.

> Nor sleep, nor sanctuary,
> Being naked, sick, nor fane nor Capitol,
> The prayers of priests, nor times of sacrifice—
> Embargements all of fury—shall lift up
> Their rotten privilege and custom 'gainst
> My hate to Martius. Where I find him, were it
> At Home upon my brother's guard, even there,
> Against *the hospitable canon*, would I
> Wash my fierce hand in's heart.
> (1.10.19–27; my emphasis)

One would say that in writing these lines, Shakespeare had vividly in mind Tacitus's report of the terrifying civil strife between Galba and Otho; the war which, as never before, was fought within the walls and in the sacred edifices of Rome and which finally brought to the destruction in 69 CE of the Capitol and Jupiter Temple: "Neither the sight of the Capitol nor the sanctity of the temples which towered above them, nor the thought of emperors past and to come, could deter them from committing a crime which any successor to the imperial power must punish (*Histories*, I.40).[11]

Tacitus's anaphorized list of profaned sacred thresholds seems to resonate in Aufidius's way of strengthening his revengeful oath. War will be as absolute as the unwritten law which forbids it within the walls of city, the home, or the temple, the places where the wayfarer, the poor, the stranger, even the enemy ought to be given asylum and sheltered as one would a welcome guest. War, however, is not just that between the two hostile cities of Rome and Antium. Shakespeare's *Coriolanus*—the most Roman of [his] Roman plays[12]—is also the play where Rome is depicted as the epitome of a ruinous and self-destructive city, the play of a forgetful humanism, that is of a dismembered and lost citizenship.

How then shall we regard this unexpected mention, or memory, of a hospitable city (or citizenship) which appears to be discarded as a "left-over" in *Coriolanus*? And how, double folded in as it is at the borders of the text, might it contribute to reassess the terms according to which we are asked to look at this play? For it is undeniable that the displacing and engaging question of *Coriolanus* is precisely the opposite one, and namely, "Who does the wolf love?" (2.1.7); a question which, as Stanley Cavell has brilliantly argued, by means of its grammatical incorrectness or ambiguity, highlights "the circle of cannibalism, of the eater eaten by what he or she eats" which "runs through the play" and which sucks in patricians and plebeians, mother and son, Rome and its children.[13]

One might strengthen Cavell's argument by adding that Shakespeare's intention in *Coriolanus*, as critics have already noted in relation to other plays,[14] seems to have been that of representing the predatory humanity of the age of iron, the age of war and destructive appetites as Ovid recounts it in his *Metamorphoses*. But if this is so, this is also the place from which the interrelated, if contrastive theme of violated hospitality might arise. In fact, hospitality takes centre stage in Ovid's enumeration of the forgotten obligations of the "human", in his Iron Age: "Vivitur ex rapto; non hospes ab hospite tutus / non socer a genero, fratrum quoque gratia rara est".[15] Meaningfully to my argument, in his 1567 translation of Ovid's *Metamorphoses*, Golding used a well-developed chiasmus to underscore the disrupted bond of mutuality between guest and host:

> Men live by ravine and by stealth. The wandering guest doth stand
> In danger of his host, the host in danger of his guest,
> And fathers of their son-in-law; yea, seldom time doth rest
> Between born brothers such accord and love as ought to be.
>
> (I.162–65)

Shakespeare knew that the ancient gods used to test the heart of human beings by visiting them disguised as wayfarers.[16] He also knew that the Iron Age was the age of enmity between gods and men. "*Terras Astraea reliquit*; be you remembered, Marcus, / She's gone, she's fled", Titus cries in the eponymous play *Titus Andronicus* (4.3.4–5), Shakespeare's first and most Ovidian Roman play, a tragedy inhabited (not differently from *Coriolanus*, his last Plutarchan Roman tragedy) by a metal-like humanity ("metal . . . steel to the very back", 4.3.48) and teeming from beginning to end with impious burials, not to mention anthropophagous banquets.

Shakespeare had learned from Ovid (or Golding's Ovid) that Astraea, the goddess of justice, had deserted the blood-soaked earth and ascended once again to the heavens. "All godliness lies underfoot. And Lady Astrey, last / Of heavenly virtues, from this earth in slaughter drownèd passed", we read in Golding's Ovid (I.169–70). But from Ovid, Shakespeare had also learned—and more decisively, I argue, in relation to the wolfish appetites of the play—that Jupiter had punished the belligerent and inhospitable humanity of that age by sending a deluge (Golding, I.186–363). The playwright must have been inspired by the fact that Jupiter had first turned Lycaon—the cruel Arcadian king who had deliberately refused to acknowledge him—into a wolf. In fact, Lycaon had ignored the "sign" he was given "that god was come" (Golding, I.257) and even dared to challenge Jupiter by offering him an anthropophagous banquet prepared with the roasted limbs of a hostage slaughtered for the occasion. The rift between human beings and gods in this myth, which was familiar to Shakespeare and to most of his contemporaries, is depicted as a refusal of acknowledgement, a sacrilegious disowning of the guest, or of the hostage for that matter.

But there were also other sources which may have propelled and fuelled Shakespeare's subterranean theme of hospitality. From Plutarch's "Life of Romulus" he may have derived the knowledge that granting "asylum"—in a mingle of obedience to a godly injunction and practical wisdom—was of a piece with the foundation of Rome. Many of its first inhabitants were refugees and Rome owed to them—and to raped women—the city's quick growth:

> Furthermore, when the cittie beganne a little to be settled, they made a temple of refuge for all fugitives and afflicted persones, which they called the temple of the god Asylæus. Where there was sanctuarie and safety for all sortes of people that repaired thither, and could not deliver any bonde man to his master, nor deter to his creditor, no murtherer to the justice that was fled thither for succor, because the oracle of Apollo the Delphian had expressely enjoyned them to graunte sanctuary to all those that would come thither for it. So by this meanes in short space their citie flourish, & was repleanished, where at the first foundation of it, they saye there was not above one thousand houses.
>
> (North's Plutarch, 15)

But why is it precisely this offence—the disowning of the human duty of giving "asylum" or "sanctuary"—that ever since outrages the alliance between gods and human beings? Would it not be because, in this way, one betrays the ethical perspective, the possibility of "counting on"—as one might say borrowing from Paul Ricoeur: for him, the Golden Rule of a "good" life?[17] In *Coriolanus*, a community (a "goodly city", 4.4.1) tied together by a "good" life appears by means of its ruinous residues and a number of impaired gestures.

Arguably in a number of his tragedies, Shakespeare was rediscovering Ovid in the light of the Senecan horror made popular in Renaissance Italy and Europe by Renato Dolce and Giraldi Cinthio in their highly Senecan tragedies. One need only mention Giraldi's *Orbecche* (1541), a tragedy famous for being the quintessential representation of impiety: a succession of violated parental bonds and sacrilegious crimes among kinspersons, most of them acted on stage, in a crescendo of mutual acts of "retributive retaliation".[18] Among these is the most hostile gift of the chopped body parts of Orbecche's husband and children, carefully arranged for her on silver platters by her father, the king Sulmone. "O spettacol crudele", the playwright makes her cry repeatedly at such a sight (5.2),[19] fuelling (as if necessary) the same dismayed reaction on the part of the audience.

Shakespeare was participating in this prevailing interpretation of tragedy when he set out to contrive the overheated temperature of *Titus Andronicus*. But, when it comes to *Coriolanus*, as I will show in a while, he seems to be less concerned with the strong theatrical effects one might obtain by competing with Seneca—the tragedian—and his Italian Renaissance followers and rather more preoccupied with the loss of an ethical community which was longed for, as the other side of the coin and a contrastive yearning, both in Ovid's narrative of the four ages of man and Seneca—the moral philosopher.

As in Ovid's Iron Age, there is no such heartfelt obligation in *Coriolanus* to respond to other people's call, nor any possibility that one may "count on" other people's welcome. Shakespeare seems to have kept well in mind the earlier quoted Plutarchan statement (that "in those days valliantness was honoured in ROME above all other vertues") when dealing with the impoverished tissue of civic virtues in the wolfish scenario of his republican Rome. Hospitality is cast aside in Aufidius's raging invective against Coriolanus, as a residual virtue, the thwarting fetter of "rotten privilege and custom" (1.10.23).

However, this is by no means the only place in the text where the offended memory of hospitality surfaces as if archaeologically from the crevices of a remote age, nor are enmity and hatred the only agencies for such a blasphemous disowning of the traditional bonds of piety and civility. For, in the previous scene of the same first act, in an episode which seems negligible in respect to the main course of the events, a banal form of amnesia has just prevented Coriolanus from repaying his debt of gratitude for the hospitality he received in the past from a Volscian soldier (1.9.77–89).

How might we interpret this amputated, or unresolved, gesture of gratitude? How does the alien or alienated matter of this scene relate to the rest of the play? And how does it call attention, for all its irrelevance, to both Coriolanus's tragic self and to his public role as a governor? These are the questions I will be dealing with in this chapter. In so doing I intend to foreground hospitality and benefit exchange as motives of great import in *Coriolanus*, which are no less crucial for being dealt with obliquely and presented as failed goals by Shakespeare. I want to show how the subterranean theme of hospitality in *Coriolanus*—so far fairly overlooked—relates to such issues as memory and gratitude, self-sufficiency and reciprocity at a crucial moment of historical and cultural change in Shakespeare's England.

My suggestion is that Seneca's treatise *De Beneficiis* (translated by Arthur Golding into English in 1578 and then again by Thomas Lodge in 1614) can offer us a way to understand the extent to which such issues were part of Elizabethan culture, and hence the part Seneca's treatise may have played as the metabolized source of an aporetic if pervasive concern in Shakespeare's drama.[20] Seneca's moral philosophy may also describe how classics could be used as a repository of values which might sound as both old and new, residual ("rotten" in Aufidiusus's words) and emerging or re-emerging, in the way Shakespeare makes them surface in the Iron Age context of *Coriolanus*. In this light I deem it useful to underline, as a start, the radical nature of the issues elicited by Shakespeare, by briefly considering the ways in which they have been or are being retrieved and catalyzed in our contemporary critical debate. For, as Greenblatt would say, "the questions I ask of my material and indeed the very nature of this material are shaped by the questions I ask of myself".[21]

In conceptualizing the idea of autonomy and the ways in which the autonomy of the self encompasses a dialogic structure and hence the field of ties and obligations—or what he terms solicitude for the "call of the other"—Ricoeur has written:

> Just as solicitude is not an external addition to self-esteem, so the respect owed to persons does not constitute a heteregenous moral principle in relation to autonomy of the self but develops its implicit dialogic structure on the plane of obligation, of rules.
>
> This thesis will be justified in two stages: first, we shall show the tie by which the norm of respect owed to persons is connected to the dialogic structure of the ethical aim, that is precisely to solicitude.[22]

In conjunction with what has been variously brought to the fore as a renewed philosophical reflection on the ethical dimension of the self, and hence on obligation as a positive form of "mutual indebtedness" and "disinterested interest" (Ricoeur, 227)—or also as "philosophical anthropology of the gift", "gift theory", or "gift studies"[23]—the themes of hospitality, solicitude, and gratuitousness have been widely rediscussed in recent years as a way of interrogating our encounter with otherness in the dislocating milieu of our new millennium. The herald of a problematized retrieval of hospitality was Derrida. In his valuable short book *Of Hospitality* (1997), he launched a reflection on this topic by taking the notion to its limit: the limit of a "utopia", which "can nowadays only be audible because it breaks its way in from the other, from the unexpected and always disturbing guest", as Anne Dufourmantelle writes in her dialogue with the philosopher, or the limit of "hospitality turning into hostility, starting from the always possible perversion of the Law".[24] The hyperbolic problematization of hospitality is all the more evident in Derrida's later article "Hostipitality" (2000). In fact, the very title of this article foregrounds in the form of an oxymoron the problem of hospitality, namely, the irresolvable contradiction (the *double bind* in Derrida's words) of rights and limits, of welcoming and mastery, which lies at the core of its performance:

> Hospitality is certainly, necessarily, a right, a duty, an obligation, the *greeting* of the foreign other [*l'autre étranger*] as a friend but on the condition that the host . . . remains the *patron*, the master of the household, on the condition that he maintains his own authority *in his own home* . . . and thereby affirms the laws of hospitality as the law of the household, . . . the law of a place (house, hotel, hospital, hospice, family, city, nation, language, etc.), the law of identity, . . . thus limiting the gift proffered and making of this limitation . . . the condition of the gift and of hospitality. This is the principle, <one could say, the aporia>, of both the constitution and the implosion of the concept of hospitality.[25]

The complex notion of hospitality, as set forth by Derrida, can be adopted as a workable category of analysis in addressing the imperial and cosmopolitan setting that characterizes the other Roman plays by Shakespeare (*Titus Andronicus, Julius Caesar, Antony and Cleopatra, Cymbeline*).[26] But what concerns us more in the case of *Coriolanus* is the way in which the theme of hospitality, with its interplay of sameness ("the law of the household", "the law of the place", "the law of identity") and otherness (friend, foreigner, enemy, etc.), interpellates the protagonist's anachronistic monologic structure of the self, a character immediately depicted at the outset of the play, self-reflexively, as he who "pays himself with being proud" (1.1.30). But what is Shakespeare suggesting when, in a flash, he links Coriolanus's imperfect performance of social virtues with a moment of amnestic disorder?

Coriolanus's Tired Memory

The reflection on the role played by memory in a positive reciprocating community is of pivotal importance in Seneca's often translated treatise *On Benefits*. As such it had its uses in early modern ethics and imagination.

As such, I also want to argue, it may have had a bearing on the telling, if fleeting characterization of Coriolanus as an absent-minded subjectivity. But let us go in order.

Coriolanus fails twice with respect to the "hospitable canon", as it is called by Aufidius. His first time is in Act 1, scene 9, soon after the victorious battle of the Romans, guided by Cominius, over the Volscians: as a reward for his high military valour he requests not war spoils or gifts but the benefit of freedom in favour of a poor Volscian who has been taken prisoner and who, poor though he is, has in the past received him with generous hospitality.

> CORIOLANUS The gods begin to mock me:
> I, that now refused most princely gifts,
> Am bound to beg of my lord general.
> COMINIUS Take't, 'tis yours. What is't?
> CORIOLANUS I sometime lay here in Corioles,
> At a poor man's house: he used me kindly.
> He cried to me; I saw him prisoner.
> But then Aufidius was within my view,
> And wrath o'erwhelmed my pity. I request you
> To give my poor host freedom.
> COMINIUS O, well begged!
> Were he the butcher of my son, he should
> Be free as is the wind. Deliver him, Titus.
> LARTIUS Martius, his name?
> CORIOLANUS By Jupiter, forgot!
> I am weary; yea, my memory is tired;
> Have we no wine here?
>
> (1.9.77–93)

Asking, as we know, is no easy task for Coriolanus, and Shakespeare makes us appreciate it here as a special endeavour. But the prisoner suddenly disappears from his sight. And something else intervenes to prevent him from returning a benefit he has received: Coriolanus cannot remember the Volscian's name.

Coriolanus's second failure occurs in the fourth act, scenes 4 and 5, when he asks to be admitted into his enemy's house, and is addressed with a question he cannot answer: "What's thy name?" Interestingly, in both cases the name takes centre stage in activating the disturbance which prevents or perverts the acknowledgement of the other or self, that is the positive circle (Seneca), the formation of the "dialogic structure" (Ricoeur), and ultimately the good performance of hospitality.

But let us first tackle the issue of Coriolanus's tired memory, a sin which is utterly intriguing for its being so venial, or at least so it appears. Freud would call it a "faulty achievement", *Fellheistung*, an unconscious defensive strategy on the part of the self, which by means of a memory lapse effaces what it sets to achieve, thus determining a collapse of the action: the action which, if achieved, would create a further and even more intolerable form of indebtedness of Coriolanus to his general Cominius.[27]

Must we say that there can be no gratitude, no *reciprocity*, without memory? In Italian, the term *riconoscenza* (gratitude) has the same root as *riconoscere* (recognize): as if gratitude (*grata beneficii memoria*) committed first of all to a relationship, an acknowledgement, which draws the other out of his anonymity, thus making us enter into an alliance, a community, a connective system of shared expectations and obligations. But Coriolanus does not remember his host's name. His poor host is left to his state of merely being caught sight of, his cry unanswered. Salvation (Redemption) is put in brackets, as if under suspension. Is Shakespeare elliptically foregrounding in this apparently marginal scene what leads his hero to the final disaster, that is, his difficulty to transfer himself from his patrician and solipsistic *virtus* to the much more complex sphere of social and civic virtues?

We should note that there is no such amnesia in the same episode told by Plutarch. Moreover, in his text, the Volscian is referred to by Coriolanus as a friend and a "wealthie man", a man easily identifiable, one would imagine, by his name.[28] So even though we are not given the Volscian's name, there is nothing in Plutarch's episode which can induce us to assume that Coriolanus doesn't remember his name, or that this may have hindered the achievement of his grateful gesture. On the contrary, the way Shakespeare rewrites it, that episode figures much more as a sort of aporia within the play, opening as it were a space of human and textual forgetfulness, or of wonder, perhaps, as if assuming the enigmatic character of a ruin. We will never know if Coriolanus ever succeeded in honouring the unwritten *reciprocity* clause, a clause as much Roman as Coriolanus's disregard for any other Roman value apart from those urged by the military code.

Now, the reciprocity clause was the articulating tenet in Seneca's treatise *On Benefits*. Indeed, he was well aware that in advocating a community put under the aegis of benefits, he was tackling "a thing that most of al other knitteth men togither in fellowship" (Book I.4).[29] In discussing how the several duties are divided between one who has proved generous and one who has benefited by it, Seneca persistently returns to the role played by memory in securing gratitude, and hence reciprocity: "Unto him wee haue inioyned forgetfulnesse, and vntoo too thee wee haue commaunded myndfulnesse" (Book VII. 22). "But wee ought too labour for nothing more, than that the remembraunce of good turnes, may alwayes sticke fast in our myndes: which must bée newe burnished from tyme to tyme, because none can requite a good turne, but he that beareth it in mynde" (Book II.24).

Repeatedly in his treatise Seneca indicates disregard as the sin which most atrophies the connective social value of gratitude, for, he argues, we only forget what is little esteemed. Arguably, Seneca had already understood the astute defensive strategies of the Freudian "faulty achievements", if then he puts the blame more on those who are ungrateful because they forget a benefit than on those who deny having received it. "Unthankfull is he that denieth the receiuyng of a good turne whiche he hath receiued. . . . But moste vnthankfull of all, is he that hath forgotten it" (Book III.1).

It is an involuntary deficiency of memory, to which Coriolanus adds as a justification a stronger distraction or passion, that is his warfare *agon* with Aufidius, that prevents him from accomplishing his noble intention. His memory "is tired", he says, and as to pity, this is a feeling he cannot indulge in, because it can damagingly divert from wrath: "I saw him prisoner. / But then Aufidius was within my view, / And wrath o'erwhelm'd my pity" (1.9.83–85). Shakespeare, however, does not allow him any chance to train his memory, as Seneca thought it ethically advisable with people whose "assurednesse . . . in requiting kyndnesse, dooth not cease, but faint: and these must wee iog" (Book V.23). As an illustration of his belief, Seneca offered an episode concerning Julius Caesar and one of his soldiers, which can be of great import if compared with the way Shakespeare contrives, by means of ellipsis and reversal, Coriolanus's memory lapse:

> One *Publius Militio* an old souldyer of *Iulius Caesars*, had a sewt before him ageinst his neyboures, and was like to haue gone by the woorse. Capteine (quoth he) remember you not how you sprent your ancle once about *Sucro* in Spayne? Yis sayed *Caesar*. Then you remember also, that when you went too sit doune vnder a certeine tree that cast verie little shadow, (for the sonne was exceeding whot and the place very rough in whiche that only one tree grew out from among the sragged cliffes): one of your souldyers did spred his cloke vnder you. When *Caesar* had answered, yea marrie, why should I not remember it? for when I was nygh dead for thirst: bycause I was not able too goo too the next spring by reason of my foote, . . . a souldyer of myne, a tall stout felowe, brought mée water in his burganet. Capteine (quoth he) and doo you knowe that man, or that burganet if you see them ageine?
>
> (Book V.24)

Caesar was unable to recognize in the aged and disabled man who was appealing to him his strong rescuer, but the man finally succeeded in awakening Caesar's sleeping memory and in obtaining his help in return. But in Seneca one could find also references to governors who did not like to be reminded of good deeds received: Tiberius is among them. To those who approached him with the expression "Remember you?" the emperor "stopped [their] mouth" by opposing forms of extreme "forgetfulnesse": "I remember not . . . what I haue bin" (Book V.25). Does Seneca's *On Benefits* lie beneath the episode of Coriolanus's deficient memory? And if so, why doesn't Shakespeare come to his aid with a reminder, or "jog", as Seneca thought it expedient to do with people suffering from failing memory?

It is not my intention to enter into the intense debate over Seneca's influence on Shakespeare, a debate which over the years has repeatedly shifted in favour of one position or the other. For our purposes, it would be enough to know that Seneca's moral treatise *On Benefits* was highly influential in medieval and Renaissance European culture; that (in Golding's and Lodge's translations) it was part of the Latin-based canon of the English Renaissance culture; that *actio ingrati*, expounded as a decried vice in Book 3, offered itself as a typical theme fit for grammar school imitative practice in rhetoric, as it was already customary in the Roman law schools according to what Seneca himself takes care to tell us (Book III.6), in his endeavour to stress the ethical relevance of his topic. But we also know that Seneca's ideas on benefits modelled the 1601 Crown discussion on the concession of patents, and that they provided a vocabulary for the theory of benevolence and reciprocity that underpinned the Elizabethan commonwealth.[30]

Interestingly, in *Coriolanus*, "benefit" is the word used by Menenius Agrippa when he champions the redistributive role played by the belly in his improbable alimentary metaphor of the State (1.1.147–54). Most importantly Coriolanus is the first to be mentioned by Seneca when he comes to the list of those who have committed the sin of ingratitude against their own country by assailing, with an unholy war, "[their] Wives . . . Children . . . Churches . . . houses, & . . . Goddes" (Book V.15). But what concerns us most is also the fact that Seneca's abhorrence of this internecine ferocity is given force by his reference to the four verses from Ovid's *Metamorphoses* which I introduced in the first part of this chapter and which are specifically devoted to the disrupted laws of civil and domestic ties in his Iron Age: "The Guest may scarsly trust his hoste, nor yet the hoste his Guest, etc." (Seneca, Book V.15–16).

Shakespeare may have drawn precisely on this authoritative association established by Seneca in Book 5 of his treatise, when he dramatized the Plutarchan tragedy of Coriolanus, as a parallel pervading story of Ovidian violated hospitality. But, rather than adding elements to prove Seneca's work as a direct source, a job persuasively done by John M. Wallace,[31] I deem more profitable to see how elements of a wider coeval textual system are catalyzed in Shakespeare's play, complicating the range of its issues with a radical ethical preoccupation. For, what we find in Seneca's treatise, and almost in the same terms used by our present theorists of "gift studies", is the memory or envisaging of a community as a hospitable and reciprocating place, a "goodly", if ghostly "place", as is the city (and the house) almost ironically evoked by Coriolanus when he arrives—the wayfarer of an incumbent wasteland—at the gates of Antium, home to the enemy.

The House of Grace and the Bond Value

If we look up the term "goodly" in the *OED* we will be referred to "gracious" as a coterminous word used to indicate a thing or character "endowed with grace or charm", or "likely to find favour", or also "condescendingly kind, indulgent and beneficent to inferiors". "Gracious" conveys many of these meanings when it occurs as a courteous epithet in relation to kings, queens, or dukes ("Your gracious Lord", etc.). All of these connotations were extensively debated in Castiglione's *Libro del Cortegiano* (1528) where *grazia*—conceptualized as an empowering virtue in the courtier's self-fashioning enterprise—occurs profusely as noun and root of a variety of sociably valuable epithets and predicates: *gratia, gratioso, aggraziato, grato, gratissimo*. "[F]or by the vertue of the worde (*"per la forza del vocabulo"*) man may saye, that whoso hath grace is Gracious" the Elizabethans could read in Hoby's translation.[32] What a pity that the reader of *The Book of the Courtier* magnificently Englished by Hoby in 1561 (a bestseller in Shakespeare's time) should at times miss the strengthening network of mutual resonances established by Castiglione's deliberate playing with a common root, when *grato* and *gratissimo*, in their meaning of "agreeable", were rendered by Hoby with "acceptable" and "most acceptable".

Castiglione dedicated most of the first book to circulating an idea of *gratia* as the completion of all other virtues possessed by the perfect courtier as a man of war and a humanist: "But principallye lette hym accompanye all his mocion wyth a certayne good judgemente and grace, yf he wyll deserve that generall favour whiche is so muche set by" (Hoby, 39). Grace was promoted as a quality of his physical aspect, manners, gestures, voice, the way he performed in the military arts and sport, as well as the way he participated in the highly valued Renaissance "civile conversazione" on art and letters. Moreover, as *gratia* (grace) exchanged with *gratia* (favour), it was conceptualized as essential to the negotiating economy of the courtly ambience.[33] But this is not a quality of things or persons one would expect to find evoked by Coriolanus. Grace is beyond his scope, if not once, when during his triumph, he is fantasized by the tribunes in the arrested "graceful posture" of a deity, his only moment of grace (2.1.215).

Now, what I think might have appealed to a poet's mind (as well as to those involved in the Renaissance fashioning of the ideal governor) is exactly the fact that in Seneca's treatise his theory of benefits is expounded as both an ethics and an aesthetics, an aesthetics of *grace*, as it appears most significantly in his digression on the three Graces, the mythological personification, in his illustration, of a joyful reciprocating community, as in a dancing ring:

> I will tell thee what the force and propertie of [benefites] is, if thou wilt first giue me leaue too ouerronne these thynges that pertaine not too the matter: namely why there bee three Graces, why they bee sisters, and why they go hand in hand: why they looke smyling, why they bee yoong, and why they bee maidens, and appareled in looce and sheere raiment. Some would haue it ment thereby, that the one of them bestoweth the good turne the other receiueth it, and the thirde requiteth it. . . . Why walkes that knot in roundell hand in hand? It is in this respect, that . . . the grace of the whole is mard, if it bee any-where broken of·but is most beautifull, if it continew toogether and kéepe his course. . . . Yoong they bee, bycause the remembraunce of good turnes must neuer wex old. . . . there ought too bee no bondage nor constreint. And therfore they weare looce garmentes.
>
> (Book I.3)

We should note that this digression on the three Graces is by no means digressive: *gratia* in Latin means not only "a benefit", a gift, a grace that has been bestowed upon us, but also the gratitude (*gratiam habere*) which is due for it. That is, the capacity, as it were, of welcoming and hosting the gift proffered. It also predicates, as we have seen in Castiglione, the quality of a person who makes himself agreeable and welcome (*gratus*), indicating the act "of ingratiating oneself", one might say borrowing from Derrida's nice probing into the multifaceted meanings of hospitality, "having or letting oneself come, coming well, welcoming [*se faire ou se laisser venir: bien venir*], greeting, greeting one another as a sign of welcome".[34] *Gratia*, as we can see, refers us to the common etymological root of grace, gratitude, grateful, ungrateful, agreeable, and greeting, and as such the memory of its mythological imagery far from being foreign is substantial to Seneca's subject.

But what I think is also worth noting in Seneca's introduction of the three Graces is that it makes evident what Derrida would call the *double bind* of conditions and disinterestedness which lies at the heart of any conceptualization of benefits, as well as of the overlapping sphere of hospitality; a *double bind* in respect to which Seneca tries to keep himself in balance as on a tightrope. As with hospitality, in so far as benefits serve not so much philanthropy or generosity as a social necessity of cohabitation and bonds, they call for rules, obligations, and mutuality, at the risk of imploding any moment into a utilitarian bargaining regulated by a logic of power. But the inner nature of benefits, Seneca stresses, is that they serve the virtue of giving with no guarantee of being returned. In so far as they serve the transparency of unconditioned giving and receiving, they should also be unbound and unrestricted as the beautiful flowing robes of the Graces. Not differently from our present theorists of "gift studies", Seneca is looking for a positive state of indebtedness based on a third value beyond those of material use and exchange. This is *le lien*, the bond value, a value grounded in the interest in entering the social relationship.

The beauty of giving is so much celebrated by Seneca as to be figured as a work of art arrested in its gratuitousness, that is, in the moment preceding its socio-economic realized profitability:

> *Phidias* makes an Image. The frute of his woorkmanship is one, and the frute of his woork is another. The end of his woorkmanship is too haue made the thing that he ment too make. The end of his woorke is too haue doone it too some profit. *Phidias* hathe finished his woorke, though he haue not sold it. . . . Likewyse of a benefyte or good turne, let the firste frute be the frute of a mans owne conceyte. This hath he reaped whiche hath brought his gift thither as he would. . . . Therfore when a good turne is accepted freendly, he that bestowed it hath alredie receiued recompence, but not reward.
>
> (Book II.33)

Similarly, there is a beauty of receiving for Seneca that, while excluding the return of the benefit as its condition, depends however on its being suspended, no matter how long, in the readiness of a gesture to be accomplished. But only if one is capable of hosting the joy (and hence the memory) of the gift received. What Coriolanus is unable to do.

Coriolanus is made to decline all this sophisticated social art of cohabitation, which is all the more tragic for his being a candidate consul, a leader of a state, a precursor of an empire to come; an art that any Elizabethan tutor, schoolmaster, or secretary of state would have suggested as the useful accomplishment of a cultivated and virtuous governor or gentleman. As Daryl W. Palmer has written, "[t]hroughout England's age of expansion, aesthetic achievement, and civil revolution, hospitality existed as a code of exchange between competing, often conflicting, orders of society". Royal hospitable practices—and especially the ritual of gift giving—responded to a precise ideological program of consensus and domination. Indeed, "the life of power [was] coextensive with the custom of donation".[35] As for Elizabeth herself, she had learned only too well the extent to which that art could help in knitting her state and her people's hearts into unity with the queen's. Her "Golden Speech" devised to sedate the heated debate over the Crown's concession of monopolies is a case in point.

> There will never queen sit in my seat, with more zeal to my country, care for my subjects . . . And though you have had and may have princes, more mighty and wise sitting in this seat, yet you never had

or shall have any that will be more careful and loving. Shall I ascribe anything to myself and my sexly weakness? I were not worthy to live then.[36]

As the historian David Harris Sacks has shown, her way of framing the issue of patents within a Senecan larger economy of benevolence, gratitude, and moral bonds is crucial in turning the question of patronage and taxation into a "ritualized exchange of gratitude given for gratitude received, . . . binding queen and subject, as she says, in 'sympathy'". The whole ritual of the discussion between the parts, Sacks argues, with the speaker of the Commons proffering thanks and devotion for "Benefitts receyued", and the Queen graciously bestowing her favours with "a Kingly heart" attested to this.[37]

Was the ensuing sovereign as "careful and loving" as Elizabeth? As we know, *Coriolanus* was written between 1607 and 1608, under the reign of James I, a reign which—because of the plague and as if ironically foreshadowing the Stuarts' fate—had started in 1603 with a series of curtailed ceremonies. The king made his solemn entry into the Tower of London without passing through the City, and when the delayed coronation ceremony took place, Westminster was barred by road and river, to the disappointment of the multitudes who had flocked to London to acclaim him and enjoy the feast in spite of the plague. The sumptuous pageants and arches which had been prepared in honour of his progress from the Tower through the streets of the City were also left unacknowledged until March 1604 when the "Triumphant Passage" finally took place. We do not know whether and to what extent the memory of those maimed and deferred rites may have influenced Shakespeare while writing of Coriolanus's abhorrence of crowds and of ritualized renewals of bonds with his Roman subjects. But certainly by 1607 James I had already made a reputation among European ambassadors as a king who manifested "no taste for the [people] but rather contempt and dislike".[38] And Shakespeare on his part was evidencing a disease of the social body for which Coriolanus had no care and no medicine, let alone a language (be it a "lawful" grammar for "asking", a ceremony of investiture, or "a pretty tale", like that of Menenius), to rearticulate according to a healthy circle the disarticulated relationship between the people and himself. The people are and remain a "herd of—boils and plague" (1.4.32) to him all along the play, as much as he remains an ungracious and inhospitable governor to them.

But let us go back to Seneca's theory of benefits, and to the way it seems to resonate contrastively, as a sort of ethical and aesthetic counterpoint, to Coriolanus's inner nature itself. For, Coriolanus does not know either the rules or the joy and the beauty of humanist giving and receiving, of taking in return, as Cominius reminds him in a remarkable piece of introspection (soon after the victorious battle against the Volscians), insightfully hinting at a man who is not at home with himself, and hence even incapable of making one's self come, of "well-coming", to himself and to one's city.

> Too modest are you,
> More cruel to your good report than grateful
> To us that give you truly. By your patience,
> If 'gainst yourself you be incensed, we'll put you
> Like one that means his proper harm, in manacles,
> Then reason safely with you.
>
> (1.9.52–57)

The point is that in so doing, in denying himself the pleasure of receiving, Coriolanus is transgressing an obligation imposed by that very patrician code he seems to perform so well. In fact, "through this process of conferring and receiving honour, the individualistic pursuit of 'nobility' or *magnitudo animi* [was] tied to the service of the Roman state".[39] But Coriolanus refuses to ceremonialize his virtues, an art, pageantry, brought to superlative excellence by the Tudor dynasty. He is unable to spend his military virtues in the forum.

Significantly, one is tempted to say, it is precisely here (after the victorious battle against the Volscians), that he will be assigned with the *addition* of another name, that of Coriolanus (1.9.64), a foreign country and another home. The *addition* in fact rewards the conqueror with a title, a "benefit" (as it is called in North's Plutarch),[40] which finds no way of becoming exchangeable in the geography of the play, not even, as it should, among Coriolanus's countrymen to rekindle their sense of Romanness. On the contrary, starting from Caius Martius's triumphal return from Corioles as Coriolanus, the audience will have to witness a frustrating succession of abortive dealings with deputations of his countrymen, none leading to a lasting pact, a mutually binding hospitality.

Obedient only to the patrician code of military *virtus*, Coriolanus has always refused to accept the superior law of reciprocity—the law, that is, that originates in the forum, the quintessential interconnective space of the city, as the rioting citizens remind him during the troubled ceremonies which, following protocol, precede his investiture as consul. The city is not its hierarchical architecture, whose "unbuilding", for those who are in power, is "to lay all flat" and "bury all which yet distinctly ranges / In heaps and pile of ruin". To the contrary: "The people are the city". For "What is the city but the people?" (3.1.198–200), the populace and tribunes argue: an assertion seemingly shaped, I suggest, by repurposing the speech of the emperor Otho to mutinous people and legions in Tacitus's *Histories*.[41]

When Coriolanus promises his mother that he will go to the forum, to him it is as if he were being sent to the gallows. And once there, he does not cooperate. He presents himself as a body that is deserving, but lacks desire, the very principle of motion, interaction, and change.

CORIOLANUS You know the cause, sir, of my standing here?
3 CITIZEN We do, sir. Tell us what hath brought you to 't.
CORIOLANUS Mine own desert.
2 CITIZEN Your own desert?
CORIOLANUS Ay, but not my own desire.
3 CITIZEN How, not your own desire?
CORILANUS No, sir, 'twas never my desire yet to trouble
the poor with begging.
3 CITIZEN You must think, if we give you anything, we
hope to gain by you.
CORIOLANUS Well then, I pray, your price o'th' consulship?
1 CITIZEN The price is, to ask it kindly.

(2.3.62–74)

Indeed, what seems to be put to the test here is the very intimate "dialectic of *self* and the *other than self*" (Ricoeur) of which desire is an instance. In Ricoeur's philosophy, "sameness", namely the "identical", is at odds with the reciprocal indebtedness of the ethical perspective, as well as being an obstacle to a full development of the Self. For "If another were not counting on me, would I be capable of keeping my word, of maintaining myself?" Coriolanus is the *idem* Ricoeur speaks about in *Oneself as Another*.[42] And such an impossibility "to be other than one thing, not moving" (4.7.42), as clearly remarked by Aufidius, is substantial to his nature and his tragedy.

What in the end is successfully conveyed to us is the tragedy of the man who is not able to start or maintain the "beneficial" circle, the Senecan interlocked and continuous dancing ring. There is no *grace* in Coriolanus to make him welcome among his countrymen as much as there is no *grace*, no salvation, to recall and to reunite him to his hospitable Volscian. His gesture of gratitude is not suspended in the readiness of a possible return as in Seneca's beautiful imagery of gift giving. It is abortive. As such I see that episode as having a great bearing in defining Coriolanus as the strange guest we meet later in the play.

"The Feast Smells Well, But I / Appear Not Like a Guest"

In Act 4, scene 5, when the state of necessity that Aufidius has foreshadowed has effectively begun, we meet Coriolanus, né Martius, banished from Rome and seeking refuge under false pretences among the Volscians, in his enemy's house. "A goodly house", he says, "the feast smells well, but I / Appear not like a guest" (4.5.5–6).

In his *Parallel Lives*, Plutarch compares him to Ulysses penetrating the walls of Troy to walk among his enemies disguised as a servant (*Odyssey*, IV.244 *et passim*).[43] In Plutarch's story, Coriolanus then proceeds unimpeded until he reaches the very heart of Tullus Aufidius's home, well protected by the solemnity of his bearing, which his humble wanderer's rags cannot hide. Such is not the case in Shakespeare, who envisions at this point a scene of great dramatic scope, which he develops, as has been noticed, through allusions to the succeeding cantos of Homer's narration, which tell the story of Ulysses's journey dressed as a lowly beggar; the same Ulysses who fears he might be pelted with stones as he makes his way home, in Ithaca, and who must then pause on a threshold which will prove difficult to cross, with the suitors mocking him at length as they continue to feast in his palace (*Odyssey*, XVII–XVIII).

Clearly, this is what Shakespeare needed most: the image of an undesirable guest, repeatedly rejected from the dinner table, abandoned on a threshold. But why? It seems to me that as the play moves towards its tragic epilogue, Shakespeare wishes to incorporate a number of meanings into the figure of an unknown traveller seeking refuge in Antium and admission to Aufidius's food-laden table, which point to a reversed mythical representation of the figure of recognition, an issue which haunts the whole tragedy: the question of an identity that knows no welcome, that cannot recognize and is not able to recognize itself, until it crumbles away like a forgotten part in the hands of a bad actor, as Coriolanus himself must finally admit, in the last act ("Like a dull actor now, / I Have forgot my part", 5.3.40–41).[44]

Fittingly, when he reaches Antium and stands on the threshold of a house whose servants insolently deny him entrance, Coriolanus is insistently asked questions he cannot answer: "Whence are you?, "Where dwell'st thou?", and in an increasingly urgent and dangerous tone, "What are you?", "What's thy name?" (4.5.8–65). But his name, the name he has acquired on the battlefield in Corioles, is precisely what he cannot pronounce. And yet, say his name he must in order to cope with "the law of the house"; a law perverted and taken to its extreme by the logic of power triggered by his name, and thanks to which the two ancient foes will become not so much host and guest as, rather, two hostages of a destructive reciprocity. Coriolanus knows only too well that he is asking for hospitality in a state of exception:[45] "Now this extremity / Hath brought me to thy hearth, not out of hope—Mistake me not—to safe my life" (4.5.80–82).

In fact, the *mensa hospitalis* to which Coriolanus is eventually welcomed and given the seat of honour next to Aufidius, who shows his guest the same tender care one would reserve for a lover ("[Aufidius] makes a mistress of him", 4.5.197–98), is the scene of a deadly game—an end game. For the guest dispossesses his host in his own home, cutting him "i'th' middle" (4.5.200) and "cannibally" (4.5.191) eating one half with the other guests' approval, as the servant observes—"for the other has half by the entreaty and grant of the whole table" (4.5.201–02); but what Coriolanus in his turn serves up is the body of Rome on a platter, which he has sacrilegiously promised to "mow down", placing himself at the head of the Volscian army.

Hospitality is here indistinguishable from hostility, one might say with Derrida. Paradoxically, however, Coriolanus is here forced to employ a contractual language from which he has always kept his distance in Rome. Until now he has always abhorred what he calls "a beggar's tongue" (3.2.118). It is only derogatorily, if not contemptuously, and to no avail, that, urged by Menenius, he has performed the "custom of request" (2.3.140) provided for the candidate to consulship. And if he has lost Rome, his own "goodly city" and his own "goodly house", it is because he has never accepted "to ask . . . kindly" (2.3.75), "mildly", or with "a gentler spirit" (3.1.56).

Coriolanus's sense of self-sufficiency has been discussed at length and most powerfully by Janet Adelman and Stanley Cavell.[46] What I would like to point out is that in Antium, in his enemy's house, for the first time he is forced out of his independence, forced as he is to perform (though scornfully, a coherent style for him throughout the play) a long and drawn-out begging to gain access to the "goodly house", that is, to the domestic, friendly values of the household, which, however, only causes him to fail for the second time to conform to the hospitable canon. For it is only as a strange guest that he will cross the threshold of the "goodly house", a guest whose name is as insistently asked as it is deferred in its utterance, Coriolanus's name being an unutterable name, "a robbery" (5.6.91), a name stolen from a place he has conquered, as he knows only too well, by widowing the place as well as its women: "City / 'Tis I that made thy widows" (4.4.1–2).

As the overriding question addressed to the foreigner, the question of the name ("What is your name?"), Derrida has argued, is tantamount to the question of hospitality itself, the one around which rights, limits, and responsibilities are generated: "In telling me what your name is, in responding to this request, you are responding on your own behalf, you are responsible before the law and before your hosts, you are a subject in law".[47]

Now it is exactly the question of the name as the question Coriolanus cannot comply with, which is given the centre stage in the play. "A name unmusical to the Volscians' ears", he says to Aufidius, "And harsh in sound to thine" (4.5.60–61). A name which bears inscribed in itself the "memorie and witness" of hostility, as we read in Plutarch,[48] and which in the scene devised by Shakespeare keeps Coriolanus arrested at length, as Homer's beggar-king, at the threshold of Aufidius's house. But only to enter into a bond of reciprocity with the enemy, his only bond. After all his name is ironically his only debt, one might want to observe, his name being the Roman way of assimilating the memory of conquered lands into a parading imperial annexationist lineage.

This must have brought into the play a pause for reflection, at a time when the names of the British royal family were being imprinted on the new territories of America. Jamestown, for example, had just been founded in 1607. Whether appropriating other people's names, or giving one's own to them, naming continued to be a strategy of no little account in beheading and incorporating the history of the other.

It is just as ironically appropriate that the Volscians' *mensa hospitalis* should be the only place of reciprocation and restitution for Coriolanus—but in a tragic and useless way. For here, in Antium, Coriolanus, *né* Martius, undergoes the ultimate dispossession, the dispossession of his name. This, as he says, is the only thing he is left with after having been banished from Rome ("Only that name remains", 4.5.75), and yet this is, importantly, the very thing in which his valour and identity—his very *Romanitas*—are condensed. Meaningfully, the loss of his name is experienced by Coriolanus as a loss, or death, of the self to the self. Shakespeare shows his character as he faces this bereavement first as a difficulty in pronouncing his name on Aufidius's threshold, then as his own incapacity to respond to that call.

> COMINIUS   "Coriolanus"
> He would not answer to, forbade all names.
> He was a kind of nothing, titleless,
> Till he had forged himself a name o'the'fire
> Of burning Rome.
> $$(5.1.11–15)$$

"Coriolanus" has become a sound for which he has no ears. It is a relict, an alienated linguistic substance which crumbles down away from him like a mute ruin. Amputated of that name, he is now a stranger to himself, a guest or hostage of his own anger, like his mother.

"He shall have a noble memory", Aufidius proclaims after he has killed him, thus having his "good turn". We feel that what we are left with is the contradictory memory of an exile, for it is only at the cost of a betrayal to both his mother country and his hosting country that he can reciprocate what he owes them both: the body claimed by his mother,[49] the name persistently thrown back at him until the end by Aufidius.

> Dost thou think
> I'll grace thee with that robbery, thy stolen name
> Coriolanus, in Corioles?
> $$(5.6.90–92)$$

Yet, even in this play about a banished and banishing humanity, Shakespeare, as he sometimes does before his ineluctable tragic epilogues, lets us feel—though only for a moment—the relief, if not the bliss, of a possible different story. This happens in the fifth scene of the last act, when he has his audience join the crowd in *greeting* the delegation of ladies (Volumnia, Virgilia, Valeria) as they re-enter Rome after their mission of peace—the

only successful negotiation of the play, though "most mortal" to Coriolanus (5.3.189), the invincible Mars, the "engine" (5.4.19). "Welcome,
ladies, welcome!" ALL. "Welcome, ladies, Welcome!"

Notes

1. Quotations refer to *Coriolanus*, ed. Peter Holland (London: Bloomsbury
   Arden Shakespeare, 2013).
2. Claudia Corti, "The Iconic Body: *Coriolanus* and Renaissance Corporeality",
   in Del Sapio Garbero, Insenberg and Pennacchia, eds, *Questioning Bodies*,
   p. 57. On Coriolanus's corporeality, see also Michele Marrapodi, "*Mens
   Sana in copore sano*: the Rhetoric of the Body in Shakespeare's Roman and
   Late Plays", in Del Sapio Garbero et al., eds, pp. 198–205. Maurizio Calbi,
   "States of Exception: Auto-Immunity and the Body Politic in Shakespeare's
   Coriolanus", in Del Sapio Garbero et al., pp. 77–94; Isabella Norton, "'He
   Was a Thing of Blood': Blood, Wounds, and Memory in Shakespeare's *The
   Tragedy of Coriolanus*", *Litterae Mentis: A Journal of Literary Studies*, 1
   (2014), 6–14. On *Coriolanus*'s theatrical transcodification of its Plutarchan
   sources, see Claudia Corti, "*Coriolanus*: presentazione, tabulazione e commento", in Alessandro Sepieri et al., eds, *Nel Laboratoro di Shakespere. I
   drammi romani*, vol. 4 (Parma: Pratiche, 1990), pp. 251–342.
3. See Janet Adelman, "'Anger's My Meat': Feeding, Dependency, and Aggression in *Coriolanus*", in Murray M. Schwartz, ed., *Representing Shakespeare:
   New Psychoanalytic Essays* (Baltimore and London: The John Hopkins
   University Press, 1980), pp. 129–149, then absorbed in *Suffocating Mothers*
   (1992).
4. North's Plutarch, "The Life of Coriolanus", p. 238.
5. On the connection of Volumnia with the founding myth of Romulus and
   Remo, see Janet Adelman, "Shakespeare's Romulus and Remus: Who Does
   the Wolf Love?", in Del Sapio Garbero, ed., *Identity, Otherness and Empire*,
   pp. 19–34. On Volumnia as "the arbiter of virtus", see Kahn, *Roman Shakespeare* (especially her chapter "Mother of Battles: Volumnia and Her Son in
   Coriolanus", pp. 144–159). But see also Michela Compagnoni, "Blending
   Motherhoods: Volumnia and the Representation of Maternity in William
   Shakespeare's *Coriolanus*", in Domenico Lovascio, ed., *Roman Women in
   Shakespeare and His Contemporaries* (Kalamazoo: Medieval Institute Publications, 2020), pp. 39–58.
6. Giorgio Agamben, *L'uso dei corpi. Homo sacer*, IV (Vicenza: Neri Pozza
   Editore, 2014), pp. 78–87.
7. Edwards, *Writing Rome*, p. 71.
8. For more on Fiennes's film, see Peter Holland, "Introduction", in Shakespeare, *Coriolanus*, pp. 133–141.
9. "In the shower scene", Tom Hiddleston has recently said, "Josie wanted the
   audience to be able to see the wounds that he refuses to show the people
   later on, but we also wanted to suggest the reality of what those scars have
   cost him privately. We wanted to show him wincing, in deep pain: that
   these wounds and scars are not some highly prized commodity, but that
   beneath the exterior of the warrior-machine, idealised far beyond his sense
   of his own worth, is a human being who bleeds". Chris Wiegand, "Tom
   Hiddleston on Coriolanus: 'There Was Nowhere to Hide—That's Exciting'",
   The Guardian, 3 June 2020, www.theguardian.com/stage/2020/jun/03/
   tom-hiddleston-coriolanus-donmar-warehouse-josie-rourke.

10. T.S. Eliot, *The Waste Land* (1922), V. 415–416, in *Collected Poems*, 1909–1962 (London: Faber & Faber, 1963), p. 79.
11. Tacitus's *Works*, The Loeb Classical Library, 5 vols (London and Cambridge, MA: Harvard University Press, 1925–1937), vol. 2. "From the houses the fire spread to the colonnades adjoining the temple; then the 'eagles' which supported the roof, being of old wood, caught and fed the flames. So the Capitol burned with its doors closed; none defended it, none pillaged it. This was the saddest and most shameful crime that the Roman state had ever suffered since its foundation". *Id.*, III.71–72.
12. See Manfred Pfister, "Acting the Roman: *Coriolanus*", in Del Sapio Garbero, ed., *Identity, Otherness and Empire*, p. 37.
13. Stanley Cavell, "'Who Does the Wolf Love?': *Coriolanus* and the Interpretations of Politics", in Patricia Parker and Geoffrey H. Hartman, eds, *Shakespeare and the Question of Theory* (New York and London: Routledge, [1985] 2004), pp. 250–251.
14. See Miola on *Titus Andronicus*, in *Shakespeare's Rome*, p. 62 *et passim*.
15. Ovidio, *Metamorfosi*, I.144–145.
16. See the episode of Baucis and Philemon in Ovid's *Metamorphoses*, Latin-Italian edition, VIII.626 *et passim* (Golding, VIII.801 *et passim*).
17. Paul Ricoeur, *Oneself as Another*, transl. Kathleen Blamey (Chicago and London: The University of Chicago Press, [1990] 1994), p. 341. See also the chapters "The Aim of the 'Good' Life and Obligation" and "Solicitude and the Norm", pp. 204–227.
18. Michele Marrapodi, "Retaliation as an Italian Vice in English Renaissance Drama: Narrative and Theatrical Exchanges", in Michele Marrapodi, ed., *The Italian World of English Renaissance Drama: Cultural Exchange and Intertextuality* (Newark: Delaware University Press, 1998), p. 195. See also Mariangela Tempera, "'Horror . . . Is the Sinews of the Fable': Giraldi Cinthio's Works and Elizabethan Tragedy", in Yves Peyré and Pierre Kapitaniak, eds, *Shakespeare et l'Europe de la Renaissance* (Paris: Société Française Shakespeare, 2005), pp. 235–247, https://journals.openedition.org/shakespeare/33.
19. The reference is from the Biblioteca Italiana online edition of the play (Roma: Biblioteca italiana, 2003), www.bibliotecaitaliana.it/xtf/view?docId=bibit000565/bibit000565.xml&doc.vi.
20. Seneca's language of benefits in Shakespeare's plays was first pointed to by John M. Wallace in "*Timon of Athens* and the Three Graces: Shakespeare's Senecan Study", *Modern Philology*, 83 (1986), 349–363, and "The Senecan Context of 'Coriolanus'", *Modern Philology*, 90:4 (1993), 465–478. But it was only after I had published two earlier versions of this chapter ["'A Goodly House': Memory and Hosting in Coriolanus", in Marta Gibinska and Agnieszka Romanowska, eds, *Shakespeare in Europe: History and Memory* (Cracow: Jagiellonian University Press, 2008), pp. 225–238, and "Disowning the Bond: Coriolanus Forgetful Humanism", in Michele Marrapodi, ed., *Shakespeare and the Italian Renaissance: Appropriation, Transformation, Opposition* (Farnham: Ashgate, 2014), pp. 73–91] that I discovered it. It was a pleasure to be confirmed on my idea that *De Beneficiis* represents a pervasive hypotext in Shakespeare's play, as well as to see that we both contribute to strengthening such an idea (even though) by pursuing different lines of investigation.
21. Greenblatt, *Renaissance Self-Fashioning*, p. 5.
22. Ricoeur, "Solicitude and the Norm", in *Oneself as Another*, p. 218.
23. See Jacques Derrida, *Donner le temps* (Paris: Galilée, 1991); Alain Caillé and Jacques T. Godbout, *L'esprit du don* (Paris: Éditions la Découverte, 1992);

Jacques T. Godbout, *Le Langage du don* (Montréal: Éditions Fides, 1996); Alain Caillé, *Le tiers paradigme. Anthropologie philosophique du don* (Paris: Éditions la Découverte, 1998).

24. Jacques Derrida and Anne Dufourmantelle, *Of Hospitality: Anne Dufourmantelle Invites Jacques Derrida to Respond* (Stanford: Stanford University Press, [1997] 2000), pp. 74–76 and 94.

25. Jacques Derrida, "Hostipitality", *Angelaki*, 5:3 (2000), 3–18 (pp. 4–5).

26. See Del Sapio Garbero, "Fostering the Question 'Who Plays the Host?'".

27. See Freud, *Opere*, vol. 8, pp. 251–256. Coriolanus's absent-mindedness and its Freudian implications have not gone unnoticed so far, but the episode tends rather to be underrated, especially in the way it refers us to an early modern understanding of these topics. See Jonas Barish, "Remembering and Forgetting in Shakespeare", in R.B. Parker and Sheldon P. Zitner, eds, *Elizabethan Theater: Essays in Honor of S. Schoenbaum* (Newark: University of Delaware Press, 1996), pp. 214–221.

28. North's Plutarch: "Among the Volsces there is an olde friende and hoste of mine, an honest wealthie man, and now a prisoner, who living before in great wealth in his owne countrie, liveth now a poore prisoner in the handes of his enemies: and yet notwithstanding all this his miserie and misfortune, it would doe me great pleasure if I could save him from this one daunger: to keepe him from being solde as a slave" (p. 242).

29. This and subsequent quotations are taken from *The Woorke of Lucius Annaeus Seneca Concerning Benefyting, That Is Too Say the Doing, Receyuing, and Requiting of Good Turnes*, transl. Arthur Golding and John Day (London: John Kingston for John Day, 1578), facsimile edition, Theatrum Orbis Terrarum, 1974.

30. See David Harris Sacks, "The Countervailing of Benefits: Monopoly, Liberty, and Benevolence in Elizabethan England", in Dale Hoak, ed., *Tudor Political Culture* (Cambridge: Cambridge University Press, 1995), pp. 272–291.

31. See note 20.

32. References are from the following editions: Baldassare Castiglione, *Il Cortegiano* (Venezia: Comin Trino, 1573), p. 34, and *The Book of the Courtier*, transl. Thomas Hoby [1561], ed. Walter Alexander Raleigh (London: David Nutt, 1900). University of Oregon edition online: Renascence Editions, 1997, p. 40.

33. Castiglione took also great pains to defend the performance of grace from the excesses of either affectation (*"affettatione"*), or *"sprezzatura"*, a new word for the ancient motto, *ars est celare artem*. For a gender-coded reading of these terms and their relation with the courtly art of dissimulation, see Harry Berger Jr., *The Absence of Grace: Sprezzatura and Suspicion in Two Renaissance Courtesy Book* (Stanford: Stanford University Press, 2000).

34. Derrida, "Hostipitality", p. 11.

35. Daryl W. Palmer, *Hospitable Performances: Dramatic Genre and Cultural Practices in Early Modern England* (Indiana: Purdue University Press, 1992), pp. 4, 8. See also Felicity Heal, *Hospitality in Early Modern England* (Oxford: Clarendon Press, 1990).

36. Elizabeth I, *Collected Works*, eds. Leah S. Marcus et al. (Chicago: The University of Chicago Press, 2000), pp. 339–340.

37. Sacks, "The Countervailing of Benefits", p. 286.

38. See Barbara L. Parker, *Plato's Republic and Shakespeare's Rome: A Political Study of the Roman Works* (Newark: University of Delaware Press, 2004), pp. 70–71.

39. Miles, *Shakespeare and the Constant Romans*, p. 155.

40. North's Plutarch: "For I never had other benefit, nor recompence . . . but this only surname" (p. 249).

41. "Tell me, do you think that this fairest city consists of houses and buildings and heaps of stone? Those dumb and inanimate things can perish and readily be replaced. The eternity of our power, the peace of the world, my safety and yours, are secured by the welfare of the senate. This senate, which was established under auspices by the Father and Founder of our city and which has continued in unbroken line from the time of the kings even down to the time of the emperors, let us hand over to posterity even as we received it from our fathers. For as senators spring from your number, so emperors spring from senators." Tacitus, *Histories*, transl. Clifford H. Moore, Loeb Classical Library, vol. 2 (Cambridge, MA: Harvard University Press, 1925), Book I.84. As a matter of fact, this is a speech he devised to justify the destructions caused by his own greed of power and which had turned into an uncontrollable state of emergency.

42. "*Oneself as Another* suggests from the outset that the selfhood of oneself implies otherness to such an intimate degree that one cannot be thought of without the other". Ricoeur, *Oneself as Another*, p. 3 and 341.

43. Homer, *Odyssey*, transl. A.T. Murray, rev. George E. Dimock, Loeb Classical Library, 2 vols (Cambridge, MA: Harvard University Press, 1919).

44. For a "performative" reading of the play, see Pfister, "Acting the Roman: *Coriolanus*", pp. 35–47.

45. For a reading of the whole play as a state of exception, see Calbi, "States of Exception", pp. 77–94.

46. See Cavell, "'Who Does the Wolf Love?'", and Adelman, "'Anger's My Meat'". But see also John Kerrigan's compelling interpretation of Coriolanus's tragedy in terms of "fidelity", "promise", "oaths", "warrants", and the discovery of their contradictions as Roman values. *Essays on Criticism*, 62:4 (2012), 319–353.

47. Derrida and Dufourmantelle, *Of Hospitality*, p. 27.

48. North's Plutarch, p. 249.

49. Volumnia: "Alack, or we must lose / The country, our dear nurse, or else thy person, / Our comfort in the country" (5.3.109–111). Revealingly Volumnia springs up in a flash as "the only true criminal" to the eye of a great writer like Giorgio Manganelli: "E quella madre ('la dicono un pò pazza') perfetta creatura giocastea, di cui 'l'orgoglioso' Coriolano non è che un budello. Altissimo e sordido. Spazzato via a un cenno della madre—l'unico autentico criminale della *pièce*" ["And that mother ('she is said to be a bit crazy'), a perfect Jocasta-like creature, of whom 'the proud' Coriolanus is but an entrail. Both lofty and sordid. Swept away at a nod of his mother's—the *pièce*'s only true criminal"]. Quoted in Viola Papetti, *Manganelli legge Shakespeare* (Roma: Edizioni di Storia e Letteratura, 2018), p. 30 (my transl.).

5 "Caesar's Wing"

Negotiating the Myth of Rome in *Cymbeline*

"Caesar's Wing"

At the temporal distance that Shakespeare chooses for the writing of *Cymbeline*, his late questionable historical play (the last in the first Folio), his main and parenthetically heightened thought still goes to Rome and its spectral ineludible embodiment, Caius Julius Caesar: Caesar "(whose remembrance yet / Lives in men's eyes, and will to ears and tongues / Be theme and hearing ever)", claims the Roman ambassador Lucius in demanding tribute and tributes with recognizable, self-quoting Shakespearean lexicon (*Cym.*, 3.1.3–4);[1] and Cymbeline, the Britons' king, on the rebound: he whose "ambition, / . . . . swelled so much that it did almost stretch / The sides o' th' world" 3.1.49–51), thus partaking of the same ongoing mythologizing process as he proudly rejects that claim. Heminges and Condell may have taken as a simple matter of fact the centrality of such a theme and such an agon in Shakespeare's canon when they decided to give *Cymbeline* the importance of a closure in their Folio: the place and role, that is, of a conclusive act in Shakespeare's lifelong engagement with the model of authority represented by Rome, the last battle. They may have been led by the same motivation in listing it as a tragedy (*The Tragedie of Cymbeline*), and among "Tragedies", the haughty genre of history, which Shakespeare in his last ironic close-up shot on Rome's tragic matter releases, as I would like to show, in its aspect of a modern and untragic struggle for meaning between two nations. In this Caesar remains a model.

Caesar is not so much a myth in Shakespeare's plays as rather the object of mythmaking, the object of a historically grounded signifying practice, by which I mean the production of symbolic meaning in a contending space: a practice through which opposing agencies, factions, and cultures negotiate their own idea of Rome and its values. This is best exemplified in *Julius Caesar*, where we are called upon to see Caesar's power—advisedly rendered metonymically as "Caesar's wing" (1.1.73)—as either "swelling" or deflating, depending on whether we decide to follow the crowd's acclaiming shouts rising from the market place or Cassius's deconstructive

DOI: 10.4324/9781003259671-7

anatomy of Caesar's body within the aristocratic circle of his senatorial friends (Act 1, scenes 2–3.). *Cymbeline* is teeming with wings and birds, and we will ask why.

Shakespeare overtly showed his concern with the dynamics of the Caesarean imperial myth when, by forcing his sources, he chose to temporally conflate Caesar's triumph with the festival of the Lupercal in the same period,[2] thus heightening the ceremonial climate he needed as the proper context for his play. For indeed, mythmaking seemed to be the theme and argument he wished to propose to his audience's reflection as the counterpart of Caesar's pitiful tragedy.

"Disrobe the images. / If you do find them decked with ceremonies", orders the tribune Flavius:

> Let no images
> Be hung with Caesar's trophies. I'll about,
> And drive away the vulgar from the streets.
> So do you, where you perceive them thick.
> These growing feathers plucked from Caesar's wing,
> Will make him and ordinary pitch,
> Who else would soar above the view of men,
> And keep us all in servile fearfulness.
>
> (1.1.64–70)

This is the republican precautionary intention from the very outset of the play. But rituality, and the empowering paraphernalia of ceremonies, signs, and symbols—as kings (and Elizabeth) well knew[3]—is precisely what Caesar needs. "Set on, and leave no ceremony out" (1.2.11), he commands, well aware that his imperial project is one with mythmaking, or else with "the growing feathers" of his wing. In addressing the ways in which festive time and rituality relate to tragedy as a genre, Naomi Conn Liebler has written, "*Julius Caesar* is grounded in this context of ceremonies and rituals . . . .: some observed, some ignored, some twisted to suit particular interests. The social rituals traced within the play occur within the larger context of the Lupercalia as a perennially observed religious ritual".[4] Indeed, religious rituality is coextensive with his image as a *triumphator* and the construction of a personal divine aura.

My concern in this chapter on *Cymbeline* is to bring to the fore Shakespeare's concern with the wider formative agency of symbolic production and the way theatre itself contributes to the way early modern England negotiates its relationship with the authority of Rome, and through it, with the national past. In this sense the assassination of a father figure at the core of *Julius Caesar*, and the way it is manufactured into a piece of controversial if viable collective memory, may well be perceived as a metaphor of revered and opposed fatherhood, a paradigm of how the memory of Rome itself is hosted by a peripheral and belated Renaissance

England. But it is in *Cymbeline*'s Augustan time and in its hybrid spatial and generic context—half ancient Rome, half Renaissance Italy, half history, half fable: a historical fantasia, a romance as it will be later defined—that such an issue, soon introduced in his first Roman play (*Titus*) to be latently present in the rest of his Roman plays, was overtly addressed and accomplished by Shakespeare. In fact (as it was already clear to Wilson Knight), it is in this play—the play where Shakespeare's two long-standing historical interests for Rome and Britain finally "meet for the first time"—that the haunting ancestry of Rome is safely appropriated by Britain in a logic of over-exhibited *translatio imperii*.[5] But this is an attempt (action, move) which is worked out, I argue, at the level of a political antagonism as well as that of an agonistic empowering production of mythical imagery: the very substance of this chapter.

Giambattista Vico would say that myth (e.g. a sensory imaginative apprehension of the world) comes before intellect (e.g. philosophy), and that philosophers "inherited from the poets" the wisdom on which they developed their "lofty philosophical topics". He would say, "all the histories of the pagan nations had mythical origins", and "the first wise men were theological poets".[6] For all his being a very secular poet, Shakespeare would arguably agree with this, aware as he was (see his *Coriolanus*) that the power of nations (and of those that are in power) is constitutively ingrained in the capacity to produce legitimizing symbolic meaning. As for his early modern audience, in an epoch in which history had not yet acquired a status which could be perceived as distinct from that of poetical genres, such an intermingling of history and myth was a mix that they would have taken as a natural way of understanding and appropriating the past.[7]

In developing my argument, I will show how the warlike confrontation which takes place anachronistically in the Augustan time stands for almost five centuries of Roman rule and rebellions, and mostly if obliquely for Claudius's "real" conquest (43 CE), when Britain was transformed into a province of Rome. But it is only in the strategic, pacificatory context of Augustan time that the antagonism towards a conquering if mythical powerful ancestry can be staged as a contrast to be healed and translated into a plausible brotherly and loyal agonism between sovereigns of equal standing: "Set we forward. Let / a Roman and a British ensign wave / Friendly together. So through Lud's town march, / And in the temple of great Jupiter / Our peace we'll ratify" (5.5.478–82).

"In Shakespeare's hands", Anderson observes, referring to issues raised by *Titus Andronicus*, "Roman inheritance is not a *thing* already passed on to England and possessed by its citizens. Instead, inheritance resemble a promise still to be completed, a transaction that can, therefore go violently and unpredictably awry".[8] *Cymbeline* aims at that completion, at that pact, which in fact Cymbeline will "ratify", without getting it go awry.

In this it met, as abundantly shown by topical readings of the play, at least since Emrys Jones, James's conciliatory policy in redefining enlarged borders at home as well as England's place in Europe and an early modern expanding world.[9] But it also brought to the fore the actuality of Rome's history as such, I argue, in the way it encapsulated the urge to come to terms with the question of the nation's origins, or better, as pervasively remarked in this book, the nation's anxiety about an origin grounded in ruin, more than in fables, and increasingly discovered as a field of unsettling encounters with "barbarism" and ethnic intermingling.[10] As I have shown earlier in "The Ruins of England" (Intro. Part 2), Camden was among those historians (or antiquarians) who most cogently drew attention to these issues. He also invited, however, a pacifying negotiation with one's past in his (1607) last version of *Britannia* dedicated to James I, "*perptuae paci fundatori*", as he calls him (the previous editions being dedicated to Elizabeth). In fact—in a period in which his current dedicatee was composing into a unified nation what ages had shaped by way of violent fractures and "engrafting" of different cultures and identities— Camden advocated a reflection on "what *they* [their ancestors] were", in order to understand what "*we* ought to be":

> When we shall read these reports let us not be offended and displeased with good Gildas, for his bitter invectives against either the vices of his owne countreymen the Britans, or the inhumane outrages of the barbarous enemies, or the insatiable cruelties of our Fore-fathers the Saxons. But since that for so many ages successively ensuing, we are all now by a certain *engraffing or commixtion* become one nation, *mollified and civilized* with Religion, and good Arts, let us meditate and consider, *both what they were, and also what we ought to be*: lest that for our sinnes likewise, the supreme Ruler of the world, either translate other nations hither, when wee are first rooted out, or incorporate them into us, after we are by them subdued.
>
> (*Brit* 1, 110; my emphasis)

Without Freud, Camden was aware that confronting the ghosts of one's past could be healing for the present and future life of a nation by now "mollified and civilized with Religion, and good Arts"; verbs—"mollified and civilized"—which deserve to be picked up and remembered when we come to *Cymbeline* and the soothsayer's pseudo-etymological Latin disquisition on "*mollis aer*" (5.5.446–49), for the way such an exercise in etymology at the court of Cymbeline puts (or re-puts) reconciliation under the aegis of the sweetening (e.g. civilizing) cultural authority of Rome.[11] But Camden's pacifying exhortation also makes us understand that Britain's past was a field of still open wounds and contentious ancestry. In fact, once excluded, the Galfridean Brutus legend, the written Roman path towards Britain's "antiquity" put forward by the new historiography, led no further than to the Druids, Cassivellaun or Cassibelin (in Caesar's first mention), and then later Cunobellin, Caractacus, Prasitagus, and Boudicea (or Bonduica). It was no small thing. But the implication was that before that there was darkness, and legend. After there was "the insatiable cruelties of our Fore-fathers the Saxons". This made the matter of Rome and origins, "civility" and "barbarism", an issue of no little import in post-Reformation construction or reconstruction of national identity.

Meaningfully, such a historical and cultural crux takes on ironic overtones in *Cymbeline* in the way it is dynamically staged by means of a plurality of voices. It is first the unrooted but Romanized and well-travelled Posthumus, whom Imogen (or Innogen hereafter) meaningfully associates to an "eagle" (1.1.140), who voices Britain's competing anxiety (an anxiety of overdoing *Romanitas*) when, after the blazon-making context which ends with the wager on the princess's body (1.4.28–72), he hears, as an exile in Rome, rumours of an impending war with his country due to tributes claimed and denied: "Our countrymen / Are men more ordered than when Julius Caesar / Smiled at their lack of skill, but found their courage / worthy his frowning at. Their discipline, / Now wing-led with their courages, will make known / To their approvers they are people such / That mend upon the world" (2.4.20–26). Then, tainted with increased antagonism, the patriotic motif is handed over to the very insular nameless Queen and her son Cloten—the rough (or barbarian) side of Cymbeline's court—who, however, seem to be assigned the role of truthful chroniclers, as heralds of a revanchist nation-proud historiography capable of excavating at the roots of a local genealogy, the names of those kings who contrasted the myth of an invincible imperial Rome: "A kind of conquest / Caesar made here, but made not here his brag / Of 'Came, and saw, and overcame' . . . The famed Cassibelan, who was once at the point— / O giglot Fortune!—To master Caesar's sword, / Made Lud's town with rejoicing fires bright, / And Britons strut with courage" (3.1.22–24 and 30–33).

Cymbeline, so far such a negligent king in so many respects, will be astute enough to take advantage of this for his no less patriotic performance: "We do say then to Caesar, / Our ancestor was that Malmutius which / Ordained our laws, whose use the sword of Caesar / Hath too much mangled, whose repair, and franchise / Shall, by the power we hold, be our good deed, / Though Rome be therefore angry" (3.1.53–58). But he will be just as shrewd in dropping the authors of such a narrative when after a won war he feels it expedient to renegotiate his country's ties to the Roman empire:

CYMBELINE   Well,
My peace we will begin. And Caius Lucius,
Although the victor, we submit to Caesar,
And to the Roman empire, promising

To pay our wonted tribute, from the which
We were dissuaded by our wicked queen,
Whom heavens in justice both on her, and hers
Have laid most heavy hand.

(5.5.458–64)

It is plausible to feel that such a wobbling statement of the nation's relation to Rome could only be understood or shared by Shakespeare's audience, in the light of the rather heated coeval debate on England's origins which, as mentioned earlier (Introduction, Part 2), had been ignited precisely by the antiquarian studies in the previous few decades, a debate which starting from the dismantlement, but not quite, of Geoffrey of Monmouth's fabulous Trojan beginnings, had made origins and identity, whether that be Trojan, Roman, or Saxon, into a contested issue. Holinshed's compilative *Chronicles of England, Scotland, and Ireland* (1577/1587), for instance, didn't refrain from extensively reporting the Galfridian Brutan beginning of Britain, while also referring to Polydore Vergil, the author of its first refutation in Henry VII's time.[12] Holinshed was not alone in ensuring continuance to Monmouth's legend. In early modern England the group included (among the others) people like Caxton, Bale, Drayton, Stow, but it had gradually taken on ideological meaning with the Reform. "We are not Brittons, we are Brutans". As in Richard Harvey 's *Philadelphus, or A Defence of Brutes, and the Brutans History* (1593), where this statement comes from, the defence of the Trojan ancestry served to assert a cultural antagonism between Brutus and Caesar, Troy and Rome's inheritance, no matter whether there was no mention of a British Brutan origin in the writings prior to Monmouth. For,

> It is not *number*, nor *money* that make a Conquerour, it is good successe, which commeth of a good forecast, that is in a *Grecian* more than in a *Roman*, and why not in Brute more than *Caesar*? If *Brutes* Chronicles had been preserved as well as *Caesars*, I doubt not of this matter and of *Brutes* immortalitie in all writings, then *Caesar* had beene halfe a *Brute*.[13]

Harvey's *Defence* was a response that aimed at going beyond documentation and Camden's distinction between legend and history. As Heather James has observed, "Increased sophistication in historical methods both weakened the legend and made its continued viability an article of faith".[14]

In *Cymbeline*, the confrontation with Rome's heritage in relation to the issue of national identity conjures all this up in the form of a pervasive tension and investigating anxiety, a tension and an anxiety which, as I argue in the ensuing sections, are perceivable in the way the rediscovered Latin sources (Caesar, Plutarch, and Svetonius among them, but mostly Tacitus) and the domestic ones (mostly represented by Holinshed's compilation) compete with each other in the characters' performance of identity and the production of symbolic meaning.

Simon Forman's 1611 famous synopsis and only memory of *Cymbeline*'s performance doesn't tell where and when he saw it. First published in the 1623 Folio edition, the dating of *Cymbeline*'s writing is traditionally placed on the broad span of 1606–11. Stanley Wells and Gary Taylor suggest the first half of 1610. In a more recent reconstruction, considering the centrality of the Welsh scenes and other topical evidences, Ros King has suggested late 1609, when festivities for the imminent investiture of Henry as Prince of Wales (1610) were being prepared.[15] Be that as it may, the equally topical cluster of issues regarding the nation's past and present relation to Rome—the subject of my following section—may have made Shakespeare's international and intercultural Roman play relevant to a Globe as well as a Court or Blackfriar audience. Certainly those issues had been rekindled by Camden's Latin-written *Britannia* (1586–1607), just translated into English in 1610. Theatres had been closed repeatedly between 1603 and 1609 because of the plague, the last time for more than one year from July 1608 to December 1609. Shakespeare may have had time to browse, perhaps not for the first time, Camden's Latin version of *Britannia* (if not Holland's 1610 translation), and felt elicited to provide his own meditation on ancestry: namely on "both what they were, and also what we ought to be", as Camden put it (*Brit* 1, 110).

Defaced History and the Play of Identity: "Here Comes the Briton" (1.4.28)

Cymbeline's often noted palimpsestic temporalities of Augustan Rome and Renaissance Italy, Roman Britain and early modern culture, historical setting and pastoral *non-lieu*, contribute to make it the proper, if confusing platform for the deployment of the congeries of issues involved in the Rome-Britain intercultural topic in its relation with that of national identity.[16] Such a mixture of times, genres, history, myths, and sources, or conflated fragments of them, seems to share with the work of the antiquarians, Camden among them, the archaeological condition of the already quoted hybrid table of contents of his 1605 *Remains Concerning Britain* (Languages, Names, Surnames, Allusions, Anagrams, Armories, Moneys, Impresses, Apparel, Artilleries, Wise Speeches, Proverbs, Poesies, Epitaphs). Bacon would say that this was the condition of the inventoried materials of history, caught at the stage which is prior to completeness, and whose perfect understanding is still a wish:

> 1. For civil history. . . . So of histories we may find three kinds, memorials, perfect histories, and antiquities; for memorials are history unfinished, or the first draft of history; and antiquities are history defaced, or some remnants of history which have casually escaped the

shipwreck of time. 2. Memorials, or preparatory history, are of two sorts; whereof the one may be termed commentaries, and the other registers. Commentaries are they which set down a continuance of the naked events and actions, without the motives or designs, the counsels, the speeches, the pretexts, the occasions and other passages of action. . . . History, which may be called just and perfect history, is of three kinds, according to the object which it propoundeth, or pretendeth to represent: for either representeth a time, or a person, or an action.[17]

The philosopher's own anxious grappling with the notion of history, and a conceptualization which is able to satisfy inclusion (of the all "book of nature") as well as motivation and design, is an instance of the effort which is being enacted in Shakespeare's time to cope with a "discovered" richness of old and modern history, and the attendant epistemological uncertainty. Bacon's history gets lost in histories, in categories and under-categories. Holinshed's compilative *Chronicles* of England's past didn't escape the unsettling condition of the Baconian "memorials" or "antiquities", or else "history unfinished". Crumley is absolutely right, when in underpinning the epistemological issues raised by *Cymbeline* and in focal-izing Holinshed's import as its main inspiring source, he draws attention to his frequent opposed versions of the same event, or else his "multiple perspectives on history".[18] But the critic overlooks the distinction between legend and history forcefully introduced by Camden's new historiography and the way it consciously redefines the space of origins and identity as a space deficient, aporetic, and fragmentary, but not fabulous. Holinshed's history of England on the contrary is strikingly aimed at sounding histori-cally plausible precisely where it is at the most fabulous, namely in its initial narrative of Britain's Trojan descent.[19]

Imbued with the playful if disruptive agency of "sedimentary strata", "dispersed" or "survived" and fragmented events and bodies (Foucault/ Bacon), *Cymbeline*'s performance of identity seems to thrive on the anxi-ety engendered by the fortuitous, damaged, heterogeneous, and untimely condition of its materials: an epistemological instability which character-izes the whole play—or else its sources and "models of authority" (H. James)—and which, as I want to show, is ironically sanctioned by the hired and final divinatory scenario which ought to dispel it.

Meaningfully, the play's incipit belongs to a disquisition on origins, the prompt for a deployment of identity definitions oscillating between forget-ful geology and unrecoverable genealogy. The problematic embodiment of this is Posthumus: a Briton worthy of all praise when we first meet him, but of uncertain loyalty, a sort of geological "stratified" artefact (we might say with Foucault), curiously forgetful of "Britain"/"And himself" (1.6.112). He will remain such: "to himself unknown" (5.4.108–109), an alien to himself and to his own birth/place, until the final *anagnorisis* ("from me was Posthumus ripped", 5.4.38),[20] seemingly invested with the task of reconstituting the surgically chopped off or dispersed (-wandering) bodies of the play (Posthumus, Guiderius, Arviragus) according to an economy regulated by the organic metaphor of trees, branches, and roots. William Camden comes to mind, when in presenting his *Britannia* to the reader he highlighted the goal of his commitment as that of disclosing the country (a motherland) to persons who were in the paradoxical condition of being "strangers in their own soile, and forrainers in their owne City" ("To the Reader", n.p.). Posthumus has a long way to go before he can boast a land and a citizenship. He has to gradually descale himself of his Roman "bark" before he is pacified with his roots. But roots in the play, apart from the king's two lost sons, symbolically confined in an uncontaminated, atemporal, and precultural state of nature, are to be intended according to Camden's acceptation: they are rhizomatic, mingled and interwoven at the origins. Indeed, as coeval new historiography argued, "the originalls of nations are obscure by reason of their profound antiquitie, as things are seen very deepe and farre remote". And, like "the courses, the reaches, the confluents, and the out-lets of great rivers are well knowne, yet their first fountains and heads lie commonly unknown" (Camden *Brit* 1, 4; see also this volume's Introduction, Part 2).

Cymbeline has attracted considerable attention in the last decade or so by criticism concerned with the plurality of the English identity and the writing or construction of early modern Great Britain. This has led to investigate materials which go beyond Holinshed, or Monmouth via Holinshed, for long assumed as the play's primary source (at least as regards the pseudo-historical plot), to gradually highlight the way the play is imbricated with the coeval revisionist historiography, typically marked by Camden's *Britannia*.[21] I refer to its alternative document-grounded methodology as my main guide in exploring *Cymbeline*'s sceptical way of dealing or playing with myths and history. As I argue, one can feel Camden's *Britannia* and *Remains Concerning Britain* resonate in Shakespeare's play with the freshness of a recent reading or rereading: one propelled by a shared, problematized concern with "digging" (see Camden, "To the Reader", *Brit* 1, 4) or "delv[ing]" origins "to the root" (*Cym.*, 1.1.27), and rewarded with a wealth of first-hand condensed Latin documentation (preferably by Caesar, Tacitus, or Seneca, but also Strabo or Dio Cassius) on ancient Roman Britain, together with Camden's records of its non-linear and hybridized archaeological remains. But when we come to the imaginary setting of *Cymbeline*, the question is not that of checking the extent to which these rediscovered original sources can intervene as a correction of the fairly inventive knowledge provided by the acknowledged traditional sources (Holinshed's *Chronicles*, *The Mirror for Magistrates*). The point is to ask how they contributed to enlarge the range of materials through which Shakespeare as well as his audience could filter, or forge, their respective way of addressing or re-envisaging their past, and to speculate on how this may have influenced the audience's experience of the play: a "puzzling" play, in Marcus's definition. The point is also that of observing the extent to which Shakespeare playfully makes traditional and new sources interact in his play, thus heightening to its very limit the degree of undecidability of its main difficult topic: national identity and its related over-determining process of mythmaking.

As in *Titus*, Shakespeare uses sources as *ruinae* or "remains". Sources seem to enjoy the material and visible condition of archaeological and desituated *objects trouvés*, a condition which in *Cymbeline* invests, with the same alienating effect, "Shakespeare" itself, namely the entirety of his textuality which the playwright seems to use as an archive for apt self-quotations, infratextual resonances or remakes, as for instance with the comic version of the classical tragic stuff of women's rape he deals with in *Titus* and *The Rape*. *Cymbeline*'s infratextuality, at least since Skura and Miola, has often been noted by critics.[22]

What I would like to bring to the fore, however, is the distancing effect that is thus achieved, for sources are sometimes part of a dynamics in which, like ruins, they can be fitting as well as defective, proper as well as aporetic and displacing. This comes out most strikingly, I argue, in the scene of the Milford Haven battle, a battle won thanks to the courage of Cymbeline's two lost sons and the old Belarius, but which is told with fragments taken from another story: that famously provided by Holinshed's chronicle of a victorious battle of the Scots against the Danish invaders, and which is won thanks to a husbandman and his two sons' valiantness. Here *Cymbeline*'s archaeological play of identity shows how freely it can touch for the atemporal "sedimentary strata" of national memory. But the story belongs to events which occurred in 976 CE, a millennium after the play's historical setting.[23] Did the play's decisive battle against Rome really deserve to be narrated with an exhibited incongruous borrowing or forgery? This is a question which has rarely been addressed in terms of willed textual inconsistency. For Leah Marcus who, following Emrys Jones,[24] reads the play as a Stuart political allegory, Posthumus is "the analogue of the exiled Scots", and the borrowing from the Scots history is viewed as part of his identification with their valiantness and claims in the nascent Great Britain.[25] It is plausible. In recording the anachronism, Mary Floyd-Wilson has observed, "the allusion frames Arviragus and Guiderius as anachronistic figures in Roman Britain. With one swift reference, the play shifts its history forward to the period of Anglo-Saxon rule".[26] Right. In fact, direct and undirect source hybridism in the play (spanning from Latin authors to Holinshed, Boccaccio, Frederyke of Jennen, Machiavelli, and others) seems to be endowed with the task of pushing the play both backwards, towards its antiquity, and forward, towards a medieval or Renaissance contemporaneity. But what is brought to light by this borrowing is also the extent to which a traditional, domestic historiography playfully interacts with the scepticism stemming from the coeval new historiography and its rediscovered Latin sources, activating, as I suggest in the course of this chapter, a pervasive economy of allusions, deflections, counterfeiting, erasures, and reversal, in the way one's roots are reimagined, or remythologized.

But before that, it may be useful to premise the special place held by Tacitus in this context and in relation to issues of national identity. The Latin author has long since been indicated as one of *Cymbeline*'s classical sources, at least in so far as the meddling of Roman and Britain's ancient history is involved. In claiming *Cymbeline*'s status as a Roman play a few decades ago, David M. Bergeron remarked that Shakespeare might have used "*The Annales of Cornelius Tacitus*, translated by Richard Greenway (1598), Suetonius's *Historie of Twelve Caesars, Emperours of Rome*, translated by Philémon Holland (1606), and Plutarch's *Lives of the Noble Grecians and Romanes*, translated by Thomas North (the 1603 edition of a book originally published in 1579)". He also argued, "of course he need not have used all three, since there is duplication of material".[27] In sharing his emphasis on Tacitus, I would add that Tacitus had a special interest in dealing with Britain. He was Agricola's son-in-law, a governor in Britain in the years that followed Claudius's invasion (43 CE), and he could rely on first-hand knowledge when, consistently in *Agricola* (the eponymous biography he devoted to him) as well as the *Annales* (covering the larger span of time going from August to Nero), he describes Britain's nation as inhabited by indomitable tribes and valiant commanders who, with no distinction of sex, shared the prerogative of war and government. Tacitus was returned with the same interest in Shakespeare's time when the discovery of Rome was one with the excavation of one's origins. As already mentioned in this volume, practically all of Tacitus's extant works were translated in 1590s.[28] Pervaded by a nostalgia of republican values and a critique of the post-Augustan tyrannical imperial Rome, they were proving indispensable in early modern England for those concerned with the issue of republicanism *versus* empire, as well as Rome's declining virtues (eventually in a logic of *translatio imperii*). Tacitus was also proving to be useful to those interested in the nation's origins and the engaging debate on notions of "civility" and "barbarism". Meaningfully, Camden made Tacitus into one of his *Britannia*'s favourite sources. And Shakespeare may have found him inspiring while writing *Titus* as well as (for different reasons) *Cymbeline*.

Cymbeline owes partly to Holinshed and partly to Tacitus the Latin name of Posthumus ("Born after his fathers death", Camden elucidates in his philological section on "Names"; *Remains*, 108). In Holinshed's fabulous Trojan lineage of Britain's origins, Posthumus is Brutus's grandfather, Silvius Posthumus, one of Aeneas's direct scions (as reminded by most);[29] in Tacitus (as pointed out by few), this is also, historically, the name of Augustus's son in law: Agrippa Posthumus.[30] The name's etymology with the two opposite sources is an issue in itself. In *Cymbeline*, for a start, it literally hints at his posthumous birth (her mother "deceased / As he was born", 1.1.39–40): the birth of a survivor, a leftover, in Patricia Parker's words, a person who like Aeneas has escaped destruction[31] and the ruin of an ancestry he carries on his shoulders. But Posthumus—perhaps obliquely paying homage to Camden's anti-Brutus new historiography— is also a character that in profile and name stands alone as a figure of a Camden-like belated and layered identity. In this case, he has no Aeneas on his shoulders. As Curran observes, "Posthumus's family tree extends not beyond his father, Sicilius who fought under Cassibelan. . . . With the Brute myth exploded, British history was now understood to begin with Julius Caesar's invasion".[32] But this didn't make the question of roots any easier, complicated as it was by the attendant issue of civility and barbarity, an issue that Shakespeare tackles by means of the Guiderius and Arviragus parallel plot.

But let us return to Posthumus: "delv[ing] him to the root" (1.1.27), his name leads to a double fatherhood, each equally bifurcated in terms of belonging and loyalty: on one hand we find a biological father (Sicilius Leonatus, a Briton with a Latin name who valiantly fought against the Romans); on the other a putative father (Cymbeline, a king who while claiming freedom and autonomy boasts Roman titles and upbringing as a charisma of cultural authority, 3.1.70–72). No doubt Posthumus's genealogy enables him to stand for more than one character in the play. Forcing the argument, one might even view Posthumus as an ironic embodiment of Camden's very project. Which was famously that to "restore antiquity to Britaine, and Britain to his antiquity", and whose method he defined as being conspicuously "etymological" in character, aiming as it did at recollecting some of the nation's antiquity by tracking (in ancient Welsh, Saxon, Latin) the impervious and deviating vicissitudes of names. And this, he said, in compliance with the commandment of the ancients "that the name be consonant to the nature of the thing, and the nature thereof to the name" (see "To the Reader"). As for more intriguing details, which would warrant Posthumus's somewhat faltering loyalty in his double "commixtion" with Rome and Britain, Tacitus's *Annals* may have proved again worth browsing. For apart from Agrippa Postumus, Augustus's grandson by him exiled, with obscure motivations, to the island of Planasia in front of Tuscany, we find another Postumus. This is Poenius Postumus, a much less prominent figure, but one which Shakespeare could have easily come across, mentioned as it was in a point of the *Annales* that could not be missed by a playwright engaged in the writing of a play on British ancestry: this is soon after Boodicia (whom hereafter I mention with Camden's spelling), Queen of the Iceni tribe (now East Anglia)—no less courageously than a Roman—is said to have committed suicide for having suffered defeat in her valorous battle against the Romans. Poenius Postumus, Tacitus explains, was the camp-prefect of the Roman second legion who after the same battle he himself commits suicide, but for the different reason that he feels guilty for having disobeyed his commander's orders, thus depriving his legion of the glory enjoyed by the rest of the Roman army (*Annals*, Book XIV.35–37).[33] Theatregoers will meet him in Fletcher's *Bonduca* (ca. 1613), a play set in the years of uninterrupted rebellions that followed Claudius's conquest and revolving around the two characters of Boudica and Caratach.

But Tacitus's bearing is also intriguingly discernible in the way (so far unnoticed) he inspires the aforementioned *Cymbeline*'s decisive battle of Milford Haven: one contrived by exploiting, I suggest (problematizing the exclusivity and strangeness of its traditionally acknowledged Holinshed source), all the suggestions that could be derived from the Latin author's narration of Claudius's invasion (43 CE). For this was the "real" conquest, the piece of truth that underpins the Queen's loudly contested "a kind of conquest / Caesar made here, but made not here his brag / Of 'Came, and saw, and overcame'" (3.1.22–24). Arguably, the queen's statement had been given new authority in Shakespeare's time. In Seneca's words, which Camden's readers could find quoted at *Britannia*'s page 45: "Claudius might make his boast that he first vanquished the Britans: for Julius Caesar did but shew them only to the Romans". Lucan and Tacitus (equally quoted by Camden) had been even more to the point. Lucan in *Pharsalia* had ascribed Caesar's incomplete conquest to cowardice ("He fought the Britans, and for feare to them his Backe he show'd"). Tacitus in *Agricola* invited a distinction between discovery and conquest: "he [Caesar] discovered onely, but delivered not unto the Romanes, Britaine" (*Brit* 1, 38).

In addition to this, Camden provided ample passages of Tacitus's description of Claudius's invasion in *Britannia* (see 43–44), making it perhaps tempting for Shakespeare to take a look at, especially because that was the very memory he had to cancel or compensate in constructing a battle that, in being favourable to the Britons, could be an honourable prelude to pacification. But to do this he had to temporally anticipate the warlike hostilities between Rome and Britain to the time of Augustus when Rome—as Camden's readers could read on pages 39–40—although imposing tributes to Britain by menacing war, still considered the tributes' negotiated alternative more convenient than a warlike conquest and a consequentially costly garrisoned province. That there was no significant military action in Augustus's times is also recorded by Holinshed, who locates the war with Rome on the issue of tributes not in Cymbeline's but in Guiderius's succeeding reign.[34]

Now, if Shakespeare strategically has Augustan diplomacy overlap with Claudius's warlike rule of Britain, it is because, I surmise, it was mainly during Britain's long-lasting resistance to Rome's accomplished conquest— a resistance guided by such legendary commanders as Caractacus, Commander (or King) of the Silures; Cartimandua, Queen of the Brigants; and then (in Nero's times) Boodicia, or Bunduica Queen of the Iceni—that its inhabitants, even though defeated, confirmed their fame of courageous and indomitable warriors in Rome's eyes: first of all in Tacitus's *Annals* (Book XII), and certainly more unconditionally than in Caesar's *Gallic Wars*. That there is a relationship (via Tacitus) with Claudius's conquest is also witnessed by the Welsh location of Shakespeare's battle and its topography. In fact, the symbolism of the Welsh Milford Haven derived its force not simply, as customarily maintained at least since Emrys Jones, by events regarding the origin of the Tudor dynasty and James I's unionist politics, but also by events regarding the Roman Britain. In fact, Wales provided the topography where the most valorous battle of the ancient Britons against Claudius's army was fought and lost. In Tacitus (as reported by Camden) the battlefield occurs twice, accurately described first (in the land Iceni) as "a place to fight in, compassed about with a rude and rusticall rampire having a narrow entrance of purpose to hinder the coming in of horsemen" (*Brit* 1, 43); and then again, as the war moves from the Iceni (East Anglia) to the Silures and the Ordovices (Wales), as a field with purposely obstructed passages. This merits extensive quotation both for its valiant if defeated commander Caractacus and for the topographical centrality of "narrow" passages—a feature that Shakespeare (maybe concomitantly inspired by Holinshed's "fensed lane")—amplifies into a highly symbolic figure of impenetrability (5.3.1–52).[35]

> Then went the Romanes from thence against the Silures, who besides their owne stoutness trusted much in the strength of Caractacus. . . . But hee in subtill craft, and knowledge of the *deceitfull waies, having the advantage of us, though otherwise weaker in strength of soldiers,* translate the warre into the country of the Ordovices: and there, joyning to him as many as feared our peace, resolveth to hazard the last chance, *having chosen a place for the battell, where the coming in, and going forth, with all things else might be incommodious to us, but for his very Advantageous. Then against the highhills, and wheresoever there was any easy passage, and gentle access, he stopped up the way with heaps of stones raised in maner of a rampier:* withal there ranne hard by a river, having a doubtfull soord, and the severall companies of his best souldiers had taken their standing before the fortifications. Besides all this, the leaders of every nation went about, exhorted and encouraged their men, by making less all causes of feare: and kindling in them good conceits of hope, with all other motives and inducements to warre. *And verily Caractacus bestirring himself, and coursing from place to place, protested, That this was the day, this the battell, which should begin either the recovery of their libertie for ever, or else perpetuall bondage. And here, he called upon his ancestors by name, who had chased Caesar the Dictator from hence, through whose valour were freed from the Roman axes, and tributes, and enjoyed still the bodies of their wives, and children undefiled.*
>
> (Tacitus, qtd *Brit* 1, 43–44; my emphasis)[36]

Caractacus was "the ancient Prince called by the Romans Caracatus (happily in his own tongue Caradoc) who flourished in the parts now called Wales", Camden writes in *Remains* (1605) in reporting the famous, skilful speech—the first in the section "Wise Speeches"—he pronounced before Claudius once he was brought in Rome as a prisoner (*Re*, 300). Wales, as Camden explains in *Britannia*, was that part of England "called in Latin Cambria, or Wallia, where the ancient Britans have yet their seat and abode". But it has "long since beene engraffed and incorporate with us into our Comon-wealth". Their ancient inhabitants, the Silures, he continues quoting Tacitus, "were a nation very great . . . fierce, valiant, given to war, impatient of servitude, forward to adventure with a resolution (the Romanes call it *Pervicacia*)", which, guided by Caractacus, was best proved during their memorable long-lasting resistance to Claudius' conquest (*Brit* 1, 615–16).

Hence, we speculate: this is the scene, the mythical anteriority to which Shakespeare's Milford Haven brings us to. Here is the hero, *The Valiant Welshman*,[37] who inspires Shakespeare's "valour / That wildly grows . . ., but yields a crop / As if it had been sowed" (*Cym.*, 4.2.178–80). And here is the battle, I argue, which still waits to be completed and imaginatively won. In this, the land of the Silures (Wales in Shakespeare's times) seems to have functioned as the inner catalyst in the over-determined conflation of times which characterizes *Cymbeline*, and the layered mnemonic dimension of places, facts, and characters. In addition to this memorable and identifying conjunction of land and valiantness, what is also interesting to note is that in Dio Cassius's record of those event (quoted by Camden), Cinobellinus's two sons are identified as Caractacus and Togodumnus (*Brit* 1, 41).

As Caractacus in Tacitus's battle, *Cymbeline*'s Belarius, Guiderius, and Arviragus have "th' advantage of the ground" (*Cym.*, 5.2.11), and as in *Cymbeline*, Tacitus's topography suggests a symbolic connection between narrow passages and the defence of an unpolluted integrity of nation and women. Furthermore, even though without a proper army and proper armours, Caractacus alone—not dissimilarly from Arviragus's "A rider like myself, who ne'er wore rowel, / Nor iron on his heel" (*Cym.*, 4.4.39–40)—knows how to take "advantage" (*Cym.*, 5.3.15) of the enemy and foster courage and alliance in his countrymen. Like the three of them, but also like Posthumus, Caractacus's soldiers are all the more praiseworthy for being able to face the enemy with no proper protection. In fact, compared with the Romans' "heavy corselets" and other proper lighter armours, the Britons "had neither head-peece nor coat of fence", Tacitus observes, in describing their combat techniques (*Brit* 1, 44). This is a feature, however, that Shakespeare interestingly transforms into an insisted upon nobler mark of primitive valour and recoverable "true" identity. Let us just consider Posthumus: "the poor soldier that so richly fought, / Whose rags shamed gilded arms, whose naked breast /

Stepped before targes of proof" (5.5.3–5); or also Guiderius and Arviragus, whose nature-compared "nakedness" stands for "royalty unlearned, honour untaught, / Civility not seen from other, valour / That wildly grows in them" (4.2.177–80).[38]

Thus, to return to the far-removed Holinshed's borrowing, the battle scene and the whole issue of Britain's valiantness in *Cymbeline* may well have been cast with the ready-made materials provided by an incongruous battle of the Scots against the Danes, but it would be wrong to think that Shakespeare wasn't aware of equally handy but more consonant and significant sources. On the contrary, it is legitimate to speculate that, in blatantly disseminating traces of his postiche (Holinshed) source, Shakespeare was involving his audience member in a construction which called for its deconstruction, one which played at displacing them with an impropriety which prompted a reflection on the arbitrariness of history and the interchangeability, or relative autonomy or fitness, of its dowels. He was also showing off, perhaps, how one might make a legend, a myth, out of a borrowed and unsituated fragment of history, an odd *object trouvé*. "This was strange chance: / A narrow lane, an old man, and two boys" (5.3.51–52), the Lord ironically synthesizes at Posthumus's first chronicle of the battle, provoking him into a repetition which turns what is serious and momentous into the sarcasm of a rhymed and mocking second version—a popularized refrain—a piece of comic and objectified textuality: "Will you rhyme upon't, / And vent it for mock'ry? Here is one: / 'Two boys, an old man twice a boy, a lane, / Preserv'd the Britons, was the Romans' bane'", Posthumus says on the rebound (5.3.55–57). Mythmaking comes out as the production of the myth's iterability, a theatrical prop. But this is done as if sharing with the interlocutor (and the audience) the knowledge that they are forging it with an improper and second-hand textuality. Seriousness doesn't exclude levity, and myths do not disdain their trivialization, which however makes their status both strong and fragile. This encourages more than discourages the suggestion that *Cymbeline*'s mythologized battle is deeply underwritten by other battles, and specifically, I argue, by the spectral and traumatic memory of Claudius's invasion and in the (Tacitan) dramatic relevance it had been invested with in Caractacus's previously quoted speech to his army: "*this was the day, this the battell*, which should begin either the recovery of their libertie for ever, or else perpetuall bondage" (my emphasis).

Caractacus's defeat marked Claudius's fame as the real conqueror of Britain. But Shakespeare's upturning of that final defeat into a victory, imbued as it is with ancient Britain's renown valiantness, is the compensating response which allows for pacification in his play. Significantly, the battle's narration is bestowed on the Romanized Posthumus, a figure of transit and intermediation, who seems to be assigned the pivotal task of transferring the writing of history from Rome (Tacitus, etc.) to Britain (Holinshed).[39] In this he seems to confusedly participate in the coeval tremendous work that antiquarians, chorographers, philologists, poets, and playwrights were doing in "writing the nation into existence" (Helgerson; see also this volume's Introduction, Part 2), namely in rearticulating the relation between time and space, the progress of time, and the material bemusing profundity of its ruins. But in Posthumus's case this is accomplished, I argue, by means of a narrative which stands out for being, with the same degree of seriousness and comedy, the repetition of another story, another battle; a repetition destined to remain forever deferred from the irreplaceable and irretrievable *"this was the day, this the battle"*. Like Camden's "strangers in their own soile, and forrainers in their owne City", the "forgetful" Posthumus is too posthumous to rightly remember. In fact Shakespeare makes him inhabit the realm of the ruins, the reuse, the "inappropriate". Nay, he is himself a ruin. In this he can be tragically funny, and hence powerful, Derrida would say, fascinated as the philosopher was (and as Nicholas Royle aptly highlights) "by the notion that what is most powerful is 'often the most disarming feebleness'".[40]

The theatrical enactment of the Milford Haven battle is a metatheatrical indicator of how sources in the play activate a layered textual economy which is pervasively authoring and disauthoring. Interestingly, such a peak of spectral and troubled authorship is coincident with one of the most frantic and confusing performances of identity ever seen. Freeing oneself of any "commixtion" with an Italianate Romanness means undergoing a disguising vertigo which keeps Posthumus busy throughout the battle, before the dream which finally restores him to himself and his ancestors: "the old stock", whatever this means (5.4.112). Exiled to Rome in the first act to be kept there for the ensuing three acts, we see him arriving in Britain as a soldier of the Roman army in the fifth act. But hardly have we met him that he "disrobes" himself of his classical armour (suggestively declassed to "Italian weeds") to "suit myself / As does a Briton peasant. So I'll fight / Against the part I come with" (5.1.23–25). But he then returns again to his previous clothes to play the part of a Roman in "bondage" (5.4.3), in whose apparel he awaits the last disclosure: a trial for whoever in the audience would feel inclined to keep a record of this indefatigable disguising activity and the details of its motivation. But before all that, if only symbolically and *in absentia*, his body undergoes the ordeal of (an equally tragicomic) absolute defacing. This is when, mistaken for the beheaded Cloten disguised as Posthumus, he is exposed to the condition of a "garment" with no head, a reversal from identity into anonymity, or more precisely from wholeness into body parts, which in turn activates an anatomizing and archaeologizing activity. He appears as a beheaded classical "ruin" to Lucius's Roman sight: "The ruin speaks that sometime / It was a worthy building"(4.2.353–54); an image which for the educated audience could sound allusively reminiscent of the beauty of the *Torso of Belvedere*, complete as it was with an incorporated, fleeting hint at a (sonnet-like) meditation on "devouring time" (see this volume's Introduction, pp. 28–32, and Chapter 1, p. 92). Innogen, on the other hand, is up to the task. The trunk is made the object of an eroticized and unsettling blazon under her eyes' scrutiny, one which, while zooming on and X-raying his anatomy (Martial thigh, Herculean chest, Mercurial foot, 4.2.308–10), makes the mythologized trunk unidentifiable and derisively exchangeable with that of Cloten, his opposite. "O Posthumus, alas, / Where is thy head? Where's that? Ay me, where's that?" (319–20), Innogen cries in the improbable tragic posture of Hecuba. More than being the proud eagle to which she had previously compared him (1.1.140), she unaware discovers that Posthumus's wings are but on his feet, perhaps.

"Is there a Posthumus in his clothes?", one is tempted to ask, joining in Innogen's despair. Indeed, to the eyes of the audience, Posthumus is literally and metaphorically, ambiguously and persistently, in and out of his "garments", whether those be Roman or British, as well as being in and out of the battle, and in and out of its diegetic delivery. Indeed, like a true "counterfeit", the creation of a "coiner" (2.5.5–6), he is persistently divided from himself, persistently at odds with the "part I come with", persistently haunted by the "woman's part" in him (2.5.20), as well as being persistently afar and displaced from the sources or textuality conjured up for the performance of identity (whether those be the native Holinshed's *Chronicles* or the Latin grounded new historiography). In this he seems to epitomize the condition of most of the play's characters. Posthumus is to all appearances a (quintessential) Mercurial character, a messenger among places and cultures, a figure of the play's continuous shifting place and perspective, and the difficult job the playwright is accomplishing in negotiating or renegotiating the relationship with Rome in the multitemporal and multicultural geography of the play, and in his contemporary post-Reformation passage from Elizabeth to James.

In sum, the more one projects the play's pseudo-historicity onto the coeval writing or excavation of the nation's antiquity, the more *Cymbeline* appears as a viable Jacobean response to the cultural inheritance of almost five centuries of Roman rule: a layered antiquity indeed, one in which Claudius's final conquest and bondage—"the greatest spurn" (*Titus*, 3.1.102)—is both effaced and archaeologically surfacing. Shakespeare's great art heightened its cogency by making it disappear into the antedated and compressed temporality of his Augustan pacifying play. However, he endowed his play with a porosity that makes it emerge with persistent allusiveness. This is thanks to a play where, as in *Titus Andronicus*, sources and time are handled archaeologically and suggestively more than according to historical authenticity and linearity. But differently from the completely fictional and yet profoundly Roman *Titus Andronicus*, *Cymbeline*'s mixture of romance and ostentatious Roman-Britain history elicited a form of cooperation on the part of its audience and readers that allowed for illusion and disillusion, belief and disbelief. In reading the play as a Stuart political allegory, Leah Marcus observes how its topicality, namely its "embeddedness in contemporary affairs", doesn't make it "more palatable". *Cymbeline* is a puzzle, she says, a continuous riddle, a forest of emblems whose deciphering is like entering a labyrinth.[41] Criticism and audience are met with the same challenge. "An incredible *tour de force* of theatrical skill" for its author, Ros King has observed, "This is a play, which in performance requires from the audience member a peculiarly high level of active, imaginative engagement: a conscious interplay of knowledge, fore-knowledge, second guessing, and reading between the lines, which excites the imagination in a quest for meaning and significance".[42] I couldn't agree more, while focalizing my attention on the play's excavating play of identity and its related agonistic mythmaking.

"A World by Itself": Insular Mythmaking, and Desires of a Larger World

Cymbeline excels in seducing his audience in a playful exercise of recognition and deflection. It artfully constructs the illusion of a shared historical authenticity. But dealing with memory, myths, and roots is not rewarded with the immediate and unquestioned recognition one would expect: the excavation and the excitement of discovery is more often met with varying degrees of ambiguity. In the play's meddling of history and romance, characters and the part they play in the performance of identity are defined by the same ungraspable remoteness and depth underlined by the earlier quoted Camden's notion of "antiquity". They are constantly more and less than such an abysmal profundity. And their "antiquitie" is persistently other than the sources that, like ruins of a textual layered conglomerate, we may conjure up to explain them.

Looking at its Roman plot closely, some of Shakespeare's heterogeneous audience could discover that Cymbeline's way of loudly proffering the names of one's ancestors in front of the Roman enemy (3.1.53–61) was rather similar to that of Caractacus's, who proudly and theatrically (in Tacitus's earlier quotation), "called upon his ancestors by name, who had chased Caesar the Dictator from hence". But disillusion steps in, if still guided by Tacitus mediated by Camden, one set on to unravel, for instance, the bizarre diversity of attitude of king and queen in relation to the Romans. In fact, if Cymbeline is given an attitude and a lexicon which invites comparison with Caractacus (the proud and valiant king of the Silures), it also turns out that, for his compliance with Rome, he could be likened to Prasutagus, king of the Iceni, Boodicia's weak husband, who (Tacitus writes) after yielding his reign for free to the Romans, left her alone to conduct a war against them in defence of their country and their raped daughters (Camden, *Brit* 1, 457. *Annals*, Book XIV.31–37). And so, conversely, if *Cymbeline*'s nameless Queen could stand for the virile Boodicia ("whom Gildas seemth to call the crafty Lionesse", Camden observes, *Brit* 1, 457), as well as an ancestry-wise Caractacus, it is also true that her contrivance as a fairy-tale potion-making wicked queen makes her quite an ironic candidate for those roles. Nevertheless, her self-inflicted death by venom continues to be subtly allusive of the historical and courageous self-poisoning Boodicia: the spectre, in the early modern construction of the nation, of a pre-Roman, savage past dominated by powerful women.[43] Interestingly, in Melly Still's 2016 RSC production of *Cymbeline*, such a displacing, elusive, and uncategorizable status of the Queen's identity was rendered by conflating two characters in one. There was no queen in the play's cast, her role being absorbed in that of Cymbeline for the first time played by a woman (Gillian Bevan): a cross-gendered commander-in-chief wearing combat fatigues all along the play and impersonating both king and queen.

As in *Titus*, Shakespeare's first Roman play, *Cymbeline*'s playwright is pressed by an excess of history and textuality—the mark of his own belatedness or "posthumousness". But this is all the more true in *Cymbeline*, where the Roman issue is brought home to England and where the playwright has to imaginatively multiply space, plots, and characters. The characters are many and misleading, considering also their own indefatigable self-doubling activity and, in Ruth Nevo's words, "replicative configurations".[44] And yet, with different degrees of irony, they are all doing their job in the play's complex dramaturgy of shifting perspectives and agonistic mythmaking. A case in point is the stolid Cloten, invested with the important task of wittily asserting the myth of Britain as a separate, self-sufficient world, which he performs firmly and loudly at the right moment: "There be many Caesars / Ere such another Julius. Britain's a world / By itself" (3.1.11–13); two statements in one which act as the prompt for the Queen's famous patriotic tirade on England's inviolability and the defensive role played by its natural geographical boundaries.

The image of Britain as a fortified and self-sufficient world had become a cliché in Jacobean time, Ros King has observed. She asks, "to what extent does it reflect James's aspirations?". James himself had exploited the trope of "a little World within it selfe" in "his first speech to parliament . . . as part of his argument for the union" of England and Scotland, she adds.[45] Francis Bacon partook of the same rhetoric with his authoritative "And now last, this most happy and glorious event, that this island of Brittany, divided from all the world, should be united in itself".[46] But as is well known, a decade earlier Shakespeare himself had provided an earlier version of the Queen's speech by assigning it to Gaunt in *Richard II* (2.1.31–68).

Where did this myth come from, I want to ask, a question which is worth relaunching in the context of a play deeply imbricated with the coeval revisionist approach to Rome. That at the origin of it all was Caesar's ambition of joining together what "nature had severed" (Camden, *Brit* 1, 34) is well known. Caesar's memory of a conquest hindered by

Britain's hostile geographical boundaries had made its coasts mythical (see Introduction, Part 2). Equally known is the fact that, starting from Monmouth, the memory of Caesar's "incomplete" conquest had been inventively transmitted to—and then by—such Renaissance chroniclers as Holinshed or the editors of the *Mirror for Magistrates*.[47] But the myth of an inviolable country seems invigorated with new force, and a more definite lexicon, in the way it is reworked in *Cymbeline*'s Roman context, one which seems to be indebted to the materials made available by the new historiography.

In a period in which the entire matter of Rome was being excavated and its ruins reappropriated, this was a trope of great import in its ideological implications and imaginative suggestiveness. In Shakespeare's *Cymbeline* it gestures towards an invasion, both literal and metaphorical, which is pervasively feared in the play, but which is consistently removed, as argued earlier in this chapter, as an accomplished historical fact, by the strategic antedated Augustan chronology of the play. The effacement turns up in the way it ironically bears on the construction of the Cloten-Queen speech in Act 3. Cloten's first part of his assertion ("There be many Caesars ere such another Julius.") may have sound dramatically right in the way it alludes to its historical contrary. Shakespeare's educated audience knew that it wasn't all that long ere another Caesar attempted what "none assaied to doe since the time of Julius Caesar", and this was Claudius, Camden reminded with Dio Cassius's words (*Brit* 1, 40). In the porous and allusive temporality of the play, Cloten's second part of his assertion ("Britain's a world / By itself") is equally constructed as if remindful of its historical future reversal: when as a consequence of Claudius's conquest, the privilege of that natural condition was infringed upon and symbolically swept away.

Now, what is worth being considered in this respect is the fact (so far fairly overlooked by critics) that such a mythology of Britain as a "world by itself", even though partly stemming from Caesar's narration of a "conquest" in some measure hampered by nature, was mostly linked to the Latin literature which revolved around Claudius's conquest; one which, in beholding or extolling the might of Claudius's achievement, had a specific concern in heightening the equivalence between Rome and World. The conquest of that isolated world was its sanctioning corollary in the rhetoric one could come across in reading the literature made available by Camden's *Britannia*.

Among the wealth of Latin authors who recorded the monumentality of Claudius's achievement, apart from the aforementioned Tacitus and Seneca, Camden quotes Aegesippus (a second-century Christian chronicler) who wrote, "Witness hereof is Britaine, which living without the world, is by the might of Romans reduced into the world" (*Brit* 1, 45). One may feel this resonate in Innogen's divided feelings, uncertainly and unfaithfully desirous of both worlds: "Hath Britain all the sun that shines? Day,

Night / Are they not but in Britain? I' th' world's volume / Our Britain seems as of it, but not in't, / In a great pool, a swan's nest. Prithee think / There's livers out of Britain" (3.4.136–40). But interestingly enough, Camden also reports (*Brit* 1, 46–47) a poem by a Latin "most learned Poet though unknown" resuscitated from its dust, he remarks, by the renowned humanist Joseph Scaliger, who included it in his *Catalecta* (1575). The poem celebrates Claudius's achieved union of two worlds, which are not physically one: "But now the Ocean interflow's two worlds by double shore" (stanza A, v. 4, *Brit* 1, 47), and emphasizes the extraordinariness of the endeavour with a rhetoric which seems to be the reversed blueprint of the Queen's speech.

That Britain from our clime far set and thence excluded quite,
Conquered of late is washed yet, with water ours by right.
Britain, I say, far set apart, and by vast sea dijoin'd,
Wall'd with inaccessible banks and craggy clifts behind;
Which father Nereus fensed had with billows most invincible
An Ocean likewise compassed with ebs and flowes as fallible.
Britain that hath a wintry clime allotted for her seat
Where cold North-Beare shines always bright with stars that never set
Even at thy sight and first approach o' Caesar soone subdu'd,
Submitted hath her necke to beare strange yoke of servitude.
Behold, the earth *unpassable* of nations makes commixtion,
What heretofore was world and world is now conjoind in one.
(stanzas E–F, *Brit* 1, 47; my emphasis, except line 2)[48]

The imagery of the first six italicized verses (the dignifying Nereus-Neptune included) is too similar to that deployed by the Queen ("The natural bravery of your isle, which stands / As Neptune's park, ribbed and paled in / With oaks unscalable and roaring waters", *Cym.*, 3.1.18–20) to discourage the speculation that this might be a direct debt. But let us note for a start the reciprocity of the two (Rome's and Britain's) myths: the way one thrives upon the other in the poet's rhetoric. The greater the emphasis on Britain's geographical isolation and its natural defensive "walls" provided by Nereus's (Neptune's) embrace, the greater the entity of Claudius's enclosing achievement and the enormity of Rome's *hýbris*. The more the island of Britain is defined as "unpassable" ("unscalable" in *Cymbeline*), the more the value of what Rome has achieved, or "completed": the trespassing of the last northern frontier of the World, one placed in defence of the very notion of the unknown, and the unification of two worlds.

But Shakespeare refunctionalizes the ancient poem's content to the end of fashioning a counter myth: a myth of insular inviolability whose dramatic energy is better deployed if framed by Julius Caesar's "kind of conquest", and the Augustan, less martial context. In fact, it is within a more strategic policy of tributes and transfer of cultural authority that it can be safely claimed and honourably negotiated.[49] Ironically, that myth is constructed with Rome's textual ruins, fittingly provided by the lost (and recovered) verses of a poet unknown. But what the playwright may have found inspiring in the ancient poem is a rhetoric of worlds disjointed and conjoined by the same sea, a trope which in and of itself was perfect for contriving the plot and poetics of a whole play. What was once a world of its own, "excluded", "set apart", "disjoin'd" from the world (the ancient poet writes), encircled now by Roman temperate waters, is part of the World: enough to fuel, concomitantly, Innogen's vacillating insular outlook with a desire of a wider world. For if Britain is "In a great pool, a swan's nest . . . There's livers out of Britain" (*Cym.*, 3.4.139–40). Not for nothing Shakespeare has furnished the small space of her bedroom with paintings, tapestries, books, mythological images, and valuable objects (2.2; 2.4.66–91), an enclave of classicism invested with a desire that leads to Rome and a large humanist world. Let us remember that in those same years, perhaps inspired by the same sources, Shakespeare was working at or had just finished working at the infiniteness of the physical, cultural, and emotional geography of *Antony and Cleopatra*'s. As I argue in my next and final chapter, this had engaged him in a not dissimilar set of reflections on world and margins, and the attendant gamut of negotiations between centre and peripheries. The original Latin materials (whether prose or poetry) that the new historiography drew attention to were prompting precisely such a set of concerns. As for *Cymbeline*, they were such as to endue with new life Cloten and the Queen's contentious claims, while envisaging, concomitantly, the possibility of making them negotiable. They also bring to light the extent to which Shakespeare's Britain builds upon the invader's authority to define its myth of resistance and inviolability. At the same time, the interrogative potential implicated in the couple "world *versus* World", or conversely "two worlds in one", is such as to underpin the Rome-Britain intercultural pacification plot and to make it topical in the Elizabethan and Jacobean understanding of *translatio imperii*.

Meaningfully, Shakespeare's way of addressing history and the complex cluster of issues of Britain's relation to Rome in *Cymbeline* is the distancing, fabulous, and anti-tragic mode of his late plays—*Pericles*, *The Winter's Tale*, *The Tempest*—the late dreams of a (Nietzschean-) Apollonian "naïve artist", as I have suggested earlier in this volume (p. 96). Which doesn't mean that such a fantastical mode of coping with reality or history makes knowledge any simpler. For the Greeks, "naïveté" (or else the Apollonian impulse towards a harmonious fusion with the surrounding world) is born of the will, Nietzsche observes; illusion is a struggle, a rose slowly budding from thorny bushes, the thorns being those of an origin marked by tragedy.[50] As—more to the point—Heather James has observed, *Cymbeline* provides a "romance solvent to its various conflicts"; conflicts stemming from "the status of Britain's emergent nationhood, particularly as it relates to . . . models of authority". My analysis so far is compatible with her conclusion: "Through its unstable 'mingle-mangle' of sources and historical periods, *Cymbeline* threatens to dissolve rather than ratify the emergent British nation along with its Jacobean political iconography".[51] Except that more than viewing the play as a "mingle-mangle" (a pun which she critically takes from John Lily), I see it as the product of an archaeological digging or *bricolage*, one marked by the epistemological instability emerging from both Bacon's notion of "defaced history" and Camden's ruin-grounded vision of history, a vision however that, for both of them, can be left behind in James's times.

Interestingly, in Francis Bacon's *The Advancement of Learning* (1607), this is metaphorically figured as the end of an Aeneas-like "peregrination" in search of the ancient and common mother-name of the nation— "Brittany"—a passage from variety to stability which—after a long "prelude"—the author sees accomplished in James's politics of pacification and unification.[52] Shakespeare's *Cymbeline* seems to celebrate this same achievement of stability and harmony—a typical Jacobean ideal— with its closure officiated by Philarmonus. As a matter of fact, what the playwright is mostly concerned with is its "prelude", the "peregrination": the (literally) perambulant or chorographic performance of the nation's identity that he, in tune with his contemporaneity, telescopes in the moment in which the production of legitimizing symbolic meaning agonistically interacts with a problematized vision of Rome and its inheritance. For Britain's discovery of its own origins cannot avoid making peace with one's Roman past. Inheritance is a tragic theme in *Titus*, as we have shown. The culturally authoritative Augustan context in *Cymbeline*, and its sanitizing "romance solvent", e.g. Apollonian tongue-in cheek "naïveté", make inheritance possible. And yet this is done ambiguously.[53] The rituality massively conjured up to celebrate the transference in the last two acts, subtly disarticulated as it is by undecidability or error, the argument of my concluding section, is just an instance of this.

Remythologyzing the Flight of Birds

"ô Cæsar, lay along:/ The Ocean seeth beyond it selfe thine altars, to adore", the unknown Poet declaims in Camden's reported poem (*Britannia*, 46). With Claudius, the Roman altars trespass the known borders of the world to mark with their sight and their rites a new sacralized outpost in an imperial geography which extends itself beyond the sea with "a double shore", an edge beyond the edge. As in Giambattista Vico's age of poetical wisdom and poetical geography, gods and auspices—"an essential principle of civilization" in the rise of nations—belong to the conquerors: "This was entirely encompassed by the heroic formula of surrender, such as that used by Tarquinius Priscus at Collatia, by which the conquered people relinquished all their sacred and secular institutions to the victors".[54] In *Cymbeline's* strategic setting, however, the victors are the Britons, and the Roman gods are appropriated to liturgically serve an antagonistic and self-empowering signifying practice: "Laud we the gods, / And let our crooked smokers climb their nostrils / From our best altars", says the king in his concluding speech (5.5.475–77).

The victory is achieved through sweat and blood, resulting in a hard-won honourable peace with Rome, but the transference of the Roman *imperium* to the western territories of Britain is legitimized by vision and divination: it is sanctioned by the favour of the Roman gods, a favour expressed by the flight of birds. Shakespeare in this outpaces the model. In fact he conjures up all his imaginative resources to mythologize the event by recourse to a soothsayer and the westward trajectory of the Roman eagle, which we are invited to see as abandoning the "spongy south" and vanishing into a radiant western sky (4.2.348–51), perhaps pointing even further (as Shakespeare's audience may well have assumed) towards promising lands on the other side of the ocean.

Meaningfully, as noted by Parker, this is accompanied by a physical movement of its characters towards Milford Haven: a movement "From east to occident", in the innocent if suggestive words used by Innogen in search of her Posthumus (4.2.371), which appropriates and repurposes the Virgilian "westering of the empire".[55] But what we should foreground here is the rituality that is conjured up to sanction it: a triumph of pre-dictions, recognitions, and theophanies modelled on Roman ceremonies whose apotheosis—an oversized Jupiter landing on the wings of an eagle—is also the most difficult to envisage in terms of theatrical imple-mentation. The fact that all this was, seemingly, the playwright's parody-ing submission, or tongue-in-cheek "tribute" to the cultural authority of Rome, makes it all the more interesting with respect to the degree of ambivalence with which Rome is appropriated by and performed from the periphery of the empire.

Transference as it is handled in *Cymbeline* overtly works as both an event and a signifying practice, a cultural field of contentious metaphorical signification.[56] Indeed, the imperial destiny of Britain is given an aura by a mythmaking Roman ceremony, an act of divination which is one with what we would now intend (and likely Shakespeare himself did) as the community's production of cultural meaning. Administered by auspices, divination was the originary form of knowledge, in Vico's discussion, the poetical and "popular wisdom of all nations. This popular wisdom con-templated God in the attribute of His providence, so that from *divinari*, to divine, His essence was called divinity".[57] Interestingly, though, this ceremony in *Cymbeline* has literally migrated from Rome to the periphery of the empire, where in fact it is officiated by a domesticated soothsayer who arrived with the hostile legions of Rome; an augur called Philarmo-nus, a name marked by the language of the invader and yet utterly suited to the appeasing and reconciling role he is called to perform.

In accordance with Homi Bhabha, cultural and postcolonial theorists could feel that we are presented here with "the problem of the ambivalence of cultural authority: the attempt to dominate in the *name* of a cultural supremacy which is itself produced only in the moment of differentiation."[58] It is thus pertinent to note that the "moment of differentiation" is inscribed in the play as a momentary difficulty of the signifying process, an element hinting at a pervasive condition of "textual instability", as has been noted by Crumley.[59] Twice, before and after the fierce battle which concludes the contention between Rome and Britain over the question of tributes, Philarmonus perceives the will of the gods in the trajectory of the Roman eagle, the first time erroneously as favourable to Rome ("Last night the very gods show'd me a vision / . . . / which portends / (Unless my sins abuse my divination) / Success to th' Roman host", 4.2.345–51). Tellingly, the second and positive auspice for Britain is the result of an act of reinterpretation, the deferred result of a readjustment which highlights the cultural combativeness of the appropriative logic.

> The fingers of the powers above do tune
> The harmony of this peace. The vision,
> Which I made known to Lucius ere the stroke
> Of yet this scarce-cold battle, at this instant
> Is full accomplished. For the Roman eagle,
> From south to west on wing soaring aloft,
> Lessened herself and in the beams o'th' sun
> So vanished; which foreshadowed our princely eagle,
> Th' imperial Caesar, should again unite
> His favour with the radiant Cymbeline,
> Which shines here in the west.
>
> (5.5.465–75)

Shakespeare must have been aware that the mythmaking flight of birds was decisive in the story of the foundation of Rome, the fratricidal legend of Romulus and Remus. As Janet Adelman has marvellously shown, the motif of male rivalry and "wolfish hunger" is pervasively underwritten by the legend of the quarrelling twins in Shakespeare's late Roman plays (*Coriolanus, Antony and Cleopatra, Cymbeline*). As she argues, even though never mentioning it, "Shakespeare psychologizes the fundamental elements of the founding legend of Rome—exile, hunger, hyper-masculinity, and fratricide—dispersing them throughout the late classical plays and giving them full articulation in *Coriolanus*". As for *Cymbeline*, she discovers this legend as standing behind both the rivalry between Rome and Britain and its sanitized resolution, mainly provided by the King's two lost sons in the second plot.[60] In my reading of the play, divination and the ambiguity embedded in the Romulus and Remus flight of birds plays has no secondary role as a resonance of an empowering, if problematic, foundational story. Shakespeare may have used Ovid's *Fasti* in conceiving his bird-grounded prophetic finale for *Cymbeline*:

> Which would erect the wall was open to question.
> "No need to quarrel," Romulus said. "Augury is quite
> Reliable, so let's resort to augury."
> The idea was attractive. One of them ascended the well-wooded Palatine,
> The other climbed the Aventine peak in the morning.
> Remus spotted six birds, Romulus, twice six in a row;
> The bargain was kept and Romulus got control of the city.
>
>   (*Fasti*, IV.8.12–18)[61]

Cymbeline's repeated and revised interpretation of the trajectory of "Jove's bird", however, seems to be remindful of "sins" which ever since destabilize the divinatory practice. ("Unless my sins abuse my divination"), the soothsayer has parenthetically warned in his first interpretation of the eagle's flight (see 4.2.345–51 and 5.5.466–75). Arguably, Shakespeare may have had other sources in mind. In that, whereas Ovid is evasive in matters of "abuses" which may have concurred in deciding for Romulus's "control of the city", in Livy's *Roman History* and Plutarch's *Lives* ("Life of Romulus"), Romulus's overwhelming vision of the 12 birds is told as a story of intended lie, a cheat, one which disturbs at the core Rome's founding myth. Here is Plutarch:

> When they came nowe to the building of their cittie, *Romulus &*
> *Remus* the two brethern fell sodainly at a strife together about the
> place where the cittie should be builded. For Romulus built ROME,
> which is called foure square, and would needs it should remaine in the
> place which he had chosen. *Remus* his brother chose another place
> very strong of situation, upon mounte *Aventine*, which was called after
> his name *Remonium*, and nowe is called *Rignarium*. Notwithstanding,
> in the ende they agreed between them selves this controuversie should
> be decided, by the flying of birds, which doe geve a happy divination
> of things to come. So being sett in divers places by them selves to
> make observation, some saye that there appeared unto *Remus* sixe,
> and to Romulus twelve vulturs. Other saye tha *Remus* truely sawe
> sixe, and *Romulus* feigned from the beginning that he sawe twise as
> many: but when *Remus* came to him, then there appeared twelve in
> deede unto *Romulus*. . . . And when *Romulus* knewe howe his brother
> had mocked him, he was very angry with him. And when Romulus
> had cast a dytche, as it were for the wall about his cittie, *Remus* dyd
> not only scorne it, but hindered also his worke, and in the ende for
> a mockerie lept over his wall. To conclude, he dyd so much, that at
> the last he was slayne there by *Romulus* owne handes as some saye.[62]

What Shakespeare needed, in the moment he was mythologizing the birth of a new Rome in Britain, was an agonism clean of any taint of fraud, and this was more easily offered by Ovid. Yet, the memory of suspect augurs in *Cymbeline* is perceivable in the way the augural vision of birds innervates a prevailing sense of equivocation, deferments, expectancy, and undecidability.

Divination in *Cymbeline*, with its relative degree of unreliability, is subtly exploited by Shakespeare to mythologize the combativeness between the two distant but related geographies of Britain and Rome. It is, however, wrought in a way that is not meant to rekindle a war against "the Roman host" (4.2.352), but rather to rearticulate the conflict in terms of negotiation of political and cultural authority. Significantly, divination, as a self-empowering signifying practice, is eventually relocated to the court of Britain. As to the founding and enabling function of divination in ancient Rome, this was incisively testified by Suetonius, a familiar author in Jacobean England, especially after Holland's translation of *The Twelve Caesars* in 1606. Places consecrated by augural rites were called "august", and it was on this basis, Suetonius explains, that the title of Augustus was conferred on Octavius:

> Some senators wished him to be called Romulus, as the second founder of the city; but Plancus had his way. He argued that "Augustus" was both more original and a more honourable title, since sanctuaries and all places consecrated by the augurs are known as "august"—the word being an enlarged form of *auctus*, implying the "increase" of dignity thus given such places, or a product of the phrase *avium gestus gustusve*, "the behaviour and feeding of birds", which the augurs observed. Plancus supported his point by a quotation from Ennius' *Annals*:

> "When glorious Rome had founded been, by augury august."[63]

The ending of *Cymbeline* is massively framed by images of transference of cultural authority, an "increase of dignity", grounded on appropriative acts of vision, interpretation, and re-signification: among these the reading of Jupiter's oracle written on the tablet Posthumus finds on his bosom at his awakening after the victorious battle against the Roman legions. This is also the occasion for the Roman soothsayer to deploy an art of interpretation based on the authority of Latin etymology, or better its late, corrupt, and misinterpreted *ruinae*; but good enough to demonstrate the extent to which the Latin tongue could be usefully employed to safeguard the necessity of the present, which in *Cymbeline* is, importantly, the newly recovered nation-based and male-defined identity of the court.

SOOTHSAYER (*Reads*) *Whenas a lion's whelp shall, to himself unknown, without seeking find, and be embraced by a piece of tender*

air; and when from a stately cedar shall be lopped branches which,
being dead many years, shall after revive, be jointed to the old stock,
and freshly grow, then shall Posthumus end his miseries, Britain be
fortunate, and flourish in piece and plenty.
Thou, Leonatus, art the lion's whelp,
The fit and apt construction of thy name,
Being *leo-natus*, doth impart so much:
[*To Cymbeline*] The piece of tender air, thy virtuous daughter,
Which we call *mollis aer*; and *mollis aer*
We term it *mulier*: which *mulier* I divine
Is this most constant wife, who even now,
Answering the letter of the oracle,
[*To Posthumus*] Unknown to you, unsought, were clipped about
With this most tender air.

(5.5.434–50)

As with the battle, the interpretation of the tablet (of which, curiously, it is an anagram) is a deferred act. It deploys itself according to a dramaturgy which requires two temporally divided phases; one which, in the hiatus between the two—the time of suspension and expectancy—allows for the unfolding of the events which make the prophecy sound true, right, and providential. In the long hiatus which elapses between Posthumus's awakening from his dream in the fourth act and the soothsayer's interpretation of the tablet that Jupiter has left on his bosom at the end of the fifth act, many things happen at Lud's Court and on Cymbeline's Romanized divining "altar". For a moment, the playwright makes us fear that the dead asking for remembrance may be appeased by the same vengeful and slaughtering rites which are deserved to Rome's enemy in *Titus Andronicus*'s opening. In fact, precisely as in *Titus*, Cymbeline announces that the kinsmen of the Britons who honourably lost their life in war "have made suit / That their good souls may be appeased with slaughter / Of their captives, which ourself have granted" (5.5.71–74). But the play has already veered towards its comic solution; the King is too busy keeping track of the dense deciphering and disentangling activity which allows for the dispersed royal family to finally come together again, and the language of Christian repentance and forgiveness easily replaces the scenario of human sacrifices. Even though not completely. For what also happens at Lud's divining court is the sacrifice of two women.[64] The first is the unnamed queen, the spokeswoman of a non-negotiable, radical patriotism, whose suicide is hailed as the enactment of retributive justice. Like Tamora in *Titus* she is the alien female body to be expelled, in a male redefinition of the nation, the spectre of those powerful women recalled by Tacitus, women who like Boodicia shared with men the government of the land; and an allusion, perhaps, to England's recent progeny of queens, all tainted by either a slight or serious discrediting fault in the Jacobean memory: the "illegitimate" (and for Bacon)[65] "masculine" Elizabeth, the Catholic "bloody" Mary, the "lewd", abdicating, and executed Mary Stuart. The second and interrelated sacrificial victim is Innogen, whose expunction from the line of a male-reordered dynasty is the by-product of a *diminutio* from the status of hereditary princess to that of tender and constant wife; a domestication sanctioned by an improbable etymological drift from *mollis aer* to *mulier*, the work of a hired soothsayer, whose inclination to comply with the winner has been sufficiently tested on occasion of the battle.

Soothsayers and acts of dubious interpretation were the corollary of the emperors' temptation—hardly resisted in the history of ancient Rome—of casting one's imperial authority in sacral terms. Julius Caesar's self-fashioning as a *Divus* is well known. He was also famous for over-crediting soothsayers and their prophetic claims. Prophecy and a plethora of gods, Jupiter in chief, sacralize the destiny of Rome and the place of August in it as a peace-maker, in Virgil's *Aeneid:* "Then wars shall cease and savage ages soften; hoary Faith and Vesta, Quirinus with his brother, shall give laws: The gates of war, grim with iron and close-fitten bars, shall be closed" (Book I.292–294 and 204f). But prophecy, as Shakespeare well shows in the tragic scenario of *Julius Caesar*, encapsulates equivocation as its inner threat in the classical world. Which doesn't mean that error and misinterpretation make it less sacral. As aforesaid, Rome's founding myth itself—the competitive augural vision of birds between Romulus and Remus—is grounded on an act of misinterpretation, a fraud (at least following Plutarch and Livy), which while highlighting the connate combativeness of mythmaking, destabilizes it at the core with an original mark of undecidability.

Shakespeare was secularly playing with all this, I suggest, when in manufacturing his *Cymbeline*'s *translatio imperii* final as a sacral founding pact, he completed it by selling an etymologizing commonplace for a riddle. The association between *mollis aer* and *mulier* was wrong, if ancient. But was Shakespeare aware of this? And is it legitimate to speculate that he was intentionally exploiting a defective etymology? Perhaps he was even signalling its inner error, encapsulated as it was in the quasihomophonic *aer* and *err*. If we respond positively to this, he was suspending and troubling the ongoing male reordering of the nation with a flaw which scattered a veil of scepticism on his ritualized triumphant final. Or, perhaps, he was providing a double final: one of them to be taken at face value, fulfilling as this was for the credulous (and unquestioning) members of his audience; the other aimed at prompting the educated part of his heterogeneous audience to push further the etymological exercise. In the tablet's first enigmatic occurrence, "*mollis aer*" is the sweetening property of a tender and embracing nature (air, climate). From the Latin "*mollio*", "*mollire*", "*mollificare*" came the English verbal form "to mollify" (to make soft, to make tender, to reduce the hardness or harshness of a thing, body, or word), but also to mitigate, to calm, to pacify, to appease. It seemed a fitting constellation of meanings for James's time. "To mollify" catalyzes all these meanings when Camden uses it in relation to the Jacobean prospective unified nation in his afore-quoted *Britannia*, and to which I will return in a while.

The *OED* traces back to a surgery treatise (1425) the first appearance of the verb in the English language, where it refers to therapeutic practices (to mollify the belly or fist, for instance). Its metaphorical potential grows in the ensuing occurrences. It is exploited by Lydgate (1430), Caxton (1490), Puttenham (1589), Donne (1624), and others. In Caxton's *Eneydos*, XV.59, it refers to the action of sacrificial rituality: "The erth . . . was all made fatte and molyfyed wyth the blode of the bests that were there Immolated". In Puttenham's *Arte of English Poesie*, I.3,4, it is the property of persuasive language: "The mollifying of hard and stonie hearts by . . . sweete and eloquent perswasion". In John Donne's *Devotions*, XIII.323, it is a Heaven's prerogative: "Thou rainiest upon us and yet doest not always mollifie all our hardness". But I found no record in the *OED* of the occurrence in Camden, who, interestingly, in his last version of *Britannia* (1607) dedicated to James I, made recourse to this verb—to mollify—to highlight the achieved sweetening and civilizing effects of Religion and Art, in a nation which he viewed as born of tragic fractures and ruins: "But since that for so many ages successively ensuing, we are all now by a certain *engraffing or commixtion* become one nation, *mollified and civilized* with Religion, and good Arts"; my emphasis; see earlier, p. 71). We find a shorter and slightly different version of this in Camden's *Remains* (*Re*, 16) where however the "mellowing" and "mollifying" agency is not that of Religion and Arts on Britain but that of England's "mildness of the soyle and sweete aire", on its stout Anglo-Saxon ancestors.[66] The difference is not uninfluential: whereas Arts (if not Religion) lead to Rome's civility, the "mildness of the soyle and sweete aire" circumscribes an insular circuit. In either case the relation with *Cymbeline*'s set of issues is evident. Nay, Shakespeare's soothsayer seems to have incorporated the lexicon of both in his unravelling of the oracle.

Britannia's latent acknowledgement of James's pacified nation is one with Camden's invitation to a pacified confrontation with one's past, one which conjured up all the therapeutic and metaphorical intentionality of "mollification". He was also inadvertently awakening its underlying unsettling connotations—to enervate, to enfeeble, to weaken, to effeminate, the rumoured characteristics of James's court. Similarly the "*mollis aer*" of Cymbeline's court could even hint at an encapsulated shared— more than opposed—kinship with Rome's southern "spongy" climate and declining values. But Shakespeare may have also had in mind that *mollitia* (grace, mellowness, suppleness) is the gift that the Muses bestow on poets: "*molle atque facetum Vergilio adnuerent gaudentes rure Camenae*"

["To Virgil the Muses, delighting in rural scenes, have granted the delicate and the elegant"] Horace writes in his *Satires* (I.10.44–45).[67]

The soothsayer's dubious association between *"mollis aer"* and *mulier* leads part of his audience to the limits of its meaning and applicability. Misinterpretation is productive. It questions the privileged ownership of divination and relaunches the interpretative act by making it rebound from scaffold to the stalls, and from playhouse to Court. It provides space(s) for speculation and connections. For the oblique etymological fluidification of *"mulier"* and its related sanitizing connotations of tenderness and "constancy" releases a ludic energy, an imaginative disorder, which allows for the return, or persistence, of the feminine as a threat (as "air"). Namely the feminine as an unfirm and unconfinable principle, which in *Cymbeline* stands for things as disparate and unsettling as Posthumus's fear of his "woman's part", as well as boy actors playing the "woman's part". The soothsayer itself, a figure of fraud and ambivalence at Cymbeline's court, disturbs at the core, with his very Roman (-Catholic) effeminating vestments (an object of stigma in the not-too-remote invectives against theatre), what he is called to officiate and license: the new pact between Rome and Britain, and the sanitized order of bodies and family.[68] From beginning to end Shakespeare doesn't seem so much to want to make sense of all this, as rather to make these elements cohabit on the scaffolds of his theatre, and more contradictorily than ever at the King's court. As Jonathan Dollimore rightly states, with the words of Raymond Williams's *Marxism and Literature* (1977): "the dominant culture . . . at once produces and limits its own forms of counter-culture".[69] Or vice versa.

Placed at the intersection of a crucial historical juncture between Augustan Rome and the emergence of an assertive nation-based awareness, and marked as it is by a sense of historical and cultural belatedness, *Cymbeline* allows us to foreground the combative, emulative intention in respect to "the Roman host" which we can see at work in the rest of Shakespeare's Roman plays. *Cymbeline* also clearly evokes the related complex gamut of ideological concerns which were at stake in the confrontation with Rome in Tudor and Jacobean England.

Shakespeare started his theatrical dealings with ancient Rome with a gesture of freedom. Dismissing any constraint deriving from historical or philological exactitude in *Titus Andronicus*, and as if starting with the ending, he began by introducing his audience to the fantastic geography of a declining imperial scenario where Caesarean *triumphalia* are as important as dismembered bodies and textuality. As if invading an authoritative centre from the margins, Rome is reduced to its archive or ruins (texts, signs, spaces, rituals) in the hands of a playwright eager to work out his own version of it, or to win his own trophies in the appropriative logic of *translatio imperii*. When Shakespeare resumed the imperial theme in his Plutarchan plays, he did it with a different degree of accuracy. His sources are well acknowledged (Plutarch, Appian, Livy, etc.). But again Shakespeare seems interested in a number of ways in which Rome's body can be mastered or cannibalized for the purposes of his own Renaissance times.

In *Cymbeline* the historical geography of Rome, the ruins of its declining values and its myth, served overtly as a world-scale stage on which to project the performance of the Tudors' and Jacobeans' growing sense of national identity and their nascent imperial ambitions in the redefined space of England, Europe, and the world. However, Rome's reinvented space and chronology also served, by means of erasures, appropriations, misinterpretation, and reversals—the stuff of memory in its never-ending negotiating activity with the past—to turn the Benjaminian "lament from history" of his Roman tragedies into late baroque comedy and romance: a provisional or suspended world of contained invasion, contained violence, and escaped rape.[70] One which, in distancing Rome, made Rome's inheritance possible.

Notes

1. Quotations from *Cymbeline* are taken from the Arden edition, ed. Valerie Wayne (London and New York: Bloomsbury, 2017). But I have consulted also the Arden edition, ed. J.M. Nosworthy (rpt London and New York: Methuen, [1955] 1986), and the Oxford Shakespeare *Cymbeline*, ed. Roger Warren (Oxford: Oxford University Press, 1998), with its first Folio Imogen emendated into Innogen. On the first Folio "error", see Stanley Wells and Gary Taylor, eds, *William Shakespeare. A Textual Companion* (Cambridge: Cambridge University Press, 2000), p. 604. See also Wayne, "Appendix 1: The Text of *Cymbeline* ('Innogen or Imogen'?)", in Shakespeare, *Cymbeline*, pp. 391–401. In this volume I refer to the British princess as Innogen.
2. As often noticed, Caesar's triumph was held in October, five months before.
3. For a reconstruction of the cultural climate which in the late years of the Elizabethan kingdom made the combination of politics, conspiracy, and religion something which (in spite of the play's pagan context), "Shakespeare's audience would have taken for granted", see James Shapiro's fascinating chapter "Is This a Holiday?", in his *A Year in the Life of William Shakespeare: 1599* (New York: Harper Perennial, 2006), p. 138 *et passim*. Among the factors analyzed by Shapiro, there was the earlier Reformist vehemence in the effacement of both Catholic imagery and festivities; a loss of communal life and visual enjoyment which Elizabeth—farsighted governor as she was—addressed with a well-balanced political ambivalence, and a calculating, spectacularized cult of her person. Shakespeare alike contributed to fill the vacuum with his theatre. As reminded by Shapiro, Shakespeare was seven when (in 1571) together with the Stratford townsfolk he saw (from his next door grammar school) Gild Chapel's stained-glass windows with their coloured sacred images being smashed, to be replaced with plain white glass.
4. See for all Liebler, *Shakespeare's Festive Tragedy*, pp. 105 and 98–99.
5. G. Wilson Knight, *The Crown of Life* (London and New York: Routledge, [1937] 2002), pp. 130 and 165–166.
6. Giambattista Vico, *New Science*, p. 135.
7. As Paulina Kewes reminds us, "To recover the uses of the past in a variety of genres is essential for the understanding of early modern historical

culture since, even if many of those genres are no longer recognized as history, early modern writers and readers treated them as such. Readers and writers, expected, and were expected, to make comparison across a spectrum of texts dealing in one way or another with the national or the foreign past. Furthermore, a poem or a play could raise questions about a historical event that a prose narrative could not, or could not as easily" ("History and Its Uses", in Paulina Kewes, ed., *The Uses of History in Early Modern England* (San Marino, CA: Huntington Library, 2006), p. 5.

8. Anderson, *Performing Early Modern Trauma*, p. 33.
9. See Emrys Jones, "Stuart *Cymbeline*", *Essays in Criticism*, 11 (1961), 84–99; Leah S. Marcus, *Puzzling Shakespeare: Local Reading and Its Discontents* (Berkeley: University of California Press, 1988), pp. 106–148; Ros King, *Cymbeline: Constructions of Britain* (Aldershot and Burlington: Ashgate, 2005); Hopkins, *The Cultural Uses of the Caesars*, pp. 111–126.; Linda Woodbridge, "Palisading the Elizabethan Body Politic", *Texas Studies in Literature and Language*, 33:3 (1991), 327–354; James, *Shakespeare's Troy*, pp. 151–188), Andrew Hadfield, "Shakespeare's Ecumenical Britain", in Andrew Hadfield, ed., *Shakespeare, Spenser and the Matter of Britain* (New York: Palgrave Macmillan, 2004), pp. 151–168, and others, who have variously discussed the topicality of the Augustan theme (and Pax Augusta) in relation to James I's unionist and pacifying times.
10. In this I agree with David D. Bergeron who, following Wilson Knight, fosters the view that the play should "be regarded as an historical play" ("*Cymbeline*: Shakespeare's Last Roman Play", *Shakespeare Quarterly*, 31:1 (1980), 31–41 (p. 32). I also agree with J. Clinton Crumley who understands *Cymbeline*'s historicity not in terms (or not just in terms) of topicality, namely mirroring of James contemporary history, as rather in terms of a confrontation with the sense of history ("Questioning History in *Cymbeline*", *Studies in English Literature*, 41:2 (2001), 297–315. Differently from Crumley, however, I see mostly in Camden's new historiography the method that interacting with traditional chronicles sceptically complicates *Cymbeline*'s response to its Roman past.
11. In the famous classically framed frontispiece of his *Theatre of the Empire of Great Britaine* (London: William Hall, 1611), John Speed seemed to provide the visual version of such a healing geo-genealogical tension at work in the epochal geo-historiography. Significantly (see the upper edge of the classical arch), the niches of his classical arch assigned to the diverse ethnicities are crowned by the presiding over gender-coded hospitable encounter between two yearning figures: an earth-goddess with a bountiful cornucopia and a conquering civilizing Roman.
12. Raphael Holinshed and Abraham Fleming, *The Historie of England, From the Time That It Was First Inhabited, Vntill the Time That It Was Last Conquered* [1587], ed. Henry Ellis (London: J. Jonson, 1807). Electronic Edition ("Of Brute and His Descent"), Book II.1, and ("Of Cassibellane"), Book III, 10. Perseus Digital Library, www.perseus.tufts.edu/hopper/text?doc=Perseus: text:1999.03.0084.
13. Richard Harvey, *Philadelphus, or a Defence of Brutes, and the Brutans History* (London: John Wolfe, 1593), pp. 2–3.
14. James, *Shakespeare's Troy*, pp. 88 and 87–88.
15. Wells and Taylor, eds, *William Shakespeare. A Textual Companion*, p. 132; King, *Cymbeline*, pp. 37–42.
16. See for all James, *Shakespeare's Troy*, pp. 151–152.
17. Bacon, *The Advancement of Learning*, pp. 71–72.
18. Crumley, "Questioning History", p. 301.

19. Holinshed and Fleming, *The Historie of England* ("Of Brute and His Descent"), Book II.1, Perseus Digital Library, www.perseus.tufts.edu/hopper/text?doc=Perseus:text:1999.03.0084.

20. For a full discussion of Posthumus's surgical birth—a Ceasearean section—and its early modern gender-coded implications, see Iolanda Plescia, "'From Me Was Posthumus Ript': *Cymbeline* and the Extraordinary Birth", in Del Sapio Garbero et al., eds, *Questioning Bodies*, pp. 135–147.

21. Among those who have directly and variously addressed the play in the light of early modern historiography, not always distinguishing between traditional and new historiography, see Jodi Mikalachki's gender-angled "The Masculine Romance of Roman Britain: *Cymbeline* and Early Modern Nationalism", *Shakespeare Quarterly*, 46:3 (1995), 301–322; John E. Curran's focalization of ennobling savagery in his "Royalty Unlearned, Honor Untaught: British Savages and Historiographical Change in *Cymbeline*", *Comparative Drama*, 31:2 (1997), 277–303. Mary Floyd-Wilson's foregrounding of ethnicity in "Delving to the Root: Cymbeline, Scotland, and the English Race", in David J. Barker and Willy Maley, eds, *British Identities and English Renaissance Literature* (Cambridge: Cambridge University Press, 2002), pp. 101–115, and *English Ethnicity and Race in Early Modern Drama* (Cambridge: Cambridge University Press, 2003), pp. 161–183; Willy Maley's focalization of the empire issue in the light of post-coloniality in *Nation, State and Empire in English Renaissance Literature: Shakespeare to Milton* (Houndmills: Palgrave Macmillan, 2003), pp. 31–44; Andrew Escobedo's redefinition of roots in terms of "newness" in "From Britannia to England: *Cymbeline* and the Beginning of Nations", *Shakespeare Quarterly*, 59:1 (2008), 60–87; Ronald J. Boling's foregrounding of the Welsh stance in "Anglo-Welsh Relations in *Cymbeline*", *Shakespeare Quarterly*, 51:1 (2000), 33–66. Moreover: H. James hints at the play's relation with the work of the antiquarians, but she doesn't explore it (*Shakespeare's Troy*, p. 152); Ros King, with whom I share the conviction that Shakespeare "had looked [or relooked, I would add] very carefully at the version of Camden's *Britannia* that was published in 1607" (*Cymbeline*, p. 64), limits her interest to Camden's ancient coins.

22. See Meredith Skura, "Interpreting Posthumus' Dream From Above and Below: Families, Psychoanalysts, and Literary Critics", in Murray M. Schwartz and Coppélia Kahn, eds, *Representing Shakespeare: New Psychoanalytic Essays* (Baltimore and London: The John Hopkins University Press, 1980), p. 203 and Miola, *Shakespeare's Rome*, p. 207 *et passim*. But see also Ros, *Cymbeline*, p. 75 *et passim*.

23. R. Holinshed, *Chronicles. The History of Scotland* (section "Kenneth"). An Electronic Edition. Perseus Digital Library. www.perseus.tufts.edu/hopper/. For such a borrowing, see W.G. Boswell-Stone, *Shakespeare's Holinshed: The Chronicle and the Historical Plays Compared* (London: Chatto and Windus, 1907), pp. 15–17. But see also Geoffrey Bullough, ed., *Narrative and Dramatic Sources of Shakespeare*, vol. 8 (London: Routledge and Kegan Paul, 1975), and Nosworthy's "Introduction", *Cymbeline*, Arden edition [1955] 1986 (pp. XVII–XIX and Appendix A, pp. 189–191).

24. In Jones's reading of the play, Milford Haven's symbolism is linked to the Tudor myth. In fact, this was the port from where Henry of Richmond's army (later Henry VII) arrived to free England from Richard III's tyranny. "Stuart *Cymbeline*", pp. 84–99. But see also Boling, for whom Milford Haven stands for an ambivalent set of Anglo-Welsh issues. "Anglo-Welsh Relations in *Cymbeline*", pp. 33–66.

25. Marcus, *Puzzling Shakespeare*, pp. 131–134.

26. Floyd-Wilson, "Delving to the Root", p. 112.
27. "*Cymbeline*: Shakespeare's Last Roman Play", pp. 33–34. In agreeing with Wilson Knight, Bergeron thinks "that the heart of the play is its historical basis, both ancient Britain and ancient Rome, and that the romance elements are not incompatible with this perspective", p. 32.
28. For more on Tacitus's popularity in Elizabethan England, see this volume's Chapter 1, note 30.
29. See Boswell-Stone, *Shakespeare's Holinshed*, p. 18. See also Roger Warren, "Introduction" to William Shakespeare, *Cymbeline*, The Oxford Shakespeare (Oxford: Oxford University Press, 1998), pp. 37–38. Among those who have elaborated on this, see Patricia Parker's "Romance and Empire: Anachronistic *Cymbeline*", in George M. Logan and Gordon Teskey, eds, *Unfolded Tales: Essays on Renaissance Romance* (Cornell: Cornell University Press, 1989), pp. 189–207. Drawing on the identification of Posthumus with some of Aeneas's traits, she shows how this bears on the play's exploitation of the Virgilian theme of the westward translation of empire. But for an exhaustive Virgilian reading of Posthumus, see James, *Shakespeare's Troy*, pp. 151–188.
30. See Bergeron, "*Cymbeline*", p. 36. Differently, Marcus has hypothesized that Posthumus may have been inspired by the "Post Nati" case, namely the debate aroused by James's decision to proclaim citizens of Britain all Scotsmen born after his ascension to the English throne, in accordance with the Roman code. *Puzzling Shakespeare*, p. 124.
31. Parker, "Romance and Empire", pp. 191.
32. Curran, "Royalty Unlearned", p. 293. Curran notes how the acceptance of a barbaric ancestry foregrounded by the new historiography leads to a revaluation of the "standards for judging the past" and a disposition "to locate virtue in savage forebears and obscure origins" (p. 278).
33. Cornelius Tacitus, *Annals*, transl. John Jackson, 1937, Loeb Classical Library, vol. 5 (London and Cambridge, MA: Harvard University Press, 1925–1937).
34. Boswell-Stone, *Shakespeare's Holinshed*, pp. 9–10.
35. The topographical configuration of the "narrow lane" has been often symbolically associated to Innogen and her womanly body, sexually threatened by invasion and pollution. See Woodbridge, "Palisading the Elizabethan Body Politic", pp. 334–336. But see also Kahn's postscript on *Cymbeline* in her *Roman Shakespeare*, p. 164.
36. Holinshed provides a free and less inspiring version of Tacitus on Caractacus's battle in *The Historie of England*, Book 4.6–7.
37. Shortened title of a coeval play by R. A., *The Valiant Welshman, or The True Chronicle History of the Life and Valiant Deeds of Caradoc the Great, King of Cambria, Now Called Wales* (1615).
38. On Northern Britons' nakedness as a sign of strength and valour, see also Camden's section on "Apparels", in *Remains*, p. 249.
39. The battle has received a considerable critical attention. In Mikalachki's "The Masculine Romance of Roman Britain" (pp. 314–316), it is insightfully discussed as a male-defined "entry into history" on the part of Guiderius and Arviragus, but one which concomitantly excludes women. Posthumus's historicizing role has been noted by Mikalachki as well as Curran (in "Royalty Unlearned", p. 298), but the destabilizing agency introduced by his personal story as well as the improper Holinshed's source (which is at the core of my analysis) is overlooked. In Leah Marcus's "puzzling" *Cymbeline*, the battle is signalled as an arcane episode, one which, with its insistent and incantatory repetition, contributes to the play's many riddles of interpretation, all leading to a prevailing "Jacobean line". In her historicist and topical approach, the use of Holinshed's Scottish battle is coherent with James's unionist project

and the related Scottish issue. I do not exclude her interpretation. However, my reasoning aims at foregrounding the way in which the play, here as elsewhere, eludes its topicality with an "impropriety" which interrogates more widely the sense of history and its epistemological aporia. The issue of history and its writing is also raised in Fletcher's *Bonduca*. See on this Curran, "Royalty Unlearned", pp. 281–282. But see also Di Michele, who emphasizes Posthumus's dramatist skill in the way he visualizes the field/stage of the battle. "Shakespeare's Writing of Rome in *Cymbeline*", in Del Sapio Garbero, ed., *Identity, Otherness and Empire*, pp. 162–163.

40. Nicholas Royle, *Jacques Derrida* (London: Routledge, 2003), p. 29. Derrida's quotation is from Jacques Derrida and Derek Attridge, *"This Strange Institution Called Literature": An Interview with Jacques Derrida* (London: Routledge, 1992).

41. Marcus, *Puzzling Shakespeare*, pp. 109–110.

42. King, *Cymbeline*, p. 37.

43. As Mikalachki has written, "Powerful females loomed large in early modern visions of national origins . . . Like the unruly women who challenged the patriarchal order of early modern England, these powerful and rebellious females in native historiography threatened the establishment of a stable, masculine identity for the early modern nation". "The Masculine Romance of Roman Britain", pp. 302–303. Floyd-Wilson is in the same vein when, in underlining the queen's composite character within what she sees as Shakespeare's wider concern for questions regarding "the generative roots of civility and barbarism", she observes: "As a second wife and 'step-dame', the queen is marked as an outsider who has infiltrated a formerly exclusive domain, and her historical perspective simultaneously represents Caesar's Britons, Geoffrey's Britons, the meddling Scottish historians, and the ancient rebellious Scots". "Delving to the Root", pp. 107–108. On the issue of powerful women on early modern English stage, see also Lovascio, ed., *Roman Women*.

44. Ruth Nevo, *Shakespeare's Other Language* (New York and London: Methuen, 1987), p. 62.

45. King, *Cymbeline*, pp. 76–77.

46. Bacon, *The Advancement of Learning*, p. 74.

47. As has been shown by Harold F. Brooks, Shakespeare may have used both the 1578 Blennerhassett and the 1587 Higgins editions of *The Mirror for Magistrates* for the construction of Act 3, scene 1. There he might have found Cassibellane's phrase apparently used against Caesar: "though Gods have giuen, thee all the world as thine; That's parted from the world, thou getst no land of Britain"; the closest to Cloten's "A world by itself" in Brooks's reconstruction. There he may have found other portions of phrases which he may have plausibly made his own for the queen's speech. See Appendix (*d*), "Act III, Scene I and *The Mirror for Magistrates*", in Nosworthy's Arden edition of *Cymbeline*, pp. 205–209.

48. It may be useful here to report Gibson's 1695 translation: "Britain, excluded from our warmer clime, / Is now surrounded with a *Roman* stream; Whose horrid cliffs, unfathom'd seas inclose, / And craggy rocks contemn invading foes. / By *Neptune*'s watry arms, with walls supplied, / And ever wet with the insulting tide. / Where frozen fields eternal winter mourn, / And Stars once risen, never can return. / By thee, great *Caesar*, with a look 'tis won, / And bears thy yoke, a burden yet unknown. / Thus friends in lands impassable we find, / Thus the two worlds are in one Empire joyn'd" (*Brit* 2, p. L).

49. This, I suggest, is what makes the difference in the group of coeval plays (William Rowley, *A Shoemaker, A Gentleman*, ca. 1609; John Fletcher, *Bonduca*, ca. 1613; R. A. *The Valiant Welshman, or The True Chronicle History of*

the Life and Valiant Deeds of Caradoc the Great, King of Cambria, Now Called Wales (1615), which similarly deal with the topic of the Romans in Britain and which also end with a reconciliation with Rome. In fact, in their Claudian, Nero's, or Dioclesian colonizing contexts, reconciliation inevitably turns into a less honourable submission. For their relevance to *Cymbeline*, see Mikalachki, "The Masculine Romance of Roman Britain", pp. 311–312; and Curran, "Royalty Unlearned", pp. 280–282.

50. Nietzsche, *The Birth of Tragedy*, pp. 23–24. For more on the suggested relation between Shakespeare's romance and the Nietzschean problematized notion of the Apollonian, see Del Sapio Garbero, "Shakespeare's Maternal Transfigurations", pp. 112–113.

51. James, *Shakespeare's Troy*, pp. 151–152.

52. Bacon writes, "And now last, this most happy and glorious event, that this island of Brittany, divided from all the world, should be united in itself: and that oracle of rest given to Aeneas, *antiquam exquirite matrem* [Search out your ancient mother], should now be performed and fulfilled upon the nations of England and Scotland, being now reunited in the ancient mother name of Brittany, as a full period of all instability and peregrinations. So that it cometh to pass in massive bodies, that they have certain trepidations and waverings before they fix and settle, so it seemeth that by the providence of God this monarchy, before it was to settle in your majesty and your generations (in which I hope it is now established for ever), it had these prelusive changes and varieties". *The Advancement of Learning*, pp. 74–75.

53. As if to hint at such an important link between the two plays, the characters endowed with the task of sealing the pact for the rise of a new or resurgent nation, questionable as it is in both plays, have the same name—Lucius. In the ruinous and equally hybrid setting of *Titus*, the general Lucius—Titus's only surviving son—has the controversial role of reestablishing order in Rome at the head of an army of Goths. In *Cymbeline*, another Lucius (Caius Lucius) seems to recast with the same degree of complexity and ambiguity, I suggest, the peace that, as Augustus's emissary, he is called to seal with Cymbeline's Britain. I agree with Lisa Hopkins when, dealing with language and national identity in Shakespeare's Roman plays, she observes, "*Titus Andronicus, King Lear*, and *Cymbeline* are in some sense all essentially part of the same story. That story is about the origins of Britain and how they continued to impact on early modern English identities". *From the Romans to the Normans on the English Renaissance Stage*, pp. 47–48.

54. Vico, *New Science*, p. 462.

55. Parker, "Romance and Empire", pp. 192–193 and 200–201.

56. Here I am drawing on Julia Kristeva's notion of "signifying practice" as the "establishment and the countervailing of a sign system" (*Desire in Language*, p. 18) as well as on Foucauldian discourse theory concerning the ways in which countries, cultures, or people negotiate power relations. See Foucault, "The order of discourse", pp. 51–76, in conjunction with *The History of Sexuality: An Introduction*, vol. 1 (Harmondsworth: Penguin, 1978).

57. Vico, *New Science*, p. 137.

58. Homi K. Bhabha, *The Location of Culture* (London and New York: Routledge, 2002), p. 34. For the way Rome—an opposed Rome—ideologically serves as a model of identification in the construction of a Stuart notion of the empire, see Maley, *Nation, State and Empire*, pp. 31–44.

59. Crumley, "Questioning History", pp. 307–308.

60. Adelman, "Shakespeare's Romulus and Remus", pp. 30 and 19–34. In her inspiring essay, Adelman doesn't extend her reflection to divination and mythmaking, but I owe to her the origin of my speculation.

61. Ovid, *Fasti*, transl. Betty Rose Nagle (Bloomington: Indiana University Press, 1995).
62. North's Plutarch, *The Lives*, pp. 25–26.
63. Suetonius, *The Twelve Caesars*, transl. Robert Graves (Harmondsworth: Penguin, [1957] 2003), p. 48. But see also Ovid's *Fasti* (I.608–12): "Augustus shares an epithet with Jupiter most high. / Our elders term hallowed things 'august', and 'august' is the term / for temples duly dedicated by priestly hands. / The word 'augury' is another related derivation, / and whatever Jupiter 'augments' with his might."
64. See on this Adelman's groundbreaking psychologized discussion of the reconciliation with Rome as a prevailing male bond grounded on the rejection of the female element, in *Suffocating Mothers*, pp. 198–218. But see also the aforementioned Mikalachki, "The Masculine Romance of Roman Britain", pp. 309–312.
65. Bacon, *The Advancement of Learning*, p. 74.
66. The *Remains'* occurrence and its relation with *Cymbeline* was first noted by Mary Floyd-Wilson ("Delving to the Root", pp. 112–113). But she overlooks (at least in this article) *Britannia*'s similar and different occurrence.
67. Horace, *The Works of Horace*, ed. C. Smart and Theodore Alois Buckley (New York: Harper & Brothers, 1863), Perseus Digital Library, www.perseus.tufts.edu/hopper/text?doc=Perseus:text:1999.02.0063. In a note to the Loeb edition of Horace's *Satyres* (1966), H. Rushton Fairclough who translates *"molle atque facetum"* as "simplicity and charm" takes pains to underline: "Professor C. N. Jackson has won wide acceptance for his view that in *molle atque facetum*, commonly rendered as 'tenderness and grace', Horace refers to the distinctive features of the *genus tenue*, or plain style of writing" (p. 119).
68. In saying this I diverge from Mikalachki's clear-cut bynarism on which her otherwise insightful argument is grounded: on the one hand an all-male searched-for alliance between Britain and Rome; on the other the primitive and nationalistic stance of powerful women (famously embodied by Boodicia) whose claim is subdued in the name of civility against savagery. "The Masculine Romance of Roman Britain".
69. Jonathan Dollimore, "Shakespeare Understudies: The Sodomite, the Prostitute, the Transvestite and Their Critics", in Jonathan Dollimore and Alan Sinfield, eds, *Political Shakespeare: Essays in Cultural Materialism* (Manchester: Manchester University Press, [1985] 2000), p. 130.
70. In saying this I am agreeing with Woodbridge's conclusion: "The British Empire, like the Roman, would thrust deep into the world's virgin territories; many read *The Tempest* as a document heralding that advance. But while Jacobeans helped invent English colonialism, the play does not fully inhabit that discourse. . . . Toward the end of his career, Shakespeare, living in a charmed moment in a changing culture, envisioned a society neither invaded nor invader, neither raped nor rapist, neither polluted nor polluter". "Palisading the Elizabethan Body Politic", p. 348.

6   World and Ruin in *Antony and Cleopatra*. An Epilogue

What a Richness in a Small Room. Innogen's Desire of a Larger World

As Robert Miola has written,

> *Cymbeline* stands as Shakespeare's valedictory to Rome, the city that long engaged his attention and inspired his art. . . . The seriousness of Shakespeare's previous Roman efforts, resulting from an abiding interest in character and politics, here yields to a cavalier nonchalance that tolerates inconsistencies, eschews political analysis, and trumpets its own artifices. Yet, Rome is undeniably present in *Cymbeline*.

And the analysis of the Roman elements, Miola further elaborates, "reveals the conclusion of Shakespeare's Roman vision. *Cymbeline* demonstrates that Britain can meet Romans on Roman terms—on the battlefield", as well as the sphere of values.[1] My take on this is that the battlefield resumes all its literal and metaphorical implications as a figure of agonism; a life-long agonism which in this last Roman play looks for differentiation and distinction at the different levels of war and politics, as well as those of heritage and the nation's own production of symbolic meaning.

Shakespeare, however, had envisaged a different and (quasi) coex-isting conclusion for his trafficking with Rome's ruins and myth, one erotically mediated by desire and female agency. This was in *Antony and Cleopatra*, the play he composed around 1606–7, or perhaps 1608, if we consider the entry into the Stationers' Register, in this date, of a work with that title on the part of the publisher Edward Blount, the only evidence on record in Shakespeare's lifetime, since there is no witness of performance, or printed text, until the posthumous 1623 first Folio.[2] Arguably, Shakespeare wanted to complete his three-pillars Plutarchan Roman cycle (*Julius Caesar*, 1599, *Coriolanus*, 1606–8, *Antony and Cleopatra*, 1606–8) with a tragic love affair which was also a grandiose funeral of Rome's might. Heminges and Condell, the editors of the first Folio, placed it just before the closing *Cymbeline*,

DOI: 10.4324/9781003259671-8

as if implying a chronological proximity in terms of composition, or inviting comparison between perspectives of Rome experienced from two opposed margins of the world: a calculating north-western Britannia against a desiring south-eastern Egypt. Interestingly, the two plays are historically linked by the same intercultural Augustan context. In the trajectory designed by the two opposite poles, Octavius Caesar (the "universal landlord", *Ant.*, 3.13.76) stands as its fixed and balancing centre. But, as hinted at in the previous chapter, Shakespeare makes some of *Antony and Cleopatra*'s destabilizing desiring energy circulate in *Cymbeline*'s landscape by maliciously encapsulating it in the bedchamber of his British princess, a closet fraught with the precious stuff, paintings, images, stories, and dreams of a larger cosmopolitan world: a pictured Cleopatra and "her Roman" among them, who in Shakespeare's (almost) coeval *Antony and Cleopatra* has just shown how a woman can transform her life as well as that of "her Roman" into a piece of art: "one such, / It's past the size of dreaming", as the Egyptian queen proclaims at the end of her story (*Ant.*, 5.2.95–96).

What a difference between Imogen and Cleopatra, William Hazlitt observes in the middle of romanticism:

> The character of Cleopatra is a master-piece. What an extreme contrast it affords to Imogen! One would think it almost impossible for the same person to have drawn both. She is voluptuous, ostentatious, boastful of her charms, haughty, tyrannical, fickle. The luxurious pomp and gorgeous extravagance of the Egyptian queen are displayed in all their force and lustre, as well as the irregular grandeur of the soul of Mark Antony.[3]

And yet when we come to *Cymbeline* (or from *Cym.* we go back to *Ant.*), we are startled by the fact that the two women are not so far apart. For Shakespeare has stealthily furnished Innogen's northern bedchamber with some of what Hazlitt describes as Cleopatra's "luxurious pomp and gorgeous extravagance". He has classicized its interior with riches of incommensurable value and incalculable risk. With baroque excess he has crowded its space with Venus's swarming messengers of love—cherubs, cupids (2.4.87–90)—and he has concealed there Cleopatra's boastful picture and charms. Indeed, he has "lodged" there, in its secret bodily places, *Antony and Cleopatra*'s similarly fantasized, unquenchable desire, one which is hungered by being satisfied. IACHIMO "under her breast— / Worthy the pressing—lies a mole, right proud / Of that most delicate lodging. By my life, / I kisse'd it, and it gave me present hunger / To feed again, though full" (*Cym.*, 2.4.134–38); Enobarbus has just used the same chiastic figure of speech in describing Cleopatra's infiniteness: "Other women cloy / The appetites they feed, but she makes hungry / Where most she satisfies" (*Ant.*, 2.2.246–48).

In Tudor and Jacobean regimes of surveillance, the aesthetics and politics of the closet emerges as a "symbol of the inaccessible, hidden places, either of religious belief or treacherous design", Knowles has observed (but see also Maus's discussion of secrecy and inaccessibility). It is associated with inwardness, meditation, and secrecy as well as heresy, treason, and menaced invasion.[4] But images, as well known, were offensive in themselves in the Reformed problematized and policed visual regime. The mere fact that as a copy of reality they could be mistaken for the real thing was enough to be stigmatized as conducive to heresy.[5] Meaningfully, under the combined scrutinizing and judicial gaze of Iachimo and Posthumus, Innogen's closet is accurately constructed as a place of inner "treacherous design", or else guilty desire: the revealing place of the unexpressed. In front of an equally inspective gaze of the audience, the proof—the "circumstance"—is visually collected and theatrically produced. Shakespeare stages it concomitantly as it were the inspector's or an infiltrate's report in a regime of surveillance ("But my design-- / To note the chamber"); the shrewd "inventory" of the emerging Jacobean art collector and well-travelled connoisseur ("Such and such pictures . . ., the arras, figures, / Why, such, and such"); the enthralled ekphrasis of a lover or spectator in love with deceptive (Italian) art and "the contents o'th' story" (2.2.23–30). The "story"—a potential treason story—is first of all inscribed on the bedchamber's walls and pictures, before leading us, anatomically and for "confirm", to an increasingly secret bodily place—a mole "under her breast", a "stain" (2.4.134, 139). By exchanging place with Enobarbus, Iachimo recounts it as a story of luxury and seduction: "First, her bedchamber, . . . / it was hang'd / With tapestry of silk and silver, the story / Proud Cleopatra, when she met her Roman / And Cydnus swelled above the banks, or for / The press of boats or pride. A piece of work / So bravely done, so rich, that it did strive / In workmanship and value; which I wondered / Could be so rarely and exactly wrought, / Since the true life on't was—" (*Cym.*, 2.4.66–75).[6] Interestingly, Innogen's classical closet is also framed as the place of a conflicting and hence suspect textuality, in the way the narrative of a gorgeous Cleopatra cohabits with that of "the chimney-piece, / Chaste Dian, bathing" (2.4.81–82), a cohabitation which calls for disambiguity and surveillance. In fact, Diana's nakedness also stands for an interiority, forensically turned inside out like a glove and violently made known and public; the violence and publicity of a criminalized interior which Gertrude in *Hamlet*'s famous closet scene rejects as that of a gaze coercively forced to introvert its direction ("Thou turn'st my very eyes into my soul", 3.4.89). Indeed, before "the cognizance" of a more secret and "more evident corporeal sign" (2.4.127; 119–20), the knowledge of Innogen's bedchamber is the effraction that exposes the princess to the potential violence of the invader (Iachimo's), as well as that conveyed (as for Cleopatra) by the appellative "whore" (see for all *Ant.*, 3.6.68;

Cym., 2.4.128), a stigma significantly conducive to a judicial sentence of death (Posthumus's).

Shakespeare precludes access to the British princess's bedchamber through her own eyes. The audience beholds its interior by sharing the combined predatory and judicial male gaze of both Iachimo and Posthumus. Innogen's body is sucked into such gaze by the set of meanings established by Iachimo's trunk, an instance of avidity and pillage. And yet Innogen's classical (Roman-Alexandrian) closet, with its inset narrative of the two famous lovers, stands as a concealed subversive space, I argue, a space of female disobedience and resistance in the overall sanitizing intentionality of *Cymbeline*.[7] Made rich by Cleopatra's bold tapestry and cherubs, it stands as a space of beauty and potentially tragic desire, a space which defines the topic of Rome and its larger world as one of allure and risk, not to say of secret infra- and extratextual alliance among women, one which Shakespeare's audience could trace by following the thread which, among omission and allusion, the two plays (*Cym.* and *Ant.*), in conjunction, seem to weave by means of their women's jeopardized riches and rivalry, turning into bonds, gratitude, and gifts.

Let us think of Cleopatra's preposterous thought for Octavius's and Antony's wives, Livia and Octavia (in *Ant.*), at the critical moment of her final defeat, when self-locked and sheltered by the walls of her funeral monument—her closet—she tries to conceal some of her riches from the obtruding eye of the winning Octavius, motivating her gesture as a gift for the two women's hoped-for "mediation" (5.2.163–70). But Plutarch's readers knew that it was rather Fulvia—Antonius's dead wife, famous for being masterly at ease with politics, generals, and armies—, the woman to whom Cleopatra owed most gratitude, and not for nothing, since Fulvia had shaped Antony into the kind of man who suited her. In Plutarch's words Fulvia was,

> a woman not so basely minded to spend her time in spinning and housewivery, and was not contented to master her husband at home, but would also rule him in his office abroad, and command him, that commanded legions and great armies: so that *Cleopatra* was to give *Fulvia* thankes for that she had taught *Antonius* this obedience to women, that learned so well to be at their commaundement.
>
> (North's Plutarch, "Life", 975)

As for Octavia, she certainly deserved Cleopatra's generosity, but not so much for eventually interceding in her favour with Octavius, as for her loyalty—and perhaps with a presentiment of what she couldn't know— because, as Plutarch (not Shakespeare) tells us in concluding his "Life of Antony", she would take on the role of mother for some of her and Antonius's children, those who escaped Octavius's carnage at their death. Cleopatra's prismatic figure in her connection with other women gestures

towards an unsettling figure of woman who interprets the lover, the warrior, and the mother, across the distant geographies of Egypt, Rome, and
Britannia.

In deciding to conclude this volume with *Antony and Cleopatra*,
I intend to bring to the fore what I see as Shakespeare's twofold way
of coming to terms with the memory of Rome and classical humanism.
Against the ideological and circumscribed nationalist framework of *Cymbeline*'s claim, I suggest viewing the geographically dilated, transnational,
or global vision of *Antony and Cleopatra* as the representation of Shakespeare's everlasting fascination with Rome. In both plays a struggle for
mastery between conquerors and conquered, centre and periphery, defines
their common international theme. But in Shakespeare's Egyptian-Roman
play, such a conflict is unsettled and blurred from the margins of a desired
and desiring female Otherness, where "the Roman host" (as Rome is
mentioned in *Cym.*, 4.2.352) is by no means represented by Iachimo (a
derisive Italianate Roman) or Posthumus (a second-hand interpretation
of Romanness), as rather by the "Asianized" Antony and his Alexandrian
monumentalized memory officiated by Cleopatra: a figure of the author
as I take it, and his/her never-ending leave-taking from Rome.

As argued in my previous chapters, the playwright's reflection on nation
and World emerges as a pivotal topic in *Cymbeline* and as a surfacing
link between *Cymbeline* and *Antony and Cleopatra*; one which secretly
fuels Innogen's timid desire of an expanded "elsewhere" (let alone the
concomitant Coriolanus's "world elsewhere", 3.3.134). It is the other side
of Britain's early modern nationalistic endeavour in defining borders and
claiming to be "a world by itself". Plausibly the playwright is relying on
the same sources while writing or projecting these late Roman plays, and
while "ruminating" on worlds jointed and disjointed, insularity and universality, national and transnational, measurable and immeasurable. He is
undoubtedly reading Plutarch's *Lives* (in North's 1579 translation), where
the "Life of Antony" and the two lovers' story coincide with the gorgeous
display of an endless list of Western and Eastern territories inclining on
the Mediterranean.[8] But he seems also interested in the contemporary
new historiography represented by Camden's *Britannia* (1586–1609), a
work which (as underlined in this volume's Introduction, Part 2) with its
problematized exploration of the link between history and space, and its
sceptical discussion of origins as an excavated story of recurrent ruination
and intermingling, played quite a role in the new geographical "writing" (Helgerson) of the nation. The playwright has also read or heard
of Bruno's infinite universe, as has been suggested most persuasively by
Gilberto Sacerdoti.[9]

In supposing that the earthly and heavenly universe of *Antony and
Cleopatra* may have been Shakespeare's favourite space for staging his
farewell to Rome, I am not alone. At least this certainly seems to have
been a temptation for many. Elicited by its uncertain chronology, the

dating of the play has been stretched back to 1599 as well as postponed to 1608 or even further to 1610, according to a variety of speculations. Invoking the play's glittering originality, Coppélia Kahn postulated "that *Antony and Cleopatra*, rather than *Coriolanus*, was Shakespeare's last Roman experiment".[10] In the case of Geoffrey Miles, ending his book on the "constant Romans" with *Antony and Cleopatra*'s spacious scenario and Cleopatra's "liberating" death, seemed to make more sense than the (perhaps) later-dated *Coriolanus* with its confining walls and its protagonist's "futile death".[11] But this decision was also made easy by the fact that the author restricted his enquiry to the three Plutarchan plays. Forcing the dating of the play further to bring it closer to *Cymbeline* (whose date though is just as uncertain) may seem less defendable. But I insist upon having *Antony and Cleopatra* as the concluding chapter of this book on different grounds: because in conjunction with *Cymbeline*, the play allows us to envisage two conflicting—and hence self-annulling—ways for Shakespeare of bidding farewell to Rome. Which is precisely my point.

Defining a Scale

"Greatness" is Rome's defining mark in early modern perception of the ancient city. Let us consider Du Bellay/Spenser's way of imagining it:

> Who list the Romane greatnes forth to figure,
> Him needeth not to seeke for usage right
> *Of line, or lead, or rule, or square, to measure*
> Her length, her breadth, her deepnes, or her hight
> But him behooves to view in compasse round
> All that the Ocean graspes in his long armes;
> Or where colde Boreas blowes his bitter stormes.
> Rome was th' whole world, and all the world was Rome;
> And if things nam'd their names do equalize,
> When land and sea ye name, then name ye Rome;
> And naming Rome, ye land and sea comprize:
> For th' ancient Plot of Rome, displayed plaine,
> The map of all the wide world doth containe.
> > (*Ruines of Rome*, son. 26; my emphasis)

We might well be on Pompey's galley, with the captain Menas in the clothes of a Renaissance geographer or astronomer—a globe nearby, a compass in his hand, as in Vermeer's paintings—at pains to measure for his lord "Whate'er the ocean pales or sky inclips" (*Ant.*, 2.7.68–69). But measurement is not an unproblematic pursuit. As in the new early modern cartography, whose discursivity Du Bellay's geographical sonnet heavily exploits, it is measurement itself that is put to the test. Rome is highlighted as a space which is not conceivable in terms of a measurable, flat geography, but rather in those of an all-encompassing round planet. You need a compass, and even so, or perhaps precisely because of the spherical circumference it draws, you have to rely on the dematerializing force of poetry to conceive the extension of the world it evokes.[12] Rome's name alone, like Antony's in Shakespeare's play, has the power needed to sustain the equivalence with the world itself. Rome stands for land and sea, and for a three-dimensional "greatness"—an incommensurability, a scale in Du Bellay's sonnet—which we may feel resonate in *Antony and Cleopatra* from the very beginning, I suggest, in the way it sets up the form of the "overflowing measure" of Antony's passion as well as the protagonists' characterization: their stature, manners, emotions, and language.[13]

Critics have often focalized the two lovers' stunning lifestyle and the search for a transcending measure for their passions as a challenge framed by a binary opposition between the two cultures of Rome and Egypt. Not without cause. The Roman order is threatened with dissolution by Egypt's "space". And the contrast is made evident by Octavius's language of measure on one side and the pair's language of excess and hyperbole on the other.[14] In parallel, however, starting from the discovery of the play's "multilinearity" which brought Ernest Schanzer (1963) to propose the play's inclusion in the group of the "problem plays", and continuing with Janet Adelman's critical move (*The Common Liar*, 1973) which powerfully highlighted the play's structure as one marked by "the achievement of simultaneous perspectives" and "uncertainty of judgement", the play has been increasingly addressed by paying attention more to blurred polarities than unambiguous oppositions.[15] As Coppélia Kahn has insightfully observed in resuming this debate, "To view the play, then, as organized by the contrast of independently constituted cultural value systems is to ignore the profound bias at work in the construction of that opposition *per se*".[16] Indeed in *Antony and Cleopatra*, a central issue is the way in which the two paradigms of contrast and interaction are coexistent in defining the space as well as the language of the play, historically overdetermined as they are by an imperially prevailing, Rome-centred culture and the struggle for power within it between Antony and Octavius. In fact, one might say that the oppositional dynamic is in many respects less a contrast between the two cultures of Rome and Egypt than one between the two Romes represented by Antony and Octavius. Significantly, Antony's death is lamented as a loss of specularity on the part of the winning Octavius. When obliged by the mirror metaphor introduced by Maecenas ("When such a spacious mirror's set before him, / He needs must see himself"), he (Octavius) admits: "O Antony . . . We could not stall together / in the same world. But yet let me lament / With tears as sovereign as the blood of hearts / That thou, my brother, my competitor / In top of all design, my mate in empire, / Friend and companion in the front of war, / The arm of mine own body, and the heart / Where mine his thoughts did kindle, that our stars, / Unreconciliable, should divide / Our equalness to this"

(5.1.34–48). The more the greatness of Rome is emphasized, the smaller its space becomes for the rival (but equally insatiable) ambition of the two male "brotherly" competitors: quite an intricacy of sameness and otherness within the same Rome, or "difference within *virtus*" in Kahn's homosocial reading of the play.[17] In this Octavius's encomium of Antony reveals its encapsulated, fratricidal legend which stands at the origins of Rome. It also refers us to their common condition of elective or adoptive sons in relation to Julius Caesar, in Adelman's psychic-analytical understanding of the play. In such a typically Roman masculine story of male bonds and fatherly lineage, the critic has insightfully argued, "Cleopatra turns out to be oddly inessential", and the insisted "official Roman line—that Antony was destroyed by Cleopatra's entrapment—begins to look like a cover-up", a way of inhibiting the memory of a father-like heroic figure. So much so that "if Cleopatra had not been there, Caesar's Rome would have had to invent her too".[18] Indeed, the Egyptian queen's Otherness functions as an expedient if pivotal triangulation in the play's mimetic logic of desire, as we might say borrowing from the Girardian "theatre of envy":[19] a triangulation that complicates with a powerful gender (or transgender) mark any clear-cut binarism that the play may seem to state, and makes it explode in its tragic dimension, as well as the possibilities it lays bare in reinterpreting the book of history with the heretic voice of a woman.

What concerns me primarily in the context of this volume is to readdress the hyperbolic world imagery of the play in the light of the belated Renaissance view of Rome's imperial space, and hence the way early modern Rome's discursivity permeates Antony's ruinous grandeur as both a challenge to Rome and a mark of Romanness. As mentioned, Shakespeare relies on Plutarch's *Lives* for this. But Rome in early modern culture was a topical reference in connection with themes of imperial pride and excess, vanity and ruin, time and decay, eternity and mutability: a set of topics which take centre stage in the poetics of his sonnets (see 65) and which, charged with contemporary moral judgement, emerge with dramatic force in *Antony and Cleopatra*.

The dramatic contraposition between Egypt and Rome is soon introduced by Philo's puritan opening lines on one hand, and Antony's defiant "Here is my space" (1.1.35) on the other; the latter reiterated in the ensuing act as "I'th' East my pleasure lies" (2.3.39). But the polarization of the two geographies of Rome and Egypt—the former standing as often said for measure and temperance, the latter for overflowing dissipative pleasure—is strategic: for the playwright from the very outset of the play consistently undoes with a plurality of voices what—through Octavius's monological gaze, but not only—he exceedingly constructs as an unsurmountable difference. Meaningfully, Shakespeare tries his most to give Octavius reason for maintaining the line between Rome and Egypt. Deviating considerably from Plutarch's "Life of Antony", a widely read stuff in his times and his main source for his play, the playwright not only omits Antonius's youthful revelries in Rome and Greece, but he also sanitizes Rome's space and manners by moving all banquets to Egypt. The only exception is Miseno's extraterritorial frolic on Pompey's galley in Act 2.7, but significantly this is passed off as nothing but a *copia*, a *facsimile*, the parodied one-time performance of an Egyptian prompt book. Conversely, bacchanals are made so prevalent at Alexandria that they are tantamount to the construction of a female Oriental Otherness by which Antony's masculine Roman *virtus* is both menaced and defined. The problem is that such a revelry-free imperial Rome, if dramatically shrewd in fuelling a moralizing logic of reversals, may have sounded unlikely both to well-read theatregoers and those in the audience who were rather familiar with the fostered imagery of the imperial city as a site of prevailing debauchery and dissolution (see the ensuing section). Unless they decided that, in the economy of the play, such a teetotal Rome, all honour and Augustan coolness, could stand for a Puritan England in its post-Reformation contraposition with an immoral Egyptian Rome.

Plutarch's readers knew that in his "Life", *pace* Octavius, there is no such uncontaminated Rome, and that Antony's fondness for excess dates back to his youth, well before the encounter with Cleopatra and the discovery of his many affinities with her. In fact, prior to his campaign in Egypt, Antony was already famous in Rome for his revelries as well as his honour as a soldier, both attitudes pursued beyond limits, namely with an excess which was all too "Roman".[20] In fact, if Alexandria precipitated his fall, this didn't mean that it was at the origin of his ill-fated intemperance. In Plutarch's unbiased narrative of the couple's story, Cleopatra is Antony's "last and extreamest mischiefe of all other" (North's *Lives*, 981), not his first ruinous one.

In this I agree with those critics who point out that "Octavius's is not the only Rome we see". As observed by Janet Adelman,

> Although Octavius is the spokesman for measure, he is by no means the spokesman for the idea of Rome itself: our sense of ancient Roman virtue comes not from Octavius but from the descriptions of Antony as he used to be. And in these descriptions, Rome itself is hyperbolic.

Antony's heroic past as a soldier, epitomized by his savage, uncanny way of coping with thirst and hungriness in times of necessity (1.4.56–72), is as excessive as his life in "the Egypt of overflow". "They are both equally excessive and equally inimical to the measure Rome of the present", the critic observes.[21] As an instance of this, one could recall that power itself in imperial Rome could be hyperbolically interpreted in a way that made it coincide with its opposite: namely with an ostentatious excess of *magnanimitas*, which is precisely Antony's prevailing virtue. This is noticed by Montaigne in a brief essay entitled "Of the Roman

Greatness" where (quoting Plutarch) he underlines: "Marcus Antonius said 'The greatness of Romane people was not so much discerned by what it tooke as by what it gave'". And this, Montaigne continued, could be observed in the way they disposed of conquered kingdoms which were either "restored to those who had lost them, or presented strangers with them". The Romans, he also added relying on Tacitus, "were from all antiquity accustomed to leave those kings they had vanquished in the possession of their kingdoms under their authoritie, 'That they might have even Kings also for instruments of their bondage'".[22] In Shakespeare's play we can feel echoes of this in Dolabella's words when, in observing Antony's *débacle*, he sarcastically weighs the enormity of his fall by the diminished rank of his emissaries: a position now assigned to schoolmasters by him who "had superfluous kings for messengers" (3.12.5).

In sum, whether Shakespeare's audience was referred to Plutarch's *Lives*—which insistently underline Antony's hyperbolic proficiency in both vices and virtues (a captivating Greek eloquence among the latter)—or to an ampler early modern discursivity on Rome's grandeur, Shakespeare's hero fully responded to the profile of a person who as a Roman is used to act and think big when he arrives at the luxurious Alexandrian court. Paradoxically he is Roman enough to feel at home in Alexandria, or in other words, he is Roman enough to ignore the boundaries that it is Octavius's task to create and maintain. Indeed, Antony is nothing but faithful to his Romanness when, challenged by Cleopatra to set a perimeter for their love, he overdoes her by prospecting a scale that, as Rome's "greatness" in Du Bellay's poetry (see the quoted son. 26), projects the play's space into the sphere of the unlimited, the exceeding, the unmeasurable: "Then must thou needs find out new heaven, new earth" (1.1.17; 37).

What kind of complication does this two-faced Rome introduce in the play's basic opposition between Rome and Egypt? Certainly it is one that blurs borders and categories and allows for the audience's oscillation between judgement and fascination, suspicion and desire. In this, as I see it, the Cydnus scene in Act 2 is paradigmatic. It functions in a way that gestures towards Cleopatra's painting in Innogen's northern bedchamber.

Dissolving the logic of opposite spaces and cultures the playwright has just staged in the first act, he strategically figures out the couple's encounter, not live by choosing Antony's privileged perspective, but by making it resound through the doubly deferred and desiring tale of Enobarbus: a second Roman beholder, whose mesmerizing picture of the Egyptian queen has far travelled with him from Alexandria to Rome to become the object of a dazzled cosmopolitan Roman audience. As such his tale is invested with the force which is proper to a device of infinite repetition and multiplied appropriations. Thus—by making Cleopatra's tale travel across sea and lands—Shakespeare transforms what seems like just love at first sight into a cross-cultural and desiring encounter. It is from such a far positioned, if widening and pluralized perspective that as audience members we are made to know and remember Cleopatra and "her strong toil of grace" (5.2.347). It is no coincidence that this is defined by "infinite variety" (2.2.246), variety being less Cleopatra's quality, as it has been argued by Harris, than an effect "created by a panoply of subject-position" in the play's "process of narcissistic displacement" and never wholly satisfied desire.[23] It is by skilfully deferring sight, voice, and judgement, or better by keeping them always on the move on the spaciousness of the world's stage, that the playwright, here as elsewhere in the play, undoes the contraposition he seems to state between Rome and Egypt. In fact, if Octavius's propaganda is at pains to create borders by Egyptianizing Antony's excess and ruin, Enobarbus—together with the play's formidable mass of messengers, envoys, scrolls, dispatches, letters—interfaces Egypt and Rome with a tale, or tales, which stealthily unfasten rigidity with a chain of fascination which allows and stands for continuing displacement, repetition, and difference: or *différance* in Derrida's acceptation.[24]

"Kingdoms Are Clay!": Allegories of the World's Inconstancy

As Hazlitt observed, *Antony and Cleopatra* is "the finest of [Shakespeare's] historical plays, that is, of those in which he made poetry the organ of history".[25] This is also the play, I argue, in which ruins, by which I intend their resilience as a deconstructive agency, are more forcefully part of such a poetry.

Meaningfully, the two lovers' passion both defies and complies with the early modern view of Rome as an allegory of the "World's Inconstancy", a view which, as discussed in my Introduction, was epitomized by the drowning force of the Tiber "hastening to his Fall": Rome's only remain in Du Bellay's sonnet 3, and a reminder, "That which is firm, doth flit and fall away / And that is flitting, doth abide and stay", 11–14). "Let Rome in Tiber melt, and the wide arch / Of the ranged empire fall! / Here is my space! / Kingdoms are clay!" we hear resounding early in the play (1.1.34–36)[26] in Antony's mouth, with an expression in which the jubilatory and long emphasized "Here is my space" is encapsulated within an often overlooked meditation on decay, or sceptical awareness of an ontological impermanence. From a dramatic point of view, this has been introduced a few verses earlier by Philo's bathetic image of Antony as the shaky "triple pillar of the world transformed / Into a strumpet fool". This is all the play is about for levelheaded minds: a fool's ruin for effect of a strumpet (and/or fortune). "Behold and see", Philo forewarns (1.1.12–13).

And yet Philo's classic marble image, later resumed by Octavius's "three-nooked world" (4.6.6)—suggesting a three-pillared round architecture, a temple—is in tune with the overall grandeur of the play. Cleopatra seems to be equally eager to give up her Egypt for love: "Melt Egypt into Nile, and kindly creatures / Turn all to serpents!" (2.5.78–79), she rails echoing Antony's imagery of the catastrophes of nations, amply visualized in contemporary emblems. Images of liquefaction and down-razing calamities occur again, hyperbolically, when at the moment of misfortune, Cleopatra does not hesitate to figure out petrified storms of acid hail, that may dissolve her together with her Egyptian progeny and subjects (3.13.164–72). In this they seem to be both imbued with the poet's "fearful" meditation on "devouring" time and collapsing architectures, as they paradoxically ground in a self-destructive *voluptas* of the end the construction of an enduring personal myth of transcendence.[27]

As in our contemporary Mitoraj's defaced sculptures, permanently exhibited in Pompey's ancient city (see also Figure 0.1, internal title page), Antony and Cleopatra seem to enjoy the condition of triumphant ghostly visitors conjured up to repeat their story forever on the background of a landscape of ruins.

Differently from *Titus*'s unburied and "lamentable" bodies, they are indeed constructed as the epitome and the protracted spectacle of both majestic ruin and self-monumentalizing transcendence. They are "the perdurability and eternity of ruins, their victory on the inexorable flow of time", we might say borrowing a language which has been used to suggestively define Rome itself and the city's paradigmatic ruin, the Coliseum, ever since Bede's times perceived as "a gigantic wreck continuously dying,

Figure 6.1 Igor Mitoraj (1944–2014), bronze sculptures

Source: Photo Luca Pizzi, courtesy of Atelier Mitoraj

and yet . . . still alive".[28] They also seem to represent in full the Renaissance emergent archaeological understanding of past civilizations as an instance of discontinuous and ruinous temporality, an awareness which corrodes at the root the assertion, "Here is my space", and makes heroic, as well as tragic, their search for a place where *to stay*. Antony's "Kingdoms are clay" is one with the poet's "fearful meditation" on ruins (son. 62). It is also one with Lucrece's meditation on Time as an all-encompassing altering agency: "Time's glory is . . . / To ruinate proud buildings with thy hours, / And smear with dust their glitt'ring golden towers; / To fill with worm-holes stately monuments, / To feed oblivion with decay of things, / To blot old books and alter their contents" (*The Rape*, vv. 939–48).

Antony's is the disordering time of archaeology, the form that it assumes in its ruination, when "Time in time shall ruinate" (Du Bellay/Spenser, 7.10). In this light the play's time—often accelerated to the point of its pulverization—appears, indeed, as that of a humanity urged as well as in "war with time" (Shakespeare, son. 15.13). As argued by many, time has a special importance in the play. For Tony Tanner, "time and place move and change so quickly that the whole world seems in a 'hurry' and in a state of flux—fluid, melting, re-forming".[29] For David Kaula, dramatic action develops "at almost confusing speed". "The turbulent flux of events is matched, on the human side, by the instability of desire". And on the longer course of history, it encompasses Antony's past, Cleopatra's present, and Octavius's future:[30] a conflated and overlapping archaeological temporality to my view which accounts for the insecure status of action, language, and feelings. Montaigne's *Essays* had been made available in English by Florio's 1603 translation. And the philosopher's sceptical rewriting of the Roman concepts of constancy and inconstancy, which had brought him to think that mutability could be a virtue as well as a motif of fall, had certainly a part in Shakespeare's play. *Antony and Cleopatra*, Shakespeare's "most Montaignian play", Geoffrey Miles has observed, "shows a world in which Roman constancy dissolves into flux, and the mutability of the outside world is matched by the mercurial changes of the characters' mind".[31] But *Titus Andronicus*'s anachronistic ruined monastery bears witness to the fact that the physical sight of ruins is as much inspiring to Shakespeare's imagination as the coeval reflection on impermanence and its development into a new philosophy. Arguably, their conjoined epistemic pressure is crucial in making the ruin of Shakespeare's Egyptian-Roman pair stand, so consistently and emblematically, as an unsettling menace and destabilizing agency in Octavius's imposed universal order.[32] Namely at the moment of Rome's apical parable, when prophetically (in Virgil's *Aeneid*, VI.851–3) and teleologically (in Horace's *Odes*, IV.14, 15), Octavius was turning into the imperially pacifying Caesar Augustus.[33]

"The time of universal peace is near", Octavius Caesar says in Act 4, before the final battle which decides of his destiny as the only master of the world, "Prove this prosp'rous day, the three-nooked world / Shall bear the olive freely" (4.6.5–7). It is in the face of such an underwritten Virgilian assurance (and Horacian sanction) that Shakespeare devotes a good part of Act 4 and the whole fifth act of his play "to do that thing that ends all other deeds / Which shackles accidents and bolts up change" (5.2.4–6), namely to deploy the two lovers' art of dying, a protracted if partly ironic interminable dying however—"O make an end" (4.14.106)—which dramaturgically "labours" at their sacralized spectralization (e.g. durability). "Now all labour / Mars what it does – yea, very force entangles / Itself with strength: Seal then, and all is done: / Eros! – I come, my queen. – Eros! – Stay for me. / Where souls do couch on flowers we'll hand in hand / And with our sprightly port make the ghosts gaze. / Dido and her Aeneas shall want troops, / And all the haunt be ours. Come Eros! Eros! (4.14.48–55), Shakespeare has Antony say, word playing with "Mars" and "mar". Indeed Shakespeare's Antony seems to be determined to conjure up all the strength he mythically shares with the demi-god Hercules in Plutarch's *Lives* (North's Plutarch, 999) to "mar" its own force, or else paradoxically construct his ruin as an enduring "haunting" status for him and Cleopatra, hereafter an anti-Virgilian competing couple in the pagan Pantheon and its world of shadows.[34]

This he achieves according to a logic which undoes what is done. And yet in its protracted undoing, it does, or else does by undoing, like Cleopatra's refreshing fans in the Cydnus synesthetic scene, where "what they undid did" (2.2.15), and in the same way in which Cleopatra's love famously "makes hungry / where most she satisfies" (2.2.47–48). Everything in *Antony and Cleopatra* seems to be strengthened by its opposite. Everything functions according to a logic which undoes what is done and vice versa, namely according to a chiastic figure of speech which establishes itself as an overall figure of thought in the play, one which "gives one value to one side of the opposition only to load it with the value to which it had been initially been opposed".[35] Signalled by a structuring returning syntax grounded on chiastic inversion and reciprocity, it actually affirms itself as a pattern of overlapping construction and deconstruction, a conceptual paradigm, which we are forced to recognize as the defining rhythm of desire, passions, and action, a dynamism which from beginning to end in the play sets the pace of life in its indissoluble relation with death. Indeed, this is the movement which defines the way meaning itself is produced in the play, characterized as it is by a continuous mirroring and chiastic reversal of one opinion into another, one term into another. Cleopatra welcomes it as a "well-divided disposition!", "O heavenly mingle" (1.5.56, 62), she concedes, when she gets to know that this is Antony's way during his negotiation with Octavius far in Rome. He swings between opposite but nonexclusive feelings, in a messenger's (Alexas) report. So much so that paradoxically he is neither this nor that: "Like to the time o'th' year between the extremes / Of hot and cold, he was not sad and not merry" (1.5.54–55); a very Montaignian state-ment[36] which can be also taken, self-reflexively, as a consideration on the play's generic status itself, oscillating between the extremes of tragedy and comedy.

We may well view such an unresolved movement as the rhythm of impermanence, an ontological if vital instability which both complies with and resists change and which courts and absorbs the end ("that thing that ends all other deeds", 5.2.5) as a possibility of a "marble-constant" fixity and eternity.[37] In the last two acts, this becomes the defining movement of the "labour" the two lovers accomplish in order that they may ghostly eternize their ruin. "She looks like sleep", Octavius Caesar acknowledges on Cleopatra's dead body at the end of the play, "As she would catch another Antony / In her strong toil of grace" (5.2.345–47). Interestingly, if differently, the playwright had similarly taken a long dramatic time to work at Julius Caesar's transformation into a spectralized figure of heritage.

Van Der Noot's Apocalypse

But let us pause for a moment on the two lovers' hyperbolic envisaging and enacting of their earthly and transcending "world", a world which, surprisingly, Antony has prospected at the outset of the play with due Roman grandeur, but in displacing biblical terms. In fact, before show-ing the extent to which Cleopatra—as the worthy queen of an anterior hegemonic Egypt—can outdo Antony in this, Shakespeare has assigned to "her Roman" the task of setting a "measure": a measure which "nobly", for Antony, consists in a denial of measure. "There's beggary in the love that can be reckoned", he says, magnanimously. And Cleopatra: "I'll set a bourn how far to be beloved". "Then thou needs find out new heaven, new earth" (1.1.15–17) Antony rebounds, anachronistically transferring the notion of "greatness" traditionally associated with Rome into the visionary transcendence of the verses from Revelation (21:1). What a leap for Shakespeare's audience at the very outset of a Roman play! The quotation, as mentioned, has been variously commented on as an oblique reference to the discoveries of the Renaissance new geography, as well the astronomic infinitude of the universe philosophically envisioned by Giordano Bruno.

But what about the relation with Rome? The congruity was revealed to me by the earlier discussed *Theatre for Voluptious Worldlings* by Van Der Noot (see my Introduction, pp. 33–34), the illustrated and popular miscellany of verses on *vanitas*, which included Du Bellay's visionary son-nets on Rome (*Songe*) anonymously Englished by Spenser. In Van Der Noot's comment, Rome's ruins, as already was the case but less militantly in the Catholic Du Bellay's imagination, received a strengthened moral-izing treatment. The illustrated catastrophe of Rome's greatness elicited a meditation on world's vanities and divine retribution, grounded in a biblically feminized and chastised contraposition between the earthly and the heavenly city, the old and the new Jerusalem, the "prostitute" and the "chaste spouse". The chastisement found its eschatological climax in the collection's added Revelation sonnets (perhaps by Noot, or Spenser himself), and especially in the final one: a sonnet specifically devised to replace the original last sonnet that in Du Bellay's *Songe* hermetically alluded to the 1527 sack of Rome, with Saint Joan's prophecy of a "new Earth, new Heauen". Here are the first four lines:

> I Saw new Earth, new Heauen, sayde Saint Iohn.
> And loe, the sea (quod he) is now no more.
> The holy Citie of the Lorde, from hye
> Descendeth garnisht as a loued spouse.[38]

In the framework of Van Der Noot's collection, this last sonnet enforced with overheated moral evaluations its religious side and its specific Protestant concern with Rome's myth of greatness and ruins. But it is precisely for this reason, I argue, that it may have proved inspiring to a playwright who was working at his *Antony and Cleopatra* and its exceedingly controversial eponymous protagonists. In front of a prospective audience which was more than probably familiar with Van Der Noot's *Theatre*, the overt association between Rome and the punitive eschatology of the holy scriptures may have been challenging. It offered the possibility of obliquely encapsulating an inflamed morality while concomitantly deflating it by an overturned use of the famous prophecy. In this, Shakespeare strikingly departed from other coeval dramatic renderings of Cleopatra's story. In fact, with his elliptical recontextualizing reuse of the famous biblical verses, the playwright outstrips the morality of opposites (announced in Philo's opening utterance), and right from the outset of his play, in the span of four lines (1.1.14–17), transforms the contraposition into hyperbolic continuity: the blasphemous if jubilatory continuity of one world into the other, of one city into the other, according to a drive which was proper to Rome's all-too-earthly city and the proud and highly symbolic upward tension of its architecture. As Great Babylon's "sharped steeples high shot up on ayre" (Du Bellay/Spenser, *Ruines of Rome*, son. 2.2), Rome's architecture was alike typically fantasized as competing with the sky, in early modern Rome's discursivity ("She whose high top above the starres did sore" (son. 4.1).

From now onwards, Shakespeare's audience is asked to cope with a play which is marked by a reshuffled moral perspective and with a space aiming at enacting in the here and now of the play the transfiguration of the earthly city (whether it is Rome, Alexandria, or both) into a complicated earthly/holy city. Indeed the apocalypse consists in the transformation of love into a mystique, or else sexuality into a "blessed" rite

(2.2.248–50), a destabilizing reversal which subtly eschews the regime of surveillance entailed in the kind of literature epitomized by Van Der Noot's collection. In sum, whether we decide to consider this collection a direct or an indirect thought-provoking source, it is certainly one which demands our attention as a co-textual coincidence, and in terms of the play's problematized interaction with Puritan topics of vanity, ruins, and symbolic geographies.

Writing of the desiring and desired female body in Jacobean theatre in a way in which sexuality is not separated from politics, Tennenhouse has conjured up Bakhtin's notion of the grotesque body to address the inter-rogation it raises in relation to the resurgent masculinity of the court in James's reign. In the context of what he calls "the theater of punishment", Cleopatra's sexual body is constructed as an essentially other and external "source of pollution", a Bakhtinian carnivalesque body, "the antithesis to aristocratic power", and a "threat to the body politic": the epitome of a polluted and punished body in the reinstated patriarchal order of James I.[39] On the backdrop of paradigmatic visions of violently opposed moral worlds, however, Shakespeare creates the space of "simultaneous perspec-tives" brought to the fore by Adelman: the dramatic enlarged space where Cleopatra's kaleidoscopic set of images (Egyptian, Roman, enchantress, gipsy, strumpet, whore, actress, soldier, loved and loving spouse, mother) as well as Antony's mingled body (Roman, Egyptian, soldier, lover, colos-sus, strumpet's fool, reveller, husband) can be put in play.

A&C's Hyperbolic (Postal) Space

"The structure of *Antony and Cleopatra* is the structure of paradox and hyperbole", Janet Adelman has observed in defining the language of the play, and the act of belief it requires, as it appeals "to our doubt". "Only the contradictions of paradox" are capable of expressing the "contradic-tions of love", she argues. But "in embracing contradictions, love tran-scends the limits of the intellect and of reality as the intellect normally perceives it: and no figure more vehemently asserts this transcendence than hyperbole".[40] That "the hyperbolic" also belongs to the world the lovers inhabit has become a truism over the years. But which world, whose world? is still worth asking. "World" is a word which amounts to 42 occurrences in *Antony and Cleopatra*, the highest count in Shakespeare's Roman canon—and more than in *Julius Caesar* where it occurs 16 times. "These thick-scattered 'world' references all suggest imperial magnificence and human grandeur", Wilson Knight wrote years ago. "The setting is not, in fact, our little world at all: it is either (i) the Mediterranean empire idealized beyond all rational limits; or (ii) the universe". Knight is not concerned in contextualizing all that much Shakespeare's hyperbolic space and language. But nobody better than he has so unconditionally extolled the unlimited vision of *Antony and Cleopatra* and the role played by the joined imagery of "world" and "sea" in the transfiguring action of the play, or its "ascending scale", as he phrases it.

> Continued reference to the sea helps to vitalize this effect. Like so many images here it serves a complex purpose: it enlarges, varies, and enriches our geographical vision. Adds light to glisten with other more concrete symbols of scintillating brilliance; and, finally, with other elements—earth, air, fire—it stresses the play's peculiarly universal scope.[41]

Caroline Spurgeon's remarks are in the same vein:

> The group of images in *Antony and Cleopatra* which, on analysis, immediately attracts attention as peculiar to this play, consists of images of the world, the firmament, the ocean and vastness generally. That is the dominating note in the play, magnificence and grandeur, expressed in many ways, and pictured by continually stimulating our imaginations to see the colossal figure of Antony;

a "vastness of scale" for the critic, and a suggestiveness of the play's imagery which foretells a quality which will be at the core of "romantic" art.[42] Others equally interested in the world theme envisage a distinction in the use of the world image—"the most general pattern of imagery in the play" for Charney—which establishes an opposition between the lovers' symbolic and infinite world identified by Egypt and a material, quantitative world represented by the Roman Empire.[43] Right, but only in so far as we take this as a provisional statement, ready to be readjusted by the fact that geographical greatness and self-destructive *hýbris* were of a piece with the myth of Rome in early modern perception. Shakespeare is no exception when we consider that the impulse at transgressing physical and symbolic boundaries in his play is as Roman as its counterbalancing Augustan values of countenance and temperance.

This makes us return to Plutarch's "Life of Antony", Shakespeare's main source for his cross-cultural love story. With its profuse enumeration of Western and Eastern territories insisting on the Mediterranean and beyond, Plutarch's is not just a "Life". It also provides a geography of the imperial Rome which hints at a cosmopolitan dilated world, an uncontained and mobile space of clashing as well as co-habiting diversity which confirmed the current image of Rome as *urbs et orbis*.[44] The play largely capitalizes on this in providing a map of the imperial Rome whose hugeness is underscored by the overwritten and uninterrupted come and go of kings, legions, generals, and their emissaries: the movement of history in its making. But routes and borders are continually redesigned by such a movement, and the circulation of persons and language brings to the fore the question of communication and manipulation. As well known, "The expanding empire was marked out and defined by the construction of roads". Their role was pivotal in ensuring "military control, communication and administration".[45] Interestingly, Montaigne showed his interest for ancient empires' postal systems in a short note entitled "Of Running Posts, or Couriers". What attracted him was speed and readiness, the way post rested "on stations to be set up. And men to have fresh horses ready for al such as came to him. And some report this swift kind of running answereth the flight of cranes".[46]

Shakespeare seems to be well aware of the richness and risks to which language was exposed in what we would, nowadays, call a global world. In fact in *Antony and Cleopatra* (and to some extent in *Cymbeline* too), he insistently dramatizes Rome's space as a postal space, the space of omnipresent messengers and interconnective correspondence, envoys, and reports, but also the problematized space of equivocation and provisional truth. Rightly, the play's conspicuous number of messengers has not gone unnoticed. In fact, they feature as a real dramatic persona. In Adelman's subtle and inspiring interpretation, they are an instance of the play's "breakdown in direct and reliable communication".[47] For Macdonald they are "an empty conduit for the flow of information" all too ready, however, to transform themselves into active and malleable producers of complacent and delusive meaning in the tangle of unstable communicative acts that characterizes the play.[48] But in our digital era it is also tantalizing to look at messengers as an instance of the play's double geography: a physical one made up of identifying borders and names, and a second incorporeal one, made up of a trespassing network of messages and the alienation which is peculiar to fluid and disembodied language. In such a landscape of hyper-connective if intermediated language, which is peculiar to our global digitalized world, feelings themselves undergo the triangulation and unreliability of the indirect message. This is revealed dazzlingly and beautifully in the play, when Cleopatra's attendant Alexas (coming from Antony) is asked to guarantee for the truth of the general's proffered affection: "His speeche sticks in my heart", he swears. And Cleopatra: "Mine ear must pluck it thence" (1.5.43–44). Ear and heart must struggle to align themselves with language, or more precisely with the scenario of reported speech which, as highlighted by Adelman, characterizes the play.

Rome's huge geography, which in the expanding imperial Rome was held together by its formidable and highly symbolic network of roads, in Shakespeare's play is pervaded by an anxiety of connection and "misaligned"[49] language, manipulated dispatches, self-falsified reports, creating comedy as well as tragedy. Inspired by Derrida, we might say that the play's language flirts (as already in *Titus*) with the volatile condition of the "envoy" that the philosopher explores in *The Postcard*: the message of agents (addressers and addressees) "accustomed to the movement of the posts . . . and to everything that they authorize as concerns falsehoods, fictions, pseudonyms, homonyms, or anonyms".[50] The movement authorizes for everything, namely for all manner of substitution and troubled destination which define the Derridean scene of writing (and inspiration), for him the scene of a "repeated" word, the word "inspired by an *other* voice", which as such is also the scene of theft, manipulation, and difference.[51] Misalignment reaches its tragic apex with Mardian's false information of Cleopatra's death. But it also includes the regret of omitted and never dispatched messages, I would add: the message that Octavia has never addressed, to announce her return to Rome, and which her brother Octavius has never received, causing him to experience a moment of imperially "ostentated" and yet touching brotherly care, a regret for failed hospitality with its embedded sentiments of longing and expectancy, in every sense unique in the context of his typical unemotional disposition. Caesar's sister and "The wife of Antony", he says lamenting Octavia's solitary voyage,

> Should have an army for an usher, and
> The neighs of horse to tell of her approach
> Long ere she did appear. The trees by th' way
> Should have borne men, and expectation fainted,
> Longing for what it had not. Nay, the dust
> Should have ascended to the roof of heaven,
> Raised by your populous troops. But you are come
> A market maid to Rome, and have prevented
> The ostentation of our love which, left unshown,
> Is often left unloved. We should have met you
> By sea and land, supplying every stage
> With an augmented greeting.
>
> (3.6.44–66)

The emotional as well as the public life of those who are in power theatricalizes itself in palaces as well as, conspicuously, along the populated highways (or sea routes) that connect the imperial space, designing a map which is defined by the speed of galloping horses and the incessant dubious plotting of the messengers. In this, readiness and alertness is all, as for Hamlet. Shakespeare's *theatrum mundi* requires that the audience collaborates in such a live and mobile weaving of space and meaning.

The early modern perception of Rome as a quintessential "greatness" is not a minor problem when we come to performance and the staging of the play's fluid spatiality which, as often said by critics, is hardly containable in a succession of linear clear-cut scenes. "Space, in particular, is managed with such elasticity in Shakespeare's playtext", Maddalena Pennacchia observes, "that it seems to 'overflow the measure' of the stage—the action shifting from one corner of the Mediterranean to the other—as if heralding its future treatment in a medium yet unborn: cinema".[52] If anything, such a peculiarity of the play has certainly fostered a more sophisticated way of using the space of the stage, which in the last century has been increasingly consonant with the evocativeness allowed by the round and empty space which characterized the Elizabethan and the (not for long) Jacobean theatres. Take the amplifying effects created by the use of a cyclorama in the pioneering 1922 Old Vic production, or the circular suggestiveness of revolving platforms, as it was in the 1951 New York production directed by Michael Benthall, and in the recent 2018 British National Theatre staging of the play directed by Simon Godwin, with Sophie Okonedo and Ralph Fiennes in the title roles. Here the stage was occupied by a round platform manoeuvred as if it were a revolving door. It made actors move rapidly through the play's shifting main scenarios of a marble-cold efficient Rome and the enveloping honey-warm cromatism of Alexandria, while allowing freedom for imagining the imperial spaciousness of the Mediterranean world which we relentlessly hear evoked in the play: a space which actually stands for the world *tout court* and whatever the "sky inclips" (*Ant.*, 2.7.69). Perhaps complying with the pervading world theme and the continuity of an undivisible world map, the only available printed text, the 1623 Folio edition, has just one act-scene division: *Act Primus. Scaena Prima.*

Antony and Cleopatra's performance history, at least until the opening of the twentieth century, is one of dissatisfying adaptations, eager as they were to meet the increasing realism of the theatre scenery and especially in the nineteenth century. Such a pretence of realistically coping with the play's fluidity of locations and their unstable relation with the characters on stage has long been dropped, fostered by Granville-Baker's influential *Preface* (1930), and later studies of the play underpinned by a growing understanding of the Elizabethan and Jacobean stagecraft and its symbolic rather than realistic use of space.[53] Twentieth-century dramatic aesthetics—from the principle of continuous staging notably foregrounded by Granville-Barker, to stylized multiple settings, up to modern notions of "empty space" (Brook)—has very much contributed to favour an evocative enactment of the play's world theme.

Rome: World and Tomb

As Gillies has pointed out in considering the inseparable association of theatre and world maps in late-sixteenth-century atlas titles, *"theatrum"* is not "an idle metaphor. . . . Ortelius derives the figurative logic of his 'theatre' from the deep relationship between geography and history". In fact he "established that geography is the 'eye of history' . . . an all-seeing *eye* commanding the spatial and temporal immensities of history". But this was made evident only in the *Parergon* which Ortelius added to the ensuing editions of his 1570 *Theatre of the World*—a supplement with histories of expeditions, peregrination, travels, shifting nations, "things done . . . as if they were at this time present and in doing"—in the author's words, designed, as Gillies remarks, "to tell the reader as much about peoples and heroic *characters* as about places". In this, in spectacularizing its discoveries as well as (iconically) its protagonists and their toolboxes, the "new" geography showed to be "conscious of having exploded ancient paradigms".[54]

Antony and Cleopatra's spaciousness seems to be shaken by the same explosion. Indeed the play makes us experience Plutarch's geography of imperial Rome as a space of shifting geopolitics, contacts, negotiations and conflicts, ambitions, power and misfortune, but also—nourished by the euphoria of the early modern discovery of geographic and astronomic new worlds—a Renaissance world map which weaves itself with a movement that cartographically continually readjusts and rewrites itself. Or, said otherwise: a world continually doing and undoing its form and boundaries, as "water is in water" we might say, borrowing from the mocking "pageant" of figures designed by the clouds that Antony catches sight of at the moment of his fall (4.14.2–11).

In fact, this is also a world aware of its vulnerability and imminent catastrophe, a world imagined in the mythologizing terms of an unlimited "greatness" which, precisely for this reason, was deeply disturbed by the vertigo or anxiety of its collapse. This was a matter of reflection in Augustan times and a matter of concern in Shakespeare's England. It is no coincidence, as Camden reminds us, that the historical Octavius Caesar himself—the "universal" *per antonomasia*—in considering whether it was expedient to invade Britannia,

> seemeth of purpose, and with good advise . . . as Tacitus saith, that is . . . safest for the State, *That the Romane Empire should be kept, & held within bounds* . . . set by nature, to the end it might be a State Adamantine . . . that is invincible; and lest, as a ship of exceeding great bulke, it might not possibly be well governed and managed, but endangered through the own unweldy hugeness sinke anone, and fall down at once, which usually befalleth unto over great States.
>
> (*Brit 1*, 39)

Does Enobarbus's desecrating and bathetic image of Antony as a "leaky" ship at the unhappy moment of his misfortune draw from here (3.13.67–70)? And also: could we perceive in this a further relationship with Cleopatra's insistence on Antony's unwieldy "heaviness" during the protracted and cumbersome dying scene (4.7–42)?

Shakespeare captures all the dialectical and dramatic relevance of Rome's huge and potentially ruinous dimension in the way he makes it interact, as a shaping rhetoric, with the story of his two lovers. For what they stand for in Shakespeare's play is the world, an enlarged and spacious world as that which could be fantasized by contemporary Renaissance men and women and which the imperial Rome, with its *urbs* and *orbis* discursivity, made it possible to stage.[55] They have the "greatness" of the world and the aura of demigods and goddesses (Atlas, Hercules, Venus, Isis) in the play's incessant process of mythmaking (see 1.5.24; 2.2.210; 3.6.16–18). Indeed as in contemporary anthropomorphized maps (see for all Münster's "Cosmographia", or also Elizabeth's Ditchley Portrait), they are both body and geography. And together, in their (Octavius's) abhorred transgendering fusion, they represent the very idea of a cosmic (Platonic) wholeness: "[Antony] is not more manlike / Than Cleopatra, nor the Queen of Ptolomy / more womanly than he" (1.4.5–7). But what Antony and Cleopatra also stand for is the excess of world which exposes them to their fall.

If "world" is a word which amounts to more than 40 occurrences in Shakespeare's play, "fall" (in association with world) occurs some 20 times, as both a noun and a conjugated verb: more than in *Julius Caesar* where the lemma appears 11 times, and more than in any other Roman play. World and ruin are the two sides of the same coin, in the sense that the extension of the protagonists' world defines the size of their life and desire as well as their fall, according to a principle of "proportion" majestically and knowingly announced by Cleopatra when at the news of Antony's death, she claims, "comforts we despise. Our size of sorrow, / Proportioned to our cause, must be as great / As that which makes it" (4.15.4–6). Ruins speaks for Rome's greatness and vice versa in Renaissance culture. In this the two lovers' destiny well catalyzes the early modern perception of ancient Rome as a map of the world, as well as the map of its ruins, the map of a greatness that sinks under the weight of its own age and weight.

Let us take Du Bellay/Spenser's sonnet 29, one of the last in *The Ruines of Rome* collection:

> All that which Aegypt whilome did devise,
> All that which Greece their temples to embrave,
> After th' Ionicke, Atticke, Doricke guise,
> Or Corinth, skill'd in curious workes to grave;
> All that Lysippus practike arte could forme,
> Apelles Wit, or Phidias his skill,
> Was wont this ancient Citie to adorne,
> And the heaven it selfe with her wide wonders fill;
> All that which Athens ever brought forth strange,
> All that which Asie ever had of prise,
> Was here to see. O mervelous great change!
> *Rome living, was the worlds sole ornament;*
> *And dead, is now the worlds sole moniment.*
>
> (my emphasis)

Rome is here viewed as a world which defiantly exceeds the measure of the earth with the aspiring verticality of its beauties. It is also understood

as a unique example of a universal city, a cosmopolitan inclusive hugeness, the equivalent of what we would nowadays call a globalized world.[56]
Its space is defined by the hyperbolic enormity of its extension, the variety
of cultures, the palimpsestic richness of previous hegemonic civilizations
that it has culturally incorporated—the Greek and the Egyptian first of all.
But its greatness is also defined by the enormity of its fall: the "mervelous
great change", by whose effect "the World's sole Ornament" is now "the
World's sole Moniment", a wonder in itself, the spectacular sight of a
self-devouring pride, as Du Bellay writes in sonnet 3, a void, which stands
for the "World's Inconstancy".

Rome, for Du Bellay and Renaissance Europe, is the world's monumental sepulchre, or as we might say according to the Humanist excavating
episteme (discussed in this volume's Introduction), the entombed archive
of the World.

> She, whose high top above the starres did sore,
> One foot on Thetis, th' other on the Morning,
> One hand on Scythia, th' other on the More,
> Both heaven and earth in roundnesse compassing,
> Jove fearing, lest if she should greater growe,
> The old Giants should once again uprise,
> Her whelm'd with hills, these seven Hills, which be nowe
> Tombes of her greatnes, which did threate the skies.
>
> (son. 4.1–8)

Du Bellay's ancient Rome is here imagined as a colossus stretching its
body across an unlimited geography: a cosmos. It is also a punished body,
a corpse, an anatomy archaeologically buried under its own "greatness"
and its own trespassed natural geographical edges (the Seven Hills). Sonnet after sonnet in Du Bellay's collection, Rome displays its myth as the
story of unappeased ambition and infringement of boundaries—of city,
world, sky—and pride buried under the debris of the natural *termini* it
has sacrilegiously challenged to its very limits.

It will be Cleopatra's task in Shakespeare's Roman-Egyptian play to
officiate the burial of such a cumbersome world/body. By which I intend
to suggest that the coeval discursivity of Rome's ruins may have played a
no lesser role in providing the world-size dimension of Shakespeare's protagonists as well as in conceiving the *grand* tonality of the play. Mostly,
it may have proved inspiring in conceiving Cleopatra's sumptuous dream,
when left alone on the stage of History represented by Octavius—now the
only Lord of the world—hers is the posthumous duty of taking care of
Antony's memory. Which she does with a blazon which is indeed "past the
size of dreaming". Framed by the disproportioned cosmographic incipit,
it maintains intact the heroic proportion between body and world, or
cosmos associated with Rome.

His face was as the heavens, and therein stuck
A sun and moon which kept her course and lighted
The little O, the earth.
. . .

His legs bestrid the ocean; his reared arm
Crested the world; his voice was propertied
As all tuned spheres, and that to friends;
But when he meant to quail and shake the orb,
He was as rattling thunder. For his bounty,
There was no winter in't; an autumn it was
That grew the more by reaping. His delights
Were dolphin-like: they showed his back above
The element they lived in. In his livery
Walked crowns and crownets; realms and islands
As plates dropped from his pocket.

                                                        (5.2. 81–91)

Antony has become indeed—on a par with Rome—"Whate'er the ocean pales or sky inclips" (2.7.68–69), an unsubstantial object of poetry and desire.

"The Noble Ruin of Her Magic": Cleopatra's Re-Creation of Antony

As Hazlitt trenchantly remarked in his essay on *Cymbeline*, "Posthumus is the ostensible hero of the piece, but its greatest charm is the character of Imogen. Posthumus is only interesting from the interest she takes in him".[57] We can't say exactly the same of Cleopatra and "her Roman" (as they are mentioned in *Cymbeline*, 2.4.70). Like Cleopatra, Innogen generously mythologizes her lover alive and dead by inscribing him in a classical Pantheon—he is a hero, her eagle, her Mars—no matter how undeservedly and how ironical this may sound. As has been observed, "Infinite variety of the imagination is the privilege of the lovers".[58] But if Innogen can plausibly, if unconsciously and naively, aspire to be Cleopatra, Posthumus is decidedly no Antony. For if the two men can be associated on the ground that they are both figures of mixed alliances and menaced identity, we also know that the similarity is maintainable only by excluding its implicit and conspicuous degree of irony. The theme of Cleopatra and "*her* Roman", on the contrary, is made to stand as a more complicated interpellation, as argued earlier in this chapter, in the way it proleptically gestures forward to the bedchamber of the British princess as a site of richness, dreams, and violated secrecy.

Cleopatra's dream-like blazon of *her* Antony represents the climax in a play characterized by an explosion of imagination. But it is all the more so for being part of a process of mythmaking which is brought to completion in the inviolable space of Cleopatra's magnificent sepulchral monument. Plutarch provided interesting pieces of information which may have been inspiring to Shakespeare in defining Cleopatra's monument as a female composite space of riches, inheritance, memory, and strenuously eluded surveillance:

> Cleopatra had long before made many sumptuous tombes and monuments, as well for excellencie of workemanshippe, as for height and greatness of building, ionying hard to the temple of Isis. Thither she caused to be brought all the treasure & pretious things she had of the ancient kings her predecessors: as gold, silver, emerods, pearles, ebbanie, ivorie, and sinnamon, and besides all that, a marvellous number of torches, faggots, and flaxe. So Octavius Caesar being affrayed to loose such a treasure and masse of riches, and that this woman for spight would set it a fire, and burne it every whit: he always sent some one or other unto her from him, to put her in good comfort, whilest he in the meane time drewe neere citie with his armie.
>
> (North's Plutarch, 1005)

Initially a shelter from Antony's fury, Cleopatra's monument in *Antony and Cleopatra* acquires increasing relevance as a female space of asylum and resistance, self-seclusion, surveillance, and profanation after Octavius's victory of Actium. In this context Proculeius, Dolabella, and their guards become prominent figures in the play's two last acts ("Guard her still Caesar come", 5.2.36, etc.). But so do Cleopatra's "women", who differently from Plutarch's "two women only, she had suffered to come with her into these monuments" (1006), remain numerically undefined in Shakespeare's play, as if envisaging a female choric dramaturgy for the couple's end: "Oh, see my women" (4.15.64). Ah, women, women! / Our lamp is spent, it's out" (4.15.88–89). "Ah women, women! Come, we have no friend / But resolution and the briefest end" (4.15.94–95).

As has been written, the closet in early modern culture "is constructed as a place of utter privacy, of total withdrawal from the public sphere of the household—but it simultaneously functions as a very *public* gesture of withdrawal, a very public sign of privacy", or "privacy exhibited in public".[59] One might argue that Egyptian funeral monuments represent the enactment *per antonomasia* of such a paradoxical condition: that of a publicized secrecy. Starting from Cleopatra's self-locking scene in Act 4, scene 13, Cleopatra's monument becomes the exhibited, prevailing location of the last two acts, the sumptuous architectural frame of the protagonists' death. But if the monument might be taken as an instance of a play, where the world, in Ian Kott's pessimistic appraisal, "gets smaller and smaller", actually a "gate", a prison,[60] it is also true that confinement heightens its force as space of resistance and transcendence. As Neill has remarked, Cleopatra's monument, is not confined to one of those tomb-properties that appeared in so many plays, but has expanded to encompass the entire stage—dominated by that façade which bore more than a passing resemblance to a Roman triumphal arch. It is a setting that embodies, more completely than in any other play, the idea of poetry-as-monument;[61]

a trope that Shakespeare, as earlier discussed in this volume, had exploited at length in his sonnets of immortality and most famously in sonnet 55.

In *Antony and Cleopatra* the agency of poetry as a transcending and vast monument, but also the monument as a closet, namely a tomb of secret (or should-be secret) riches and beauty, is temporally and spatially dilated in the play's two last acts, so as to coincide with the stage and hence the maximum of exposure and the maximum of suspicion and control. Cleopatra's setting also embodies Camden's cultural understanding of the "monument" (discussed earlier in my Introduction) as a token of cultural heritage in the way it enacts the conjunction of material things and the act of recollection embedded in the things remembered. Let us remember Camden' *Remains of Britain* and the composite kind of documents which makes up the list of its contents: *Languages, Names, Surnames, Allusions, Anagrams, Armories, Moneys, Impresses, Apparel, Artilleries, Wise Speeches, Proverbs, Poesies, Epitaphs*.[62] Interestingly, Cleopatra's monument is shaped as an antiquarian space, a space of collection and recollection of her ancient world, which turns into the repository of alienated objects and merchandised humanity destined to hang—as in a Mantegna's Roman triumph—on the triumphal arches (or stalls) of History as the confused and theatricalized spoils of the winner: "we, / your scutcheons [shields with coats of arms] and your signs of conquest, shall / Hang in what place you please", Cleopatra reproaches, speaking to Octavius. "This is the brief of money, plate and jewels / I am possessed of. 'Tis exactly valued, / Not petty things admitted" (5.2.133–35; 137–39), she claims lying on the conspicuous part of the treasure she has hidden, but which is anything but concealed from Octavius's absolute eye when servants are all too ready to disown loyalty with the shifting of fortune.

To some in the audience this may have sounded variously allusive to the many Catholic remains, whose burial had been providential to save them from the Reformist iconoclasm, and the relevant dynamics of secrecy and spying that this had activated. This may have also pointed out to their gradually re-emerging as the disquieting, objectified, and marketable ruins of a dismembered and dis-remembered cultural heritage. Perhaps this is also the status—the status of ruins that have escaped the deluge—which is enjoyed by the two paintings of Cleopatra and Diana, together with other refined items and books of a classical past, that Shakespeare has placed in Innogen's northern bedchamber.

What Shakespeare's Cleopatra is called to do in his play is to remember: even if "All's but naught", at Antony's death, when the world has been stolen of "our jewel", and she cannot throw any longer her "sceptre at the "injurious gods / To tell them that this world did equal theirs" (4.15.80–83). Prevailing on transient riches, however, Cleopatra transforms her monument into the stage of Antony's and her own triumph on time and its devastations. Perhaps inspired by the pharaonic art of conceiving burial sites and memory, Shakespeare bestows on her the task of taking care of Antony's body. Cleopatra "offers herself as a custodian of Antony's heroic masculinity, and of Rome itself", Nadia Fusini has observed.[63]

But it is under guard that she attends to his burial and then, as in a dream, to his resurrecting apotheosis: "I dreamt there was an emperor Antony" (5.2.73–75). Craftily, her sumptuous dream contemptuously circumvents Octavius's censuring listening (she will talk only "beggarly" business with him) to be trusted on ears which, as in Shakespeare's romances, and most significantly in *Pericles* and *The Winter's Tale*, are supposed to be capable of a suspension of disbelief. "You laugh when boys or women tell their dreams; / Is't not your trick?" (5.2.73–74), she asks Dolabella, Octavius's more malleable guard. Indeed Cleopatra's dream is so disproportioned as to require an act of faith on our part: that which is urged by dreams and poetry. Antony's ruins—or "the noble ruin of her magic", as Scarus sarcastically comments on the defeated and dishonoured warrior of the Actium battle (3.10.18)—allow for no other term of comparison than the "world" or the "universe" in Cleopatra's past-tense vision: "His face was as the heavens . . . His legs bestrid the ocean". Indeed the anthropomorphic geography of her dream encapsulates the uncompromising awareness of a Queen that she is burying a world: a world which is rewritten and re-authored as she buries it. In the moment in which, literally and metaphorically, the world with its champion, Antony, is lost, dissolved as Antony has it, "as water is in water" (4.14.11), it explodes as spaciousness and plenty in Cleopatra's surveilled space of her monument: namely as a resisting if doubtful object of desire and imagination. If Antony, as often said, has lost himself in Egypt's element—water[64]—Shakespeare's Cleopatra is asked to reciprocate him, I suggest, by reconfiguring, or reshaping, his ruins as quintessentially Roman.

There is no such dream in Plutarch, Shakespeare's main source. We are told that, as allowed by Octavius Caesar, Antony's funerals were held in great pomp by Cleopatra, but there is no mention of a funeral speech on her part. She then visited his tomb in the coming days for a last "oblation" when the horrifying prospect of being brought to Rome as Octavius's captive queen materialized as a real threat to her. On this occasion she pronounced a brief speech addressed to Antony whose core was her most lamentable decay from the status of a free woman to that of a prisoner and a slave. Her main disquiet, however, was the irony of her eventual dying in Rome:

> they will make us change our countries. For as thou being a Romane, hath bene buried in Aegypt: even so wretched creature I, an Aegyptian shall be buried in Italie, which shall be all the good that I have received by thy countrie. If therefore the gods where thou art now have any power and authoritie, sith our gods here have forsaken us: suffer not thy true frend and lover to be carried away alive, that in me, they triumphe of thee: but receive me with thee, and let me be buried in one selfe tombe with thee.
>
> (North's Plutarch, 1009)

This is beautiful, and beautifully said, in Plutarch, but it is different from the expanded memorializing part Cleopatra takes over in Shakespeare's play, before orchestrating the spectacle of her own death. Departing from his main source, the playwright makes her stand as a prevailing female agency of transforming memory and triumph on ruins. Indeed, competing with a part (the honours of war) which dramaturgically, and according to the Roman fashion, should belong exclusively to the triumphant Octavius—who in the meantime, in fact, is accurately theatricalizing his late benevolence as a winner—she engages defiantly in the work of restoring Antony to his *measure*, namely as it appears to me, his equivalence with the "world/universe" and hence with Rome, their Alexandrian Rome. For it is only when Antony is "Antony" that she can be "Cleopatra" (3.13.191–92).

In this, I suggest, Shakespeare makes the most of the Renaissance poetics of ruins and the understanding of Rome as an abstraction, a "greatness" which defies exact definition, unless it is by means of a hyperbole—Rome's proper rhetorical figure in the way it aims at authenticating the early modern perception of Rome as an aporetic magnitude. As Rome's name in Du Bellay/Spenser's earlier quoted sonnet 26,[65] Antony's name in *Ant.* is hyperbolically coterminous with world. As Du Bellay/Spenser's Rome in the earlier quoted sonnet 3, Antony is a colossus which "bestrid" his body parts on the geography of the entire world.[66] As in this same sonnet 3, Antony is tomb and monument of his own greatness. Comprehensively in Cleopatra's protracted burial and desiring epicedium, Antony realizes the early modern representation of Rome as a unique conjunction of "ornament" and "moniment"; a conjunction unconditionally stated in the closing couplet of Du Bellay/Spenser's sonnet 29: "Rome living, was the worlds sole ornament; / And dead, is now the worlds sole moniment".

"Here I Am Antony / Yet Cannot Hold This Visible Shape"

Like Benjamin's angel, Antony's face is turned backward, towards the fragmented landscape of his ruin after the catastrophe of the Actium battle: "See / How I convey my shame out of thine eyes / By looking back what I have left behind / 'Stroyed in dishonour" (3.11.51–54). "Where we perceive a chain of events", Benjamin writes, the angel

> sees one single catastrophe which keeps piling wreckage upon wreckage and hurls it in front of his feet. The Angel would like to stay, awaken the dead, and make whole what has been smashed. But a storm . . . irresistibly propels him into the future to which his back is turned, while the pile of debris before him grows skyward. This storm is what we call progress.[67]

As discussed in my chapter on *Titus Andronicus*, Benjamin's angel is an inspiring and illuminating metaphor of a notion of history grounded in ruins, but it can be summoned here again to account for Antony's blown-up world, and the way the hugeness of that explosion propels him violently into a future which is not his own. "I am so lated in the world that I / have lost my way for ever" (3.10.3), he says as he indulges in, more than resisting, the drift of that all confusing storm: one which abolishes distinctions and the temporally ordered "chain of events". If Hamlet's problem is a world "out of joint", Antony's is a misaligned world, a misalignment which defines the play's language as well as Antony's belatedness as a mismatch with a temporality which exceeds him, and in respect to which he discovers to be residual, as only a ruin ("the noble ruin of her magic") can be. Indeed, he is "lated" with respect to the time of history that he cannot arrest. History, or progress (in Benjamin's acceptation), goes arm-in-arm with the young Octavius, but this is historically grounded in ruins: Antony's time. "Now I must / To the young man send humble treaties; dodge / And palter in the shifts of lowness, who / with half the bulk o' th' world played as I pleased" (3.11.61–64).[68]

What he is forced to look at, backwards like Benjamin's angel, is the ruin of his world, which is also the wreckage of "what he was" (3.13.47–48), the ruination of his overinscripted Roman body, namely his symbolic body, strongly defined by his masculine honour. His state of "lowness" (3.11.63) and "baseness" (4.14.58) is in many respects a repetition of Hamlet's self-reproached effeminating cowardice. But Antony is a soldier, and what he is forced to confront in his pre-mortem anatomy of the self is the shame of "the sword, made weak by my affection" (3.11.67), namely the shame of his disarticulation as "a man of steel (4.4.33)—his committing, "visible shape", which he sees collapsing, alienated from the self, "as water is in water": "Here I am Antony / Yet cannot hold this visible shape" (4.14.13–14).

"Here I am . . . Yet": interestingly Antony's detachment from his "shape" (body/self) has been musically anticipated as a Nietzschean/ Wagnerian "twilight of the gods", a scenario of deserting gods marked by the ominous oboe music wafting from the underworld to the ear of the soldiers, on the night that precedes the last disastrous battle: "List, list! / Hark! . . . What should this mean?" 'Tis the god Hercules whom Antony loved / Now he leaves him", one of them hazards (4.3.16–22). Framed by a *mensa hospitalis* which is both a Dionysian bacchanal and a Christological "last supper" ("Tend me tonight" Antony invites speaking to his "hearty friends". "Haply you shall not see me more, or if, / a mangled shadow", 4.2.24–27), the music introduces a loss of identifying simulacra. It thus opens up a space of sensuous drifting, or forgetfulness of the self, which returns as the malignant and abysmal side of the many Dionysian revelries of the play.

Antony's carapace can hold no longer. His "man of steel" identity should be kept together by the armour that symbolically, if ironically, Cleopatra has herself tightly "buckled" on his body for the inauspicious final clash with Octavius (4.4), but his identifying martial "visible shape" explodes in a storm of alienated fragments. "Unarm, Eros", he orders when all is lost. "The long day's task is done / And we must sleep . . . / The sevenfold shield of Ajax cannot keep / The battery of my heart. O, cleave, my sides! / Heart, once be stronger than thy continent; /Crack thy frail case! Apace, Eros, apace! /No more a soldier; bruised pieces go; / You have been nobly borne" (4.14.39–46). The image is that of a fragmented statue, or at least this is the noise—a steely and stony noise—that Shakespeare makes us hear. Mirrored by the powerful metaphoricity of the clouds' liquid and silent pageant of fashioning and unfashioning forms, armour and body coalesce in dramatizing Antony's *voluptas* of self-disarticulation. Images of undoing—from the mythical to the musical to the anatomical to the pictorial and the archaeological—are profusely conjured up in this part of the play. They are preparatory to his suicide, the final self-cancellation. For "There is left us / Ourselves to end ourselves" (4.14.21–22).

Under the ocular absolutism of Octavius Caesar's state of emergence ("Observe how Antony becomes his flaw", he orders, "And what thou think'st his very action speaks / In every power that moves", 3.12.34–36),[69] Antony enacts, before dying, the show of his "outward" and "inward" ruination: the fragmentation of a hero who has abandoned himself and who can expect little more than this from either gods or lieutenants. "Let that be left / Which leaves itself" (3.11.7, 19–20), he reflects as he pitilessly works at definitely "empting" himself of all qualities after the final defeat at the hand of the "full Caesar". Earlier the choric and ever discerning Enobarbus has been ruthlessly lucid in comparing the confrontation between the two agonists as a lost battle between emptiness and fullness: "That he should dream, / Knowing all measures, the full Caesar will / Answer his emptiness" (3.13.34–36). Indeed it is Antony himself who, throughout, works at constructing himself as an object of loss and desire. As observed by Adelman:

> No one is more keenly aware of his absence than Antony himself, who watches his status as "Antony" dissolve and become as indistinct as water is in water; his peculiar pain turns in part on his awareness of himself as the standard against which his own loss of heroic masculinity must be measured.[70]

The disintegration of Antony's heroic self, as we might say, is the void, the emptiness which allows for Cleopatra's desiring and transcending recreation.[71] In this, Cleopatra, like Isis with Osiris, as has been observed, "restores, memorializes and consecrates Antony's male identity: in the womblike receptive space of her female memory".[72] Cleopatra's dream, however, is also representative of a Renaissance myth of rebirth, I suggest, a myth that in the Italian visual arts (and not only) had been profusely shaped by the sacred subject of the resurrection and ascension. As I have argued elsewhere, Shakespeare's theatre powerfully contributed to the theme in his late plays with his secular tales of death and resurrection (*The Winter's Tale*, *Pericles*): mainly stories of maternal transfiguration organized according to a bipartite structure of the play which was close to the pictorial treatment of resurrections and the typical subdivision of the canvas in a lower and a higher part.[73] We may perceive a same structuring principle in the quasi-coeval *Antony and Cleopatra*.

What is extraordinary, though, is that it is a woman who plays the role of the artist, the dramaturg, and the preserving memorialist (even though we shouldn't forget Paulina's gallery in *The Winter's Tale*). As in Raphael's *Transfiguration* commented by Nietzsche, it is Cleopatra's task to work out the visible miracle of Antony's Apollonian transfiguration. Which she does by rescuing Antony's "mangled shadow" from the contingency and turmoil of reality and by assigning it to the eternity and fixity of the myth: the same goal which she pursues soon after for herself, as she stages her "marble-constant" death as a rite of stoic courage and artistic transfiguration. "I am fire and air; my other elements / I give to baser life" (5.2.288–89), she claims, in her (perhaps Baconian) humoral squeezing of her sensorial body into the noble aetherial elements of her soul.[74] "I have immortal longings in me", she states as she sumptuously prepares herself as a queen and as a wife for the final triumphant reunion with Antony: "Husband, I come! / Now to that name my courage prove my title" (5.2.286–87).[75]

But even though gesturing towards the dreamy, transfiguring, and reconciliatory mode of Shakespeare's coming tragicomedies, *Antony and Cleopatra* is not a *romance*.[76] In fact, the lovers' final apotheosis doesn't bring us out of the grip of contradictions in which the play is enmeshed. At the theatrical and existential level, we might rather try to explain the play's insistent asking for a mixed emotional response in the terms of an unresolved coexistence of the contrasting categories of the Apollonian and the Dionysian, a coexistence that, speaking of Greek tragedy, Nietzsche understands as the reciprocating excitement of *dream* and *intoxication*, "inciting one another to ever more powerful births" (*Birth*, 14). Then, in working out the link of the ancient tragedy with the modernity of Wagner's musical drama, Nietzsche imagined the way we are expected to respond to it as that of an ideal passionate "friend" who, helped by music, "beholds the transfigured world of the stage and yet denies it. He sees the tragic hero before him, in epic clarity and beauty, and yet rejoices in his destruction. He understands the dramatic events to their very depths, yet he is happy to escape into incomprehension. . . . He looks more keenly, more deeply than ever, and yet wishes for blindness" (*Birth*, 105).[77] Nietzsche had in mind to extend his reflections to Shakespeare's theatre, which he didn't, but for a brief consideration on *Hamlet* (*Birth*, 39–40). But the audience's reaction to *Antony and Cleopatra* might be imagined in the same terms. Which means, as Nietzsche intends it, remaining in the grip of such a "marvellous division of the self", an unreconciled mixture of profound Dionysian darkness and the optical illusion of light provided by the representational capacity of the Apollonian dream.

As we know, in Plutarch's "Life" Antony's identifying gods are Hercules and Bacchus. Favoured by the cleavage opened up by the "strange" sub-terranean music heard by the soldiers in Shakespeare's play, the drowning experience of ruin, pleasure, and waste in the lower level of the representation continues to release its Bacchic or Dionysian potential of disruptive emotions and meanings. This reverberates not just on the couple's last and self-annihilating bacchanal on the night that precedes the battle of Antony's final ruin, but even more suggestively, to my view, on the way Antony's lacerated name drowns in Cleopatra's self-lacerating scream. This happens in Cleopatra's "other" death, the death she contrives to defend herself from Antony's fury after the disastrous Actium events, and whose meaning in the play's economy of interchangeability between truthfulness and acting (or dissembling), is no less true for being fictitious. The "truth" is contained in Mardian's short, if finely re-elaborated report of the queen's false death as well as in Cleopatra's poetical report of her dream. "The last she spake / Was 'Antony! Most noble Antony!' / Then, in the midst, a tearing groan did break / The name of Antony; it was divided / Between her heart and lips. She rendered life, / Thy name so buries in her" (4.14.29–34).

What we are here encouraged to share with Antony ("And bring me how he takes my death", 4.13.10) is not simply Cleopatra's death but also the way his name dies in her, strangled with/in her, in this producing, I suggest, the archaeological view of a broken marble inscription with a name dismembered in its two enigmatic and estranging halves: ANT · ONY—a defaced inscription inviting pietas, deciphering, completeness.

Thus it stands in Cleopatra's bodily sepulchre: an instance of obfuscated or divided identity as Antony has always been, a man of conflicting if "well-divided disposition" in Cleopatra's embracing vision of her lover's "mingled" or layered personality. Throughout the play the audience has been familiarized with the idea that Antony's name is coterminous with Rome's hugeness. In gathering and entombing in herself Antony's fragmented name, Cleopatra makes it live operatically in the contradictory immanence of her own living body, divided between heart and its hindered access to lips, word, symbol.[78] And hence, if in Cleopatra's dream Antony's name seems to be transferred entirely to the eternal and limpid time of myth, in her fictional death it remains scattered in the "realm of things" (we might say with Benjamin, *Origin*, 178–79), namely in the dismembered and aporetic landscape of wrack and human woe. In this Cleopatra is imagined as tomb and womb, a site of interment as well as rebirth, a monumental shelter as well as re-creative recollection.

Hosting Rome: Restoring Antony to Himself From the Margins of the Empire

"How can words capture the exhausted plenitude of antiquity?" Hui has asked speaking of Du Bellay, and how does he cope with "the oximorons that describe Rome—eternal and vanished, infinite and incomplete?" The problem is that of bringing back to form what lies in ashes, Hui argues; which the French poet does by addressing in each sonnet "a myth of catastrophe, a different account of Rome's grandeur and subsequent fall".[79]

Perhaps more than in any of Shakespeare's Roman plays, I argue, language in *Antony and Cleopatra* is faced with such an early modern crux of shaping Rome's grandeur and catastrophe into words. But Shakespeare takes up the gauntlet, knowing that he can rely on the unbounded language of love and desire. In fact it is Cleopatra's task to lovely host and administer, in such a paradigmatic mode, Antony's riches and ruins ("O see, my women, / The crown o'th' earth doth melt", 4.15.64–65). She does this by withholding Antony's mangled body from Octavius's jurisdiction and by reshaping its spoils according to a scale of their own. As Adelman has observed: "In thus giving Cleopatra the last word, Shakespeare robs Caesar of his 'triumph', his attempt to arrange how these events will be remembered; in effect she displaces his play with her own. And through this gesture, revises both the agent and the site of memory"; a gesture which to Adelman seems "the great generative act of the play".[80]

In this Shakespeare is not at all relinquishing his unsparing anatomizing insight he has sharpened in his previous Roman plays. Hyperbole allows for assent as well as scepticism; pathos as well as bathos, an assertive as well as a fluid, Montaignian staging of identity. And this is coherent with the play's structure which, as has been said, is comprehensively grounded in "continuous staging" (Granville-Barker) and "simultaneous perspectives" (Adelman), "discontinuous identity" (Dollimore),[81] and "simultaneous truth" (Neill).[82] In fact if Cleopatra labours at the recon-struction of Antony's final apotheosis as a Herculean heroic myth and a champion of unbounded *magnanimitas*, the play has worked at dis-seminating throughout, with a plethora of important and less important secondary characters (lieutenants and soldiers, Philo, Canidius, Ventidius, Scarus, Agrippa, Enobarbus—the true artificers of Rome's greatness), a disenchanted critique of Rome and those in authority (see especially 3.1 and part of 3.2).[83] We have heard Antony's parallel with Jupiter played down with finely dissimulated irony by some of them (3.2.9–10). And Enobarbus, the choric and rational presence in the play,[84] shows he has never skimped on his mistakes when, after the Actium battle, in one of his cynic asides conversant with the audience, he has bluntly likened Antony to a doomed leaking vessel (3.13.67–70). Cleopatra herself is by no means unaware of Antony's declining *virtus* as a soldier. A crowd of informers and messengers has kept her continually posted on the bad press they have in Rome: Antony is shamed for his dishonourable "levity", and the story goes that war at Alexandria has become the occupation of women and eunuchs (3.7.12–14). As she helps him wearing his heroic armour—for the last time in the Actium battle—it must have not escaped her that Antonius has put on weight (as Julius Caesar himself had "with feasting" in Egypt, 2.6.64), and that tying and untying his armour's buckles—bungling with them ("False, false! This, this!")—means more and less than it used to be (4.4.5–11). Nor has Cleopatra forgotten her political responsibilities as queen of an occupied country, for which reason perhaps (we will never know!) she has betrayed her lover in view of a facilitated negotiation with the winning Octavius. Switching from the calculating queen to the truly passionate lover comes easy to her. And the view that sexual desire is "potentially redeeming" cannot induce us to ignore, as Dollimore has argued, that what is dramatized in *Antony and Cleopatra* is "the connec-tion between desire and power; or more exactly, sexual love and political struggle".[85] It is a fact that she has always resisted Rome's power by being irresistible to its generals—Pompey, Caesar, Antonius—namely by play-ing at emasculating them and in jeopardizing their reputation. This has proved catastrophic to Antony.

But if she has been restless in precipitating his ruin, restlessly and loy-ally, she sets at work to monumentalize his ruins. First of all she doesn't leave his body to Octavius after his botched suicide. With ropes and the sole help of her women, she draws his heavy body up through a window in her firmly locked monument: this is far from being solemnly tragic. The scene is awkward and bathetically worked out, with Cleopatra who insists on remarking Antony's heaviness: "Here's sport indeed! How heavy weighs, my lord! / Our strength is all gone into heaviness; that makes the weight" (4.15.17). Tragicomically, Antony's all-too-earthly heaviness precludes ascension, literally and symbolically, to Cleopatra's monument and the lofty realm of the gods, thus echoing Enobarbus's ruthless and unmerciful image of Antony as a heavy and sinking ship (a current image, as earlier mentioned, for the Rome of *finis imperii*).

But soon after Cleopatra is grand and merciful as Isis,[86] or as a Michelangiolesque "Pietas", I would say, in the way, helped by her women, she welcomes and attends to Antony's bruised body and identity:[87] his crucified, "mangled shadow", dying but not dead (4.2.27; 4.15.6). For this is Antony's preoccupation as he agonizes: his having come short of a successful Roman death, after having fantasized it in the terms of an erotic mystique: as that of a "bridegroom" who "run[s] into't / As to a lover's bed" (4.14.101–102).[88] His failure in dying makes him doubt he has been up to his identity as a Roman, and on this he needs assurance: "Not Caesar's valour hath o'erthrown Antony, / But Antony's hath triumphed on itself" he claims from the outside of the monument's basement, where he has hardly arrived born by his guard, eliciting an assent, a warrant. In this Cleopatra is prodigal: "So it should be", she assures, "that none but Antony, / Should conquer Antony, but woe 'tis so" (4.15.15–18). Such he had willed his death to be when, confronted with Cleopatra's courageous (if deceptive) death, he had announced he didn't want to be less noble than a woman in crying: "I am conqueror of myself" (4.14.63).

Insistently, Antony returns on this as he breathes his last: "and do now not basely die / Not cowardly put off my helmet / To my countryman; a Roman by a Roman / Valiantly vanished" (4.15.58–60). But in this last occurrence, his "Roman by a Roman / valiantly vanished" refers us ambiguously both to Antony conqueror of himself and to Rome conqueror of itself. In fact, the implications of the Roman "noble" art of dying reverberate ironically from the personal onto the political fratricidal context of the empire which is being represented on stage: a war between "countrymen". In this the "noble" death is corrosively displayed as fuelling the myth as well the problem of Rome, the suicidal gesture being as much a proud affirmation of unmatchable power—for which only Rome is a menace to Rome—as the cause of an announced self-destruction. Indeed honour in Rome is the effect of a fatal, narcissistic game. And Shakespeare's Octavius seems to be well aware of its collective psychic content when perversely he exploits it as an arm of his military strategy against Antony: "Go charge Agrippa / Plant those that have revolted in the van / That Antony may seem to spend his fury / Upon himself" (4.6.8–10). By redoubling Antony's self-annihilation before it actually takes place, Octavius's theatre of cruelty—with those who have deserted Antony lined up as a mirror in front of him—dramatizes on the all-too-real dislocated scenario of the battlefield the split image of the same, and of self-inflicted death.

But let us return to Cleopatra who in pitifully assuring Antony of his Romanness, conveys all the meanings that in early modern Europe were associated to a conquering if self-destructive Rome. Once again,

Du Bellay/Spenser's *Ruines of Rome* is worth quoting for the role it may have had in defining the play's belated vision of a heroic Rome: a Rome looked at from the author's contemporary standpoint of its ruins.

> Behold what wreacke, what ruine, and what wast,
> And how that she, which with her mightie powre
> Tam'd all the world, hath tam'd herselfe at last,
> The pray of time, which all things doth devowre.
> Rome now of Rome is th' onely funerall,
> And onely Rome of Rome hath victorie.
>
> (son. 3.5–10)

"Only Antony, of Antony hath Victory", we are prompted to paraphrase, where not for the fact that Antony's unheroic botched suicide doesn't exactly harmonize with such a myth of Rome. But Shakespeare's Cleopatra mercifully takes upon herself the duty of re-establishing the equivalence between Antony's name and Rome: "Ah, women, women! Look, / Our lamp is spent, it's out . . . / We'll bury him, and then what's brave, what's noble, / Let's do't after the high Roman fashion" (5.1.88–92). Hers is the task of burying him according to the Roman fashion. Hers the task of restoring him to the complex nobleness and greatness of a Roman. Miola is right in remarking that "Least Roman of all Shakespearean women, Cleopatra is, paradoxically, most Roman as well".[89]

"After Antony's death", Dollimore has observed, "the myth of autonomous *virtus* is shown as finally obsolescent; disentangled now from the prevailing power structure, it survives as a legend. Unwittingly Cleopatra's dream about Antony helps relegate him to this realm of the legendary".[90] Right, but this happens not without the awareness on the part of Cleopatra that legend making is part of the same struggle for power. In fact what she is there for, starting from the dilated time of Act 4, scene 15, is to gather the ruins of that world, and to reinvent them poetically: a political gesture in itself in so far as this is a task which she performs by usurping Rome's authorship. She has always been remarkable in fictionally constructing the reality she wants; a conscious art of self-deception that she has displayed throughout the play, for effect of which everything around her has been despotically called to bend down to her will of loving and desiring control of reality. She doesn't surrender her inclination—a queenly prerogative—now that the world is lost.

On the contrary, Shakespeare makes her regain her art by repositioning her as a peripheral and yet powerful figure of reconstruction and hosting memory, a move that signifies *per se*. Since the outset of her encounter with Antony, Cleopatra has asserted her right to give hospitality as a possible means to maintain her majesty: "Upon her landing, Antony sent to her; / Invited her to supper. She replied / It should be better he became her guest, / Which she entreated" (2.2.229–32). Mind you, she has hardly finished being an object in somebody's else spectacular and desiring pageant (Enobarbus's tale) when, as if aware of the power relation regulating the sphere of representation between conqueror and conquered, she has readily readjusted the perspective, by claiming (as Derrida would say) the right of "*being-oneself in one's own home*". This is not without consequence. It lays bare the inner nature of "welcoming" as a question of mastery—namely, of "who plays the host"—which, in the economy of the play, means the possibility of reversing hierarchies: that between conqueror and a female subjugated other, that between Rome and its provinces, that between a masculine and a feminine culture, but also that between subject and object of history and mythmaking. In fact, if Enobarbus's mesmerizing picture of Cleopatra has positioned us in Rome to share with the Romans an "orientalist" imperial gaze,[91] Cleopatra's claim makes us return to Egypt and to her perspective of an empress who, however vanquished, asserts her right to give hospitality. Up to the end when Cleopatra will take centre stage as a figure of hosting memory (and self-representation), Antony will be Cleopatra's guest and vice versa in a struggle for power fought on the polysemic ground of the *mensa hospitalis*.

As I have argued elsewhere, hospitality, in the way it is problematized by the question "Who plays the host?" is a shaping agency in Shakespeare's Roman plays, in matters regarding identity, otherness, memory, and representation;[92] one which invites investigation in the light of Derrida's notion of "hostipitality". Born out of a conflation of hostility and hospitality which is remindful of an originary etymological cohabitation of opposites (*hostis/hospes*), Derrida's coinage highlights the conditionality of such an ethical duty and the fact that its inner core of benevolence and limits determines "its constitution as well its implosion". "[The] law of hospitality" the philosopher argues,

> violently imposes a contradiction on the very concept of hospitality in fixing a limit to it, in determining it: hospitality is certainly, necessarily, a right, a duty, an obligation, the *greeting* of the foreign other [*l'autre étranger*] as a friend but on the condition that the host, the *Wirt*, the one who receives, lodges or *gives asylum* remains the *patron*, the master of the household, on the condition that he maintains his own authority *in his own home* . . . and thereby affirms the laws of hospitality as the law of the household, *oikonomia*, the law of his household, the law of a place (house, hotel, hospital, family, city, nation, language, etc.).[93]

What concerns us in relation to Shakespeare's Rome is the interplay in the practice of hospitality, as expounded by Derrida, between *ipseity* ("the law of the place", "the law of the household", "the law of identity") and otherness (friend, enemy, foreigner, woman); and hence the fact that greeting the foreign other always opens up a contradictory field of benevolence and mastery, a field regulated by the impending cause of its implosion.

The theme of hospitality with its related question—"who plays the host?"—may be traced to cover a variety of issues in the Roman Shakespeare. As I show in this volume, it is a motif of great import in *Coriolanus*, not the less so for being a failed goal. Indeed, the failure of the "hospitable canon" is what makes the hero into an element of discord in the construction of the social fabric. Not only: from *Titus Andronicus* to *Antony and Cleopatra* and *Cymbeline*, hospitality is a pervading concern in Shakespeare's Roman plays, whether he deals with the sphere of civil virtues in the contained space of early republican Rome or the worldwide geography of the imperial Rome and its complex system of cohabitation with the conquered Other.

Interestingly, from *Titus Andronicus* to *Antony and Cleopatra*, the literal and metaphorical presence of the *mensa hospitalis* looms large on Shakespeare's Roman plays as the site where friends can easily turn into enemies and vice versa, or guests turn into wives/husbands and vice versa. But it is mainly the female body that in both plays spectacularizes the practice of hospitality as a vulnerable process of otherness turning into sameness, and incorporation turning into implosion and rejection. Meaningfully in both *Titus Andronicus* and *Antony and Cleopatra*, the victory upon a defeated female enemy takes on (or is prospected in) the forms of the festive welcome which awaits the triumphator upon his arrival from his military campaigns, thus provoking a disturbing proximity of hostility and hospitality. Consider the way the captive queen Tamora "beautifies" (1.1.110) the triumph of the general Titus, acting as food for the imperial gaze of a community to feed on, or for a collective dream of control; a wish for power, one might say, through the visual consuming of a captive foreign female body.[94] It is precisely this that is most dreaded by the defeated Cleopatra: playing the part of a disempowered guest at the Roman "master's court" (5.2.52), being a "brooch", in her own words, an ornament in Octavius Caesar's "imperious show" (4.15.24–26), or worse, seeing her seductiveness transformed into monstrosity, "a most monster-like" phenomenon, a freak offered to the eyes of "shouting plebeians", as she is reminded by Antony at his worst (4.12.32–37).

Captive female members were a recurrent feature in the triumphs of imperial Rome, and Shakespeare's Cleopatra or Tamora seem to be all too knowledgeable about what Rome's triumphs stood for. The enemy was magnificently "greeted" as a domesticated guest in the streets of the imperial city and made the object of contrasting sentiments, pride, horror, piety, manifestations of hostility and empathy, or hostipitality.[95] Gender, or "the convertible body of women", in Ania Loomba's words, is what allows Shakespeare to unsettle the perspective of the dominating gaze in respect to the subordinated other. "The exchange of women", she observes, "has always signalled the vulnerability of cultural borders". Take *Titus*: here "one Roman subdues Tamora in war, while another marries her".[96] In this, she is hostage, guest, and host, the troubling sexual threshold between cultures and races, and between self and other.

Hospitality is handled in such a way as to raise crucial ethnic and gender issues in the cosmopolitan context of *Antony and Cleopatra*; a play where, as noticed, banquets are so prevalent as to be tantamount to the construction of an Oriental Otherness by which Antony's masculine Roman *virtus* is both threatened and defined. But disrupting both the patriarchal laws of hospitality and the laws of the victor, it is Cleopatra who remains "the master of the household", which entails, in Derrida's expansion of this prerogative, "*the being oneself in one's own home*", maintaining the privilege of legislating about "the condition of the gift and of hospitality."[97] Intermingling with the cross-cultural negotiation of the play, the banqueting and drinking rituals of hosting are a continual framing of a gender-coded struggle for mastery, as shown in Cleopatra's most revealing playing with cross-dressing and gender roles: "I drunk him to his bed, / Then put my tires and mantles on him, whilst / I wore his sword Philippan" (2.5.21–23). Indeed, in the multiple perspective of the play triggered by its cross-cultural geography, the gender-coded dialectic between self and other also elucidates a two-directional encoding process. Cleopatra is envisioned as a go-between: a host as well as a guest. She stands for a masterful as well as a mastered vilified Otherness, a hostage in other people's country and imagination, and within a complex representational paradigm, which includes theatre itself.[98]

Memory in the play cannot be isolated from the question of representation—a recurrent preoccupation in the play—in its relation with gender and the framing semantics of power and negotiation which regulates the imperial geography of the play. Consistently throughout the play Cleopatra is as much aware of her place as the captive object of a voracious transforming fantasy at the Roman "master's court" (5.2.52) as of herself in the world of her present and afterlife representations. It is an element of the ironical metatextual awareness of the play that Cleopatra will mention precisely her *mensa hospitalis*, namely what stands for exchange and reciprocity, as the stuff of an iniquitous theatrical replica of her and Antony's story, for future generations of spectators to feed on: "Saucy lictors / Will catch at us like strumpets, and scald rhymers / Ballad us out o' tune. The quick comedians / Extemporally will stage us and present / Our Alexandrian revels; Antony / Shall be brought drunken forth: and I shall see / Some squeaking Cleopatra boy my greatness / I'th' posture of a whore" (5.2.213–19).

Thus, when we come to the last two acts, the fact that Cleopatra steals the spotlight as a memorializing and self-memorializing figure shouldn't come as a surprise. It is coherent with an ongoing struggle for "*being one-self in one's own home*". All along the play Shakespeare has kept her alert on matters of hosting and representation, while intertwining her story with that of her "Roman host" on the backdrop of Rome's cosmopolitan space. This is relevant for more than one reason. Firstly because, as I take it, Cleopatra's dream—*her* authorial statement—is also an act of appropriation in respect to Rome's discursivity. Secondly, because it signals a cross-cultural exchange between centre and periphery which undoes what seems to be raised as an opposition. Thirdly, because it authenticates the play's diffuse self-reflexiveness.

From the question "Who plays the cook?" sardonically raised in *Titus Andronicus*, to that of "Who plays the host?" provocatively insinuated in *Antony and Cleopatra*, Shakespeare, I argue, consistently gestures in his Roman works towards his own belated and negotiated relation with Rome's authority and its complex inheritance. Cleopatra shares with her author ("cook", "host", guest, foreigner, latecomer) the task of gathering and appropriating Rome's mangled body, in a ruinous scenario marked by the anxiety of absent (murdered) fathers and the responsibility of memory. Memory (in the form of revenge) has been claimed as an accomplished duty by Antony at the moment of his most debasing exposure as a soldier. "[A]t Philippi . . . I struck / The lean and wrinkled Cassius, and 'twas I / That the mad Brutus ended" (3.11.35–38). Cleopatra is invested with a similar duty of remembrance when she engages with Antony's rehabilitating apotheosis. She refers us to a dissolved world of heroism and a precedent generation of mythic fathers, a world in which, as Adelman has observed, "men were more than men", when "the greatest Romans themselves overflowed the measure", and "Rome and Egypt were not irreconcilable" as it is now in the Rome of the younger Caesar's.[99]

Cleopatra's epicedium is of a piece with the past tense of her dream. But she is meanwhile producing herself as a present writing subject. In fact she is aware of the constructedness of her illusion ("I dreamt there was an emperor Antony", 5.2.75), which she, consistently, exposes to sceptical interrogation ("Think you there was or might be such a man / As this I dreamt of? 5.2.92–93). Not only: Cleopatra's poetry works at both constructing and dissolving her object of desire, by laying bare the raw materials her dream is made of, namely by determinately maintaining her dream and her listener(s) within the signifying intentionality of representation, the space of the hyphen between the signified and the signifier. Indeed, we cannot overlook the fact that Cleopatra's re-vision of Antony is ostentatiously pieced together with *Julius Caesar*'s textual *spolia*. Antony's colossal size, and its world-like metaphoricity, has already belonged to him—Caesar—before returning in Cleopatra's dream of her "emperor"—underwritten by Cassius's unsparing anatomy—as a world of loss and desire: "His legs bestrid the ocean; his reared arm / Crested the world" (5.2.81–82). A shattered universe of fixed stars is equally evoked in both plays at the death of their protagonists. Octavius himself, the master of measure, is forced to follow suit at Antony's death, but tellingly, the world imagery is subtly rewritten as a residual and misaligned rhetorical formula. Remindful of the annihilating prodigies on the night of the conspiracy narrated by Caska (in *JC*), to Octavius (in *Ant.*) "The breaking of so *great* a thing should make / A *greater* crack. The round world / *Should have* shook lions into civil streets / And citizens to their dens" (5.1.14–17; my emphasis). "Should" but *hasn't*. Octavius Caesar's new era announces itself as a world without portents and without prodigies or miracles: his is an era which distinguishes between "great" and "greater", an era of untragic temperance, as that which we find celebrated in Horace's Ode 4, Book III.

But if so, this also means (as often noticed) that the same generic status of tragedy is put to the test, in a way that makes it border on a variety of forms, from romance to the operatic—and not without an excess of reuse, I would say—that Susan Sontag would define as "camp".[100] In *Antony and Cleopatra*, what was Julius Caesar's in the eponymous play is returned to Antony, out of love or calculated rhetorical strategy. Cleopatra's dream is steeped in the textual materiality of Rome's overflowing rhetoric of colossal greatness. And such a desiring re-creation of Antony plays at defying the "censuring Rome" (5.2.56) with the language of Rome, in a way that ironically deflates its legislating imperial role. In this she competes with her author in pillaging Caesar's hyperbolic features, the imagery that Cassius has already contributed to liquefy and dismantle in *Julius Caesar*. But such a spectral presence of a previous Shakespearean textuality, I argue, cannot be done away as mere pillage or self-pillage, an example of easy self-quotation, or the narcissistic indulging of a mature and self-assured playwright. Or rather: it may be so, but there is more in it. It foregrounds the importance that Caesar has assumed as a sign of fatherly power (he whose "ambition, / . . . . swell'd so much that it did almost stretch / The sides o'th' world"), we are still reminded for the last time in *Cym.*, 3.1.49–51): a fatherly ghost *per antonomasia* in Shakespeare's canon and the origin of many forms of *iterability*—namely a drifting, differing, and altering repetition in its Derridean acceptation.[101] Indeed in migrating from one character onto another, and from one context into another, the Roman heroic script reveals its condition of a language whose force is inversely proportional to the loss of a stable and monologic authority: one which as such opens up to spoliation and a variety of appropriations. And of course Caesar's ghost has a haunting relevance in the couple's love story itself, a relevance which emerges horribly in Antony's words as a nauseated sense of leftovers and things repeated: "I found you as a morsel, cold upon / Dead Caesar's trencher—nay you were a fragment / Of Gnaeus Pompey's" (3.13.121–23).

Antony, however, becomes Caesar's most extraordinary and seductive repetition in Cleopatra's hands, both in ironic reconstructed grandeur and in ruination.[102] Shakespeare assigns to Cleopatra's funeral rites and posthumous dreams the task of translating, with accrued magnificence,

Rome's mythic prerogatives epitomized by Caesar into Antony's bodily features and manners. It is Antony who swells into the imperial shape of a colossus in her dream. It is Anthony who best interprets the eroticized ideal of an unbounded, ecumenical, and magnanimous geography ("In his livery / Walked crowns and crownets; realms and islands / As plates dropped from his pocket", 5.2.89–91). But Antony's bounty and their plenty is autumnal ("an autumn it was / That grew more by reaping", 5.2.86–87). Shakespeare makes them both aware of their belatedness: namely that they are performing the last act of a run-out story of grandeur, a belatedness which is signalled by the very contradictory language of the play, by its hyperbolic (*and* poetic) mode—a mark of past excess and heroism as has been noticed[103]—as well as, I argue, of displayed desiring repetition.

Plutarch tells us that Cleopatra was 39 at her death and Antony 53 or 56. Shakespeare makes the most of this by making the couple indulge on the signs of their aging. Compared with the young Octavius Caesar, the blossoming "rose / Of youth" (3.13.20–21), they know that theirs is the time of "blown" roses (3.13.41) and "grizzled" hair (3.13.18), the time of decline and heaviness. But more profoundly, the playwright makes them feel that they are tragically "lated in the world" (3.11.3). Indeed, they are both "peerless" (1.1.41) in theatrically embodying the eclipse and in yielding to the fascination of the ruin (3.13.54–56; 5.2.50).

Skeletons and Patterns: An Epilogue

> Yet these olde fragments are for paternes borne.
>
> (Du Bellay)

As discussed in my Introduction, in the Renaissance poetical discovery of Rome's ruins the interchangeable role of poetry with music and masonry was essential in providing the resuscitating visual imagery of Rome's cadaver. The enterprise is cast as an Orphic ritual of descent into darkness and bringing forth to light of those who are dead. It is also visualized as a masonry skill, a capacity to bring back to order the stones of the City's crumbled walls. The imagery is mythical, but it is revisited with a spirit which, modernly, is sceptical and archaeological: "O that I had the *Thracian* Poets harpe, / For to awake out of th'infernall shade / Those antique Cæsars, sleeping long in darke, / The which this ancient Citie whilome made: / Or that I had *Amphions* instrument, / To quicken with his vitall notes accord, / The stonie joynts of these old walls now rent . . . Or that at least I could with pencill fine, / . . . To builde with levell of my loftie style, / That which no hands can evermore compyle" (Du Bellay writes in his *Ruines*, 25.1–7). The effort to dig it up to light was necromantic, as Thomas Greene has suggested in discussing the relation between the Renaissance theory of imitation and the discovery of ancient ruins.

Ruins, he argues, gestured not only towards the impermanence of history but more cogently towards a cultural distance, remoteness, and "historical solitude".[104]

For humanists, philologists, epigraphists, archaeologists, or poets like Poggio, Biondo, or Du Bellay, Rome is a corpse, an uncanny archaeological vision of a "disjointed" architecture and disarticulated temporality. And the aim at deciphering the elliptical sense of its ruins is imbued with the humanist awareness that the endeavour is rewarded with only partial understanding. You need art—you need "magic"—to draw the corpse out of its tomb and make it whole: "*Rome n'est plus, & si l'architecture / Quelque umbre encore de Rome fait revoir, / C'est un corps par magique sçavoir*". "*Rome* is no more: but if the shade of *Rome* / May of the bodie yeeld a seeming sight, / It's like a corse drawne forth out of the tomb / By Magicke skill out of eternall night", Du Bellay sounds in Spenser's translation (5.5–8). And then on a longing vein: "this nothing, which have thee left, / Makes the world wonder, what they from thee reft" (13.11–14). Indeed, ruins are an instance of aporetic knowledge. They refer us to a world of signification which is both visible and invisible, one which acquires epistemic relevance in the light of the Foucauldian archaeological view of knowledge and the related notions of "vacant spaces" and discontinuous strata of events.

Starting from Poggio's archaeological spectacle of a "fallen world", Rome as an empty place, a dismembered corpse as it appears to him on the Capitoline Hill, "this nothing" (in Du Bellay's poetry) had become a truism in humanist and Renaissance culture, a culture which was haunted by the notion of the classical past as a vacant place. For Poggio as for Du Bellay, ancient Rome was a "pouldred corse" (son. 27.14), which with its spectral "naked arms" (son. 28) promised a totality that could be experienced only as *spolia*: relics, traces, "olde markes to see, / Of which all passersby doo somewhat pill" (son. 30.11–12). And "Yet these olde fragments are for paternes borne: / Then also marke, how Rome from day to day, / Repayring her decayed fashion, / Renewes herself with buildings rich and gay", Du Bellay writes in sonnet 27.8-11. Rome's "naked" ruins disclosed a form, a "pattern" to early modern sight which implied inheritance, namely the possibility of transmission and creative rearticulation. In this, in signalling a model of repetition and refunctioning, they signified *per se*. Indeed they were the generative ground of the Renaissance aesthetics of rebirth. We can appreciate such a revolutionary impact of the ruinous past to the end of Shakespeare's contemporaneity, and of modernity as such, by commenting it with Benjamin's reappraisal of the German *Trauerspiel* of the seventeenth century:

> The legacy of antiquities constitutes, item for item, the elements from which the new whole is mixed. Or rather: is reconstructed. For the perfect vision of this new phenomenon was the ruin. The exuberant

subjection of antique elements in a structure which, without uniting them in a single whole, would, in destruction, still be superior to the harmonies of antiquity, is the purpose of the technique which applies itself separately, and ostentatiously, to realia, rhetorical figures and rules. Literature ought to be called *ars inveniendi.* The notion of the man of genius, the master of the *ars inveniendi*, is that of a man who could manipulates models with sovereign skill.

(*Origin*, 178–79)

Borrowing from Eagleton's inspiring interpretation of Benjamin's theory of history and literary phenomena, we might say that Rome's material and textual corpus becomes a "non-intentional constellation" in Shakespeare's art. As the Scripture for "the revolutionary reader", it is "sacred" in so far as it is "autonomous": "autonomous not of history, but like the Bible, of authorial intention ('Truth', [Benjamin] writes, 'is the death of intention') and so of a single exhaustive interpretation". But truth can be "redeemed" as previous artefacts are "strategically reconstructed" and "reinscribed in new social practices".[105]

"Rome"—a name for both a void and an excess of greatness and meaning—was essential to the Renaissance's explosion of creative energy; essential in the way it enacted and foretold an idea of the classical which, as Settis understands it in our own days (see my Introduction), is tantamount to the eternity of a paradigm of decay and mutability, or else an organism capable of being appropriated and reinterpreted in a diversity of times and places.

Ruins had been turned into a widely circulated pictorial and poetical theme in Humanist and Renaissance Europe. Shakespeare catalyzes all of such a ruin-based culture, I argue, when departing from his sources, he makes his Cleopatra affirm her role as a preserving tomb/memory of Antony's "noble ruin"; or, more precisely, "[T]he noble ruin of her magic" (3.10.18), in Scarus's sarcastic conclusive view of the Actium's dishonoured hero, who thus, in imagining him as Cleopatra's defaced statue, forcefully contributes to highlight Cleopatra's role as a destructive as well as a reconstructive figure. Cleopatra's dreamt Roman hero springs out of Antony's fragmentation, the work of many. And he seems to be recreated, I suggest, as if piecing his image up together with the recycled noble marbles of his (and as aforementioned) Julius Caesar's debris. Such a spoliative/recycling phenomenon, as reminded by Vasari to his contemporaries (see chapter on *Titus*), was a visible ongoing process in the physical space of Renaissance Rome, as displayed by its architectural and visual arts. *Spolia*, "the practice of exploiting older structures for building materials", in Hui's discussion of ruins, "is a material and metaphorical *translatio*—a transfer from one place to another as well as one discourse (pagan) to another (Christian). One can see how this is a material analogue to the literary practice of imitation, citation, and allusion".[106]

In such a context, I argue, Cleopatra becomes a figure of competing authorship.[107] Ironically though: for if she can be seen as a gatherer, the symbol of a recovering if pillaging early modern authorship, she is also the last pharaoh of an older Greek-Egyptian civilization. And thus if the Tiber's imperially devouring "mouth"—*ostium* in Latin, as the name of Rome's harbour (Ostia)—has incorporated the world starting from its Greek-Asian part, the Nile strikes back in Shakespeare's rewriting of the Plutarch's couple by incorporating and authoring the spoils of Rome. In the archaeological distance and catastrophic temporality of ruins, Shakespeare's Cleopatra stands as a transversal and disordering spectrality: an agency (and paradigm) of a hyper-mediated remoteness, a haunting and haunted figure of repetition, one which redoubles itself on the same Shakespearean stage on which she is being performed: "The quick comedians / Extemporally will stage us and present / Our Alexandrian revels; Antony / Shall be brought drunken forth; and I shall see / Some squeaking Cleopatra boy my greatness / I' th' posture of a whore" (5.2.215–20).

"Let Rome in Tiber melt, and the wide arch / Of the ranged empire fall!" we have heard Antony exclaim at the beginning of the play (1.1.34), prefiguring a catastrophe which the playwright wants us to feel as already impending there, from the very beginning. Thus, if we look at the play backwards from the mangled and dying body of Antony—his broken name buried in Cleopatra's body/tomb/womb—we discover that Shakespeare has made us enter the spaciousness of the imperial Rome's through a ruined monumental arch, namely archaeologically, in the same way he has made us enter Rome in his first Roman play, *Titus Andronicus*. But if in *Titus's finis imperii* Rome, excavating among Rome's bodily and textual debris brings forth, as I have shown, the issue of a broken tale among generations and the way this is tragically interwoven with a crisis of inheritance, in *Antony and Cleopatra* ruins are met with rebirth, namely with an explosion of elegiac transcending poetry. The weight of a lost, unattainable, and yet overconnoted past doesn't turn into a nightmare (as in Titus's library/cookery) or disowned humanism (as in *Coriolanus's* desolate land). It turns into richness, multiplicity, and playfulness. With his Cleopatra, Shakespeare has buried Rome and has turned its over-determined void into inheritance: that of a poet creatively at ease with his debt to tradition, a tradition which at theatre tests and renegotiates every time its actuality—namely its Benjamin's heliotropic and dialectical cogency—in the contact with the living presence of the audience: "How many ages hence / Shall this our lofty scene be acted over in states unborn and accents yet unknown?" (*JC*, 3.1.111–12).

And yet the luxurious, hyperbolic grandeur of *Antony and Cleopatra* is marked by the same excess of signification and the same void that starting from *Titus Andronicus* characterizes Shakespeare's Roman canon. Indeed, as I like to view it, Shakespeare's Cleopatra is sitting in the same vacant place that Poggio Bracciolini established as a powerful icon of melancholic belatedness and loneliness at the outset of *Ruinarum Romae Descriptio* (1448), the first book of his meditation on ruins and on fortune as the engine of history:

> The hill of the Capitol on which we sit, was formerly the head of the Roman empire, the citadel of the earth, the terror of kings; illustrated by the footsteps of so many triumphs, enriched with the spoils and tributes of so many nations. This spectacle of the world, how is it fallen! how changed! how defaced!
>
> (see my Introduction, p. 18)

Ruins, loss, longing, and acts of interment and aporetic disinterment are strictly interwoven in Poggio's materially situated perspective. With his early modern numerous contemporaries, he bequeaths to us an idea of Rome's grandeur which is one with the literal and metaphorical colossal size of its elliptical ruins and the call for interpretation moving from them, whether those be marbles or texts: a by no means simple idea of Rome as an allegory of the "varietate fortunae" (Poggio) or the "World's Inconstancy" (Du Bellay). As argued in my Introduction and first chapter on *Titus*, ancient Rome stands as the petrified representation of an ontological crisis in Shakespeare's time, the lost referent *per antonomasia*, impermanence being its only ontology. For all his exhaustive Plutarchan sources, *Antony and Cleopatra* places itself in the same sceptical if overconnoted space, thus becoming contemporary to Shakespeare's early modern present, an epoch in which the allegoric and moral acceptation of inconstancy was giving ground to impermanence as a new philosophical understanding of the world and the human.

If Antony embodies and epitomizes the sense of the end and of his self-empting, Cleopatra is a figure of reinventive memory. In this, Shakespeare's play both complies with and defies Montaigne's sceptical assertion:

> that the knowledge he had of it [ancient Rome] was altogether abstract and contemplative, no image of it remaining to satisfy the senses; that those who said that the ruins of Rome at least remained, said more than they were warranted in saying; for the ruins of so stupendous and awful a fabric ["*si espouvantable machine*"] would enforce more honour and reverence for its memory; nothing he said remained of Rome but its sepulchre.[108]

The couple's "sepulchre" is a site of commemoration and resurrection in Shakespeare's play, the pulsating heart of the world, *the* immeasurable world itself, in the here and now of the play. In resurrecting Rome and their two most famous ghosts from their ashes, a common trope in Renaissance culture as argued in this volume, Shakespeare's play satisfies the senses and the imagination, the body and the soul, the real and the abstract, scepticism and its poetical transcending. In this the two lovers acquire the size of Rome itself, their enlarged Alexandrian Rome: that is an imagined and abstract spaciousness that allows for the possibility of conceiving variety and the cohabitation of reconciled spheres and worlds, one in which they can claim the eternity "in [their] lips and eyes" (1.3.36) and the same colossal and spherical size of the world: what is "past the size of dreaming".

Cleopatra's loving and transfiguring perception of Antony seems to build, all along the play, on an idea of Rome—its space, its heroes, its myth—as one which can be dug out of its oblivion in the form of the unimaginable. A field of possibilities springing out of a field of ruins. Cleopatra's Antony is both ruin and myth: his broken name calls for sceptical hermeneutics (the work of passers-by, lovers, archaeologists, epigraphists, philologists) on one side, as well as desirous and transcending poetry on the other. In this Cleopatra is a figure of burial, melancholy, memory, and authorship as well as of unquenchable desire: the same which fuels the eroticism of her theatrical reunion with him. I like to cherish the thought that Shakespeare decided to entrust the Egyptian queen—more than Cymbeline's court of Britannia—with the task of helping him take his leave from Rome. But it is a leave-taking act that—as for Cleopatra, and as for Innogen perhaps—will forever nurture desire.

Notes

1. Miola, *Shakespeare's Rome*, pp. 206–207. But see also, "Past the Size of Dreaming?"
2. See John Wilders, "Introduction", in William Shakespeare, *Antony and Cleopatra* (London: Bloomsbury Arden Shakespeare, 2005), pp. 69–75. Quotations are from this edition. Throughout I have consulted also *Antony and Cleopatra*, The Oxford Shakespeare, edited by Michael Neill ([1994] 2000) and *Antony and Cleopatra*, The New Cambridge Shakespeare, edited by David Bevington ([1990] 2005).
3. William Hazlitt, *The Round Table and Characters of Shakespeare's Plays* (London: Dent, 1969), p. 228.
4. James Knowles, "'Infinite Riches in a Little Room': Marlowe and the Aesthetics of the Closet", in Gordon McMullan, ed., *Renaissance Configurations: Voices/Bodies/Spaces, 1580–1690* (Houndmills and London: Macmillan, 1998), p. 9 and 3–29. For an in-depth discussion of the relation between the rhetoric of inwardness, "inward truth", and its relation with phenomena of secrecy, heresy, treason, and surveillance, see Katharine Eisaman Maus, *Inwardness and the Theater in the English Renaissance* (Chicago: The University of Chicago Press, 1995), pp. 1–34 and 104–127.
5. For a full discussion of the Reformist theological content of these issues, see Clark, *Vanities of the Eye*. For more on art as an instance of fictive and suspect truth in Shakespeare, see also Del Sapio Garbero, "Be Stone No More".
6. See also later, in the description of Diana's sculpture, Shakespeare's long-felt fascination with the way art and nature compete for truth (*Cym.*, 2.4.80–85). This refers us to *The Rape*'s ekphrasis as well as the playwright's later concern for Giulio Romano, "that rare Italian Master", he mentions in *The Winter's*

Tale as the artist who had succeeded in the "rare" achievement of showing "life as lively mock'd as ever" (5.3.18–20).

7. In this I both agree and depart from Janet Adelman when in foregrounding the play's "circumscription of the female" and its overall sanitizing project, she observes, "The tapestries of Imogen's bedchamber tell the story of 'proud Cleopatra, when she met her Roman . . .'; but *Cymbeline* is the undoing of that story, the unmaking of female authority, the curtailing of female pride". *Suffocating Mothers*, pp. 211 and 199–219.

8. For Shakespeare's theatrical transcodification of his Plutarchan source, see Keir Elam, *Antony and Cleopatra. Presentazione, Tabulazione, Commento"*, in Alessandro Serpieri et al., eds, *Nel Laboratorio di Shakespeare. Dalle fonti ai drammi*, 4 vols, vol. 4, *I drammi romani* (Parma: Pratiche Editrice, 1988), pp. 133–247. For more on direct sources see Geoffrey Bullough, ed., *Narrative and Dramatic Sources of Shakespeare*, vol. 5 (London: Routledge and Kegan Paul, 1964).

9. Gilberto Sacerdoti, "*Antony and Cleopatra* and the Overflowing of the Roman Measure", in Del Sapio Garbero, ed., *Identity, Otherness and Empire*, pp. 107–119. See also Gilberto Sacerdoti, *Nuovo cielo, nuova terra. La rivoluzione copernicana di Antonio e Cleopatra di Shakespeare* (Roma: Edizioni di storia e letteratura, [1990] 2008).

10. Khan, *Roman Shakespeare*, p. 110.

11. Miles, *Shakespeare and the Constant Romans*, p. 188.

12. For an in-depth approach to the early modern "new geography" in the light of a Vichian notion of poetical geographies, see Gillies, *Shakespeare and the Geography of Difference.*

13. Antony's grandeur, which I refer to Rome's world-like geography and the way it is constantly undermined by the early modern perception of its colossal ruins, has been deeply discussed in terms of "exorbitance" by John Gillies. "Exorbitance" is a quality which he refers to Antony's transgressive moral code as well as his political ambitions of creating an anti-Augustan competing and Egypt-centred Eastern empire. He demonstrates how this was supported by Caesar Augustus's propaganda, as witnessed by Virgil's mention of Antony's fuelling the conflict between Rome and the East (*Aeneid,* VIII.685–88) in terms which envisage a clash of civilizations. Gillies adds that this is not so in Plutarch's cosmopolitan Rome. But this pre-Plutarchan vision of Antony accentuates the political and cultural implications of the opposition between Egypt and Rome. *Shakespeare and the Geography of Difference*, pp. 112–115.

14. See respectively Sacerdoti, "*Antony and Cleopatra* and the Overflowing of the Roman Measure", p. 107, and Tony Tanner, "*Antony and Cleopatra*: Boundaries and Excess", *Memoria di Shakespeare*, 4 (2017), 1–19 (pp. 2–3). But see also Maurice Charney, *Shakespeare's Roman Plays: The Function of Imagery in the Drama* (Cambridge, MA: Harvard University Press, 1961), p. 110 *et passim.*

15. See Adelman, *The Common Liar*, pp. 48 and 14–52. Apart from Granville-Barker's groundbreaking "Preface" to the play (*Prefaces to Shakespeare*, 4 vols (London: Batsford, [1927–47] 1972), see Schanzer, *The Problem Plays of Shakespeare*, p. 132, who for this refers us to H.T. Price's *Construction in Shakespeare* (1951).

16. Kahn, *Roman Shakespeare*, p. 112. For an incisive synthesis of the state of art in matters regarding the way the play's Egypt/Rome presumed "binarism" has been approached by criticism, see pp. 110–111. On male emulation, pursued by the Roman elite, see her chapters on both *Julius Caesar* and *Antony and Cleopatra*, pp. 88–96, 112–137.

17. Kahn, *Roman Shakespeare*, p. 111. For an upturning of the contrast between Egypt and Rome in terms of Rome's narcissistic doubling of itself, see Jonathan Gil Harris, "'Narcissus in Thy Face': Roman Desire and the Difference It Fakes in *Antony and Cleopatra*", *Shakespeare Quarterly*, 45:4 (1994), 408–425.

18. Adelman, *Suffocating Mothers*, pp. 182–183. But see also the link she discovers with the Romulus and Remus's male dynamics in her "Shakespeare's Romulus and Remus".

19. Girard, *A Theatre of Envy*.

20. Garrett A. Sullivan makes a similar point in addressing the issue of stable opposite identities in terms of mystified and shifting forms of constructedness and appropriation. *Memory and Forgetting*, pp. 96–99.

21. Adelman, *The Common Liar*, p. 131, 132. But see also Rosy Colombo: "Excess belongs mainly to Antony . . . but it is taken over by Cleopatra to make up for his loss, in her imaginative recreation of his heroic status". "Introduction", *Memoria di Shakespeare*, 4 (2017), VII–XIV (p. XIV).

22. Florio's Montaigne, "Of the Roman Greatness", *Essays*, II.24, p. 677.

23. Harris, "'Narcissus in Thy Face'", p. 422.

24. Jacques Derrida, *Writing and Difference*, transl. Alan Bass [1967] (Chicago: The University of Chicago Press, 1978). See mainly, the chapter "Freud and the Scene of Writing", pp. 196–215.

25. Hazlitt, *The Roundtable and Characters of Shakespeare's Plays*, p. 228.

26. The "wide arch" mention may be associated to the romanizing colonnade of the Elizabethan theatres, but also to the proscenium arch introduced by the transformed Jacobean theatre. For a discussion of the visual issues raised by such an innovation, which implied the passage "from rounded multi-dimensionality to the frontality of perspective", see Richard Wilson, *Free Will*. As he observes, "In *Antony and Cleopatra*, it seems, the war of the world is between the two regimes of sense concretized by the circular amphitheatre and the proscenium arch" (p. 323).

27. For a reflection on the seventeenth-century concern with mutability, chaos, and cosmic decay as a ubiquitous critique of providentialist belief or Platonic universalisms, see Jonathan Dollimore, *Radical Tragedy: Religion and Power in the Drama of Shakespeare and His Contemporaries* (Brighton: The Harvester Press, 1984), pp. 92–99. As he observes, "the Jacobean obsession with disintegration may reveal, directly or undirectly, some of the real forces making for social instability and change . . . it was an obsession which could be used subversively as well as conservatively" (pp. 93–94).

28. Settis, *Futuro del 'classico'*, p. 85. See my Introduction, p. 16.

29. Tanner, "*Antony and Cleopatra*", p. 10.

30. David Kaula, "The Time Sense of *Antony and Cleopatra*", *Shakespeare Quarterly*, 15:3 (1964), 211–223 (pp. 212, 213).

31. Miles, *Shakespeare and the Constant Romans*, p. 108. See also his chapter on "'Infinite Variety': *Antony and Cleopatra*", pp. 169–188. Montaigne developed his revision of the Stoic value of constancy mainly in "Of Constancie", "Of the Inconstancie of Our Actions" (I.12 and II.1), "Of Diverting and Diversions" (III.4), but also in his essays on dying and moral knowledge.

32. Other previous dramatic treatment of the two lovers' story, such as Samuel Daniel's *The Tragedie of Cleopatra* (1594), the French Estienne Jodelle's *Cléopatra Captive* (1552), or Robert Garnier's *Marc Antoine* (1578) translated by the Countess of Pembroke as the *Tragedie of Antoine* (1592), had no such wide historical and epistemic insight. For their relation to Shakespeare's play, see Chernaik, *The Myth of Rome*, pp. 140–144, and Schanzer, *The Problem Plays of Shakespeare*, pp. 167–183.

33. For a reading of the play in the light of a bivalent historical reception of Octavius's pacifying but dictatorial Rome in Shakespeare's times, see Heinemann, "'Let Rome in Tiber Melt'".

34. As Ramie Targoff observes, here Antony rewrites Virgil by transforming the "tragic scene in the underworld into a moment of public triumph, where the lovers will be forever on display as they were in the streets of Alexandria". "Love and Death in Egypt and Rome", *Memoria di Shakespeare*, 4 (2017), 461–472 (p. 65).

35. David Quint, "Virgil's Double Cross: Chiasmus and the *Aeneid*", *The American Journal of Philology*, 132 (2011), 273–200 (p. 274).

36. See the essay "How we weepe and laugh at one self-same thing", Florio's Montaigne, *Essays*, Book I.37.

37. The "doing and undoing" pattern of the play has been commented on according to a variety of approaches. See for all Neill, "Introduction", pp. 100–107. But see also Adelman, *The Common Liar*, throughout. Neill recognizes "two distinct uses of paradox in the play. . . . in one, which we might loosely call Roman, it expresses only self-devouring contradiction; in the other, more typically "Egyptian" use, it figures the inalienable doubleness of things" (p. 102). But see also Peter Berek, "Doing and Undoing: The Value of Action in *Antony and Cleopatra*", *Shakespeare Quarterly*, 32:3 (1981), 295–304.

38. Noot, *A Theatre Wherein Be Represented*, EEBO edition, unnumbered page. But see also Spenser, "A Theatre for Wordlings", son. 15, 1–4, in Spenser, *The Yale Edition of the Shorter Poems*, p. 484.

39. Tennenhouse, *Power on Display*, pp. 144–146.

40. Adelman, *The Common Liar*, pp. 113 and 112. Others, from different perspectives, have noticed the play's prevalence of this figure. See for all Benjamin T. Spencer, "*Antony and Cleopatra* and the Paradoxical Metaphor", *Shakespeare Quarterly*, 9:3 (1958), 373–378; Madeleine Doran, "'High Events as These': The Language of Hyperbole in *Antony and Cleopatra*", *Queen's Quarterly*, 72 (1965), 25–51; Charney, *Shakespeare's Roman Plays*; Tanner, "*Antony and Cleopatra*".

41. Wilson G. Knight, *The Imperial Theme* (New York: Routledge, [1931] 2002), pp. 206–207 *et passim*.

42. Caroline Spurgeon, *Shakespeare's Imagery and What It Tells Us* (Cambridge: Cambridge University Press, [1935] 2001), pp. 350, 354.

43. Charney, *Shakespeare's Roman Plays*, pp. 93, 83.

44. This didn't mean that the comparison Rome = world presumed a real equivalence. As Gillies points out in his discussion of Rome's understanding of the "orbic frame", *orbis* was a cultural construct which didn't coincide with all the known world. In ancient Rome *Orbis* was defined by boundaries, terminal lands (*termini*), which seen in the logic of a Vichian poetical geography were meant to defend from disastrous transgressiveness and confusing otherness (*Shakespeare and the Geography of Difference*, pp. 10–12). For a discussion of natural "terminal" borders used as symbolic and mythologized places of violation and transgression, as well as identity, difference, and exclusion in the classical world, see pp. 7–12.

45. Richard Hingley, *Globalizing Roman Culture: Unity, Diversity and Empire* (London and New York: Routledge, 2005), p. 78.

46. Montaigne, *Essays*, transl. John Florio, Book II.22, p. 669.

47. Adelman, *The Common Liar*, p. 34.

48. Ronald R. MacDonald, "Playing Till Doomsday: Interpreting *Antony and Cleopatra*", *English Literary Renaissance*, 15:1 (1987), 78–99 (p. 85).

49. I owe this term to Adelman, *The Common Liar*, p. 36.

50. Jacques Derrida, *The Postcard*, 1980, transl. Alan Bass (Chicago and London: The University of Chicago Press, 1987), p. 5.

51. "Inspiration is the drama, with several characters, of theft, the structure of the classical theater in which the invisibility of the promptor [*souffler*] ensures the indispensable *différance* and intermittence between a text already written by another hand and an interpreter already dispossessed of that which he receives", "La parole soufflée", in his *Writing and Difference*, p. 176. But see also in *Writing and Difference*, "Freud and the Scene of Writing", pp. 196–231.

52. Maddalena Pennacchia, "Performance History", in Domenico Lovascio, ed., *Antony and Cleopatra: A Critical Reader* (London: Bloomsbury Arden Shakespeare, 2020), p. 55.

53. The play's performance history is one of severe cuts, the problem being mainly Shakespeare's disregard of the Aristotelian dramatic units and the incessant fading of one scene into anther, for long seen as a "defective method", as Bradley's reassuming statement stands to prove. A.C. Bradley, *Shakespearean Tragedy* (1904), pp. 71, 260. Qtd in Schanzer, *The Problem Plays of Shakespeare*, p. 132. In his 1709 edition of the play, Nicholas Rowe deemed it expedient to "remedy" this by subdividing the play's continuity into acts and scenes, and by geographically defining each scene, according to the increasing illusionism of the theatre scenery. In performance, "Some adaptation of the text had therefore to be made in order to reduce the number of scenes and to avoid frequent scene changes, a process which went on up to the end of the nineteenth century" (Wilders, "Introduction", pp. 15 and 12–43). For more on the difficulty of the play's staging and the actor's performances, see David Bevington's "Introduction" to his edited *Antony and Cleopatra*, pp. 42–67; Neill's "Introduction" to his edited *Antony and Cleopatra*, pp. 23–88. In connection with the world theme, see M. Charney, *Shakespeare's Roman Plays*, pp. 93–96.

54. Gillies, *Shakespeare and the Geography of Difference*, pp. 71–72, 34.

55. In Bernard Klein's words, "spatial hyperbole shapes the characters' speech in every act". "Antony and Cleopatra", in Neill and Schalkwyk, eds, *The Oxford Handbook of Shakespearean Tragedy*, p. 453.

56. For a reappraisal of ancient Rome in the light of our current notion of a global world, see Hingley, *Globalizing Roman Culture*.

57. Hazlitt, *The Round Table and Characters of Shakespeare's Plays*, p. 180.

58. Klein, "Antony and Cleopatra", p. 463.

59. Alan Stewart, "The Early Modern Closet Discovered", *Representations*, 50 (1995), 76–100 (p. 82).

60. Ian Kott, *Shakespeare our Contemporary* (1961), qtd in Neill, "Introduction" to *Antony and Cleopatra*, p. 39.

61. Neill, *Issues of Death*, pp. 327 and 308. But see also in the Introduction to my volume the section, "'Not Marble, nor the Gilded Monuments': Ruins and Poetical Power".

62. Camden, *Remains Concerning Britain*.

63. Nadia Fusini, *Donne Fatali: Ofelia, Desdemona, Cleopatra* (Roma: Bulzoni Editore, 2005), p. 76.

64. On the play's imagery of dissolution and self-loss, see for all Neill, "Introduction" to *Antony and Cleopatra*, pp. 107–111; Charney, *Shakespeare's Roman Plays*, pp. 136–141; Agostino Lombardo, *Il fuoco e l'aria. Quattro studi su Antonio e Cleopatra* (Roma: Bulzoni, 1995), pp. 41–67.

65. "Rome was th' whole world, and all the world was Rome; / And if things nam'd their names do equalize, / When land and sea ye name, then name ye Rome; / And naming Rome, ye land and sea comprise" (Du Bellay/Spenser, son. 26).

66. This doesn't exclude other sources. See Adelman (*The Common Liar*, p. 98) for the suggested similarity with Jove's description in Lyon's *Imagines Deorum* (1581); see Bevington (*Antony and Cleopatra*, n. 79, p. 253) for the comparison with Marlowe's *Tamburlaine* (2.1). Antony's colossal size is also customarily referred to the Colossus of Rhodes. See Wilders's notes 78–90 of his edited *Antony and Cleopatra*, pp. 281–282.

67. Benjamin, "Theses on the Philosophy of History", in *Illuminations*, p. 249.

68. In Tanner's discussion, Octavius "is in time with Time. Antony and Cleopatra are out of time". With which he means that theirs is the time of eternity. "Egypt is a timeless present", the present of poetry and a perpetual holiday in its double sense of "vacancy" and "waste". Octavius's time on the contrary is "full of history". "*Antony and Cleopatra*. Boundaries and Excess", pp. 9 and 16–17.

69. For a reading of the play in the light of the absolutist visual paradigm of baroque culture, see Richard Wilson's chapter "Your Crown's Awry", in his *Free Will*, pp. 310–370. For related issues of visuality in Shakespeare and the late-sixteenth-century redefinition of the eye, see Del Sapio Garbero, "A Spider in the Eye/I", pp. 133–155 and "Troubled Metaphors", pp. 43–70.

70. Adelman, *Suffocating Mothers*, p. 177. On Antony's dissolving self and its relation with contemporary feminist notions of melancholy (Judith Butler, Julia Kristeva), see Cynthia Marshall, "Men of Steel Done Got the Blues: Melancholic Subversion of Presence in *Antony and Cleopatra*", *Shakespeare Quarterly*, 44:4 (1993), 385–408. For more on "fullness" and "emptiness", see Neill's insightful "Introduction", pp. 75–76.

71. See Dollimore, *Radical Tragedy*, p. 207.

72. Adelman, *Suffocating Mothers*, p. 184.

73. Del Sapio Garbero, "Shakespeare's Maternal Transfigurations", pp. 93–117. For a discussion of the eschatological theme in its relation with medieval double-tiered funerary sculptures, see John M. Bowers, "'I Am Marble-Constant': Cleopatra's Monumental End", *Huntington Library Quarterly*, 46 (1983), 283–297 (pp. 290–291).

74. The reference is to Virgil, *Aeneid* VI.747 ("*Plurumque reliquit / Aetereum sensum atque aurai simplicis ignem*" / "Pure and unmixed the aetherial sense is left, mere air and fire"). What has gone unnoticed, at least to my knowledge, is that Bacon's readers could find this quoted and discussed in his *Advancement of Learning* (1607) in conjunction with man's "confounded mass" and "infinite variations". "The soul on the other side is the simplest of substances" as well expressed by the poet, Bacon states. "So that it is no marvel though the soul so placed enjoy no rest, if that principle be true, *that Motus rerum est rapidus extra locum, placidus in loco*", e.g. (The motion of things is rapid out of their place, quiet in their place). Hence "poets did well", he continues, "to conjoin music and medicine in Apollo, because the office of medicine is but to tune the curious harp of men's body and to reduce it to harmony" (p. 106). It is legitimate to speculate, I argue, that this humoral/medical distinction between body and soul, heavier and lighter elements, may have been an inspiring source to Shakespeare in imagining Cleopatra's death as an Apollonian final search for harmonious poetry and transcending rest.

75. On Cleopatra's suicide, see Neill's chapter "*Finis coronat opus*: The Monumental Ending of *Antony and Cleopatra*", in *Issues of Death*, pp. 305–327. For a feminist criticism of women's lunar variety, and the way Cleopatra's "marble-constant" suicide transgresses the patriarchal "system of differences", see Catherine Belsey, *The Subject of Tragedy: Identity and Difference in Renaissance Drama* (London and New York: Routledge, 1985), p. 184. On suicide as the achievement of the "unbounded totality" through art, see Rosy

Colombo, "Cleopatra's Roman Death", *Memoria di Shakespeare*, 4 (2017), 73–86. But see also Gray, *Shakespeare and the Fall of the Roman Republic*, chapters 3 and 4.

76. For more on the play's oscillation between tragedy and comedy and their union "on an epic scale", see Barbara C. Vincent, "Shakespeare's *Antony and Cleopatra* and the Rise of Comedy", in Drakakis, ed., *Antony and Cleopatra*, pp. 212–247.

77. For more on this, see Gary Shapiro, *Archaeologies of Vision: Foucault and Nietzsche on Seeing and Saying* (Chicago and London: The University of Chicago Press, 2003), p. 128.

78. For a discussion of love in afterlife, and the way this can only be fulfilled by the perpetuating power of poetry in the context of a Protestant redefinition of the afterlife, see Ramie Targoff, *Posthumous Life: Eros and Afterlife in Renaissance England* (Chicago: The University of Chicago Press, 2014). But see also her "Love and Death in Egypt and Rome".

79. Hui, *The Poetics of Ruins*, p. 159.

80. Adelman, *Suffocating Mothers*, p. 183.

81. Dollimore, *Radical Tragedy*, pp. 30 and 3–50. His is a challenging discussion of both dramatic modes and identity in the light of a subversive notion of discontinuity which stems from Montaigne's ideas. As Dollimore observes, the bathetic in the play "makes for an insisting cancelling of the potentially sublime in favour of the political realities which the sublime struggles to eclipse or transcend" (p. 212).

82. In line with the critical move represented by Adelman (*The Common Liar*) and Dollimore (*Radical Tragedy*), Neill has incisively deconstructed the binary opposition between "female/Egyptian mutability and male/Roman self-consistency", by expanding on Montaigne's problematization of a coherent selfhood and its bearing on Shakespeare's couple, independently from gender. Who is the true Antony? And who is the true Cleopatra? Their restless "oscillation of mood", he argues, refers us to *Hamlet* and *Troilus and Cressida*, where Shakespeare "had already shown a fascination with the discontinuous and histrionic nature of identity explored in Montaigne's *Essays*". "Introduction", pp. 82–85.

83. On the pivotal role of minor characters in matters of Roman *virtus*, especially in the play's Ventidius scene, see Giorgio Melchiori's essay, "'They That Have Power': The Ethics of the Roman Plays", in Del Sapio Garbero, ed., *Identity, Otherness and Empire*, pp. 203–205.

84. On the multifaceted figure of Enobarbus (chorus, but also artist, and seer), see Agostino Lombardo's extensive study, *Ritratto di Enobarbo* (Pisa: Nistri-Lischi, 1971).

85. Dollimore, "Shakespeare Understudies", p. 144.

86. On the relation with the regenerative myth of Isis, see Adelman, *Suffocating Mothers*, pp. 183–185. As suggested by Adelman, Shakespeare may have read Plutarch's essay "Of Isis and Osiris" in his *Moralia* translated into English by Philomen Holland in 1603.

87. This just meets Antony's expectation when earlier in addressing his soldiers he elicits: "You have shown all Hectors. / Enter the city; clip your wives, your friends; / Tell them your feats, whilst they with joyful tears / Wash your congealment from your wounds, and kiss / The honoured gashes whole" (4.8.7–10).

88. For a reading of Antony's death as a feminized sacrificial rite consumed on "Cleopatra's altar", see Little, *Shakespeare Jungle Fever*, pp. 114 and 112–122.

89. Miola, *Shakespeare's Rome*, p. 161.

90. Dollimore, *Radical Tragedy*, p. 212.

91. I am using "orientalist" according to the colonialist implications brought to the fore by Edward Said: for him a Western situated and dominating way of representing and authorizing the Orient, *Orientalism* (New York: Vintage, 1978), pp. 72–73.

92. Del Sapio Garbero, "Fostering the Question".

93. Derrida, "Hostipitality", pp. 4–5. See also, Derrida and Dufourmantelle, *Of Hospitality*, pp. 41–45.

94. Arguably Shakespeare, here as in *Titus* (1.1.113), apart from Plutarch's captive Cleopatra who "would marvelously beawtifie and sette out [Octavius's] triumphe" (North's Plutarch, 1007), was echoing Horace on ancient Britannia's hostages ("Or *Britains* yet untouche'd, in chains shou'd come, / To grace thy triumph, through the streets of *Rome*"). The poet's verses, addressed to Octavius Augustus, had been reported in Camden's *Britannia* (*Brit 2*, p. XLII), and the fact that Cleopatra's claim could be perceived as underwritten by the memory of "Britains . . . in chains" may have sounded all the more disturbing to those in Shakespeare's audience who were familiar with Camden or Horace.

95. See for all Dio Cassius's description of one of Julius Caesar's triumphs. *Roman History*, vol. IV, pp. 245–247.

96. See respectively Loomba's "'Delicious traffick': Racial and Religious Difference on Early Modern Stages,' in Catherine M.S. Alexander and Stanley Wells, eds, *Shakespeare and Race* (Cambridge: Cambridge University Press, 2000), pp. 218–219, and *Shakespeare, Race, and Colonialism*, p. 88.

97. Derrida, "Hostipitality", p. 4.

98. For a reading of Cleopatra in the light of her image's nomadism across time and geographies see Keir Elam, "'Cleopatra a Gypsy': Performing the Nomadic Subject in Shakespeare's Alexandria, Rome and London", *Memoria di Shakespeare*, 4 (2017), 35–60.

99. Adelman, *The Common Liar*, p. 134.

100. Susan Sontag, "Notes on Camp", in Susan Sontag, ed., *Against Interpretation and Other Essays* (New York: Farrar, Straus and Giroux, 1966).

101. See earlier note 24 (on Derrida). For a discussion of iterability as the essence of imitation and its confines, see Greene, *The Light to Troy*, pp. 10–11.

102. As Agostino Lombardo has observed, *Julius Caesar* features in *Antony and Cleopatra* as the "theatrical past, as well as the historical past". "A Tragedy of Memory", *Memoria di Shakespeare*, 4 (2017), 103–111 (p. 104).

103. Adelman observes: "[I]f hyperbole is the rhetorical figure appropriate to excess, it is also the remembrance of time past, when the hyperbole was still available to man". *The Common Liar*, p. 12. Neill interprets Antony's belatedness in terms of obsolescence and nostalgia. For him Antony is "the last survivor of a heroic age, whom the play bathes in the glow of admiring retrospection". "Introduction", pp. 93–96.

104. See Greene, *The Light to Troy*, pp. 8 and 4–27.

105. Terry Eagleton, *Walter Benjamin, or, Towards a Revolutionary Criticism* (London: Verso Editions, 1981), pp. 116–117. Benjamin's quotation is from *Origin*, p. 36.

106. Hui, *The Poetics of Ruins*, p. 56.

107. On theoretical questions of author and authorship, see Stephen Orgel's chapter "What Is a Text?", in Stephen Orgel, *Authentic Shakespeare: And Other Problems of the Early Modern Stage* (New York and Abingdon: Routledge, 2002).

108. Montaigne, *The Journey Through Germany and Italy*, in Montaigne, *The Complete Works*, p. 572 (see earlier extensive discussion, Introduction, Part 1).

Bibliography

Primary Sources

A., R., *The Valiant Welshman, or The True Chronicle History of the Life and Valiant Deeds of Caradoc the Great, King of Cambria, Now Called Wales* (London: George Purslowe, 1615). Early English Books Online.

Ascham, Roger, "The Schoolmaster", in G. Gregory Smith, ed., *Elizabethan Critical Essays*, 2 vols, vol. 1 (London: Oxford University Press, 1950), pp. 1–45.

Bacon, Francis, *The Advancement of Learning* [1605] *and New Atlantis*, ed. Arthur Johnston (Oxford: Clarendon Press, 1974).

Benedetti, Alessandro, *Historia corporis humani sive Anatomice* [1502], Latin / Italian bilingual edition, ed. Giovanna Ferrari (Firenze: Giunti, 1998).

Biondo, Flavio, *Roma ristaurata, et Italia illustrata di Biondo da Forlì* [1444–46], transl. Lucio Fauno (Venezia: M. Tramezino, 1542).

Bracciolini, Poggio, *De fortunae varietate et Urbis Romae & de ruina eiusdem descriptio* (1448).

Bracciolini, Poggio, *Les Ruines de Rome. De Varietate Fortunae. Livre I*, transl. Jean-Yves Boriaud, Introduction by Philippe Coarelli and Jean-Yves Boriaud (Paris: Belle Lettres, 1999).

Bullough, Geoffrey, ed., *Narrative and Dramatic Sources of Shakespeare*, 8 vols (London: Routledge and Kegan Paul, 1957–1975).

Bulwer, John, *Chirologia: Or the Natural Language of the Hand and Chironomia: Or, the Art of Manual Rhetoric* (London, 1644).

Caesar, *The Gallic War*, transl. H. J. Edwards, Loeb Classical Library (Cambridge, MA: Harvard University Press, 1917).

Camden, William, *BRITANNIA: A Chrorographicall Description of the Most Flourishing Kingdomes, ENGLAND, SCOTLAND, and IRELAND, and the Ilands Adioyning, Out of the Depth of ANTIQUITIE, Written First in Latine by William Camden, Translated Newly into English by Philémon Holland* (London: G. Bishop and I. Norton, 1610).

Camden, William, *Remains Concerning Britain* [1605], ed. John Philipot and W.D. Gent (London: Charles Harper, 1674).

Camden, William, *Britannia, Newly Translated to English by Edmund Gibson* (London: F. Collins, 1695).

Castiglione, Baldassare, *Il Cortegiano* (Venezia: Comin Trino, 1573).

Castiglione, Baldassare, *The Book of the Courtier*, transl. Thomas Hoby [1561], ed. Walter Alexander Raleigh (London: David Nutt, 1900). University of Oregon edition online: Renascence Editions, 1997.

Chaucer, Geoffrey, *The Poetical Works of Geoffrey Chaucer*, 10 vols (London: William Pickering, 1845).

Ciardi, Roberto Paolo and Lucia Tongiorgi Tomasi, eds, *Immagini anatomiche e naturalistiche nei disegni degli Uffizi, Secc. XVI e XVII* (Firenze: Olschki, 1984).

Cicero, *The Oratore* (Books I, II), transl. E.W. Sutton and H. Rackham, Loeb Classical Library (London and Cambridge, MA: Harvard University Press, 1947).

Cicero, *The Oratore* (Book III), *De Fato, Pradoxa Stoicorum, De Partitione Oratoria*, transl. H. Rackham, Loeb Classical Library (London and Cambridge, MA: Harvard University Press, 1948).

Crooke, Helkiah, *Microcosmographia: A Description of the Body of Man* (London: William Jaggard, 1615).

Daniel, Samuel, *The Tragedie of Cleopatra* (1594), in *The Complete Works in Verse and Prose*, 4 vols, ed by Alexander B. Grosart, 1885.

Dee, John, *Mathematicall Preface to Elements of Geometrie of Euclid of Megara* (London: John Daye, 1570). (The Project Gutenberg Ebooks, 2007).

Dio Cassius, Lucius, *Roman History*, 9 vols, transl. Earnest Cary, Loeb Classical Library (London and Cambridge, MA: Harvard University Press, 1961).

Donne, John, *Devotions Upon Emergent Occasions* (London: Thomas Jones, 1624).

Donne, John, *Poesie*, bilingual edition, ed. and transl. Alessandro Serpieri and Silvia Bigliazzi (Milano: Rizzoli, 2009).

Du Bellay, Joachim, *Les Antiquitez de Rome contenant une generale description de sa grandeur, et comme une deploration de sa ruine: plus un songe ou vision sur le meme subject* (Paris, 1558).

Du Bellay, Joachim, *'Les antiquitez de Rome' et 'Les regrets'* (Genève Lille: Droz Giard, 1960).

Du Bellay, Joachim, *Ruines of Rome* [1558], transl. Edmund Spenser, in E. Spenser, *The Yale Edition of the Shorter Poems*, ed. William A. Oram et al. (New Haven and London: Yale University Press, 1989).

Eliot, T. S., *The Waste Land*, in *Collected Poems, 1909–1962* (London: Faber & Faber, 1963).

Elizabeth, I., *Collected Works*, ed. Leah S. Marcus et al. (Chicago: The University of Chicago Press, 2000).

Estienne, Charles, *De dissectione partium corporis humani libri tres* (Paris, 1545).

Euripides, *Hecuba*, transl. Edward. P. Coleridge (London: G. Bell and Sons, 1910). The Internet Classical Archive, http://classics.mit.edu/Euripides/hecuba.html.

Gibbon, Edward, *The History of the Decline and Fall of the Roman Empire*, 12 vols, ed. J. B. Bury (New York: Freed De Fau & Company Publishers, [1776–1789] 1907).

Giraldi Cinthio, Giovanbattista, *Orbecche* [1541] (Roma: Biblioteca Italiana, 2003), www.bibliotecaitaliana.it/xtf/view?docId=bibit000565/bibit000565. xml&doc.vi.

Golding, Arthur, *Ovid's Metamorphoses*, ed. Madeleine Forey (London: Penguin Books, 2002).

Harvey, Richard, *Philadelphus, or a Defence of Brutes, and the Brutans History* (London: John Wolfe, 1593).

Henslowe, Philip, *The Diary, 1591–1609*, ed. J. Payne Collier (London: The Shakespeare Society, 1845).

Henslowe, Philip, *The Diary, 1591–1609*, ed. Walter W. Greg (London: A.H. Bullen, 1904).

Holinshed, Raphael, *Chronicles: The History of Scotland* (section "Kenneth"). Perseus Digital Library. www.perseus.tufts.edu/hopper/.

Holinshed, Raphael and Abraham Fleming, *The Historie of England, from the Time That It Was First Inhabited, Vntill the Time that It Was Last Conquered* [1587], ed. Henry Ellis (London: J. Jonson, 1807).

Homer, *Odyssey*, transl. A.T. Murray, rev. George E. Dimock, Loeb Classical Library, 2 vols (Cambridge, MA: Harvard University Press, 1919).

Horace, *The Works of Horace*, ed. C. Smart and Theodore Alois Buckley (New York: Harper & Brothers, 1863), www.perseus.tufts.edu/hopper/text?doc=Per seus:text:1999.02.0063.

Horace, *Odes*, transl. Charles E. Bennet [1914], Loeb Classical Library edition (London and Cambridge, MA: Harvard University Press, 1964).

Horace, *Satyres, Epistles and Ars Poetica*, transl. Rushton Fairclough [1926], Loeb Classical Library edition (London and Cambridge, MA: Harvard University Press, 1966).

Livy, *The Romane Historie Written by T. Livius of Padua*, transl. Philemon Holland (London: Adam Islip, 1600).

Livy, *The Rise of Rome: Book One to Five*, transl. T. J. Luce (Oxford: Oxford University Press, 1998).

Lomazzo, Giovanni, *Trattato dell'arte, della pittura, scultura ed architettura*, 7 Libri (Milano: Paolo Gottardo Ponzio, 1584).

Lomazzo, Giovanni, *A Tracte Containing the Artes of Curious Paintinge, Carvinge, and Buildinge* [1584], abridged transl. Richard Haydocke [1598], facsimile (Amsterdam and New York: Capo Press, 1969).

Lucan, M. Annaeus, *The Civil War (Pharsalia)*, transl. J. D. Duff, Loeb Classical Library (Cambridge, MA: Harvard University Press, 1928).

Montaigne, Michel de, *The Journey through Germany and Italy* (or, *Diary of a Journey*), in Montaigne, *The Complete Works of Michel de Montaigne*, 4 vols, transl. Charles Cotton, ed. William Hazlitt (London: John Templeman, 1842), pp. 527–629.

Montaigne, Michel de, *Essays*, transl. John Florio (1553–1625), 3 Books (University of Oregon: Renascence Editions online, 1999).

Müller, Heiner, *Anatomy Titus Fall of Rome (1985)*, transl. Carl Weber and Paul David Young, in *Heiner Müller after Shakespeare: Macbeth and Anatomy Titus Fall of Rome* (New York: Paj Publications, 2012).

Nashe, Thomas, *The Unfortunate Traveller or the Life of Jack Wilton* (London: T. Scarlet for C. Burby, 1594).

Ovid, *Tristia*, transl. Arthur Leslie Wheeler. Revised G. P. Goold. Loeb Classical Library [1929] (London and Cambridge, MA: Harvard University Press, 1965).

Ovid, *Fasti*, transl. Betty Rose Nagle (Bloomington: Indiana University Press, 1995).

Ovidio, *Metamorfosi*, ed. and transl. Piero Bernardini Marzolla (Torino: Einaudi, 1979).

Plutarch, *The Lives of the Noble Grecians and Romanes, Englished by Thomas North* (London: Thomas Vautroullier and Ion Wight, 1579).

Puttenham, George, [1589] *The Arte of English Poesie: A Critical Edition*, ed. by Frank Whigham and Wayne A. Rebhorn (Ithaca, NY: Cornelll University Press, 2007).

Rowley, William, *A Shoemaker, A Gentleman* (ca. 1609), ed. Trudy Laura Darby (London: Globe Quartos, Nick Hern Books, 2002).

Seneca, Lucius Annaeus, *The Woorke of Lucius Annaeus Seneca Concerning Benefyting, That Is Too Say the Doing, Receyuing, and Requiting of Good Turnes*, transl. Arthur Golding (London: John Kingston for John Day, 1578).

Seneca, Lucius Annaeus, *The Workes of Lucius Annæus Seneca*, transl. Thomas Lodge (London: William Stansby, 1614).

Serpieri, Alessandro, Claudia Corti, and Keir Elam, eds, *Nel laboratorio di Shakespeare. I drammi romani* (Parma: Pratiche Editrice, 1988).

Shakespeare, William, *Cymbeline*, ed. J.M. Nosworthy (London and New York: Methuen, [1955] 1986).

Shakespeare, William, *Sonetti*, ed. and transl. Alessandro Serpieri (Milano: Rizzoli, 1991/1998).

Shakespeare, William, *Cymbeline*, ed. Roger Warren (Oxford: Oxford University Press, 1998).

Shakespeare, William, *The Tempest*, eds, Virginia Mason Vaughan and Alden T. Vaughan (London: Bloomsbury Arden Shakespeare, 1999).

Shakespeare, William, *Antony and Cleopatra*, ed. Michael Neill (Oxford: Oxford University Press, [1994] 2000).

Shakespeare, William, *Poemetti*, ed. and transl. Gilberto Sacerdoti (Milano: Garzanti, 2000).

Shakespeare, William, *Antony and Cleopatra*, ed. David Bevington (Cambridge: Cambridge University Press, [1990] 2005).

Shakespeare, William, *The Poems*, ed. John Roe (Cambridge: Cambridge University Press, 2006).

Sidney, Philip, "An Apologie for Poetry" (1595), in G. Gregory Smith, ed., *Elizabethan Critical Essays*, vol. 1 (London: Oxford University, 1950), pp. 148–207.

Speed, John, *The Counties of Britain. A Tudor Atlas (The Theatre of the Empire of Great Britain*, 1611-12), eds, Nigel Nicolson and Alasdair Hawkyard (London: Pavilion, 1995).

Spenser, Edmund, *The Yale Edition of the Shorter Poems*, ed. William A. Oram et al. (New Haven and London: Yale University Press, 1989).

Spenser, Edmund, *The Faerie Queene*, ed. Douglas Brooke-Davies (London: J.M. Dent, 1997).

Stow, John, *Survey of London, Reprinted From the Text of 1603*, ed. C. L. Kingsford (Oxford: Clarendon Press, 1908).

Stubbes, Philip, *Anatomie of Abuses* (London: Richard Jones, 1583).

Suetonius, *The Twelve Caesars*, transl. Robert Graves (Harmondsworth: Penguin, [1957] 2003).

Tacitus, Cornelius, *Works*, transl. Clifford H. Moore and John Jackson, Loeb Classical Library, 5 vols (London and Cambridge MA: Harvard University Press, 1925–1937).

Van Der Noot, Jan, *A Theatre Wherein Be Represented as Wel the Miseries & Calamities That Follow the Voluptuous Worldlings as Also the Greate Ioyes and Plesures Which the Faithfull Do Enioy* (1569) [*A Theatre for Voluptious Worldlings*]. EEBO.

Vasari, Giorgio, *The Lives of the Painters, Sculptors and Architects*, 4 vols, transl. A. B. Hinds (London and New York: Dent, 1980).

Vesalius, Andreas, *De Humani Corporis Fabrica libri septem* (Basilæ: Ioannis Oporini, 1543).

Virgil, *Aeneid*, transl. Henry Rushton Fairclough, rev. G. P. Goold, Loeb Classical Library (London and Cambridge, MA: Harvard University Press, 1999).

Vv.Aa., *The Mirror for Magistrates*, ed. Thomas Blennerhassett (1578).

Vv.Aa., *The Mirror for Magistrates*, ed. John Higgins (1587).

Webster, John, *The Duchess of Malfi*, ed. J.R. Brown, The Revels Plays (London: Methuen, 1964).

Wells, Stanley and Gary Taylor, *William Shakespeare: A Textual Companion* (Oxford: Oxford University Press, 1997).

Secondary Sources

Adelman, Janet, *The Common Liar: an Essay on Antony and Cleopatra* (New Haven: Yale University Press, 1973).

Adelman, Janet, "'Anger's My Meat': Feeding, Dependency, and Aggression in *Coriolanus*", in Murray M. Schwartz, ed., *Representing Shakespeare: New Psychoanalytic Essays* (Baltimore and London: The John Hopkins University Press, 1980), pp. 129–149.

Adelman, Janet, *Suffocating Mothers: Fantasies of Maternal Origin in Shakespeare's Plays, Hamlet to the Tempest* (New York: Routledge, 1992).

Adelman, Janet, "Shakespeare's Romulus and Remus: Who Does the Wolf Love?", in Maria Del Sapio Garbero, ed., *Identity, Otherness and Empire in Shakespeare's Rome* (Farnham and Burlington: Ashgate, 2009), pp. 19–34.

Agamben, Giorgio, *L'uso dei corpi. Homo sacer*, IV (Vicenza: Neri Pozza Editore, 2014).

Anderson, Thomas P., *Performing Early Modern Trauma from Shakespeare to Milton* (Aldershot and Burlington: Ashgate, 2006).

Arendt, Hannah, *Between Past and Future: Eight Exercises in Political Thought* (New York: The Viking Press, [1954] 1961).

Aston, Margaret, "English Ruins and English History: The Dissolution of the Sense of the Past", *Journal of the Warburg and Courtauld Institutes*, 36 (1973), 231–255.

Aston, Margaret, *England's Iconoclasts: Laws Against Images* (Oxford: Clarendon Press, 1988).

Barish, Jonas, "Remembering and Forgetting in Shakespeare", in R.B. Parker and Sheldon P. Zitner, eds, *Elizabethan Theater: Essays in Honor of S. Schoenbaum* (Newark: University of Delaware Press, 1996), pp. 214–221.

Barkan, Leonard, "Making Pictures Speak: Renaissance Art, Elizabethan Literature, Modern Scholarship", *Renaissance Quarterly*, 48:2 (1995), 326–351.

Barkan, Leonard, *Unearthing the Past: Archaeology and Aesthetics in the Making of Renaissance Culture* (New Haven and London: Yale University Press, 1999).

Barthes, Roland, *The Pleasure of the Text*, transl. Richard Miller (New York: Hill and Wang, [1973] 1998).

Bassi, Shaul, *Shakespeare's Italy and Italy's Shakespeare: Place, 'Race', Politics* (London: Palgrave Macmillan, 2016).

Bate, Jonathan, *Shakespeare and Ovid* (Oxford: Clarendon Press, 1993).

Bate, Jonathan, "Introduction", in William Shakespeare, *Titus Andronicus*, ed. Jonathan Bate (London: Thomas Learning, 2003).

Belsey, Catherine, *The Subject of Tragedy: Identity and Difference in Renaissance Drama* (London and New York: Routledge, 1985).

Belsey, Catherine, "Tarquin Dispossessed: Expropriation and Consent in *The Rape of Lucrece*", *Shakespeare Quarterly*, 52:3 (2001), 315–335.

Belsey, Catherine, "Invocation of the Visual Image: Ekphrasis in *Lucrece* and Beyond", *Shakespeare Quarterly*, 63:2 (2012), 175–198.

Benjamin, Walter, "*Central Park* (1938–1939), transl. Lloyd Spencer with Mark Harrington", *New German Critique*, 34 (1985), 32–58.

Benjamin, Walter, *Illuminations*, ed. and with an Introduction by Hannah Arendt, transl. Harry Zorn (London: Pimlico, 1999).

Benjamin, Walter, *The Origin of German Tragic Drama*, with an Introduction by George Steiner, transl. John Osborne (London and New York: Verso, 2003).

Benjamin, Walter, "Paralipomena on the Concept of History", in *Selected Writings*, vol. 4, 1938–1940, eds, Howard Eiland and Michael W. Jennings, transl. Edmund Jephcott et al. (Cambridge, MA: The Belknap Press of Harvard University Press, 2003), pp. 401–411.

Berek, Peter, "Doing and Undoing: The Value of Action in *Antony and Cleopatra*", *Shakespeare Quarterly*, 32:3 (1981), 295–304.

Berger, Harry, Jr., *The Absence of Grace. Sprezzatura and Suspicion in Two Renaissance Courtesy Book* (Stanford: Stanford University Press, 2000).

Bergeron, David D., "*Cymbeline*: Shakespeare's Last Roman Play", *Shakespeare Quarterly*, 31:1 (1980), 31–41.

Berns, Ute, "Performing Anatomy in Shakespeare's *Julius Caesar*", in Maria Del Sapio Garbero, Nancy Insenberg, and Maddalena Pennacchia, eds, *Questioning Bodies in Shakespeare's Rome* (Göttingen: V&R Unipress, 2010), pp. 95–108.

Berry, Ralph, "*Julius Caesar*: A Roman Tragedy", *Dalhousie Review*, 61:2 (1981), 324–336.

Bevington, David, *Action Is Eloquence: Shakespeare's Language of Gesture* (Cambridge, MA: Harvard University Press, 1984).

Bevington, David, "Introduction", in William Shakespeare, *Antony and Cleopatra*, ed. David Bevington (Cambridge: Cambridge University Press, [1990] 2005), pp. 1–80.

Bhabha, Homi K., *The Location of Culture* (London and New York: Routledge, 2002).

Bigliazzi, Silvia, "Romanity and *sparagmos* in *Titus Andronicus*", in Maria Del Sapio Garbero, ed., *Rome in Shakespeare's World* (Roma: Edizioni di Storia e Letteratura, 2018), pp. 87–106.

Blumenberg, Hans, *Shipwreck with Spectator: Paradigm of a Metaphor for Existence*, transl. Stephen Rendall (Cambridge MA and London: The MIT Press, [1979] 1997).

Boling, Ronald J., "Anglo-Welsh Relations in *Cymbeline*", *Shakespeare Quarterly*, 51:1 (2000), 33–66.

Boswell-Stone, W.G., *Shakespeare's Holinshed: The Chronicle and the Historical Plays Compared* (London: Chatto and Windus, 1907).

Bowers, John M., "'I Am Marble-Constant': Cleopatra's Monumental End", *Huntington Library Quarterly*, 46 (1983), 283–297.

Bromley, Laura, "Lucrece's Re-Creation", *Shakespeare Quarterly*, 34:2 (1983), 200–211.

Brook, Peter, *The Empty Space* (London: Penguin Books, [1968] 1990).

Buci-Glucksmann, Christine, *Baroque Reason: The Aesthetics of Modernity* (London: Sage Publications, 1994).

Burrow, Colin, "Shakespeare and Humanistic Culture", in Charles Martindale and A.B. Taylor, eds, *Shakespeare and the Classics* (Cambridge: Cambridge University Press, 2004), pp. 9–27.

Burrow, Colin, *Shakespeare and Classical Antiquity* (Oxford: Oxford University Press, 2013).

Caillé, Alain, *Le tiers paradigme. Anthropologie philosophique du don* (Paris: Éditions la Découverte, 1998).

Caillé, Alain and Jacques T. Godbout, *L'esprit du don* (Paris: Éditions la Découverte, 1992).

Calbi, Maurizio, *Approximate Bodies: Gender and Power in Early Modern Drama and Anatomy* (London and New York: Routledge, 2005).

Calbi, Maurizio, "States of Exception: Auto-Immunity and the Body Politic in Shakespeare's *Coriolanus*", in Maria Del Sapio Garbero, Nancy Insenberg and Maddalena Pennacchia, eds, *Questioning Bodies in Shakespeare's Rome* (Göttingen: V&R Unipress, 2010), pp. 77–94.

Campi, Riccardo, D. Messina and M. Tolomelli, *Mimesi, Origine, Allegoria* (Firenze: Alinea, 2002).

Camporesi, Piero, *The Incorruptible Flesh: Bodily Mutation and Mortification in Religion and Folklore* (Cambridge: Cambridge University Press, 1988).

Caporicci, Camilla and Armelle Sabatier, eds, *The Art of Picture in Early Modern English Literature* (New York and London: Routledge, 2020).

Carron, Jean-Claude, "Imitation and Intertextuality in the Renaissance", *New Literary History*, 19:3 (1988), 565–579.

Carruthers, Mary, *The Book of Memory: A Study of Memory in Medieval Culture* [1990] (Cambridge: Cambridge University Press, 2013).

Cavell, Stanley, "'Who Does the Wolf Love?': *Coriolanus* and the Interpretations of Politics", in Patricia Parker and Geoffrey H. Hartman, eds, *Shakespeare and the Question of Theory* (New York and London: Routledge, [1985] 2004), pp. 245–272.

Charney, Maurice, *Shakespeare's Roman Plays: The Function of Imagery in the Drama* (Cambridge, MA: Harvard University Press, 1961).

Chernaik, Warren, *The Myth of Rome in Shakespeare and His Contemporaries* (Cambridge: Cambridge University Press, 2011).

Ciardi, Roberto Paolo, "Il corpo, progetto e rappresentazione", in Roberto Paolo Ciardi and Lucia Tongiorgi Tomasi, eds, *Immagini anatomiche e naturalistiche nei disegni degli Uffizi, Secc. XVI e XVII* (Firenze: Olschki, 1984), pp. 9–30.

Clark, Stuart, *Vanities of the Eye: Vision in Early Modern European Culture* (Oxford: Oxford University Press, 2007).

Clewell, Tammy, "Mourning Beyond Melancholia: Freud's Psychoanalysis of Loss", *Journal of the American Psychoanalytic Association*, 52:1 (2004), 197–223.

Coarelli, Philippe and Jean-Yves Boriaud, "Introducion" in Poggio Bracciolini, *Les Ruines de Rome. De Varietate Fortunae. Livre I*, transl. Jean-Yves Boriaud (Paris: Belle Lettres, 1999), pp. XI–LXXI.

Collinson, Patrick, "History", in Michael Hattaway, ed., *A Companion to English Renaissance Literature and Culture* (Oxford: Blackwell, 2003), pp. 58–70.

Colombo, Rosy, "Cleopatra's Roman Death", *Memoria di Shakespeare*, 4 (2017), 73–86.

Colombo, Rosy, "Introduction", *Memoria di Shakespeare*, 4 (2017), VII–XIV.

Compagnoni, Michela, "Blending Motherhoods: Volumnia and the Representation of Maternity in William Shakespeare's *Coriolanus*", in Domenico Lovascio, ed., *Roman Women in Shakespeare and His Contemporaries* (Kalamazoo: Medieval Institute Publications, 2020), pp. 39–58.

Corti, Claudia, "*Coriolanus*: presentazione, tabulazione e commento", in Alessandro Sepieri et al., eds, *Nel Laboratoro di Shakespere. Dalle fonti ai drammi. I drammi romani*, vol. 4 (Parma: Pratiche Editrice, 1988), pp. 251–342.

Corti, Claudia, "The Iconic Body: *Coriolanus* and Renaissance Corporeality", in Maria Del Sapio Garbero, Nancy Insenberg and Maddalena Pennacchia, eds, *Questioning Bodies in Shakespeare's Rome* (Göttingen: V&R Unipress, 2010), pp. 57–76.

Cottegnies, Line, "Of the Importance of Imitation: Du Bellay, Shakespeare, and the English Sonnetteers", *Shakespeare Studies*, 48 (2020), 41–47.

Craddock, Patricia B., "Edward Gibbon and the 'Ruins of the Capitol'", in Annabel Patterson, ed., *Roman Images* (Baltimore and London: The John Hopkins University Press, 1984), pp. 63–82.

Cranston, Philip E., "'Rome en Anglais se prononce room . . .'. Shakespeare Versions by Voltaire", *Modern Language Notes*, 6 (1975), 809–837.

Crowe, Jonathan, *Trials of Authorship: Anterior Forms and Poetic Reconstruction From Wyatt to Shakespeare* (Los Angeles and Oxford: University of California Press, 1990).

Crumley, J. Clinton, "Questioning History in *Cymbeline*", *Studies in English Literature*, 41:2 (2001), 297–315.

Cunningham, Andrew, *The Anatomical Renaissance: The Resurrection of the Anatomical Projects of the Ancients* (Aldershot: Scholar Press, 1997).

Curran, John E., "Royalty Unlearned, Honour Untaught: British Savages and Historiographical Change in *Cymbeline*", *Comparative Drama*, 31:2 (1997), 277–303.

D'Amico, Jack, "Shakespeare's Rome: Politics and Theatre", *Modern Language Studies*, 22:1 (1992), 65–78.

d'Amico, Masolino, *Scena e parola in Shakespeare* (Roma: Edizioni di Storia e Letteratura, [1974] 2007).

Daniel, Drew, *The Melancholic Assemblage: Affect and Epistemology in the English Renaissance* (New York: Fordham University Press, 2013).

Daniell, David, "Introduction", in William Shakespeare, *Julius Caesar*, ed. David Daniell (London: Bloomsbury Arden Shakespeare, 1998), pp. 1–148.

Del Sapio Garbero, Maria, *Il bene ritrovato. Le figlie di Shakespeare dal King Lear ai Romances* (Roma: Bulzoni, 2004).

Del Sapio Garbero, Maria, "'A Goodly House': Memory and Hosting in *Coriolanus*", in Marta Gibinska and Agnieszka Romanowska, eds, *Shakespeare in Europe: History and Memory* (Cracow: Jagiellonian University Press, 2008), pp. 225–238.

Del Sapio Garbero, Maria, "Fostering the Question 'Who Plays the Host?'", in Maria Del Sapio Garbero, ed., *Identity, Otherness and Empire in Shakespeare's Rome* (Farnham and Burlington: Ashgate, 2009), pp. 91–104.

Del Sapio Garbero, Maria, ed., *Identity, Otherness and Empire in Shakespeare's Rome* ([Farnham and Burlington: Ashgate, 2009] rpt New York and London: Routledge, 2016).

Del Sapio Garbero, Maria, "Translating *Hamlet*/Botching Up Ophelia's Half Sense", in Harold Bloom, ed., *William Shakespeare's Hamlet*, new ed. (New York: Infobase Publishing, 2009), pp. 135–150.

Del Sapio Garbero, Maria, "A Spider in the Eye/I: The Hallucinatory Staging of the Self in Shakespeare's *The Winter's Tale*", in Ute Berns, ed., *Solo*

Performances: Staging the Early Modern Self in England (Amsterdam: Rodopi, 2010), pp. 133–155.

Del Sapio Garbero, Maria, "Disowning the Bond: Coriolanus Forgetful Humanism", in Michele Marrapodi, ed., *Shakespeare and the Italian Renaissance: Appropriation, Transformation, Opposition* (Farnham: Ashgate, 2014), pp. 73–91.

Del Sapio Garbero, Maria, "'Be Stone No More': Maternity and Heretical Visual Art in Shakespeare's Late Plays", *Actes des congrès de la Société française Shakespeare*, 33 (2015), 1–13, http://shakespeare.revues.org/3493.

Del Sapio Garbero, Maria, "Shakespeare's Maternal Transfigurations", in Karen Bamford and Naomi J. Miller, eds, *Maternity and Romance Narratives in Early Modern England* (Farnham and Burlington: Ashgate, 2015), pp. 93–118.

Del Sapio Garbero, Maria, "New Visual Paradigms in Shakespeare's Times", in Maria Del Sapio Garbero, ed., *Shakespeare and the New Science in Early Modern Culture* (Pisa: Pacini, 2016), pp. 5–24.

Del Sapio Garbero, Maria, ed., *Shakespeare and the New Science in Early Modern Culture* (Pisa: Pacini, 2016).

Del Sapio Garbero, Maria, "The Illness of Shakespeare's Rome: An Introduction", in Del Sapio Garbero, ed., *Rome in Shakespeare's World* (Roma: Edizioni di Storia e Letteratura, 2018), pp. vii–xxii.

Del Sapio Garbero, Maria, ed., *Rome in Shakespeare's World* (Roma: Storia e Letteratura, 2018).

Del Sapio Garbero, Maria, Nancy Isenberg and Maddalena Pennacchia, eds, *Questioning Bodies in Shakespeare's Rome* (Göttingen: V&R Unipress, 2010).

De Rosa, Andrea, "Prefazione: Giulio Cesare, il tiranno", in Fabrizio Sinisi, *Giulio Cesare. Uccidere il tiranno* (Gorgonzola, MI: Nardini Editore, 2017), pp. 5–6.

Derrida, Jacques, *Writing and Difference*, transl. Alan Bass [1967] (Chicago: The University of Chicago University Press, 1978).

Derrida, Jacques, *La carte postale* (Paris: Flammarion, 1980).

Derrida, Jacques, *The Postcard*, transl. Alan Bass [1980] (Chicago and London: The University of Chicago Press, 1987).

Derrida, Jacques, *Donner le temps* (Paris: Galilée, 1991).

Derrida, Jacques, "By Force of Mourning", *Critical Inquiry*, 22:2 (1996), 171–192.

Derrida, Jacques, "Hostipitality", *Angelaki*, 5:3 (2000), 3–18.

Derrida, Jacques, *Specters of Marx* (New York and London: Routledge, [1993] 2006).

Derrida, Jacques and Derek Attridge, *"This Strange Institution Called Literature": An Interview with Jacques Derrida* (London: Routledge, 1992).

Derrida, Jacques and Anne Dufourmantelle, *Of Hospitality. Anne Dufourmantelle Invites Jacques Derrida to Respond* (Stanford: Stanford University Press, [1997] 2000).

Di Michele, Laura, *La scena dei potenti. Teatro politica spettacolo nell'età di W. Shakespeare* (Napoli: Istituto Universitario Orientale, 1988).

Di Michele, Laura, "Shakespeare's Writing of Rome in *Cymbeline*", in Maria Del Sapio Garbero, ed., *Identity, Otherness and Empire in Shakespeare's Rome* (Farnham and Burlington: Ashgate, 2009), pp. 157–173.

Dobson, Michael, *The Making of the National Poet: Shakespeare, Adaptation and Authorship, 1660–1769* (Oxford: Clarendon Press, 1992).

Dobson, Michael, "Nationalism, National Theatres and the Return of *Julius Caesar*", in Daniela Guardamagna, ed., *Roman Shakespeare: Intersecting Times, Spaces, Languages* (Oxford: Peter Lang, 2018), pp. 33–56.

Dollimore, Jonathan, *Radical Tragedy: Religion and Power in the Drama of Shakespeare and his Contemporaries* (Brighton: The Harvester Press, 1984).

Dollimore, Jonathan, "Shakespeare Understudies: The Sodomite, the Prostitute, the Transvestite and Their Critics", in Jonathan Dollimore and Alan Sinfield, eds, *Political Shakespeare: Essays in Cultural Materialism* (Manchester: Manchester University Press, [1985] 2000), pp. 129–153.

Donaldson, Ian, *The Rapes of Lucretia: A Myth and Its Transformations* (Oxford: Clarendon Press, [1982] 2001).

Doran, Madeleine, "'High Events as These': The Language of Hyperbole in *Antony and Cleopatra*", *Queen's Quarterly*, 72 (1965), 25–51.

Drakakis, John, ed., *Antony and Cleopatra: William Shakespeare* (Houndmills: Macmillan New Casebooks, 1994).

Drakakis, John, "'Fashion it Thus': Julius Caesar and the Politics of Theatrical Representation", in Richard Wilson, ed., *Julius Caesar: William Shakespeare* (Houndmills and New York: Palgrave New Casebooks, 2002), pp. 77–91.

Duffy, Eamon, *The Stripping of the Altars* (New Haven and London: Yale University Press, 1992).

Duncan-Jones, Katherine and H.R. Woudhuysen, "Introduction", in William Shakespeare, *Poems*, eds, Katherine Duncan-Jones and H.R. Woudhuysen (London: Thomson Learning, 2007), pp. 1–124.

Dundas, Judith, "Mocking the Mind: The Role of Art in Shakespeare's *Rape of Lucrece*", *The Sixteenth Century Journal*, 14:1 (1983), 13–22.

Eagleton, Terry, *Walter Benjamin, or, Towards a Revolutionary Criticism* (London: Verso Editions, 1981).

Eaton, Sara, "A Woman of Letters: Lavinia in *Titus Andronicus*", in Shirley Nelson Garner and Madelon Sprengnether, eds, *Shakespearean Tragedy and Gender* (Bloomington and Indianapolis: Indiana University Press, 1996), pp. 54–74.

Edwards, Catherine, *Writing Rome: Textual Approaches to the City* (Cambridge: Cambridge University Press, 1996).

Elam, Keir, "*Antony and Cleopatra*: Presentazione, Tabulazione, Commento", in Alessandro Serpieri et al., *Nel Laboratorio di Shakespeare. Dalle fonti ai drammi, I drammi romani*, vol. 4 (Parma: Pratiche Editrice, 1988), pp. 133–247.

Elam, Keir, "'Cleopatra a Gypsy': Performing the Nomadic Subject in Shakespeare's Alexandria, Rome and London", *Memoria di Shakespeare*, 4 (2017), 35–60.

Elam, Keir, *Shakespeare's Pictures: Visual Objects in the Drama* (London: Bloomsbury, 2019).

Elet, Yvonne, *Architectural Invention in Renaissance Rome* (Cambridge: Cambridge University Press, 2018).

Eliot, T.S., "Seneca in Elizabethan Translation", in T.S. Eliot, *Selected Essays* (London: Faber and Faber, 1934).

Enterline, Lynn, *The Rhetoric of the Body From Ovid to Shakespeare* (Cambridge: Cambridge University Press, 2000).

Enterline, Lynn, *Shakespeare's Schoolroom: Rhetoric, Discipline, Emotion* (Philadelphia: University of Pennsylvania Press, 2012).

Ernst, Wolfgang, "Radically De-Historicising the Archive. Decolonising Archival Memory from the Supremacy of Historical Discourse", in *Decolonising Archives* (L'Internationale Online, www.internationaleonline.org, 2016), pp. 10–16.

Escobedo, Andrew, "From Britannia to England: *Cymbeline* and the Beginning of Nations", *Shakespeare Quarterly*, 59:1 (2008), 60–87.

Fawcett, Mary Laughlin, "Arms/Words/Tears: Language and the Body in *Titus Andronicus*", *ELH*, 50:2 (1983), 261–277.

Ferguson, Margaret, "'The Afflatus of Ruin': Meditation on Rome by Du Bellay, Spenser, and Stevens", in Annabel Patterson, ed., *Roman Images* (Baltimore and London: The John Hopkins University Press, 1984), pp. 23–50.

Ferrara, Fernando, *Shakespeare e le voci della storia* (Roma: Bulzoni Editore, 1994).

Ferrara, Fernando, *Il teatro dei re: saggio sui drammi storico-politici di Shakespeare* (Bari: Adriatica Editrice, 1995).

Ferrari, Giovanna, "Public Anatomy Lessons and the Carnival: The Anatomy Theatre of Bologna", *Past and Present*, 117 (1987), 50–106.

Fineman, Joel, "Shakespeare's *Will*: The Temporality of Rape", *Representations*, 20 (1987), 25–40.

Fiorentino, Francesco, "Introduzione", to Heiner Müller, *Anatomia Tito Fall of Rome. Un Commento Shakespeariano*, ed. and transl. Francesco Fiorentino (Roma: L'Orma Editore, 2017), pp. 7–35.

Floyd-Wilson, Mary, "Delving to the Root: Cymbeline, Scotland, and the English Race", in David J. Barker and Willy Maley, eds, *British Identities and English Renaissance Literature* (Cambridge: Cambridge University Press, 2002), pp. 101–115.

Floyd-Wilson, Mary, *English Ethnicity and Race in Early Modern Drama* (Cambridge: Cambridge University Press, 2003).

Foucault, Michel, *The Archaeology of Knowledge and the Discourse of Language*, transl. A.M. Sheridan Smith (New York: Pantheon Books, 1972).

Foucault, Michel, *Discipline and Punish: The Birth of the Prison*, transl. A.M. Sheridan Smith (Harmondsworth: Penguin Books, 1977).

Foucault, Michel, *The History of Sexuality: An Introduction*, vol. 1 (Harmondsworth: Penguin, 1978).

Foucault, Michel, *Le parole e le cose: un'archeologia delle scienze umane* [1966], transl. Emilio Panaitescu (Milano: Rizzoli, 1978).

Foucault, Michel, "The Order of Discourse", in Robert Young, ed., *Untying the Text: A Poststructuralist Reader* (London: Routledge and Kegan Paul, 1981), pp. 51–76.

Freud, Sigmund, *Civilization and Its Discontents*, transl. Joan Riviere (London: The Hogarth Press, 1930).

Freud, Sigmund, *Opere*, vol. 8 (Torino: Bollati Boringhieri, 1989).

Fusini, Nadia, *Donne fatali: Ofelia, Desdemona, Cleopatra* (Roma: Bulzoni Editore, 2005).

Fussner, Frank Smith, *The Historical Revolution. English Historical Writing and Thought* (London: Routledge, [1962] 2010).

Garber, Marjorie, *Shakespeare's Ghost Writers: Literature as Uncanny Causality* (New York and London: Methuen, 1987).

Genette, Gérard, *Figure III: discorso del racconto*, transl. Lina Zecchi (Torino: Einaudi, 1976).

Gentili, Vanna, *La Roma antica degli elisabettiani* (Bologna: Il Mulino, 1991).

Gillies, John, *Shakespeare and the Geography of Difference* (Cambridge: Cambridge University Press, 1994).

Girard, René, *A Theatre of Envy* [1990] (South Bend, IN: St. Augustine's Press, 2002).

Godbout, Jacques T., *Le Langage du don* (Montréal: Éditions Fides, 1996).

Goldberg, Jonathan, "'The Roman Actor': *Julius Caesar*", in Richard Wilson, ed., *Julius Caesar: William Shakespeare* (Houndmills and New York: Palgrave New Casebooks, 2002), pp. 92–107.

Golinelli, Gilberta, *Il testo shakespeariano dialoga con i nuovi storicismi, il materialismo culturale e gli studi di genere* (Bologna: Emil, 2012).

Gombrich, E.H., *Art and Illusion: A Study in the Psychology of Pictorial Representation* (London: Phaidon, 1962).

Grady, Hugh, *Shakespeare and Impure Aesthetics* (Cambridge: Cambridge University Press, 2009).

Granville-Barker, Harley, *Prefaces to Shakespeare*, 4 vols (London: Batsford, [1927–47] 1972).

Graves, Robert, *The Greek Myths* (London: Penguin Books, [1955] 1960).

Gray, Patrick, *Shakespeare and the Fall of the Roman Republic: Selfhood, Stoicism, and Civil War* (Edinburgh: Edinburgh University Press, 2019).

Greenblatt, Stephen, *Renaissance Self-Fashioning: From More to Shakespeare* (Chicago and London: The University of Chicago Press, 1980).

Greenblatt, Stephen, *Shakespearean Negotiations: The Circulation of Social Energy in Renaissance England* (Berkeley: University of California Press, 1988).

Greenblatt, Stephen, "Shakespeare and the Exorcists", in Patricia Parker and Geoffrey Hartman, eds, *Shakespeare and the Question of Theory* (New York and London: Routledge, 1990), pp. 163–186.

Greenblatt, Stephen, *Hamlet in Purgatory* (Princeton: Princeton University Press, 2001).

Greenblatt, Steven et al., *Cultural Mobility: A Manifesto* (Cambridge: Cambridge University Press, 2010).

Greenblatt, Stephen, *The Swerve: How the Renaissance Began* (London: The Bodley Head, 2011).

Greenblatt, Stephen, *Tyrant: Shakespeare on Politics* (New York and London: Norton, 2018).

Greene, Thomas M., *The Light to Troy: Imitation and Discovery in Renaissance Poetry* (New Haven and London: Yale University Press, 1982).

Greene, Thomas M., "Resurrecting Rome: The Double Task of the Humanist Imagination", in P. M. Ramsey, ed., *Rome in the Renaissance: The City and the Myth* (Binghamton: Medieval and Renaissance Texts and Studies, vol. 18, 1982), pp. 41–54.

Guardamagna, Daniela, ed., *Roman Shakespeare: Intersecting Times, Spaces, Languages* (Oxford: Peter Lang, 2018).

Guillory, John, "Monuments and Documents: Panofsky on the Object of Study in the Humanities", *History of Humanities*, 1:1 (2016), 9–30.

Gurr, Andrew, *The Shakespearean Stage, 1576–1642* (Cambridge: Cambridge University Press, 1992).

Hadfield, Andrew, "Shakespeare's Ecumenical Britain", in Andrew Hadfield, *Shakespeare, Spenser and the Matter of Britain* (New York: Palgrave Macmillan, 2004), pp. 151–168.

Hadfield, Andrew, *Shakespeare and Republicanism* (Cambridge: Cambridge University Press, 2005).

Hadfield, Andrew, "Edmund Spenser's Translations of Du Bellay in Jan van der Noot's *A Theatre for Voluptuous Worldlings*", in Fred Schurink, ed., *Tudor Translation* (Basingstoke: Palgrave Macmillan, 2011), pp. 143–160.

Hadfield, Andrew, "Renaissance England's View of Rome", in Maria Del Sapio Garbero, ed., *Rome in Shakespeare's World* (Roma: Edizioni di Storia e Letteratura, 2018), pp. 127–146.

Halpern, Richard, "The Classical Inheritance", in Michael Neill and David Schalkwyk, eds, *The Oxford Handbook of Shakespearean Tragedy* (Oxford: Oxford University Press, 2016), pp. 19–34.

Hampton, Timothy, *Writing From History: The Rhetoric of Exemplarity in Renaissance Literature* (Ithaca and London: Cornell University Press, 1990).

Harrington, John, "*A Preface, or Rather a Briefe Apologie of Poetrie* prefixed to the translation of *Orlando Furioso*, 1591", in G. Gregory Smith, ed., *Elizabethan Critical Essays*, vol. 2 (London: Oxford University Press, 1950), pp. 194–222.

Harris, Jonathan Gil, "'Narcissus in thy Face': Roman Desire and the Difference it Fakes in *Antony and Cleopatra*", *Shakespeare Quarterly*, 45:4 (1994), 408–425.

Harris, Jonathan Gil, *Untimely Matter in the Time of Shakespeare* (Philadelphia: University of Pennsylvania Press, 2009).

Hazlitt, William, *The Round Table and Characters of Shakespeare's Plays* (London: Dent, 1969).

Heal, Felicity, *Hospitality in Early Modern England* (Oxford: Clarendon Press, 1990).

Hegel, Georg Wilhelm Friedrich, *The Philosophy of History*, transl. J. Sibree (New York: Cosmo Classics, 2007).

Heinemann, Margot, "'Let Rome in Tiber Melt': Order and Disorder in *Antony and Cleopatra*", in John Drakakis, ed., *Antony and Cleopatra: William Shakespeare* (Houndmills and London: Macmillan New Casebooks, 1994), pp. 166–181.

Helfer, Rebeca, *Spenser's Ruins and the Art of Recollection* (Toronto: University of Toronto Press, 2012).

Helgerson, Richard, *Forms of Nationhood: The Elizabethan Writing of England* (Chicago: The University of Chicago Press, 1992).

Hell, Julia and Andreas Schonle, eds, *Ruins of Modernity* (Durham and London: Duke University Press, 2010).

Hieatt, A. Kent, "The Genesis of Shakespeare's *Sonnets*: Spenser's *Ruines of Rome: by Bellay*", *PMLA*, 98:5 (1983), 800–814.

Hiles, Jane, "A Margin for Error: Rhetorical Context in *Titus Andronicus*", in Philip Kolin, ed., *Titus Andronicus. Critical Essays* (New York and London: Garland Publishing, 1995), pp. 233–248.

Hillman, David, *Shakespeare's Entrails: Belief, Scepticism and the Interior of the Body* (Houndmills and New York: Palgrave Macmillan, 2007).

Hillman, David, "The Pity of It. Shakespearean Tragedy and Affect", in Michael Neill and David Schalkwyk, eds, *The Oxford Handbook of Shakespearean Tragedy* (Oxford: Oxford University Press, 2016), pp. 135–150.

Hillman, David and Carla Mazzio, eds, *The Body in Parts: Fantasies of Corporeality in Early Modern Europe* (New York and London: Routledge, 1997).

Hingley, Richard, *Globalizing Roman Culture: Unity, Diversity and Empire* (London and New York: Routledge, 2005).

Hodges, Devon L., *Renaissance Fictions of Anatomy* (Amherst: The University of Massachusetts Press, 1985).

Hoenselaars, Ton, ed., *Shakespeare's History Plays: Performance, Translation, and Adaptation in Britain and Abroad* (Cambridge: Cambridge University Press, 2004).

Holderness, Graham, *Shakespeare Recycled: The Making of the Historical Drama* (New York and London: Harvester, 1992).

Holderness, Graham, "*Julius Caesar*: Shakespeare and the Ruins of Rome", in Michele Marrapodi, ed., *Shakespeare and the Visual Arts. The Italian Influence* (London and New York: Routledge, 2017), pp. 341–355.

Holderness, Graham, Brian Loughrey and Andrew Murphy, eds, *Shakespeare: The Roman Plays* (London: Longman, 1996).

Holland, Peter, "Introduction", in William Shakespeare, *Coriolanus* (London: Bloomsbury Arden Shakespeare, 2013), pp. 1–141.

Holland, Peter, ed., "Shakespeare and Rome", thematic issue of *Shakespeare Survey*, 69 (2016).

Hopkins, Lisa, *The Cultural Uses of the Caesars on the English Renaissance Stage* ([Farnham: Ashgate, 2008] rpt London and New York: Routledge, 2016).

Hopkins, Lisa, *From the Romans to the Normans on the English Renaissance Stage* (Kalamazoo: Medieval Institute Publications, 2017).

Hopkins, Lisa and Domenico Lovascio, eds, "The Uses of Rome in English Renaissance Drama", thematic issue of *Textus: English Studies in Italy*, 29:2 (2016).

Howard, Jane E. and Phyllis Rackin, *Engendering a Nation: A Feminist Account of Shakespeare's English Histories* (London and New York: Routledge, 1997).

Hui, Andrew, *The Poetics of Ruins in Renaissance Literature* (New York: Fordham University Press, 2016).

Hulse, S. Clark, "Wresting the Alphabet: Oratory and Action in *Titus Andronicus*", *Criticism*, 21:2 (1979), 106–118.

Hulse, S. Clark, *Metamorphic Verse: The Elizabethan Minor Epic* (Princeton: Princeton University Press, 1981).

Hults, Linda C., "Dürer's 'Lucretia': Speaking the Silence of Women", *Signs*, 6:2 (1991), 205–237.

Irigaray, Luce, *Speculum With the Other Woman*, transl. Gillian G. Gill (Ithaca: Cornell University Press, [1974] 1985).

Irigaray, Luce, *Marine Lover of Friedrich Nietzsche*, transl. Gillian G. Gill (New York: Columbia University Press, [1980] 1991).

Ivic, Christopher and Grant Williams, eds, *Forgetting in Early Modern English Literature and Culture* (London and New York: Routledge, 2004).

Jacobs, Frederika, "(Dis)assembling: Marsyas, Michelangelo, and the Accademia del Disegno", *The Art Bulletin*, 3 (2002): 426–448.

Jaffé, Michael, "Rubens and Optics: Some Fresh Evidence", *Journal of Warburg and Courtauld Institutes*, 34 (1971), 362–366.

James, Heather, "Dido's Ear: Tragedy and the Politics of Response", *Shakespeare Quarterly*, 52:3 (2001), 360–382.

James, Heather, *Shakespeare's Troy: Drama, Politics, and the Translation of Empire* (Cambridge: Cambridge University Press, [1997] 2006).

Jones, Emrys, "Stuart *Cymbeline*", *Essays in Criticism*, 11 (1961), 84–99.

Kahn, Coppélia, *Roman Shakespeare: Warriors, Wounds and Women* (London: Routledge, 1997).

Kantorowicz, Ernst H., *The King's Two Bodies: A Study in Mediaeval Political Theology* (Princeton: Princeton University Press, 1957).

Karmon, David, *The Ruin of the Eternal City: Antiquity and Preservation in Renaissance Rome* (Oxford: Oxford University Press, 2011).

Kaula, David, "The Time Sense of *Antony and Cleopatra*", *Shakespeare Quarterly*, 15:3 (1964), 211–223.

Kendall, Gillian Murray, "'Lend Me Thy Hand': Metaphor and Mayhem in *Titus Andronicus*", *Shakespeare Quarterly*, 40:3 (1989), 299–316.

Kerrigan, John, *Motives of Woe: Shakespeare and 'Female Complaint': A Critical Anthology* (Oxford: Clarendon Press, 1991).

Kerrigan, John, *Revenge Tragedy: Aeschylus to Armageddon* (rpt Oxford: Clarendon Press, [1996] 2001).

Kerrigan, John, "Shakespeare. Elegy, and Epitaphs *1557–1640*", in Jonathan Post, ed., *The Oxford Handbook of Shakespeare's Poetry* (Oxford: Oxford University Press, 2013), pp. 225–244.

Kerrigan, John, *Shakespeare's Originality* (Oxford: Oxford University Press, 2018).

Kewes, Paulina, "History and Its Uses", in Paulina Kewes, ed., *The Uses of History in Early Modern England* (San Marino, CA: Huntington Library, 2006), pp. 1–30.

King, Ros, *Cymbeline: Constructions of Britain* (Aldershot and Burlington: Ashgate, 2005).

Klein, Bernard, "Antony and Cleopatra", in Michael Neill and David Schalkwyk, eds, *The Oxford Handbook of Shakespearean Tragedy* (Oxford: Oxford University Press, 2016), pp. 452–467.

Knight, Wilson G., *The Imperial Theme* (London and New York: Routledge, [1931] 2002).

Knight, Wilson G., *The Crown of Life* (London and New York: Routledge, [1937] 2002).

Knowles, James, "'Infinite Riches in a Little Room': Marlowe and the Aesthetics of the Closet", in Gordon McMullan, ed., *Renaissance Configurations: Voices/Bodies/Spaces, 1580–1690* (Houndmills and London: Macmillan, 1998), pp. 3–29.

Kolin, Philip, "Performing Texts in *Titus Andronicus*", in Philip Kolin, ed., *Titus Andronicus: Critical Essays* (New York and London: Garland Publishing, 1995), pp. 249–260.

Kolin, Philip, "*Titus Andronicus* and the Critical Legacy", in Philip Kolin, ed., *Titus Andronicus: Critical Essays* (New York and London: Garland Publishing, 1995), pp. 3–58.

Kristeva, Julia, *Desire in Language: A Semiotic Approach to Literature and Art*, transl. Leon S. Roudiez et al. (Oxford: Blackwell, 1989).

Lake, Peter, "Tragedy and Religion. Religion and Revenge in *Titus Andronicus and Hamlet*", in Michael Neill and David Schalkwyk, eds, *The Oxford Handbook of Shakespearean Tragedy* (Oxford: Oxford University Press, 2016), pp. 167–183.

Lake, Peter, *How Shakespeare Put Politics on the Stage: Power and Succession in the History Plays* (New Haven and London: Yale University Press, 2017).

Lake Prescott, Anne, "Du Bellay and Shakespeare's Sonnets", in Jonathan F.S. Post, ed., *The Oxford Handbook of Shakespeare's Poetry* (Oxford: Oxford University Press, 2013), pp. 134–150.

Laqueur, Thomas, *Making Sex: Body and Gender From the Greek to Freud* (Cambridge, MA: Harvard University Press, [1990] 1992).

Liebler, Naomi Conn, *Shakespeare's Festive Tragedies: The Ritual Foundations of Genre* (London and New York: Routledge, 1995).

Little, Arthur L., Jr., *Shakespeare Jungle Fever: National-Imperial Re-Visions of Race, Rape, and Sacrifice* (Stanford, CA: Stanford University Press, 2000).

Lombardo, Agostino, *Ritratto di Enobarbo* (Pisa: Nistri-Lischi, 1971).

Lombardo, Agostino, *Il fuoco e l'aria. Quattro studi su Antonio e Cleopatra* (Roma: Bulzoni, 1995).

Lombardo, Agostino, "A Tragedy of Memory", *Memoria di Shakespeare*, 4 (2017), 103–111.

Loomba, Ania, "'Delicious Traffick': Racial and Religious Difference on Early Modern Stages", in Catherine M.S. Alexander and Stanley Wells, eds, *Shakespeare and Race* (Cambridge: Cambridge University Press, 2000), pp. 201–222.

Loomba, Ania, *Shakespeare, Race, and Colonialism* (Oxford: Oxford University Press, 2002).

Lovascio, Domenico, *Un nome, mille volti. Giulio Cesare nel teatro inglese della prima età moderna* (Roma: Carocci, 2015).

Lovascio, Domenico, ed., "Shakespeare: Visions of Rome", special issue of *Shakespeare*, 15:4 (2019).

Lovascio, Domenico, ed., *Roman Women in Shakespeare and His Contemporaries* (Kalamazoo: Medieval Institute Publications, 2020).

Lovascio, Domenico and Lisa Hopkins, eds, "The Uses of Rome in English Renaissance Drama", thematic issue of *Textus: English Studies in Italy*, 29:2 (2016).

Luis-Martinez, Zenòn, "Shakespeare's Historical Drama as *Trauerspiel*: *Richard II* and After", *ELH*, 75 (2008), 673–705.

Lupic, Ivan, "The Mobile Queen: Observing *Hecuba* in Renaissance Europe", *Renaissance Drama*, 46:1 (2018), 25–56.

MacDonald, Ronald R., "Playing Till Doomsday: Interpreting *Antony and Cleopatra*", *English Literary Renaissance*, 15:1 (1987), 78–99.

MacFaul, Tom, "A Theatre for Worldlings", in Richard A. McCabe, ed., *The Oxford Handbook of Edmund Spenser* (Oxford: Oxford University Press, 2010).

Magnusson, Lynne, "Shakespearean Tragedy and the Language of Lament", in Michael Neill and David Schalkwyk, eds, *The Oxford Book of Shakespearean Tragedy* (Oxford: Oxford University Press, 2016), pp. 120–134.

Maley, Willy, *Nation, State and Empire in English Renaissance Literature: Shakespeare to Milton* (Houndmills: Palgrave Macmillan, 2003).

Marcus, Leah S., *Puzzling Shakespeare: Local Reading and Its Discontents* (Berkeley: University of California Press, 1988).

Marenco, Franco, *La parola in scena. La comunicazione teatrale nell'età di Shakespeare* (Torino: UTET, 2004)

Marrapodi, Michele, "Retaliation as an Italian Vice in English Renaissance Drama: Narrative and Theatrical Exchanges", in Michele Marrapodi, ed., *The*

Italian World of English Renaissance Drama: Cultural Exchange and Intertextuality (Newark: Delaware University Press, 1998), pp. 190–207.

Marrapodi, Michele, "*Mens Sana in copore sano*: The Rhetoric of the Body in Shakespeare's Roman and Late Plays", in Maria Del Sapio Garbero, Nancy Insenberg and Maddalena Pennacchia, eds, *Questioning Bodies in Shakespeare's Rome* (Göttingen: V&R Unipress, 2010), pp. 198–205.

Marrapodi, Michele, ed., *Shakespeare and the Visual Arts: The Italian Influence* (New York and London: Routledge, 2017).

Marrapodi, Michele, ed., *The Routledge Research Companion to Anglo-Italian Renaissance Literature and Culture* (New York and London: Routledge, 2019).

Marshall, Cynthia, "Men of Steel Done Got the Blues: Melancholic Subversion of Presence in *Antony and Cleopatra*", *Shakespeare Quarterly*, 44:4 (1993), 385–408.

Marshall, Cynthia, *The Shattering of the Self: Violence, Subjectivity, and the Early Modern Text* (Baltimore: The John Hopkins University Press, 2002), pp. 106–216.

Martindale, Charles and Michelle Martindale, *Shakespeare and the Uses of Antiquity* (London and New York: Routledge, 1990).

Martindale, Charles and A.B. Taylor, *Shakespeare and the Classics* (Cambridge: Cambridge University Press, 2004).

Maus, Katharine Eisaman, "Taking Tropes Seriously: Language and Violence in Shakespeare's *Rape of Lucrece*", *Shakespeare Quarterly*, 37:1 (1986), 66–82.

Maus, Katharine Eisaman, *Inwardness and the Theater in the English Renaissance* (Chicago: The University of Chicago Press, 1995).

Maus, Katharine Eisaman, "Introduction" to *Titus Andronicus*, in Stephen Greenblatt et al., eds, *The Norton Shakespeare*, 3rd ed. (New York and London: Norton, 2016), pp. 491–498.

Mazzocco, Angelo, "Rome and the Humanists: The Case of Biondo Flavio", in Paul A. Ramsey, ed., *Rome in the Renaissance: The City and the Myth* (New York: Center for Medieval & Early Renaissance Studies, 1982), pp. 185–193.

McDonald, Michael, "Ophelia's Maimèd Rites", *Shakesepeare Quarterly*, 37:3 (1986), 309–317.

Meek, Richard, *Narrating the Visual in Shakespeare* (Farnham and Burlington: Ashgate, 2009).

Mehlman, Jeffrey, "'The Floating Signifier': From Lévi-Strauss to Lacan", *Yale French Studies*, 48 (1972): 10–37.

Melchiori, Giorgio, *Shakespeare. Genesi e struttura delle opere* (Bari: Laterza, 1994).

Melchiori, Giorgio, "'They That Have Power': The Ethics of the Roman Plays", in Maria Del Sapio Garbero, ed., *Identity, Otherness and Empire in Shakespeare's Rome* (Farnham and Burlington: Ashgate, 2009), pp. 191–205.

Melehi, Hassan, "Antiquities of Britain: Spenser's *Ruines of Time*", *Studies in Philology*, 102:2 (2005): 159–183.

Melehi, Hassan, *The Poetics of Literary Transfer in Early Modern France and England* ([Farnham: Ashgate 2010] rpt London: Routledge, 2016).

Mikalachki, Jodi, "The Masculine Romance of Roman Britain: *Cymbeline* and Early Modern Nationalism", *Shakespeare Quarterly*, 46:3 (1995), 301–322.

Miles, Geoffrey, *Shakespeare and the Constant Romans* (Oxford: Clarendon Press, 1996).

Minier, Márta, "The 'Contemporary Past' in Retakes on the Roman Plays", in Maria Del Sapio Garbero, ed., *Rome in Shakespeare's World* (Roma: Storia e Letteratura, 2018), pp. 234–235.

Miola, Robert S., *Shakespeare's Rome* (London and New York: Cambridge University Press, 1983).

Miola, Robert S., "*Julius Caesar* and the Tyrannicide Debate", *Renaissance Quarterly*, 38 (1985), 271–289.

Miola, Robert S., *Shakespeare and Classical Tragedy* (Oxford: Clarendon Press, 1992).

Miola, Robert S., "Past the Size of Dreaming? Shakespeare's Rome", *Shakespeare Survey*, 69, thematic issue on "Shakespeare and Rome", ed. Peter Holland (2016), 1–16.

Mottram, Stewart, *Ruin and Reformation in Spenser, Shakespeare, and Marvell* (Oxford: Oxford University Press, 2019).

Muir, Tom, "Without Remainder: Ruins and Tombs in Shakespeare's *Sonnets*", *Textual Practice*, 24:1 (2010), 21–49.

Mullaney, Stephen, "'Do You See This?' The Politics of Attention in Shakespearean Tragedy", in Alexander Nagel and Christopher S. Wood, eds, *Anachronic Renaissance* (New York: Zone Books, 2010).

Mullaney, Steven, *The Place of the Stage: License, Play, and Power in Renaissance England* (Ann Arbor: The University of Michigan Press, [1988] 2004).

Neill, Michael, "'Amphitheatres in the Body': Playing With Hands on the Shakespearean Stage", *Shakespeare Survey*, 48 (1996), 23–50.

Neill, Michael, "Introduction", in William Shakespeare, *Antony and Cleopatra*, ed. Michael Neill (Oxford: Oxford University Press, [1994] 2000), pp. 1–130.

Neill, Michael, *Issues of Death: Mortality and Identity in English Renaissance Tragedy* (Oxford: Oxford University Press, [1997] 2005).

Neill, Michael, *Putting History to the Question: Power, Politics, and Society in English Renaissance Drama* (New York: Columbia University Press, 2001).

Neill, Michael and David Schalkwyk, eds, *The Oxford Handbook of Shakespearean Tragedy* (Oxford: Oxford University Press, 2016), pp. 151–166.

Nevo, Ruth, *Shakespeare's Other Language* (New York and London: Methuen, 1987).

Newman, Jane O., "'And Let Mild Women to Him Lose Their Mildness': Philomela, Female Violence, and Shakespeare's *The Rape of Lucrece*", *Shakespeare Quarterly*, 45:3 (1994), 304–326.

Nietzsche, Friedrich, *The Birth of Tragedy, or Hellenism and Pessimism*, transl. Shaun Whiteside (London: Penguin Books, 2003).

Nietzsche, Friedrich, "On the Uses and Disadvantages of History for Life", in *Untimely Meditations*, transl. R. J. Hollingdale (Cambridge: Cambridge University Press, 2007), pp. 57–123.

Norton, Isabella, "'He Was a Thing of Blood': Blood, Wounds, and Memory in Shakespeare's *The Tragedy of Coriolanus*", *Litterae Mentis: A Journal of Literary Studies*, 1 (2014), 6–14.

Nosworthy, J.M., "Introduction", in William Shakespeare, *Cymbeline*, Arden edition (London and New York: Methuen, [1955] 1986), pp. XI–LXXXIII.

Orgel, Stephen, *Authentic Shakespeare: And Other Problems of the Early Modern Stage* (New York and London: Routledge, 2002).

Orgel, Stephen, *Spectacular Performances: Essays on Theatre, Imagery, Books and Selves in Early Modern England* (Manchester and New York: Manchester University Press, 2011), p. 162.

Orgel, Stephen, *The Reader in the Book: A Study of Places and Traces* (Oxford: Oxford University Press, 2015).

Pagetti, Carlo, "Shakespeare's Tales of Two Cities: London and Rome", in Maria Del Sapio Garbero, ed., *Identity, Otherness and Empire in Shakespeare's Rome* (Farnham and Burlington: Ashgate, 2009), pp. 145–155.

Palmer, Daryl W., *Hospitable Performances. Dramatic Genre and Cultural Practices in Early Modern England* (West Lafayette, IN: Purdue University Press, 1992).

Panofsky, Erwin, *Meaning in the Visual Arts* (New York: Doubleday, 1955).

Panofsky, Erwin, *Renaissance and Renaissances in Western Art* (Stockholm: Almqvist & Wiksells, 1960).

Papetti, Viola, *Manganelli legge Shakespeare* (Roma: Edizioni di Storia e Letteratura, 2018).

Park, Katherine, "The Criminal and the Saintly Body", *Renaissance Quarterly*, 47 (1994), 1–33.

Parker, Barbara L., *Plato's Republic and Shakespeare's Rome: A Political Study of the Roman Works* (Newark: University of Delaware Press, 2004).

Parker, Patricia, *Literary Fat Ladies: Rhetoric, Gender, Property* (London and New York: Methuen, 1987).

Parker, Patricia, "Romance and Empire: Anachronistic *Cymbeline*", in George M. Logan and Gordon Teskey, eds, *Unfolded Tales: Essays on Renaissance Romance* (Cornell: Cornell University Press, 1989), pp. 189–207.

Parker, Patricia, "Othello and Hamlet: Dilation, Spying, and the 'Secret Place' of Woman", *Representations*, 44 (1993), 60–95.

Parry, Graham, *The Trophies of Time: English Antiquarians of the Seventeenth Century* (Oxford: Oxford University Press, 2007).

Paster, Gail Kern, *The Body Embarrassed: Drama and the Discipline of Shame in Early Modern England* (Ithaca: Cornell University Press, 1993).

Paster, Gail Kern, "'In the Spirit of Men There Is No Blood': Blood as Trope of Gender in *Julius Caesar*", in Richard Wilson, ed., *Julius Caesar: William Shakespeare* (Houndmills and New York: Palgrave New Casebooks, 2002), pp. 1–169.

Paster, Gail Kern, *Humoring the Body: Emotions and the Shakespearean Stage* (Chicago: The University of Chicago Press, 2004).

Paster, Gail Kern, Katherine Rowe and Mary Floyd-Wilson, eds, *Reading the Early Modern Passions: Essays in the Cultural History of Emotions* (Philadelphia: University of Pennsylvania Press), 2004.

Pennacchia, Maddalena, "Antony's Ring: Remediating Ancient Rhetoric on the Elizabethan Stage", in Maria Del Sapio Garbero, ed., *Identity, Otherness and Empire in Shakespeare's Rome* (Farnham and Burlington: Ashgate, 2009), pp. 49–59.

Pennacchia, Maddalena, *Shakespeare intermediale. I drammi romani* (Spoleto: Editoria & Spettacolo, 2012).

Pennacchia, Maddalena, "Performance History", in Domenico Lovascio, ed., *Antony and Cleopatra: A Critical Reader* (London: Bloomsbury Arden Shakespeare, 2020), pp. 55–87.

Pfister, Manfred, "Acting the Roman: *Coriolanus*", in Maria Del Sapio Garbero, ed., *Identity, Otherness and Empire in Shakespeare's Rome* (Farnham and Burlington: Ashgate, 2009), pp. 35–47.

Pfister, Manfred, "The Romes of *Titus Andronicus*", in Maria Del Sapio Garbero, ed., *Rome in Shakespeare's World* (Roma: Edizioni di Storia e Letteratura, 2018), pp. 149–166.

Platt, Michael, "*The Rape of Lucrece* and the Republic for Which it Stands", *The Centennial Review*, 19:2 (1975), 59–79.

Plescia, Iolanda, "'From me Was Posthumus Ript': *Cymbeline* and the Extraordinary Birth", in Maria Del Sapio Garbero, Nancy Isenberg and Maddalena Pennacchia, eds, *Questioning Bodies in Shakespeare's Rome* (Göttingen: V&R Unipress, 2010), pp. 135–147.

Plescia, Iolanda, "Expressions of Futurity in Early Modern Dramatic Dialogue: A Case Study", in Gabriella Mazzon and Luisanna Fodde, eds, *Historical Perspectives on Forms of English Dialogue* (Milano: Franco Angeli, 2012), pp. 99–115.

Pollard, Tanya, "What's Hecuba to Shakespeare?", *Renaissance Quarterly*, 65:4 (2012), 1060–1093.

Pope, Stephanie L., "Gestures and the Classical Past in Shakespeare's *Titus Andronicus*", in Domenico Lovascio, ed., *Shakespeare: Visions of Rome*, *Shakespeare*, 15:4 (2019), 326–334.

Prescott, Anne Lake, "Du Bellay and Shakespeare's Sonnets", in Jonathan F. S. Post, ed., *The Oxford Handbook of Shakespeare's Poetry* (Oxford: Oxford University Press, 1916), pp. 134–150.

Presner, Todd Samuel, "Hegel's Philosophy of World History via Sebald's Imaginary of Ruins: A Contrapuntal Critique of the 'New Space' of Modernity", in Julia Hell and Andreas Schonle, eds, *Ruins of Modernity* (Durham and London: Duke University Press, 2010), pp. 193–211.

Pugliatti, Paola, *Shakespeare the Historian* (London: Palgrave Macmillan, 1996).

Quint, David, "Virgil's Double Cross: Chiasmus and the Aeneid", *The American Journal of Philology*, 132 (2011), 273–300.

Rackin, Phillis, *Stages of History: Shakespeare's English Chronicles* (Ithaca: Cornell University Press, 1990).

Rackin, Phyllis, "History into Tragedy: The Case of *Richard III*", in Shirley Nelson Garner and Madelon Sprengnether, eds, *Shakespearean Tragedy and Gender* (Bloomington and Indianapolis: Indiana University Press, 1996), pp. 31–53.

Ravenscroft, Edward, "To the Reader", in Philip Kolin, ed., *Titus Andronicus. Critical Essays* (New York and London: Garland Publishing, 1995), pp. 375–376.

Ricoeur, Paul, *Oneself as Another*, transl. Kathleen Blamey (Chicago and London: The University of Chicago Press, [1990] 1994).

Rifkin, Benjamin A., "The Art of Anatomy", in Benjamin A. Rifkin, Michael J. Ackerman and Judith Folkenberg, eds, *Human Anatomy: Depicting the Body from the Renaissance to Today* (London: Thames & Hudson, 2006), pp. 7–67.

Ronan, Clifford, *"Antike Roman": Power Symbology and the Roman Play in Early Modern England* (Athens: University of Georgia Press, 1995).

Rowe, Katherine A., "Dismembering and Forgetting in *Titus Andronicus*", *Shakespeare Quarterly*, 45:3 (1994), 279–303.

Royle, Nicholas, *Jacques Derrida* (London: Routledge, 2003).

Ruffini, Franco, *Teatri prima del Teatro. Visioni dell'edificio e della scena tra Umanesimo e Rinascimento* (Roma: Bulzoni, 1983).

Sacerdoti, Gilberto, *Nuovo cielo, nuova terra. La rivoluzione copernicana di Antonio e Cleopatra di Shakespeare* (Roma: Edizioni di storia e letteratura, [1990] 2008).

Sacerdoti, Gilberto, "*Antony and Cleopatra* and the Overflowing of the Roman Measure", in Maria Del Sapio Garbero, ed., *Identity, Otherness and Empire Identity, Otherness and Empire in Shakespeare's Rome* (Farnham and Burlington: Ashgate, 2009), pp. 107–119.

Sacks, David Harris, "The Countervailing of Benefits: Monopoly, Liberty, and Benevolence in Elizabethan England", in Dale Hoak, ed., *Tudor Political Culture* (Cambridge: Cambridge University Press, 1995), pp. 272–291.

Said, Edward, *Orientalism* (New York: Vintage, 1978).

Sawday, Jonathan, *The Body Emblazoned: Dissection and the Human Body in Renaissance Culture* (London and New York: Routledge, 1995).

Schanzer, Ernest, *The Problem Plays of Shakespeare: A Study of Julius Caesar, Measure for Measure, Antony and Cleopatra* (London and New York: Routledge, [1963] 2005).

Schoenfeldt, Michael C., *Bodies and Selves in Early Modern England: Physiology and Inwardness in Spenser, Shakespeare, Herbert, and Milton* (Cambridge: Cambridge University Press, 1999).

Schwyzer, Philip, *Archaeologies of English Renaissance Literature* (Oxford: Oxford University Press, 2007).

Serpieri, Alessandro, *I sonetti dell'immortalità* (Milano: Bompiani, 1975).

Serpieri, Alessandro, "*Julius Caesar*. Presentazione, Tabulazione, Commento", in Alessandro Serpieri, Claudia Corti and Keir Elam, eds, *Nel Laboratorio di Shakespeare. Dalle fonti ai drammi*, 4 vols (Parma: Pratiche Editrice, 1988), vol. 4, pp. 15–129.

Serpieri, Alessandro, "Reading the Signs: Towards a Semiotics of Shakespearean Drama", in John Drakakis, ed., *Alternative Shakespeares* (New York and London: Routledge, 1992), pp. 119–143.

Serpieri, Alessandro, "Prefazione", in William Shakespeare, *Giulio Cesare*, transl. Alessandro Serpieri (Milano: Garzanti, 1994), pp. XXXII–XLVII.

Serpieri, Alessandro, "Body and History in the Political Rhetoric of *Julius Caesar*", in Maria Del Sapio Garbero, Nancy Isenberg and Maddalena Pennacchia, eds, *Questioning Bodies in Shakespeare's Rome* (Göttingen: V&R Unipress, 2010), pp. 219–236.

Settis, Salvatore, *Futuro del 'classico'* (Torino: Einaudi, 2004).

Settis, Salvatore, "Arte classica, libertà, rivoluzioni", *Sei lezioni di Salvatore Settis*. https://www.raicultura.it/arte/articoli/2020/06/Winckelmann--ebc1eef9-20f3-421f-813d-04fde0f00130.html.

Shapiro, Gary, *Archaeologies of Vision: Foucault and Nietzsche on Seeing and Saying* (Chicago and London: The University of Chicago Press, 2003).

Shapiro, James, *A Year in the Life of William Shakespeare: 1599* (New York: Harper Perennial, 2006).

Siemon, James R., "Introduction", in William Shakespeare, *King Richard III*, ed. James R. Siemon (London: Bloomsbury Arden Shakespeare, 2009), pp. 1–123.

Sinisi, Fabrizio, *Giulio Cesare. Uccidere il tiranno* (Gorgonzola, MI: Nardini Editore, 2017).

Skura, Meredith, "Interpreting Posthumus' Dream From Above and Below: Families, Psychoanalysts, and Literary Critics", in Murray M. Schwartz and Coppélia Kahn, eds, *Representing Shakespeare. New Psychoanalytic Essays* (Baltimore and London: The John Hopkins University Press, 1980), pp. 203–216.

Sontag, Susan, "Notes on Camp", in Susan Sontag, *Against Interpretation and Other Essays* (New York: Farrar, Straus and Giroux, 1966).

Spencer, Benjamin T., "*Antony and Cleopatra* and the Paradoxical Metaphor", *Shakespeare Quarterly*, 9:3 (1958), 373–378.

Spencer, Terence John Bew, "Shakespeare and the Elizabethan Romans", *Shakespeare Survey*, 10 (1957), 27–38.

Spring, Peter, *The Topographical and Archaeological Study of the Antiquitie of the City of Rome, 1420–1447* (University of Edinburgh, unpublished PhD thesis, 1972).

Spurgeon, Caroline, *Shakespeare's Imagery and What It Tells Us* (Cambridge: Cambridge University Press, [1935] 2001).

Stewart, Alan, "The Early Modern Closet Discovered", *Representations*, 50 (1995), 76–100.

Stolberg, Michael, "A Woman Down to Her Bones. The Anatomy of Sexual Difference in the Sixteenth and Early Seventeenth Centuries", *Isis*, 94:2 (2003), 274–299.

Sugg, Richard, *Murder After Death: Literature and Anatomy in Early Modern England* (Ithaca and London: Cornell University Press, 2007).

Sullivan, Garrett A., *Memory and Forgetting in English Renaissance Drama* (Cambridge: Cambridge University Press, 2005).

Summit, Jennifer, "Reading Reformed: Spenser and the Problem of the English Library", in Christopher Ivic and Grant. Williams, eds, *Forgetting in Early Modern English Literature and Culture* (London and New York: Routledge, 2004), pp. 165–178.

Tanner, Tony, "*Antony and Cleopatra*: Boundaries and Excess", *Memoria di Shakespeare*, 4 (2017), 1–19.

Talvacchia, Bette, *Taking Positions: On the Erotic in Renaissance Culture* (Princeton: Princeton University Press, 1999).

Targoff, Ramie, *Posthumous Life: Eros and Afterlife in Renaissance England* (Chicago: The University of Chicago Press, 2014).

Targoff, Ramie, "Love and Death in Egypt and Rome", *Memoria di Shakespeare*, 4 (2017), 461–472.

Tempera, Mariangela, "'Horror . . . is the Sinews of the Fable': Giraldi Cinthio's Works and Elizabethan Tragedy", in Yves Peyré and Pierre Kapitaniak, eds, *Shakespeare et l'Europe de la Renaissance* (Paris: Société Française Shakespeare, 2005), pp. 235–247.

Tempera, Mariangela, "*Titus Andronicus*: Staging the Mutilated Roman Body", in Maria Del Sapio Garbero, Nancy Isenberg and Maddalena Pennacchia, eds, *Questioning Bodies in Shakespeare's Rome* (Göttingen: V&R Unipress, 2010), pp. 109–119.

Tennenhouse, Leonard, *Power on Display: The Politics of Shakespeare's Genres* (New York and London: Routledge, [1986] 2005).

Tricomi, Albert H., "The Aesthetics of Mutilation in 'Titus Andronicus'", *Shakespeare Survey*, 27 (1974), 11–20.

Tricomi, Albert H., "The Mutilated Garden in *Titus Andronicus*", *Shakespeare Studies*, 9 (1976), 89–105.

Velz, John W., "The Ancient World in Shakespeare: Authenticity or Anachronism? A Retrospect", *Shakespeare Survey*, 31 (1978), 1–12.

Vickers, Brian, "Francis Bacon and the Progress of Knowledge", *Journal of the History of Ideas*, 53:3 (1992), 495–518.

Vickers, Nancy, "'The Blazon of Sweet Beauty's Best': Shakespeare's *Lucrece*", in Patricia Parker and Geoffrey Hartman, eds, *Shakespeare and the Question of Theory* (New York and London: Routledge, 1991), pp. 95–115.

Vico, Giambattista, *New Science. Principles of the New Science Concerning the Common Nature of the Nations* [1744], transl. David Marsh (London: Penguin Books, 2013).

Vienne-Guerrin, Nathalie and Sarah Hatchuel, eds, *Shakespeare on Screen: The Roman Plays* (Mont-Saint-Aignan: Publications des Universités de Rouen et du Havre, 2009).

Vincent, Barbara C., "Shakespeare's *Antony and Cleopatra* and the Rise of Comedy", in John Drakakis, ed., *Antony and Cleopatra: William Shakespeare* (Houndmills: Macmillan New Casebooks, 1994), pp. 212–247.

Waith, Eugene M., "The Metamorphosis of Violence in *Titus Andronicus*", rpt in Philip Kolin, ed., *Titus Andronicus: Critical Essays* (New York and London: Garland Publishing, [1957] 1995), pp. 99–114.

Wallace, John M., "*Timon of Athens* and the Three Graces: Shakespeare's Senecan Study", *Modern Philology*, 83 (1986), 349–363.

Wallace, John M., "The Senecan Context of 'Coriolanus'", *Modern Philology*, 90:4 (1993), 465–478.

Warren, Roger, "Introduction", in William Shakespeare, *Cymbeline*, ed. Roger Warren (Oxford: Oxford University Press, 1998), pp. 1–136.

Watt, Gary, "The Art of Advocacy: Renaissance of Rhetoric in the Law School", *Law and Humanities*, 12:1 (2018), 116–137.

Wayne, Valerie, "Appendix 1: The Text of *Cymbeline*", in William Shakespeare, *Cymbeline* (London and New York: Arden Bloomsbury Shakespeare, 2017), pp. 378–401.

Weiss, Roberto, *The Renaissance Discovery of Classical Antiquity* (Oxford: Basil Blackwell, 1969).

Wells, Marion A., "'To Find a Face where All Distress Is Stell'd': Enargeia, Ekphrasis, and Mourning in *The Rape of Lucrece* and the *Aeneid*", *Comparative Literature*, 54:2 (2002), 175–198.

Wells, Stanley, *Re-editing Shakespeare for the Modern Reader* (Oxford: Clarendon Press, 1984).

Westeweel, Bart, ed., *Anglo-Dutch Relations in the Field of the Emblem* (Leiden and New York: Brill, 1997).

Wiegand, Chris, "Tom Hiddleston on Coriolanus: 'There Was Nowhere to Hide—that's Exciting'", *The Guardian*, 3 June (2020). www.theguardian.com/stage/2020/jun/03/tom-hiddleston-coriolanus-donmar-warehouse-josie-rourke.

Wilders, John, "Introduction", in William Shakespeare, *Antony and Cleopatra* (London: Bloomsbury Arden Shakespeare, 2005), pp. 1–84.

Williams, Raymond, *Marxism and Literature* (Oxford: Oxford University Press, 1977).

Wilson, Richard, "Introduction to *Julius Caesar*", in Richard Wilson, ed., *Julius Caesar: William Shakespeare* (Houndmills and New York: Palgrave New Casebooks, 2002), pp. 1–27.

Wilson, Richard, "'Is This a Holiday?' Shakespeare's Roman Carnival", in Richard Wilson, ed., *Julius Caesar: William Shakespeare* (Houndmills and New York: Palgrave New Casebooks, 2002), pp. 55–76.

Wilson, Richard, ed., *Julius Caesar: William Shakespeare* (Houndmills and New York: Palgrave New Casebooks, 2002).

Wilson, Richard, *Free Will: Art and Power on Shakespeare's Stage* (Manchester: Manchester University Press, 2013).

Womersley, David, "Sir Henry Savile's Translation of Tacitus and the Political Interpretation of Elizabethan Texts", *The Review of English Studies*, 42:167 (1991), 313–342.

Woodbridge, Linda, "Palisading the Elizabethan Body Politic", *Texas Studies in Literature and Language*, 33:3 (1991), 327–354.

Wynne-Davies, Marion, "'The Swallowing Womb': Consumed and Consuming Women in *Titus Andronicus*", in Valerie Wayne, ed., *The Matter of Difference: Materialist Feminist Criticism of Shakespeare* (Ithaca and New York: Cornell University Press, 1991), pp. 129–151.

Yates, Frances, *The Art of Memory* (London: The Bodley Head, [1966] 2014).

Index